HEROES OF THE GAEL

Heroes of the Gael

A HISTORY OF FIONN AND THE FIANNA

NATASHA SUMNER

PRINCETON UNIVERSITY PRESS
PRINCETON & OXFORD

Published by Princeton University Press
41 William Street, Princeton, New Jersey 08540
99 Banbury Road, Oxford OX2 6JX

press.princeton.edu

GPSR Authorized Representative: Easy Access System Europe - Mustamäe tee 50, 10621 Tallinn, Estonia, gpsr.requests@easproject.com

ISBN 9780691204734
ISBN (e-book) 9780691278698

Library of Congress Control Number: 2025930724

British Library Cataloging-in-Publication Data is available
Editorial: Anne Savarese and Emma Wagh
Production Editorial: Sara Lerner
Jacket Design: Heather Hansen
Production: Erin Suydam
Publicity: William Pagdatoon and Charlotte Coyne
Copyeditor: Lachlan Brooks

Jacket Credit: Inge Johnsson / Alamy Stock Photo

This book has been composed in Arno

Printed in the United States of America

10 9 8 7 6 5 4 3 2 1

MIX
Paper | Supporting responsible forestry
FSC® C008955

CONTENTS

ILLUSTRATIONS

ACKNOWLEDGEMENTS

BRINGING THIS BOOK to completion was a more substantial feat than I could have predicted, and I certainly did not accomplish it unaided. The heroes who facilitated research trips, commented on conference papers and chapter drafts, and helped in myriad other ways at various points over more than a decade are too numerous to list in full, but some are worthy of special recognition. I extend heartfelt thanks to Rob Dunbar and Críostóir Mac Carthaigh for repeatedly welcoming me to the University of Edinburgh and University College Dublin and smoothing the way to consult collections; Mícheál Briody, Domhnall Uilleam Stiùbhart, and Matthew Knight for generously sharing their own research materials and providing access to rare sources; Kevin Murray, Joseph Falaky Nagy, and Domhnall Uilleam (again) for reading work in progress and remedying gaps in my knowledge; my former colleagues and advisors at Harvard, Tomás Ó Cathasaigh, Catherine McKenna, William Gillies, and Barbara Hillers, for their initial and ongoing guidance; my talented editor at Princeton, Anne Savarese, and the press's anonymous readers for helping tie up loose ends; and friends and family whose Fenian generosity frequently ensured a roof overhead while archive hunting, and who graciously put up with long evenings in the office and nearly finished sections secreted away on holiday. Without such considerable support, far more errors and omissions would remain than reviewers are sure to point out. I preemptively thank my critics for their dedication to Fenian scholarship, for I hope to have laid a foundation on which others may continue to build.

HEROES OF THE GAEL

Introduction

> The greatest heroes acknowledge his superiority; his enemies tremble at his name; and the highest encomium that can be bestowed on one whom the poet would most exalt, is to say, that his soul was like the soul of Fingal.
>
> —HUGH BLAIR, "A CRITICAL DISSERTATION ON THE POEMS OF OSSIAN" (1763)[1]

FIONN MAC CUMHAILL could well be considered the greatest Gaelic hero—and there has certainly been no shortage of great Gaelic heroes. But unlike Cú Chulainn or Cormac mac Airt, who also once enjoyed wide renown, Fionn and his roving warrior band, the Fianna, have retained their popularity into the modern period. Their stories have enthralled audiences for well over a millennium—longer, even, than the British King Arthur and his knights.[2] Indeed, prose and poetry about the Fianna comprise a prolific body of 'Fenian' narrative that spans roughly 1,400 years from the earliest written sources in Old Irish to modern literature and folklore originating in Ireland, Scotland, the Isle of Man, and the North American diaspora. That they have long held the Gaelic imagination is no small thing, but what is more, they have also made a substantial cultural impact well beyond their Gaelic point of origin. The names of these heroes have graced the lips of presidents, emperors, and kings: Thomas Jefferson found versions of their tales "the source of daily and exalted pleasure"; Napoleon Bonaparte admired their martial valor, envisioning himself as a modern Fenian warrior; and Napoleon's godson, upon whom the French emperor bestowed a heroic Fenian name, became the first King Oscar of Sweden.[3]

This burst in international popularity was something of a historical fluke, since it was due not to any mass exposure to the Gaelic stories themselves, but to a series of eighteenth-century creative adaptations in English, collectively known as *Ossian*, which James Macpherson claimed to have translated from manuscript and oral sources. Macpherson's adaptations had a great impact on the way the tradition was viewed and the uses to which it was put in the following centuries; yet, his efforts were by no means the first historically significant reformulation of this lengthy tradition, and they would not be the last. This book explores the changing fortunes and altering perceptions of the Fenian tradition from its earliest extant witnesses in the seventh century, through its eighteenth-century Ossianic debut on the world stage and the reverberations of that newfound renown in the Gaelic world, and finally into the modern period of nation-building, national image formation, and folklore collecting.

Our Heroes

Aspects of the representation of heroes are international. While not generally portrayed as deities, heroes' abilities typically broach or exceed the ordinary limits of human possibility. People—usually men—of action, they tend to exhibit physical strength, martial excellence, and a commitment to defending or upholding the social order. More specific heroic characteristics may be socially and culturally dependent, and there is variation from one hero to another.[4] In a present-day Western Anglophone milieu, for instance, it can be observed that Superman, Spider-Man, Iron Man, Batman, and Black Panther all fill socially protective roles, but exhibit different backgrounds, outlooks, and skills. The same can be said for the Fianna.

The hundreds of stories and songs that make up the Fenian tradition depict a legendary early medieval golden age when Gaeldom is justly ruled and the Fianna are its defenders. Patrolling the Irish and Scottish wilderness, they alternate among temporary encampments, sustaining and entertaining themselves by hunting. Their pastoral idyll is frequently interrupted, however, for peace is hard won in an age when the fabric separating this realm from the otherworld is thin, and powerful invaders are eager to encroach on Gaelic territory. Ever watchful, our capable heroes successfully keep upstart otherworldly lords at bay and shield their shores from attack, but not all antagonism is external. At the height of the tradition, the warriors over whom Fionn presides hail from two long-embattled kindreds—Clann Bhaoiscne and Clann Mhorna—whose truce is wont to waver when tensions run high. Amid regular threats to their group and the broader society they protect, there are thus ever-present overtones of internal strife.

Fionn himself belongs to Clann Bhaoiscne. Indeed, the earliest texts frequently introduce him as *Finn ua Baíscne*, 'Fionn, descendant of Baoiscne.'[5] His connection with this kindred is maintained across the centuries, although from the late medieval period until the present day he has more commonly been called either Fionn mac Cumhaill (i.e., Fionn, son of Cumhall) or simply Fionn, his renown being such that no patronymic is needed to clearly identify him.[6] That Fionn is, in fact, a descriptive sobriquet rather than an original name is another point of commonality he shares with heroes worldwide.[7] Various sources give his birth name as either Deimhne or Glais Díge and attribute the bestowal of the name Fionn, 'fair-haired,' to unacquainted or poorly acquainted observers of his innate superiority.[8] In one instance, in a competition against other boys, an adult witness to his childhood strength dubs the fair lad 'Fionn,' while in another, a poet named Fionn File—the hopeful beneficiary of prophetic knowledge imbued in the salmon of Fecc—realizes that the 'Fionn' foretold to receive this gift is not himself, but rather our young protagonist and rechristens him.[9]

On the Clann Bhaoiscne side of the Fianna, Fionn is joined early on by his son Oisín and nephew Caoilte, and later (from circa 900–1200) by others including Diarmaid ua Duibhne and Oisín's son Oscar, while the most prominent members of Clann Mhorna, Goll, Garadh, and Conán enter the written record around the same time. As in the case of Fionn, several of the Fianna's birth names differ from their heroic monikers. Caoilte, 'slender-warm,' receives his name when an otherworldly smith comments on his appearance in a hot forge; Oscar, 'agility, strength,' is found to have some strength left in him after a harrowing encounter, according to modern folklore; and Goll, 'one-eyed,' is so called due to his loss of an eye in a long-ago battle.[10] Like modern superheroes, moreover, each is associated with one or more unique traits, such as Fionn's unnatural wisdom, Caoilte's incredible speed, and Goll's great might. But the Fianna are not stock characters; their portrayals are complex. These and other aspects of their characterization develop over the centuries, and notable personality traits wax and wane.

The diverse stories about them include accounts of great victory, fascinating adventure, harrowing rescue, steadfast love, and heart-rending betrayal. A narrative tradition long in the making, its origins are shrouded in the mystery of prehistoric Ireland, and its oral and written aspects have been entwined from the earliest extant sources. Sparsely surviving early medieval accounts of our heroes suggest that circulation continued to be predominantly oral until the tenth century when an initially slow trickle of Fenian ink swelled to a lively rivulet, preserving longer and more copious texts that shed increasing light on our developing characters and their exploits. A surge in the early thirteenth century produced the longest extant Gaelic medieval text, *Acallam na Senórach* (The dialogue of the elders), and subsequent centuries witnessed a veritable deluge of Fenian compositions as the Fianna attained the premodern equivalent of bestseller status. They were the most prevalent topic of literature in Early Modern Gaelic (c. 1250–1650), and they maintained this prestige for centuries, occupying considerable space on manuscript pages even into the eighteenth and nineteenth centuries.[11] Thanks to the efforts of modern folklorists, thousands of orally collected accounts show their ongoing prominence not just in the Gaelic languages, but also among English speakers in the former 'Gaelic world' and its diasporas. Composition has continued, moreover, in both Gaelic and English. Reimagined not only by Macpherson, but also by proponents of the late nineteenth- and early twentieth-century Celtic Revival, not to mention numerous twentieth- and twenty-first-century authors, composers, screenwriters, and the like, our heroes' storied renown persists to the present day.

Fenian Studies

Despite the Fianna's widespread and enduring popularity, this book is the first full-length, comprehensive analysis of Fenian stories and songs and their place in society. Until relatively recently, scholarly concentration largely fell on other bodies of Gaelic heroic literature—primarily texts concerning Cú Chulainn and other legendary Ulster warriors—none of which were as long-lasting or prolific. Although scholars are beginning to rectify this situation, the vastly important Fenian narrative tradition remains marginal to the received history of Celtic, and by extension, Western literature. Multiple Fenian texts lack editions and translations, let alone sustained critical analysis, and Fionn and the Fianna continue to receive only a fraction of the attention that their heroic British counterparts, Arthur and his knights, do. But the winds of change are blowing. Since the early 2000s, more scholars than ever before have turned their attention to Fenian topics, and the fruits of their labors can be observed in conferences organized, grant-funded projects initiated, courses offered, theses supervised, and articles and books published. Through their efforts, we are witnessing the emergence of an academic field of Fenian studies, the continued growth of which will undoubtedly result in ever diminishing gaps in knowledge and a greater awareness of the importance of this prolific corpus to our understanding of Gaelic, Celtic, and broader Western written and oral narrative traditions.

The present swell of Fenian scholarship is rooted in a wave of publications in the final decades of the last century when our heroes captured the attention of a small but dedicated academic cohort. A foundational triad of monographs appeared in the 1980s, which included Joseph Nagy's *Wisdom of the Outlaw* (1985), analyzing accounts of Fionn's youth from a Lévi-Straussian structuralist perspective; James MacKillop's *Fionn mac Cumhaill: Celtic Myth in English Literature* (1986), documenting major English-language engagements with the tradition; and Dáithí O hÓgáin's *Fionn mac Cumhaill: Images of the Gaelic Hero* (1988), providing a nonspecialist introduction to a broad range of material, including several rarely considered texts in Early Modern Gaelic. These were supplemented by articles by these and other scholars, among them notably Máirtín Ó Briain, Alan Bruford, and Donald Meek, and two substantial essay collections dedicated to Fenian material, *Fiannaíocht: Essays on the Fenian Tradition of Ireland and Scotland* (1987), edited by Bo Almqvist, Séamas Ó Catháin, and Pádraig Ó Héalaí, and *An Fhiannaíocht* (1995), edited by Pádraig Ó Fiannachta. This body of scholarship—the first modern critical examinations of the Fenian tradition—illuminated a languishing corpus for the inspiration of a new scholarly generation.[12]

The academics entering the field in the present century have trained under and worked alongside the aforementioned pioneers, and are responsible for the current unprecedented vibrancy of Fenian studies. Under their stewardship, a series of Fíanaigecht conferences has taken place,[13] first at the University of Cambridge in 2009, then the University of Glasgow in 2014, Sabhal Mòr Ostaig on the Isle of Skye in 2018 (in conjunction with the Ulidia [Ulster cycle] conference), and, most recently, Mary Immaculate College in Limerick in 2022. These have produced three new essay collections, *The Gaelic Finn Tradition* (2012), edited by Sharon Arbuthnot and Geraldine Parsons, *The Gaelic Finn Tradition II* (2022), edited by Sharon Arbuthnot, Síle Ní Mhurchú, and Geraldine Parsons, and *Proceedings of Ulidia-Finn 2018* (forthcoming), edited by Ralph O'Connor, Abigail Burnyeat, Geraldine Parsons, and Domhnall Uilleam Stiùbhart. Topical symposia have also generated essay collections dedicated to specific Fenian collections and texts, including *Duanaire Finn: Reassessments* (2003) and *Tóruigheacht Dhiarmada agus Ghráinne: Reassessments* (2018), emerging from the Irish Texts Society's annual seminars in Cork in 2002 and 2017 and edited by John Carey and Kevin Murray respectively, and *In Dialogue with the Agallamh: Essays in Honour of Seán Ó Coileáin* (2014), emerging from a conference at University College Cork in 2012 and edited by Aidan Doyle and Kevin Murray. Two publications in preparation by myself and Joseph Nagy have resulted from a series of workshops at Harvard's

Radcliffe Institute in 2018 and 2021, moreover, the first an essay collection featuring representative work in each period of the tradition and the second a textual reader for classroom and nonspecialist use.

Since the essay has long been the predominant critical medium in the discipline of Celtic Languages and Literatures, as Arbuthnot and Parsons point out, the significance of these collections is undeniable.[14] They have begun to be supplemented by single-author studies, moreover, including Kevin Murray's *The Early Finn Cycle* (2017), a guide to the primary and secondary sources for early Fenian literature (c. 600–1225) intended for university students, but reflecting the most current scholarship and therefore also of specialist interest. Murray's companion booklet, *The Early Fenian Corpus*, which followed in 2021, supersedes Kuno Meyer's considerably earlier survey of the same corpus in his *Fianaigecht* (1910), while Joseph Flahive's booklet *The Fenian Cycle in Irish and Scots-Gaelic Literature* (2017) provides an up to-date introduction to the field for students and nonspecialists and Tadhg Ó Síocháin's *Caoilte sa Luath-Fhiannaíocht* (2021) offers new insight into the earliest depictions of a single character. Such resources make Fenian narrative more approachable, enabling newcomers to more easily situate themselves within this sizable textual tradition, and improving scholars' ability to teach and work with the material.

Work is also underway to improve the accessibility of the primary corpus. In addition to the textual reader mentioned above, which will contain new translations in cases when existing resources are outdated or the texts have never been translated, the past few decades have seen the publication of an attractive new translation of *Acallam na Senórach* (1999), edited by Ann Dooley and Harry Roe; a consolidated edition of the later, longer *Agallamh na Seanórach* (2014), edited by Nessa Ní Shéaghdha; and a new edition of *Lige Guill / The Grave of Goll: A Fenian Poem from the Book of Leinster* (2009), edited by Diarmuid Ó Murchadha. While the number of Fenian texts still needing first or new editions and translations extends into the hundreds, the publication of a handful of additional texts edited as thesis projects is likely in coming years. We have also seen the recent commencement of major digital initiatives, including the Fionn Folklore Database, launched in 2023 and directed by me, which provides the first comprehensive classification system for Fenian folklore, and Kevin Murray's newly funded project to produce a digital critical edition of the *Acallam*, which promises to far surpass the current standard edition published in 1900.[15]

These rapid advances are enormously significant, but given the emergent state of the field, considerable gaps remain. Fenian criticism to date has concentrated primarily on texts in Old and Middle Irish, examined the much larger body of Early Modern Gaelic texts less frequently, and, with some notable exceptions, tended to sidestep Macpherson's *Ossian* and its reverberations and overlook the modern oral corpus. The tendency to prize earlier texts over later compositions reflects a longstanding bias in the study of Gaelic literature, but this ground is shifting, and genres once out of favor, like so-called 'bardic' poetry and heroic romance (including Fenian romance), have begun to receive increased attention.[16] With regard to the oral corpus, the absence of a reliable finding aid prior to the launch of the Fionn Folklore Database long hindered Fenian folklore scholarship, although scholars like Ó Briain and Bruford did make major contributions in this area in the latter third of the twentieth century. Recent work inspired by the database has begun to emerge, however, and considerable further advances can be expected in this area too in years to come.[17] Regarding *Ossian*, academics in non-Gaelic disciplines have ushered in a new wave of scholarship that views the momentous historical controversy over Macpherson's epics not as a stark case of fraud or authenticity, but rather as the result of complex social, political, and cultural conditions motivating multiple parties to act in highly principled, if sometimes morally ambiguous ways.[18] Even so, apart from Derick Thomson's 1952 study *The Gaelic Sources of Macpherson's 'Ossian'*, which provides firm evidence for the adaptation of parts of Macpherson's text from Gaelic Fenian and heroic lays, few modern Gaelic scholars have tested the Ossianic waters.[19] Similarly, although the late nineteenth and early twentieth-century Celtic Revival has been subject to reassessment in recent years, almost no attention has been given to revivalists' engagement with and contribution to the Fenian narrative tradition. That the work of Macpherson and the revivalists is predominantly in English may be the primary deterrent, although new compositions in the Gaelic languages from the nineteenth century to the present day have also received limited attention. There is therefore considerable room for expansion of the field of Fenian studies, and several areas exist in which growth is particularly wanting.

A New Approach

Although this book cannot address every remaining gap in the scholarly record, its scope is considerably broader than any previous study of the corpus. More anthropological than philological, it explores Fenian narrative in its multilingual cultural contexts, tracing the emergence and development of prominent aspects of the tradition from the early medieval to the modern periods, with the aim of better understanding not only how our heroes' stories have been told, but why.

Irish philosopher Richard Kearney writes that "telling stories is as basic to human beings as eating. More so, in fact, for while food makes us live, stories are what make our lives worth living. They are what make our condition *human*." Without stories, not only would life be unbearably boring, but much of what we deem to be human would be impossible. This is because, as critical thinkers dating back to Aristotle have observed, we process our very existence through story. Not only does the narrativized "creative redescription" of the world in story reveal "patterns and hitherto unexplored meanings" that help us understand our everyday reality, but stories also provide the conceptual distance necessary to imagine alternate modes of existence.[20] In whatever medium it is communicated—oral, written, or otherwise—a story is never just a story. In its reflection of one's thoughts, it invites a response from another. It is a mode of entertainment, certainly, but also of contemplation, of communication, and, laterally, of action. It is indeed no coincidence that technological innovations from photography to the mobile phone were first conceptualized in stories.[21]

The Fenian tradition provides ample space for imaginative engagement with the narrative past, the historical present, and the aspirational future. Part (pseudo)historical fiction, part (proto)fantasy, stories about Fionn and the Fianna project their creators' and interlocutors' perceptions of a bygone Gaelic heroic age through the lens of their contemporary realities. In doing so, whether intentionally or not, they encode pressing concerns of their day and elicit reactions from their listeners, readers, and viewers. Some among their audience then go on to compose new accounts of our heroes, or to present renewed versions of well-known storylines from their own unique perspectives. An ever-expanding multiform tradition proliferates. And it does so justifiably, for as folklorist Alfred Nutt wrote about Fenian tales in 1899, "No literature can, for so many centuries, maintain itself and preserve its plastic vitality without good and sufficient reason."[22]

In what follows, I trace the fates of Fionn and the Fianna across the centuries and throughout the Gaelic world and undertake to explain their persistent popularity. My approach intermingles distant and close reading practices, scanning the breadth of the corpus to identify emergent patterns and focusing in on different moments to elucidate the contemporary significance of individual texts.[23] Because the entirety of the tradition has yet to be adequately expounded, the book is necessarily as descriptive as it is analytic, and it engages only sparingly with theoretical interventions. My objective here is narrative history; I examine these Fenian stories in order to tell *their* story. And I find that they have engaged audiences from the seventh century to the present day not just because they are entertaining tales, but also because they are relevant to people: they reflect the aspirations and concerns of diverse groups responding to historical changes both within and without. I explore this premise in three chronologically ordered parts.

The first part details the development of the Fenian narrative from its earliest extant textual records through the medieval and early modern creation of its greatest literary achievements. Tracking the evolution of persistent themes and characters across multiple forms and genres over the course of centuries, I demonstrate how the cycle has adapted to meet the needs and expectations of successive generations.

The second part devotes groundbreaking attention in a study of the Fenian tradition to the fiery controversy stirred by James Macpherson's adaptation of Fenian characters and plots in his international bestseller *Ossian* (1761–63). A Gael himself, Macpherson's engagement with this material was unique. The controversy, moreover, aroused a wave of interest in genuine Fenian narrative and led to the preservation of some of the most important Fenian texts. Exploring this cultural phenomenon from a Gaelic perspective, I consider the Fianna's journey to international fame, and examine the controversy's impact on the transmission and reception of Fenian narratives in Ireland and Scotland in the century following *Ossian*'s publication.

The third part addresses the position of Fionn and the Fianna in the modern Irish and Scottish nations from the beginning of the Celtic Revival period (c. 1860) until the present day. I explore how the fascination with both nations' Gaelic heritage contributed to the publication of medieval and early modern primary source texts, the composition of new adaptations, and the collection of a vast corpus of folklore. I investigate, too, the use of Fenian tales and tropes in the push for Irish independence and the symbolic expression of ethnocultural identity, as well as the reinterpretation of the Fianna in schoolbooks and children's literature, where they remain a popular topic to this day.

The image of the Fenian tradition that emerges from this tripartite consideration is one of a dynamic and multifaceted body of story and song that has remained relevant over the centuries due to constant adaptation. Throughout the lifespan of the tradition, multiple population groups have embedded their contemporary concerns in the stories and songs in ideologically significant ways, so that Fenian narrative not only has a long history—it has affected that history and been affected by it.

Technical Matters

SOME PRELIMINARY ATTENTION to editions and translations, dating, and terminology is warranted, particularly given the breadth of material considered in this book.

Editions and Translations

When multiple editions of a text exist, I use the current scholarly standard. Translations are my own unless otherwise attributed.

Dating

While taking into account the difficulties outlined by Kevin Murray in dating early Fenian sources, I provisionally accept Gerard Murphy's revised dating of all eighth- to twelfth-century texts for which more thorough attempts at dating have not been made. In some cases, the most recent attempt at dating remains that of Kuno Meyer over a century ago.[1] I adhere to the most widely accepted date of later texts but acknowledge that considerable work remains to be done to securely date much of the corpus. By necessity, broad date ranges are often given.

Names and Titles

For the sake of consistency, I use modern spellings of characters' names throughout, regardless of the period under discussion. A pronunciation guide is provided after the epilogue. Titles of texts and names of premodern authors and places have not been modernized.

Corpus-Specific Terminology

Fianna

The name of Fionn's fighting force does not derive from his name, although such a folk etymology has been recorded: "Long ago, there was a renowned commander of the army of Ireland called Fionn mac Cumhaill, and the army that was under his command were called Fianna, from the name of that hero."[2] In actuality, the derivation of *fían* has been tentatively traced to Indo-European **wēd-*, 'wild,' but the meaning of the word has varied over time.[3] In the earliest Gaelic written records, *fían* (plural *fíana*) refers to a warrior band on the margins of society, and the later iteration *fiann* can be read simply as 'soldier(s)' or 'army.' These terms can refer to our heroes, but they are not specific to them. From the late medieval period onward, however, we can observe the use of *An Fhiann, Na Fianna,* and the Fianna as collective proper nouns in Irish and English referring to the specific group of elite warriors under Fionn's leadership. While this usage is fairly consistent in Ireland, in Scottish Gaelic our heroes are more commonly known as *an Fhèinn, an Fhìnn,* or *na Fiantaichean.*[4] In Scottish English, they may also be called Fingalians, from Macpherson's redesignation of Fionn as Fingal. I retain early medieval terminology when discussing the earliest extant texts in chapter 1. I use the term Fianna throughout the rest of the book.

Fenian

The word 'Fenian' can be used as a noun or an adjective. The earliest printed use of the term occurs in Bishop John O'Brien's 1768 Irish-English dictionary, in which he translated "Béarla na féine" as "the Fenian Irish," alluding not to our heroes but to the Féni, a posited early Irish population group said to descend from Fenius Farsaid in *Lebor Gabála Érenn* (The book of the taking of Ireland).[5] Sylvester O'Halloran, in his 1772 *Introduction to the Study of the History and Antiquities of Ireland,* referred to the Féni as "Phenians" and further claimed that the Irish translation of the Latin name Fenius was "Fion." While he went on to note later uses of the name, including "Fion Mac Cumhal," he did not extend the meaning of Phenians to refer to Fionn's Fianna.[6] The translation of Féni as "Phenian" was again adopted by Charles Vallancey, who used the word in 1782 to refer to a dialect of Irish "known only to the learned" in the second edition of his *Grammar of the Iberno-Celtic, Or Irish Language.*[7] By 1786 we find the use of "Finian" with reference to Fionn's warriors in Joseph Cooper

Walker's *Historical Memoirs of the Irish Bards,* indicating either a transfer of meaning from the Féni to Fionn's Fianna or the formation of an analogous homonym from the name "Fin" (Walker's spelling of Fionn)—or perhaps a combination of both.[8] Charlotte Brooke addressed the term's emergent dual meaning in her 1789 *Reliques of Irish Poetry,* writing that "the Irish in general were frequently called *Fenians,* or *Phenians,* from their great ancester [*sic*] *Phenius Farsa.* . . . But the Leinster legions [i.e., Fionn's Fianna] proudly arrogated that name entirely to themselves, and called their celebrated body, exclusively, *Fenii,* or *Fiana Eireann.*"[9] The word came to commonly refer to the Fianna on account of these eighteenth-century publications, which together represent some of the earliest Anglo-Irish engagements with the Fenian narrative tradition.[10] We soon find it in Scotland too, for example in Walter Scott's 1816 novel *The Antiquary.*[11] The word took on a derogatory quality in the mid-nineteenth century due to its association with Irish revolutionary activity, however, and it has negative connotations to this day in parts of Britain and Northern Ireland.[12] Yet for those on the side of revolution, it connoted an ethnic heritage to be celebrated, and due, no doubt, to the success of the Irish independence movement, the term has persisted there as the common English referent to the Fenian narrative tradition. I use the term over other less regionally controversial alternatives because it is topically limited to the Fianna, is inclusive of a variety of forms and media, and avoids privileging one Gaelic language over another.

Ossianic

In Scotland the word 'Ossianic' is more commonly used than Fenian to describe this narrative corpus. Because 'Ossianic' derives from Macpherson's mid-eighteenth-century adaptations rather than with reference to the native narrative tradition, I only use it in relation to characters and texts created by or in the style of Macpherson.

Gaelic Terminology

The Gaelic terms most commonly used to refer to Fenian narrative are *fianaigecht* (Old Irish), *fiannuigheacht* (Early Modern Gaelic), *fiannaíocht* (modern Irish), and *sgeulachdan na Féinne* (Scottish Gaelic). The Scottish Gaelic term refers specifically to material about Fionn's Fianna, and the meaning of *fianaigecht* is also exclusive. The Irish word has evolved to be structurally rather than characterologically delimited, however, and now means "any long prose tale, generally with implications of a magical and heroic content."[13] Modern Irish *fiannaíocht* is therefore not a synonym for the Fenian tradition, but rather refers specifically and exclusively to hero tales: long, winding stories that relate the intrepid adventures of diverse martial heroes including, but not limited to, the Fianna. A variety of forms of Fenian narrative are discussed in this book including, but not exclusive to, *fiannaíocht*.

Conceptual Terminology

Gaelic

When addressing the Fenian tradition in Ireland, I use 'Irish' and 'Gaelic' interchangeably. While the modern preference for Irish over Gaelic is comprehensible with regard to the struggle for language rights, the broad spectrum of meaning of the word can lead to lexical confusion in discussions of Irish literature and folklore, particularly when context does not clearly indicate whether the word refers to ethnicity, nationality, or language.[14] Confusion can also result from the use of the term 'Gaelic' in a discussion that encompasses more than one Gaelic language, of course. Using the terms 'Irish Gaelic,' 'Scottish Gaelic,' and 'Manx Gaelic' in every instance would be tedious, however, especially when it is contextually apparent which language is meant. For these reasons, I have not limited myself to specific language terminology. Rather, I have endeavored to choose the most appropriate term in each instance to provide clarity yet avoid tedium.

Narrative

I frequently use the word 'narrative' rather than 'literature' to refer to the Fenian corpus because, while 'literature' can refer to orally composed or circulating texts (i.e., oral literature), it is more commonly understood to mean written texts, whereas I wish to recognize the inherent orality of the reception of this material throughout much of the premodern and modern periods.[15] Derived from the Latin *narrare* (to tell), the word 'narrative' can also refer to stories told nonverbally through images and sound.[16] The Fenian narrative corpus encompasses verbal and nonverbal forms of storytelling.

Nationalism

Benedict Anderson defines the nation as "an imagined political community—and imagined as both inherently limited and sovereign." For him, nationalism thus entails the pursuit of a "sovereign state."[17] While this definition broadly reflects the current understanding of political nationalism within the structure of the modern nation state, the promotion of unique national identities predates the modern era and does not always align with the pursuit of political sovereignty. As John Hutchinson recognized some time ago, "nations or ethnic groups, if defined in terms of myths of common origins, distinctive cultural characteristics, and attachments to specific territorial homelands, have existed from time immemorial."[18] The early Irish were by no means politically unified, but they conceived of themselves as a distinct nation. Such identities change over time, moreover. By the seventeenth century, the delineation between Irish Gael and Gall 'foreigner' was religious, linguistic, and territorial, and by the eighteenth century we can see the emergence among the Protestant Anglo-Irish ascendency of a Gaelic-informed national consciousness. In early modern Scotland, too, Scots and Scottish Gaelic speakers promoted distinctive communal identities, while united under Scottish and British political polities to which many also expressed collective allegiance.[19] We can observe in all of these instances cultural forms of nationalism that privilege the celebration of a posited community's unique heritage over political sovereignty. Cultural nationalism may coincide with political nationalism, as it often did during the early modern and modern struggles for Irish nationhood, but it can also be expressed separately from the pursuit of political sovereignty.[20] I use the terms 'nationalism' and 'cultural nationalism' interchangeably, generally without a political connotation.

Tradition

I use the word 'tradition' to signal the interdependence of Fenian material. While individual Fenian compositions and depictions can certainly be interpreted without reference to other material in the tradition, some of their inherent meaning derives from their relationship with one another. I do not here draw the distinction that John Miles Foley does between traditional works with "active dependence on an oral tradition" and post-traditional works "whose meaning derives chiefly from a single text created by a single author."[21] Varieties of both sorts of composition exist within the Fenian tradition, which I am here defining as all textual and extratextual creations that feature the Fianna. I also use the term 'cycle' (for which see chapter 2) to refer to this narrative corpus.

PART I

The Fianna in Gaelic Literature, c. 600–1760

1

Fionn and the Fianna

WHAT MAKES A WARRIOR FENIAN? How did Fionn and the Fianna come to occupy their longstanding position as the foremost champions of the Gael? This chapter seeks answers to these questions in the literary record of early medieval Ireland (c. 600–1200). Scattered references to *fénnidi*, 'fenian warriors,' occur among the earliest extant Irish texts. Many of the referents are now understood to be fictional—and it is the fictional Fenians whom this book principally concerns and to whom the proper noun refers. But in several instances, the *fénnidi* in question are manifestly real. Important clues to the nature of the early Fenian literary tradition may therefore be sought, and found, in the social practice that underpins it. As our period progresses and more sources become available, the stories and poems themselves present new angles from which to approach these questions. Already in mid- to late Old Irish literature (c. 700–900), themes and modes of characterization can be discerned that begin to distinguish the tradition. The development of these emerging traits, and the nature of Fenian literature's relationship with the martial elements of society, are crucial points of inquiry that contribute to our understanding of the tradition. The fast-growing narrative corpus concerning Fionn, Oisín, and their companions at the close of the Middle Irish period (c. 900–1200) is a testament to the Fianna's enduring appeal.

Fenians in Early Society and Literature

Sufficient evidence exists to suggest that the *fían*, 'fenian warrior band,' was, at the time of Christian conversion and for some time thereafter, an integral institution in Irish society. It is thought that such fenian bands consisted primarily of those young men of the propertied class who had aged out of fosterage, but had not yet met the qualifications entitling them to the full rights of citizenship in their *túath*, 'petty kingdom,' according to early Irish law, namely reaching the age of majority and coming into their landed inheritance.[1] Until such time, these men would have led transient lives of hunting and raiding in frontier lands, and might also have acted as mercenaries. They would generally have maintained few ties with their *túath*, although there is evidence that suggests some senior *fénnidi* may have been assigned legitimate law enforcement duties by their local king.[2] References to such historical fenian warriors can be found in early Irish ecclesiastical literature and hagiography, in which any such legitimate roles they may have held are elided. The church denounced them as *díberga*, 'brigands,' likely reflecting both an ideological and a practical opposition to the practice, given that monastic settlements tended to be erected in the very borderlands fenian bands would have been wont to traverse—and ravage.[3] Despite centuries of negative campaigning against what the church clearly perceived as an unruly remnant of the pre-Christian past, however, a record in the Annals of Ulster for the year 847 evidences the continued, although surely greatly attenuated, existence of this social institution in the mid-ninth century.[4]

Aspects of this fenian social reality naturally contribute to the representation of legendary, but fictional, *fénnidi* in Old Irish literature. The earliest surviving reference to a body of story about *fían* leaders and their bands occurs in Tírechán's seventh-century account of the missionary itinerary of Saint Patrick, which mentions a *fían* under the leadership of a pseudohistorical, fourth-century *fénnid* of Munster descent. According to Tírechán, while traveling through Mayo, Saint Patrick resurrected a century-dead royal swineherd who attributed his violent death to this *fían*—a claim reflective of the brutality accorded to ransacking fenian warriors, particularly in ecclesiastical sources. The *fénnid* in question is said to have been the son of the erstwhile Irish high king, Lughaidh Mac Con.[5] This is not the only mention of Mac Con in early Fenian literature. An eighth- or ninth-century story about the legendary leader reflects the historical relationship between the ruling elite and select fenian warriors. Here, none other than Fionn mac Cumhaill appears in Mac Con's service; according to the text, "is Find ba fhénnid do suidiu" ("Fionn was his fenian warrior").[6] Fionn makes his entrance only after Mac Con has lost the high kingship and been treacherously murdered by the *fénnid*, Fearchess mac Commáin, at the behest of Mac Con's foster father, Munster king Oilill Ólom. Fionn exacts vengeance by killing Fearchess.[7] Neither Fionn nor Fearchess is entirely detached from settled society. Rather, the duties they perform on behalf of Mac Con and Oilill Ólom approximate protection and enforcement positions that legal texts suggest senior *fénnidi* could have occupied in early medieval Irish society.[8]

The Fenian tradition eventually coalesced around Fionn mac Cumhaill, but in the earliest literature Fionn was one of a number of literary *fénnidi,* some of whose stories have undoubtedly been lost. Like their historical counterparts, these were sons of the propertied elite. Fionn's descent is traced to powerful rulers from the earliest extant version of his genealogy, ascribed to the seventh-century poet Senchán Torpéist.[9] Mac Con's son likewise belongs to the ruling class, and Mac Con himself led a *fían* prior to taking the high kingship, according to one version of his story.[10] In fiction, as must have been the case in reality, when living the Fenian lifestyle these men have an uneasy relationship with settled society; sometimes they are depicted as menaces, while at other times they perform services for society. Historically, this ambiguous state would usually have been temporary, lasting only so long as a young man remained propertyless. Not all early literary *fénnidi* are so fortunate. Some remain in the *fían* their entire lives and, as in the case of Fionn, amass a narrative corpus. Aspects of the lifestyles of these perennial *fénnidi* may even reflect the settled, aristocratic society they will never rejoin.

The eighth- or ninth-century story *Bruiden Átha Í* (The contention of Áth Í) presents an alternative society in which settled social customs are mirrored in the Fenian sphere. Of principal interest is the fact that in this story, Fionn is married. The way he acquires his wife—via abduction—is in keeping with the lifestyle of a warrior in exile. Yet Fionn clearly does not consider the abduction a mere fleeting interaction, as might be expected of a roving *fénnid;* he seeks a more enduring arrangement. Such a relationship adds new complexity to the literary Fenian lifestyle, introducing bonds of kinship not generally applicable to *fénnidi,* given their detachment from the *túath* and historical ineligibility for marriage.[11] In an atmosphere of chronic unrest, kinship bonds can be dangerous, and they emerge here as the root of a bitter animosity between Fionn and another lifelong *fénnid,* Fothadh Canainne. Through his wife, Badhamair, Fionn becomes embroiled in a blood feud with Fothadh Canainne's half-brother, Cuirreach Life, over the murder of Badhamair's foster brother, Dubh. When Fionn pursues Cuirreach to exact vengeance, Cuirreach kills Badhamair.[12] Fionn succeeds in beheading Cuirreach and avenging both his wife and her foster brother,[13] but in doing so, he enters into a blood feud with Fothadh Canainne. After some time, they make peace, and Fionn arranges an ale feast to mark the agreement. Before the date of the feast arrives, however, Fionn unwittingly kills Fothadh Canainne's sister and her husband, permanently recommencing the feud.[14] Both Fionn and Fothadh Canainne have remained in the *fían* long enough to develop and maintain complex kinship networks similar to those within settled society. While perhaps not reflective of the usual experiences of historical *fénnidi*, this situation makes for engaging, socially relevant literature. Judging by the prevalence of blood vengeance in early medieval Irish tales more generally, the Fenian topic matter of *Bruiden Átha Í* echoes a social concern of its *túath*-bound audience.

Fothadh Canainne meets his end not at the hand of Fionn, but in a battle between his Connacht-based *fían* and that of a Munster *fénnid* named Oilill mac Eoghain. Given their aggressive, unsettled lifestyle, conflict between different fenian bands is likely to have been commonplace. Rather than portraying such conflict in a negative light, the Old Irish accounts of this battle underscore the *fénnid*'s honor and heroism. Like Fothadh Canainne's feud with Fionn, a woman features in this contention, but the principal concern here is the relative social standing of the two *fían* leaders. An early prose text explains how Fothadh Canainne woos Oilill's wife and convinces her to elope with him, upon payment of her *tinnscra*, 'bride price,' because she is more beautiful than his own wife.[15] Not singularly driven by desire, Fothadh Canainne seeks the woman as a symbol of his power. Although he fails to validate his martial superiority—he and Oilill slay one another in the ensuing battle—a record of his valor survives for posterity.[16] The elegiac poem *Reicne Fothaid Canainne* (The *reicne* of Fothadh Canainne) is voiced either by his spirit or, as the prose text would have it, by his own severed head in the absence of any survivors.[17] It celebrates his *fían*'s awe-inspiring and deadly achievements on the battlefield,[18] and bears witness to his success as a *fían* leader. Just as the deeds of his loyal followers reflect favorably on him, so do the many valuable possessions he leaves behind. Evidence of the success of his exploits, these are symbols of wealth and power: fine clothing and weaponry, well-crafted jewelry, a valuable ornamental casket, a resplendent serving cup, an elaborate *fidchell* set, and brilliant candles to illuminate an evening's noble entertainment.[19] With their enumeration, Fothadh Canainne sends a clear message: he has lived, and died, well. His deeds were great and his way of life honorable—indeed, enviable. Although the church registered its opposition to the practice, the lifestyle of this legendary *fénnid* represents everything for which a young nobleman embarking upon this way of life might strive. In the *fían* he could hone his martial skills and seek fame and glory. Perhaps he might return with spoils to augment his inheritance; or perhaps he might die a worthy and heroic death in battle. Whatever the relationship between fenian ideology and reality, the practice had its heroes, and clearly Fothadh Canainne was one.[20]

Emerging Themes

Fenian heroes spend much of their time hunting and fighting in the wilderness landscapes they traverse. While these aspects of the literature may have initially mirrored the social role of the *fénnid,* they persist across all periods and can be considered definitive themes of the tradition. Significant and long-standing tropes of Fenian narrative less directly reflective of a historical fenian practice can also be discerned in the earliest extant literature. Many of these contribute to the characterization of Fionn mac Cumhaill as he emerges as the central figure in a narrative cycle with a growing textual record.

Fionn is known not only for his martial skill against conventional aggressors, but also for his ability to negotiate the boundary between the natural and supernatural worlds, enabling him to know the typically unknowable and guard against the ordinarily unassailable. The earliest portrayal of his interactions with the supernatural world occurs in an eighth-century story about an otherworldly aggressor named Cúldubh.[21] Despite the best efforts of Fionn's *fían,* Cúldubh has been stealing their nightly meal and carrying it away to a *síd,* 'otherworldly residence.'[22] Fionn, the greatest of the warriors, chases and slays the thief, but in the process his thumb gets slammed in the door to the *síd.*[23] Upon placing the injured digit in his mouth, he gains supernatural knowledge. Fionn's thumb of knowledge is a distinguishing attribute of his character at every stage in the history of the tradition, and this is not the only story about its derivation. By the twelfth century, an account had emerged that would supersede it. The later version backdates Fionn's acquisition of his unique gift to a period of apprenticeship during his youth. While cooking a supernaturally endowed salmon for his mentor, Fionn burns his thumb. Reflexively raising it to his mouth, he receives the enlightenment sought by another but destined for him. The method by which he can subsequently access his gift is the same in both stories. To reveal that which is hidden—either obscure information or a sought-after entity—he need only return his specially tempered thumb to his mouth.[24] The early account illustrates the method with an example concerning a young man named Dearc Corra who has been expelled from the *fían.* When Fionn encounters him again with a much-altered appearance, he is able to discern Dearc Corra's true identity by using his thumb of knowledge.[25] While Fionn excels in every way as a warrior, the thumb gives him access to a higher realm of understanding through which he supersedes the role of a mere *fénnid*.

The events preceding Dearc Corra's expulsion hark to another persistent trait in Fionn's characterization. Fionn is often portrayed as a lover of women, if not always a successful or even a suitable lover. In this instance, he desires a woman who would prefer the company of Dearc Corra. Even though the young man declines her advances in deference to Fionn, the incident results in his banishment. This episode resembles a much more disruptive love triangle in the popular legend about Diarmaid, a young man in Fionn's *fían*, and Gráinne, the young daughter of Irish high king Cormac mac Airt. Fionn seeks to marry Gráinne, but Gráinne turns her attention to Diarmaid and convinces him to elope with her, prompting a contention that ultimately results in Diarmaid's death. The direct textual descendent of the earliest complete version of this tale may not be older than the fourteenth century,[26] but there is evidence that a form of the story was known from a much earlier date. The title, *Aithed Gráinne ingine Corbmaic la Díarmait húa nDuibni* (The elopement of Gráinne, daughter of Cormac, with Diarmaid ua Duibhne), is included in two medieval tale lists believed to derive from a tenth- or eleventh-century original,[27] and to each of the two principal characters has been attributed a stray Middle Irish quatrain quoted in the commentary to the *Amra Choluim Chille* (The wonders of Colm Cille).[28] A circa eleventh-century poem set during the elopement has Gráinne recommend sleep to the watchful Diarmaid,[29] while in the tenth- or eleventh-century story known as *Úath Beinne Étair* (The cave of Howth), the pair are discovered hiding in a cave, but they manage to escape capture.[30] Diarmaid's subsequent death is first reported in *Acallam na Senórach* (The dialogue of the elders, c. 1225).[31] The love triangle at the heart of this story, as in its early precursor, portrays Fionn as the less desirable of two men—a status he certainly does not relish, and which prompts him in each case to lash out against his lower-ranking competitor. By these actions he shows himself to be a powerful commander, but the perception of him as a less-than-ideal mate remains unchanged at the close of these stories.

The theme of Fionn as a somewhat problematic lover is developed in *Tochmarc Ailbe* (The wooing of Ailbhe), a circa tenth-century composition related to the Diarmaid and Gráinne tale.[32] The earliest extant Fenian story of any substantial length, *Tochmarc Ailbe* explores the issue from a different perspective. Rather than spurning Fionn, Ailbhe actually wants to marry the *fían* leader. The voice of opposition belongs to her father, who tries to dissuade her by highlighting Fionn's unsuitability as a husband for a young, aristocratic woman—which, as a daughter of Cormac mac Airt, she certainly is.[33] By this point, her sister Gráinne has already chosen Diarmaid over Fionn, but their elopement and Fionn's pursuit are not recounted. Instead, *Tochmarc Ailbe* follows an alternative narrative arc in which Gráinne and Fionn were married for a short time, but legally divorced.[34] Cormac objects to a match between Fionn and Ailbhe not because he fears Fenian retribution for a betrayal Gráinne did not, in this case, commit, but rather out of concern for Ailbhe's wellbeing as the wife of such a man. He would prefer her to remain within the safety of *mur Temrach*, 'Tara's rampart,' rather than join Fionn in a transient Fenian camp.[35] She has already considered the disagreeable aspects of unsettled life, however, and concluded that she would prefer wild boar to an elaborate feast, bedding of birch to down, and birdsong to musical instruments. She would give up everything, she avers, for the wilderness idyll of which she dreams.[36] Cormac's imagery may hint at greater stakes than Ailbhe's physical discomfort, however.

Cormac has ample cause for concern, as the early Fenian corpus demonstrates. In the discussion of *Bruiden Átha Í* above, I suggested that, in practical terms, marriage is not very compatible with the transient, hostile Fenian lifestyle. The complex loyalties of kinship can augment the violence not just of a *fénnid*'s life, but also of those around him, and the lifespans of Fenian wives like Badhamair can consequently be rather short. Of the eight wives accorded to Fionn in the circa twelfth-century *Banshenchas* (Lore of women), three are said to have met violent deaths.[37] Indeed, the *fían* is more commonly a site of aggressive sexual license than marital bliss, and many women fall prey to Fenian warriors, rather than becoming their lovers. The woman Fionn desires in the Old Irish story about Dearc Corra is one of a number of female captives abducted during a raid on a Déise settlement.[38] More overt aggression features in a late Middle Irish account of Fionn's grandson Oscar's loss of a testicle when he and eight other members of Fionn's *fían* are caught attempting to rape a woman. Rather than reflecting negatively on Oscar, the rape attempt allows him subsequently to assert his social dominance over the woman's shamed husband.[39] Even when violence is not attested, loose sexual arrangements are the norm. According to a ninth-century text, "indeed in every mountain region and every forest that Fionn used to frequent with his *fían*, there would be a particular woman waiting for him in the nearest inhabited land."[40] While Ailbhe presents a romanticized rather than a realistic view of life as a Fenian wife, the notion that Fionn may be an unsuitable spouse by dint of the fact that he is a *fénnid* lurks beneath the surface of her discourse on the *fían* and her uncertainty about whether Cormac will consent to the marriage.[41]

Yet Cormac's primary objection is not to Fionn qua *fénnid*. What concerns him most is Fionn's advanced age in comparison with Ailbhe's youth. The issue of an aging principal character is yet another preoccupation of the tradition, particularly in the early medieval period, and different texts grapple with it in different ways. In the stories of Dearc Corra and Diarmaid and Gráinne, Fionn's intended female conquests' rejection of him for younger men strikes at the heart of his warrior identity. His reduced appeal suggests a perception of declining sexual virility and diminishing martial prowess. Such concerns are aired openly in *Tochmarc Ailbe* in Cormac's objections to Ailbhe's attraction to the *fían* leader. Cormac advises his daughter that "grey-haired men are not to be listened to. Although they croon finely, they do not perform their duties."[42] He then makes a comparison that explicitly links the sexual and martial aspects of the *fénnid*'s characterization. As in the case of raiding warriors, he suggests that a young woman ought to prefer a horse that is *sedlach*, 'vigorous, lively,' to one that is old.[43] Similar rhetoric turns up in a circa eighth-century account of a quarrel between Fionn and his son Oisín. Having parted company for a year, Oisín does not immediately recognize Fionn when they meet again, and filial compassion does not prevent him from taunting the older, possibly hostile warrior about his age. Like Cormac, he questions the reliability of Fionn's self-testimony, claiming that "the grey-haired man is wont to talk from behind the boss of his shield."[44] Yet when the time comes for action, the skills needed for his survival may forsake the older *fénnid*: "When tremors have overtaken every bone, the spear from his hand is not bitter."[45] For a martial hero like Fionn, even unfounded speculations about diminished performance, either on or off the battlefield, could be potentially damaging.

The serious threat aging poses is evident, but despite such derisive conjecture, Fionn's actual physical condition remains shrouded in ambiguity in these texts. In his quarrel with Oisín, Fionn answers the younger man's mocking criticism with claims about the superior skills of an experienced warrior. Although each speaks well enough to satisfy the other and they resolve their dispute, neither wins a clear victory in this meeting of minds.[46] Similarly, for every argument Cormac levels against Fionn's advancing age, Ailbhe offers a counterargument. Like those of a seasoned horse, she claims, the keen judgement and sure step of an older man are more dependable.[47] Her argument inverts established wisdom against May–December marriages, which Cormac makes a point to mention: "I have heard of an arrangement that is not wise: a young woman going to a great warrior"—the *laec liathaínech*, 'grey-bearded warrior,' of his sustained complaint—"Ill is what I fear will come of it."[48] In the literary record, disaster does indeed generally ensue from such matches, and one might therefore expect Cormac to hold firm to his position.[49] Ailbhe is persistent, however, and wins her father's grudging support. What is more, neither she nor Fionn suffers the tragic fate that literary precedent might suggest is in store for them. Rather, this story about Fionn's later life shifts the focus from the physical to the intellectual sphere, thereby enabling its (possibly) flagging hero to continue to merit the affections of a desirable young woman. Their courtship consists of a lengthy series of riddles posed by Fionn and readily answered by Ailbhe.[50] Through this interaction the aging *fían* leader establishes that he and the high king's daughter are well matched for wit and intelligence, and we are given to believe that their subsequent marriage is successful on account of their complementary personalities. Despite the ambiguity surrounding Fionn's physical condition, he is able to maintain his social status in both *Tochmarc Ailbe* and the story about his quarrel with Oisín, but his age places him in a compromised position.

A handful of early medieval texts treat the issue of the aging Fenian hero with less ambivalence. In these, Fionn's declining physical state is addressed, and the narrative problem it poses is ultimately resolved by his death. These sources give two different extended descriptions of Fionn's death. The first, a fragmentary tenth- or eleventh-century account dubbed *Aided Finn* (The violent death of Fionn), treats the matter with candor and concision. When members of Fionn's *fían* begin to desert him on account of his age, he decides to attempt a leap between two distant points on the river Boyne in order to prove his continued agility or die trying. He dies.[51] The second and more commonly referenced story has the timeworn hero die in battle with the Luaighne of Tara.[52] Appearing in the twelfth-century *Tesmolta Cormaic ui Chuinn ocus Aided Finn meic Cumaill* (The praise of Cormac ua Cuinn and the violent death of Fionn mac Cumhaill), this account draws a reverent but pointed contrast between the hero at the peak of his strength and his condition at the time of his death. In his younger years, it is said that there never was a better warrior. While his earlier aptitudes were many, however, the story is set "after old age and venerability have come upon him" and his time of glory has passed.[53] Although venerated for his former deeds, Fionn's strength and therefore his worthiness as a warrior-protagonist is gone, and his impending death is presented as an inevitable event. Much like the first account, in which he went bravely to his almost certain death performing a feat requiring the strength of youth, in this story the aged and weakened Fionn enters into a battle with the Luaighne knowing by way of a prophecy that he will not emerge from it. He is thus granted the honor of a warrior's death in battle, with the shame of loss mitigated by the inexorability of fate.[54] The circa eleventh-century record of his decapitation by the Luaighne in the Annals of Tigernach for the year 283 legitimizes Fionn's fated, heroic demise in the accepted historical record.[55]

The Middle Irish death tales are significant not only because they bring the issue of an aging martial hero to a satisfactory resolution, but also because they reflect an impetus to document the major events of Fionn's life. The tendency for a biographical corpus to form around a legendary hero has been recognized internationally. Such biographical material chronicles the hero's notable deeds and final demise, and, crucially, explains how he came to be a hero in the first place. Within early Irish literature, heroic biographies can be traced for iconic characters like Cú Chulainn and Cormac mac Airt, and so it is hardly surprising that Fionn's life should have received similar attention.[56] Birth and boyhood accounts dating to the Middle Irish period function as Fionn's heroic résumé, clearly establishing the remarkable challenges he has confronted to become Ireland's preeminent *fían* leader. His youthful acts of martial prowess are sketched in the late eleventh-century *Macgnímartha Finn* (Boyhood deeds of Fionn) alongside the acquisition of his characteristic thumb of knowledge.[57] His hereditary right to his position, and unjust alienation from it, are explained in greater detail in the early twelfth-century *Fotha Catha Cnucha* (The reason for the Battle of Cnucha).[58] The account of Fionn's extraordinary birth, this story describes the abduction of the daughter of the high king's druid by Fionn's father, Cumhall, and Cumhall's death in the resultant Battle of Cnucha. When the druid subsequently rejects his visibly pregnant daughter, she finds shelter with Cumhall's sister, Bodhmall. Raised by Bodhmall, Fionn goes on to regain his mother's hereditary land (the Hill of Allen in present-day County Kildare, Ireland) and, it can be inferred from other textual sources, his father's position at the head of the *fían*—but this restoration of order does not fully mend the rift opened in the Battle of Cnucha.[59] Echoes of the contention surface throughout the Fenian corpus in the uneasy relationship between members of the *fían* belonging to Clann Mhorna, who fought against Cumhall, and Clann Bhaoiscne, Cumhall's family.[60] Resolution is only achieved with Fionn's death at the hands of a cohort of Luaighne men composed of the sons and grandson of the principal rival for Cumhall's position prior to the Battle of Cnucha.[61] Fully mapped in literature by the twelfth century, the life of Fionn thus forms the scaffolding for a contemporary cycle of Fenian narrative.

An Early Fenian Oral Tradition

A poem attributed to a mid-twelfth-century author suggests that a poet who is master of his craft ought to be able to recite one hundred and twenty Fenian stories.[62] The extant Fenian literary corpus from the seventh to twelfth centuries, thematically diverse as it is, falls far short of this number. Sources have undoubtedly been lost, but even so, Fenian narrative is not well represented in surviving early Irish literature. Much more common are stories and poems relating the deeds of the Ulster hero Cú Chulainn, the godlike Tuatha Dé Danann, or early Irish kings. While the poet's statement may be somewhat hyperbolic, the wide referential field in the early Fenian corpus is suggestive of a more extensive oral tradition than was ever recorded in early literature. Allusions to persons and events not elsewhere discussed abound. We might look, for instance, to the approximately one hundred and seventy names recorded in the eleventh-century list of Fionn's principal men titled *Fiannshruth* (*Fían* lore). Although few of these characters are known from other sources and some were undoubtedly invented to augment the list, others may have been heroes of tales that are now lost, and that may have never found their way onto parchment.[63] The likelihood of such a scenario is suggested by the author's designation of them as those whom "the common people refer to as the *fíana* of Fionn."[64]

Allusions to the popularity of Fenian tales among ordinary Irish men and women strengthen the conviction that alongside the early literary stratum of the tradition, a wealth of oral Fenian material existed. To the *Fiannshruth* author's statement can be added the claim, made in a late eleventh-century onomastic poem, that the entertainment at the *óenach*, 'assembly,' at Carmun included "the *fían* lore of Fionn, an inexhaustible subject."[65] Given the limited number of extant literary texts, we might posit that this inexhaustible store of Fenian narrative would not only have been read aloud from the manuscripts of professional litterateurs, but also performed by entertainers proficient in oral storytelling. Credence is lent to this premise by the later depiction in *Acallam na Senórach* (c. 1225) of an *airfitech*, 'professional musician / poet,' who seeks out an aged member of Fionn's *fían* in order to hear Fenian tales and commit them to memory so that he, in turn, may tell them—perhaps even at an assembly like the one held at Carmun. Joseph Falaky Nagy sees reflected in this episode "the apparent fact that it was the lower orders of oral performers, such as the *airfitech*, who in story and song sustained the Fenian tradition" into the period when Fenian literature was to become eminently fashionable.[66]

Such oral performers would have contributed to a vibrant and multifaceted early oral Fenian tradition that appears to have spanned all levels of Gaelic society. At the same time, their world would have been one in which the oral and written were in constant interaction. The early medieval oral tradition in which they would have participated would have included orally composed folklore texts, as well as texts not originally oral in their composition, but transmitted and refashioned orally, and also written texts read aloud. The manuscripts containing our extant early Fenian literature, in turn, certainly hold, reference, or adapt material also performed orally.[67]

Swapping the literary lens for the oral and panning away from Fionn (the protagonist of most of the early texts) to the subsidiary characters, the scope of the early Fenian tradition comes more clearly into focus. The surviving material about these characters barely scratches the surface of what must have been known, yet it is informative. Specifically, the early references to a handful of younger members of Fionn's *fían* suggest that in the oral sphere, if not in the written, biographical traditions were developing for these heroes just as they were for Fionn. Diarmaid turns up in a limited number of texts, yet there was clearly a body of story about him. He is consistently assigned the patronymic by which he is known at all stages of the tradition (ua Duibhne), and his illicit relationship with Gráinne was known, although no complete early version of the story survives.[68]

Details about Caoilte from before his rise to literary prominence suggest that scribal authors also knew more about him than they placed on parchment. Given his longstanding association with the Fenian tradition, this is hardly surprising. He is listed alongside Fionn as a descendant of Baoiscne as early as the seventh century, and both he and Oisín regularly accompany Fionn throughout the early corpus.[69] By the Middle Irish period he was known as the *fían* leader's nephew, and his unusual birth to Fionn's sister during a foot race with a horse is mentioned twice.[70] Although a version of this story is nowhere to be found in the earliest literature left to us, it is surely no coincidence that Caoilte has always been known for his speed. A depiction of his running ability survives from the Old Irish period, and he is accorded the epithet *coslúath*, 'fleet-footed,' in tenth- and eleventh-century texts.[71]

Defining moments in the lives of Oscar and Oisín are also noted, but rarely elaborated on in the early medieval Fenian corpus. Oscar makes his first literary appearance in the Middle Irish period. His heroic death in *Cath Gabhra* (The Battle of Gabhair), which receives extended treatment in later literature, is succinctly recorded in an eleventh- or twelfth-century poem. The related *dinnshenchas*, 'onomastic lore,' alludes to otherwise undocumented circumstances of his upbringing, identifying the place where his foster mother Glas died while mourning his death. Although his descent from Oisín was known, no early birth tale survives.[72] Nor is an early story of Oisín's birth extant, but there are two marginal quatrains referencing just such an account. Also dated to the eleventh or twelfth century, these record Oisín's extraordinary conception while his mother was in the shape of a deer.[73] The referenced story would have served to explain Oisín's name (a diminutive form of the word *os*, 'deer'[74]), in addition to forming an aspect of his heroic biography. That the quatrains about Oisín's birth survive is particularly fortuitous because they provide the sole premodern evidence for the story. Even given the extensive body of later Fenian literature, no mention of this tale is made between the eleventh-century reference and an eighteenth-century version. Yet Oisín's birth to a mother who can take the form of a deer is well attested in modern Fenian folklore, and it has been suggested that both of the earliest literary accounts derive from oral tradition.[75] In all likelihood, the medieval marginal quatrains give us a rare glimpse of a continuous, predominantly oral tradition about Oisín at a much earlier date than we might otherwise have known.

The Development of the Early Fenian Tradition

While early tales of Fionn and his men appear to have had a primarily oral existence, they were to explode onto the literary scene between the thirteenth and eighteenth centuries, soon becoming the most popular topic in secular Gaelic literature. The preconditions allowing for this rapid increase in Fenian literature form a subject of scholarly inquiry. The negative attitude of the church to the historical fenian practice surely contributed to the scarcity of early medieval texts about *fénnidi*. Monastic scholars would have had ample cause to spurn their unwelcome neighbors' lifestyle. Nor would they have had many practical reasons to laud the deeds of Fenian heroes. Since *fénnidi*—real and fictional—were detached from settled society, their tales could not well serve the historical, genealogical, or religious functions characteristic of literature in Old Irish. (In contrast, the social relevance of Ulster Cycle stories, which relate the legendary history of celebrated dynasties, likely accounts for their much greater prevalence.)[76] Yet by the early thirteenth century, Fenian literature had not only attained scholarly acceptability, it was thriving. To reach that point, it has been posited that over the course of the early Middle Ages, changes were occurring in two interrelated areas: the literati's attitudes to tales about *fían* warriors, and the nature of the tradition itself.

Lack of evidence clouds our view of the earliest stages of the Fenian tradition, but this has not precluded learned speculation. Mid- to late twentieth-century scholarship tended to favor the premise that Fionn originated as a pre-Christian Celtic deity, **Vindos*, and that the extant narrative tradition about him began taking shape in Ireland during the euhemerization process.[77] Doubt has since been cast on the status of **Vindos* as a deity, but Fionn's name and some aspects of his character almost certainly derive from an older body of insular Celtic tradition also echoed in Welsh sources.[78] Among modern scholars, only Dáithí Ó hÓgáin has advanced a specific developmental model. He proposes that a cult to an Irish derivative of **Vindos* flourished in the Boyne Valley,[79] and that Fionn mac Cumhaill emerged as an avatar of this figure localized to the Hill of Allen during a campaign by the occupants of the surrounding territory, the Uí Fhailghe, against Uí Néill expansion in the late fifth to early sixth centuries. According to this theory, the military campaign would have rendered Fionn (<**Vindos*) an attractive figure for development, his presumably already-established martial and wisdom characteristics allowing him to become "a medium of lore through which young men could be trained and prepared for the function which invariably fell to them—that of defending in arms the interests of their sept."[80] After being raised to this iconic position within local Uí Fhailghe ideology, Ó hÓgáin further proposes that Fionn became a symbolic hero for all of Leinster in the course of the sixth century, and thereafter became known as the protector of Ireland.[81]

Ó hÓgáin's detailed, but highly speculative theory should be treated with caution. Only a handful of extant tenth- to thirteenth-century sources link Fionn with the Uí Fhailghe.[82] While these could, in theory, reflect a several-centuries-old tradition in which Fionn was a local Uí Fhailghe hero, the connection could also have been made in conjunction with, or after, the establishment of Fionn's residence at the Hill of Allen (fig. 1) in Fenian narrative. It is unknown when this might have occurred, but no definitive association between Fionn and the Hill of Allen predates the tenth century.[83] What is more, although early Fenian texts are scarce, they are widespread, situating Fionn not just in Uí Fhailghe territory in Leinster, but also within the ambit of the Déise and Corca Laoidhe in Munster, and the Dál nAraidhe in Ulster.[84] Given this broad geographical range, scholars generally agree that it is not now possible to determine precisely where the character originated. The proposed scenario is likely inaccurate—yet the foundational assumptions of the theory

FIGURE 1. Hill of Allen, Co. Kildare, Ireland. (Michael Anderton Photography.)

are perceptive. These are, first, that tales about Fionn could have gained prominence in response to a specific, political need for a hero around whom to rally; and second, that the body of tradition about Fionn was sufficiently malleable to become politicized in new ways as it spread throughout Ireland.

In the early medieval period, Fionn was probably one of several legendary *fénnidi* about whom bodies of story existed. The extant record of these heroes is poor, and some may never have found textual representation. Among Fionn's counterparts, the legendary Connacht *fían* leader Fothadh Canainne looms largest in the surviving corpus, perhaps due to his contention with Fionn. Only scattered references to others remain, such as Fothadh Canainne's killer Oilill mac Eoghain, or Mac Con's killer Fearchess mac Commáin, both from Munster.[85] These references suggest the existence of a potentially large number of such characters whose traditions faded away with the decline of the historical fenian practice, leaving only the corpus of material relating to Fionn for posterity. Fionn's continued appeal may have had to do with the corpus's potential openness to ideological investment, as Ó hÓgáin has highlighted.

We have seen that the earliest extant literary references to Fionn penned by monastic literati depict the hero behaving much as a fenian warrior might be expected to behave, according to the ecclesiastical and legal sources. From the eighth-century story about the altercation with Dearc Corra, we will recall a Fionn whose sphere is wholly separate from society. When this Fionn emerges from the wilderness, it is to lead raiding parties and abduct women. When he appears allied with the deposed high king Mac Con in an eighth- or ninth-century text, the act of violence he commits is more socially acceptable in that it can be legally justified, yet it still appears to correspond with actual fenian activity. In this instance, Fionn avenges the murdered Mac Con, fulfilling the role of a senior *fían* member appointed as a king's champion or enforcer. In the tenth century, however, Fenian material began taking on new meanings, in the process shedding its association with aspects of the practice deemed disreputable by the church, such as raiding and the abduction of women, and becoming more encompassing.

Once culturally accepted outlaws, Fionn and his men progressively came to be seen as the military arm of the law—the *Fianna Éireann*, 'Fenians of Ireland,' still celebrated in Irish popular culture today.[86] This development entails a shift in characterization that is first apparent in their description in the circa tenth-century *Tochmarc Ailbe*: "They were known as *fíana* because they were the fenians and soldiers of the king."[87] *Fíana* has a more specific meaning here than in earlier texts. Whereas any number of disparate *fíana*, 'fenian warrior bands,' might have traversed the earlier narrative landscape, these *fíana* are interconnected, and the node linking them is the king whom they all serve. No longer merely loose collectives of displaced young men, they now constitute a royal defense force—and not for just any king. With *Tochmarc Ailbe*, Fionn and his men come into the ambit of the legendary third-century high king, Cormac mac Airt. Fionn's relationship with Cormac in this text is complicated by his marriages to Cormac's daughters. Indeed, Fionn arguably maintains something like an old-style, marginal *fían* during a period of estrangement preceding his divorce from Gráinne: at that time "anyone among the men of Ireland who was at odds with the king would be in the household of Fionn."[88] But by the eleventh century, the narrative tradition evidences a strong connection between the *fénnid* and the high king. An account of Cormac's allocation of Ireland's defense forces holds that after selecting his soldiers, "he appointed thrice fifty generals [*rígfeindidh*, '*fían* leaders'] over them to maintain his rule and his discipline and his hunting. He gave the headship of all and the grand stewardship of Ireland to Fionn ua Baoiscne."[89] Fionn thus comes to occupy the most powerful military position in the land, commanding 150 *fían*-like companies charged with the protection of all of Ireland. Needless to say, this is far removed from the enforcement position he once held under Mac Con, in which he had the limited responsibility of exacting legal vengeance for a specific crime. The prominent role he is accorded under the high kingship of Ireland is a tenth- to eleventh-century innovation.

Fionn's association with Cormac mac Airt comes at a time when the literati's interests—and indeed their language—were noticeably shifting. The Middle Irish literary corpus (c. 900–1200) reflects a monastic scholarly community actively seeking to record knowledge that was formerly the purview of the pre-Christian learned classes and the broader oral tradition. Their project was both documentary and synchronistic, reworking stories hitherto disregarded in literary contexts and fitting them together to form something of a national record of the Irish people. While dynastic concerns still warranted attention, this expanded frame also brought place into focus. The wide-roaming Fianna feature time and again in the emergent corpus of *dinnshenchas*.[90] In the place name origin stories we learn numerous events in the lives of major and minor Fenian characters for the first time. The extant early accounts of Fionn's birth and death also date to this period, and some of this is reflected in the *dinnshenchas*.[91] It is alongside and in conjunction with this growing body of Middle Irish Fenian literature that Fionn's association with Cormac mac Airt emerges.

Cormac loomed large in Uí Néill propagandist literature of the Old Irish period, when branches of that kindred held sway in much of the northern half of the island. Although their power began to wane by the late tenth century, the legendary king found a place in the new historical schema, coming to symbolize pan-Irish, rather than specifically Uí Néill, might. Having long been acclaimed for his supposed providential rule over all of Ireland, Cormac continued to be upheld as a paragon of kingship—the exemplar of *fir flathemon*, 'the king's justice.'[92] In the newly synchronized narrative, however, he was joined by the Fianna, whose duty was to maintain order in this golden age. Thus, the eleventh-century *Fiannshruth* relates that when *cain Cormaic*, 'Cormac's law,' extended throughout Ireland, Fionn was his right-hand man, entrusted with a large, stratified defense force: "Fionn mac Cumhaill was captain of the household to Cormac and head of his mercenaries and hired soldiers and the rest of his kerne."[93]

That this important development in Fenian tradition resulted from a deliberate consolidation of the sources about Ireland's history is not in question, but the motivation for the combination is worth investigating. The idea that Fionn might be an appropriate companion for the paragon of kingly justice would seem to run counter to the negative portrayal of fenian warriors in earlier writings—but times had changed. The dearth of recorded encounters after the last annalistic reference to *fíana* in the ninth century suggests the practice was then nearly defunct. When safely relegated to the past and no longer reflective of an actual societal threat, fictional *féinnidi* appear to have become as acceptable to Irish monastic scholars as Sir Walter Scott's Jacobites were to the nineteenth-century British establishment.[94] Yet this alone does not account for Fionn's association with Cormac mac Airt.

If we shift our focus to contemporary military practices, it becomes apparent that changes in defensive strategy rendered Cormac and the newly legitimized character of Fionn an ideal match. Historians note a growing tendency among kings of the period to employ standing armies and hire mercenaries.[95] By bringing Fionn under Cormac mac Airt's sway and placing him in charge of vast armies in place of a simple *fían*, the stories of both Cormac and Fionn were updated to reflect contemporary practices. Such a modernization could conceivably have enabled the traditions to remain relevant to the "rising class of landless nobles in military service to kings" by representing their "ideals and aspirations."[96] The widespread body of early Fenian narrative was sufficiently malleable to accommodate such a shift, while traditions about other, more geographically delimited characters might not have been.[97] This factor, combined with the likely popularity of Fenian material in the oral tradition, would have made Fionn well suited for the role of leader of the high king's military forces. In taking it on, Fionn shed the negative overtones of the historical fenian practice and adopted the integrity of Cormac. No longer a local hero, in these and later texts Fionn features as the national protector of Ireland, defending against external invasion and symbolically, if not explicitly, upholding the peace and justice of Cormac's rule.

The Fianna's enduring appeal springs from their ability to adapt to changing social structures and value systems, yet remain familiar. Although the Fionn of the earliest literature undoubtedly shares more in common with the *féinnidi* of old than his twelfth-century counterpart does, aspects of Fenian characterization bridge the centuries. He and his men are consistently depicted as martial heroes who traverse the wilderness landscape of the social margins. They subsist by hunting, and distinguish themselves with great feats against powerful adversaries, both human and otherworldly. Fionn, in particular, maintains a close connection to the supernatural realm, whence different accounts say he acquired his distinctive thumb of knowledge. But gifted as he is, this lifelong *fénnid* is repeatedly depicted as a problematic lover for whom transient relationships with women are the norm. His son Oisín descends from one such relationship. That Fionn has a son, and in time, a grandson, underscores a persistent issue that early medieval literati struggled to address—Fionn's advancing age. While some sources shroud the aging martial hero's physical condition in ambiguity, others offer the final resolution of a valiant death.

The death tales emerged during a period of sustained growth of the Fenian literary corpus, which occurred in conjunction with a Middle Irish trend toward historical consolidation. Surviving Fenian narrative from this time appears to draw broadly from literary sources and a thriving oral tradition. As the personal histories of Fionn and, to a lesser extent, members of his family found their way onto the manuscript page, new facets of the tradition took shape that would themselves become established tropes. The internal conflict between Fionn's own Clann Bhaoiscne and the competitive Clann Mhorna, for instance, came to prominence in Middle Irish texts detailing the beginning and end of the celebrated *fían* leader's life. The most fully developed character in extant early sources, and the fulcrum of a burgeoning narrative cycle, Fionn also underwent a shift in portrayal. From a comparatively humble position, tenth-century literati brought him into the ambit of high king Cormac mac Airt and elevated him to the command of a national defense force. In doing so, they reinvigorated the Fianna. Now reflective of a contemporary standing army, rather than the all-but-forgotten historical *fénnidi*, and established as the champions of a unified, golden-age Ireland, their popularity mounted in later Middle Irish literature. On the cusp of yet another moment of cultural shift, the Fenian tradition had revealed itself as an ideal vehicle for Gaelic cultural expression, the Fianna's easy adaptability and familiar heroism rendering them eminently capable of meeting the creative needs of coming eras.

2

Saint Patrick and the Pagans

THE FIANNA WERE POISED to take their place as the Gaelic world's martial heroes par excellence by the mid-1100s, having displayed a remarkable ability to adapt to societal change over the course of the early medieval period. Momentous new challenges were on the horizon, however, to which they would need to respond if they were to continue their expansionary crusade across the literary landscape. The effects of the Anglo-Norman invasion, which began in 1169 and heralded the long colonization of Ireland, reverberated across every aspect of Gaelic life in subsequent decades (and centuries, as later chapters will explore). Nearly simultaneously, Irish monasteries—the centers of literary production—began facing intense pressure to conform to renewed ideals imported from the European continent. To accommodate the social, cultural, and political impact of these events on the creators and consumers of Fenian narrative, the scope of the tradition would broaden, yet again, in form, subject, and application. In what follows, we shall briefly examine the structural framework that enables the tradition's seemingly perpetual expansion, before embarking upon our primary investigation of the critical Fenian literary developments of the decades on either side of the turn of the thirteenth century. A significant transitional period, it is at this point that we witness the growing literary presence of the poetic lay, which brings the Fianna into direct conversation with Christianity and sets the stage for *Acallam na Senórach* (The dialogue of the elders). One of the most celebrated Fenian compositions and the longest extant early medieval Gaelic text, the *Acallam* is both atypical of the tradition as a whole, and immensely socially relevant.

A Cycle, a Saint, and a Swelling Literary Tradition

Stories about the hero Fionn mac Cumhaill accrued over the first six centuries of Irish literary history, as we have seen. From a minimal early textual record, the literary presence of Fionn and his Fianna expanded more rapidly in the tenth to twelfth centuries, when literati documented traditions about Fionn's birth and death and elevated him from a simple *fían*-leader to the command of Ireland's national defense force. I have referred in passing to the body of Fenian narrative that took shape around this biographical framework as a *cycle*.

The term 'cycle' has been used in different ways since its nineteenth-century emergence as a literary-critical concept. The way I employ the term, and the way many Celticists have historically employed it, aligns with Erich Poppe's description of an "immanent cycle"—that is, an interrelated body of narrative that authors and audiences understand implicitly to cohere.[1] As Poppe explains, coherence among stories in a cycle is maintained by "their setting at a particular time and the overlap of their narrative personnel and geographical focus." Moreover, they "ideally cluster around a common, fixed point of reference," in other words the central hero(es) of the cycle.[2] The Fenian cycle began to develop around the biography of Fionn, and as it grew, its point of reference expanded to incorporate the principal members of Fionn's *fían*, sometimes called the *gnáthfhiann*, 'standing *fían*.'[3] These include several characters with whom we are already familiar—Oisín, Oscar, Caoilte, Diarmaid—and others whose rise to prominence is observable in the late medieval period. This central cast of heroes traverses an Irish and, as we will see in subsequent chapters, Scottish wilderness landscape, and in the stories we have thus far encountered, shares a third-century temporal setting. These dramatis personae, locus, and tempus are the fundamental components of the Fenian heroic world—or, to draw a more timely comparison, the Fenian narrative universe, for the cycle rivals the modern Marvel and DC 'universes' for complexity and productivity, and certainly surpasses them in longevity.[4]

Moving beyond the fundamentals, structural elements further serve to maintain unity in a large and complex narrative cycle. Thematic iteration is helpful for sustaining intertextual cohesion; several persistent Fenian themes came to light in the previous chapter, and others will soon emerge, as we will see in chapter 3. Also important is the establishment of fixed events that individual texts can cross-reference, helping audiences better locate stories within the loose timeline of the cycle.[5] Some of the coalescing details of Fionn's biography are fixed events, including Fionn's conception and the subsequent

Cath Cnucha, 'Battle of Cnucha,' in which the recurrent dynastic conflict between Clann Mhorna and Clann Bhaoiscne is rooted; Fionn's assumption of control of the Fianna under high king Cormac mac Airt, by which position he is commonly known; and *Cath Gabhra*, 'the Battle of Gabhair,' the scene not just of Oscar's death, as noted in chapter 1, but also of the Fianna's ultimate defeat.[6] The standardization of these events would have helped the cycle cohere, thereby promoting its growth. However, the explosion of Fenian narrative in the period under discussion in this chapter was likely aided most by the emergence of another fixed event: the encounter between members of the Fianna and Saint Patrick, the widely reputed bearer of Christianity to Ireland.

As the Fenian cycle gained popularity over the course of the Middle Irish period, it might have seemed only natural that the foremost warriors of the Gael, who were partnered with Ireland's greatest high king as early as the tenth century, should also have encountered the island's most venerated cleric. And just as the Fianna's connection with Cormac mac Airt corresponded with a shift in characterization, Saint Patrick's integration into the cycle occasioned change. This development was significant for a few reasons. First, it necessitated an extension of the Fenian timeline, since Saint Patrick was believed to have arrived in Ireland in the year 432, approximately 150 years after Fionn's recorded death in the annals.[7] Second, whereas Fionn generally took center stage in the early literature, other characters move to the forefront by necessity in this emergent postmortem strand of Fenian narrative. (As we shall see, however, the activities of Fionn and other deceased members of the Fianna are by no means neglected.) And third, unlike most of the literature we have explored thus far, the accounts involving the saint consist largely of first-person narrative verse.

The premise of the new Christian-era strand of the cycle is this: one or more exceptionally long-lived Fenian warriors—usually Oisín or Caoilte or both—encounters Saint Patrick on his circuit to convert Ireland, and an interaction ensues in which the pagan and Christian parties share their unique worldviews. The dialogue format reflects the influence of hagiological literature, in which saints are regularly depicted querying potential pagan converts.[8] The earliest extant texts in this strand are Middle Irish poems that convey the Fenian ancients' recollections of their glory days in response, either explicitly or implicitly, to Saint Patrick's inquiries. Thus, the late eleventh- or early twelfth-century poem beginning *Óenach indiu luid in rí* ("Today the king went to a fair") preserved in the Book of Leinster, has Oisín, now elderly and blind, relate the peculiar events that transpired when he, Fionn, and Caoilte unwittingly sought hospitality in an unfriendly otherworldly dwelling after an impromptu horse race carried them far from their comrades. The narrative unfolds over fifty-four quatrains that trace the sequence of events in detail, from the exuberance of the race, to their hosts' increasing hostility, to the heroes' safe return to their wonted wilderness at daybreak.[9] At no point is the story's silent clerical listener named, yet his identity would have been self-evident to an audience familiar with the cycle's most recently established fixed event.[10]

Chronological investigation and genre classification of such narrative verse has evolved over time. Gerard Murphy, the most prolific twentieth-century editor of the Fenian poetic corpus, posited that the genesis of the form was linked with the twelfth-century rise in narrative balladry across Western Europe, and he and others referred to such poems as Fenian 'ballads.'[11] However, more recent analysis suggests that some of the extant poems date to the eleventh or perhaps even the late tenth century, concurrent with the earliest known non-Fenian narrative poetry in Gaelic and predating European balladry.[12] The Fenian poems also differ topically from ballads in that they invariably celebrate a heroic past, while ballads need not be heroic and might even look to a speculative future. In fact, close examination of both corpuses shows Fenian narrative poetry to have been largely resistant to influence from European balladry, which is now seen as a more recently imported genre.[13] To allay confusion, many scholars today refer to these poems as *laoithe*, 'lays,' a term often accorded them not only by scribes, but also by modern oral tradition bearers.[14]

Like so much of the early material in the cycle, the Fenian lays may have emerged from an older, primarily oral tradition. Indeed, it is plausible that they had precursors among the repertoires of the lower poetic grades, who would have specialized in more populist material than the high-ranking poets known as *filid* (modern Irish *filí*). But poetic practices were changing over the course of the Middle Irish period, when the *filid* are known to have adopted meters and perhaps also topics from their lower-status counterparts.[15] Fenian material is likely to have proven attractive, given the revitalization of the Fianna then taking place. (As we will recall, this is when Fionn transitioned from a simple *fían* leader to the commander of a national defense force, and the Fenian literary corpus began to expand.) Fenian lays could well have been among the popular poetic material the *filid* assimilated, and if so, it is likely that they revised and augmented them in accordance with their scholarly profession.[16] Joseph Flahive has observed that some of the earliest texts appear more learned than later lays, incorporating "lessons in history."[17] Take, for instance, the mid-twelfth-century *Laoidh Scéith Fhinn* (The lay of Fionn's shield), in which Caoilte (or Oisín, depending on the version) tells the tale of the construction, lineage, and eventual destruction of Fionn's shield, providing something of a narrative genealogy for the object. The poem finishes with an invocation of God and Mary, affirming its purported author's now-Christian milieu.[18] With regard to style, this and other early lays do not depart significantly from non-Fenian poetry of the time, although there is a preference for "vigorously straightforward composition" over academic esotericism in the lays, as befits the entertaining social function of narrative verse.[19]

The new strand of the cycle focusing on the Fenian ancients' dialogue with Ireland's patron saint proved remarkably generative. Twelfth-century lays survive in greater numbers than lays from the century or so prior, and in these, interwoven with reflections upon the days of yore, are descriptions of the heroes' interactions with the new religion. In the lay beginning *Ochtur táncamar anúas* ("We eight descended"), for example, Oisín recounts the conversion of eight surviving Fianna, and in *A bhen dén folcadh mo chinn* ("Woman, bathe my head"), after recalling a hunting excursion and enumerating Fionn's now-hidden treasures, he muses about his own baptism by Saint Patrick.[20] By the end of the century, the corpus concerning the exchange between cleric and hero had clearly become large and broad-ranging, as reflected in a scribal reference to the "agallaim éccsamail ingantaigh" ("diverse and wondrous dialogue") between Caoilte and Saint Patrick.[21] This growth crested in one of the most striking developments not just in this strand, but in the cycle as a whole, with the composition in the early thirteenth century of a prosimetrum (i.e., prose intermingled with verse) account of over eight thousand manuscript lines titled *Acallam na Senórach* (fig. 2).[22]

The longest extant medieval Irish text, the *Acallam* traces the remaining Fianna's interactions with Saint Patrick over the course of his peregrination throughout Ireland. The initial encounter expands upon conversion scenes already outlined in the lays. Whereas eight members of the Fianna were said to have survived in *Ochtur táncamar anúas*, here Caoilte and Oisín are accompanied by a retinue of roughly twice that number.[23] Saint Patrick's parallel priestly entourage is overcome with "gráin 7 egla," "horror and fear," at first sight of them, for they are quite literally larger-than-life relics of a former age of heroes: we are told that "the tallest of the clerics only came to the waist or the shoulder of any of them when they were sitting down."[24] A sprinkling of holy water by the saint banishes the priests' fear, however, along with a thousand legions of demons. Once introductions have been made, a water source located, and the party shown appropriate hospitality, Caoilte and company

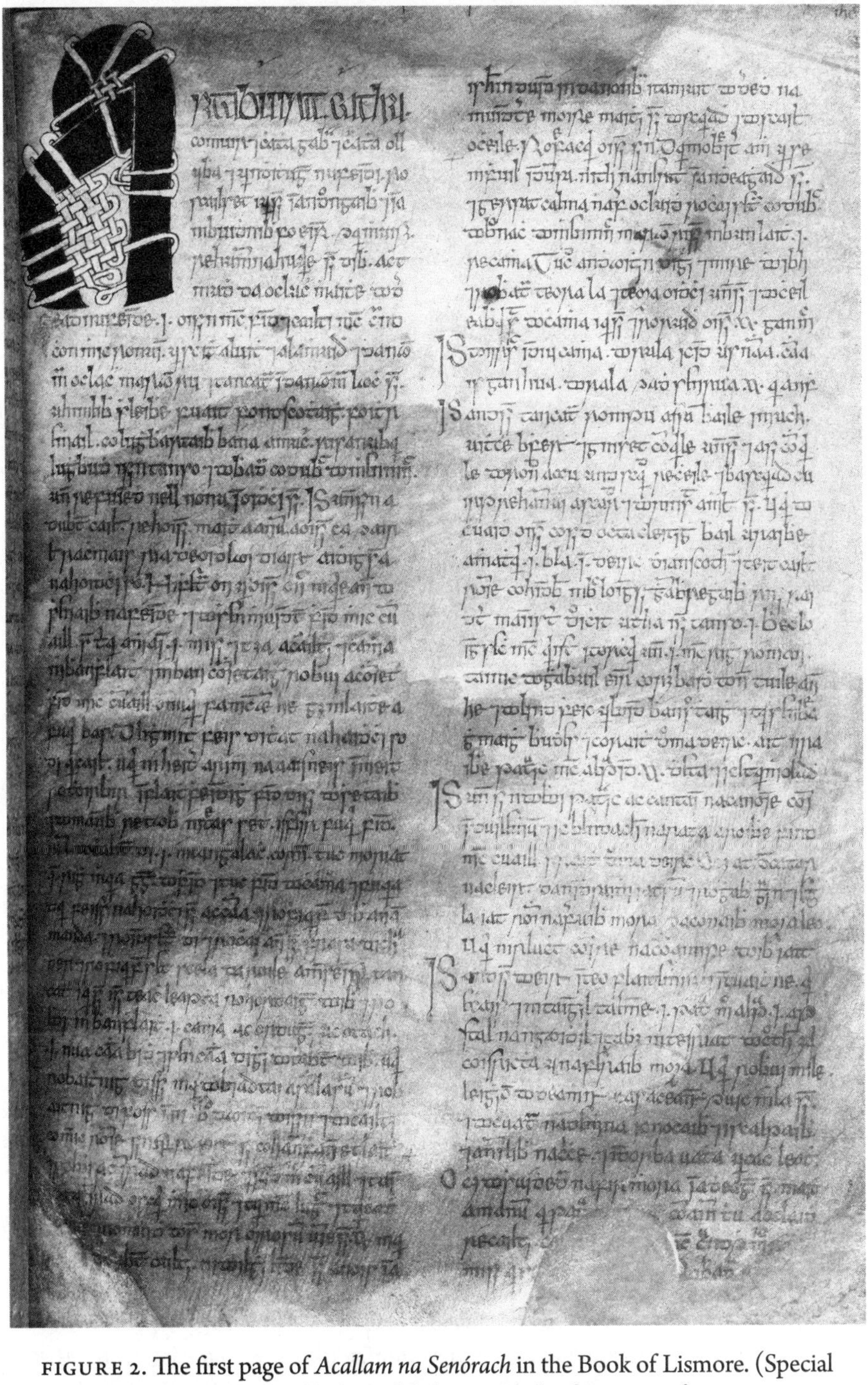

FIGURE 2. The first page of *Acallam na Senórach* in the Book of Lismore. (Special Collections, University College Cork Library, Book of Lismore, f. 201r. By permission of University College Cork and Irish Script on Screen, School of Celtic Studies, DIAS.)

submit to baptism, just as Oisín did in earlier lore.[25] They then set out on their journey, and at various locations, Caoilte relates tales of the powerful foes encountered and adventures undertaken in that region by the Fianna. Saint Patrick's reaction to these in-tales is noteworthy. After receiving a directive from his guardian angels to record the elderly warriors' knowledge "on poets' tablets, in learned language," his instruction to his scribe to write down the stories becomes a constant refrain. The reason for their preservation, as decreed by the heavenly host, is simply that "the masses and the nobility of later times would enjoy listening to those stories."[26]

Perhaps it was the angelic absolution in the *Acallam* that ultimately lent the Fenian cycle respectability among the writers of medieval manuscripts, as Kim McCone once suggested—although upon closer inspection, it may be more accurate to view this proclaimed acceptance as a reflection of an already-burgeoning esteem.[27] In any event, the *Acallam* propelled our heroes into the literary limelight. Its value to literati and their patrons is evident not only in its five extant manuscript witnesses, but also in the emergence of three alternate recensions.[28] The first of these, known as the *Acallam Bec* (Little dialogue), is approximately contemporaneous, and although considerably shorter, it follows *Acallam na Senórach* in making Caoilte its heroic interlocutor. The second, the fourteenth- or fifteenth-century Early Modern Gaelic *Agallamh na Seanórach*, is a greatly expanded version that differs from its predecessors, but accords with many of the early lays, in having Oisín as its principal discussant rather than Caoilte.[29] The third, known as the *Agallamh Nua* (New dialogue), is an abridged adaptation found in late seventeenth- to nineteenth-century manuscripts in which Caoilte is again the interlocutor.[30] The scholarly popularity of these lengthy prosimetrum texts was almost certainly entwined with a broader public interest in the shorter, more easily transmissible lays, each medium supporting the other. This is apparent from the rapidly increasing number of lays recorded in Irish and Scottish manuscripts in the late medieval and early modern period. (Indeed, a subset of lays that began to be grouped together in Irish manuscripts from perhaps the early eighteenth century even came to be known as *Agallamh Oisín agus Phádraig* [The dialogue between Oisín and Patrick].) Because the Patrician frame narrative—whether explicit, as in the recensions of the *Acallam*, or implicit, as in many of the lays—allowed for near-endless expansion, authors could provide a constant supply of new Fenian dialogue material. And judging by the written record, audiences were clamoring for it, be they elites or commoners—just as the angels predicted.

The Anomalous *Acallam*

Acallam na Senórach is both extremely important to the study of Fionn and the Fianna and unreliably representative of the Fenian cycle. It has received the most academic attention of any text within the emergent dialogue strand of the tradition, due initially to its unprecedented length and diverse content, and latterly to its high literary merit. Because it incorporates or adapts numerous preexisting compositions, including lays, many early critics chiefly regarded it as an impressive medieval compendium of lore about the Fianna.[31] However, more recent scholarship has established that the unknown author's aim was not purely or even primarily to anthologize the tradition for the entertainment of audiences to come, whatever he had his angelic host proclaim. In fact, the *Acallam* could well be considered a socially and politically motivated creative engagement with the Fenian narrative tradition. In the following discussion, we shall see in the text not only reflections of the complex historical period in which it emerged—the likes of which might be found in any contemporaneous composition—but also embedded critical commentary on the author's unique cultural moment, arguably from a specific local perspective, and often reliant upon the modification of accepted Fenian tropes and tales, or the invention of new ones.

Few moments in Irish history are marked by tranquility, but the one in which the *Acallam* emerged would have been particularly fraught for our author. Writing circa 1225, mere decades after the centuries-long conquest and colonization of Ireland began in 1169, he would have witnessed rapid change in many regions of the island over the course of his lifetime.[32] The balance of power in large swathes of the east and south, in particular, would have shifted progressively toward Cambro- and Anglo-Norman lords. Hoping to maximize the economic potential of their newly granted territories, these lords' interest was piqued by native monastic settlements, which had expanded considerably from the simple structures established centuries prior in the interstitial regions historical *fíana* once traversed. Now societal hubs, Irish monasteries presented opportunities for both trade and plunder, and so the early generations of colonial lords situated their alien castles in proximity to them, and sometimes seized them. Proceeding to develop and fortify their regions, these lords founded borough towns and cleared agricultural land for cultivation by their tenantry, who included native Gaels and immigrant laborers. In so doing, they disrupted local political systems and economic patterns and greatly accelerated the deforestation of the storied Fenian wilderness.[33]

This interruption of normative patterns of land occupation and use may well have influenced one of the most notable features of the text—its intense onomastic focus. In areas "where the landscape was transformed into clearly defined landholdings," Diarmuid Ó Murchadha and Kevin Murray explain, "the very fabric of Gaelic-style names was rudely shattered."[34] In his treatment of placenames, our author adapts preexisting *dinnshenchas* ('onomastic lore') accounts and composes new ones using the established formulae of that genre to subtly address his colonial context. The typical place name query that opens most *dinnshenchas* texts fits neatly into the dialogue structure of the *Acallam*, as do the subsequent narratives about the person or utterance for which a place is called, the offering of complementary or alternative etymologies, and the formulaic closure: 'whence such-and-such place is named.'[35] Thus, on one occasion Caoilte is asked, "why is this place called Fert Fiadmoir ['the grave of Fiadhmór'], and why is this hill to the west called Cnoc in Chircaill ['the hill of Circall'], and why is the hill next to it called Cnoc in Chongna ['the hill of Congna']," to which he responds with the story of the Fianna's beheading of three enemy warriors, closing the lengthy episode with a typical summation: "Those three heads were placed on these three hills, whence they are named."[36] While the *Acallam* borrows conventions from the *dinnshenchas* genre, however, onomastic lore typically has an impersonal, academic tone; it lacks the poignancy of the deep sorrow that Caoilte expresses in reaction to many of the changes he perceives in the land and its customs. From the aforementioned hills, for instance, the party proceeds to northern Connacht where the following exchange takes place:

> Then the hosts came to Breicslíab ['speckled mountain'], now called Slíab Formaíle ['the bare-topped mountain'] in Connacht, and to Suide Finn ['Fionn's seat'] on the summit of the mountain, and as they sat there tears fell heavily and flowed across Caoilte's cheeks, observing the place where Fionn mac Cumhaill used to sit. "And what causes you to weep, my dear Caoilte," said the King of Connacht, "and is it seeing the place where Fionn used to sit and Formaíle of the Fianna?" "It is indeed," said Caoilte, "for this mountain was the favourite hunting place of the standing *fían*, and Loch na nEillted ['the lake of the does'], now called Loch Formaíle, and Clúain na Damraide ['the meadow of the stags'], now called Cell Tulach [Kiltullagh, i.e., 'the church of hills'], and the abode of Conán Maol, son of Morna, and Ros na hEchraide ['the forest of the horse team'], now called Inn Airm [Arm, i.e., 'the place'], where there was a throng of horses of the Fianna,

> and the fortress of Saltrán Sálfhada ['long-heeled Saltrán,' once a Fenian *gilla*, 'serving boy'], now called Cell Chaímín [Kilkeevin, i.e., 'the church of Saint Caoimhín (Kevin)'] on the [River] Suck, and Móin na Fostada ['the bog of the hindering'], now called Móin in Tóchair Chonneda ['the bog of the causeway of Conned'], and Carraic ind Fhomorach ['the rock of the Fomorian'], now called Dún Mór [Dunmore, i.e., 'great fortress']."[37]

Here and elsewhere in the text, Caoilte surveys a landscape utterly transformed and grieves for a lost way of life. The party occupies a prominence from which Fionn used to oversee the hunt, in a region where every lake and meadow's significance to such Fenian endeavors was encoded in its name—designations that have been overwritten in a process of geographical redefinition not unlike what was happening in the author's own time. From this prominence, too, in addition to managing the hunt, Fionn would have been capable of scanning the countryside the Fianna kept secure, for our heroes frequently glimpse approaching adversaries from their hunting hills. In another of Caoilte's tales featuring the minor character Saltrán Sálfhada, the Fianna spot a gigantic woman seeking their aid from atop a similar mound in Munster—Saltrán is called upon to serve her water—and soon afterward they observe her enormous male pursuer, whom they wound and drive off to sea.[38] Other accounts of past glories have the Fenian hunting party intercept and vanquish foreign invaders, as in the story of the sons of the king of Lochlann (Scandinavia) who traverse the Irish Sea with hostile battalions, only to be soundly defeated at Rudraige (Dundrum Bay) in Ulster.[39] But as Caoilte, gazing out from Fionn's mountaintop vantage point, is painfully aware, the Fianna's watch has ended. Change has come from across the redefined moors and causeways, and nothing is as it was. It is not difficult to perceive in such passages the refracted anxieties of an era of conquest and colonization.

The landscape over which Caoilte casts his mournful eye is Patrician rather than post-conquest, of course, and looking beyond our interlocutor's recurrent melancholia, critics have observed a lack of overt references to the author's contemporary milieu.[40] Plausible veiled allusions to Anglo-Norman sites and personages can be identified, however, which further illuminate the text's colonial undertones. As Caoilte regards the territory surrounding Suide Finn, it is significant that his gaze settles at last upon Dún Mór, the mid-twelfth-century center of power of the king of Connacht and high king of Ireland Toirdhealbhach Úa Conchobhair, and subsequently the site of a castle erected by the de Bermingham lords during Richard de Burgh's conquest of Connacht, which began around the time of writing or shortly thereafter.[41] The recognition of shifting authority may extend beyond the text's temporal setting there, as it almost certainly does when the itinerant company is in the vicinity of Tulach na Féinne ('the assembly mound of the Fianna')—renamed Árd Pátraic (Ardpatrick)—near Cenn Abrat Sléibe Cáin (likely Suide Finn, i.e., Seefin Mountain) in the Ballyhoura Mountains of central Munster.[42] Ardpatrick had long been recognized as a significant Patrician monastic site,[43] and Richard de Burgh's father William had established a castle in its environs in 1198.[44] When Caoilte, looking out from Cenn Abrat, draws attention to a fortress and settlement (*dunad 7 degbhaile*) previously unbeknownst to him, his remark calls to mind not only the nearby Anglo-Norman stronghold, but also the ongoing disruption of the de Burgh lordship, as Anne Connon has shown.[45] In the *Acallam*, the fortress is found to belong to two sons of the local king of Fermoy who have abandoned their wives for women from elsewhere. The wives' quandary is easily resolved when Caoilte proffers a Fenian love charm to recapture their wayward husbands' attention from the unwelcome outsiders.[46] In the author's own time, there could be no similarly expedient reversal of the incursion of foreign barons like the de Burghs on the territory of former Irish kings. Contemporary tensions are reflected in such subtle gestures toward colonial lordship.

Caoilte reckons with conversion-era cultural change over the course of the narrative, oscillating between lament for what has been lost and veneration for the bringer of Christianity. In his interactions with Saint Patrick, whose foreign origins were well attested, some see an aspirational blueprint for Anglo-Norman and Gaelic relations in post-conquest Ireland. The stark difference between the way the Fenian-Patrician relationship is constructed in the *Acallam* and the roughly contemporaneous *Acallam Bec* lends considerable support to this premise. As Kristen Mills has demonstrated, the *Acallam* brings the Fenian ancients and the newly arrived clerical cohort to a near-immediate accord that supersedes their vast differences: Caoilte and his men approach the saint and his disciples confidently, engage them in amicable conversation, and accept baptism readily and without trepidation.[47] Conversely, the *Acallam Bec* has our heroes flee the priestly coterie, whose alien chanting and "aighthe bana attruagha bannda" ("pale, pitiful, womanly faces") disconcert them. Unlike in the *Acallam*, where Caoilte and company never utter a harsh word about Saint Patrick, in the *Acallam Bec* the initial consensus is that "muna marbtar iat eireochait toraind" ("if they are not killed, they will rise over us"). Only two of the Fianna—Caoilte and a lone follower—ultimately undergo baptism, and this is only accomplished by stealth, for the saint initiates the ritual as they sleep.[48] The *Acallam Bec* account reflects a wariness of foreigners that would surely have been comprehensible to a thirteenth-century audience who were themselves experiencing colonization. The *Acallam*, on the other hand, might be seen as modeling a mode of interaction for the benefit of Gael and settler alike.

At the heart of the Fenian-Patrician relationship in the *Acallam* is not simple capitulation on the Fianna's part to inevitable, externally driven cultural transformation, but rather a process of transculturation in which both parties experience change. Although Caoilte frequently longs for the days of yore, his extended engagement with the saint leads him to develop broader knowledge of the new religion than the act of baptism alone could convey, such that when, toward the end of his travels, he is offered the restoration of his youthful physique in the pagan otherworld, he declines: "It would be lamentable . . . were I to take a magical form. I will not take any form but that which my Maker, my Creator, the glorious, true God gave me, with the knowledge of belief and piety from the Adze-head [Saint Patrick], he who has come into Ireland." His choice is depicted not as an abandonment of Fenian mores, but rather as an integration of Christian and traditional values, as his otherworldly hosts' response affirms: "That is the word of a true soldier and a true warrior!"[49] The text suggests that although there can be no winding back of the clock—no return to a heroic golden age—Fenian cultural heritage is not incompatible with Christianity. The apostle to the Irish exhibits similar adaptive traits, as Amy Mulligan has established. Whilst Caoilte and the Fianna receive religious instruction from Saint Patrick, the latter actively seeks Fenian wisdom about each place along his missionary journey and, as we have seen, he endeavors to have this knowledge preserved. In the process, he gains a deeper understanding of the land, its people, and their customs, and develops a new, more integrative means of expression. Just as Caoilte comes to emulate Patrician preaching, the saint assimilates the native mode of encoding heroic deeds in the Gaelic historical record, producing poetic quatrains about his own banishment of demons and creation of holy wells with as much skill as any Fenian.[50] The Christian era is thus depicted as an adaptive continuation rather than an overwriting of Irish culture. That the historical Saint Patrick was a Briton adds further nuance to his character's sincere interest in Irish history, as Mulligan reminds us, for his proto-Welsh roots might be seen to parallel those of many colonists.[51] As an influential foreigner who "consults Irish tradition-bearers and uses his powers and technologies to support Irish literature and culture" on one hand, and learns to express himself in a traditional Gaelic mode on the other, Ireland's patron saint can be read as an exemplary 'good' settler, exhibiting respect for and adaptability to native cultural practices.[52]

The promotion of integrative settlement practices takes on further significance when it is borne in mind that *Acallam na Senórach* almost certainly emerged from a monastic scriptorium. It is, in fact, one of the last medieval Irish texts of a secular nature for which this is true. The specific location of composition is thought to have been among a network of influential native Augustinian foundations in Connacht.[53] The Augustinian order gained popularity in Ireland in the early twelfth century during the beginning of a prolonged monastic reform movement.[54] By the early thirteenth century, indigenous reformed monasteries would have been competing for patronage with newer Anglo-Norman foundations of the same orders, which appropriated monastic reform as another front in the conquest. Maintaining an uncompromisingly negative attitude toward Gaelic language and culture, these communities must have exacerbated already mounting pressure within the movement to excise secular Gaelic scholarship from religious centers of learning.[55] The contention over which sorts of intellectual activity the church should support is one of the most pivotal issues echoed in the *Acallam*, and undoubtedly the primary motivation behind the angelic affirmation of the value of Fenian lore, "even though," as Saint Patrick states, "our religious life is being disrupted and our prayers neglected" in order to record Caoilte's recollections.[56] The *Acallam* pushes back against the notion that religious literati should pay no heed to Ireland's storied past, staking a claim for the propriety of secular literature even in reformed monastic scriptoria, and implying that church patrons, whether native or settled, should emulate the saint in valuing and supporting such heritage projects.

The Patrician dialogue was an ideal form through which to take a stand, given its close relationship with hagiological literature—a prime stock-in-trade of Augustinian literati at the time.[57] Our author had only to adapt his source material to accord with the shifting intellectual priorities of his monastic milieu. He manipulated the tradition to different ends than his predecessors a few centuries earlier when they brought the Fianna into line with political literature about Cormac mac Airt, but the revisionist practice was a familiar one. If the *Acallam* portrays Saint Patrick as the 'good' settler in response to colonial pressure, the Fianna here become models of the "benevolent pagan" whose salvation was optimistically countenanced in contemporary theology, and Fenian narrative, in this guise, begins to look acceptably proto-Christian.[58] Potentially unsavory characteristics are pushed safely out of the frame in

Caoilte's depiction, and we learn that the Fianna held themselves to a moral code not entirely in keeping with their *personae* in other texts. When Saint Patrick asks what has sustained the survivors for so long, Caoilte avers: "the truth in our hearts, the strength of our arms, and the constancy of our tongues."[59] In the same exchange, the Fenian ancient proclaims Fionn, his hallowed leader, to have been so generous that:

> If the russet leaves were gold,
> Which the forest sheds,
> If the bright wave was silver,
> Fionn would give it [all] away.[60]

The laudable traits of the Fianna's pagan morality are also on display in a passage detailing Fionn's advice to his grandson Mac Lughach, in which Caoilte has Fionn recommend peaceable and polite behavior, not just toward other noblemen, but also to women, household servants, holy men, men of art, and *daescarshlúagh* ('common people'). In addition, the *fían*-leader cautions against lying, gossip, boastfulness, drunkenness, and miserliness.[61] And as Fionn counselled, so, apparently, did his men behave. According to Caoilte,

> I know of no fault with Fionn's *fíana*,
> by the King above my head,
> except, oh God who came to earth,
> that they did not adore the Son.[62]

This single fault is mediated by accounts of Fionn's inspired knowledge of the Christian God's existence, including information gleaned from his extraordinary thumb about the coming of several saints;[63] by the baptism of the surviving Fianna; and ultimately by the angels' directive.

In ensuring that the depiction of the Fenian lifestyle accorded with thirteenth-century Augustinian morality, our clerical author also had to contend with the endemic internal conflict of Fenian Ireland. The considerable degree to which Caoilte's accounts were crafted to present the legendary past in a favorable light is perhaps most apparent from this perspective. In other texts, tensions frequently erupt among factions of the *gnáthfhiann* and violent confrontations take place with denizens of an often-hostile otherworld. Contention between Clann Mhorna and Clann Bhaoiscne also appears in the *Acallam*, but here it is downplayed. For instance, the story of Fionn's youth references the Battle of Cnucha, but elides both the cause of the battle and its relevance to the hereditary feud, concentrating instead on Clann Mhorna's deference to Fionn when he assumes the leadership of the Fianna.[64] The scattered references to internal conflict under Fionn's leadership that appear elsewhere in the text tend to function not as dramatic foci, but rather as negative exempla that shed light on problems arising in the narrative present.[65] The contention is put to rest at last with the author's engineering of a Patrician-era reconciliation between the Clann Bhaoiscne survivors, Caoilte and Oisín, and a Clann Mhorna descendant, Donn mac Aoidh mhic Garaidh mhic Mhorna, who is subsequently granted the leadership of a revived Christian-era *fían*.[66] Relations between the Fianna and the Tuatha Dé Danann—the inhabitants of the otherworld—moreover, are largely friendly. Not only does Oisín disappear for a considerable time into the *sídh*, 'otherworldly residence,' where his mother lives, representatives of the otherworld also visit the travelers on their peregrination and accept Saint Patrick's teachings.[67] Any threat these powerful beings may pose is "easily controlled by Christian clerical intervention and even by the actions of a Christianized person of good-will"—in other words, Caoilte—as Ann Dooley assesses.[68] Indeed, Caoilte pays an extended visit to the *sídh* of Eas Ruadh (Assaroe, Co. Donegal), where it is as if time artificially regresses, for after crossing the threshold, he regains his ability to perform great deeds, defending Ireland's shores one last time from foreign attack. But as we have seen, the ancient Fenian rejects a full magical restoration, tempting as it might be, instead securing for his hosts a truce with long-standing enemy raiders and quelling the residual heroic-era strife that Saint Patrick's presence mitigates outside of the *sídh*.[69] Not only is potential conflict thus subdued, three narrative 'worlds'—Fenian, otherworldly, and Patrician—are uncharacteristically reconciled in the *Acallam*.[70]

This reconciliation serves a further purpose, for in the interactions among members of the three Irish polities, behavioral patterns are modeled that were clearly intended to resonate with audiences, whether clerical or lay. Prominent in this regard is the fixation some have identified in the text with lawful, monogamous wedlock—a facet of the broad societal reforms Augustinian and other monastic orders were promoting.[71] The advocation of pious adherence to marital vows is at the forefront of the exemplum-like account of the romantic tribulations of Aodh mac Muireadhaigh, king of Connacht, in whose life Saint Patrick has a vested interest, having previously resurrected him from the dead.[72] After receiving a profession of love from an otherworldly woman of the *sídh* of Brú na Bóinne in Leinster, the king is tempted to stray from his wife, the daughter of the king of Leinster—as early Irish nobility were wont to do, to the consternation of the reforming church. The would-be couple seeks Saint

Patrick's advice, however, and there is no ambiguity in his verdict: "The king has pledged to God and to me that he would be bound to a single wife, and we may not go against that pledge."[73] Resigning themselves to this judgement, their piety is later rewarded when, in a soap-operatic turn of events, the king's wife dies from natural causes and the saint himself formalizes the new union.[74]

The hardship of adhering to religious principles is, in fact, commonly rewarded in order to indicate appropriate behavior. This can be observed not only in relation to appropriate modes of personal conduct, but also contributions to church resources. In the above example, the king of Connacht offers Saint Patrick a generous land grant as *luach in posta*, 'the marriage fee,' and he receives in return a promise that three high kings of Ireland will descend from his Connacht kindred.[75] Elsewhere, on the other hand, when a Munster nobleman refuses to contribute a portion of his bounty after a successful hunt, he is cursed with abdominal pain until he agrees to issue the church its desired *luach*, 'fee,' after every hunt thenceforth.[76] The surviving Fianna, who laud generosity as a noble trait, have no difficulty accommodating the church's expectation of support, but even their heroic giving seems exaggerated. In one recollection after another, at every mention of Fenian riches—and as great warriors, we learn that the Fianna amassed considerable wealth—each treasured item is subsequently unearthed and gifted to Saint Patrick. In this way, not only is Fenian prosperity shown to underpin that of the Patrician church in yet another intermingling of pagan past and Christian present, but our heroes' generosity is also presented as a model for contemporary Christian benefactors. Such beneficence is likely so stressed—and its emulation undoubtedly desired—on account of the fierce competition for patronage in a colonial era, as noted above.[77]

An even more specific context has been suggested, moreover, for the text's promotion of reformed modes of conduct and generous support of the church. Ann Dooley and Anne Connon contend that the *Acallam* was produced within a network of Augustinian houses in present-day Counties Mayo and Roscommon under the auspices of the Mic Oireachtaigh (MacGeraghtys) and Uí Fhiannachta (Finnertys), with the aim of promoting the ambitions of the Uí Chonchobhair (O'Connor) dynasty and furthering their own interests.[78] A western bias is immediately evident in some of the text's most visible authorial interventions, including first the swapping of the traditionally accepted high king of Ireland at the time of Saint Patrick's arrival, Laoghaire mac Néill, for Diarmaid mac Cearbhaill, founder in the mid-sixth century (alongside Saint Ciarán) of the monastery of Clonmacnoise, which was patronized by

FIGURE 3. Croagh Patrick, Co. Mayo, Ireland. (Alamy. Photo by AlbertMi.)

Connacht rulers; and second, the introduction of the ahistorical doublet kings of Munster and Leinster, Eoghan Leithdhearg and Eochaidh Leithdhearg, in place of their better-known historical counterparts, in comparison with the treatment of Connacht monarchs Muireadhach mac Fiannachta and his son and successor Aodh. While also fictional, Muireadhach and Aodh appear to parallel the early thirteenth-century Úa Conchobhair kings of Connacht, Cathal Croibhdhearg (1202–24) and Aodh mac Cathail (1224–28), in whose reigns the *Acallam* was likely composed.[79] The monastic families in question would certainly have looked to the kings of Connacht—with whom they shared familial lineage—for patronage. What is more, the churches they controlled were situated on the popular and prosperous pilgrimage route to Cruachán Aighle (Croagh Patrick) (fig. 3) in County Mayo, and it follows that another aim of the text may have been to promote the regional monarchy to pilgrims through moral entertainment that advocated generous donation.[80] Contrary to this suggestion is the simple fact that much of the text does not concern itself with the pilgrimage route, and the overall itinerary—meandering and often indistinct—is hardly an effective travel plan, even if the advertisement of particular sacred places may have led to increased traffic.[81] Be that as it may, it is now clear that reflections of contemporary issues ripple beneath the surface of the *Acallam*'s masterfully crafted pages. While unreliably representative of the broader Fenian tradition, this anomalous text well illustrates the ongoing malleability of the Fenian corpus in advancing historical moments.

———

The new strand of the cycle that emerged in the later Middle Irish period and led to the composition of *Acallam na Senórach* was a highly impactful development. Not only did the introduction of the Patrician dialogue extend the cycle, adding a new fixed point of reference—Caoilte and Oisín's encounter with Saint Patrick—it also established a new frame into which a hypothetically endless sequence of stories could be fitted. What is more, this innovation united the trifecta of Irish legendary heroes—Fionn the preeminent warrior, Cormac the greatest high king, and Patrick the patron saint—in the same narrative cycle, anchoring the Fianna within a symbolic network of collective ethnic identity. Viewed in this light, it is little wonder that an early thirteenth-century Augustinian scholar in Connacht chose our heroes as the subject of his lengthy literary masterpiece.

Reflective of its contemporary colonial moment, the *Acallam* is a poignant and at times deeply sorrowful text. As we witness Caoilte and Oisín mourn a lost way of life, we cannot help but see reverberations of Anglo-Norman conquest lurking behind their repeated acknowledgements of the reorganization and onomastic redesignation of the land. As recent scholarship has shown, not only do their golden-age recollections appear to contain veiled references to specific sites of colonial authority, but the complex Fenian-Patrician relationship can also be seen to promote the transculturation and integrative settlement practices conducive to maintaining positive Gaelic / Anglo-Norman relations. If Saint Patrick can be read as an idealized settler, however, the Fianna are adapted to the role of benevolent pagans—a move likely influenced by the internal monastic anxieties of a reforming age. In his reconciliation of the Patrician, Fenian, and otherworldly narrative 'worlds,' the *Acallam*'s author grants Fionn inspired knowledge of God, introduces a Fenian moral code, downplays conflict between Clann Bhaoiscne and Clann Mhorna, and tempers the threat posed by the Tuatha Dé Danann. Pushing back against contemporary pressure to excise secular literature from monastic scriptoria, he takes a nuanced approach that accepts the necessity of lifestyle reforms—concerns about Irish marital practices are echoed in the text, for instance—while staking a claim for the propriety of traditional topics of Gaelic scholarship. The *Acallam* is thus an expansive and deeply resonant text that models the multiformity of the greater Fenian tradition, but on a tightly controlled and highly adaptive canvas. Although much literature in the subsequent period of the Fianna's greatest popularity will bear only partial resemblance to it, the significance of this early thirteenth-century tour de force cannot be underestimated.

3

Heroes of the Gael

THE FIANNA'S FAME soared throughout the Gaelic-speaking world in the period from roughly the thirteenth to the eighteenth centuries, during which time hundreds of new Fenian adventures were penned. As this thriving narrative cycle expanded, elements of continuity secured new compositions in a time-honored tradition, while aspects of innovation ensured the stories' continuing relevance in changing circumstances. In our exploration of the significant developments of this period, we will see not only the remarkable productivity of the novel Patrician dialogue, resulting in an abundance of new lays, but also the emergence of a new literary form set within the conventional pre-Christian *tempus*, the Fenian romance. Tracing our heroes' trajectory to peak popularity will also present opportunities to survey new and persistent themes, track the expansion of the *gnáthfhiann*, 'standing *fían*,' and investigate character developments crucial to our understanding of evolving group dynamics, on one hand, and audience reception, on the other. Remaining socially relevant through an era of prolonged conquest and colonization, stories about Fionn and the Fianna flourished as a preeminent mode of entertainment, while reflecting aspects of the sociopolitical contexts in which they were created and transmitted.

The Fianna, the *Filí*, and the Folk

The stand taken by literati like the author of *Acallam na Senórach* (The dialogue of the elders) against the removal of secular literature from monastic scriptoria was ultimately unsuccessful. The writing was on the wall already in the late twelfth century, which saw the emergence of hereditary learned families specializing in poetry, history, law, and medicine. By the mid-thirteenth century these nascent scholarly orders had established a new literary medium that would prove remarkably durable. Leaving behind the increasingly antiquated Middle Irish of monastic scholarship, they pioneered a standard written language—known today as Early Modern Gaelic—that was based on the contemporary oral vernacular, and that remained in use into the eighteenth century in some parts of the Gaelic-speaking (and writing) world. Into their compositions, moreover, they injected new vitality and creativity, tailoring their poetry and prose to elite patrons with tastes and interests that diverged from those of their monastic forbears.[1]

The Fianna thrived in this new literary environment, becoming predominant in the revitalized secular Gaelic literary tradition that soon sprang forth.[2] The accommodating nature of the Patrician frame narrative led to an expanded *Agallamh na Seanórach*, as well as a veritable explosion of lays detailing in vivid verbal tableaux the recollected adventures of our heroes. These were composed and copied in large numbers not only in Ireland, but also in the Gaelic-speaking Scottish Highlands and islands, which tended to look to Ireland as a cultural touchstone and shared similar learned practices, including the use of the Early Modern Gaelic literary language.[3] The two largest collections of lays predating the eighteenth century are *Duanaire Finn* (Poem book of Fionn), a compilation penned by an Irish scribe in Flanders in 1626–27, and the Book of the Dean of Lismore, a Scottish collection of lays and other poetic material assembled in Perthshire in the early sixteenth century. The former is notable for its antiquarian bent and contains many of the earliest-dated lays, while the latter generally reflects a later period of composition and contains both Scottish and Irish-authored texts. Together they hold over ninety different Fenian lays and lay fragments, with almost no overlap between them.[4] In addition to these important collections, numerous copies of variously dated lays came to rest in manuscripts written largely in eighteenth- and nineteenth-century Ireland, although some late Scottish collections also exist.[5] Indeed, the lays were by far the most productive aspect of the cycle during its period of greatest popularity, and although the complete corpus is not yet known, we can be certain that it encompasses hundreds of unique compositions, many of which have yet to receive academic attention.[6] The widespread popularity of Fenian lays in late medieval and early modern Ireland and Scotland is thus plainly evident. Their circulation in the Manx Gaelic–speaking Isle of Man can also be presumed, although lack of evidence clouds our view of the Manx Fenian tradition.[7]

Lays of this period are generally of a less scholarly nature than many of their Middle Irish predecessors, and audiences clearly enjoyed them for the entertaining stories they relate.[8] Their mode of narration is not straightforward,

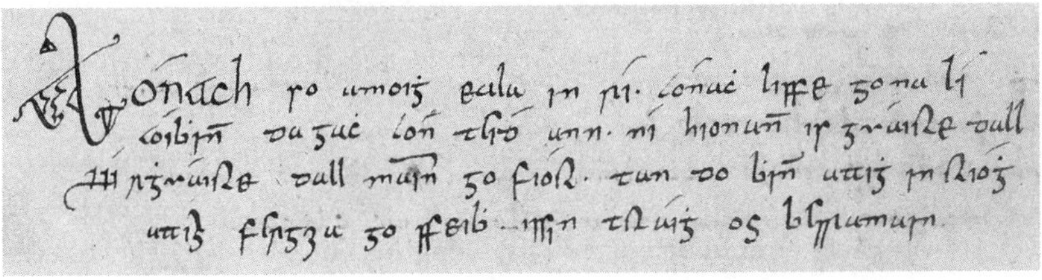

FIGURE 4. The beginning of *Aonach so a Moigh Eala* in *Duanaire Finn*. (Special Collections, University College Dublin Library, MS A20, f. 12v. By permission of UCD-OFM Partnership and Irish Script on Screen, School of Celtic Studies, DIAS.)

however. Not only is the Patrician dialogue context sometimes implicit rather than explicit, as in *Áonach so a Moigh Eala in rí* ("This was a fair in Magh Eala of the king") (fig. 4),[9] but knowledge of aspects of the story is often taken for granted rather than narrated—that is, authors tended to assume on the part of their audiences not only broad familiarity with the Fenian heroic world and its fixed events, but also prior acquaintance with the tales to which the lays pertain. Rather than imparting fully detailed storylines, Hugh Shields explains that the lays are "concerned with events chiefly as a celebration of them," and while some scenes are acutely described, others may be left to the mind's eye.[10] The lay form also came to incorporate elements of lyric, lament, and panegyric as it developed, such that several late medieval and early modern texts classed as lays are not strictly narrative verse, although their referential context may be a narrative one.[11] Take, for instance, *Lon Doire an Chairn* (The blackbird of Derrycairn), a sixteenth- or early seventeenth-century lyric about the beautiful sounds of nature in the Fianna's time. Although one can situate the poem within the general setting of the Patrician frame, and the speaker sketches the outline of a story about the blackbird, the principal focus is not narrative.[12] In a subset of Oisín's conversations with Saint Patrick, moreover, lament for fallen comrades and a lost way of life is the dominant theme, and although these lays may reference valiant exploits of the Fianna in passing, storytelling is secondary.[13] We might also look to the handful of battle incitements that gained popularity in later centuries, the dominant mode of which is panegyric. Despite the situation of these poems within the context of prominent Fenian battles, one must look elsewhere for comprehensive accounts of the conflict at hand.[14]

If the lays lack narrative specificity to a greater or lesser degree, prose compositions spare no detail. This period saw the rise of a new prose form, the heroic romance. While in many ways consistent with developments in prose narrative in other regions of Europe, Gaelic romances do not reflect a wholesale importation of conventions from the continental genre, which emerged in twelfth-century chivalric literature and continued to develop throughout the late medieval and early modern periods. Like their European counterparts, Gaelic romances tend to be episodic and lengthy, but most of them concern native heroes like Fionn and the Fianna, rather than protagonists common across Europe, such as Arthur or Charlemagne. Potential chivalric influence is perceptible—for instance, heroes tend to engage romantically with only one woman, rather than exhibiting the sort of promiscuity acceptable in the past—but continental courtly love conventions are generally not present. In fact, many of the heroes' battle tactics relate closely to earlier Gaelic literature and would be considered dishonorable according to chivalric standards. Moreover, basic elements of the stories' composition that accord with the continental tradition, including combat with foreign adversaries and voyages to lands of wonder, were already present in early Gaelic literature. In contrast with the early literature, however, the romances exhibit a loftier style, replete with elevated language, copious alliteration, a tendency toward extensive enumeration, and stock phrases that are often strung together into long formulaic passages.[15] It is these stylistic features, more than anything, that characterize the Gaelic romance genre, a significant proportion of which concerns the Fianna.

Fenian romance literature is in many ways the counterpart to the lays. There is little doubt that some lays have their roots in contemporary prose, while others led to the composition or adaptation of prose narratives.[16] It is in the romances, moreover, that detailed accounts of some of the events referenced in the lays can be found, and some even incorporate short segments of verse, although the prose form predominates.[17] The romance corpus is considerably smaller, totaling fewer than thirty full or partial extant tales largely composed between the fourteenth and seventeenth centuries, but their popularity was comparable. Well over fifty manuscript copies are still in evidence for the most prevalent Fenian romances, placing them among the preferred topics for secular prose narrative by the late early modern period.[18] Fenian romances differ significantly from the lays in their setting, however, for the Patrician frame is entirely absent from these prose compositions. Rather than harking back to a recollected golden age, they unfold entirely within the confines of a heroic era in which the Fianna are very much alive, whether in their adventurous prime or their catastrophic final decline.[19]

Into the latter category falls the earliest extant romance, a thirteenth- or fourteenth-century story about the events preceding Fionn's death, including most pertinently a hunt for an auspicious wild sow.[20] The distinguishing stylistic markers of the genre are immediately evident in the copious alliterating adjectives and the enumeration of locales and quarry in the opening description of the chase:

> They settled and arranged the hunt through the woods and wildernesses and sloping glens [*fo ḟeadhuibh 7 fo ḟásaigibh 7 fo ḟánglenntuiph*] of the lands nearest them, and through smooth, delightful plains [*muighib réidhe roáilli*], and through close-sheltering woods [*cailltib clithardlúithe*], and through broad-bushed, vast oak forests [*doiredhuib dosleathna dímóra*]. And each of the Fianna of Ireland went separately to his hunting mound, and to his [hound] releasing place [*láthair licthe*], and to his gap of danger [*berna báegail*], as they were wont to arrange every victorious chase before then. But that day was not the same for them as every other day, for the hunt failed them, such that they found neither sow nor hare nor wolf nor badger nor stag nor hind nor doe nor fawn on which any of them might redden his hand that day.[21]

The effect of such devices, which reflect pleasing sound patterns and were undoubtedly intended for oral delivery, may be difficult to appreciate from a modern perspective that takes silent reading as the norm. The reading aloud of literature was a standard practice in the late medieval period, however, and it remained common into the nineteenth century.[22] Public reading would have contributed to a wide familiarity with Fenian topics, and it is not difficult to envision Fenian romances entering into oral circulation in this way; indeed, numerous tellings of romances have been gathered by folklore collectors. Similarly, Fenian lays appear to have been designed for singing—modern recordings exist and their singing was described as early as the eighteenth century—and they would have circulated both orally and in written manuscripts.[23] It can be further assumed that the authors of romances and lays incorporated their knowledge of the undoubtedly vibrant contemporary oral tradition into their compositions. As in earlier literature, the oral-literary trajectory during the period of composition and transmission of Fenian romances and lays was most likely one of constant vacillation rather than a unidirectional progression—and both literature and folklore were experienced aurally.[24]

Like other Fenian literature, the lays and romances are generally not ascribed to named authors, but their composition likely fell under the purview of *filí*—academically trained poets whose years-long course of study prepared them to serve Gaelic lords and chieftains in a political capacity.[25] Such individuals were masters of the Early Modern Gaelic language, and they would have had a detailed familiarity with the adventures of the Fianna, as with all aspects of Ireland's legendary history.[26] That the production of Fenian literature was considered a less serious endeavor than many of the *filí*'s other undertakings is suggested not only by the lack of ascriptions, but also by the *óglachas* ('loose meter') form of the lays. Less complex than the *dán díreach* ('strict poetry') meters typical of political and scholarly verse of this period, this formal choice likely reflects the lays' role as "lighter bardic compositions" for social entertainment.[27] The Fianna do find their way into the *filí*'s more serious poetry, however, in the form of 'apologues'—short narrative passages inserted to highlight heroic attributes of the poems' panegyric subjects.[28] For instance, one such apologue compares a patron's beloved hunting hound to notable Fenian canines whose exploits are related, while another has Fionn himself foretell the coming of the poem's Scottish celebrant to deliver Ireland from her late sixteenth-century travails.[29]

When the Gaelic aristocracy fell in Ireland and the native system of learning collapsed in the seventeenth century, patronage of the *filí*'s elite panegyric poetry waned and the use of the Early Modern Gaelic language declined. Yet the Fianna—ever adaptable—retained their popularity, and Fenian romances and lays remained in manuscript and oral circulation.[30] The lays' loose metrical form no doubt helped them to persist; as Ruairí Ó hUiginn explains, "not having to show regular alliteration and, more crucially, internal rhyme, consonance and the other intricate metrical features that mark strict *dán díreach*, allowed for poems to be changed or modernized linguistically without doing violence to a complex metrical pattern."[31] The modernization of the language of older lays is thus perceptible in many collections, and several late lays were composed in modern Irish and Scottish Gaelic.[32] That the tradition remained productive after the *filí*'s decline is also evident in the grouping together of approximately eleven lays, some of them quite recent, into a compilation known as *Agallamh Oisín agus Phádraig* (The dialogue between Oisín and Patrick). This entertaining series of recollected narratives, embedded within a rather more barbed exchange between Oisín and Saint Patrick than Caoilte's interactions with the cleric in the *Acallam*, is preserved in numerous manuscripts dated from the early eighteenth century onward.[33] Romances were less frequently penned in the later period, but the Fianna put in an appearance in *Eachtra Thriúir Mhac Thoroilbh mhic Stairn* (The adventure of the three sons of Torolbh mac Stairn) by eighteenth-century author Mícheál Coimín (Michael Comyn),[34] and two additional long prose texts—*Cuireadh Mhaoil Uí Mhanannáin* (Maol [bald one] descendant of Manannán's invitation) and *Eachtra an Deirg* (Dearg [red one]'s adventure)—have also been dated to the late eighteenth century.[35] As we will see in chapter 9, moreover, oral traditions about Fionn and the Fianna remained vibrant into the twentieth century, even as literary composition ebbed.

Evolving Narratives

Any attempt at a comprehensive overview of Fenian lays and romances must necessarily be impeded by the vast quantity of primary source scholarship yet to be undertaken. The full extent of the manuscript corpus of lays remains uncertain; critical editions, let alone translations and literary studies, of numerous lays and romances are lacking; and many existing editions and translations are outdated and deficient.[36] Even so, it is possible to trace the emergence of new thematic trends, as well as the persistence of longstanding, definitive tropes of the tradition. With regard to the latter, the Fianna continue to spend a great deal of their time traversing wilderness landscapes, be they in Ireland or Scotland: stories frequently open on hunting scenes, and battles are regularly fought in interstitial zones. We can also see a return to Fionn's biography—the foundational strand of the corpus—in a handful of birth stories and a single death tale (discussed above), but this is not a major area of concentration in late medieval and early modern texts.[37] Rather, stories composed in this period, whether in the form of poetry or prose, are often fashioned around a central quest. This adventurous structure approximates the presentation of quests in oral *Märchen*, 'wonder tales,' outlined by Vladimir Propp, and indeed the quest format could be indicative of the heroic romance genre's oral structural underpinnings.[38] The nature of these quests has enabled a loose thematic organization of Fenian romances and lays into categories that sometimes coincide with the stories' titles.

Stories in which the Fianna must escape an otherworldly dwelling where they have been trapped and subjected to hostile enchantments are frequently described as *bruíon* (Early Modern *bruidhean*), 'otherworldly dwelling' tales. Since the peripatetic Fianna regularly seek lodging for the night when their exploits take them far afield, the *bruíon* escape is an unsurprisingly prevalent theme.[39] The lay *Óenach indiu luid in rí* ("Today the king went to a fair"), outlined in chapter 2, tells the earliest extant Fenian story of this type, but the best-known is undoubtedly *Bruidhean Chaorthainn* (The enchanted hall of the rowan tree). In this circa fourteenth- to sixteenth-century romance, a group of Fianna are lured under false pretenses to a hostile *bruíon* where they become magically fastened to their seats and must get word of their situation, and the means of their rescue, to their Fenian comrades.[40] The Fianna are similarly lured, entrapped, and ultimately rescued in the sixteenth- or seventeenth-century *Bruidhean Eochaidh Bhig Dheirg* (Little red Eochaidh's enchanted hall). There they are surrounded by a hostile otherworldly force and subjected to near-deadly trickery in the guise of hospitality, as when they are given caustic washing-water that burns off a warrior's toe.[41] Magical obfuscation also plays a role in *Feis Tighe Chonáin* (The feast at Conán's house), a fourteenth- or fifteenth-century frame tale, perhaps loosely modeled on the *Acallam*, in which the Fianna lodge at the house of Conán Chinn tSléibhe (Conán of Slea Head) and share a series of episodic stories in response to their host's questions. In the episode known as *Teach Cuanna* (Cuanna's House), the characters who subject our heroes to trickery, including water that turns bitter and a talking ram they cannot catch, are allegorical—an unusual attribute within the cycle.[42] Mention can also be made of *Bruidhean Chéise Corainn* (The enchanted hall at Keshcorann), in which several of the Fianna are enticed into a cave, magically incapacitated, and bound by the three monstrous daughters of a Tuatha Dé Danann lord;[43] *Cuireadh Mhaoil Uí Mhanannáin*, in which the Fianna are beguiled at Maol's otherworldly dwelling by the likes of boars they cannot catch;[44] *Seilg Sléibhe Fuaid* (The chase on Sliabh Fuaid), a lay in which the Fianna are captured using strange, sleep-inducing music;[45] *Seilg Ghleanna an Smóil* (The chase in Glenasmole), a lay in which the Fianna are lured into a *bruíon* by a shapeshifting deer-woman who demands to marry an unwilling Fionn;[46] and *Laoidh Chab an Dosáin* (The lay of Cab an Dosáin), in which a member of the Fianna is subjected to a series of harrowing magical transformations while lodging with an otherworldly host.[47]

In other stories, a person associated with the Fianna is abducted and must be recovered. These are known as *tóraíocht* ('pursuit') tales, and in their most recognizable format, they are analogous to European romance plots. Thus in the fifteenth- or sixteenth-century *Tóruigheacht Shaidhbhe* (The pursuit of Sadhbh), the Fianna's quest through fantastic foreign realms for the man who has abducted the Fenian wife Sadhbh is comparable to the Arthurians' pursuit of the oft-abducted Guinevere.[48] The circa fifteenth-century *Tóruigheacht an Ghiolla Dheacair* (The pursuit of the difficult servant) departs from the normative pattern, however.[49] Here, fifteen of the Fianna are whisked away to a foreign realm after becoming magically affixed to an unusual stranger's ill-tempered horse while trying to move it, and the remaining Fianna must locate and rescue their comrades. *Tóruigheacht Dhiarmada agus Ghráinne* (The pursuit of Diarmaid and Gráinne), dated to the fourteenth to sixteenth century, is even less conventional in that it takes the perspective of an abductor—albeit an unwilling one.[50] As we know from chapter 1, Gráinne, daughter of Cormac mac Airt, is engaged to marry Fionn, but instead elopes with Diarmaid, compelling him by means of a common motif, the *geis*, 'binding injunction,' the breaking of which is always foolhardy. This initiates a *tóraíocht*, but rather than accompany the Fianna in their pursuit, the audience follows and is implicitly led to sympathize with Diarmaid as he evades, outwits, and overcomes his Fenian comrades—and to mourn his tragic end. We will return to Diarmaid's travails below, but the nonconformity of the story to typical heroic romance plots may be further punctuated by comparison with damsel in distress tales, which were also prevalent in European romance.[51] In such stories a young woman pleads for and receives help against a malevolent pursuer. Thus, in lays such as *Cath Chnoic an Áir* (The Battle of the Hill of Slaughter),[52] *Cath Rìgh na Sorcha* (The battle of the king of Sorcha),[53] *Laoidh na h-Ighinne* (The lay of the maiden),[54] and *Suirghe Ghuill* (Goll's courting),[55] women fleeing unwanted and monstrous suitors request and receive the Fianna's aid in defeating these oppressors.[56] Diarmaid—a respected member of the Fianna—is portrayed as neither a malicious abductor nor any other stereotypical oppressor.

The damsel in distress theme is character-based, as is the theme of the magical helper—a mysterious person with special abilities whose aid is crucial to the accomplishing of a task. Stories in which such characters take leading roles have been called helper tales.[57] The helper in perhaps the most well-known tale of this sort, the sixteenth- or seventeenth-century romance *Bodach an Chóta Lachtna* (The churl in the drab coat) is a large, unkempt stranger who offers his aid in a foot race against an exceptionally fast foreign challenger when Caoilte, the Fianna's own speedster, is unavailable. Against all odds, the churl wins the race with ease and forces the foreigner to agree to pay the Fianna an annual tribute.[58] Also notable is the lengthy *Eachtra Chéadaigh Mhóir* (The adventure of Céadach the Great), which concerns a warrior of exceptional strength and skill named Céadach who takes service with the Fianna and aids them in an overseas quest. Unlike the churl, Céadach's help costs him his life, for he and the story's aggressor mutually kill one another, but fortunately for him the loss is temporary; the story closes on his magical resurrection.[59] Magical helpers can also be minor characters, as in the case of the two sons of the king of India who lend their services in *Tóruigheacht an Ghiolla Dheacair*, one of whom is an exceptional tracker and the other a conjurer of ships.[60] These helpful individuals are beneficial to the Fianna, but not unambiguously so, for their superior abilities could pose a security threat to the Fianna or even undermine the heroes' credibility as the greatest of warriors. The former issue may be addressed by tests of loyalty, as when Céadach is ordered to accomplish a series of seemingly impossible tasks shortly after his arrival, while the tradition deals with the latter by limiting helpers to cameo appearances. By generally providing task-specific aid and not appearing serially, magical helpers do not overshadow the cycle's principal heroes, despite taking leading roles in many of the quests they join.

Given the necessity of travel to many quests, the most prominent theme in the heroic literature of this period is overseas adventure. It is an aspect of many of the stories described above and the primary feature of several others, the titles of some of which even begin with the word *eachtra*, 'adventure, expedition.' These stories typically open with the arrival of a mysterious stranger who lures the Fianna abroad, as in *Eachtra Lomnochtáin* (The adventure of Lomnochtán [naked one]), in which Lomnochtán arrives aboard a ship, claims to be a friend, and invites the Fianna to accompany him to his island abode where they must inevitably overcome hardship.[61] Similarly, in *Tóruigheacht Taise Taoibhghile* (The pursuit of Taise Thaoibhgheal [soft bright-sided one]), a woman arrives by boat and places a *geis* on Fionn to abduct her from her unnamed homeland, leading to a lengthy expedition that culminates in a great battle with the forces of her husband, the king of the land.[62] The Fianna also venture overseas in numerous lays, including the popular *Suirghe Fhinn go Críocha Lochlann* (Fionn's courting in Lochlann), dated to the eighteenth century, in which an invitation to Fionn from a monstrous messenger to come court the daughter of the king of Lochlann leads the Fianna into yet another trap,[63] and the circa thirteenth-century lay beginning *Fleadh ros fúair Corbmac ó Fhionn* ("Cormac got a feast from Fionn") in which a challenge from the visiting king of Sorcha leads to an expedition through numerous lands to defeat the boastful foreigner.[64] While such meandering adventures are common across European romance literature, in the Gaelic context the theme likely builds upon that of the journey to the otherworld in early Irish literature. Although the locations on which our heroes' ships alight are now foreign rather than otherworldly, the boundary between the foreign and the supernatural is highly permeable, and their travels invariably take them to lands of wonder.[65]

Whether the action occurs at home or on foreign soil, most Fenian narratives incorporate some form of contention. The Fianna's adversaries are usually foreign and thus either implicitly or explicitly supernatural, and the conflict tends to take place outside the realm of everyday life, either in an overseas location or on the Irish (or occasionally Scottish) shoreline—the frontier between home and abroad, real and surreal.[66] Stories that focus on the breach of that frontier by a formidable foe are known alternatively as invasion or battle tales.[67] There are numerous such stories, among the oldest of which is *Cath Fionntrágha* (The Battle of Ventry), which is mentioned in twelfth-century lays, briefly outlined in the *Acallam*, and presented in expanded form in a popular fifteenth-century romance. In this tale, the Fianna successfully defend against an attack at Ventry Bay (fig. 5) by Dáire Donn (Brown-haired Dáire), the king of the world, occasioned by the prior elopement of the king of France's wife and daughter with Fionn.[68] The Fianna are also forced into defensive mode in copious lays, prominent among which are *Cath na bPunann* (The Battle of the Sheaves), in which the Fianna overcome an invading army that surprises them while they are uncharacteristically harvesting grain;[69] *Laoidh an Airghinn Mhóir* (The lay of Airgheann the Great), in which the Norse king Airgheann invades after his wife elopes with one of the Fianna, and the Fianna narrowly defeat his forces;[70] *Laoidh Mhághnuis Mhóir* (The lay of Mánus the Great), in which the Norse king Mánus arrives with a fleet, demands Fionn's wife and hound, and is defeated;[71] and *Duan a' Mhuileartaich* (The lay of the Muileartach), in which the Fianna rebuff a gigantic Scandinavian *cailleach*, 'hag,' intent on destruction.[72] The Fianna also overcome foreign attackers in a series of lays concerning an attempt to conquer Ireland by a warrior from the East. In *Laoidh an Deirg mhic Droichil* (The lay of Dearg son of Droicheal), Dearg tries to force Cormac mac Airt to submit, but the Fianna overcome his forces and kill him. Dearg's son Conn then comes to avenge his father in *Laoidh Choinn mhic an Deirg* (The lay of Conn son of Dearg) and is also slain.[73] The Fianna's prowess is on full display in these blow-for-blow accounts of martial conflict. Either outnumbered or disadvantaged by the supernatural abilities of their opponents, our heroes typically suffer grave losses, but achieve glorious victory in the end.

The glory of some Fenian battles is complicated by the theme of internecine strife, which occurs frequently in late medieval and early modern Fenian narrative. While contention between Clann Mhorna and Clann Bhaoiscne is downplayed in the *Acallam*, it finds full expression in *Bruidhean Bheag na hAlmhaine* (The little brawl at Allen), a fifteenth- or sixteenth-century tale

FIGURE 5. Ventry Bay, Co. Kerry, Ireland. (Alamy. Photo by David Collins.)

about a fight between the two factions over who has the right to collect a tribute from Lochlann—Fionn mac Cumhaill or Goll mac Morna, head of Clann Mhorna. The topic of the Battle of Cnucha is broached, old wounds are reopened, and considerable blood is shed before a resolution is reached.[74] Clann Mhorna privileges are also to the fore in lays about a conflict between Goll and Caireall, a contrarian member of Clann Bhaoiscne typically associated with Scotland. Tempers flare when Caireall questions Goll's right to the prized marrow bones at a feast. The Battle of Cnucha is once again referenced—a typical pattern—and a fight breaks out that results in Caireall's death, according to modern Scottish Gaelic sources.[75] The battle itself gets fuller treatment in an expanded prose *Cath Cnucha,* and nearly all accounts of this period agree that it was Goll who killed Fionn's father Cumhall.[76] The special privileges Goll and his kindred enjoy are intended to promote peaceful coexistence, but the tensions between the two groups are never far below the surface, and conflict is all but inevitable. It is hardly surprising, therefore, that Goll meets his unfortunate end at the hands of Clann Bhaoiscne. The causes of this final contention are variously given, but most sources agree that the mortally wounded Goll is driven onto a lone rock in the sea where he dies accompanied only by his wife, who witnesses his final words.[77] While in the early medieval material, the tension between Clann Bhaoiscne and Clann Mhorna is bookended by tales of Fionn's death, later authors focus instead on Goll's demise, and indeed the downfall of the Fianna (discussed below), as an ultimate resolution.

Considerable topical expansion within the Fenian corpus is thus apparent during the late medieval and early modern period. In copious and varied new compositions, authors engaged with broader European heroic romance themes while continuing to develop tropes already well-entrenched in the cycle. Into the weft of stories centering newly popular motifs like foreign adventure and incursion, overarching concerns such as the contention between Clann Bhaoiscne and Clann Mhorna are threaded seamlessly. This trend carries over into the academic treatment of these narratives. Although the non–mutually exclusive categories of *bruíon*, *toraíocht*, overseas adventure, damsel in distress, helper, invasion / battle, and internecine strife into which these tales and lays are grouped are modern and should not be mistaken for a native taxonomy, they resemble early medieval categorizations in their thematic delineation, and sometimes even overlap with early categories (e.g., *catha*, 'battles,' and *echtrada*, 'foreign adventures').[78] In approaching a period of such intense vibrancy and thematic creativity within the cycle, it is fitting that the new and the renewed are key foci of both criticism and critical vocabulary.

Heroes and Antiheroes

Just as thematic developments are observable in Fenian lays and romances of the thirteenth and later centuries, the evolving characterization of our warrior protagonists is evident. While Fionn was the preeminent hero of most of the early stories, he now presides over a formidable heroic collective, some of whom are clearly more accomplished warriors, and many of whom fulfill specific roles in a multifaceted and increasingly complex cycle. Indeed, as the Fianna expand, Fionn's principal contribution to the group is less often physical than intellectual. He may exhibit brute strength when necessary, but his qualifications as a seer, on the one hand, and a wise leader, on the other, are what storylines tend to hinge upon.

In the earliest sources, Fionn's capacity for prophecy is explicitly associated with poetic composition. When his thumb is auspiciously slammed in the door to a fairy domicile in the circa eighth-century "Finn and the Man in the Tree," he chants *imbas forosnai* ('inspired knowledge') in obscure *roscad* verse.[79] In the twelfth-century *Macgnímartha Finn* (Boyhood deeds of Fionn), he gains proficiency in three modes of poetic prophecy, including the *imbas*, upon tasting the salmon of knowledge, and displays his newfound wisdom by reciting a poem about the coming of summer.[80] Verse features irregularly in the romances, however, and two alternate accounts of Fionn's acquisition of foresight in *Feis Tighe Chonáin* draw no connection with poetic skill. The first occurs at the resolution of a conflict, when Fionn and two less prominent characters with an aptitude for prescience, Mac Reithe and Diorraing, drink from an otherworldly vessel that bestows the gifts of "fios 7 fíor-eolus" ("knowledge and true wisdom"). In the second, these same three ingest water from a well of knowledge during a struggle with the otherworldly women guarding the well.[81] Fionn's characterization as a poet persists in a small number of prophetic lays ascribed to him, but this trait largely migrates to other characters, and poetry need not feature when he accesses his special skill.[82] When he and several of his men are trapped in *Bruidhean Chaorthainn*, for instance, he uses his thumb of knowledge to learn the means of their release—the blood of their supernatural captors—but he does not communicate this inspired wisdom in verse.[83]

The Fenian poet par excellence is Oisín, the purported originator of most of the lays, although Caoilte, the narrator of much of the prose and poetry in the *Acallam*, occasionally lends his voice too.[84] Unlike Fionn, whose poetic ability was supernaturally inspired, we might assume that these two deliberately cultivated the art of verse-craft, given the requirement in the twelfth-century *Áirem Muintire Finn* (The enumeration of Fionn's people) for every member of the Fianna to be "a prime poet."[85] In Oisín and Caoilte's seniority, this skill serves to exemplify the only Fenian ability remaining to them, having ceased to be active warriors. (Oisín laments the loss of his youthful vigor and appearance, not to mention the camaraderie of his heroic brethren, in numerous lays.)[86] Their capability in the poetic realm also reinforces their social position as wisdom figures, for their use of this elevated mode of discourse bolsters their claim to accurate knowledge of the past and lends an air of authenticity to their stories. An interesting contrast can be drawn here with the literature dealing with old age, discussed in chapter 1, in which the value of an elderly Fenian warrior is queried. We have seen that as a Fenian character ages, his diminished physical strength begins to negate his warrior identity, and his desirability as a suitor becomes limited. While the solution to the quandary of old age in the early tales was simply the hero's death, the aged Oisín and Caoilte can now continue to serve a purpose, despite their physical weakness. Although they frequently reference their infirmity, death rarely seems imminent; as long as they are a source of poetic wisdom, they can go on living—and narrating.

We value these ancients as poetic wisdom-bearers only after they have outlived the collapse of the Fianna, however. The tragic fall happens under Fionn's watch, and as it approaches, there is growing ambiguity about both the extent of his domain and his effectiveness as a leader. We can assume that Fionn continues to operate within the ambit of Cormac mac Airt, whether or not this is explicitly stated in every text. As Fionn's popularity grows, however, so too does his relative standing, and at times it comes to seem as though he is Cormac's equal, rather than merely a powerful retainer. While Cormac is *ardrígh*, 'high king,' of the settled population, Fionn, as *ríghfhéinnidh*, '*fían* leader' (literally, '*fían* king'), can sometimes been seen as having jurisdiction over all the wilderness spaces—or indeed the island of Ireland itself.[87] Take, for instance, *Laoidh Laighne Mhóir* (The lay of Laighne the Great), in which Fionn cleverly negotiates with a newly arrived invader in the guise of a druid requesting immunity for his holdings in Ireland. When Fionn's request is granted and his deception revealed, the invader protests, to which Fionn responds that he is both a *draoi*, 'druid,' and "flaith na fíorFhéine" ("ruler of the true *Fían*"), and that "liomsa . . . gabhus Éire" ("Ireland belongs to me").[88] Some texts even expand Fionn's dominion beyond historically Gaelic-speaking regions, as in the thirteenth- or fourteenth-century "Slaying of the Pig of Formaoíl and the Death of Fionn," where he is styled "rígfénnid hÉrenn 7 Alban 7 Saxan 7 Bretan 7 Leódus 7 Lochlann 7 na n-ailén cendtarach" ("the *fían* leader [king] of Ireland and Scotland and the Saxons and the Britons and Lewis and Lochlann and the nearer islands").[89] In *Tuarasgabháil Chatha Gabhra* (The account of the Battle of Gabhair), moreover, Oisín claims: "Ní roibh ón Innia anoir / go Fódla iarthar an domhain / rí nach roibh fár smacht" ("From India in the East to Ireland in the West of the world, there was no king who wasn't subject to us").[90] Whatever the actual extent of Fionn's domain, the lays and romances regularly portray him as a powerful and enduring leader.

The tendency of longstanding rulers to exhibit hubris has been well-documented, and psychiatric research supports the statutory term limits many modern nations impose on elected officials.[91] No such checks on power exist in the warrior society of the Fianna, and perhaps predictably, pride comes before Fionn's fall. Although Oisín and Caoilte's lays often cast a rosy hue on his leadership, depicting him as a model of righteousness and nobility,[92] a darker side emerges that ultimately tears the Fianna asunder. The honor of Fionn's conduct is questioned in the circa sixteenth-century invasion romance

Eachtra Iollainn Iolchrothaigh (The adventure of Iollann Iolchrothach [Handsome Iollann]), in which discontent amongst the Fianna with their sometimes troublesome leader impedes their defense against Iollann Iolchrothach, the king of Spain, who has come to seek the head of the king of Ireland. Even the most loyal of Fionn's men—Diarmaid and Oisín—refuse to fight on his behalf in this story, and one of Oisín's sons reveals a serious act of treachery in which Fionn attempted to have him killed out of jealousy over a woman.[93] Fionn's overweening pride is thereby coupled with his enduring characterization as an inappropriate suitor, a motif that echoes more famously in the Diarmaid and Gráinne tradition. Following the elopement of his intended bride with one of his most trusted men, Fionn crosses the line from justifiable indignation to unwarranted animosity when his resentment persists years after peace has been brokered. Whether Fionn orchestrates the climactic hunt for the enchanted boar solely to lure Diarmaid to his death is not entirely clear in *Tóruigheacht Dhiarmada agus Ghráinne*, as opposed to the broadly contemporaneous *Laoidh Dhiarmaid* (The lay of Diarmaid), where he is unequivocally to blame.[94] His vindictive pride clearly prevents him from delivering the magical draught that would have healed Diarmaid in the romance, however, and the remaining Fianna's bitterness at their companion's preventable death is palpable. Only Oisín's wise counsel prevents Oscar from killing Fionn, while Oisín, for his part, disregards his petulant father's refusal to return Diarmaid's hunting hound to Gráinne, conveying the dog to the grieving woman himself.[95] Irrevocable distrust has been sown, even among the members of Fionn's own kindred, and there is an ominous sense at the close of the story that the collapse of the fractured Fianna is merely a matter of time.

The narratives detailing *Cath Gabhra*, 'the Battle of Gabhair,' illuminate our protagonists' antiheroic last act.[96] Set in the rule of Cormac's son Cairbre, the romance opens on a barely recognizable Fianna. Now arrogant and domineering, their demands in return for protecting Ireland have become unbearable. When they insist upon a hefty tribute after the betrothal of the high king's own daughter, as has apparently become customary in Irish marriages, Cairbre summons his forces to expel them.[97] The reason for the dispute is represented differently in the lays, which portray the Fianna in a more favorable light, but even there we learn that Cairbre perceives them as levying *cíosa cruadha*, 'harsh taxes,' and displaying *anuabhar*, 'excessive pride.' In retaliation, the disgruntled monarch demands exclusive hunting rights in Ireland in a transparent attempt to curtail their power, which is predictably met with refusal.[98] Ireland's golden age of heroes thus closes on the high king and the Fianna bent upon reciprocal and mutually foolhardy destruction. The chaotic nature of this battle is reflected in its unconventional partnerships. The Fianna—fragmented since the deaths of both Goll mac Morna and his brother Garadh (for whom see below)—ally with their traditional Scandinavian enemies under the son of the king of Lochlann, while Cairbre counts among his supporters not only the Irish provincial kings, but also the Scottish branch of Clann Mhorna under the leadership of Garadh's son Oscar.[99] Although Oisín will later recount his side's deeds to Saint Patrick as some of the Fianna's final triumphs, celebrating in particular the heroism of his own son Oscar, there are no real winners here. Oisín's son slays Garadh's son, bringing the intergenerational feud between Clann Bhaoiscne and Clann Mhorna to a violent close. The battle then culminates with Cairbre himself rounding upon Oscar mac Oisín, the Fenian champion striking off his erstwhile king's head as the latter's spear tears through his bowels—a mortal wound. What remains to the few survivors is a battlefield strewn with fallen heroes and an island bereft of leadership, left almost utterly defenseless.[100]

The tragic valor of Oscar mac Oisín—one of the Fianna's youngest members, cut down in his prime—serves as a counterpoint to the destructive behavior some texts associate with the aging Fionn. Indeed, as Fionn recedes, whether from grace or merely from action, other members of the group rise to the fore. Oscar is consistently known as one of the group's strongest combatants, and he is celebrated as such not only in accounts of the Battle of Gabhair, but also in *Cath Fionntrágha*, *Tóruigheacht an Ghiolla Dheacair*, and numerous other tales. Diarmaid, too, is renowned for his physical prowess, and his tendency to attract women has been known to benefit the Fianna in difficult situations, as in *Seilg Ghleanna an Smóil* when they escape from a *bruidhean* with the aid of a female guard swayed by the dashing Fenian.[101] Caoilte's superior running ability is on display in narratives like *Cath na bPunann*, which hinges on his speedy retrieval of the Fianna's weaponry,[102] and we see the development of an origin story for his name in *Laoidh na Ceardcha* (The lay of the smithy) when the supernatural smith fashioning the Fianna's swords asks after *in fear cailti*, 'the slender, warm man,' whose face is flushed from the heat of the forge.[103] Characters like Mac Lughach and Diorraing mac Doghair enter the Fenian inner circle in the late medieval period, moreover, and Fionn's hounds Sceólang and, more significantly, Bran are depicted as valued contributors in the hunt and on the battlefield.[104] The hounds are especially remarkable in that they are Fionn's biological cousins, born to his mother's sister after an affronted Tuatha Dé Danann woman transformed her into a dog, as we learn in *Feis Tighe Chonáin*.[105] Bran's heroism is prominently displayed in numerous stories, including *Laoidh na Con Duibhe* (The lay of the black dog) in which a stranger with a black hound arrives from Orkney and demands a dog fight. The foreigner's hound defeats nearly every Fenian canine before Bran is dispatched to finish off the evidently otherworldly beast.[106]

Other texts highlight Clann Mhorna members of the Fianna, including most notably Goll mac Morna, the head of his Connacht-based kindred.[107] From his first appearance in *Cath Slébe Cáin* (The Battle of Sliabh Cáin), a circa tenth-century anecdote about a battle with Fionn, Goll rises to prominence as a somewhat unlikely counter-hero.[108] Initially called Aodh (in early sources) or Iollann (in later sources), he came to be known as Goll, 'one eyed,' due to his loss of an eye in the Battle of Cnucha, in which he struck the fateful blow that killed Fionn's father Cumhall and initiated the contention with Clann Bhaoiscne. We might have expected him to become Fionn's sworn enemy as a result of this act, but in reaching a diplomatic compromise to maintain the unity (more or less) of the Fianna, both familial heads exemplify the wise leadership of a Fenian hero.[109] And indeed, a strand of the tradition lauding Goll as a noble and powerful warrior is already evident in the eleventh-century poem *Ligi Guill i mMaig Raigni* ("The grave of Goll in Mag Raigne").[110] In the late medieval and early modern periods, Goll is known as one of the best Fenian combatants, alongside Oscar, and he brings about numerous victories. It is Goll who saves the day in *Bruidhean Chéise Corainn*, for instance, defeating the three powerful Tuatha Dé Danann women into whose enchanted trap Fionn and several other Fianna have fallen.[111] In *Laoidh an Airghinn Mhóir* he heroically vanquishes the invading Airgheann,[112] while in *Cath Rìgh na Sorcha* he overcomes the foreign king who has been menacing a maiden under Fenian protection.[113] He takes a prominent role in *Tóruigheacht Shaidhbhe*, moreover, volunteering to lead the Fianna in their overseas quest to recover the abducted Sadhbh while Fionn is otherwise occupied at home.[114] Although he was once an aggressor to Clann Bhaoiscne, and is destined to become one again when the fragile accord between Clann Mhorna and Clann Bhaoiscne ultimately collapses, these and other texts extol Goll as an honorable member of the Fianna whose contributions are valued by the group.

Although the nobility and prowess of the other two most prominent members of Clann Mhorna, Goll's brothers Garadh and Conán, are also recognized, texts more often commemorate their least laudable actions, and it is largely on their account that Clann Mhorna's reputation suffers. Garadh may receive honorable epithets like *fial*, 'generous,' and *glan*, 'pure,' in poetry,[115] but the deed that leads to his demise, while in response to an acknowledged slight, is heinous: he barricades a group of Fenian women in a hall and burns them alive. The earliest reference to this incident in *A chaorthuinn Cluana Ferta* ("Oh rowan tree of Clonfert") associates it with the final clash of the Fenian factions. In this circa twelfth-century lay set shortly after Goll has been killed, Garadh outlines his premeditated plan to murder the Clann Bhaoiscne women in revenge and acknowledges his own prophesied death nearby—presumably in retaliation.[116] Here his dramatic, impassioned drive to exact sweeping vengeance for a kin member slain in battle is evocative of heroic epic. Later accounts, on the other hand, bear more resemblance to the exaggerated violence of modern slapstick comedy. These do away with the battle context to depict the elderly Garadh's reaction to a cruel trick played on him by the Fenian wives. He has stayed back from the hunt and fallen asleep in the Fenian camp, when the women decide to secure his hair to the side of the hall and raise a mock battle cry. He awakens and leaps into action, cartoonishly scalping himself in the process, then burns the women in retaliation and flees. When the Fianna discover Garadh's inexcusably horrific offense, they track him down and his own son Aodh beheads him before going mad with grief and drowning himself.[117] In versions of the story of Garadh's most memorable act, he thus evolves from an admirable if epically reactive warrior to a tragicomic villain abhorred even by his own son.

A trend toward the comedic is also observable in the characterization of Conán, who similarly enters the literary record around the twelfth century. Initially described as a valiant but headstrong warrior,[118] Conán cuts a less menacing figure in many of the romances and lays, which exaggerate his greed and quick temper to farcical proportions. While trapped in *Bruidhean Chaorthainn*, not only does he brazenly demand food and drink from his rescuers, but Diarmaid goes to great lengths to steal the king of the world's own dinner for him, rather than serving what is readily available, in order to avoid potential complaints from the ornery Fenian about the victuals' provenance. Conán gets his comeuppance, however, when the serum needed to break the spell magically fastening them in place runs out before he can be released. Although his brethren pull him free, he loses the skin of his heels, shoulders, and backside, thus explaining his usual epithet *maol*, 'bald.'[119] Conán is quite literally the butt of a joke that only gains in popularity, for in time, versions of these humorous motifs migrate to other compositions. *Eachtra Lomnochtáin* similarly highlights his gluttony, having him stubbornly remain on board the Fianna's docked ship to eat and drink to excess while the others disembark and continue their quest. This choice later places him in the rescuer's role, but the recompense for his aid is ironically disagreeable: in the struggle to free his companions, Lomnochtán's wife tears the skin from Conán's scalp with her long fingernails, leaving him *maol* until Diarmaid procures him a sheep's hide transplant.[120] Another close parallel to the denuding incidents in these tales appears in *Seilg Sléibhe Fuaid*. Much like in *Bruidhean Chaorthainn*, Conán becomes magically fastened to his seat, but here he pulls *himself* free when he leaps in terror at the sight of his captor, who subsequently heals his wounded buttocks—employing the same transplant method as in *Eachtra Lomnochtáin*—after he pitifully cries out for mercy.[121] *Seilg Sléibhe Fuaid* thus further exemplifies a shift in Conán's characterization toward cowardice, a trait also apparent in other late texts. In *Laoidh Mheargaigh na Lann* (The lay of Meargach of the blades), for instance, he refuses to enter the fray and merits the description: "Conán who was not severe in battle, and who required not the reputation of a warrior or [a man] of action."[122] Once a cantankerous hero, but a hero nonetheless, by the eighteenth century Conán's comic range extends to empty bravado.

The foremost members of the Fianna gain considerable definition over the course of the late medieval and early modern periods, coming to exhibit distinctive heroic traits that enable them to make unique contributions, regardless of the nature of the quest or battle on which they embark. Fionn is generally portrayed as a wisdom figure, taking a less active role than in the early literature, while Goll and Oscar, the strongest warriors of their kindreds, nearly always win the day, with the aid of others, each utilizing their special skills: Caoilte as the swiftest runner, Diarmaid the renowned lover, Bran the most accomplished hound, and, of course, Oisín the loyal companion and latter-day poet. These stock characterizations are not necessarily consistent, however, for our protagonists sometimes take on qualities of troubled antiheroes, particularly as they near their fall in the Battle of Gabhair. The aging Fionn, in particular, risks succumbing to his pride, but a shadow overhangs the entire group at times. Increasingly, too, some characters come to serve villainous or even comical roles, as we have seen in the cases of Garadh and Conán, whose heroic qualities are significantly tempered in later texts. Indeed, some commentators have identified a shift toward the burlesque in early modern Fenian literature, which corresponds well with the evolving portrayal of our principal Clann Mhorna buffoon, and which may reflect the changing literary tastes of a society that ceased to be dominated by a Gaelic warrior caste.[123] It is to the social context of the tales that we now turn.

Fenian Literature in Society

Eminently malleable, the Fenian tradition was undoubtedly used in myriad ways in this period to reflect, refract, and process not only broad societal changes, but also specific regional concerns. At this distance—and given the very minimal scrutiny to which most lays and romances have so far been subjected—many historical resonances remain unrecognized, and some are certainly lost to time. Scholars have made progress understanding the contextual development of certain aspects of the tradition, however, helping us to understand the stories' explosive and persistent popularity throughout the Gaelic world's most tumultuous era.

The theme of foreign hostility and incursion is particularly significant from a sociopolitical perspective. While the Fianna's enemies vary, their most prevalent overseas foes are Scandinavians from the imprecisely defined northern land of Lochlann. It has been suggested that the numerous appearances of these hostile *Lochlannaigh* reflect a cultural memory of the trauma of the ninth- and tenth-century Norse invasions in Ireland. Potentially troubling this theory is the fact that the Scandinavian enemy does not enter the Fenian literary tradition until the twelfth century, at which point they fulfill, in Proinsias Mac Cana's words, a "traditional" role of "violators of Ireland's sovereignty."[124] As we have seen, foreigners in these texts, including most prominently the *Lochlannaigh*, appear somewhat supernatural, being at times imbued with magical traits. Such characters could be seen as romance-era stand-ins for the Tuatha Dé Danann or Fomorian adversaries more prevalent in earlier texts.[125] Notwithstanding some of the *Lochlannaigh*'s ahistorical qualities, however, Mac Cana asserts that their role in the Fenian corpus is an "unmistakable" aspect of historical recollection, however "vague" the details.[126]

The impact of increasingly frequent and unpredictable Norse depredations must have been pronounced. As Mac Cana writes, "If their physical impact was, to say the least, not inconsiderable, there can be little doubt that the psychical repercussions which they generated among the Irish people, and notably among the learned and professional classes, went deeper still and evoked responses of self-preservation and self-vindication."[127] That collective trauma is inherently intergenerational is now well accepted, and narratives echoing, reinforcing, and renegotiating traumatic events' social significance have been observed to persist in collective memory across very broad time periods.[128] It is not just possible, but indeed probable, that the psychological effect of the Viking incursions was still present much later than the period in which they occurred. By way of comparison, we might consider the perception of Oliver Cromwell in Ireland. Roughly three hundred years after Cromwell's Irish campaign (1649–53), Irish Folklore Commission collectors were able to gather a large store of potently negative accounts about him, reflecting the continued impact of his activities, and their outcomes, on an Irish collective identity.[129] The twelfth-century first appearances of Scandinavian enemies in Fenian literature occur at a comparatively smaller remove from the perceived end to the Norse threat in Ireland in the 1014 Battle of Clontarf.[130] The lengthy memory that has been shown to exist regarding events such as Cromwell's short but brutal campaign suggests that the Scandinavian theme prevalent in the later Fenian tradition may indeed be rooted in historical collective trauma. But this alone does not explain the popularity of the motif.

The theme of an invading Scandinavian enemy likely resonated particularly strongly among Gaels in the late medieval and early modern periods due to the recurrent social upheaval of foreign incursion and colonization. In Ireland, the era of the production and transmission of Fenian lays and romances evoking this topic was certainly a fraught one, coming on the heels of the Anglo-Norman invasion and lasting throughout the waves of invasion, limited foreign control (and the lapse thereof), reinvasion, plantation, and acculturation of the thirteenth to eighteenth centuries. This was likewise a precarious time for Gaelic Scotland, encompassing multiple and often unsuccessful struggles to maintain territorial, legal, and cultural autonomy from the forfeiture of the Lordship of the Isles to the aftermath of the defeat at Culloden. While the *Lochlannaigh* in Fenian narrative likely evoked traumatic memories of early Norse invaders, concurrently and even more poignantly, they would have come to stand in for the Gaels' contemporary aggressors. Such representative identification is accounted for in modern studies of popular or 'folk' history, which find that traditions about foreigners commonly function as a means of articulating a contemporary group identity, rather than a documentary record of the past.[131] It thus matters little that the *Lochlannaigh* in Fenian narrative hardly resemble the actual Norse invaders because, while they probably originated in a persistent memory of historical trauma, their continued popularity was undoubtedly due to their representational relationship with the world of the authors and transmitters. They are the symbolic foreign foe whom the Fianna, as pan-Gaelic heroes, never fail to vanquish—an attractive and readily adaptable scenario that could easily have constituted an escapist counterpoint to a less-than-ideal reality.[132]

If the intense popularity of Fenian narrative is due, at least in part, to the successful mobilization of the theme of the Scandinavian invader as a stand-in for all-too-real contemporary aggressors, more particular social resonances may also have been at play. Close examination with an eye to political history has led academics to speculate about the composition and reception of some texts. Diarmuid Ó Murchadha has suggested, for instance, that "the conflict-laden verse saga of the career of Goll" may initially have been inspired by the reign of the mid-eleventh-century king of Connacht Aéd Úa Conchobair, whose influence grew as that of the Munster contender for the high kingship receded.[133] Caoimhín Breatnach posits, moreover, that many of the romances were crafted for patrons with specific interests in mind. The oldest manuscript copy of *Cath Fionntrágha*, written in the fifteenth century, is dedicated to a Gaelic noblewoman named Sadhbh Ní Mháille (O'Malley) who may have been married to a lord of Gaelicized Anglo-Norman stock, MacWilliam Burke (also called Riocard Ó Cuairsge) of County Mayo. Breatnach notes this text's emphasis on intermarriage between the Fianna and the Tuatha Dé Danann, and views the romance as a reinterpretation of an existing narrative to appeal to the tastes of a particular patron.[134] Strengthening the argument that *Cath Fionntrágha* was tailored to appeal to Ní Mháille and Burke is the significance to Burke of a County Sligo location of the same name as the legendary battle. Burke made a peace treaty there with the lord of Tír Chonaill (Donegal), and Breatnach suggests that the contrast between this "peaceful settlement, beneficial to both parties" and "the disastrous consequences of the battle fought at *Fionnlráigh*" in the romance was intentional, highlighting the wisdom of that treaty.[135] In a literary tradition controlled by an aristocratic elite in the habit of receiving compositions of a panegyric nature—the so-called 'bardic' poems of the *filí*, which utilized apologues to liken patrons to the heroic Fianna—it is certainly plausible that Fenian texts written for elite entertainment might include elements of referential flattery.

Contextual investigations of other texts could also prove fruitful, even when composition dates and detailed manuscript provenances are not known. By way of example, although the precise moment when the Diarmaid and Gráinne story was expanded into its popular romance format may be uncertain, the prevalence of southwestern Munster locations in *Tóruigheacht Dhiarmada agus Ghráinne* suggests that it originated in Corca Dhuibhne (the Dingle and Iveragh peninsulas)—that is, the region named for the descendants of an eponymous Duibhne, easily equated with the shadowy figure in the Fenian hero's regular patronymic: Diarmaid ua (descendant of) Duibhne. A local audience is likely to have seen the favorable portrayal of Diarmaid in the romance as a celebration of one of their own, and indeed, the manuscript history of this

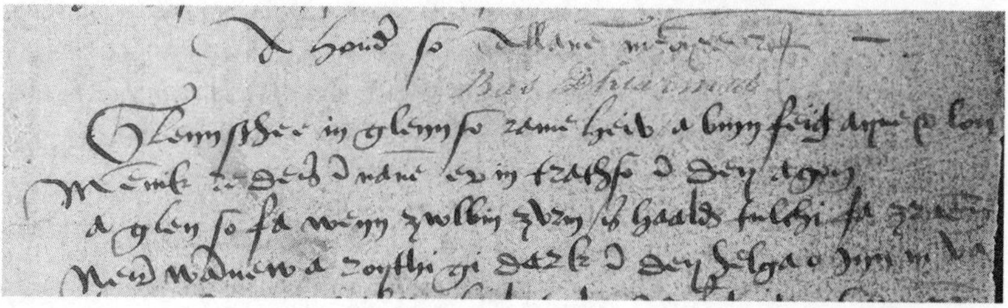

FIGURE 6. The beginning of *Laoidh Dhiarmaid* in the Book of the Dean of Lismore. (National Library of Scotland, Adv. MS 72.1.37, p. 147. By permission of the National Library of Scotland and Irish Script on Screen, School of Celtic Studies, DIAS.)

oft-copied romance reflects a strong Munster interest.[136] It is likewise possible that the composition in Scotland of the lay on the death of Diarmaid (*Laoidh Dhiarmaid*) (fig. 6)—which situates the fatal boar hunt on Beinn Ghulbain (Ben Gulabin), Perthshire, within a Campbell sphere of influence—was intended to honor a patron of that lineage, for the ascendant Campbells had begun to claim Diarmaid as an ancestor.[137] The lay's inclusion in the sixteenth-century Book of the Dean of Lismore, compiled in the cultural milieu of the Campbells, could reflect its ongoing appeal due to a perceived genealogical link with Diarmaid.[138] That it continued to be held in high esteem within the family as time progressed is best illustrated by a mid-eighteenth-century account written by Rev. Alexander Pope in Caithness. Pope describes hearing the lay from an elderly Campbell man who, out of deference to his purported ancestor, insisted upon removing his cap during its delivery.[139] One might reasonably posit, then, that personal investment rendered both *Tóruigheacht Dhiarmada agus Ghráinne* and *Laoidh Dhiarmaid* eminently palatable to their initial recipients, and that regional or familial pride played a role in their subsequent transmission.

The circumstances of textual transmission confirm that Fenian narratives continued to serve contemporary sociopolitical functions even centuries after their composition. The Fianna were again pressed into symbolic service during the early seventeenth-century disintegration of traditional Gaelic society in the wake of the Nine Years War in Ireland. Following the landmark defeat at Kinsale in 1601, several of the aristocracy departed for the continent, taking up residence in foreign courts and attaining leadership positions in continental regiments as they strove to secure foreign aid to wrest Ireland from London's grasp once and for all. Their intended aim was ultimately not realized, however, and traditional Gaelic society disintegrated in Ireland. Over the course of the century, the Gaelic elite who remained were largely dispossessed of their landholdings and the British government's reach was extended to the furthest corners of the island.[140] Such a fundamental shift in power had considerable cultural effects, among the most significant of which were the waning of literary patronage and the shuttering of the native schools of learning. Many of the literati responded by taking holy orders so that they could continue to engage in literary production in Irish monastic colleges abroad, and perhaps unsurprisingly, much of the scholarship they produced was of a reactive nature.[141] Moved by a nationalist spirit to celebrate and preserve their threatened cultural heritage, exiled Irish scholars assembled, compiled, or composed several of the great works that survive today to relate the past glories of Gaelic Ireland.[142]

It was in this atmosphere that the wholly Fenian manuscript containing both *Duanaire Finn* (the largest collection of early lays) and a recension of the *Acallam* was compiled in Ostend and Leuven in Flanders in 1626–27.[143] It is not difficult to see why the Fianna would have been an attractive subject for a volume motivated by cultural threat. Not only were stories about them still popular, they had held a prominent place within the perceived history of the Gaels since the Middle Irish period, as audience investment in the traditions of Diarmaid and Gráinne explored above reaffirms. Indeed, their historical place was formalized in the early seventeenth century by a scholar contemporaneous to the compiler of *Duanaire Finn*, historian Geoffrey Keating (Seathrún Céitinn), in his *Foras Feasa ar Éirinn* (Compendium of knowledge about Ireland), completed in 1634. Keating sheds valuable light on the contemporary understanding of the Fianna's historicity, explaining that "although many imaginative romances have been written about Fionn and the *Fían* . . . still it is certain that true credible accounts of them were also written." Notwithstanding the creative embellishment of their reported exploits, to him, and undoubtedly to many others, the heroic Fianna had existed as "hired warriors of the Kings of Ireland, to defend and protect the country for them."[144] Still widely known as the protectors of early Gaelic Ireland, the Fianna were thus ideally situated to have their texts copied and preserved at this time of political exile and cultural endangerment.[145]

In conjunction with ethnic pride, Ruairí Ó hUiginn suggests that the creation of this manuscript was driven by a personal affinity with the tradition's militant protagonists; indeed, the Fenian contents of the compilation were "singularly suitable" for Somhairle Mac Domhnaill, the patron who commissioned it.[146] Mac Domhnaill was an aristocratic member of Clann Dhomhnaill, a large and formerly powerful family with branches in Northern Ireland and Scotland. Originally from County Antrim and closely related to the head of the kindred, he was a known rebel whose activities, including his part in planning a rising in 1614 that was halted before it ever came to fruition, as well as a subsequent stint of piracy along the Scottish coast, contributed to his exile to the continent. He then transitioned to the role of captain in the Irish regiment of the Spanish army in Flanders, winning commendation in battle, and apparently still aggravating the English by his continued involvement in at least one plot concerning Ireland.[147] Whether during his itinerant spate of outlawry in familiar Gaelic environs or his military service overseas, he and his martial brethren may well have seen themselves as "latter-day *féinnithe* [Fianna]," much like generations of warriors before him.[148] In Mac Domhnaill's case, however, he sought to defend the very cultural fabric of which the Fianna were becoming emblematic. Whatever this manuscript meant to him—and one suspects it meant a lot—his commissioning of it helped the Fianna on their way, aiding the circulation of *Acallam na Senórach* and the sixty-nine lays in *Duanaire Finn*.

The thirteenth century heralded a new era in which Fionn and the Fianna emerged as the preeminent heroes of the Gael, their adventures soon becoming ubiquitous in the literature and lore of Gaelic-speaking Ireland, Scotland, and, one assumes, the Isle of Man. Having reached its maturity, the Fenian cycle burst forth with a veritable deluge of lays and romances that seamlessly melded definitive features of the narrative tradition from its inception with new aspects perfectly tailored to meet the evolving tastes of the age. While our heroes maintain their peripatetic wilderness-dwelling habits in these stories, we see topical expansion in the prevalence of new themes around which the central quests of late medieval and early modern adventure narratives are organized. The vibrant creativity of the cycle is also reflected in the expanded heroic collective over which Fionn now presides, each warrior exhibiting a unique skillset to meet the needs of diverse and challenging situations. Not all texts in this increasingly complex corpus are celebratory, however, for as the events preceding the collapse of the Fianna are fleshed out, some characters take on a sinister aspect. The death of Diarmaid on account of Fionn's overweening and vindictive pride foments irrevocable distrust, while the deaths of Goll and Garadh mac Morna in serious internal conflicts fragment the Fianna. The ultimate resolution to the long-simmering feud between Clann Bhaoiscne and Clann Mhorna occurs in their mutual defeat in the Battle of Gabhair, which some accounts take as an inevitable corrective to growing Fenian hubris, even while hailing Oisín's valorous son Oscar in his tragic final moments. More often than not, though, these dark events alternatively loom in the distant future or reside in Oisín and Caoilte's ancient and rose-hued past, with focus instead falling on our heroes' valiant deeds. In this wonted, victorious guise they continued to serve contemporary sociopolitical functions, whether to flatter patrons and presumed descendants, or as evidence of historic Gaelic greatness in a time of severe cultural threat.

Adapted versions of the Fianna would go on to attain international celebrity in James Macpherson's infamous mid-eighteenth-century Ossianic epics, but these venerable heroes had already put at least a millennium of literary and oral history behind them in the Gaelic-speaking world by that time. It is clear from our exploration of the Fianna's past incarnations in chapters 1 through 3 that this has been an adaptive and multiform body of story from its earliest appearance in textual records. At no point can the cycle be essentially defined as prose or poetry, oral or literary, entertaining or sociopolitically invested. The intense scholarly focus on Macpherson's epics tends to overshadow the earlier Fenian tradition, which is often viewed from the perspective of Ossianic scholarship as the vague, uniform, and apolitical Gaelic source material from which his compositions were creatively fashioned. In contrast, I have sought to highlight the narrative and ideological complexity of the Gaelic texts, qualities that should be borne in mind when approaching Fenian material from any historical period. As Joseph Falaky Nagy perceptively points out, "Macpherson's is but one chapter in a long-lived, and perhaps still not concluded, saga of the Gaelic use of Fenian story as a way to introduce cultural and political change, and to mediate between 'native' and 'foreign,' and 'old' and 'new.'"[149] The situation was only to get more convoluted as Macpherson's works sparked debates in the literary sphere of the Gaels' historic colonial oppressor about the quality, relevance, and national provenance of their acclaimed heroes.

PART II

The Fianna and the Ossianic Controversy, c. 1760–1860

4

From Fionn to *Fingal*

WITH THE PUBLICATION of his Ossianic epics, James Macpherson plucked Fenian narrative from its place in the Gaelic cultural sphere and thrust it into an international public consciousness, forever altering the way Fenian literature and folklore would be perceived. From the Ossianic epics' first appearance in the mid-eighteenth century until at least the mid-nineteenth century, Gaelic Fenian narrative was considered almost solely with regard to them, the claims Macpherson made about them, and the controversy that erupted surrounding those claims. This chapter considers how the Fianna's adapted personae came to be known the world over, while chapters 5 and 6 trace the long reverberations of the controversy in the Gaelic world and beyond. The epics that were to become so contentious emerged from, and might indeed be seen as symptomatic of, deep-seated tensions within their Scottish place of origin and the greater United Kingdom. Macpherson was not alone in responding to those tensions, but his efforts struck a chord that resounded within the hearts of some, and galled others to the very core. Neither Macpherson nor his Edinburgh backers could have anticipated the intense reactions his publications would engender. Few non-Gaels knew anything about Fionn, Oisín ('Oisean' in Scottish Gaelic) and their ilk when Fingal and Ossian were introduced to an English-reading public in the summer of 1760. In a matter of years—barely the blink of an eye in the Fianna's long narrative history—everything changed. Within a decade, their Anglicized alter egos were household names, and their position within Gaelic narrative tradition was hotly debated across the United Kingdom.

Outside Awareness

While knowledge of the Fenian tradition outside of predominantly Gaelic-speaking areas would not have been great prior to Macpherson's publications, there is evidence for a limited awareness in Scots and English-speaking regions. References to "Fyn Makcoull" (Fionn mac Cumhaill) and "Golmakmorn" (Goll mac Morna) by John Barbour, Gavin Douglas, David Lindsay, and an anonymous poet once thought to be William Dunbar suggest that the Fianna were not entirely unknown in Lowland Scotland from the fourteenth to sixteenth centuries.[1] Yet the scarcity and brevity of these references, and the overt association in two instances with Ireland and the Highlands,[2] indicate that the Fianna retained their Gaelic cultural identity and were neither widely imported nor fully embraced in the Lowlands. The early Scots poets depicted Fionn and Goll—sometimes satirically—as heroes of impressive stature, but they showed only minimal acquaintance with the plots of Fenian stories.[3]

Turning to learned texts circulating beyond the Gaelic sphere in the pre-Macphersonic period, we find varying degrees of familiarity with the Fenian narrative tradition. The brief account left by the sixteenth-century Lowland Scottish historian, Hector Boece (known in Latin as Boethius) suggests that he may have been better informed than his poetic coevals, for in addition to describing Fionn as a Scottish giant, he referenced a body of Fenian romance literature. Perceiving no historical merit in the tales, however, he did not recount any of them for his readers.[4] Other scholars exercised less restraint, and in the late sixteenth and seventeenth centuries, Fenian storylines began to be referenced, sketched, and adapted in English and Latin histories of Britain and Ireland. Around 1570, Edmund Campion recorded the survival to Saint Patrick's time of a giant whom he took to be "Fin Macoole,"[5] while the saint's more conventional interactions with Oisín are reflected in the contemporaneous Book of Howth. The scribe responsible for the manuscript's extended Fenian section (Hand III, writing c. 1571–72)[6] clearly had direct knowledge of his Gaelic source texts, yet his account distorts native tradition. Adapting a handful of stories and lays—including *Cath Gabhra* (The Battle of Gabhair), *Dóiteán Tighe Fhinn* (The burning of Fionn's house), *Suirghe Fhinn go Críocha Lochlann* (Fionn's courting in Lochlann), *Laoidh an Deirg mhic Droichil* (The lay of Dearg [red one] son of Droicheal), and *Cath Fionntrágha* (The Battle of Ventry)—to an alternative historical narrative, he presented the Fianna and their progenitors not as Gaelic heroes, but as unruly Danish (Viking) warriors commissioned to defend a flagging host of Irish kings from foreign invasion.[7]

The Book of Howth received moderate circulation in manuscript form among early Anglo-Irish scholars, and the Fenian material penned in the 1590s by Meredith Hanmer is closely based on it,[8] but little further interest is evident in what was then the sole protracted non-Gaelic account of the Fianna. Correctives to introduced distortions were also slow to appear in languages comprehensible to those who might not have known better. These came at last in the 1680s, in histories written by two native Gaels, Peter Walsh and Roderic O'Flaherty. Walsh countered in English that Fionn was "neither *Gyant* nor *Dane*," while O'Flaherty provided traditionally accurate synopses in Latin not just of the Battle of Gabhair, but also the elopement of Diarmaid and Gráinne, and the death of Fionn at the hands of the Luaighne.[9] Further critique subsequently appeared in English in Dermod O'Connor's 1723 translation of the early seventeenth-century history of Ireland written by Geoffrey Keating (Seathrún Céitinn).[10]

Through this meagre collection of sources, attentive readers of history could have acquired a basic, if somewhat confused, familiarity with Gaelic Fenian narrative in the period preceding Macpherson's Ossianic epics. But those not inclined to such a pursuit would have had little opportunity for exposure. Apart from these learned texts, and the few early Scots poetic references already noted, information about the Fianna accessible to non-Gaels was very limited. In early Irish poetry in English, there is only James Farewell's derogatory portrayal of Fionn and Oscar in merited damnation in Hell.[11] The sole additional reference that can be adduced, while more agreeable, would not have added greatly to readers' understanding of Fenian tradition. Although Martin Martin describes a number of topographical sites associated with "Fin Mack Coul" in his unusual English-language travel account of his native Hebrides, he decides not to "trouble the Reader" with stories about Fionn and his men.[12] We can thus safely assume that prior to the mid-eighteenth century, the Fianna were virtually unknown to the majority of non-Gaels—and they might well have remained that way, if not for Macpherson's publications.

Protecting Culture / Projecting Culture

Although most outsiders would have been ignorant of the rich and lengthy Gaelic Fenian tradition, eighteenth-century Scottish Gaels were expressing a growing interest in documenting their own traditions even before Macpherson set pen to paper. The events of eighteenth-century Scotland can, to some extent, be seen as paralleling those of seventeenth-century Ireland, when the greatest blows were struck to the Gaelic aristocracy, native centers of learning were decimated, and a reactionary cultural nationalist project got underway in continental Irish colleges as exiled literati strove to preserve centuries of native literature and scholarship from destruction. In Scotland, while several regions within the Gaelic-speaking Highlands had experienced violence and social unrest in the seventeenth century and a governmental project of Anglicization and cultural reform was underway, the native social structure remained relatively intact. However, partly as a result of alterations in trade and economic practices, and partly as a result of the legislated Lowland education (and socialization) of chieftains' children, Highland values were altering from the top down, and this was affecting Scottish Gaelic literary culture. As more and more chieftains turned their gaze toward the Lowlands, professional literary composition began to attenuate, and many of the most noted literary productions of the period originate from nonprofessionally trained authors.[13] In the late seventeenth and early to mid-eighteenth centuries the stakes of the Jacobite rebellion became seriously elevated, and not only cultural values, but the entire social structure was undermined by military defeats and the resulting penalties imposed. The Jacobites lost the Battle of Dunkeld in 1689 (shortly after a victory at Killicrankie), failed to achieve their goals at the Battle of Sheriffmuir in 1715, and suffered a final, devastating defeat at the Battle of Culloden in 1746. Following Culloden, the Highlands saw a period of massive social change as punishing as anything that had happened in Ireland a century prior: property titles of Jacobite chieftains were stripped, Gaels were forbidden to carry weapons or wear their traditional dress in the 1746 Disarming Act, and large-scale population relocation began taking place in conjunction with land improvement projects.

Examining the literary record, Derick Thomson contends that there was "a contemporary movement or awakening, no doubt closely connected with the traumatic events of the first half of the eighteenth century."[14] As the foundations of their society began to crumble beneath them, some learned Scottish Gaels, like their Irish counterparts, felt driven to preserve what they could of intangible Gaelic culture. While the greatest blows were not struck until after Culloden, cracks in the foundation were evident from the early years of the century. Even in nonviolent periods, the threat to Scottish Gaels' accustomed way of life was omnipresent as the government reacted to successive risings by constructing military roads and erecting garrisons in the Highlands. An additional impetus to assert their cultural worth comes in the form of the negative characterization of Scottish Gaelic people and culture in the Scots- and English-language spheres in which they were, by this point, regularly participating. Prejudicial distinctions between the "Wild Scots" of the Highlands and "the 'domesticated' 'house-holding' Scots" of the Lowlands had been extant for some time, as sixteenth century writings can attest.[15] The ethnic denigration was to worsen in the eighteenth century. In an English context, it has been said that Scots, in general, were "the most abused minority of that age."[16] To many in the southern part of the island 'Scottish' was analogous to 'backward,' and to many Scots and English speakers alike, 'Highlander' was akin to 'savage.'

It is in this atmosphere that the collection of Scottish Gaelic poetry, and of heroic lays in particular, began. The earliest collection was made in Caithness around 1739 by Rev. Alexander Pope. Inspired to preserve the Gaelic poetry he and his parishioners valued, Pope started writing down verses then circulating orally, including ten or so Fenian lays or fragments.[17] Whether others were similarly inspired in the fraught period approaching the final Jacobite Rising is not now known. What is clear is that as tensions rose in the Highlands and the traditional way of life grew ever more precarious, the desire for cultural preservation became more urgent. The 1746 defeat at Culloden prompted both rapid social change and an intensification of Scottish Gaels' drive to document their cultural heritage. A manuscript likely made in the Kintyre region of Argyll around the same time as the rising, possibly by a Cameron, represents the first extant Culloden-era record of Fenian texts. Called the "Turner Manuscript" after a former owner, it consists of poetry, including literary versions and fragments of eight Fenian lays.[18] Not long after the compilation of this manuscript, two of the most prolific collectors of the century, Rev. James McLagan and Rev. Donald MacNicol, began their work documenting the Gaelic poetry then circulating. Both men are conventionally said to have begun assembling their sizable collections around 1755, although it is possible that McLagan was jotting down poems even earlier than 1750.[19] In addition to a wide range of popular poetry, McLagan eventually amassed nearly ten thousand lines of heroic verse comprising forty-six different lays and related material, of which thirty-seven are Fenian.[20] Some of MacNicol's collection was apparently lost at sea during his son's lifetime, but included within the surviving portion are a few thousand lines of heroic verse comprising twenty-eight different lays, of which all but one are Fenian.[21] Also inspired to collect shortly after Culloden, although not as educated as his contemporaries, was Archibald Fletcher of Glen Orchy in Argyll. Fletcher gathered nineteen Fenian lays aurally, beginning c. 1750. Not being literate, he periodically had the material transcribed from his dictation.[22]

The importance of these collections to modern scholarship is undeniable: not only do they evidence an eighteenth-century urgency to preserve valuable cultural productions in the face of great social stress, their contents have also been extremely significant to the study of Gaelic literature in general, and the Fenian tradition in particular. However, the readership of these collections of

Fenian lays was limited by their lack of publication and their language. Only one early to mid-century collector sought to cross this barrier by presenting the translated text of a heroic lay to a non-Gaelic reading public. This was Jerome Stone, who collected Gaelic poetry, including heroic lays, in the early 1750s. Stone was a graduate of the University of St. Andrews, as were his contemporaries, McLagan and MacNicol.[23] Unlike them, he was not a native Gaelic speaker, but he is said to have had a talent for language acquisition. When he relocated to Dunkeld, Perthshire to take a position as a schoolmaster, he took the opportunity to learn Gaelic and document the culture. Of the surviving ten heroic lays Stone collected, eight are Fenian and two pertain to the Ulster cycle. In January 1756, Stone published a loose translation of one of the Ulster lays, *Bàs Fhraoch* (The death of Fraoch), in what was then Scotland's only periodical, *The Scots Magazine*.[24]

Stone's publication is reflective of the contemporary tenor of Scottish academia. Rather than representing a cultural nationalist effort at literary preservation, Stone's collection appears to have been made in support of research he was conducting into the 'primitive' origins of the Scottish Gaels.[25] Theorizing about a primitive stage in cultural development was an aspect of contemporary proto-anthropological thought. Among the most influential Scottish proponents of primitivism was Thomas Blackwell, whose *Enquiry into the Life and Writings of Homer* (1735) gained him wide acclaim. For Blackwell, the poetic genius of Homer directly correlated with the early stage of development of ancient Greek culture: "He took his plain natural Images from *Life*: He saw *Warriors*, and *Shepherds*, and *Peasants*, such as he drew; and was daily conversant among such People as he intended to represent. . . . For so unaffected and simple were the Manners of those Times, that the Folds and Windings of the human Breast lay open to the Eye; nor were People ashamed to avow Passions and Inclinations, which were entirely void of Art and Design."[26] Poetic expression—specifically of the epic variety—was natural in Homer's primitive society, Blackwell claimed; but as societies developed, heroic vision and emotive expression became inhibited by artifice and corruption, and the ability to compose poetry in the vein of Homer's epics was lost. Jerome Stone's prefatory letter to his translation reveals a similar outlook on Gaelic poetry that he proposes could be "of very great antiquity": "Several [Gaelic] performances are to be met with, which for sublimity of sentiment, nervousness of expression, and high spirited metaphor, are hardly to be equaled among the chief productions of the most cultivated nations. Others of them breathe such tenderness and simplicity, as must be affecting to every mind that is in the least tinctured with the softer passions of pity and humanity. Of this kind is the poem of which I here send you a translation."[27] Stone's high opinion of the artistic merit of Gaelic poetry is matched by that of scholars today, but Stone valued *Bàs Fhraoch* for different reasons than modern scholars do. For him, the heroic lay displayed the same sort of emotive simplicity sketched by Blackwell in the poetry of Homer. Stone went on to compare his translation with a Homeric episode, making his critical debt to Blackwell evident, and setting a precedent for the primitivist study of Gaelic lays.

In Stone's translation can be discerned a desire for *Bàs Fhraoch* to conform to the esteemed aesthetics of Homeric epic, and to accommodate the tastes of an English-language reading public. Editorial changes are immediately apparent from Stone's title, "Albin and the Daughter of Mey," where Fraoch, the Gaelic hero's name, has been replaced with a non-Gaelic moniker, Albin, "presumably on the grounds of euphony," as Howard Gaskill assesses. It could also be that Stone did not find the association of *fraoch*, 'heather,' with "bristling anger" to be "appropriate to the hero of a romantic ballad."[28] Stone further catered to the tastes of his audience in his rendering of the language of the translation, which is in the elevated style of English-language poetry and does not reflect the more straightforward mode of expression of the Gaelic heroic lay. Additionally, he expanded the poem from the original thirty-three quatrains (132 lines) to twenty ten-line stanzas each composed of two quatrains and a couplet (200 lines). This expansion allowed him to emphasize the affective and heroic elements of the poem while still reflecting the plot of the original fairly accurately. Such deviation from the original underscores the fact that the aim of translation at the time was generally not to reflect, as closely as possible, the content and register of the poem in its original form. Rather, we might see Stone's effort as an attempt to 'translate' the content and register of the original into a recognizable equivalent in an Anglophone cultural context.[29] It appears from the English-language literary world's awakening desire for such 'primitive' Scottish Gaelic poetry, that Stone, who died only months after his translation was published, knew and served his market well.

It is generally agreed that James Macpherson was influenced by Jerome Stone's translation. His own publication of original poetry in the *Scots Magazine* in May 1755, and again in October 1758, indicates that he was a reader of the periodical. He likely also began collecting in this period. As both a fellow collector and a student of the University of Aberdeen, where Blackwell still lectured and had extensive influence, Macpherson would have been drawn to Stone's topic. In fact, a comparison of Macpherson's Ossianic texts with Stone's originals suggests that Macpherson not only read Stone's translation, he also acquired Stone's Gaelic texts.[30]

Unlike Stone, but like the other early to mid-eighteenth-century collectors, Macpherson was a native Scottish Gaelic speaker. Much has been made of the fact that he was born and raised less than half a mile from the Ruthven Barracks in Badenoch. Built to establish control over the Jacobites, in 1746 these barracks were the site of the disbanding of the defeated Jacobite army—an army in which his relatives had fought. In all likelihood, he was prompted to collect by an interest in cultural preservation amidst rapid social change and a newfound knowledge of the primitivist trend in contemporary literary and proto-anthropological theory. From Stone's published translation, he may also have come to appreciate how his own cultural productions could reflect the values so admired by contemporary intellectuals and artists.[31] Yet he did not initially intend to follow in Stone's footsteps. While questions abound regarding the creation of the English-language epics that Macpherson would eventually publish, the scholarship of the past half century or so shows that he did not enter into the project with the intention of committing fraud, nor is the end result best described as 'fraudulent,' however far from the Gaelic texts much of Macpherson's work is. Indeed, the kernel of the *Poems of Ossian* rests in the collection of heroic poetry that he had already begun to make, prior to any hint of translation.

The initial idea for the project was not, in fact, Macpherson's at all, but owes its genesis to a group of prominent Edinburgh literati keenly interested in Highland poetry like Stone's translation but lacking the linguistic capability to find and appreciate it in the original. Among these was the Lowland poet John Home. After a stay in London at the turn of the year 1749–50, Home had received a curious parting gift from the English poet William Collins. This gift was the unfinished manuscript of a poem encouraging him to look to the Highlands for poetic inspiration. The task that Collins set for Home is summarized in several early lines of the poem, now known by the title, "Ode on the Popular Superstitions of the Highlands of Scotland":

Fresh to that soil thou turn'st, whose ev'ry Vale
Shall prompt the Poet, and his Song demand;
To Thee thy copious Subjects ne'er shall fail
Thou need'st but take the Pencil to thy Hand
And paint what all believe who own thy Genial Land.

> . . .
> Ev'n yet preserv'd how often may'st thou hear
> . . .
> Strange lays whose pow'r had charm'd a Spenser's Ear[32]
> At Ev'ry Pause, before thy Mind possest,
> Old Runic Bards shall seem to rise around
> With uncouth Lyres, in many-colour'd Vest,
> Their Matted Hair with boughs fantastic crown'd.[33]

Collins prefigured Stone in his intimation that if Home were simply to look, he might discover the fruits of a bygone age: the lays of bardic figures of a Homeric cast, outfitted with lyres and leafy crowns.[34] Home took his directive seriously. Conversing with the Gaelic-speaking philosopher Adam Ferguson he learned more about the format of the "Strange lays" he sought. Ferguson would later explain to the committee appointed to investigate the authenticity of Macpherson's epics that he had heard lays in his youth and had even copied one down from a tailor circa 1740—although the copy did not survive for him to show Home. It was apparently Ferguson who brought Macpherson and Home together in the autumn of 1759. Upon learning that Macpherson had already assembled a small collection of heroic lays, Home pressed the young Highlander for a translation of one. His request, initially declined, was eventually met with a translation of a lay about the death of Oscar that greatly impressed him.[35] At long last, Home had found his "Old Runic Bard."

Ossian's Dawn

The events of the next few years brought Fenian characters to the world stage in publications that would stir interest and controversy for centuries to come. At such a nodal point in history, it is not surprising that different interpretations exist of the actions that were taken and the degree of responsibility borne by each individual for the controversial results of those actions. While some commentators have placed the full responsibility for all perceived misrepresentation (or worse) in the Ossianic texts squarely on Macpherson's shoulders,[36] others view the texts as, to some extent, a collaborative project in which degrees of individual culpability are variously, and often uncertainly, assessed. My own evaluation—and that of most modern scholars who have looked closely into the production of the texts—falls within the second category.

Already at its genesis in Macpherson's translation of Oscar's death lay for Home, the Ossianic project represented multiple interests. Home, feeling he had made an important discovery, pressed Macpherson for further translations, which he then shared with a small group of Lowland authors and scholars in Edinburgh. Similarly impressed, this influential group—which included the soon-to-be University of Edinburgh Professor of Rhetoric, Rev. Dr. Hugh Blair—managed to convince a reluctant Macpherson to assemble and publish *Fragments of Ancient Poetry, Collected in the Highlands of Scotland, and Translated from the Galic or Erse Language* from material in his collection. June 1760 marks the dawn of *Ossian*.[37]

Fragments was a pamphlet containing fifteen short, rhythmic prose items topically, if not metrically, similar to Stone's "Albin and the Daughter of Mey"; each 'fragment' combined expressions of powerful emotion with natural imagery to lament a fallen hero. The work was an immediate success, and readers clamored for more. They had good reason to believe their wishes would be met, since Blair virtually promised a second, more substantial text in his short preface to the publication. In the preface, he described the project in terms familiar to an audience versed in Blackwell's work on Homer. He affirmed that the fragments were "genuine" and "of the most remote antiquity," as shown by the "ideas" and "manners" portrayed in them, which "belong to the most early state of society." He then went on to propose that:

> Though the poems now published appear as detached pieces in this collection, there is ground to believe that most of them were originally episodes of a greater work which related to the wars of Fingal. . . . It is believed, that, by a careful inquiry, many more remains of ancient genius . . . might be found in the same country where these have been collected. In particular there is reason to hope that one work of considerable length, and which deserves to be styled an heroic poem, might be recovered and translated, if encouragement were given to such an undertaking.[38]

Blair's conviction that an epic existed was so strong that he proceeded to outline what it would look like when it was found. This description can, of course, only have come from Macpherson,[39] and it indicates that even at an early period, Macpherson thought of the lays as episodes within a linear, Fenian chronology. The comparison of Gaelic heroic material with Homeric epic having already been made by Stone, it would have been no great leap for Macpherson to extend the analogy, slotting the lays with which he was familiar into an epic framework the likes of which he would have studied at Aberdeen. Already during the composition of the *Fragments*, it appears that he and his backers believed wholeheartedly—strongly enough to publish not merely a hypothesis, but a plot outline—that an original epic could be recovered.

Macpherson's apparent early belief in the feasibility of the project did not guarantee his willingness to take it on. Perhaps he recognized his weakness as a Gaelic scholar, or perhaps he hoped to make his name as an author rather than a translator. For whatever reason, despite the initial success of the *Fragments*, Macpherson again had to be cajoled into undertaking the search for and assembly of the epic. Given Blair's bold statement in his preface, which helped to secure the support and financial aid of influential people, the pressure on Macpherson from his backers would have been considerable.[40] Upon committing, he was dispatched to the Highlands to gather further evidence of the lost epic. He made two substantial collecting trips between the summers of 1760 and 1761, which were, by all accounts, highly successful. A cultural insider, and evidently quite a charismatic man, Macpherson was able to secure the loan or gift of numerous manuscripts containing Gaelic Fenian material, many of which survive today principally due to his efforts. According to his own and others' testimony, he also amassed a considerable collection of oral lays, including material gathered personally and copies of lays in others' collections; for instance, he is known to have requested and received lays from McLagan.[41] With the help of a few enlisted Gaelic scholars, he then set about collating the versions, identifying what he deemed to be accretions, and writing (or, as he would likely have seen it, reconstructing) the epic.[42] *Fingal, An Ancient Epic Poem, in Six Books* (fig. 7) was published in December 1761, with Macpherson presented as its translator. Its success encouraged him to publish a sequel in March 1763 entitled *Temora, an Ancient Epic Poem, in Eight Books*.[43] He would continue to edit these texts in subsequent editions, but all further Ossianic-style publications emerged from the pens of imitators.

Macpherson did not set out to defraud an unsuspecting public—yet his Ossianic texts are something other than the translations they purport to be. They depart considerably from the native lays in both content and style. This state of affairs is perhaps not as damning as it might seem, however, given Macpherson's goal and research methods. As we have seen, his goal from the beginning was the reconstruction of an ancient epic that he appears to have sincerely believed existed. He elaborated on his theory of the composition and transmission of the Ossianic texts in his introduction to the collected edition of *The Works of Ossian the Son of Fingal* (1765), asserting that in Ossian's time and place (third-century Scotland), bards transmitted both family records and

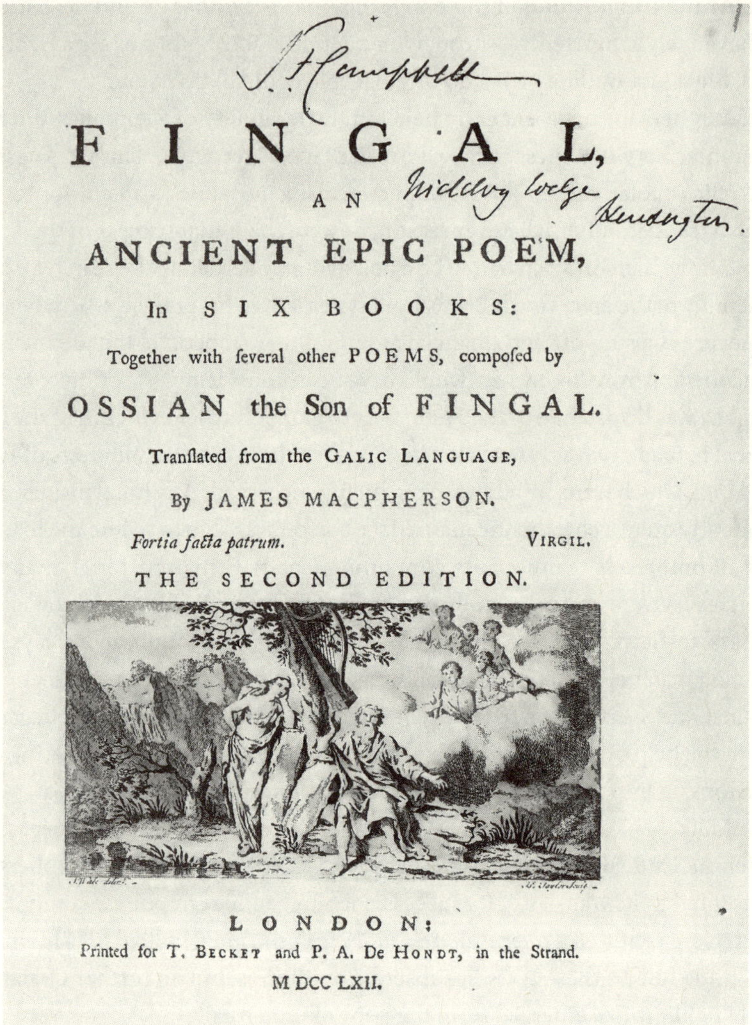

FINGAL,
AN
ANCIENT EPIC POEM,
In SIX BOOKS:
Together with ſeveral other POEMS, compoſed by
OSSIAN the Son of FINGAL.
Tranſlated from the GALIC LANGUAGE,
By JAMES MACPHERSON.
Fortia facta patrum. VIRGIL.
THE SECOND EDITION.

LONDON:
Printed for T. BECKET and P. A. DE HONDT, in the Strand.
M DCC LXII.

FIGURE 7. John Francis Campbell's copy of James Macpherson's *Fingal* (1761). (National Library of Scotland, Cam.1.b.1[1]. By permission of the National Library of Scotland.)

"ancient poems" orally from generation to generation. He went on to affirm that the oral tradition continued down to the contemporary era, and avowed that the Ossianic epics were assembled from "tradition, and some manuscripts."[44] Macpherson certainly was not alone in presuming the historicity of 'Ossian' (Oisín / Oisean) and his fellow warriors. As we have seen, the Fianna's place in a Gaelic pseudohistorical framework was established in the medieval period, and they continued to be accepted as historical in contemporary histories—including most notably those by Keating and O'Flaherty, which Macpherson had read.[45] We have also seen that the lays tend to be voiced in the first person, and both Irish and Scottish sources frequently ascribe them to Oisín / Oisean. Given the state of knowledge about Gaelic medieval society and literature at the time, Macpherson had a fairly firm basis for his initial assumptions.

Macpherson's theories about the composition and transmission of the texts, on the one hand, and the nature of the oral tradition, on the other, had great bearing on his research methods. His perception of the oral tradition also aligned well with the contemporary state of knowledge. Skepticism about the fidelity of the oral tradition and its value as a source for, or object of, academic study was common at the time. This skepticism is evidenced in John Locke's *An Essay Concerning Human Understanding* (1690), which was still influential in the mid-eighteenth century; Locke contended that "*in traditional Truths, each remove weakens the force of the proof*: And the more hands the Tradition has successively passed through, the less strength and evidence does it receive from them."[46] In his correspondence with McLagan, Macpherson conveyed a similar distrust for the reliability of the oral tradition: "Traditions are uncertain; poetry delivered down from memory, must lose considerably; and it is a matter of surprise to me, how we have now any of the beauties of our ancient Gaelic poetry remaining."[47] He well knew the late date of the manuscripts he collected, the oldest of which, the sixteenth-century Book of the Dean of Lismore, reveals its age in a number of dated entries.[48] He could thus presume that the Fenian texts in these manuscripts contained the same sort of accretions he attributed to orally transmitted texts. He gave an assessment of the fidelity of the tradition, as a whole, to the posited original epic in his introduction to *The Works of Ossian*, where he asserted that "Frequent transcription and the corrections of those, who thought they mended the poems by modernizing the ideas, corrupted them."[49] Based on his understanding of epic structure, he considered himself fully capable of spotting the textual degeneration and late accretions he presumed to exist. His task, as he perceived it, was to reassemble the epic and restore it, to the best of his ability, to its original state. The degree of liberty taken in accomplishing this task is the subject of ongoing debate.

Without becoming enmeshed in the debate, it can be said that Macpherson's Ossianic texts differ considerably from his Gaelic source material, and are best viewed as creative adaptations rather than translations.[50] The

Fragments are most closely related to the native tradition—likely because there was no need to weave them into an imposed epic structure—but even these have been manipulated to fit Macpherson's vision of what ancient poetry should look like. While parts of them identifiably derive from Gaelic lays, the derivation is loose. Likewise, by Derick Thomson's count, there are twelve segments of *Fingal* that bear some resemblance to Gaelic Fenian and heroic plots, but there is also much that appears to be original composition. Despite the already-raging controversy, Macpherson grew bolder when composing his final epic. While allowing for a pleasing parallel with the two Homeric epics, *Temora* bears far less resemblance to the Gaelic Fenian tradition than the other Ossianic publications, only showing evidence of derivation in its first book.[51]

The Ossianic Controversy

Macpherson's initial collecting was likely prompted by Gaelic pride and a sense that in such uncertain times, a valuable aspect of his own culture could disappear without a trace. When he wrote that "the compositions of Ossian would have still remained in the obscurity of a lost language" if not for his so-called translations, he revealed a fear that the Gaelic language itself might not long survive the cultural changes taking place.[52] It seems he was also driven by a desire to succeed in the Anglophone literary world and reap the incumbent economic and social benefits of such success. A degree of posturing to better represent himself and his work in his explanatory writings may partially account for the lack of clarity regarding his methodology. Some of his stylistic choices may also have had just as much to do with his assessment that the Gaelic lays were not likely to "please a polished age" as they did with establishing a primitive, epic voice.[53] Yet among his greatest motivations in taking on, and continuing with, the Ossianic project appears to have been Scottish patriotism. Just as Scottish Gaels were denigrated within Scotland and greater Britain, English prejudice against Scots of any ethnicity was particularly high at this time. As Richard Sher notes, this widespread prejudice "crossed class and party lines," and found particularly brutal expression among some of the most influential of the English literati. To some degree, it was a holdover from earlier conflict, but it found renewed ideological purpose in its contemporary expression. At precisely the time of writing of the Ossianic texts, anti-Scottish bias was heard most loudly in two arenas, the political and the literary. It surfaced in response, on the one hand, to the political rise of the third Earl of Bute, John Stuart, to become British Prime Minister (1762–63), and on the other hand, to Scottish writers' growing success in an English market, which was perceived as a challenge to "English assumptions of supremacy."[54] According to such prejudice, Scots were commonly depicted as boorish, avaricious, deceitful, and worse. It is not difficult to sympathize with Macpherson's desire to push back against the caustic denigration of his countrymen, even while maintaining a critical stance regarding the ways in which he did so.

Seeking to establish the nobility of Scotland's past and the value of Scottish literature against English claims to the contrary, Macpherson proclaimed a Scottish origin for his protagonists. In so doing, he discounted the overwhelming evidence from within the Gaelic Fenian tradition, even in Scotland, that while some of the Fianna's exploits took place on Scottish soil, the heroes were of Irish stock. Additionally, in his copious academic-style notes, he presented a version of Irish and Scottish history in which he claimed a Scottish origin for, and primacy within, early Gaelic culture.[55] While this historical model contained a number of inconsistencies and contrasted with that of Irish authors, it was firmly rooted in a Scottish historical tradition stretching back to John of Fordun in the fourteenth century.[56] The adaptation of Fenian lays to the form of wholly Scottish epics that accorded with this version of history was, moreover, an ideologically charged move. In the contemporary literary landscape, the epic was seen as the pinnacle of artistic achievement, and ever since the publication of John Milton's *Paradise Lost* in 1667, many English intellectuals had considered that text Britain's epic equivalent to the works of Homer and Virgil.[57] With his Ossianic epics, Macpherson claimed both a far greater antiquity and an artistic primacy for a body of literature of Scottish origin. Using an academic annotation style, he imbued his works, and the historical claims therein, with an aura of learned authority to which his supporters were receptive.

The group of influential Lowland Scottish literati who encouraged Macpherson's work on the project and secured for him the necessary financial support were among the most affected by English prejudice against Scottish-authored literature. John Home's play *Douglas*, for instance, was rewarded with lukewarm responses from influential critics like Samuel Johnson, despite its success in Edinburgh and London. Among their motivations for backing the Ossianic epics, then, was almost certainly a similar desire to Macpherson's to vindicate Scottish literature. In the aftermath of the publications, those to whom the national bias of the works appealed sought to secure the Scottish epics' place in the literary vanguard, and Scotland as the heartland of the elevated moral sentiment that *Ossian* reflected and contemporary society valued.[58]

Also on the minds of Macpherson's backers was the Scottish militia crisis of the Seven Years' War. In 1757 a militia bill was passed from which Scotland was excluded. The exclusion was justified by claims that Scotland could not finance a militia, but a more likely explanation is that English politicians were loath to allow weapons into Jacobite hands so soon after Culloden. Scottish fears of invasion were amplified in 1760 when a French squadron entered Scottish waters. The mood in Parliament remained the same, however, and proposed revisions to the militia bill were defeated later that year—despite the lobbying of Home, Ferguson, and others.[59] In such men's active support for Macpherson's Ossianic texts can be read an attempt to promote British unity and assuage fears of armed and dangerous Scots. Unlike their counterparts in Gaelic Fenian narrative, Macpherson's epic heroes are the picture of restraint; as Mícheál Mac Craith states, "Fingal never gives vent to unbridled anger or brute force, even in a good cause." Yet when faced with the prospect of foreign attack, they display the utmost of "martial valour." The portrayal at the end of *Fingal* of hero and enemy reconciling, moreover, can be read as a recipe for friendly relations between England and Scotland.[60] Such features, while certainly calculated to fit an epic model and make the characters more attractive to contemporary readers, also served to counter stereotypes of the wild, barbaric Highlander. Thus, ironically, what started out as a collection project driven by Gaelic pride and veneration of a lost way of life resulted, with the support of militia-oriented Lowland backers, in the production of texts so well adapted to the values and language of the dominant culture that they communicated a message of successful acculturation—a 'making safe' of the Highlands, and therefore of Scotland.

The militia crisis highlights just how charged the atmosphere between England and Scotland was at the time. If matters of ethnicity and nationality had not carried so much weight, the bitter and lengthy controversy that arose over the legitimacy of the Ossianic texts might have amounted to little more than a flash in the pan. As it was, the reaction was almost immediate. Throughout the 1760s doubts were raised about precisely the aspects upon which the patriotic claim to their being great works of Scottish literature rested: their age, their elite classification as epics of Homeric caliber, and their Scottish (as opposed to Irish) origin.[61] While the early published criticism was sometimes vehemently anti-Scottish, at this point the works were generally accepted as authentically Gaelic in origin.[62] In the 1770s, however, the controversy advanced into a new, more scathing stage as the question of forgery took over and attacks took a more personal turn.

The tenor of the late eighteenth-century criticism is well captured in the commentary of Samuel Johnson, the most influential Ossianic critic of this era. Johnson presented an alternative view of Scottish Gaelic language and culture to the noble vision advanced by Macpherson. Repeating a common ethnic stereotype, he avowed that Scottish Gaelic was "the rude speech of a barbarous people," and he further argued that it "never was a written language; that there is not in the world [a Scottish Gaelic] manuscript a hundred years old; and that the sounds of the Highlanders were never expressed by letters" before the relatively recent translation of a few religious texts.[63] Johnson made a strict distinction between manuscripts written in Irish (of any stage) and those written in Scottish Gaelic, and he presumed the Early Modern Gaelic manuscripts that had existed longer than a century in Scotland to be of Irish extraction.[64] His thoughts regarding Gaelic manuscripts are particularly relevant because, even though Macpherson placed a heavy emphasis on his use of oral sources in the assembly of the Ossianic texts, Johnson felt strongly that nothing of length or merit could long be transmitted in oral form, and therefore the original texts, if they existed, must have been written.[65]

Johnson's comments appeared in 1775 in his *Journey to the Western Islands of Scotland,* which documented the trip he made to the Highlands, in part to seek evidence for the authenticity of the Ossianic epics. In his account, he claimed that he found all the evidence that was presented to him wanting (because no lengthy, ancient manuscript was presented), and that Macpherson's Scottish supporters were either purposely spreading lies or doing so unknowingly due to an inherent inability to think critically. He stated unequivocally, "I believe [the poems of Ossian] never existed in any other form than that which we have seen."[66] Johnson was by no means the only critic to accuse Macpherson of composing the Ossianic works himself, but he was among the first and loudest. The most famous published response is that of the early collector of Fenian lays, Rev. Donald MacNicol. In his 1779 *Remarks on Dr. Samuel Johnson's Journey to the Hebrides,* MacNicol refuted Johnson's claims about the Scottish Gaels' lack of learning and manuscripts in earlier centuries with evidence to the contrary and took umbrage at Johnson's caustic accusation of Scottish credulity. Expanding his scope, he discounted the criticism of like-minded individuals as the result of anti-Scottish bias, complaining about "men, who are unwilling to give credit to any thing calculated to reflect honour on the ancestors of the *Scotch* nation."[67] MacNicol also rebutted claims against the Ossianic texts' epic status and age. In his only concessions regarding the works' authenticity, he referenced Johnson's position that they were too long to have been preserved orally, and restated Macpherson's claim that the epics were not discovered whole, but assembled from multiple sources, many of which were oral:

> It is true, there is no man now living, and perhaps there never has existed any one person who either can or could repeat the whole of the Poems of *Ossian*. It is enough, that the whole has been repeated in detached pieces through the Highlands and Isles. Mr. *Macpherson*'s great merit has been the collecting the *disjecta membra poetae*; and his fitting the parts so well together, as to form a complete figure. . . . In the arrangement of the whole work, and even in the improvement of particular passages, the public are perhaps indebted to the taste and judgment of Mr. *Macpherson*. Being perfectly master of all the tradition relative to the *Fingalian* times, he has, no doubt, availed himself of that advantage, in placing the poems in their most natural order; and in restoring the scattered members of such pieces, as he found floating on tradition only, to their original stations.[68]

MacNicol's position that the works were authentic despite some "improvement" was typical of many supporters, just as Johnson's opinion that they contained such a copious amount of "improvement" that they were essentially original compositions was typical of many deniers. Each occupied a pole in the criticism comprising the Ossianic controversy, and each accused adherents of the opposite position of forming prejudicial views rooted in national pride. Both were to some degree correct.

The controversy continued in Britain in much the same fashion for the remainder of the century, fueled by, and in turn fueling, patriotic Scottish and English stances. The contributors were numerous, and the public spats between individuals were bitter. Johnson's Gaelic-speaking friend, the amateur lexicographer William Shaw, was the principal initiator of several such quarrels. Remarks and accusations published in Shaw's *An Enquiry into the Authenticity of the Poems Ascribed to Ossian* (1781) prompted disputes with Macpherson's former pupil John Clark, English author and soon-to-be bishop of Dromore, Co. Down Rev. Thomas Percy, and Highland-born philosopher Adam Ferguson (mentioned above). Many others, too, published their own opinions or gave fresh voice to arguments already made.[69] Given the identity politics at play in this time of "extreme national prejudice and suspicion," it was in neither side's interest to try to see the issue from the opposite perspective, or even from a more moderate one. Deniers were resolute in their stance that the work was a forgery, and supporters, even while admitting authorial interference, were quick to justify such actions with reference to the transmission of the early modern epics. They would argue that Macpherson had emulated Homer, collecting the strands of the narrative and binding them together, or else like "those who collected the books of Homer" after the poet's death.[70]

After Macpherson's death in 1796, it was hoped by both sides that the issue could finally be put to rest. In 1805, the Highland Society of Scotland published a comprehensive report on the texts' authenticity. In the preparation of this report, committee members had access to the surviving manuscripts gathered by Macpherson. Additionally, inquiries were made to acquire testimony and correspondence from as many parties with whom Macpherson had been in contact in the course of the Ossianic project as possible. The committee published irrefutable evidence of a Gaelic oral and written Fenian tradition, and noted significant differences in style and content between the Gaelic lays and Macpherson's works. While the authors recognized the likelihood of a great deal of adaptation and addition, however, they were reluctant to deliver a harsh verdict without being able to consult all of the same oral texts Macpherson did.[71] Even so, the report on the authenticity of *Ossian* likely represents the most balanced treatment of the issue possible at the time, and it was certainly the fairest effort made to resolve the controversy.

The other two major contributions to the controversy in the early years of the nineteenth century took the form of editions. Malcolm Laing's critical edition was published in 1805, the same year as the Highland Society's report. Laing sought to expose Macpherson's fraud by illustrating, sometimes creatively, that nearly every element of the Ossianic works could be traced to a non-Gaelic literary source. While he may have had some insight into Macpherson's motivation, his lack of knowledge about the Gaelic literary and oral traditions is obvious, and many of his comparisons are tenuous.[72] The other important edition consists, allegedly, of *The Poems of Ossian, in the Original Gaelic* (1807). There is evidence that concurrent composition of at least some of the Gaelic text was taking place during the creation of *Fingal*, and that it was something of a group effort. All of the persons whose names have been associated with the Gaelic version are also thought to have aided with the English one. In addition to James Macpherson, these are Rev. Andrew Gallie, Lachlan Macpherson, and Capt. Alexander Morison.[73] In the advertisement preceding the first edition of *Fingal*, Macpherson asserted that "there is a design on foot to print the Originals," but admitted the possibility that "this publication [may] not take place."[74] It did not, according to the publisher, due to a lack of subscribers. In 1779 the preparation of the Gaelic text for publication was again advertised in MacNicol's *Remarks on Dr. Samuel Johnson's Journey to the Hebrides*. If Macpherson found renewed interest in the project in the wake of Johnson's criticism, however, he seems to have lost it again. The Gaelic version of the Ossianic epics had to be recovered from his papers after his death and remains incomplete, lacking eleven poems.[75] Those responsible for finally bringing the edition into print likely believed that it would prove the Ossianic supporters' case beyond a doubt. For those receptive to such a message, it was seen to have done so, just as Laing's edition was considered revelatory by many authenticity deniers. Neither edition was widely accepted by adversaries as conclusive proof.[76]

Macpherson's Ossianic epics were monumental publications that penetrated to the heart of Scottish identity and, as the coming chapters will demonstrate in greater detail, forever altered the perception of the Gaelic Fenian tradition in Scotland and beyond. Emerging from social tension, they in turn stoked controversy. In their creation, the young and ambitious Macpherson sought to elevate public perception of his oft-denigrated culture, and to make a name for himself in the process. Whatever liberties he is seen to have taken with his source material—well-intentioned or otherwise—he certainly did not seek to kindle a contentious debate. But kindle it he did, and the critical fires raged throughout the latter part of the century, turning up ever more fodder. By 1805, copious amounts of information had been brought to light without a definitive verdict, ensuring that *Ossian* would remain contentious for years to come. The intense scrutiny does not seem to have troubled Macpherson overmuch, however. Withdrawing entirely from the controversy, he let the allegations against him go unanswered. What mattered to him were his Highlands, not his critics. Although he departed the familiar crags and glens of Badenoch when he took up *Ossian*, passing many successful years in London and abroad, he acquired a large estate there later in life. In 1796 when he drew his last breath in his Highland abode, he was elegized in Gaelic.[77] Fittingly memorialized in the oral medium of song, his legacy was also to be etched in stone above his grave in London's Westminster Abbey. Johnson, having preceded him there, did not object to the honor.

5

Romantic Highlands and Godly Fingalians

AS *FINGAL* and *Temora* rose to the status of international bestsellers, the world turned its gaze upon Scotland. Western popular culture was soon awash with translations and inspired creations, the adapted Fenian heroes appearing in diverse media and speaking languages more foreign to them than English. As international readers' fascination deepened, some were motivated to learn Gaelic and many others embarked on Highland tours, seeking to experience the sublime scenes that haunted *Ossian*'s pages for themselves. In the epics' homeland from the mid-eighteenth to the mid-nineteenth centuries, however, the Ossianic spotlight was characterized by "ideological ambivalence."[1] Scottish Gaels cannot have universally welcomed a stream of tourists whose romanticized preconceptions encouraged them to view their hosts in a primitivist light—and yet there is no denying that Macpherson's portrayals contributed to a revitalization of the Highlands' image. Indeed, the texts were sources of great pride for Scottish Gaels, and Highland ministers, in particular, defended them passionately, finding faith in *Ossian* to be quite compatible with religious belief. The attention the epics received also supported the preservation and publication of much traditional Fenian narrative and stimulated Gaelic literary production in the Ossianic mode. In the century after Macpherson's texts debuted, the Highland region and its culture thus came to be viewed through an Ossianic lens from both within and without.

Ossian's Widespread Appeal

Readers' interest may have been piqued initially by *Fingal* and *Temora*'s presentation as ancient epics, but it was Macpherson's compellingly unique content and emotive style that held his audience's attention, regardless of the authenticity controversy emanating from ivory towers.[2] Within Britain, authors, playwrights, musicians, and artists began expressing their admiration almost immediately in modes ranging from stylistic imitation to inspired creation. Numerous versified editions were published, first of individual 'fragments' and eventually of the complete works, and poets took Ossianic themes in new directions. Dramatic and musical adaptations with varying degrees of resemblance to Macpherson's epics were also common, and took the form of plays, closet dramas, pantomimes, operas, and chorales.[3] The 1768 operetta *Oithóna*, for instance, closely followed Macpherson's text, while the 1791 ballet pantomime *Oscar and Malvina* was an inspired creation in the Ossianic mode.[4] In the visual arts, a massive bust of Ossian (now lost) graced the gateway of a London statuary workshop from circa 1770, and in 1772 painter Alexander Runciman created "the first sustained visual response to *Ossian*," an elaborate ceiling mural of seventeen compositions in the drawing room of Penicuik House near Edinburgh (lost to fire in 1899).[5]

The heated controversy among the British literary elite about *Ossian*'s authenticity had even less relevance to the reading public on the European continent, where the texts were most often experienced in translation. There were multiple and varied translations to be had, although in many regions it was a few decades before the fully translated works hit the market. Among the earliest and most influential were Melchiorre Cesarotti's Italian editions (1763, partial; 1773, full), Michael Denis's German edition (1768–69), and Pierre Le Tourneur's French edition (1776–77). These were followed by, and used in the production of, many others.[6] Even being a translator of *Ossian* could bring renown, as in the case of Cesarotti, who adopted the moniker 'Padre Ossian' and basked in the admiration of the likes of French Emperor Napoleon Bonaparte and King Stanislaus of Poland.[7] The availability of the texts in translation prompted a spate of poetic imitation on the continent, which was soon accompanied by inspired creative works.

Johann Wolfgang von Goethe is among the most important of Macpherson's continental adherents, since he concurrently played a role as an Ossianic translator, and it was through him that many enthusiasts got their first taste of *Ossian*. The tormented protagonist of his 1774 breakout novel *Die Leiden des Jungen Werther* (*The Sorrows of Young Werther*) identifies so strongly with Ossian that he translates a lengthy extract from *Fingal*.[8] Vastly better than Denis's translation, in Howard Gaskill's estimation this extract "contributed mightily to raising *Ossian* to the status of a cult text both in Germany and beyond."[9] What is more, Goethe was driven to learn to read *Ossian* in Gaelic. Macpherson's

Temora included a Gaelic version of the seventh book, which was likely intended to allay any early doubt about his sources, but which Denis omitted. Upon encountering the Gaelic text in an English edition, Goethe attempted to translate it with the encouragement of his friend, Johann Gottfried Herder.[10] While the thirty-eight lines he produced in August and September 1771 were not entirely accurate, they represent an impressive accomplishment, given the likelihood that he neither had adequate resources nor a native speaker to hand for consultation.[11] Goethe also published a pirated four-volume English edition of *Ossian* with Johann Heinrich Merck in 1773–77, which further increased the epics' reach and contributed to their popularity.[12]

As Goethe's literary career took off, Herder was on his way to becoming the philosophical dynamo of German romanticism. His receipt of a review copy of Denis's *Ossian* in 1769 proved influential.[13] In his response, published in 1773, he critiqued Denis's work and outlined his own perspectives on translation. Poetic form, he argued, was integral to meaning, and Denis's polished metrical hexameter stripped *Ossian* of "Ausrüfe über das Wilde, oder Sanfte, oder Feierliche oder Kriegerische" ("the feeling of wildness, gentleness, celebration, [or] war") so that it no longer sounded like the poetry of "eines ungebildeten sinnlichen Volks" ("an uneducated but sensitive people") transmitted across the ages.[14] As a translator, he declared, "Hätte ich gewiß auf andern Wegen ähnliche Schritte thun wollen, die jetzt—Denis nicht gethan hat" ("I should surely have wanted to follow a different path, that is, to do what Denis did not do").[15] No idle threat, with his own principles in mind, Herder went on to revise two of Goethe's Gaelic-derived poems and translate another from English for his landmark 1778–79 collection of 'folk' songs, the *Volkslieder*.[16] Like his friend, he was eager to experience the Scottish bard in the supposed original language, and it seems he hoped to supersede Denis by translating the complete Gaelic *Ossian* when it was finally published.[17] It came too late for him, however, and the task fell to another.[18]

Like Macpherson, Herder was interested in concepts of cultural primitivism put forward by Blackwell and others. William Wilson and Howard Gaskill have suggested that his ideas about culture were both reinforced and developed through his reading of Denis's edition of *Ossian*, despite his disapproval of the translation style. In notes to the text that Denis derived from Cesarotti, Herder encountered Giambattista Vico's premise that "each historical epoch forms an independent cultural entity whose various parts are integrally related to form an organic whole."[19] Denis's edition also included Rev. Dr. Hugh Blair's "Critical Dissertation on the Poems of Ossian," which reiterated

Blackwellian ideas about the "primarily emotional origin" of language and the fundamentally emotive qualities of 'primitive' poetry, and extended them to so-called primitive societies in less ancient epochs than that of Homer—including, of course, third-century Scottish Gaels, but also contemporary Sámi people.[20] Aspects of these ideas can be traced in the formulation of Herder's premises that each nation is unique and organically formed by its environment, and that the vitality of a nation rests in its recognition and developmental expression of its own national character.[21] For him, this national character was to be sought in history and accessed through the contemporary vestiges of the nation's history: its vernacular language and its folk songs.

To Herder, *Ossian* offered "a model for national regeneration" in its creative evocation of the history, the spirit, and the voice of a nation.[22] It bears pointing out, as Gaskill has done, that unlike some continental readers, Herder was well versed in the authenticity debate and suspected early on that Macpherson's source material had been adapted to conform to an epic structure.[23] This was immaterial. For Herder, the designation *Volk* ('folk' or 'people,' but also 'nation') had to do with nationality. Such diverse figures as Aeschylus, Sophocles, Homer, Shakespeare, and Ossian were folk poets because their works captured the spirit of their nations. Germans had turned away from their vernacular culture, Herder claimed, for which reason there were no contemporary literary 'folk' or 'national' poets. However, the spirit of the nation could still be recovered from orally preserved peasant songs. Only these songs remained largely untainted by foreign influence, and so it was on them that German literature should be modeled.[24] He therefore encouraged his fellow literati to collect folk songs, as Macpherson had done:

> We Germans should also have many more such poems as I indicated when speaking of Scottish romance. . . . In more than one province I am acquainted with folksongs, regional songs, peasant songs that certainly would lack nothing when it comes to liveliness and rhythm, naïveté and strength of language; but who is there to collect them? to care about them? to care about the songs of the people? from streets and alleys and fishmarkets? in the traditional roundelays of the country folk? about songs that are often unscanned and poorly rhymed? who would collect them?[25]

Goethe answered his mentor's call, sending Herder a selection of orally gathered Alsatian ballads, and he and fellow writers of the *Sturm und Drang* movement took up the gauntlet to create the contemporary vernacular literature that Herder believed the nation lacked. With the spontaneous, expressive vigour of their language and phrasing, identified by Herder as typical of folk poetry, these writers ushered in a new literary era.[26] It is on their foundation that German romanticism rests.

As romanticism swept across the continent and beyond, so too did appreciation for Macpherson's *Ossian*. Indeed, the list of writers gripped by Ossianism in the late eighteenth and early nineteenth century reads like a directory of the literary elite—Goethe, of course, and also Schiller, Novalis, and Hölderlin in Germany, Chateaubriand, Staël, and Lamartine in France, Foscolo and Leopardi in Italy, and Pushkin and Lermontov in Russia, just to name a few.[27] Ossianic dramas, operas, and musical compositions took shape in France, Germany, Austria, the Netherlands, Italy, Spain, Denmark, and Russia.[28] Major political figures enjoyed *Ossian*, as well. Napoleon found the epics so inspiring that he carried a copy with him on campaign and commissioned thematic artwork by prominent painters, including François-Pascal-Simon Gérard, Anne-Louis Girodet, and Jean-Auguste-Dominique Ingres (fig. 8).[29] Napoleon's Ossianic passion is also responsible for the royal King Oscars in Sweden, since the boy destined to become Oscar I was named by his godfather, who was none other than the French emperor.[30] The texts gained popularity and elicited a creative response overseas too, and the future American president Thomas Jefferson declared Ossian "the greatest Poet that has ever existed."[31] Like Goethe and Herder, Jefferson's interest was both intense and scholarly. In 1773 he wrote to Macpherson to request the Gaelic originals, along with a grammar and dictionary with which he might study them. His request was rewarded with the Gaelic New Testament and a vocabulary compiled in 1741 by the prominent poet and schoolteacher Alasdair mac Mhaighstir Alasdair, but no Gaelic *Ossian*.[32] As we know, this had yet to be completed.

Burgeoning romanticism also bolstered Ossianic appreciation on the shores of the epics' birth, even after Malcolm Laing's critical edition cast further doubt on the works' authenticity in 1805. Indeed, many of the early nineteenth-century Lowland and English literary greats fell under the Macphersonic spell, or at the very least succumbed to *Ossian*'s topical influence, even while disapproving of its creator's methodology.[33] Sir Walter Scott, for instance, accepted the arguments against authenticity, yet still praised the epics' beauty, lauded their international reach, and adopted traits from them into his own writing style.[34] Fellow literary Lowlander, Robert Burns counted *Ossian* among his favorite works, and both Samuel Taylor Coleridge and Lord Byron, leading figures in English romanticism, published poems openly evoking Macpherson's epics. Even William Wordsworth, who railed against *Ossian*'s popularity, can be shown to have derived aspects of his style from Macpherson.[35] British artists also took Ossianic inspiration, the most celebrated being the English romanticist painter J.M.W. Turner.[36]

FIGURE 8. Jean-Auguste-Dominique Ingres, *Le Songe d'Ossian* (1813). (Alamy. Owned by Musée Ingres Bourdelle, Montauban, France.)

The Highlands' New Image

As *Ossian* took the world by storm, winds of change were blowing in Scotland. While the Highlands were once denigrated by Lowlanders and English alike, Highland heritage now began to be celebrated. The Highland Society of London was an early contributor to this shift. Founded by Scottish expatriates in

1778, James Macpherson among them, the society declared its dedication both to the social betterment of Highlanders and to the maintenance of their unique culture. Pursuant to its cultural goals, it established annual piping competitions, which were held in Falkirk from 1781 to 1783 and in Edinburgh from 1784 to 1844, in conjunction with the newly founded Highland Society of Scotland.[37] In 1780, a Society of Antiquaries of Scotland also formed, which initiated archaeological fieldwork and artifact collecting. These activities led to the establishment and popularization of recognized symbols of Highland heritage. Jewelry makers drew inspiration from historical depictions and artifacts to produce Celtic-inspired markers of Scottishness, and tartan, which had been banned as seditious between 1746 and 1782, grew popular.[38]

In different circumstances, such cultural nationalism in an upstart region might have fanned the flames of sociopolitical grievance, strengthening the cultural divide and prompting pushback, but in this instance it remained in the romantic realm. The punitive measures of the post-Culloden period and the ongoing mass evictions to enable rural economic development effectively eliminated the threat of further rebellion.[39] Consequently, even the Highland uprisings, relegated as they were to the past, could be rendered safe topics. Scott's sentimental neo-Jacobitism in his popular first novel *Waverley* (1814) is a case in point. Depicting the valorous but ill-fated rebels in a primitivist light, Scott established an implicit contrast between them and contemporary, rational, nonrebellious Scots.[40] The British integration of Scottish Gaelic cultural nationalism is further apparent in King George IV's 1822 visit to Scotland. This was the first time in nearly two hundred years that a reigning monarch had passed north of the border, and it was a powerful recognition of Scotland's place within the United Kingdom. The occasion was marked by Highland-themed pageantry orchestrated by Scott, and famously, the king donned a kilt.[41]

The attention generated by Macpherson's epics contributed to the revitalization—and romanticization—of the image of the Highlands. As Nigel Leask observes, "the publication of Ossian reinvented the Highland landscape as the scene of heroic Fingalian resistance" of foreign incursion.[42] Of course, Highlanders well knew theirs was a heroic land, having recounted the adventures of Fionn and his followers in every corner of the region since time immemorial—but now all of Britain and beyond knew their peaks, valleys, and islands as the haunts of the Fianna's celebrated doppelgängers. Macpherson's emotive descriptions of this landscape engendered pride among its modern denizens, like the fourth Duke of Atholl, who in 1782–83 transformed a structure on his Dunkeld, Perthshire estate into a veritable shrine to the epics.

Ossian's Hall, as it is still known, overlooks a waterfall not unlike the resounding cataracts of the popular publications, and for several decades housed a painting of the ancient bard.[43] Among outsiders, Macpherson's scenes awakened new interest in the Scottish Highlands.

Growing curiosity coincided with the expansion of transportation infrastructure throughout Scotland. As remote parts of the country became more easily accessible to travelers, Highland tourism grew popular. The new cultural tourists sought the Ossianic experience of awe-inspiring, sublime scenery, which the topographical ambiguity of Macpherson's notes enabled them to discover almost anywhere they went.[44] Those of more particular taste were aided by the provision in the first edition of the Gaelic *Ossian* (1807) of a "Map of Ancient Selma, the residence of Fingal, with part of the Fingalian Territories in the Shire of Argyle" (fig. 9) by the statistical geographer Sir John Sinclair, alongside topographical descriptions by other notable scholars.[45] It is this landscape that Dorothy Wordsworth described as "inviting to the fancy" and voyagers like Welsh naturalist Thomas Pennant and London *Times* editor John Stoddart explored in popular travelogues replete with Ossianic references.[46] The Macphersonic heroes even turned up in fictionalized accounts of Highland tours, beginning with Lowland author Tobias Smollett's epistolary novel, *The Expedition of Humphrey Clinker* (1771). Indeed, the description Smollett's character Jeremy Melford pens of his Inveraray surroundings well captures the romantic outlook of many contemporary travelers: "We have had princely sport in hunting the stag on these mountains—These are the lonely hills of Morven, where Fingal and his heroes enjoyed the same pastime: I feel an enthusiastic pleasure when I survey the brown heath that Ossian wont to tread; and hear the wind whistle through the bending grass—When I enter our landlord's hall, I look for the suspended harp of that divine bard, and listen in hopes of hearing the aerial sound of his respected spirit."[47]

Visitors to the Highlands not only observed (and described) their newly sublime surroundings, they also left their mark on them. As a symptom of Ossianic tourism, some locations that had no prior connection with either the Fenian tradition or Macpherson's Ossianic texts were imbued with Ossianic resonance, soon becoming standard stops on increasingly regular routes. Sites like Ossian's cave in Dunkeld (near the Duke of Atholl's storied hall), Ossian's grave north of Creiff, the graves of Oscar and Malvina on the Isle of Arran, and Loch Ossian east of Fort William all likely emerged from Ossianic rather than traditional roots.[48] Some such identifications issued from tourists' pens and were reified through subsequent iterations. Fingal's Cave on the Isle of Staffa

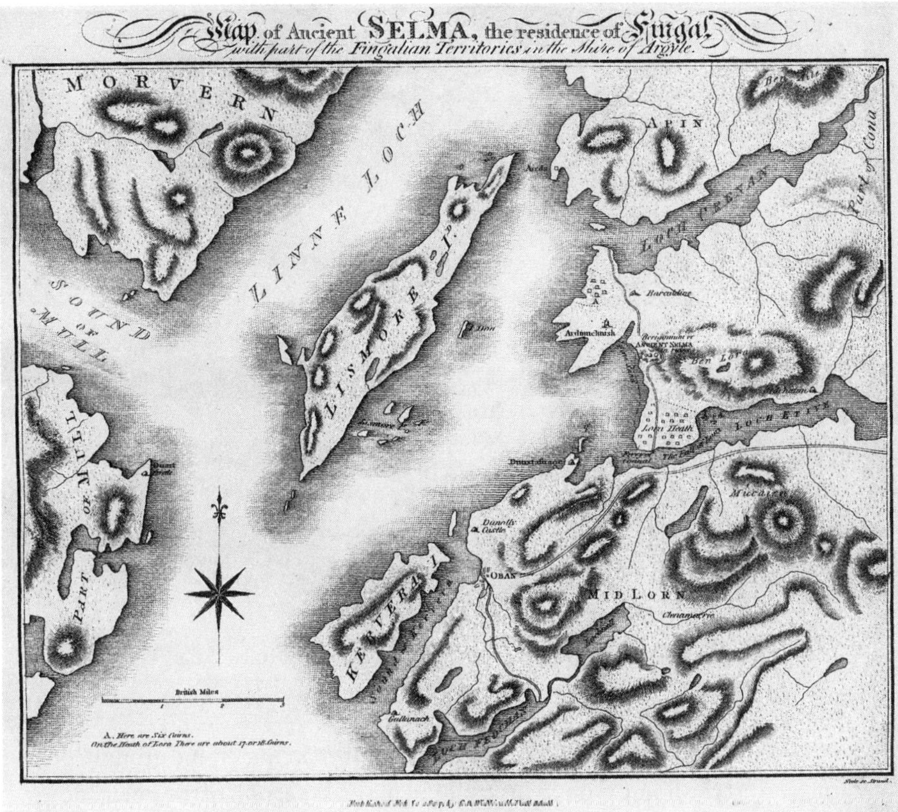

FIGURE 9. Map of Selma in the first edition of the Gaelic *Ossian* (1807). (Widener Library, Harvard University.)

(fig. 10) is a prominent case in point. Sir Joseph Banks first called the popular site by that name in 1772, citing the authority of a local guide. While the actual name may have been *an uamh bhinn*, 'the melodious cave,' and not the homophonous *uamh Fhinn*, 'the cave of Fionn,' it is significant that neither the Fenian nor the non-Fenian version was selected for inclusion on the Ordnance Survey map.[49] Rather, the Ossianic name coined by Banks and publicized by countless others became the official designation and remains current today. This altered nomenclature can be seen to parallel the economic 'improvement' projects on which Ossianic tourism was dependent for the modes of transportation that they brought, but which altered the very landscape tourists came to see.[50]

Indeed, the overwriting of place names serves as a reminder of the implicit colonialism of the Highland tour. As Paul Baines notes, "The tourist

FIGURE 10. Fingal's Cave, Staffa, Scotland. (Alamy. Photo by Allan Wright.)

appropriation of Ossian enacted the poem on its national home ground, or rather, recast the home ground in an all-but limitless version of the poem, not so much researching or supporting the authenticity of what Macpherson had published, but identifying it with the Highlands, or even Scotland as a whole in a colonial gesture which acts as a kind of literary evacuation."[51] Tourists did not come to experience the region as it was, but to claim the Highlands as their Ossianic playground, and to view the Gaelic-speaking inhabitants as native-exotic remnants of a posited past. They longed for caves that were once frequented by Ossianic heroes; for halls that echoed with the memory of ancient bardic odes; and for rustic locals who could recite all the poems of Ossian "in the original Gaelick," as Smollett's tourists exalted in finding.[52] For Highlanders, *Ossian* thus proved both a blessing and a curse.

Ossian the Blessed

Among those Highlanders most invested in *Ossian* were Presbyterian ministers. The clergy's interest in Macpherson's epics is somewhat ironic, given the earliest mention of the Fenian heroes by a representative of the Church of

Scotland. This occurred in the first book printed in a Gaelic language, John Carswell's *Foirm na n-Urrnuidheadh* (1567), an Early Modern Gaelic translation of John Knox's *Book of Common Order* (1556). In his preface, Carswell described Fenian stories, among other genres of traditional Gaelic narrative, as "eachtradha dīmhaoineacha buaidheartha brēgacha saoghalta" ("vain, seductive, lying and worldly tales") and cautioned avoidance of them.[53] In the eighteenth century, however, many clergy came to see great value in both the traditional Gaelic tales and the adapted English epics. After the publication of *Ossian*, Highland ministers were among Macpherson's most vehement supporters, upholding an emergent perception of the Fianna—in their Ossianic guises—as the ultimate expressions of honorable Scottish ideals.

The clerical passion for *Ossian*'s pagan heroes is partially explicable by the large involvement of members of the clergy in bringing the epics into being. Rev. Dr. Hugh Blair occupied his chair at the University of Edinburgh concurrently with his appointment to Saint Giles Church, and he was known as much for his academic work as for his sermons. Also within the inner Ossianic circle were John Home and Adam Ferguson, both ordained ministers.[54] The degree to which Blair and his clerical brethren influenced the form *Ossian* took is unclear—after all, Macpherson himself studied divinity—but they certainly saw nothing vain, seductive, or otherwise objectionable in the epics. Indeed, Blair concluded his 1763 "Critical Dissertation" with the declaration that Ossian "is always moral. Though his merit were in other respects much less than it is, this alone ought to entitle him to high regard, that his writings are remarkably favorable to virtue. They awake the tenderest sympathies, and inspire the most generous emotions. No reader can rise from him without being warmed with the sentiments of humanity, virtue, and honour."[55] The moral virtue the learned reverend perceived in the texts also met with subsequent ministers' approval, providing ethical grounds for continued clerical endorsement. As Rev. Dr. Thomas McLauchlan would later quip in the preface to his 1859 edition of the Gaelic *Ossian*, "The purest mind may come in contact with [the poems] without repugnance, or the danger of pollution. They may not be religious; they are certainly not immoral."[56] In remarks reminiscent of Saint Patrick's absolution of Fenian audiences in the *Acallam*, elevated clerical commentators thus authorized and reauthorized consumption of these purportedly pagan texts as religiously defensible.

The intellectual atmosphere in which late eighteenth- and early nineteenth-century Highland ministers operated also likely predisposed them toward *Ossian*. Notwithstanding the Scottish and Gaelic pride the epics evoked, there were ecclesiastical reasons for ministers to concern themselves with matters of ancient Scottish history. Like other Protestant denominations in the wake of the Reformation, Scottish Presbyterians had engaged in historical investigations to establish pre-Reformation roots for their faith.[57] From the mid-seventeenth century, a perception of early Gaelic Christianity gained currency according to which Gaelic Christians were less Romanized due to the influence of native tradition.[58] The publication of *Ossian* would have been opportune for proponents of this medieval proto-Presbyterianism. While Macpherson and Blair both stressed the Ossianic heroes' lack of religious beliefs, Blair praised their dignity and sublimity—the latter evoking "the highest ideas of human perfection"—at a time when other European ethnic groups were thought to tend toward barbarism.[59] The version of early Scotland depicted in *Ossian* thus suggested an inherent virtuosity worthy not only of ethnic pride, but also of evangelical emulation. What is more, as Donald Meek has asserted, under the influence of *Ossian*, Highland Presbyterians' conception of early Gaelic Christianity took on a sublime, naturalistic aspect, and "spiritual romanticism" thrived, particularly after 1800.[60]

When it came to the Ossianic controversy, Highland ministers affirmed without reservation the authenticity convincingly argued by Blair.[61] As Gaelic speakers, they were well able to recognize differences between orally circulating lays and Macpherson's epics, but what concerned them most was not establishing a precise textual correspondence. They were far more interested in the ability of traditional narrative to uphold the desirable image of the Fianna established in *Ossian*. They could clearly perceive a similarity of characters and themes, and they considered this to be adequate evidence; after all, Macpherson's sources were not known and could contain different material than they themselves had encountered. This attitude is evident in letters to the Highland Society of Scotland's committee on authenticity by ministers who stressed the difficulty in adjudicating "the degree of liberty used by Mr. Macpherson" in the absence of his field notes.[62] Steadfast in their conviction that the texts were, on the whole, genuine, these officiants' faith in *Ossian* resembled religious belief. The texts were reportedly even used in a formal capacity to support church teachings: Donald MacPhie of Barra told a folklore collector in the 1860s that his local catechist used to read *Ossian* to the congregation.[63] Perhaps influenced by such ministrations, other Highlanders also came to share the clergy's Ossianic devotion. As Rev. John MacDonald of Ferintosh, Ross and Cromarty reported in 1805, the texts' authenticity was "as firmly believed in the Highlands as the truth of any tradition whatever. Learned and unlearned, young and old, agree in this." According to MacDonald, when he asked one elderly Lochalsh man whether he believed Ossian's poems were genuine, the man countered with a retort: "Do I believe the Bible?"[64]

Ossian and the Collection and Publication of Scottish Lays

MacDonald of Ferintosh belonged to a cohort of Highland folklore collectors, many of them ministers, who were spurred to action in the period following the publication of Macpherson's *Ossian*. Fired as much by pride in the rejuvenated image of the Highlander as by indignation at Johnson's portrayal of Gaelic Scotland as a nonliterary culture, these individuals took it upon themselves to document a massive amount of orally circulating poetry, including many Fenian lays.

The drive to collect began almost immediately. As early as 1767, the religious poet Rev. Dugald Buchanan (Dùghall Bochanan), clearly inspired by *Ossian*, sought funding for a trip to gather "the Poems of the antient & modern Bards . . . to inform [Scots] of the heroic valour the love of Liberty the tender Passion the natural Description, the sublime Sentiment and unparalelled [*sic*] Hospitality of their great forefathers."[65] Buchanan's proposed venture does not appear to have been sponsored or undertaken, but others were engaged in less formal collecting activities. Rev. James McLagan and Rev. Donald MacNicol, who began gathering Gaelic verse prior to Macpherson's literary success, were still active at this time, and Rev. Ewen MacDiarmid of Comrie, Perthshire began noting down poetry, including Fenian lays, around 1762.[66] The following decades saw Duncan Kennedy of Argyll and Ranald MacDonald (Raghnall Dubh) of Eigg join the fray. While Kennedy was a schoolmaster rather than a minister, the notes accompanying the numerous lays he collected in Argyll, Lochaber, Mull, and Eigg between 1774 and 1783 are dotted with biblical passages, and like the ministers, "he seems to have considered the historicity of the [lays] as 'gospel truth,'" as Anja Gunderloch surmises.[67]

Ranald MacDonald was the son of the celebrated poet Alasdair mac Mhaighstir Alasdair, whose 1741 Gaelic vocabulary found its way into Thomas Jefferson's hands. To MacDonald we owe the first Gaelic poetry anthology, *Comh-chruinneachidh Orannaigh Gaidhealach* (A collection of Gaelic songs), published in 1776 and colloquially known as the Eigg Collection. Although motivated by the Ossianic controversy, this volume does not contain any Fenian verse, but it paved the way for subsequent projects.[68] One decade later, in 1786, Perth bookseller John Gillies published the largest eighteenth-century anthology of Gaelic poetry, *Sean Dain, agus Orain Ghaidhealach / A Collection of Ancient and Modern Gaelic Poems and Songs*, known as the Gillies Collection. This tome is still one of the most important sources for the study of Scottish Gaelic heroic narrative, significant both for its early publication date and for the sixteen orally collected Fenian lays—many of them lengthy—that it contains.[69] While Gillies oversaw the project, his opening advertisement indicates that he was not conversant in Gaelic and he did not gather the material himself.[70] The greatest contributor was the redoubtable McLagan, who one can imagine was more than happy to support this landmark volume of Gaelic poetry, just as he had readily contributed to Macpherson's venture.[71]

By this time, the controversy over *Ossian*'s authenticity had grown heated and popular interest in Macpherson's texts was exploding. As outsiders like Goethe, Herder, and Jefferson pined for the purported originals of restored ancient epics, others grew curious about the Gaelic lays. The Gillies Collection included no translations, so it did not have a significant impact among this demographic. However, burgeoning Highland tourism made it easier for the inquisitive to seek firsthand knowledge of the Gaelic Fenian tradition, and some individuals went so far as to publish their findings. Notably, in 1782 and 1783 a small collection of heroic verse gathered by Thomas F. Hill, an English Quaker, appeared in the widely circulated *Gentleman's Magazine*. Hill visited Argyll and Lochaber in 1780 and came away with seven Fenian lays, most of them provided by Alexander MacNab, the Dalmallie blacksmith, which beneficent Gaels translated for him.[72] Hill's publication roused further curiosity, and MacNab soon became well enough known that tourists sought him out for his accounts of the Fenian heroes and his opinions about *Ossian*.[73] They also scoured crags and glens in the hope of discovering new reciters, and boasted in their journals and travelogues about hearing the songs of Ossian, despite the lays' incomprehensibility to them.[74]

Ossian was also the driving force behind a new wave of collecting by Highlanders around the turn of the nineteenth century, when the Highland Society launched its investigation into the epics' authenticity. In order to prepare the most comprehensive report possible, the appointed committee circulated a request for orally collected Fenian poetry throughout the Highlands and islands.[75] Not all of the texts that were submitted survive, but among those that do are twenty-four Fenian lays collected by Rev. Alexander Irvine of Little Dunkeld, Perthshire between 1797 and 1805.[76] We likewise have eight Fenian lays collected in Sutherland and Caithness by Rev. Alexander Sage of Kildonan and four gathered in the early 1800s by John Macpherson (Iain MacMhuirich), a schoolmaster on Mull, at the behest of Ranald MacDonald of Staffa, a member of the committee on authenticity.[77] Also collected at this time and furnished to the committee were thirteen poetic specimens about the Fianna's escapades procured by Peter MacFarlane in Argyll and seven somewhat less complete Fenian lays contributed by another committee member, Sir George Mackenzie of Coul, Ross and Cromarty.[78]

Other collectors of this generation worked independently of the Highland Society investigation, although they too had *Ossian* in their purview. Rev. Alexander Campbell of Portree, Skye was one such individual. Inspired by Macpherson, Campbell amassed thirteen Fenian poems around 1797.[79] A decade later, after the report on authenticity was published, he tried to sell his collection to the Highland Society, but his offer was refused, perhaps for reasons discussed in the next section.[80] Rev. John MacDonald of Ferintosh, mentioned above, was motivated by a similar spirit. In 1805 he set out on a tour of northwest Scotland, determined "to ascertain to what extent traditions of the Fingalians existed in the Highlands, and whether Ossian's poems were still remembered."[81] His trip resulted in the collection of eight Fenian lays.[82]

Collectors' ongoing interest in Gaelic heroic narrative naturally led to the inclusion of material about Fionn and the Fianna in additional anthologies of Gaelic poetry, which were becoming ever more prevalent in the early nineteenth century.[83] Not only did Alexander and Donald Stewart devote space to a handful of Fenian selections in their sizable 1804 collection *Cochruinneacha Taoghta de Shaothair nam Bard Gaëleach / A Choice Collection of the Works of the Highland Bards*,[84] in 1816 Hugh and John MacCallum printed fifteen Fenian lays in *An Original Collection of the Poems of Ossian, Orran, Ulin, and Other Bards*, a bilingual two-volume collection devoted to heroic verse. The lays in the latter anthology came from multiple contributors, including Rev. Alexander Irvine, and they complemented the copious heroic material in the earlier Gillies Collection.[85]

As with the Gaelic manuscript tradition—which by this time was quite attenuated in Scotland—the increasing presence of Fenian lays in these print collections likely helped to reinforce the orally circulating texts, while *Ossian*'s popularity surely helped them maintain their prestige. Indeed, later collecting has shown that the lays continued to be sung in the Highlands and islands throughout the nineteenth and twentieth centuries (see chapters 7 and 9). Very little Macphersonic verse has ever been orally collected, however, despite the publication of the Gaelic *Ossian*. The folk preferred the traditional texts.[86]

Ossianic Gaelic Imitation and Influence

Macpherson's creative adaptations may have proved resistant to oral circulation, but they had a significant impact on Gaelic literary production. Indeed, Donald Meek has shown that "there was a widespread desire to replicate the style of *Ossian* in Gaelic."[87] This desire was most fully realized in the 1780s by Rev. John Smith of Campbeltown, who published the supposed English translations and alleged Gaelic originals of his own Fenian adaptations, alongside a dissertation asserting the authenticity of *Ossian*. The prose poetry in his *Galic Antiquities* (1780) is stylistically similar to the earlier epics, and like Macpherson, Smith took inspiration from the Gaelic tradition. To explain the verses' omission from *Ossian*, he claimed to have encountered them in regions his predecessor did not reach: "Early struck with the beauty of some of them . . . and finding that they had escaped the inquiries of the able and ingenious translator of Ossian, whose researches were chiefly confined to the more northern parts of the Highlands, I began to collect them for my own amusement."[88] He further maintained that he published the poems only with considerable encouragement, again copying a Macphersonic model.[89] Regardless of his projected altruism, however, his motivation was at least partly monetary; piggybacking on *Ossian*'s popularity, he hoped the proceeds of the English-language volume would be sufficient to fund the publication of his Gaelic translation of the Old Testament.[90] Unfortunately for him, his fundraising effort was unsuccessful, even though his purportedly ancient poetry amassed a large international following. Sales of unauthorized foreign editions and translations of *Galic Antiquities* were abundant, but Smith received no revenue from these.[91] His subsequent publication of the Gaelic versions of his poems in 1787 may have been a defensive move in light of the Ossianic controversy, since a Gaelic volume certainly could not be expected to generate many sales. If so, it worked; Smith was well respected, and the authenticity of his collection was generally accepted.[92]

Inspired by Smith and Macpherson, some of the folklore collectors discussed above were also prone to embellishing their texts, including most notably Kennedy and Campbell of Portree. Kennedy left two collections, the second of which contains somewhat altered versions of several poems included in the first. In total, he has thirty-three different poems, formed via collation and interspersed throughout with embellishments, some of which are in keeping with the style of the Gaelic lays, and others that are Macphersonic in style. But unlike Smith and Macpherson, Kennedy admitted to adding passages of his own composition.[93] Campbell of Portree, on the other hand, went to great lengths to authenticate his texts, getting them signed by a Justice of the Peace and producing affidavits from reciters. Of the twenty-nine poems in his collection, however, only approximately half are unaltered in any substantial way, while the rest are either reworked or wholly invented in the Macphersonic style.[94] Other collectors were largely faithful to the Gaelic tradition, although occasional editorial interference has been detected.[95]

Kennedy intended to publish his lays, which helps to account for his stylistic and editorial choices. His prefixing of each poem with a prose "argument" in English and his use of Macphersonic names like Fingal and Ossian are in keeping with the publication norms established by Macpherson and retained by Smith.[96] Unsurprisingly, Ossianic influence can also be detected in the early published anthologies, which do not distinguish between Macphersonic and traditional heroic verse. Gillies included five poems reminiscent of *Ossian,* while about a third of the heroic material in the Stewarts' collection is Macphersonic, and the MacCallums' collection is, in Derick Thomson's words, "a curious mixture" of the traditional and the adapted.[97] Like Kennedy, the MacCallums and their contributors prefixed several of their poems with short summaries and adopted Macphersonic nomenclature. They also translated into the elevated prose style preferred by Macpherson and Smith, and they used their preface to argue for the antiquity of the anthologized verse and the authenticity of *Ossian,* professing to have "contemplated both sides of the question, and weighed the balance with reason and justice."[98] Their inclusion of a short section describing the Isle of Staffa and Fingal's Cave further indicates that they envisioned an audience of *Ossian* enthusiasts. Perhaps they even hoped to capitalize on Ossianic tourist traffic, given that they closed the section by noting the location of an inn where visitors to Staffa could be comfortably entertained.[99]

New and reworked verse along Ossianic lines was thus readily welcomed into the canon of purportedly ancient Gaelic poetry. Some of the newer Macphersonic poems even attained prominent positions in published collections that did not otherwise promote heroic verse. For instance, Rev. Duncan MacCallum opened his 1821 *Co-chruinneacha Dhan, Orain, Etc., Etc.: A Collection of Original Poems, Songs, Etc.* with two such pieces before transitioning to other genres, and John Mackenzie similarly launched his celebrated *Sar-Obair nam Bard Gaelach: or, the Beauties of Gaelic Poetry* with three purportedly ancient heroic poems in 1841.[100] The success of such anthologies—Mackenzie's in particular—suggests an increasing acknowledgement among a broad readership of the value of a wide variety of Gaelic verse. Yet the fronting of these Macphersonic poems signals that part of contemporary Gaelic poetry's perceived legitimacy derived from its lineage—that is, its emergence out of the dignity and artistry of an age of bards and heroes. It is significant that *Ossian*'s popularity soared to new heights during this time, with approximately twenty-five English-language editions appearing in Britain in the first three decades of the century alone.[101] A revised Gaelic edition was published in 1818, moreover, and distributed for free to Highland Gaels "so that, by the pleasing eloquence of your own Bard, [your] magnanimity may be nurtured, matured, and perpetually awakened in the centuries to come, until it rises to the highest peak of sublimity."[102] If contemporary Gaelic poetry could be seen to move readers with its beauty, its supposed antecedent, in the presumed original language, was not simply enjoyable, it was morally improving.

Given *Ossian*'s reputation and gratis circulation, it should come as little surprise that its influence on Gaelic literature extended further than patriotic imitation. Just as in other literary traditions around the world, Macpherson and his imitators had "a remarkably stimulating effect" on both poetry and prose.[103] As Meek has demonstrated, late eighteenth- and early to mid-nineteenth-century authors adapted the sublime sensibility of *Ossian* to diverse genres, embracing the fresh perspective of the Macphersonic mode. Ossianic imagery seeped into Rev. Dugald Buchanan's religious poetry, while William Livingston imitated both the style and content of the popular epics in his versified accounts of battles, and popular poets like Neil MacLeod made generous use of motifs such as "the blind bard; the aged survivor of the vanished kindred; the heroic age of an earlier day; and the Arcadia which preceded the death of the heroes."[104] In prose, Ossianic themes and motifs surfaced in the essays of Rev. Dr. Norman MacLeod ('Caraid nan Gàidheal'), the pioneer of Gaelic periodical publishing, whose writings well exemplify the naturalistic, spiritual romanticism that flourished at that time. The Macphersonic-romantic style was enlisted by MacLeod and others, moreover, to capture the mood of emigrants savoring the final glimpses of their mountainous homeland as they set off for North America, and to lament the state of affairs that brought about their departure.[105] The "joy of grief" that Macpherson so aptly adapted from the Gaelic narrative tradition to suit his fractured post-Culloden moment thus gained prolonged relevance in an era of mass migration.[106]

Gaelic Scholarship beyond the Controversy

While *Ossian* continued to captivate audiences and inspire creative engagement within the Gaelic sphere and beyond well into the nineteenth century, a shift in scholarly activity is perceptible in Scotland. In the late eighteenth century, much energy was devoted to debating the epics' authenticity, and the fervor of Gaelic-speaking intellectuals—many of them ministers—for oral collecting was fueled in no small part by the ongoing controversy. By the early nineteenth century, however, people had largely made up their minds about *Ossian,* and the need for collecting to support claims for or against authenticity declined. For most, the publication of the Highland Society's report, Laing's critical edition, or the Gaelic *Ossian* had settled the matter one way or the other. The controversy, though not resolved, was effectively shelved.[107]

New avenues of investigation opened in 1803 with the Highland Society of Scotland's acquisition of the manuscripts Macpherson had collected. These nineteen manuscripts enabled the society to countenance more scholarly tasks than those in which it had previously been engaged. After evaluating the material in conjunction with the *Ossian* investigation, a Standing Committee for literature and music was established in 1806, among the principal undertakings of which was the compilation of a dictionary to aid in the study of Gaelic manuscripts. Regrettably, however, this promising project was fraught with contention; the dictionary was not completed until 1828, and the discord created by the venture left its mark.[108] Despite continuing to accrue Gaelic manuscripts, the society took on no new cultural projects, shifting its focus heavily toward economic development. Yet all was not for naught, for in 1850, at the instigation of William Forbes Skene, the bulk of the Highland Society's manuscript collection was deposited in the Advocate's Library in Edinburgh—now the National Library of Scotland.[109] There, in the period between the demise of the society's interest in Gaelic and the flurry of activity that would accompany the approaching Celtic Revival, concentrated scholarship on Macpherson's manuscripts at last began to take place. What is more, this labor produced Fenian fruit: in 1862, at the dawn of a new age in Gaelic scholarship, Rev. Dr. Thomas McLauchlan published the first edition and translation of a selection of poems from the Book of the Dean of Lismore.[110] A devotee of Macpherson, he printed the bard's name as Ossian.

Ossian enthralled audiences the world over. No baseless fad, the worldwide craze for the books' Highland heroes generated translations and imitations, and drove eager tourists to purportedly Ossianic locations. The epics inspired a French emperor and an American president. They influenced a wide swathe of Western literature in the century following their publication. And in the land of their birth, they engendered Scottish Gaelic pride. Indeed, *Ossian*'s importance among some of the Highland clergy appears to have approached that of scripture. Here were texts that not only validated, but also elevated Gaelic cultural identity, exemplifying the morality and honor of Highlanders' ancient past and demonstrating a behavioral model for the present. Fired by ethnic pride and keen to validate the epics' authenticity, clerics and other intellectuals engaged in a spate of collecting that added greatly to the preservation efforts of earlier collectors. As the bounty of the Gaelic oral tradition filled notebooks and furnished published anthologies, numerous traditional Fenian lays were ushered into print for the first time. With the repatriation of Macpherson's manuscript collection at the turn of the nineteenth century, moreover, the scene was set for Gaelic textual scholarship to begin. But progress was halting, and it would be nearly sixty years until the appearance of McLauchlan's partial edition of the Book of the Dean of Lismore. Nor would Macpherson's *Ossian* undergo any serious textual scrutiny in the half century following the publication of the Highland Society's report. For elucidation of the Fenian manuscript record and *Ossian*'s relationship to it, the world would have to look to Ireland.

6

Ireland's Own *Fianna Éireann*

THE IMPACT OF *OSSIAN* in Ireland was significant and sustained. With James Macpherson's Ossianic debut, a gauntlet was thrown down—or to use a more suitably Gaelic metaphor, a challenge pole was struck; Scottish hegemony over *Fianna Éireann*, 'the Fianna of Ireland,' had to be challenged. For a century, in the midst of widespread cultural change, the controversy raged, subsided, and raged again, bubbling to the surface in multiple forms and for varying purposes. Protestants and Catholics, antiquarians and novelists, Gaelic scholars and political rebels all devoted attention to Fionn, the specter of Fingal ever looming in the background. As they pushed back on Macpherson's interpretations, they ushered the first Irish Fenian texts into print, and they began to work the Fianna into the fabric of a renewed national consciousness. In the period between the mid-eighteenth and mid-nineteenth centuries, Ireland would come to be seen as a distinct modern nation with its own unique cultural heritage to be explored, (re)interpreted, and celebrated, and the Fianna would take their place in a national symbolic network.

Hibernian Perspectives and Correctives

The initial Irish response to *Ossian* predates cultural nationalism à la Herder, although a version of this ideology was to have a profound effect in Ireland in the late nineteenth and early twentieth centuries. Mid-eighteenth-century Irish scholars had, in fact, begun to explore their cultural heritage before either Macpherson or Herder and the Romanticists presented them with new impetuses. These scholars' research stems in part from the same burgeoning Celticism that influenced William Collins, the English author of the "Ode on the Popular Superstitions of the Highlands of Scotland," which he composed for Macpherson's initial encourager, John Home.[1] As early as 1753, Irish Catholic antiquarian Charles O'Conor published his *Dissertations on the Antient History of Ireland*, which set forth the terms according to which many would soon approach Macpherson's claims about Irish culture and history. Building on the earlier histories of Geoffrey Keating (Seathrún Céitinn) and Roderic O'Flaherty (*Ogygia*, 1685), O'Conor sought to counter the Celtic origin theory most attractive to colonialists that the Irish Gaels descended from barbarous Celtic tribes that had passed from Northern Europe to Britain and Ireland. According to this position, the civilizing effects of colonization had been beneficial to the Irish. O'Conor's counterclaim, derived from native Gaelic sources, denied that the early Irish had lacked civility and instead followed the pattern set out in the eleventh-century *Lebor Gabála Érenn* (Book of the taking of Ireland), whereby the Gaels descended from the Biblical figure Japheth, son of Noah, and their ancestors migrated to Ireland via Phoenician outposts in the Mediterranean. These early Irish Gaels, according to O'Conor, brought with them Phoenician literacy and cultivated an advanced society, which fell at the destructive hands of Ireland's Anglo-Norman colonizers.[2]

While Macpherson and O'Conor adopted very different strategies, one advocating a primitive Gaelic golden age based on a Homeric model and the other claiming a civilized Gaelic golden age based on a Phoenician model, both were reacting against similar socially, politically, and culturally damaging forms of ethnic prejudice. Irish Gaels had been depicted as barbaric from the earliest colonial commentary, Giraldus Cambrensis's *Topographia Hibernica* (1188). However, the text that likely had the most influence on later writers was a product of the second wave of the long conquest of Ireland. Edmund Spenser's *A View of the Present State of Ireland* (c. 1596) resembles an ethnographic tract detailing those Irish customs most reflective of their barbarism—customs that needed to be eliminated in order for English civility to prevail. These included "their form of agriculture, modes of land holding and government, religion and rituals, clothes, [and] even hairstyles."[3] Such all-encompassing notions of Irish depravity served to justify conquest and plantation to English colonialists, settlers, and their descendants, and were sustained over a long period of time. In the mid-seventeenth century, Anglo-Irish antiquarian James Ware edited and published commentary on Ireland by both Giraldus Cambrensis and Spenser, making their views widely available for the first time.[4] In the mid-eighteenth century when O'Conor was writing, many English and Anglo-Irish commentators were still "sustained by [a] vision of themselves as the bearers of law to the regions of barbarism."[5] Such a view was not difficult to maintain in an Ireland in which Catholics were barred from holding governmental positions and their social advancement was frustrated by laws limiting their access to property. The situation of O'Conor, a Catholic and one of the few descendants of the former Gaelic nobility who still possessed some status and means, was far from representative.[6]

To lend a veneer of learned authenticity to his texts, Macpherson employed a complex critical apparatus that included dissertations and footnotes comparable to those found in classical editions. In this apparatus, which was most prominent in *Temora*, he claimed a Scottish origin for the Gaelic-speaking peoples and stressed the ability of *Ossian* to shine a light on an early period in Scottish and Irish history. Bolstering himself against Irish counterclaims, he rejected "the improbable and self-condemned tales of Keating and O'Flaherty" in no uncertain terms, calling them "credulous and puerile to the last degree" and claiming that they had "disgraced the antiquities they meant to establish."[7] Presenting his own interpretation of those "antiquities," Macpherson outlined a scenario in which, as Scottish Gaelic society grew weaker than its Irish counterpart under England's power, Irish poets "assumed to themselves the character of being the mother-nation of the Scots." At the same time, he asserted, these poets began to "appropriate Ossian and his heroes to their own country." Claiming, rather unwisely, to have "all that remain" of Irish Fenian compositions "just now, in my hands," he declared them all to have originated in the fifteenth century.[8] His version of events was therefore to be seen as older and more reliable. In 1771, he expanded on these views in *An Introduction to the History of Great Britain and Ireland*.[9]

Macpherson's cavalier treatment of Ireland and Scotland's shared ethnic history could not go unanswered, especially given the potential damage such views, expressed in such popular publications, threatened to do to the native Irish argument against ethnic discrimination. Irish scholars reacted immediately and with justifiable indignation. The earliest Irish response to Macpherson's historical claims was that of Catholic antiquarian Sylvester O'Halloran, who published reactions to each of Macpherson's epics in the *Dublin Magazine*. While O'Halloran accused Macpherson of meddling with the text of *Fingal* (the basis for which he believed to be Irish) and printing mere "fables" in *Temora*, his primary interest lay in refuting Macpherson's alternative view of the past.[10]

O'Halloran was followed closely by Bishop John O'Brien (Seán Ó Briain) of Cloyne, whose extended commentary appeared over six issues of the *Journal des Sçavans* in Paris in 1764. O'Brien was well connected within the Gaelic literary world and may even have been a poet himself. He was certainly a competent Gaelic scholar, and he had amassed a sizable manuscript library.[11] The focus of the bulk of his commentary in the *Journal* was on Macpherson's treatment of Irish history, which he firmly refuted with substantial evidence.[12] Unusually among prominent early Irish commentators, moreover, he devoted some space to a literary consideration of *Ossian*. Like O'Halloran, he criticized Macpherson for meddling with his source texts, but O'Brien evidenced his case much more thoroughly, pointing out similarities with three Irish Fenian texts, *Cath Fionntrágha* (The Battle of Ventry), *Bruidhean Chaorthainn* (The enchanted hall of the rowan tree), and *Laoidh an Deirg mhic Droichil* (The lay of Dearg [red one] son of Droicheal). His verdict was that Macpherson's history was deficient and his misuse of Irish sources constituted plagiarism.[13]

The two most influential responses were somewhat slower to appear. The first of these was authored by Charles O'Conor, from whom a reaction would be expected, given the status his *Dissertations* had gained in Ireland as a standard historical text.[14] O'Conor appended a pamphlet on *Ossian* to the second edition of his history, published in 1766. In it, he asserted that Fingal and Ossian were Macpherson's own creations, adapted from the "vulgar Stories" of the Irish Fenian and Ulster cycles, which Macpherson had ahistorically conflated.[15] He pointed out numerous historical and topographical inaccuracies, examined and discredited Macpherson's likely sources, and reaffirmed his own premise that an advanced early Irish society had colonized Scotland. If O'Conor hoped to silence Macpherson's supporters with the weight of his counterarguments, he was not successful, but his rebuttal proved to be influential in Ireland.

Following in O'Conor's footsteps, Sylvester O'Halloran again broached the topic in 1772 in a history he was inspired to write by the Ossianic controversy.[16] O'Halloran's *Introduction to the Study of the History and Antiquities of Ireland* was published in London and directed at a broad Anglophone audience. In his final chapter he expanded upon his earlier criticism of *Ossian*.[17] The most interesting and influential aspect of this publication is not the part that directly addressed Macpherson's historical framework, however, but rather O'Halloran's conception of early Irish history. Although he adhered to the same model of migration via Phoenician locales as O'Conor, O'Halloran stressed that not only were the early Irish learned,[18] their society was chivalrous. Appearing at times reminiscent of Macpherson's idealization, O'Halloran's early Ireland was populated with knights adhering to a code of conduct that he derived, via such authorities as Keating, from Irish romance literature.[19] He argued that chivalry elsewhere in Europe could be traced back to an Irish model.[20] Indeed for him, all of "the most distinctive and civilized of the military customs and laws and manners of Europe" originated in an advanced early Irish civilization.[21] This proved an attractive theory in the decades to come as interest in Ireland's cultural heritage grew to unprecedented levels.

Emerging Anglo-Irish Interest

Macpherson's epics, and the early responses of Ireland's Catholic historians to them, were important factors in the growing attention of members of the Anglo-Irish ascendancy to Ireland's native history. In an earlier period, Ireland's colonial inhabitants tended to perceive themselves as English. By the late eighteenth century, however, that identity had shifted, both in the eyes of the colonists' descendants, and from the perspective of the English. As Lesa Ní Mhunghaile explains, the resulting impact of this collapse of earlier identity categories was that "the term 'barbarous Irish,' once reserved for the Gaelic Irish only, now also referred to [the Anglo-Irish]"; it thus "became imperative to challenge this slur."[22] With Irish history in the limelight and reputations on the line, many turned a friendly eye to the glorious Irish past of O'Conor and O'Halloran.

The newfound Anglo-Irish desire to uphold the valorous heritage of their shared land led to increased antiquarian research. In 1772, a Select Committee was formed by the Dublin Society, primarily for the purpose of acquiring and translating Gaelic manuscripts.[23] In an unprecedented move, both O'Conor and the Catholic Archbishop of Dublin, Rev. Dr. John Carpenter, were elected to the Committee in 1773, and Fr. John Connery (Seán Ó Conaire) of Cloyne, formerly a scribe for O'Brien, was appointed an honorary member. But this state of affairs was not to last; the Select Committee was dissolved in 1774 after the acquisition and translation of only one manuscript, apparently due to waning interest.[24] It was followed, from 1779 to 1783, by the Hibernian Antiquarian Society, of which O'Conor appears to have been the only Catholic member. Although responsible for the publication of a number of papers and the commissioning of many drawings of monuments, this society collapsed due to a disagreement, carried out in print, about the origin of the Irish Gaels; not all Anglo-Irish antiquarians had taken up O'Conor and O'Halloran's position.[25] The formation of a more permanent body was already underway, however. Out of a group of scholars that had been meeting since 1782 at Trinity College, Dublin arose the Royal Irish Academy in 1785. The remit of this organization was wider than that of previously established organizations, extending to sciences and "polite" literature in addition to antiquities, and its membership was much larger.[26] Notably, both prominent Catholic antiquarians O'Conor and O'Halloran were admitted to sit as members alongside their Protestant peers.[27]

The Royal Irish Academy's success can be gauged in its accomplishments, including not only publications and the gathering of general antiquities, but also the establishment of a sizable manuscript collection. Much of this growth happened slowly, however, and substantial purchases and donations would not occur until the mid-nineteenth century.[28] In the early years, Royal Irish Academy scholars and other interested parties alike were reliant on Irish speakers to copy texts. The vast majority were also reliant on these scholar-scribes to translate the texts; despite growing Anglo-Irish enthusiasm for Gaelic culture, few ever learned, or even desired to learn, the Irish language. Thus, men like Muiris Ó Gormáin, who was employed by both the Royal Irish Academy and the Select Committee to the Dublin Society, as well as numerous private individuals, produced copies and translations of texts of all sorts.[29] While the involvement of these Gaelic literati in antiquarian projects often goes unnoticed in commentary, records of many of them exist, and it is evident that they were also affected by the contemporary vogue for antiquarianism.[30] From the manuscripts they produced, it is clear, too, that the Fenian tradition was of great interest to them and their patrons. Indeed, most extant Irish witnesses of Fenian lays and romances were copied in the post-*Ossian* period, from the mid-eighteenth to the mid-nineteenth centuries.[31]

The Irish Fianna in Print

The increased copying of Fenian texts indicates the attention the Ossianic controversy drew not only to historical matters, but also to the Irish Fenian tradition. O'Halloran, O'Brien, and O'Conor all suggested that Macpherson's sources had been Irish rather than Scottish, and O'Brien even provided some textual commentary. It was left to others, however, to seek out and publish the Irish-language Fenian texts that would ultimately discredit Macpherson. This process began in the final decades of the eighteenth century, but the task was not always undertaken by those most qualified to do it. While we might expect such publications to have originated among the Gaelic literati, much of the interest expressed in print at the time flowed from the pens of Anglo-Irish writers. These individuals often lacked a complex understanding of the Gaelic tradition, but like countless others across Europe and the Americas, they were drawn to *Ossian*'s sentimental, heroic idealism. They were, moreover, eager to wrest this powerful national symbol from the grasp of the Scots. For them, the question of the provenance of Fenian narrative was paramount. Because there was little conception of the continuous development and dispersal of the texts over time and space, it was thought that there must be a single authoritative version of each lay or tale.[32] The strong case made by Irish historians for the primacy of Irish language and culture over that of Scotland suggested that the authoritative Fenian texts were Irish. All that remained for Anglo-Irish patriots to do was to 'discover' and publish them.

The first Irish Fenian lay to find its way into print appeared in 1786 in Joseph Cooper Walker's *Historical Memoirs of the Irish Bards*. Walker was a member of the Royal Irish Academy's Antiquities Committee and a friend and younger colleague of the leading historians of the day.[33] Tinged with romance, his book attempted to trace the history of the by-then famed figure of the Celtic 'bard' in Ireland. While adhering to the image of a sophisticated early Irish society put forward by O'Conor and O'Halloran, his depiction of the mannerisms of poets during the ancient period was, however reluctantly, reliant on Macpherson.[34] To differentiate his material, however, Walker drew attention to a second early poet, Oisín's brother Fearghus Finnbhéil. Later commentators would go on to discuss and anthologize lays attributed to both Fearghus and Oisín.[35] He included one Fenian lay to exemplify the authentic, early Irish Fenian tradition, and it is significant in light of the Ossianic controversy that he printed the Irish text and only a short synopsis in English.[36] Although incomplete, Walker's version of *Laoidh na Seilge* (The lay of the hunt) was among the earliest traditional Fenian texts to be published, appearing in the same year as the landmark Gillies Collection in Scotland.

Also notable is the extension of Walker's concentration to the contemporary period, and thus the inclusion of vernacular poems by the modern 'bard' Turlough Carolan (Toirdhealbhach Ó Cearbhalláin). The growing celebration of Carolan reflects the "cultural defiance" inherent in the Irish reclamation of the past: the roots of a soon-to-be politicized cultural nationalism.[37] It is here that the difference between Macpherson's approach to the Gaelic 'bardic' figure and that of the Irish is apparent. Macpherson's elegiac, epic bard was relegated to the past, and with him, the vibrant and sometimes violent aspects of Gaelic culture that he described. In this way, the Highlands—recently rebellious, but quelled and under development—were, in effect, sanitized of their primitive, uncontrollable, and even barbaric associations. Thus, *Ossian* could be used both to celebrate a heroic cultural past and to promote Scottish interests within the union.[38] In the Irish depiction of continuity between the ancient Oisín and the relatively recently deceased Carolan, however, Luke Gibbons argues that we can see "the transition from the image of the bard as an elegiac figure, sighing over the passing of the old order, to being a source of regeneration in a newly awakened nation."[39] Walker may well have perceived the recent granting of legislative independence to Grattan's Parliament as a sign of renewed hope for the future of Ireland, as others of his countrymen did.[40] At times of discouragement of this hope over the course of the next century, the desire for regeneration—with its associated cultural symbols—would turn rebellious and even revolutionary. Such notions were certainly not on Walker's mind, but their seeds had been planted for others to nourish. Thus, while his contribution to the search for Fenian originals was minor, the ideas Walker put forward influenced the changing ideological atmosphere of the nineteenth century.

In 1787, another Anglo-Irishman contributed more substantially to the search for the originals of Macpherson's *Ossian*, albeit in a very different way. Matthew Young, a Protestant clergyman and Trinity College fellow who had been taught some Irish by the prominent Gaelic scribe Muiris Ó Gormáin, published a collection of Scottish Gaelic lays with facing prose translations in the first volume of the *Transactions of the Royal Irish Academy*.[41] He had traveled to the Highlands to assess the question of *Ossian*'s authenticity for himself in 1784, and his words would have been welcome to those seeking to elevate the Irish tradition over Macpherson's texts: "Mr. Mc. Pherson, I acknowledge, has taken very great liberties with [the texts]" and is also "liable to censure for having altered the date of his originals . . . having given them a much higher antiquity than they are really entitled to."[42] He went on to echo Johnson's assertion that Scottish Gaelic only recently became a written language, implying that all written Scottish texts of lays must be late. Those of the "mother country," it could be extrapolated, must be authoritative.[43] The numerous printed poetic references tying the Fianna to Ireland, which Young claimed Macpherson omitted or obscured, would have contributed to such a reading, as would the reassertion of Saint Patrick's prominence in Young's collection. As Young noted, references to Saint Patrick were among the elements of the native tradition that Macpherson discarded.[44]

1787 was also the year that Edmund de Harold, a Co. Limerick-born Protestant who had relocated to the continent, responded to the popularity of Macpherson's text by publishing his own collection of Ossianic 'translations'—purportedly from Irish originals—into English and German.[45] Unlike Young, Harold made no attempt at translating literally, but unlike Macpherson, he openly admitted that in 'translating' the stories, he had embellished them:

"They are all founded on tradition; but the dress they now appear in is mine."[46] While his was thus as much a creative venture as an edifying one, his ideological bent was clear: he emphasized the primacy of the Irish tradition.[47]

Although Harold's volume was relatively popular in northern regions of the European continent, in Ireland the most influential publication containing Fenian texts, alongside Walker's *Historical Memoirs of the Irish Bards*, was Charlotte Brooke's *Reliques of Irish Poetry* (1789).[48] Brooke was the daughter of Irish author Henry Brooke, and she had received from him an elite education not usually available to those of her gender.[49] She also gained familiarity with the Irish language and learned tradition in her youth, which Walker asserts enabled her to readily discover Macpherson's embellishments in *Ossian*.[50] Macpherson appears to have been to the fore in her mind when she was preparing her anthology, given that seven of the sixteen Irish-language poems she included were heroic lays—five of them Fenian and two concerning Ulster cycle heroes. All but one of these "have direct relevance" to *Ossian*, which "can hardly have been fortuitous," as Mícheál Mac Craith notes.[51] Brooke devoted greater concentration to these lays than the other poems in the collection, following Macpherson's lead in accompanying each with an introduction and notes.[52] As in Young's and Walker's collections, moreover, she included originals in addition to translations, silently claiming greater accuracy and authority than Macpherson, whose Gaelic text did not appear in his lifetime.[53] She thus evoked *Ossian* without ever actually mentioning the famed Scottish epics.

The translations are given pride of place in the first section of Brooke's anthology, indicating that despite her choice to publish bilingually, her primary projected audience was English-speaking. In part, this was because, like the antiquarians who preceded her, she sought to address the negative perception of Ireland. She wrote with pride about the regularity of mixed Anglo- and Gaelic Irish bloodlines and complained about "modern writers" who depicted "our early ancestors" as "*barbarians, descended from barbarians, and ever continuing the same*." Such prejudice, she deemed, was due to the simple fact that "we are too little known to our noble neighbour of Britain."[54] In aspiring to make Ireland's literary heritage known in Britain, it seems likely, as Clare O'Halloran deduces, that Brooke intended "to produce a volume of poetry which would achieve the same effect as Macpherson had for the image of Scotland." Indeed, Brooke's lack of open rebuttal of Macpherson may reflect a desire for her book to be viewed as "a companion piece rather than a rival to *Fingal* and *Temora*"—and O'Halloran adds that "this was indeed how the English reviewers perceived it."[55]

Brooke did not preserve the integrity of the Gaelic stanzas in her translations. Without deviating from the plots of the lays, she added descriptive material at will. Her alterations lent an air of refinement to her heroes, polishing away "the robustness, even coarseness, which was a characteristic of the material she was handling" until they resembled Ossian and Fingal.[56] As her recent editor, Lesa Ní Mhunghaile, attests, she "'domesticated' the Gaelic texts of her originals by rewriting them using concepts with which her readers could identify."[57] Her preference for Sylvester O'Halloran's version of early Irish history also indicates a propensity toward this sort of topical assimilation. In accordance with O'Halloran's depiction of a chivalrous early Irish culture, Brooke's heroes are referred to as knights.[58] Much like *Ossian*, then, Brooke's mode of portraying heroic material seems to have been designed for maximum impact in a non-Gaelic sphere. *Reliques of Irish Poetry* is thus exemplary of the role Anglo-Irish authors and antiquarians played, and would continue to play for some time, in bringing issues surrounding Gaelic culture "out of the confines of antiquarian debate and into a wider literary milieu."[59] This they did for the perusal of the public—but through an Anglicized cultural lens.

Brooke built not only on the ideological scaffolding erected by O'Halloran, but also on that of Walker. The influence of the latter is apparent in her inclusion of poetry composed by the near-contemporaneous 'bardic' figure Carolan toward the end of the book. In her celebration of Carolan, she contributed to the same promotion of cultural continuity as Walker,[60] and indeed surpassed Walker by also including orally collected folksongs—an early indication of the penetration into Ireland of Herderian ideas about the spirit of the nation residing in 'folk' poetry. Brooke approached the folksongs she included with the romanticizing treatment characteristic of this ideology, associating them with the peasantry, praising their "simplicity" and "beauty," and stressing the corruptible act of memory required to bring such compositions of a former era to presence.[61]

Reliques of Irish Poetry was important for the creation of a public interest in Gaelic literature and culture. Its impact is apparent in the increased circulation in manuscript form of versions of the poems it contained, increasingly with scribal references to Brooke's texts. Direct transcriptions from the book even began circulating via manuscript, sometimes accompanied by Brooke's commentary, granting them a republication of sorts.[62] While statistics are not readily available, it is probably safe to say that Brooke's book bolstered the growing popularity of the Irish Fenian tradition, while concurrently stoking the Ossianic fires. As Clare O'Halloran observes, "It can hardly be coincidence that in the year following the appearance of *Reliques of Irish Poetry* a new edition of Macpherson's Ossian was published in Dublin; the first in thirty-five years."[63] Two years after that came the publication of a handful of loosely translated lays by Charles Henry Wilson, a London-based Anglo-Irishman who clearly took inspiration from Macpherson and would certainly have been familiar with *Reliques of Irish Poetry*.[64] Due to the efforts of Brooke and others, Fionn and his Fianna were coming to be considered part of the cultural patrimony not just of the Gael, but of the Irish nation.

Ancient Irish Heroes, New Irish Politics

The Anglo-Irish ascendancy's interest in Fenian texts in mid- to late eighteenth-century Ireland—a time, it should be noted, when some Gaelic material (e.g., Jacobite poetry) was avoided—is indicative of the Fianna's relative ideological neutrality. In the tense political atmosphere of the 1790s, this neutrality gave way for the first time as the Fianna made their way into the network of symbols of Irishness utilized by the United Irishmen.[65] Inspired by the 1789 French Revolution, the United Irishmen sought to free Ireland from England's yoke. In 1792 one supporter intent on inciting his countrymen to action published a poem in the Belfast United Irish newspaper the *Northern Star*, proclaiming:

> O cou'd I glow with Ossian's living fire,
> I wou'd a thousand warriors yet inspire,
> With all their father's love of deathless fame,
> While tyrants trembled at their awful name,
> . . .
> Must you Hibernians ever wear the chain?[66]

In 1795 the United Irishmen tried to start a periodical titled *Bolg an Tsolair* [*sic*]*: Or, Gaelic Magazine* (fig. 11).[67] The only published volume gave pride of place to *Laoidh na Seilge*, the first of eight poems extracted from Brooke's anthology, all given in translation and then in the original Irish.[68] Mary Helen Thuente has pointed out the thematic significance of *Laoidh na Seilge*, which tells of the Fianna overcoming internecine strife and uniting against a common foe—the Tuatha Dé Danann of *Sliabh gCuillinn*, 'Slieve Gullion.'[69] The volume also included an abridged Irish grammar, and its editor, Co. Down scholar and schoolmaster Patrick Lynch (Pádraig Ó Loingsigh)—a native Irish speaker—expressed his hope that *Bolg an Tsolair* would remedy "the total neglect" of the language.[70] Both the periodical's association with the United Irishmen and the

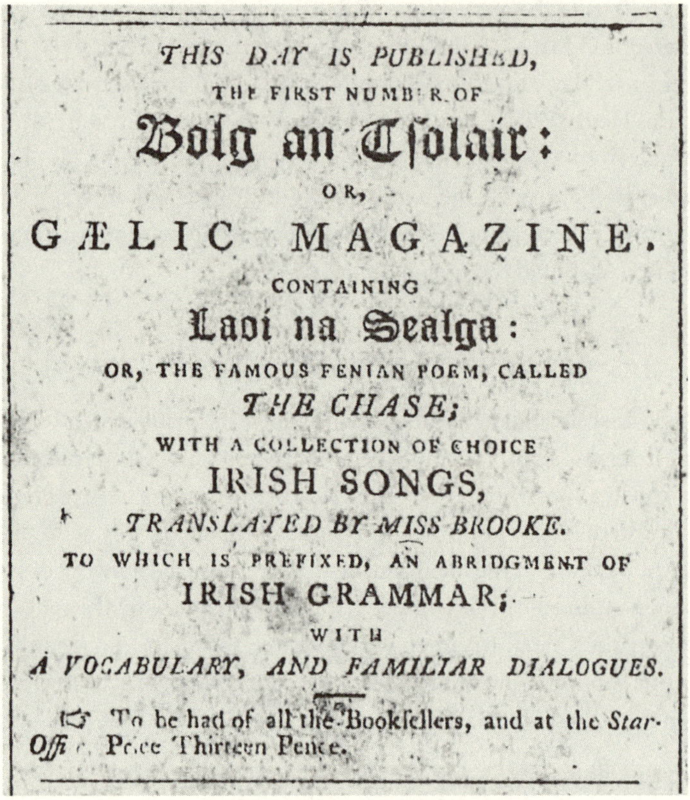

FIGURE 11. Advertisement for the periodical *Bolg an Tsolair* [*sic*] in the Belfast *Northern Star*, August 31, 1795, p. 1. (Newspapers.com.)

type of material it contained indicate that the aim was not merely to support the needs of a neglected linguistic community, however. In *Bolg an Tsolair*, the Fianna and the Irish language itself were leveraged to promote separatist identity politics.

The United Irishmen hoped to bring about parliamentary reform and religious equality, and to improve the lot of farmers through reduced taxation and free trade. While they strove at first to achieve their goals through peaceful agitation, by 1794 many members had become disillusioned with the organization's lack of progress, and the society turned revolutionary. In 1798, with the help of a small French contingent, United Irish forces rose against the government for three months before finally being subdued. The rising resulted in an estimated thirty thousand deaths and the revocation of the Irish parliament.[71] It also politicized Gaelic cultural topics, leading many Anglo-Irish antiquarians to temper their enthusiasm or even abandon antiquarian study, rather than risk being perceived as anti-British. Thus, the Royal Irish Academy's Antiquities Committee became moribund from approximately the 1801 Act of Union.[72]

Popular interest in the nation's cultural heritage had been nurtured by this time, however, and it did not simply disappear with the study of antiquities. Rather, it found expression in the early nineteenth-century 'national' novel, in which Anglo-Irish authors embraced romanticism and dotted their pages with sublime landscapes, ruins, and native-exotics in "ancient costume."[73] One of these novels, Sidney Owenson, Lady Morgan's *The Wild Irish Girl* (1807), even rehashed the antiquarian arguments of the Ossianic controversy—supporting, of course, the Irish origin claim, and advocating Sylvester O'Halloran's chivalrous, learned model of early Ireland.[74] That Owenson would look to O'Halloran is unsurprising, given her romantic bent. In her choice of subject, she was no doubt also influenced by the appearance of the Highland Society's report on the authenticity of *Ossian* in 1805. Ossianic influence also turned up regularly in the poetry of the period. Indeed, Clare O'Halloran finds that "by the first decade of the nineteenth century the language of Macpherson's Ossian had become part of the popular consciousness of the Irish past," even while "the charge of theft continued to be made against Macpherson."[75]

As time passed, academic interest in Irish language and heritage was gradually rekindled. The Gaelic Society of Dublin was founded in January 1807 with the aim of translating manuscripts texts, and the first (and only) volume of its journal included two Fenian lays—*Cath Chnoic an Áir* (The Battle of the Hill of Slaughter) and *Lon Doire an Chairn* (The blackbird of Derrycairn)—and a stanza on the coloring of Fionn's hound Bran. These were edited by Theophilus O'Flanagan, a Gaelic scholar known to have aided both Walker and Brooke, who incorporated commentary on "Mr. McPherson's pretended translation."[76] The Gaelic Society of Dublin was short-lived, as was the Iberno-Celtic Society, which had a similar aim and only published one volume of its *Transactions* in 1820.[77] Nonetheless, scholarly attention to Fenian texts was increasing. Provincial printers had begun to emerge in the post-Union period, and in 1819 a translation of *Cath Fionntrágha* was published in Cork. The story was evidently popular in the southwest, connected as it was to the region's heritage, and the translation was reprinted many times; a short excerpt even found its way into Limerick-born novelist Gerald Griffin's *The Invasion*, printed in London in 1832.[78] In the 1820s, three poetry anthologies emerged that featured several Fenian lays; these were *Reliques of Irish Poetry*, published anonymously in 1825,[79] as well as *An Duanaire: Fiannaigheacht, Danta, agus Ranna* and *An Duanaire: Fonna Seanma, Danta, agus Ranna*, both published in 1829 and edited by Co. Sligo Gaelic scholar and schoolteacher Thaddaeus Connellan (Tadhg Ó Coinniálláin).[80] While some of the lays included had appeared elsewhere, several were first printed in these collections. The Royal Irish Academy also turned its attention back to Gaelic culture at the end of the decade with an essay competition on the authenticity of *Ossian*. This resulted in a sizable journal segment dedicated to detailed investigations by two prominent scholars, Rev. William Hamilton Drummond and Edward O'Reilly, who lent their authority, and that of the venerable society, to the by-then standard Irish argument that Macpherson falsely presented the Fianna as Scottish, pilfering from Irish tradition to create his epics.[81]

Folklore Collectors and Historians

While the Ossianic controversy had inspired a generation of Scottish folklore collectors to document the rich stores of narrative verse circulating in the Highlands and Islands, in Ireland, native and Anglo-Irish scholars alike turned predominantly to the abundant manuscript record to elucidate the nation's Gaelic heritage. Some antiquarians also looked to oral resources, however, as we saw in Charlotte Brooke's inclusion of orally collected folksongs alongside the manuscript derived Fenian lays in her anthology. Early fieldwork of this nature accords with the Herderian impetus to connect the present with a more culturally 'authentic' past. The 1798 United Irish rebellion complicated such endeavors, but it did not wholly thwart folklore collecting. Although information about the provenance of much manuscript material is wanting, early nineteenth-century references to orally gathered Fenian narrative can be found. For instance, both the Royal Irish Academy and the British Museum hold copies of a collection of Fenian lays gathered in 1812 by one William Kelly (Uilliam Ó Colla) from an unnamed Co. Mayo shepherd; this was presented the following year to the Irish Archaeological Society, to which he sought entry, and James Hardiman published one of the lays in a poetry anthology in 1831.[82] Thaddaeus Connellan also claimed on his title pages to have used both manuscript and oral sources. He did not document the specific provenance of anything in his anthologies, but according to correspondence, he had begun collecting Fenian lays in Cos. Sligo and Mayo by 1807.[83] Another folklore collection was made in the late 1820s by Belfast antiquarian Robert Shipboy MacAdam (Roibeard Mac Ádhaimh). MacAdam gathered oral traditions and manuscripts throughout rural Ulster, where he traveled in connection with his family's ironworking and saddlery business.[84] His papers in the Belfast Central Library include three fragmentary lays and two proverbs about the Fianna that appear to have been taken down from recitation.[85]

Despite this early evidence of orally collected Fenian narrative, however, the first folklore anthology assembled in Britain and Ireland had no Fenian content. In 1825 Thomas Crofton Croker, a London-resident civil servant from Cork city, was inspired to publish *Fairy Legends and Traditions of the South of Ireland* by the continental vogue for folklore. He took as his model Jacob and Wilhelm Grimm's *Kinder- und Hausmärchen*, which had appeared in English translation to great acclaim two years previously. While the Grimms saw the spirit of the nation in the peasantry's customs and beliefs, such Herderian notions did not sit well with Croker; rural unrest had periodically erupted in localized violence since the turn of the century, and he felt that the unruly Irish peasantry were neither wholly possessed of "civilization" nor of "the nobleness of savage nature."[86] His heavily adapted characters thus served to reinforce rather than rebuff negative stereotypes. Designed for and hailed as a success within the Anglophone market, his anthology set the tone for early Irish folklore publishing.[87] When the first orally collected Fenian tales did come to print, their heroic protagonists may not have been as condescendingly drawn as Croker's Irish peasants, but they did undergo stylistic modification to meet the conditioned expectations of an Anglophone reading public. While printing presses were far from inundated with Fenian folklore in the first half of the nineteenth century, Dublin-resident writers Caesar Otway, originally from Co. Tipperary, and William Carleton, originally from Co. Tyrone, penned literary retellings in 1827 and 1845 respectively of *Conán agus Piast Locha Dheirg* (Conán and the monster of Loch Dearg), *Macgnímartha Finn* (The boyhood deeds of Fionn), and *Fionn sa Chliabhán* (Fionn in the cradle).[88] Adapted translations also occasionally turned up in popular magazines and newspapers beginning in the 1830s.

As creative writers began tentatively exploring Fenian folktales, academic awareness of orally circulating narrative about the Fianna grew and scholarly approaches to Gaelic history and culture became more rigorous. The commencement of the Ordnance Survey in 1824 marks a new era in which more advanced methodologies than those of the early antiquarians began to be utilized in Gaelic scholarship. In the 1830s and early 1840s the survey employed a small number of Irish-speaking fieldworkers to aid in topographical research. Their letters contained remarks about Fenian place names and sometimes included tale summaries.[89] According to both Irish-speaking and non-Irish-speaking fieldworkers, tales about the Fianna were prevalent. In May 1835, for instance, a rather disapproving assistant surveyor for the parish of Layd in the Glens of Antrim related that: "The writer has spent much time in listening to the innumerable legends, stories and traditions which are recited in the more remote parts of this parish. They mostly refer to nothing but the fabled deeds of Fin McCoul, Ossian and the many other giants and enchanters who made Glenariff and Lurigethan hill the scene of their exploits. They are inconsistent, contradictory and absurd."[90] Some of the most substantial accounts of the Fianna reported to Ordnance Survey fieldworkers come from Ulster, the first province surveyed, and are contained in an accompanying set of memoirs. The production of the memoirs was discontinued in later stages of the project.[91]

Considerable research was required on account of the decision to include historical landmarks in the survey, and thus the enterprise had a historical department.[92] This was headed by the archaeologist George Petrie, under whom worked two of the most reputable Gaelic scholars of the period, John O'Donovan (Seán Ó Donnabháin) and Eugene O'Curry (Eoghan Ó Comhraí). As Jeanne Sheehy remarks, "by providing regular salaries for Petrie, O'Donovan and O'Curry, [the Ordnance Survey] permitted antiquarian research on a scale which might not otherwise have been possible."[93] It led to intensified manuscript collecting and an increase in the publication of editions and translations by scholars associated with both the Ordnance Survey and the Royal Irish Academy.[94] The interest generated by the survey led, as well, to the founding of archaeological and historical societies outside of the urban, Dublin center, which began publishing findings in their own journals.[95] Of greatest consequence to us, though, is the contribution O'Curry would go on to make to Fenian scholarship.

O'Curry was primarily engaged in manuscript research for the Ordnance Survey. He was subsequently hired to catalogue manuscripts in the Royal Irish Academy and the British Museum, gaining extensive familiarity with the Gaelic manuscript tradition. In recognition of his expertise, he was inducted into the Royal Irish Academy in 1853 and appointed the first professor of Irish History and Archaeology at the newly founded Catholic University in Dublin in 1854. On the heels of his university appointment, he undertook a series of public lectures on the Irish manuscript corpus that were of monumental importance within the field of Irish history.[96] The Fenian narrative tradition featured in his fourteenth lecture, delivered on July 7, 1856. He affirmed the Irish origin of the Fianna early in the talk, citing the medieval Irish textual record as evidence, but he did not belabor the point; the Ossianic controversy was not his intended topic, and his audience was hardly going to disagree with him.[97] He then launched into a description of the corpus, pondering the authenticity of poetic ascriptions to Fionn, Oisín, and Fearghus Finnbhéil and summarizing a wide selection of narratives from across historical periods. He aimed to communicate a deeper understanding of Fenian literature than any listener was likely to possess, given how few texts had yet been published, and to encourage people to learn the language and study the stories' considerable "literary merits" for themselves.[98] The published lecture—one of the first academic overviews of the Fenian cycle—indeed proved influential to the philologists and historians who succeeded O'Curry.[99]

From Fingal to the Fenian Brotherhood

By the mid-nineteenth century, academic attention to Ireland's Gaelic heritage was flourishing, buoying the public interest that had swelled even in the wake of the 1798 rebellion. Long simmering tensions would soon come to a head, however, and Irish cultural nationalism would again take on a political tone that would color perceptions of the Fianna. While rural Ireland witnessed intermittent violence in connection with agrarian and sectarian grievances in the early decades of the century, some of this discontent was redirected into populist politician Daniel O'Connell's successful fight for Catholic emancipation in the 1820s and his unsuccessful campaign to repeal the Act of Union in the 1830s and '40s.[100] Despite O'Connell's oft-cited approval of anglicization, he maintained an active interest in Irish history and culture. He was a member of the Irish Archaeological Society and he deliberately planned monster meetings in "places that had a historic resonance for the public," such as the Hill of Tara (the reputed ancient seat of the high kings of Ireland), "to stress the possibility of the return of the golden age if repeal were granted."[101] Yet O'Connell was careful to avoid overt gestures toward cultural nationalism. Young Ireland, the radical nationalist organization that emerged in the early 1840s, differed in this respect. This group's popular patriotic newspaper, the *Nation*, openly celebrated Ireland's distinctiveness, printing antiquarian commentaries and original poetry—some of which emulated Macpherson's Ossianic verse—alongside news of the repeal movement's progress.[102] As the repeal movement faltered, a group of Young Irelanders staged an ill-conceived rising in 1848 that was quickly quashed. In ironic consequence of their failure, their activities were substantially less damaging to the growing enthusiasm for Gaelic heritage than the 1798 United Irish rebellion had been. The groundwork had thus been laid for further politicization of the nation's cultural symbols.[103]

Although the great famine of 1845–48 dealt a massive blow to the poverty-stricken, rural Irish speakers to whom the patriotic literati increasingly looked for their literature and folklore,[104] a strong national awareness nonetheless persisted throughout the 1840s and '50s. University-based Irish language studies had been born in 1840 with the founding of a chair of Irish at Trinity College, and this was followed by the establishment of similar chairs in 1848–49 at the newly formed Queen's Colleges of Belfast, Galway, and Cork.[105] Interest in the Fianna—and their relationship with *Ossian*—kept pace with these developments, yielding two English-language collections of Fenian lays in the 1850s.[106] The latter of these issued from the pen of John Hawkins Simpson, a Derbyshire native whose five-year sojourn in Co. Mayo resulted first in a pamphlet describing the ravages of the famine and arguing vehemently for a tenants' rights bill,[107] and then in an anthology titled *Poems of Oisin, Bard of Erin* (1857). The "poems" were prose translations of lays from "old MSS" and oral tradition, and they were intended to illustrate Macpherson's imposture.[108]

Like many of the Anglo-Irish antiquarians, Simpson relied upon Irish speakers to locate and decipher his primary source material. Rev. W. H. Drummond's *Ancient Irish Minstrelsy* (1852), on the other hand, consisted almost entirely of his own original verse translations of Fenian lays. Although intended for "the general reader," it was in many ways a belated companion to his prize-winning Royal Irish Academy essay on the authenticity of *Ossian*, published two decades prior and recapped in his preface.[109] His use of the Macphersonic form of Oisín's name, while calling the Fenian leader 'Finn,' betrays his Scottish referent. Scattered throughout the book, moreover, are Scottish Fenian lays derived from Matthew Young's collection and the Highland Society's report on *Ossian*—including three of Duncan Kennedy's texts—in what looks like a misguided attempt at repatriation.[110] Drummond sourced his Irish lays from published anthologies, manuscript copies, and in at least one instance, oral tradition.[111] His efforts impressed upon him "the importance and necessity of collecting and comparing all the different copies which can be procured of our ancient Irish compositions—a task worthy of some competent and properly qualified Irish Aristarchus."[112]

Drummond's wish for further scholarship in this area was fulfilled in short order. The period of optimism immediately preceding the famine had resulted in considerable institutional manuscript acquisitions, and by 1853 sufficient source material was available for the formation of a learned society intent upon "saving from the wreck of time, the songs, poems, and legends of Oisin, Erin's ancient bard and minstrel"[113]—that is, editing and translating Irish Fenian literature. Included in the Ossianic Society's six published volumes were the earliest editions of three romances: *Cath Gabhra* (The Battle of Gabhair) and *Feis Tighe Chonáin* (The feast at Conán's house), edited by Gaelic scribe and poet Nicholas O'Kearney, and *Tóruigheacht Dhiarmada agus Ghráinne* (The pursuit of Diarmaid and Gráinne), edited by the society's president, Standish Hayes O'Grady; two volumes of lays edited by the society's secretary and publisher John O'Daly; and an edition of the early medieval *Macgnímartha Finn* (The boyhood deeds of Fionn) by one of the society's vice presidents, Queens College, Belfast professor and former Ordnance Survey researcher John O'Donovan.[114] In a refreshing turn away from recent practice, contributors largely maintained their focus on Ireland in their critical apparatuses, offering only occasional glimpses of Macpherson's shadow—apart from one glaring exception. In 1860, the centenary year of the *Fragments of Ancient Poetry*, another of the society's vice presidents, Queen's College, Cork professor Owen Connellan, dragged Macpherson into broad daylight again, rehashing the Irish case against *Ossian* in an eloquent if unoriginal essay. Connellan's celebration of Irish scholars' reclamation of "their old hero Fionn" from "the disguised semblance of Fingal" is tinged with irony, given the society's own adopted moniker.[115]

The Ossianic Society's volumes were intended to have widespread appeal, and care was taken to ensure they were affordable to scholars and laborers alike. In this respect, the society has been described as "a forerunner of the popular Gaelic revival associations founded later in the nineteenth century."[116] Also similar to later revival associations, the Ossianic Society placed great store in publishing in the language. Its officers, all of whom were, by regulation, Gaelic scholars, expressed their aim to furnish "a satisfactory and practical answer to the often-repeated question—'Is there anything to read in Irish?'"[117] Facing-page translations ensured equal access to readers of both Irish and English, and the society does not appear to have countenanced sacrificing text in either language to address emerging budgetary concerns. Seeing their venture as a patriotic one, they encouraged the support of "all Irishmen, whether at home or abroad, who love their country."[118] Irish people, for their part, responded with gusto. By 1860, membership numbered over seven hundred and satellite societies had been founded in Philadelphia and New York City—a sure testament to the contemporary popularity of Fenian topics amid a strengthening national awareness.[119]

Although officially apolitical, the Ossianic Society attracted not only cultural, but also political nationalists. Indeed, its last president, William Smith O'Brien, was a former Young Ireland leader who had served a sentence in Van Diemen's Land (Tasmania) for his role in the failed rising. Other Young Irelanders also appeared on the society's rolls, as did members of a new underground revolutionary organization founded in 1858, the Irish Republican Brotherhood (IRB).[120] While these individuals' political views did not seep into the society's publications, a connection can be drawn between the Ossianic Society and the IRB's concurrently established North American branch, the Fenian Brotherhood. Indeed, it might be said that the Ossianic Society was indirectly responsible for the American organization's name, given the significant role it played in the renewed cultural permeation of Fenian literature in the 1850s.

Like Smith O'Brien, the New York-based Fenian Brotherhood's leader, Co. Limerick-man John O'Mahony, was both a former Young Ireland rebel and a Gaelic scholar. His familiarity with the Ossianic Society's work is apparent from his 1857 translation of Keating's *Foras Feasa ar Éirinn* (Compendium of knowledge about Ireland). There, alongside annotations of Keating's discussions of the Fianna, he called for readers to support the Ossianic Society so that "our Fenian literature will soon be placed within the reach of Irish students."[121] To that end, he is said to have helped establish the New York Ossianic Society, which distributed "several cases of books" in 1860.[122] As acting secretary at one of the society's meetings, he reported that he and founding member David O'Keeffe had read Gaelic poetry aloud from Ossianic Society volumes, and that he had offered his own premises as a regular location to meet "for instruction or literary entertainment in [our] native tongue."[123]

O'Mahony elucidated his decision to call the Fenian Brotherhood after the Fianna in the first issue of the organization's newspaper, the *Phoenix*, explaining that "the duties of the contemplated organization are nearly the same as those of the Fenian Order," namely, "to defend the country from foreign invaders, to put down domestic tyrants and plunderers, and to assist . . . in maintaining order and justice."[124] For the imagery on their flags and banners, moreover, the organization adopted Fionn's own *Gal Gréine* ('sunburst') standard (fig. 12), described in the lays.[125] The legendary heroes' status as national guardians certainly made the name and sunburst imagery astute branding strategies, but O'Mahony's literary activity strongly suggests that the evocation of the Fianna held deeper meaning for him, as it surely did

FIGURE 12. Fenian sunburst flag (modern recreation). (Alamy.)

for the considerable number of his brethren who also joined the Ossianic Society.[126] One well-known legend with particular resonance holds that the Fianna are not dead, but merely resting in enchanted slumber, destined to reemerge one day to save Ireland from its oppressors.[127] In adopting the Fenian name and imagery, O'Mahony and his followers cast themselves in the role of the returning Fianna in a bid to engineer the phoenix-like resurrection of an independent Ireland.

Neither the Ossianic Society nor the Fenian Brotherhood were destined for lasting success. The momentum of the former was hampered by contentious relations with members of the elite Royal Irish Academy, including Eugene O'Curry, who was highly critical of the society's work.[128] Internal strife also arose, and publication delays led to defaults in membership payments. Officers were eventually forced to accept the unlikelihood that additional planned editions would reach a timely completion, and in 1863, like the Gaelic Society and the Iberno-Celtic Society before it, the Ossianic Society folded.[129] The Fenian Brotherhood's movement would also ultimately fail, just as those of the United Irishmen and Young Irelanders had. After a series of failed raids on Canada, the organization disbanded in 1886.[130] As one antirepublican commentator taunted, "the right time had not come, and the genuine Fenians would not rise."[131] Unlike their predecessors, however, both midcentury organizations had lasting effects for the reception of Fenian narrative. The Ossianic Society's efforts greatly increased the promulgation of printed texts about Fionn and the Fianna, and as Irish attention drifted away from Macpherson's epics, the society's volumes remained popular for years to come.[132] Due to the renown of the Fenian Brotherhood, moreover, the word Fenian came to be associated more readily with political nationalism than Ossianic disputation.[133]

Over the course of a century, Fionn and the Fianna were thus firmly established as national symbols. Fenian texts were not the ideological point of departure, however; *Ossian* was. The first to react to the international literary phenomenon, the Catholic literati, hotly refuted Macpherson's alternative historical scheme because of the negative implications it had both for their own ethnic identity and the way members of the dominant English and Anglo-Irish culture identified them. The Anglo-Irish themselves followed in the latter decades of the eighteenth century, evidencing a shift in their own collective self-perception. Identifying now as fully Irish and developing an interest in the history and cultural heritage of their land, they began to study and write about Irish antiquities, and were the initial mediators of Irish Fenian texts to an Anglophone public. The interest taken by these relative cultural outsiders in Fenian matters affected the way they were perceived; for instance, Charlotte Brooke's popular lays, which appeared in English in a decidedly Macphersonic dress, encouraged the further romanticization of the Fianna. In the manuscript collecting and copying for which many early Anglo-Irish enthusiasts were responsible, however, they can be credited with rescuing numerous books from oblivion and thus enabling later scholarly research.

By the nineteenth century, the fact that Ireland had its own Fenian tradition was common knowledge, and interest in both the native and the Ossianic material can be discerned, in conjunction with a growing national awareness and a general curiosity about Ireland's cultural heritage. At times, this burgeoning nationalism combined with deeply felt grievances against the state, erupting in political resistance and violent rebellion. To varying degrees in each case, from the United Irishmen to the Young Irelanders to the Fenian Brotherhood, a symbolic engagement with Fenian and Ossianic material can be detected. This is hardly surprising, given the martial focus of many of the texts, which often have to do with the defense of Ireland. This focus was highlighted and romanticized by O'Halloran, whose history proved to be popular well into the nineteenth century. The greatest advances in Irish historical and literary research occurred in the second quarter of that century, when the Royal Irish Academy returned to the question of the authenticity of *Ossian*, folklore publishing began in Ireland, and the Ordnance Survey prompted more intensive, and indeed more scholarly, investigations into the island's past than ever before. By the third quarter of the century, an Irish public could read some of the earliest published Fenian folktales, although in a polished, English guise; they could read several volumes of Fenian tales and lays translated from manuscript sources, thanks to the activities of the Ossianic Society; and they could study such topics in universities. Irish national spirit—and the interest in Fenian matters with which it had become intimately associated—had ebbed and flowed from the mid-eighteenth to the mid-nineteenth centuries, and it was to subside once again until the approach of the twentieth century. Fenian publishing would decline after the Ossianic Society's demise and academic progress would stall as the newly established university chairs were allowed to lapse.[134] When this spirit returned, however, it would do so in an all-encompassing, politicized cultural nationalist movement reminiscent of similar occurrences on the continent, but the likes of which Ireland had never before seen.

PART III

The Fianna and the Modern Nation, c. 1860–2025

7

Scottish Gaelic Folklore in an Ossianic Shadow

THE MODERN PERIOD, in terms of Fenian narrative, encompasses roughly the past century and a half of popular and scholarly engagement with Fionn and his Fianna, and is marked by a shift in focus. The century following the publication of *Ossian* saw the recognition of Fenian literature as an important element within the national heritage of both Ireland and Scotland, with considerable concentration in Scotland on orally collected lays. While the written record was hardly ignored in either country in the period under discussion in chapters 7 to 9, a pronounced feature of this era is the intense concentration on, and collection of, folktales. This chapter, which treats the second half of the nineteenth century in Scotland, thus begins with, and largely concerns, folklorist John Francis Campbell (1821–85). The most prominent figure in the story of modern Scottish engagement with the cycle, Campbell not only amassed a considerable Fenian oral corpus, his writings on *Ossian* constitute the first concentrated, source-based reappraisals of Macpherson's epics since the Highland Society's report on authenticity. They mark the start of a new phase of interest in Fenian and Ossianic narrative that coincided with the rise of a modern Celtic Revival in both Scotland and Ireland. As Scottish fascination with the nation's Celtic heritage grew, *Ossian*'s authenticity and the nature of Gaelic Fenian narrative became relevant questions once again.

The Beginning of Modern Folklore Collecting

John Francis Campbell is known today as the father of modern Gaelic folklore studies. Grandson of the Earl of Wemyss and cousin to the Duke of Argyll, he might at first seem an unlikely proponent of Gaelic oral tradition. Indeed, he was distanced both socially and geographically from ordinary Highlanders, working as a British government official in London. However, he spent his formative years on the Inner Hebridean Isle of Islay where his father was landlord,[1] and the young Campbell was allowed to interact freely with the island's Gaelic-speaking lower classes. He writes fondly and proudly of his countryside rambles in the care of John Campbell, bagpiper to his father, who taught him to speak Gaelic.[2] He further recalls that he heard many Gaelic stories during that time, and made some effort at collecting folklore himself around 1847 at the instigation of Rev. Dr. Norman MacLeod, editor of the first Gaelic periodicals.[3] In time and with further prompting, he would develop a concentrated interest, which would result not only in an extensive body of collected folklore, but also in the methodological advancement of Gaelic folklore studies.

As we have seen, many of the folklore collectors who preceded Campbell were induced to collect by the Ossianic controversy. In contrast, Campbell's initial interest lay not in the Fenian material, but in international folktales (*Märchen*), which were the primary focus of European folklore scholarship at the time. A direct line of influence can be traced back from Campbell to Jacob and Wilhelm Grimm in Germany. The seventh and final edition of the Grimms' immensely popular *Kinder- und Hausmärchen* was published in 1857, shortly before Campbell began his collecting project, and he was familiar with their work.[4] The Grimms were interested in theories of the origin and distribution of folktales, positing an Indo-European path of transmission for international tales, and initiating the theoretical approach to folklore as the remnants of earlier mythologies. These ideas influenced British scholar and diplomat George Webbe Dasent, who, after meeting and discussing folklore with Jacob Grimm in Stockholm in 1840, translated and published *Popular Tales from the Norse* (1859) from stories collected by the Norwegian scholars, Peter Asbjørnsen and Jørgen Moe.[5] Campbell was a friend and former traveling companion of Dasent's, and he shared with Dasent stories he recalled hearing in the Scottish Highlands in his youth. Dasent's enthusiastic response led Campbell to design his own collecting project with a view to expanding the corpus of folklore to which the Indo-European distribution theory ought to be applicable, and evaluating that and other emerging theories—which he began to do in his own later studies.[6] Continued scholarly work in this area would eventually result in the modern Aarne-Thompson-Uther (ATU) international folklore classification system.

Campbell did little collecting himself, being constantly occupied with other work and lacking experience in writing Gaelic at the beginning of the project.[7]

Instead, he designed an efficient method of gathering oral narrative, employing a number of localized folklore collectors to cover a significant portion of the Highlands.[8] In doing so, he initiated one of the first systematic folklore collecting schemes in the world and documented several hundred stories and songs over the course of only two years.[9] In the guidance he gave his collectors, he pioneered a fieldwork methodology that stressed detailed record keeping and fidelity to the oral texts.[10] He was ahead of his time in the amount of metadata he asked his collectors to record for each folklore item, requesting interviewees' names, occupations, and locales, as well as the dates of collection.[11] In the resulting four volumes of *Popular Tales of the West Highlands* (1860–62), he printed both the Gaelic texts and the most literal English translations he could produce, expressing distaste for the "freely" translated texts published by others.[12] He was also interested in gathering multiple versions of the same stories—as Dasent had advised him to do—in order to further his research into international folktales.[13] By comparing different versions with one another and with stories in published European collections, he attempted to determine which tales in his collection were of international origin.[14] He had then intended to map the incidents in his international tales across all versions to devise paradigms—"the old form of the legends," as he called them—in much the same way as later tale classification specialists would do, although he never realized this goal. Such work, Campbell presciently observed, would be a crucial step in advancing folklore research.[15]

Ossian's Long Shadow

In the introduction to the *Popular Tales*, Campbell labored the point that he had "altered nothing" and that "these really are what they purport to be—stories orally collected in the West Highland since the beginning of 1859."[16] The stress he placed on his fidelity to the orally narrated texts was an effect of the shadow still being cast by *Ossian* over folklore collecting and publishing in Scotland.[17] Campbell's fear that this shadow might attach itself to him, shading his reputation with its aura of inauthenticity, at first made him reluctant to engage in the collecting project. In a February 1859 letter to Dasent, who had by then transitioned from his diplomatic position in Sweden to become assistant editor of the London *Times*, Campbell wrote, "From what I know of the highlands and highlanders, I am sure there is a great deal to be got . . . but with the fate of Macpherson before me, I want some Saxon to see the opening of the stores of stories now locked up in wild Islands, in the minds of a race whom it is the fashion of your paper to decry, and in a language all but unknown."[18] In response, Dasent decried Macpherson, suggesting that he was "unfit for his work," and assured Campbell, "No one who is fit to collect Gaelic tales, traditions or ballads need fear abuse if his work shows his fitness for the task. . . . So if you mean to carry on the good work—and it is a good work—don't be downhearted but go at it and if, as no doubt it will be, your work be true and faithful, never fear that justice and fame . . . will fail to follow you. So don't be a McPherson, and then you needn't be alarmed at what any one may say."[19] Campbell certainly had no intention of being 'a Macpherson,' and he took great care in documenting his material to indemnify himself against accusations of inauthenticity.

The Ossianic controversy was thus in Campbell's purview from the beginning. The fact that his search turned up both international and Fenian material also meant that the controversy had some bearing on his work. Even so, throughout 1859 he maintained focus on his original object of study, international folktales, which he accurately contended had been neglected in favor of heroic verse.[20] He largely disregarded the latter, asserting that although he was aware of "men who could repeat such poems," he "took no trouble to get them" because his "business was prose."[21] The subject could not be circumvented, however; not only did the specter of *Ossian* haunt his correspondence with Dasent, others raised the topic with him. William Montagu, Duke of Manchester had developed an interest in the 1807 Gaelic *Ossian*, and requested in May 1859 that Campbell forward any Fenian lays his collectors encountered.[22] That same month a contact put him in touch with William Forbes Skene, keeper of the manuscripts at the Advocates Library in Edinburgh, who alerted him to the Fenian contents of the Book of the Dean of Lismore.[23] In June Campbell examined three manuscripts belonging to the Highland Society of London, noting the presence of orally collected lays,[24] and in September he heard a lengthy Fenian lay for himself on a visit to the Outer Hebrides, although he admitted in a letter to Dasent, "I don't know the Ossian book well enough to say if this is in it."[25] His attention had been piqued, but his primary interest and chief research goal remained the international tales.

Campbell only included five tales about the Fianna in the first two volumes of the *Popular Tales*, published in October 1860. He felt obligated to address the issue of Macpherson's *Ossian* in his introduction, but he did so in a limited fashion, reluctant to "stir up the embers of an expiring controversy, which was besprinkled with peculiarly acrid ink."[26] He had not performed any close textual comparison, and he expressed himself in terms of personal belief rather than studied certainty: "I believe . . . that the printed Gaelic is old poetry, mended and patched, and pieced together, and altered, but on the whole a genuine work," he wrote, citing the existence of manuscript evidence of early Fenian verse. Continuing in the same vein, he stated that the "rhythm" and "style" of the Gaelic lays are "altogether lost in [Macpherson's] English translation," and concluded, "I neither believe that MacPherson composed Ossian, nor that Ossian composed all the poems which bear his name. I am quite content to believe Ossian to have been an Irishman, or a Scotsman, or a myth, on sufficient evidence."[27] To this he added a brief description of the oral Fenian material he and his collectors had encountered, including poetry, stories, and place lore originating in both Scotland and the Isle of Man.[28] Campbell's opinion about *Ossian* circa 1860 thus echoes the relatively neutral conclusion of the Highland Society's report, a copy of which he had acquired in December 1859. Although he clearly maintained an open mind, he displayed little interest in engaging further with the controversial subject.

Nonetheless, Campbell quickly discovered that once broached, the topic was difficult to avoid. After perusing the first few orally collected Scottish Gaelic Fenian stories ever published, readers and reviewers clearly felt that there was more to be said about Fionn and *Ossian*, and they urged Campbell to continue his investigation.[29] His editor, David Douglas, was also keen for him to explore Fenian matters in greater depth, as Douglas was about to publish Rev. Dr. Thomas McLauchlan's edition of the Book of the Dean of Lismore and saw a marketing opportunity.[30] Spurred to action, Campbell began thinking in earnest about the nature of Gaelic Fenian verse, and sought it wherever it could be found. In 1861 he elicited Fenian material from his collectors and asked them to submit statements about the relationship between Macpherson's *Ossian* and the oral tradition in their regions.[31] Additionally, he examined every published text he could get, including not only the extremely rare 1786 Gillies collection, which McLauchlan lent him, but also proofs of McLauchlan's forthcoming edition.[32] The third and fourth volumes of *Popular Tales of the West Highlands*, published in 1862, reflect this altered focus: the third volume contains several Fenian stories and lays, and much of the fourth is taken up by a lengthy dissertation considering *Ossian*'s authenticity and Fenian narrative more generally.

With his dissertation on *Ossian* Campbell sought to clear the air. He traced the history of the controversy and investigated the historical evidence for the Gaelic Fenian tradition, engaging with contemporary scholarship emerging out of Ireland.[33] He also took stock of the orally collected Fenian material, with which he had become quite familiar, and performed a textual comparison of manuscript, print, and oral versions of one of the most popular lays, *Laoidh Dhiarmaid* (The lay of Diarmaid).[34] In so doing, he showed that oral material then circulating predated *Ossian* and that the language of the lays had been subject to change.[35] All of this evidence, alongside his collectors' statements, was provided to support his new conclusions about the authorship and literary status of *Ossian*.[36] While Campbell remained uncertain about the question of authorship and allowed for the possibility that Macpherson might have "had something which we have not," here he argued with conviction that the Gaelic *Ossian* was not "older than MacPherson's time," despite being "founded upon genuine old popular materials." Moreover, even though the authorship of *Ossian* was uncertain, he contended that it should certainly be regarded as an authored, modern text—an adaptation or "composite work" maintaining a relationship with its source material similar to that of Tennyson's *Idylls of the King* with Arthurian legend. More strongly stated, "Ossian is a fiction, but a structure founded upon facts."[37]

Given the still extant Scottish support for authenticity, Campbell surely recognized the potential for disagreement with such a conclusion, however well evidenced. Yet, having spent a great deal of time and spilled a substantial amount of ink attempting to satisfy his readers and himself on the topic of *Ossian*, he hoped against hope that the Fingalian shadow would lift from him thereafter, declaring in his final sentence, "it is my ambition to lull [the Ossianic controversy] fast asleep for good and all."[38] This did not happen, of course. Although Campbell certainly muddied the waters, Macpherson's advocates were not easily swayed.

Carmichael and Arnoldian Celticism

The tenacity of the argument for authenticity is well exemplified by Campbell's interactions with Alexander Carmichael, an excise officer in the Hebrides who did a great deal of folklore collecting both for Campbell and of his own accord. The two men maintained a friendly disagreement about the topic over the course of Campbell's research for his 1862 dissertation, and Campbell acknowledged Carmichael to be "a firm believer in Mac Pherson's Ossian."[39] Carmichael's published statement affirms his admiration for Macpherson's texts, and shows him to have wholeheartedly believed in the existence of the Fianna and the authorship of much of the Fenian material by 'Ossian.'[40] He appears to have regarded Campbell's interest in Fenian material as an opportunity to finally vindicate Macpherson. His marginalia and commentary on the folklore material he sent to Campbell show that he viewed the items he collected solely in light of *Ossian*, rather than with reference to earlier Gaelic tradition, as Campbell did. For instance, next to one lay he noted, "Surely this is somewhere in Oss. although I cannot recollect where."[41] In discussing a lay that bore no relation to *Ossian*, he remarked, "This piece is so truly ludicrous that it defies comparison," and he proposed a bizarre hypothesis about the lay being introduced into the Scottish tradition by a legendary shipwrecked Irish sea captain said to have seduced a Skye woman by telling her stories. Clearly taken aback, Campbell added his own comment: "These remarks of Carmichael's are very curious. The lay which he sends is a genuine ballad current all over the Highlands . . . Nevertheless the collector is so impressed with the authenticity of *Ossian* that he makes game of the genuine ballad."[42] Campbell attempted to disabuse Carmichael of his irrational attachment to Macpherson's adaptation, pointing out the differences between the collector's texts and the published *Ossian*, but this only seemed to strengthen Carmichael's resolve. In a response dated December 19, 1861, he wrote: "I am no less surprised than disappointed to hear that nothing of what I have sent you corresponds with Oss. as published. I did not expect that much of it would but I certainly fully hoped that there were occasional passages to correspond with the published Oss. I think I have something to suit the published Oss. this time at any rate."[43] For Carmichael and others of his disposition, the significance of Macpherson's texts as cultural symbols was blinding, even a century after their initial publication.

Carmichael's position was well aligned with that of the soon-to-emerge Celtic revivalists, whose romanticized views of Celtic cultures set the tone for the coming decades and aroused renewed interest in Celtic literatures and folklore across Britain and Ireland. One proponent of proto-revivalist thought, Matthew Arnold, with full knowledge of the criticism that had been leveled at *Ossian*, declared wholeheartedly and to great effect in 1867 in *On the Study of Celtic Literature*, "Make the part of what is forged, modern, tawdry, spurious in the book, as large as you please. . . . But there will still be left in the book a residue with the very soul of the Celtic genius in it."[44] In Arnold's view, *Ossian* did not have to be an 'authentic' translation of an ancient Gaelic epic to represent and communicate those qualities he determined to be essentially Celtic—qualities apparently carried over from Macpherson's source material regardless of how similar the source and adaptation were.

Arnold's Celt was a romanticized construct that functioned as a counterpoint to the perceived faults in modern English society. In opposition to "philistinism, utilitarianism, excessive rationalism, artificiality, [and] industrial urbanization," the posited Celt was "spiritual, impractical, rural, natural, and poetic."[45] To Arnold, *Ossian* spoke of a culture that had once been great, but had "shrunk to what we now see" as a result of being "ineffectual in politics"—a culture that had always lost its battles as a consequence of this fault. A quotation from Macpherson's epic served to illustrate this point: "'They went forth to the war,' Ossian says most truly, '*but they always fell*.'"[46] Arnold argued, however, that even though the Celtic elements of the United Kingdom had been rightfully conquered (in his opinion) by the more politically capable English, a history of ethnic intermingling had resulted in a beneficial Celtic influence on English culture. Specifically, Celtic "sensibility, the power of quick and strong perception and emotion" had combined with the other elements that constituted English culture and, when positively employed, served to mitigate English faults.[47] Thus, although principally "a Germanic people," Arnold argued that the superiority of English literature, art, and religion to that of other European nations was owing to its Celtic influence.[48]

Arnold's celebration of a visionary, natural, poetic Celtic essence was an important catalyst of revived, late nineteenth-century Celticism not just in England, but also and ultimately more potently in Ireland, Scotland, and Wales. As Patrick Sims-Williams notes, "Arnold had no intention or expectations that his ideas would lead to a literary revival . . . in the Celtic countries themselves. But this is what happened. The Celticity of the virtues which Arnold praised . . . was accepted without question; the alleged Celtic faults . . . were explained away historically or turned into hidden merits."[49] The response of inhabitants of conceptually Celtic regions to Arnoldian Celticism was, in fact, somewhat more complex than this quotation would suggest. While Arnold's mode of expression was fresh and compelling, and he was unique in suggesting that aspects of the culture of subject Celtic-speaking peoples had contributed positively to that of their subjugator, his characterization of the Celt, in both positive and negative aspects, was derivative. On one hand, he was building on post-*Ossian* celebrations of Celtic 'bardic' sentiment recently refined by Ernest Renan in *La Poésie des Races Celtiques* (1854), but also present in both Irish and Scottish cultural nationalism of the preceding century, as we have seen. People of Celtic heritage could thus accept Arnoldian Celtic "virtues" "without question" because versions of them had already come to form part of their cultural identities. On the other hand, Arnold adopted English imperialist views that had, over the first half of the nineteenth century, filtered through emergent European racial theory to coalesce in the notion of an inferior Celtic 'race.'[50]

Such negative views were compounded by periodic violent uprisings in Ireland that had led the Irish, and by association, all Celtic peoples, to be seen as "an ever present threat to peace and stability" in the United Kingdom.[51]

Returning to the case of Carmichael, it is clear from his interactions with Campbell that the culturally essentializing romanticism that arose in the late eighteenth century in the wake of *Ossian* still persisted among a segment of the Gaelic-speaking population in Scotland around the time that Arnold was formulating his views. Those aspects of Arnoldian Celticism that could be perceived as positive were well received by such romantic cultural nationalists, since they tended to align with a preexisting cultural self-image. A renewed rise in antagonistic expressions of Celtic ethnic inferiority promoted the reactive growth of such views into Celtic Revivals, and additionally motivated revivalists to reject or adapt the portrayals of negative traits—to "[explain them] away" or "[turn them] into hidden merits."[52] Indeed, this is precisely what romantic cultural nationalists in Scotland had been doing all along via their support of *Ossian*. Arnold thus contributed to the persistence of an atmosphere in which *Ossian* could continue to be celebrated even after Campbell's lengthy reappraisal in 1862.

Renewed Controversy

In this ideological milieu, steadfast supporters of *Ossian* embarked upon renewed efforts to vindicate Macpherson and with him, Scottish Gaelic culture. The first such work since the appearance of Campbell's *Popular Tales* was Colonsay-born lawyer Archibald MacNeill's *Notes on the Authenticity of Ossian's Poems*, published anonymously in 1868. MacNeill's booklet was hardly a major contribution—its circulation was limited, and despite the promise of new evidence derived from McLauchlan's 1862 edition of the Book of the Dean of Lismore, it did little more than restate the case for authenticity—but Campbell was moved to respond by the author's complete disregard for his own work on the subject.[53] Campbell's opposing view was printed anonymously in the London *Times* on October 14, 1869, reaching a much greater audience than the booklet itself.[54] An indignant reaction appeared two weeks later in the *London Scotsman*, likely written by Rev. Archibald Clerk of Kilmallie, who was then hard at work on an Ossianic project of his own.[55] In late 1870, Clerk presented the fruit of his labor to the public in the form of a new two-volume edition and translation of the Gaelic *Ossian*. He prefaced the text with a lengthy "Dissertation on the Authenticity of the Poems" in which he recognized Campbell's scholarly contribution, but failed to appreciate the Islayman's critical assessment, instead endorsing the longstanding view that the Gaelic *Ossian* was authentic, but Macpherson's English translation was unfaithful.[56] Unsurprisingly, this elicited a barbed (but again anonymous) response from Campbell in the *Times* on April 15, 1871, which was in turn answered by Prof. John Campbell Shairp of the University of St. Andrews, writing in support of Clerk in *Macmillan's Magazine* in May 1871.[57] The long-simmering controversy had thus entered a new phase, and however reluctant Campbell had previously been to join the fray, he was fast becoming a principal combatant—albeit a somewhat covert one.

To Campbell, these publications illustrated the degree to which patriotically minded Scots were willing to overlook unfavorable perspectives to pursue a cultural agenda, glossing over the only recent, relevant scholarship rather than engaging with it. In his *Times* reviews he simultaneously dismantled the authors' arguments and further developed his own position. While he had been uncertain about the authorship of *Ossian* in 1862, in 1869 he used a stylistic comparison among Macpherson's *Highlander* (an earlier, non-Fenian epic), *Ossian*, and the Gaelic Fenian lays to conclude that Macpherson authored the epic adaptations. Over the next two years, his curiosity drove him back to the Gaelic Fenian oral tradition to delve more deeply into its scope and subject matter, and he brought this research to bear in his more pointed 1871 review. There, he reiterated that Macpherson based *Ossian* on "genuine Scotch Materials, which he used as other men of genius have used early national myths," and suggested, in direct opposition to Clerk, that the Gaelic *Ossian* was "a free metrical translation" from the English. Although he offered superficial compliments to the translator for his hard work and the printer for the quality of the paper, his disdain for inferior scholarship is readily apparent, and his aggravation both at the resurgence of the controversy and at his own work being flouted is palpable in his closing paragraph:

> Those who desire to form an opinion had better read the Ossianic controversy, the Gaelic books which contain ballads, and Mr. Clerk's new edition of Ossian's poems; then converse with the most ignorant of the people of the Highlands and islands and gain their confidence. It has cost about 40 years to acquire the small amount of information of which the epitome is contained in this paper. Those who are too lazy to inquire had best follow some leader and join the fight, or leave others to fight it out to the bitter end.[58]

FIGURE 13. John Francis Campbell (center) and Hector MacLean (right) collecting folklore from Lachlan MacNeill (left) on Islay in 1870. (School of Scottish Studies Archives, University of Edinburgh, image Sx J 43. By permission of Heritage Collections, University of Edinburgh.)

In other words, anyone who was not well versed in the entire history of the controversy, the Gaelic *Ossian*, the published Gaelic lays, and the unpublished Fenian folklore still current in Western Scotland was unqualified to comment in any way, let alone to respond to his review.

Clerk's edition could only have confirmed Campbell's opinion of the necessity of his next book, and it likely spurred him on toward its completion in 1872. Compiled in a remarkably short period of time, *Leabhar na Féinne* (The book of the Fianna) presented editions of the majority of Fenian lay texts known to Campbell from collections dating back to the Book of the Dean of Lismore.[59] Alongside these, he included samples of orally collected material acquired on two folklore collecting trips to the Highlands in the autumns of 1870 and 1871 (fig. 13).[60]

In his journal entries for these collecting trips, the establishment of a Fenian chronology emerges as one of his fieldwork goals. Already in September 1870 he described hearing several different Fenian items, "all of which, joined with other knowledge and with manuscript and book versions of the poems, will easily make a connected story equal to any popular history that I know in any language."[61] A month later in an *Inverness Courier* article he noted that "no one has tried to arrange [the lays and stories] so as to mend the broken thread of the old story. That work is surely worth doing."[62] In a journal entry from the following year he documented his process in questioning a particularly prolific informant about the order of Fenian events,[63] and he took a similar approach when it came time to organize the layout of *Leabhar na Féinne*. Rather than grouping the texts according to their provenance, he sorted them categorically and printed them in what he took to be their internal "chronological sequence."[64]

Campbell's attention to chronology is likely to have been influenced both by his interest in understanding Macpherson's process in composing *Ossian*, and by a desire to produce an 'authentic,' cohesive Gaelic counternarrative as compelling as the one that so enthralled his cultural nationalist compatriots.[65] For the particular benefit of that audience, Campbell scattered comments throughout the text about the relationship—or rather, lack thereof—between Macpherson's *Ossian* and the texts of the Gaelic tradition. In these comments, he restated the positions taken in his *Times* reviews alongside textual evidence for his claim that the language, style, and contents of the two traditions differ substantially. To drive his point home, in the final section of the book he included the few texts he had discovered that imitate Macphersonic style "in order that believers in the antiquity of Mac Pherson's Ossian may compare quantity, date, and quality."[66] The evidence against Macpherson was seemingly irrefutable, and in Campbell's view, by accepting *Ossian* as a modern, composite text, cultural nationalists would gain more than they lost. What reason could there be to grasp at a defamed and tarnished symbol, when in *Leabhar na Féinne*, for the first time, the Gaelic Fenian story was told from beginning to end in all its glory?

The book did make supporting the argument for authenticity more difficult for anyone who read it. Even Carmichael admitted in a letter to Campbell, "For my own part I must candidly own that my faith in Mac Pherson's 'Ossian' is more shaken than is at all pleasant."[67] But it could have no effect on those without the will to read it. Despite the topical summaries preceding the versions of each lay, the lack of English translations was a significant deterrent, and sales were very poor.[68] This factor may help to explain the failure of the authors of the next books in support of authenticity to engage with Campbell's extensive work on the subject.

In 1874, English Classics scholar C. S. Jerram published a volume containing new translations of two of Rev. John Smith's Macphersonic lays and commentary about the Ossianic controversy. Campbell declined to write a review and complained in a letter to the author, "You quote the latest book on one side (Clerk's) and ignore the latest on the other (mine)."[69] However, his annoyance with Jerram was minor compared with his reaction to Glasgow minister Rev. Dr. Peter Hately Waddell's 1875 monograph *Ossian and the Clyde, Fingal in Ireland, Oscar in Iceland, or Ossian Historical and Authentic.* Not being a Gaelic speaker, Waddell openly disregarded all linguistic evidence.[70] Engaging only with Macpherson's English text, he claimed to have proven *Ossian*'s authenticity using topographical and geological evidence.[71] Campbell, whose journals evince a longstanding passion for historical geology,[72] was at least as competent to judge such arguments as Waddell was to make them, and he made copious and highly aggravated notes in the opening pages of his copy of the book. Deeming it "a grand fiction" founded upon nothing but "faith," he sent Waddell a copy of *Leabhar na Féinne* for his reading pleasure, and privately dubbed him "Hateful Twaddle."[73] Unfazed by criticism, Waddell continued to restate his dubious position at speaking engagements and in a number of periodicals.[74]

Campbell and the Revivalists

The persistence of the controversy and the disinterest not just of *Ossian*'s most vocal supporters, but of members of Scottish cultural societies generally in Gaelic language and literature disheartened Campbell. The Highland Society of Scotland only purchased one copy of *Leabhar na Féinne* and declined to promote the book among its members, while none of the other Scottish cultural societies purchased any copies.[75] Campbell further perceived this disinterest reflected in the publications that members of these groups supported. In a January 1874 note on a draft of an article about Highland dress, he opined, "The Inverness 'Highlander', the Glasgow 'Gael' [*An Gaidheal*] and the 'Tuam News', the 'Revue Celtique' and other papers are working at a celtic revival, but the writers generally seem to have small power and smaller knowledge, and the whole will end in smoke."[76] In 1873, Angus Nicolson, editor of *An Gaidheal* had sent him a copy of the first bound volume of the periodical and offered him advertising space for *Leabhar na Féinne,* which Campbell declined. Complaining of the limited funds of those Gaelic speakers who would be interested in the book's content and the disinterest of "Gaelic scholars who read

Mac Pherson's Ossian in English and talk as if they knew Fionn at home," he asserted, "I need not waste my own money or your space to tell the general public that I have printed a book which no fellow can understand."[77] When Rev. Dr. Alexander Cameron of Brodick, Arran wrote to him in 1878 regarding a projected new periodical for Gaelic scholarship, Campbell issued a similarly pessimistic response: "My experience leads me to advise caution. . . . I know the classes who take an intelligent interest in Gaelic lore, and I know them to be poor in purse if rich in mental gifts. . . . There is no buying public for a Celtic periodical as yet."[78]

Campbell's foray into Fenian studies, and thus into the Ossianic ring, had led him to the opinion that the study of Gaelic literature in general, and the Fenian tradition in particular, was so underappreciated that it was hardly worthwhile. He had published *Leabhar na Féinne* as the first of two volumes, and he had completed substantial work toward the planned second volume. His manuscript collection contains a lengthy general introduction to the study of Gaelic heroic narrative that he had planned to condense, some translations of individual Fenian lays, and the beginning of a chronological prose retelling in English of the traditions of the Fianna.[79] After his publication proposal for the second volume was declined by Macmillan in 1876, however, he appears to have largely given up on the project.[80] In a manuscript note written in 1881 he admitted that the volume "probably, never will be written. . . . Nobody would read such Rubbish. Nevertheless no country in Europe has such a store of Heroic tradition as the West Highlands, *orally preserved*."[81]

Campbell felt further alienated by the politicization in the 1870s and '80s of what support there was for Gaelic interests and Celtic studies. At this time, key figures such as John Murdoch, editor of the *Highlander*, and John Stuart Blackie, University of Edinburgh Professor of Greek, became strong supporters of both a revival of Gaelic language and literature and Highland crofters' rights. Murdoch fomented dissent in his newspaper, at speaking engagements at the urban cultural societies, and in localized crofters' meetings where he promoted the idea that Highland Gaels' "language and culture was just as much at stake as was their land."[82] Campbell identified with the landlord class and wanted nothing to do with the growing agitation.[83] In 1874, perceiving similar trends among Celtic revivalists in both Ireland and Scotland, he scribbled the following marginal note: "It tends towards 'Home Rule', the abolition of Game and Landlords and the promotion of Fenianism and the Commune. Therefore I keep out of this Celtic movement which is humbug."[84] Yet, he could not keep out of it completely, for during the same period, the University of Edinburgh at long last approved the establishment of a Celtic Chair, a matter that greatly interested Campbell. In 1875, Blackie became the convener of the Celtic Chair Committee and he campaigned intensely, seeking donations at every speaking engagement he could secure, and mixing promotion for the crofters' cause with his fundraising efforts.[85] Campbell maintained a correspondence with Blackie at the time and helped to publicize the campaign among his own highly influential relatives, friends, and colleagues.[86]

Campbell was concerned not only that sufficient funds should be raised for a Chair to be established, but also that an appropriate scholar should be selected as the first holder of the prestigious position. Blackie had, at one point, pressed Campbell to apply, but Campbell declined.[87] Blackie's friend, Rev. Archibald Clerk was also discussed as a possible candidate—a prospect that horrified Campbell, who noted in his copy of Clerk's *Ossian* in January 1876: "This man is utterly unfit to fill any chair from which Common Sense is to be taught. He is equally unfair + incompetent to argue rationally."[88] Campbell's preferred candidate was his former folklore collector, Hector MacLean.[89] In the end, the Scottish applicant viewed as the most likely to succeed was Rev. Dr. Alexander Cameron, who eschewed the romanticized bent of scholars like Clerk, and whose joint interests in philology and Gaelic literature aligned him more closely with continental Celtic scholarship.[90] Rev. Donald Mackinnon's appointment in 1882 thus came as a surprise to many and confirmed Campbell's negative opinion of contemporary Celtic studies, since although Mackinnon was a competent Gaelic scholar, he was both a believer in Ossianic authenticity and a supporter of the movement for crofters' rights.[91] In October 1883, Campbell reflected bitterly in the endpapers of his copy of *Transactions of the Gaelic Society of Inverness*, volume 1, that "during eleven years this Celtic revival in Ireland, Scotland, Wales, and France turned political." Its proponents had become involved with both the Irish land rights movement and the establishment of the "Crofter Parliament in Glasgow"—in other words, the Napier Commission, which was set up to evaluate crofters' grievances and which Mackinnon had joined. Campbell concluded his note by declaring, "I am out of the mess. I got out of it as soon as I saw the drift of this *Celtic Revival*. It is a curious bit of real life in which I have been mixed up with people whose names are printed in this book."[92] Had he lived to see the amelioration of the crofters' grievances and the blossoming of serious Scottish Gaelic scholarship alongside the more romanticized variety that so aggravated him, perhaps he would have returned to his Fenian studies with renewed vigor. As it was, he died in 1885, still bitter.

Later Engagements with Fenian Narrative

While no one of Campbell's intense productivity would take up the study of Scottish Gaelic Fenian narrative throughout the remainder of the Celtic Revival period, new and more diversified scholarship did finally emerge. Although many commentators continued to support authenticity, their claims were increasingly tempered by a recognition of Campbell's definitive evidence of textual difference. Among the most prominent Ossianic supporters were Blackie and Mackinnon, both of whom were staunch nationalists in the face of contemporary anti-Scottish discrimination.[93] Campbell had pressed Blackie on the matter, although he moderated his critique due to Blackie's role in securing funding for the Celtic Chair.[94] While Blackie never gave up his position, in his book on *The Language and Literature of the Scottish Highlands* he cited Campbell's findings and admitted "the possibility of [the unknown author's] having dealt in a grand style of freedom" with his source material. Yet, much like Arnold, Blackie maintained that regardless of authorship, age, or manipulation, *Ossian* was "a genuine Celtic production."[95] Mackinnon also qualified his position along Arnoldian lines, writing in an 1877 article, "No matter for the moment whether or not it was Macpherson himself who composed 'Ossian.' He was on any account a true Gael."[96] Perceiving an essential Highland spirit in the Gaelic *Ossian*, he persisted in valuing it above all other Scottish Gaelic literary production, despite the serious critiques that had been levelled.

The acceptance of "the spirit, though not the letter, of Macpherson's work" became the standard revivalist approach.[97] In 1896, in recognition of the centenary of Macpherson's death, the prolific Celtic revivalist author William Sharp edited a new edition of *Ossian*, which was printed by Patrick Geddes.[98] In his introduction, Sharp confronted "the question of the partial authenticity of Macpherson's 'Ossian,'" devoting significant space to Campbell's findings.[99] He concluded that, while *Ossian* was not "a genuine translation of authentic Dana Oisin [*sic*] mhic Fhionn," still "the ancient poetry, the antique spirit, breathes throughout this eighteenth-century restoration and gives it enduring life, charm, and all the spell of cosmic imagination."[100] One year later, a similar passion for Scotland's ancient spirit drove further creative engagement with Fenian narrative when J. F. Campbell's cousin, the Marquis of Lorne, staged his bewildering opera *Diarmid*, influenced by Gaelic, Scandinavian, and Macphersonic literature, in Covent Garden Theatre on October 23, 1897.[101]

Sharp's views were reprinted in his introduction to the 1896 poetry anthology *Lyra Celtica*, edited by his wife Elizabeth. The inclusion in this collection of a selection of medieval Fenian poetry in translation (alongside a few Macphersonic texts) reflects the academic interest in Gaelic literature that had begun to flourish within the preceding decade.[102] Underpinning this interest was the work of foreign philologists like Whitley Stokes (Indian Civil Service), Ernst Windisch (University of Leipzig), Heinrich Zimmer (University of Greifswald and Friedrich Wilhelm University, Berlin), Ludwig Christian Stern (Royal Library, Berlin), and Kuno Meyer (University of Liverpool). In the second half of the nineteenth century, these scholars edited a considerable number of primarily early Irish but also some Scottish Gaelic texts, allowing the history of Gaelic literature in general, and the Fenian tradition in particular, to be investigated with greater clarity.[103] While in Campbell's time few were engaging with early Celtic philological scholarship, in the 1880s and '90s Scottish Gaelic scholars increasingly took note of these authorities' stances on the historicity of the Fianna, the development of the Fenian narrative cycle, and the Ossianic controversy. In 1898 a translation of Stern's recently published German essay denouncing *Ossian* as a fabrication and comparing it with the Scottish Gaelic lays was even presented before the Gaelic Society of Inverness;[104] two decades prior, the same society had entertained Waddell's vehement but linguistically uninformed arguments for authenticity.[105]

One of the earliest representatives of this new era of Scottish Gaelic scholarship was Rev. Dr. Alexander Cameron, who launched the first academic journal for Scottish Gaelic Studies in 1881, the *Scottish Celtic Review*, which he modeled on continental examples.[106] Although Campbell had advised him against this venture due to a perceived lack of interest, the journal had sufficient subscribers and was discontinued in 1885 not for want of an audience, but because of Cameron's inability to regularly edit (and, to some extent, write) issues and still keep up with his ministerial responsibilities.[107] He also had another extracurricular project to occupy his time, for it is to Cameron that we owe the next, and final, major compilation of Scottish Gaelic Fenian lays from manuscript sources. Very little of his work in this area was published prior to his death in 1888, but in 1892 Alexander MacBain, school rector and coeditor of the *Highland Monthly* in Inverness, and Rev. John Kennedy of Caticol, Arran published the first of two volumes of *Reliquiae Celticae*, assembled from Cameron's extant papers. Subtitled "Ossianica," this volume largely consisted of the transcribed texts of several collections of Fenian lays, including more accurate texts from the Book of the Dean of Lismore than McLauchlan had printed, and texts from collections that Campbell had been unable to include in *Leabhar na Féinne* or had presumed lost.[108]

That MacBain would have recognized the value in making these texts accessible in print is no surprise, given his own stance on Gaelic Fenian narrative and *Ossian*; in 1885 he had argued that *Ossian* described the "sham-antique" rather than actual antiquity; that "Macpherson is as truly the author of 'Ossian' as Milton is of 'Paradise Lost'"; and, moreover, that Macpherson had been mistaken in assuming the historicity of his narrator.[109] Indeed, MacBain followed Campbell in positing that the Fianna were not historical personages, but euhemerized pre-Christian gods.[110] His work was informed by continental scholarship, as was that of his former student and the first full-time lecturer of Celtic at the University of Glasgow, Rev. Dr. George Henderson, who examined Zimmer's theory that Fionn was an actual, ninth-century person of Norse descent, and found it wanting. Like his mentor, Henderson argued for a mythological foundation for the tradition, and he brought Campbell's work toward the second volume of *Leabhar na Féinne* into his analysis.[111] Having relinquished Macpherson's Scottish-origin narrative and embraced philological scholarship (Zimmer's much-debated theory aside), such avenues could finally be investigated in mainstream Scottish academia in a way that was not possible in Campbell's time.[112]

Scholarly interest in Scottish Gaelic folklore also grew during this period, resulting in the collection of further Fenian material, particularly in Argyll. Inspired by J. F. Campbell's collecting project, Lord Archibald Campbell commissioned four ministers to gather folklore for a series called *Waifs and Strays of Celtic Tradition* (1889–95), which ran to five volumes.[113] The fourth volume of this series was entirely dedicated to Fenian material, and the second and third contain a significant number of Fenian and hero tales.[114] The general editor of the series, the prominent English folklorist Alfred Nutt, contributed significantly to the critical apparatus of the volumes. In an essay appended to the second volume he discussed recent Fenian scholarship, traced the development of the Gaelic Fenian tradition, and in a footnote dismissed *Ossian* as "absolutely worthless" for the study of Celtic narrative.[115] J. F. Campbell's work, on the other hand, he recognized in his introduction to the fourth volume as the most extensive, important, and valuable to come out of Scotland. There he appealed to Scottish scholars to extend the study of their Fenian literature and folklore for the greater glory of their nation: "Gaelic Scotland has at length organised the song- and letters-loving tendencies of her children. . . . Let the first task . . . be to promote the criticism of the one living hero-cycle of Western Europe, the tales of Finn MacCumhal and the Fian band."[116]

By the turn of the twentieth century, however, the Fianna were once again receding from prominence. Scholarship began to decline, creative engagement was minimal,[117] and folklore collectors, embracing the notion of the visionary Celt bequeathed by Arnoldian Celticism, increasingly shifted their attention to proverbs, beliefs, and charms. Alexander Carmichael, for instance, appears to have altered his focus around the time of the publication of *Leabhar na Féinne*, perhaps on account of his shaken faith in *Ossian*. As Dòmhnall Uilleam Stiùbhart explains, he "increasingly felt that the soul of the culture was not to be found in the epic prose tales tailored for public recitation" but rather in "the private, the personal, the spiritual."[118] He is now known predominantly as a collector of the latter type of lore on account of his *Carmina Gadelica* (1900–1971), a compilation of orally collected charms and prayers that was widely celebrated by his contemporaries.[119] The collector of the Fenian *Waifs and Strays* volume, Rev. John Gregorson Campbell of Tiree, is also better known for his non-Fenian material. His collection of charms and superstitions was published in two parts, *Superstitions of the Highlands and Islands of Scotland* (1900) and *Witchcraft and Second Sight in the Highlands and Islands of Scotland* (1902).[120] Such folklorists' interest in aspects of folk belief in turn influenced Anglophone revivalists like William Sharp, for whom Carmichael's charms were "proof of the supernatural affinity between the visionary, passionate, soulful, intuitive Celt and an emblematic nature, a spirited rejection of modern rationalism and progress."[121] As the supernatural sprang to the foreground in the Scottish Celtic revivalist sphere, the Fenian retreated, its *Ossian*-inspired moment in the limelight coming to an end.

The second half of the nineteenth century has been called "a golden age of Gaelic folklore collecting."[122] It was certainly a golden age for the collection and study of Fenian folklore and manuscript literature in Scotland, thanks in no small part to the efforts of John Francis Campbell. While a patriotic, kilt-clad Scot, his initial motivation was not cultural nationalism, but rather an interest in European folklore gleaned from study, travel, and interaction with others who shared the same passion. It was through his investigation of Scottish Gaelic folklore that he developed his great appreciation for the Gaelic Fenian tradition. He went on to edit and publish a significant number of lays and tales from written and oral sources, and to lead the charge to debunk Ossianic authenticity claims once and for all. These ventures were not altogether fulfilling for him, however. The timeframe of his work coincided with the rise of Celtic revivalist activity in Scotland in the 1870s and, despairing at both early revivalists' romanticized outlooks and their support of the crofters' rights movement, Campbell abandoned his Gaelic research without completing his groundbreaking work on Fenian narrative. Even so, the wheels he set in motion continued to spin, and in the final decades of the nineteenth century, his papers (both published and unpublished) inspired additional collecting and, in conjunction with the work of foreign philologists, further investigation of Scottish Fenian texts. A solid basis for the modern study of the cycle thus emerged in this moment of cultural revival, but the Fianna's time in the Caledonian sun was not to last. As a new century dawned, revivalists shifted their interest away from Scotland's Fenian heritage to embrace the visionary Celt. The remainder of the Scottish Celtic Revival was to see an outpouring of inspired creativity in the romantic Celtic mode, but minimal scholarly or creative work of importance on Fionn and the Fianna. While the early twentieth century bore little Fenian fruit in Scotland, however, matters were rather different in Ireland, as we shall come to see.

8

Fionn at the Birth of an Irish Nation

BY THE TIME John Francis Campbell began his project to gather and publish the Gaelic folktales of Scotland, Ireland had already seen the publication of a considerable number of folktales by early collectors like Thomas Crofton Croker and William Carleton. However, these were heavily edited and presented entirely in English, even when reflecting an Irish-speaking area, as was the case with Carleton's collection. Early Irish collectors also favored material concerning customs and beliefs (e.g., fairy stories), and the presence of *Märchen* and Fenian and heroic material in their publications is minimal. This remained the situation in 1861 when J. F. Campbell visited Ireland to take stock of the Gaelic tradition there. His visit led him to issue a call to arms to the Irish in 1862 in the final volume of *Popular Tales of the West Highlands*: "It is to be hoped that some Irishman will collect and publish the Irish popular tales."[1] Campbell's call was answered in due course, and his influence on Irish folklore scholarship and methodology was immense. At precisely the moment when most Scottish folklorists were turning away from collecting lengthy prose tales, Irish folklorists, with Campbell's strictures about accurate recording in mind, began to take this work in hand. By the early years of the twentieth century, a significant amount of Irish Fenian folklore had been gathered, and new, modern Irish editions of literary Fenian material were being produced by language revivalists as reading material for learners and speakers. Anglo-Irish literary revivalists also turned their attention toward Gaelic heroic narrative during this period, adding their own contributions to the published Fenian record. The decades preceding the formation of the Irish Free State in 1922 saw a further reconception and repackaging of Fenian narrative for children, particularly as Gaelic revivalists' efforts led to the teaching of language and cultural topics in schools.

Over the course of the latter half of the nineteenth century and the early twentieth century, the Fianna's place within Irish popular culture thus evolved in conjunction with, and in support of, the ideological goals of the emerging independent Irish nation.

A New Awareness

The first person to answer J. F. Campbell's call for increased Irish folklore collecting was a Wexford-born, Dublin-based bookseller named Patrick Kennedy. Kennedy had been interested in the folklore of his native region for some time. As early as 1851 he issued a request to readers of the Wexford *Independent* to send him "outlines of . . . local traditions," which he then proposed to publish alongside similar material of his own recollection.[2] Kennedy was also a regular book reviewer—a pursuit appropriate to his occupation—and from his reviews and other writings it is clear that by the 1860s, he was well aware of European trends in folklore publication. For instance, in April 1862 a review of G. W. Dasent's and J. F. Campbell's folklore publications that was likely written by Kennedy appeared in *Duffy's Hibernian Sixpenny Magazine*. The author of this review expressed approval for Campbell's new practice of publishing tales "in their unpolished simplicity," although the "worked up" and "smoothed" tales in Dasent's collection appealed to him more as a reader.[3] When publishing his own material, Kennedy reflected an understanding of the importance of minimizing structural interference to enable the comparative study of international tales; in his *Legendary Fictions of the Irish Celts* (1866), he claimed that "the greater part of the stories and legends in this volume are given as they were received from the story tellers with whom our youth was familiar."[4] Perhaps because he wrote from memory rather than conducting fieldwork, however, Kennedy was quite happy to present his tales in the literary style that he found most appealing as a reader, despite Campbell's caution that "if any one polishes the language of Irish peasants, he will most certainly spoil it."[5] Kennedy's work thus represents something of a midway point between the heavily adapted folklore material that was commonplace earlier in the century and the methodologically more modern collections that would emerge in Ireland in the decades to come.

Kennedy's work is important to the study of Fenian narrative insofar as *Legendary Fictions of the Irish Celts* was the first Irish folklore collection to include a significant amount of Fenian material. In the section on "Ossianic and Other Early Legends," he was less concerned with presenting oral Fenian tales than with giving the most appealing accounts that he had encountered, however. When he was aware that a tale was available "in an improved form . . . in MSS," he therefore made ready use of the literary source.[6] He took contemporary folklore and medieval manuscript material to be interchangeable due to the continuity of subject matter, and he was not unique in disregarding the importance of his informants' creative process—or indeed, the impact of his own, given that his folktales were recollected decades after he had heard them told.[7] The particular interest of Kennedy's collection is that the two Fenian folktales that he did include were heard in English from a boy named Jemmy Reddy who understood but did not speak Irish.[8] Kennedy thus provides an early record of the transfer of some Fenian folktales into English in Ireland during the process of language shift.[9]

Much of Kennedy's knowledge about Fenian narrative was drawn from the influential Ossianic Society volumes, the first four of which he had reviewed at length in 1859.[10] In his review he called on his readers to support the Ossianic Society's work, and on Gaelic scholars to edit and translate additional manuscript texts.[11] As it was, the Ossianic Society folded in 1863, and apart from Kennedy's own limited work for a popular audience, very little Irish Fenian material was published for the better part of the following two decades. It was not until the last quarter of the century, when Irish cultural nationalist interest surged to new heights, that Kennedy's appeal for increased primary-source scholarship on topics of national interest, including the Fenian material, was finally met.

The Intersection of Political and Cultural Nationalism

The strength that late nineteenth-century Irish cultural nationalism would acquire, and the power that would be invested in Irish Fenian and heroic narrative, were due in no small part to the increasing politicization of Ireland's symbolic cultural heritage. Such politicization had already begun to occur on a comparatively small scale in conjunction with rebellions since the 1790s. By the 1860s, the Irish Republican Brotherhood (IRB) in Ireland had adopted the Fenian moniker and flag (the *Gal Gréine*, 'sunburst') of its American branch and had attracted considerable support. Over the course of that decade, the organization's activities on both sides of the Atlantic landed several prominent members in prison, and by the 1870s the IRB's revolutionary potential appeared to be largely quashed, its energy redirected from rebellion to prison rescue missions.[12] While the organization's standing may have diminished, however, it had been highly visible for some time, and the ideological association of political nationalism with the Fianna suggested by the Fenian name had received public recognition. In 1867—the year of a failed IRB rebellion in Ireland—an unnamed reviewer of Kennedy's *Legendary Fictions of the Irish Celts* in the London *Times* veered rather off topic to denounce the "modern Fenians" at length, issuing a warning that in hindsight appears almost prophetic: "We have said enough to show that a genuine popular legend may have more power than the law of the land, and that myths may be worth the attention of statesmen. . . . Small things may work evil or do good; even nursery fictions may prop or help to upset a President or a Parliament, or set Republican shilelaghs to crack European crowns."[13] While the IRB had not then succeeded in upsetting the British parliament, it persisted as a clandestine revolutionary organization. And while its republican goals did not appeal to all, political activism was certainly on the rise, and the heroic cultural symbolism that it employed in the use of the Fenian name began to take broader root.

The 1870s saw the campaign for parliamentary devolution, the rise of land activism, and Gaelic revivalism, precipitating and paralleling similar movements in Scotland. Current and former IRB members were involved in all three movements, and the goals of land activists, in particular, were pursued by both legal and radical means.[14] From circa 1880, Charles Stewart Parnell fronted both the Land League movement and the Home Rule campaign, gaining massive public support and dominating Irish parliamentary seats with his nationalist party members. But despite his popularity in Ireland, he succeeded neither in achieving devolution nor in getting sufficient legislation passed to fully rectify Irish rural tenants' dire situation before his political downfall in 1890.[15] Both issues would rise to the fore again in the early twentieth century, when the campaign for Home Rule would cede to revolutionary republicanism. What would make such a shift possible was the rising cultural nationalism that had already begun to unite Irish people to the cause of national self-determination in Parnell's time.

The main avenue for the spread of cultural nationalism was the language movement. By 1877, the Society for the Preservation of the Irish Language (SPIL) had come into being with the goal of reviving modern Irish-language literature and creating an audience for such a literature. While the SPIL followed the lead of the earlier antiquarian societies in promoting the study of Irish as a patriotic, but nonpolitical activity in which Irish people of different parties and creeds could find common ground, the language revival movement became progressively politicized. By 1880, a splinter group called the Gaelic

Union had formed, which was also professedly apolitical, but employed stronger rhetoric than that of its parent organization; for instance, in an early publication, it equated opposition to the Gaelic language with anti-Irish sentiment.[16] The Gaelic Union in turn grew into the Gaelic League (*Conradh na Gaeilge*), founded in 1893. In principle, the Gaelic League's most radical aim was its commitment to the 'de-anglicization' of the nation, a goal that it pursued to great effect, even if it did not succeed in restoring the Irish language as the national vernacular; fifteen years after its founding, it had nearly six hundred branches throughout Ireland and had become the means through which many people of all ages began learning the language.[17] While the organization itself was nonpolitical and catered to a wide segment of society, however, its members increasingly were political, and from the intermingled ranks of the Gaelic League and the IRB would rise the foremost revolutionaries of the early twentieth century.[18] Rising alongside them, as we shall see, were the Fianna.

Fionn and the Gaelic Revival

By the final quarter of the nineteenth century, most Irish speakers were illiterate in their native tongue. Their narrative traditions circulated largely orally, and very few books were available in the language. The Gaelic revivalists sought not only to reverse language decline, but also to rectify the perception of modern Irish as a language without a literature. They succeeded in getting Irish approved as an extra, after-hours subject in schools as early as 1878, and they immediately began publishing textbooks and reading materials to encourage learners and native speakers alike to read the language.[19] Through the content of their publications, they sought to ensure a perception of cultural continuity with a once-great, self-governing early Irish society. It is therefore comprehensible that many of their publications consisted not of new creative work, but rather of editions of medieval and early modern texts.

Fenian literature proved particularly attractive to the revivalists due to the linguistic accessibility of the bulk of the corpus—the early modern prose tales and lays—in comparison with the Old Irish language of the Ulster cycle texts.[20] Among the first texts printed by the SPIL and the Gaelic Union for use as upper-level reading material were *Tóruigheacht Dhiarmada agus Ghráinne* (The pursuit of Diarmaid and Gráinne), *Laoidh Oisín i dTír na nÓg* (The lay of Oisín in the Land of Youth), and *Macgnímartha Finn* (The boyhood deeds of Fionn). Appearing in 1880–81, these had all been previously published by the Ossianic Society, but were reedited and provided with new translations and glossaries to aid learners.[21] Two of the three—*Tóruigheacht Dhiarmada agus Ghráinne* and *Macgnímartha Finn*—were immediately included on the secondary school syllabus.[22] As the movement progressed, the Gaelic League and its members brought out editions of several more Fenian texts, including *Bodach an Chóta Lachtna* (The churl in the drab coat), *Bruidhean Chaorthainn* (The enchanted hall of the rowan tree), *Bruidhean Eochaidh Bhig Dheirg* (Little red Eochaidh's enchanted hall), *Cath Fionntrágha* (The Battle of Ventry), *Tóruigheacht an Ghiolla Dheacair* (The pursuit of the difficult servant), *Eachtra Lomnochtáin* (The adventure of Lomnochtán), and numerous lays.[23] Fenian material of manuscript and oral derivation also appeared in *Irisleabhar na Gaedhilge* (the *Gaelic Journal*), founded by the Gaelic Union in 1882 and taken over by the Gaelic League in 1893; *An Claidheamh Soluis*, the Gaelic League's periodical, founded in 1899; and the *Irish-American* (New York), a mainstay of the revival movement among the North American diaspora.[24] The Fianna even found their way onto the stage at an 1898 Gaelic League event in Belfast, where they (among other heroes of Irish history and legend) were depicted for the first time in a series of dramatic *tableaux vivants*.[25] All of this contributed to a growing popularity of Fenian subjects among language revivalists, to the extent that some Gaelic Leaguers began employing Fenian pseudonyms in their journalistic and creative writing, publishing under names such as 'Conán Maol,' 'Diarmuid Ó Duibhne,' 'Diarmuid Donn,' and 'Fearghus Finnbhéil' (poet to the Fianna).[26]

While the Gaelic revivalists greatly improved access to Fenian literature, their editing standards differed from what would be considered acceptable practice today. Not only were their editions presented in modernized language to aid learners, but the texts were frequently bowdlerized or adapted to agree with an idealized image of medieval Irish society. As Philip O'Leary explains in his magisterial study of Gaelic Revival literature, the revivalists "adhered, often it seems unconsciously, to an ideology that insisted on taking the early tales as explicit, noble, anachronistically ethical and patriotic models for an emerging de-Anglicized Ireland."[27] To them, these early heroic narratives illustrated—or were made to illustrate—those aspects that were taken to be the most positively representative of the unique culture of the Irish nation.

A Herderian strain of cultural nationalism is detectable in the revivalists' activities. Herder had argued that each nation was unique and organically formed by its environment, and that the vitality of a nation rested in its recognition and developmental expression of its own national character.[28] The revivalists, like Herder, were concerned with making 'authentic' national literature available; their editing of vernacular manuscript texts celebrating the nation's glorious past can be seen in this light.[29] And like Herder, they also sought the basis for their distinctive national character in what they perceived to be the modern vestige of the nation's past: its folklore. Gaelic Leaguer Pádruig Ó Laoghaire's opening statement to his 1895 collection of Munster folklore well illustrates this: "Hearing plenty of stories when I was very young, I said that if they were collected and published it would benefit many. . . . I knew they were valuable, for they reveal to us the mind and the intellect of the Gaels more clearly and distinctly, perhaps, than anything else we now have left, and anything that sheds light on their customs should interest us."[30] Indeed, the turn toward folklore was widespread. The collection and performance of folklore formed an aspect of local Gaelic festivals (*feiseanna*) in Ireland and London from the late 1890s. In 1897, the Gaelic League also instituted its annual national festival, the Oireachtas, in emulation of the Welsh Eisteddfod. Prizes were awarded at the Oireachtas for oral storytelling, collected folklore, and modernized versions of early literary texts, and many prize-winning folktales were subsequently published in a series of proceedings volumes (*Imtheachta an Oireachtais*), adding to the growing quantity of folklore being published to help reinvigorate the weary soul of the nation.[31]

Fenian material is considerably more prevalent in these late nineteenth- and early twentieth-century Irish folklore publications than in Scottish publications of the same period. While Alfred Nutt addressed his comments to Scottish collectors, it was the Irish who responded when he wrote: "Who shall say that the Fenian hero-tales are unworthy the care, the study which every European race has bestowed upon its national traditions? Let us not forget that for hundreds of years these tales were the delight and solace of our forefathers, that they spring from the heart's blood of the race, that they have become bone of the bone, flesh of the flesh of the Gael wheresoever he has fixed his dwelling."[32] There are two likely reasons for this difference in approach. First, Ireland could lay claim to an early and vast Fenian literary heritage that Scotland could not. Tracing links between modern folklore and early literature was thus of limited benefit to Scottish cultural nationalists, whereas it became very important in the course that language revivalists took. In the words of one revivalist, modern folklore was viewed as "the natural and untainted continuation of the last literature in our great books"; the topical continuity of the Fenian tradition was an obvious means of establishing such a continuation.[33] The second likely reason for Irish revivalists' different approach to Fenian material concerns national politics. In Ireland there was a growing need to emphasize the heroic aspect of Irish culture in the period preceding the establishment of the new state when its cultural nationalism was becoming politicized to a much greater degree than in Scotland. These points will be examined in further detail in the following section.

Early Irish Fenian Folklore Collectors

It is something of an oddity, given this background, that the first major collector and publisher of Fenian folklore in Ireland since Patrick Kennedy was not Irish, but American. Jeremiah Curtin was the son of Irish emigrants from counties Limerick and Cork, and his father and others in their Wisconsin community had spoken Irish, although Curtin was not brought up speaking it.[34] He acquired a basic knowledge of the language through self-study while a student at Harvard circa 1860, and he created his own phonetic system for recording unfamiliar spoken words in many languages. These early efforts certainly must have helped him when he began collecting folklore in the Irish-speaking west of the country, but even so, he required the aid of native speakers to comprehend the stories he collected and render them into English.[35] Despite these shortcomings, however, Curtin gathered a great deal of material over the course of two extended visits in 1887 and 1891–93, much of which he published in the early 1890s in the New York newspaper, the *Sun*, and in three standalone collections.[36] His approach to Irish folklore was not out of keeping with that of Irish collectors of the period, despite lacking the specific nationalist aspect. Curtin's initial aim had been to discover orally preserved material "that would supplement and strengthen recorded mythology" in Royal Irish Academy manuscripts—about which he had presumably read in publications such as the Ossianic Society volumes, and that he discussed with contemporary experts during his visits.[37] Given that he sought the sort of 'mythological' material that might be found in both the early literary and modern oral traditions, it is not surprising that much of his collection consists of long and often heroic prose tales—nor that nineteen Fenian tales can be found in his published material.[38]

Douglas Hyde, the most significant Irish collector to gather and publish Fenian folklore since Kennedy, was both a recognized scholar and a significant figure in the language revival movement.[39] He was, in fact, the president of the Gaelic League, and some decades after the beginning of his folklore collecting career he would become the first President of Ireland. In 1890 Hyde published a collection entitled *Beside the Fire* in which he revealed his approach to folklore collecting. He acknowledged Curtin's work, finding fewer faults with it than with the work of those who preceded him.[40] Yet Hyde regretted that Ireland had not yet had its own John Francis Campbell to record Irish material not only in the Irish language, but in "the *exact language*" used by informants.[41] He took on this role himself, and in nearly all of his folklore publications he provided the original Irish text, sometimes with translations into English or French, as in *Beside the Fire* and *An Sgéaluidhe Gaedhealach* (1901), but often without.[42] He also led the way in consistently documenting his sources. His methodological practices effectively set the bar for the new Irish folklore collecting generation.

Hyde's ideological perspective is also evident in his preface to *Beside the Fire*, and bears examining as an early and concrete example of the revivalist approach to folklore summarized in the previous section. Hyde stressed the presumed antiquity of folktales—"the flotsam and jetsam of the ages, still beating feebly against the shore of the nineteenth century, swallowed up at last in England by the waves of materialism and civilization combined; but still surviving unengulfed on the western coasts of Ireland."[43] The dichotomy drawn here is interesting from the perspective of Irish cultural nationalism. England is shown to be devoid of a crucial link to its cultural heritage, having given way to materialistic modernity, whereas Ireland still retained that link.[44]

Also notable is Hyde's concentration on the "western coasts." The poverty-stricken west was seen as the heartland of Ireland's Gaelic culture, where not only the Irish language, but also vestiges of authentic, native narrative had survived the ravages of time and the materialism of modernity. Hyde went on to delineate this idea more clearly, stating that "of all the traces that man in his earliest period has left behind him, there is nothing except a few drilled stones or flint arrowheads that approaches the antiquity of these tales, as told to-day by a half-starving peasant in a smoky Connacht cabin."[45] The antiquity of folktales mattered in a cultural nationalist context because the older a story was believed to be, the freer it could be presumed to be from external contamination, and therefore the more representative of the nation's culture. In this respect, Hyde's perspective was in line with folklore studies elsewhere in this age of the delineation of modern European nation-states. As folklorist Linda Dègh explains, "it was assumed that the 'folk,' as a primitive human contingent, unwittingly preserved elements of a forgotten, superior, national poetic heritage."[46] The concentration on the western poor and on folklore in Irish rather than English saw its genesis with late nineteenth-century collectors like Hyde and was deeply rooted in both contemporary folklore theory and Irish cultural nationalism. This concentration would continue well into the twentieth century, paralleling the elevated levels of cultural nationalism in the era of the creation of the new Irish state.

The obvious topical relationship of Fenian folklore with early Irish literature led to a perception not just of its antiquity, but also of its greater cultural authenticity than other strata of folklore, as previously noted. In fact, Hyde argued that Fenian folklore was categorically different from other oral material, claiming for it "*conscious* genesis inside the shores of Ireland," in contrast with the international tales shared among many nations.[47] He stressed the importance of the Fenian material in some of his most emphatic discussions of cultural degeneration outside of the Irish-speaking west. For instance, in the notes to an early folklore collection, he described knowledge of Fenian folklore as a cultural litmus test:

> I believe, for example, that the character of the people is no longer the same in the east of the county Leitrim and in the county Longford, where Irish died out a generation or two ago. There Dermod of the Love Spot is unknown, Finn Mac Cool is barely remembered as a 'giant,' Ossian is never heard of, the ancient memories have ceased to cling to the various objects of nature; the halo of romance, the exquisite and dreamy film which hangs over the Mayo mountains has been blown away by the blast of the most realistic materialism.[48]

Similarly in *Beside the Fire*, he commented on the cultural superiority of "the man who reads Irish MSS., and repeats Ossianic poetry" over the uncultured, Anglophone Irishman.[49] Hyde also referenced Fenian and heroic narrative in his acclaimed 1892 lecture "The Necessity for De-Anglicising Ireland," which he gave to the newly formed Irish National Literary Society and which preceded the formation of the Gaelic League. There, he recognized the importance of two principal Irish heroes, the Fenian Fionn mac Cumhaill and the foremost Ulster cycle warrior Cú Chulainn—"the chief persons of our two epic cycles."[50] Given his audience, he focused more upon literature than folklore, and he lamented the fact that with the rapid decline in the ability of most Irish people to speak and read Irish, Ireland had lost "all that connected it with the era" of those Ulster and Fenian heroes.[51] Yet, as he declared in another publication, in the oral tradition he had found "vast quantities about Finn, Ossian, Oscar, Goll, and Conan."[52]

That Fenian folklore was seen as a fundamental means for reestablishing the connection with earlier Irish culture is evident in the introduction at the

1902 Galway Feis of a prize specifically for "legends relating to the Fianna of Erin."[53] This motivation can also be perceived in the amount of such folklore published in the late nineteenth and early twentieth centuries. While Hyde was most well-known for his early twentieth-century song collections, he also published an ample selection of the "vast quantities" of Fenian material he reported finding in the oral tradition.[54] Following his lead, his contemporaries added considerably to the printed Fenian folkloric record. These included collectors like William Larminie in the northwest,[55] Domhnall Ó Fotharta (Daniel Faherty) in Connemara,[56] Mícheál Ó Tiománaidhe (Michael Timony) in County Mayo,[57] and Seosamh Laoide (Joseph Lloyd) in Counties Donegal and Monaghan,[58] all of whom got their start in the end of the nineteenth century, and others like Énrí Ó Muirgheasa (Henry Morris) in County Donegal,[59] who began collecting in the early twentieth century. Some individuals, like Éamonn Ó Tuathail in Counties Donegal, Monaghan, and Tyrone,[60] Fr. Seán Mac Diarmada in County Roscommon,[61] and C. M. Hodgson in County Galway,[62] gathered Fenian material that was not published until a more formalized organ arose for such a purpose: the periodical *Béaloideas,* which got its start in 1927. In addition, private collections were gathered by other collectors of this era, which contain Fenian folklore and have never been published; some of these eventually found their way into the Irish Folklore Commission's archive.[63] Together, these myriad late nineteenth- and early twentieth-century collectors provided evidence of a Fenian folklore tradition across a large segment of what was then Irish-speaking Ireland. For cultural nationalists and nation-builders, this was easily sufficient confirmation of the western survival of a more essential Irish culture.

Fionn and the Irish Literary Revival

The spirit of cultural revival of the late nineteenth and early twentieth centuries in Ireland was not confined to the Gaelic revivalists. Emerging around the same time and flourishing concurrently was an English-medium revivalism that also engaged with Fenian topics, and did so in a highly influential way. The person whom a number of prominent Anglo-Irish revivalists traced as their inspiration was Standish James O'Grady. Cousin to the Gaelic scholar Standish Hayes O'Grady, but not an Irish speaker himself, O'Grady was an amateur historian and historical novelist of the late nineteenth century. He was educated at Trinity College Dublin in the 1860s, but he claimed that he learned nothing about Irish history there and only became interested in the field after happening upon a copy of O'Halloran's *Introduction to the Study of the History and Antiquities of Ireland* (1772) in a private library.[64] This discovery led him to explore the more scholarly work of the mid-nineteenth century, including the Ossianic Society editions and primary source-based historical scholarship by competent Gaelic scholars. O'Grady's historical narrative thus has as its basis the contemporary state of knowledge, according to which the native schema of early Irish colonization presented in *Lebor Gabála Érenn* was viewed from a mythological perspective, while the Fenian and Ulster cycle heroic literature was seen to have a historical foundation.[65] O'Grady's primary stylistic influence, however, was O'Halloran. Strongly drawn to the heroic material, O'Grady wrote about it extensively, and in his treatment can be seen the romanticized markers of the early Anglo-Irish historical school.

O'Grady's first venture into this mode of writing was his three-volume *History of Ireland* (1878–81). As Joep Leerssen notes, O'Grady's history, much like O'Halloran's before him, was "part of imaginative literature rather than of an academic, scholarly endeavour."[66] O'Grady was aware of this; he wrote with the aim of giving "a clear and vivid picture of the past," which he saw as "the true function of the historian" because until historical knowledge was "popularised," he argued, there could be no "new surge of antiquarian enthusiasm [to] again ruffle the tranquil mind of the intellectual classes in Ireland." While he did not view himself as a mere "novelist," unbeholden to "historical faithfulness," he was comfortable portraying as history a narrative whose accuracy could not be verified, so long as it had a basis in authentic, native legend.[67] "The legends," he wrote, "are that kind of history which a nation desires to possess. They betray the ambition and ideals of the people, and, in this respect, have a value far beyond the tale of actual events and duly recorded deeds."[68] With his imaginative *History of Ireland*, O'Grady achieved his goal of ruffling minds, although it was not those of an antiquarian bent whom he reached, but those for whom well-told and compelling stories were not only entertainment, but also their craft. His 'history' was essentially a fresh and vigorous retelling of the heroic material, and whatever the Gaelic scholars thought of it, a rising, young, Anglo-Irish literary class was drawn in. For them, O'Grady's repackaging of O'Halloran's chivalric heroes, both in the Fenian and the Ulster cycle narratives, was highly compelling.

These late nineteenth- and early twentieth-century literary revivalist writers would have encountered O'Grady both through his *History of Ireland* and his heroic juvenile novels, which introduced Fionn and Cú Chulainn to Irish youths. As William Butler Yeats later professed, O'Grady "made the old Irish heroes, Finn, and Oisin, and Cuchulain, alive again" and while others followed him in this endeavor, "O'Grady was the first and we had read him in our teens."[69] The novels—*Finn and His Companions* (1892), *The Coming of Cuculain* (1894), *In the Gates of the North* (1901), and *The Triumph and Passing of Cuculain* (1919)—were simplified and indoctrinating. In them, O'Grady distilled the value system he perceived in (or imposed upon) early Irish literature down to its essential parts and embedded it in contrived narratives. In the *History* and to an even greater degree in the novels, he felt no compunction about excising material that he felt did not belong; much like Macpherson, he took it upon himself to determine "instinctively" what was "canonical" or "essential" and what was not. In this, he took a moral perspective, asserting that "The nobler conception of any character, is, of course, to be preferred to the ignoble."[70] In *Finn and His Companions*, O'Grady's Fianna were depicted, following O'Halloran, as chivalric warriors upholding a code of honor that they taught to others and from which they never wavered.[71] All untoward material was excised, and details and even plot lines were modified to present the uncomplicated, 'noble,' heroic personalities O'Grady sought. As James MacKillop writes, "O'Grady's hero . . . is the warrior-hunter-poet of tradition cleaned and dressed up to meet the demands of rectitude on a Victorian Sunday."[72] What is more, O'Grady claimed that in his creative portrayal of the Fianna, the values of early Irish society were accurately reflected and modern Ireland's ancestors were shown to have been more virtuous than the celebrated Romans:

> I do not say that everything related about them is true, but when we compare these stories with what is known historically about the conquerors of the Roman Empire, we can see that the people amongst whom Ossian lived must have been very like the people of the Ossianic stories, and that Finn, who was the father of Ossian, Oscur his son, Diarmid his chivalrous cousin . . . and the rest were very brave, upright, true-hearted, and affectionate men, who in their forests and their rude simple homes preserved certain virtues which the Romans and the Romanised Britons had lost in spite of all their wealth.[73]

Implicit in this commentary is a criticism of modern materialism, and a suggestion that by adopting (or returning to, as O'Grady would have it) the values advocated in the text, the Irish could use their own culturally inherent virtue to thrive as a nation.[74] In this aspect, O'Grady's novels provided an alternative to popular contemporary English juvenile literature, which emphasized the virtues necessary to live for the greater glory of the empire.[75] His use of national patriotism to further a sociopolitical agenda also paralleled the activities of the Gaelic revivalists—although unlike a growing number of Gaelic revivalists, O'Grady held that the Irish nation should remain under the control of a unified parliament.[76]

O'Grady was likely influenced by the rising tide of Celticism, as was another soon-to-be influential person exploring Ireland's cultural heritage. Patrick Weston Joyce's 1879 book *Old Celtic Romances* was among the most popular and influential collections of his time, joining O'Grady's *Histories* as a seminal literary revivalist work. The use of 'Celtic' in his title is telling, given that the book consisted entirely of translations from Gaelic manuscript sources. Like O'Grady, Joyce made use of published translations when available, but unlike O'Grady, Joyce was an Irish speaker and he was able to access the primary sources directly. As he stated in his introduction, "in order to secure the advantage of various readings, I compared, in every case, the published text with at least one copy of the story, in the Royal Irish Academy, in Trinity College, or in my own private manuscript collection." He gave his manuscript and print sources for each item, and observed that his original translations of two of the six Fenian texts—*Bruidhean Chaorthainn* and *Tóruigheacht an Ghiolla Dheacair*—were the earliest in print.[77] His particular interest in Fenian texts can perhaps be traced to his childhood in Gleann Oisín (Glenosheen, i.e., 'Oisín's Glen') at the foot of Suidhe Finn (Seefin Mountain, i.e., 'Fionn's Seat,' in County Limerick), where "he was imbued with an intense consciousness" of the "mellifluous names" surrounding him.[78]

Given Joyce's detailed documentation of sources, which had previously been rare, it might be presumed that his texts are reliable, unlike O'Grady's more creative ventures. In reality, they were subject to the same sort of bowdlerization typical of Irish-language editions of the revival period, and stemming from a similar desire to that of O'Grady to present a noble, early Irish culture. As Caoimhín Breatnach has pointed out with regard to Joyce's translation of *Bruidhean Chaorthainn,* he embellished his sources to emphasize particular Fenian traits and excised passages not in keeping with the image of the Fianna he wished to present.[79] Like O'Grady, Joyce idealized and romanticized the Fianna in keeping with a Macphersonic image of moral Fenian heroism. Indeed, he praised both Macpherson and O'Grady for presenting "the true interpretation of the spirit of these old romances, prose and poetry," noting particularly that whatever its faults, *Ossian* was "always dignified in thought and expression."[80] While Joyce took fewer liberties than O'Grady, those that he did take would have gone unnoticed by readers competent in both English and Irish, given that he did not print his source texts. Even if he had, moreover, his liberties were such that they could have been overlooked, since he worked in an academic climate in which they would likely have been approved.

Both Joyce and O'Grady's efforts can be seen in light of the reaction to Arnoldian Celticism noted by Patrick Sims-Williams.[81] Characteristics of O'Grady's romanticized perspective, in particular, have been linked with this ethos. For instance, George Watson sees O'Grady's concentration on the "imagination of the country" as a manifestation of Celticism.[82] His reaction against materialism by retreating into a distant past can also be viewed in this light. Joyce, moreover, focused on the artistic side of the ancient "Celtic people" of Ireland, highlighting the connection between the literary texts and oral storytelling.[83] Yet even as O'Grady and Joyce espoused some aspects of the Arnoldian depiction of the Celt, they clearly rejected others. In their subject matter, both highlighted the martial heroism of the Irish Celt and implicitly countered the inherent inferiority Arnold accorded to a culture that "'went forth to war'" but "'*always fell.*'"[84] Arnold's formulation of the Celt justified English rule over Ireland. Conversely, in Joyce's portrayal of the Fianna, even the mere mention that ancient Ireland had been forced to render tribute to a foreign leader was offensive; as Breatnach shows, while the manuscript sources for *Bruidhean Chaorthainn* indicate that this was an ongoing and unrectified situation, Joyce interpolated a statement asserting that Ireland quickly overcame the foreigners and maintained its "ancient freedom."[85] Joyce and O'Grady responded to the negative aspects of the newly popular Celticism by invoking the heroic image of the early Irish formulated in the post-Macpherson period, and emphasizing traits such as martial prowess and moral probity, rather than the impractical spirituality highlighted by Arnold.

Some of the most prominent of those whom Joyce and O'Grady influenced would take a different approach. Yeats, often seen as the principal figure of the Anglo-Irish literary revival, veered away from the heroic to embrace Arnold's visionary Celt; yet he rejected any notion of ethnically inherent ineptitude and promoted the universal strength and beauty of the Celts' "'natural magic.'"[86] This perspective is clearly evident in his early poem "The Wanderings of Oisin," an 1889 epic reworking of *Laoidh Oisín i dTír na nÓg* that revels in pagan spirituality and extends Oisín's otherworldly sojourn to encompass three mystical lands.[87] Yeats's interest in the Celt as "a visionary" also drew him to folklore.[88] His two books of folktales, *Fairy and Folk Tales of the Irish Peasantry*, published in 1888, and *Irish Fairy Tales*, published in 1892, were culled and edited from other collections, and tended heavily toward the supernatural material also preferred by his revivalist counterparts in Scotland.[89] As his treatment of "The Wanderings of Oisín" indicates, Yeats saw Gaelic literature and folklore primarily as raw material from which a modern Irish literature could emerge. While he respected the exactitude of Hyde's collecting work, he expressed a hope that Hyde would "put some of his gatherings into ballads."[90] As reading material, he preferred the heavily manipulated folklore published earlier, the authors of which had "made their work literature rather than science" and had "caught the very voice of the people."[91] (The irony of speaking over storytellers in order to catch their "very voice" apparently went unrecognized by Yeats.) Over time, he became progressively more interested in the "unbounded and immortal" aspects of the heroic material, but in this respect, he wrote more often about Cú Chulainn than about Fenian topics.[92] Indeed, it is largely on account of Yeats and his fellow Anglo-Irish revivalists that Cú Chulainn became popular as a national hero—more so, even, than Fionn, although the Ulster material did not entirely usurp the place of Fenian narrative in the national consciousness.

One Anglo-Irish revivalist who concentrated a great deal on the Fenian material was Yeats's friend and cocreator Lady Isabella Augusta Gregory. Unlike many of the English-language writers, Lady Gregory learned some Irish and was able to access source material in the language. Her 1904 collection *Gods and Fighting Men* consists entirely of reworked stories about the Fianna and the early Irish Tuatha Dé Danann, who populate the Mythological tale cycle.[93] She sought to create a coherent narrative in her treatment of the Fenian material, and she edited and amalgamated accordingly. Coherence was not her only aim, however; like others before her, she engaged in bowdlerization for patriotic purposes. Maria Tymoczko has shown, with regard to her treatment of Ulster cycle material in her 1902 book *Cuchulainn of Muirthemne*, how her mode of presentation was in keeping with nationalist ideological goals. As Tymoczko asserts,

> By and large . . . the distinct cultural markers that she transposes . . . had already been selected by the nationalist movement as elements of the Irish social structure and Irish value system to be promoted as distinguishing the Irish from the English. The Irish were, for example, contrasted with the English as being more spiritual (hence open to the spirits represented by the *síd*) and also more heroic in a conventional late-nineteenth-century sense of heroism (e.g. good at war, physically valorous). . . . However, elements of the source culture that had not emerged as part of the patriotic

> definition of Irishness . . . are either assimilated in Gregory's translations . . . or diluted by being translated with multiple lexemes.[94]

Worth noting, too, is the fact that assimilation or dilution might take place not just when a cultural element had failed to emerge as a patriotic trait, but also when it was considered to be unbecoming of a patriotic narrative. Tymoczko's general findings are largely transferrable to *Gods and Fighting Men,* which would benefit from a similarly detailed investigation. Lady Gregory did not go as far as Yeats did in his spiritual celebration of Oisín, but she also did not present either Oisín or Fionn as "an inflated heroic figure," as in the works of O'Grady. Her depictions are generally recognized as being closer to their literary and folkloric sources than those of other Anglo-Irish writers of her era due to her greater knowledge of those sources—and yet, they are heavily reworked; in them, Fionn appears as "the figure from Irish and Gaelic tradition made rather more respectable."[95] Lady Gregory sought to engage a popular audience and instill them with nationalist pride. Like O'Grady before her, her stated goal in doing so was to encourage "much fine scholarship" on the Gaelic manuscript material.[96] Her implicit goal was to better the reputation and condition of the Irish via a revaluation of Ireland's cultural heritage in the eyes of both the Irish and the English.

Also like O'Grady, Lady Gregory sought to reach young people with her Fenian stories. As she asserted, "my own object . . . [is] to make a part of Irish literature accessible to many, especially among my young countrymen."[97] In his introduction to *Gods and Fighting Men,* Yeats honed in on the very young as a particular target audience. Having opened with a recollection of a trip he made to see the legendary site of the Fianna's residence on the Hill of Allen, he concluded by writing:

> When I asked the little boy who had shown me the pathway up the Hill of Allen if he knew stories of Finn and Oisin, he said he did not, but that he had often heard his grandfather telling them to his mother in Irish. He did not know Irish, but he was learning it at school, and all the little boys he knew were learning it. In a little while he will know enough stories of Finn and Oisin to tell them to his children some day. [The landowners'] children might never have known what would give them so much happiness. But now [the landowners] can read this book to their children, and it will make Slieve-na-mon, Allen, and Benbulben . . . and half the country-sides of south and west, as populous with memories as are Dundealgan and Emain Macha and Muirthemne; . . . and perhaps when many names have grown musical to their ears, a more imaginative love will have taught them a better service.[98]

Yeats's comments are indicative of the degree to which the ideological aims of the Anglo-Irish and Gaelic revivalists had become integrated, despite differing opinions regarding the most appropriate language of publication.[99] The Irish nation is here envisioned as one that has forgotten its cultural heritage—its language, its history, and its stories. By this time, youth education had come to be seen as a primary means of promulgating both linguistic proficiency and cultural knowledge. As Yeats makes clear, he and Lady Gregory supported the Gaelic League's efforts to ensure the teaching of Irish in schools. Lady Gregory, in particular, maintained close connections with Douglas Hyde and the Gaelic League throughout her literary career.[100] Her books were meant to bolster the League's cultural revivalist efforts, and the audience she envisioned and received for the collection included both young and old.

Lady Gregory's renditions of native Irish narrative were incredibly popular. Tymoczko states that they "served as the principal literary translations in English of early Irish literature not only for her generation, but also for the readers of the next half century."[101] In a missive reminiscent of Thomas Jefferson's letter to Macpherson, American President Theodore Roosevelt wrote to Lady Gregory to commend her on *Cuchulain of Muirthemne* and affirm his newfound interest in Irish literature in translation.[102] Her Fenian stories produced imitators across Ireland and beyond, many of whom directed their narratives even more toward a juvenile audience than she had, and pursued nationalist goals in their modes of presentation to an even greater degree.[103] As O'Leary has found in his study of Gaelic literature of the period, despite the efforts of the Gaelic revivalists, English publications like these were simply more accessible to a largely Anglophone populace, and were therefore more influential.[104] While they were often far from the realm of faithful translation, it was these English texts that were most commonly read, and it was versions of them that later found their way into school textbooks for even wider promulgation.[105] The image of the Fianna in popular culture since the late nineteenth- and early twentieth-century Celtic Revival has thus largely been derived from Anglo-Irish creative adaptations.

Philologists and Historians

Like their Scottish counterparts, both the Gaelic and the Anglo-Irish literary revivalists drew inspiration from the concurrent work of philological scholars. The comparatively amateur editors of early modern Fenian texts for use in the language movement took their cues from those specialists of Old Irish literature, while Lady Gregory predicted that creative English-language adaptations such as her own would result in increased primary source scholarship: "I believe the forty students of old Irish lately called together by Professor Kuno Meyer will not rest satisfied until they have explored the scores and scores of uncatalogued and untranslated manuscripts in Trinity College Library, and that the enthusiasm which the Gaelic League has given birth to will lead to much fine scholarship."[106] A native of Germany, Meyer had been working on early Fenian literature since the 1880s at the University of Liverpool, and he had completed scholarly editions of *Macgnímartha Finn, Cath Fionntrágha,* and several other texts by the time Lady Gregory's *Gods and Fighting Men* was published in 1904.[107] His 1910 collection *Fianaigecht* gathers together editions and translations of some of the earliest known literature in the cycle, and is still a useful reference today.

Other prominent scholars of Fenian literature of the revival period include Dublin-born Whitley Stokes, who edited numerous Fenian texts during and after a lengthy term in the Indian Civil Service, the most significant of which was *Acallam na Senórach* (The dialogue of the elders, 1900);[108] and Kerryman W. M. Hennessy, who first edited *Fotha Catha Cnucha* (The reason for the Battle of Cnucha) in the 1870s and served on the council of the SPIL.[109] Meyer's mentor, Ernst Windisch, Professor of Sanskrit at the University of Leipzig, also published a handful of early Fenian poems, and a partial English translation of his commentary on "Ancient Irish Legendary Literature and Ossianic Poetry" was published by SPIL cofounder and Gaelic Leaguer Thomas O'Neill Russell in Boston in 1893.[110] Ludwig Christian Stern, manuscripts librarian at the Royal Library in Berlin, similarly developed an interest in Fenian literature in the late nineteenth and early twentieth centuries, editing a number of texts including *Fiannshruth* (The Fenian genre) and an Old Irish poem on the conversion of the Fianna beginning *Ochtur táncamar anúas* ("We eight descended").[111] Notable, too, was Co. Limerick native Standish Hayes O'Grady, who had been a founding member of the Ossianic Society and had edited *Tóruigheacht Dhiarmada agus Ghráinne* in the society's second volume. His magnum opus *Silva Gadelica*, published in 1892, contained editions and translations of early texts like *Airem Muintiri Finn* (The enumeration of Fionn's people), as well as heroic romances, *Bruidhean Bheag na hAlmhaine* (The little brawl at Allen) and *Bruidhean Chéise Corainn* (The enchanted hall at Keshcorann) among them.[112] Trinity College, Dublin lecturer Edward J. Gwynn's early twentieth-century editions of the metrical *dinnshenchas*, 'onomastic lore,' which contained several Fenian episodes, were also significant.[113] These scholars' work was not as ideologically motivated as the Gaelic revivalists' educational publications, and while many of the texts they treated are now sorely in need of new editions, deficiencies largely reflect the inferior state of knowledge at the time, rather than conscious adaptation.

Experts deliberated not only the language of early Fenian literature, but also the historicity of the Fianna. Eugene O'Curry, the foremost authority in early Irish history in the mid-nineteenth century, had accepted the prevailing assessment that the Fianna were historical personages, although he acknowledged in 1856 that many of their stories were "apocryphal."[114] Decades later, in 1892, the influential French Celticist Henri d'Arbois de Jubainville also held to the traditional view that Fionn and his men were historical, but by then, questions had begun to arise.[115] In Britain, J. F. Campbell, Alexander MacBain, Alfred Nutt, Sir John Rhys, and George Henderson all came to see the Fianna as euhemerized pre-Christian gods after considering the corpus in light of contemporary mythological scholarship.[116] Scholars not inclined to entertain such arguments sought a more solid foundation for the argument for historicity. As early as 1862, Scottish historian William Forbes Skene suggested that the Fianna should be identified with early peoples not only in Ireland, but also in other regions of Northern Europe, meaning that they had existed in both Ireland and Scotland—a persistent point of Caledonian contention.[117] A few decades later, German philologist Heinrich Zimmer took a rather different approach; he thought the Fianna had lived more recently than commonly believed, claiming circa 1890 that they were the progeny of naturalized Scandinavian invaders, and identifying Fionn with a ninth-century Norse Dubliner named Caittil Find.[118] This schema was widely criticized within the scholarly community. The most influential theory in Ireland emerged in the first decade of the twentieth century and was advanced by Eoin MacNeill, cofounder, with Douglas Hyde, of the Gaelic League. MacNeill accepted the traditional view that the Fianna lived in third-century Ireland (not Scotland), and he proposed that they were army corps modelled on Roman British legions and drawn largely from subject peoples in Leinster and Connacht.[119]

Interlocuters of contemporary scholarship for popular and educational audiences were left to navigate this array of theories as best they could. Douglas Hyde's comprehensive 1899 *Literary History of Ireland* was particularly authoritative. Writing before MacNeill published his thoughts about the historicity of the Fianna, Hyde initially exercised caution when discussing the sources for early Irish history, claiming that there was "no means of determining the truth of such events as the struggle . . . between the Fenian bands and the High-king" or "the actual existence of . . . Finn mac Cumhail (Cool) and his son

Ossian and his grandson Oscar."[120] His reserve gave way in his later chapter on the Fenian cycle, however, where he staked the following claim:

> I can see . . . no sufficiently cogent reasons for viewing Finn mac Cúmhail [*sic*] with different eyes from those with which we regard his king. Cormac mac Art [*sic*] is usually acknowledged to have been a real king of flesh and blood . . . why should Finn, his chief captain . . . be a deity euhemerised? I do not see any arguments sufficient to differentiate this case of Finn . . . from that of Cormac and other kings and heroes who were the subjects of bardic stories, and whose deaths were recorded in the Annals, except the accident that the creative imagination of the later Gaels happened to seize upon him and make him and his contemporaries the nucleus of a vast literature.[121]

For Hyde, then, the Fianna existed. Not so for fellow scholar and Gaelic Leaguer Eleanor Hull in her *Text Book of Irish Literature*. Writing in 1908, the same year as MacNeill, Hull determined accounts of the Fianna to be "semi-historic," accepting the existence of fenian bands in early medieval Ireland, but finding it difficult to regard Fionn "and his followers otherwise than as products of the poetic imagination."[122] In her later *History of Ireland and Her People*, she omitted discussion of the Fianna altogether.[123] Academic opinion was thus inconclusive, with influential voices supporting opposing positions. Irish popular belief in the Fianna's historicity would nevertheless remain strong for some time, in large part due to the messages conveyed to Irish youth through literature and education. Indeed, even Hull did not differentiate between history and legend when imparting Fenian episodes in her juvenile reader *Pagan Ireland* (1904). While she stated near the end of the book that "the stories about them are so mixed with legend that is difficult to know how much is true," she followed this with an endorsement of the probability "that some such band of trained warriors as the Fianna are represented to have been, did exist in Ireland about the time of which we are speaking," and transitioned into accounts of the conditions for entry into the Fianna and the causes of their devastating final battle, *Cath Gabhra* (The Battle of Gabhair).[124] Any reader, no less a child, could be forgiven for interpreting narratives presented in such a way as historical fact.

Pearse, Fionn, and the Education of Irish Youth

In the early twentieth century, in conjunction with the rise of the Sinn Féin political party, which was founded in 1905, the Gaelic League shifted progressively toward an open revolutionary stance.[125] This position was reflected in the cultural symbolism promoted by its more radical members. In particular, scholars have detected a rise to prominence of a more 'masculine' form of Celticism than that of Yeats or Arnold. Principal among revivalists promoting a Celtic masculinity was Patrick Pearse (Pádraig Mac Piarais), whose literary influences included the moral-heroic Fenian adaptations of S. J. O'Grady and Joyce.[126] Pearse had been an active member of the Gaelic League since the 1890s—he lectured in Irish on the historicity of the Fianna at a meeting in 1900—and editor of *An Claidheamh Soluis* since 1903.[127] His cultural nationalist ideas were voiced not only in the pages of that newspaper, but also through the literature he edited and authored. In 1906 and 1908, Pearse produced editions of *Bodach an Chóta Lachtna* and *Bruidhean Chaorthainn* for the Gaelic League that exhibit bowdlerization consistent with other revivalist-edited texts.[128] In his introductions, he glorified not only the integrity of the Fianna, but also the quality of Fenian literature, writing of *Bruidhean Chaorthainn* that "it would be difficult to find anything to surpass [it] in the literature of Europe in terms of the beautiful thoughts and the mellifluous speech expressed in [it]."[129] He was also responsible for creative, moralizing adaptations of Fenian and Ulster cycle material intended for children—particularly boys.

Pearse's portrayal of Irish cultural heroes as models of ideal masculinity, which will be discussed in greater detail below, was closely connected with his work on educational reform. As we have seen, education was a key issue for language revivalists, who viewed schools as important sites "to counter the anglicizing effects of the state."[130] Since the founding of the SPIL, they had worked toward the provision in schools of Irish language classes through which the national cultural heritage could be taught and the process of language shift could begin to be reversed. The approval of Irish as an after-hours subject in 1878 had been an important symbolic victory, but it resulted in few courses due to the unavailability of teacher training before 1897.[131] The pace of progress accelerated in the twentieth century, although early advances were limited. The position of Irish was strengthened somewhat in 1900, becoming an allowable subject during school hours, and in 1904 a bilingual program was created for primary schools in Gaeltacht (Irish-speaking) regions, although by 1906 it had only been implemented in 30 percent of them.[132] A successful 1908–10 campaign resulted in obligatory Irish for entrance to the National University Colleges from 1913, but it was not until 1922 under the Free State government that Irish was made a mandatory subject in primary schools, taught for one hour per day, and Gaeltacht schools became Irish-only. Other cultural educational measures were also put in place in 1922, and Irish became compulsory in secondary schools in 1927.[133] In the interim, the most significant effort was made by Pearse. While many people weighed in on the issue in multiple nationalist publications, Pearse's commentary was among the most charged; to him, the national school system in Ireland was "the murder machine"—the agent of the death of the nation's language and culture and the enslavement of Irish people to anglicized modes of thought and behavior.[134] In 1908, in response to the meager concessions granted for the teaching of Irish language and culture to that point, he started his own school for boys outside of the national school system.[135]

The bilingual curriculum at Pearse's Scoil Éanna (St. Enda's School) was very different from the national standard. His educational goal was to bring children "to feel that they are Irish children; that this is Ireland; that they are destined to become citizens of an Irish Nation; and that their allegiance and their love are due to that Nation."[136] He was primarily interested in communicating Irish cultural nationalism, which he saw as the natural and only means through which Irish students could reach their "full perfection."[137] He had, moreover, a very particular vision of Irish culture that he sought to instill in his boys. As he wrote in 1916 in reflection on his own initiative and in anticipation of nation-wide change, "A new education system in Ireland has to do more than restore a national culture. It has to restore manhood to a race that has been deprived of it. Along with its inspiration it must, therefore, bring a certain hardening. It must lead Ireland back to her sagas."[138] Cú Chulainn and Fionn were the representatives of this saga-oriented, ideal manhood. Through the narratives that Pearse wove around them, they exemplified an early twentieth-century nationalist conception of what it meant to be male and Irish. Cú Chulainn represented chivalric honor and self-sacrifice for a noble cause, while Fionn and his Fianna were paragons of honesty and loyalty, as illustrated by the Fenian motto gracing the school's crest: "neart in ár lámhaibh, fírinne in ár dteangthaibh, agus glaine in ár gcroidhthibh" ("strength in our hands, truth on our lips, and cleanness in our hearts") (fig. 14).[139] Moreover, both Fionn and Cú Chulainn demonstrated physical prowess. The boys learned to associate such traits with these personas not only in their lessons and in the school's magazine, *An Macaomh*, but also through dramatic pageants in which they enacted events from the lives of their role models. S. J. O'Grady's *The Coming of Fionn* was performed twice at St. Enda's, in 1909 (fig. 15) and 1910, as were plays based on Fenian and Ulster material written by Pearse himself.[140] A youth branch of the Gaelic League called Na Fianna Éireann was also established at St. Enda's and elsewhere, paralleling the English and American Boy Scouts, with the purpose of communicating these native, masculine ideological

FIGURE 14. St. Enda's school crest. (Image courtesy of the Pearse Museum / OPW, Dublin.)

principles widely.[141] In the Fianna handbook, the cover of which bore the Fenian sunburst, Pearse advised that "the story of those old Fianna of Fionn should be part of the daily thought of every Irish boy, and especially of every boy of the new Fianna."[142] Indeed, he might have more accurately asserted his belief that every Irish boy should bear in mind *Pearse's interpretation* of the Fianna and what they stood for in early twentieth-century Irish society. He certainly strove to make this a reality for as many boys as he could reach.

By the time of the formation of the Irish Free State in 1922, simplified and ideologically invested images of the Fianna had emerged from both the Anglo-Irish and Gaelic revivalist camps exploring via seemingly timeless symbols,

FIGURE 15. St. Enda's student Denis Gwynn playing Fionn in S. J. O'Grady's play *The Coming of Fionn* in 1909. (*An Macaomh* 1, no. 1, 1909. Image courtesy of the Pearse Museum / OPW, Dublin.)

but in very modern terms, just what it meant to be Irish. The creation of these simplified narratives was enabled by the increased interest in Ireland's heritage generated by Celticism and popularized by the cultural nationalist activities of the language revivalist movement. From this interest came an explosion of folklore collecting and a spate of publication of Fenian folklore and manuscript texts. Bowdlerization to make source texts better accord with nationalist ideals was common, and creative, ideologically invested adaptations were prevalent.

In this multitude of new cultural productions of the Revival period, two distinctive trends in the perception of Fenian narrative in Ireland are evident. The first is the progressive transference of the projected audience of Fenian narrative from adults to children as attention turned toward the use of the educational system to curb language shift and communicate cultural nationalist ideals. This tendency would continue in the literary sphere, and in chapter 9 we will also see reflections of it in the educational curriculum of the newly independent nation. The second trend is the realization of the motivational potential of these distinctly Irish narratives in conjunction with the political radicalization of the Revival movement. The two principal sites of cultural nationalist youth inculcation, St. Enda's and Na Fianna Éireann, became recruiting grounds for both the IRB and the Irish Volunteers (later known as the Irish Republican Army), which led the campaign for independence; in fact, Pearse himself opined that "if the Fianna had not been founded in 1909, the Volunteers of 1913 would never have arisen."[143] Several youths who had been taught that they belonged to boy-troops like those of Fionn and Cú Chulainn thus proudly channeled their valiant heroes in the conflicts of 1916–21.[144] For them, and doubtless also for many adults, ideologically invested forms of Fenian narrative helped to stoke not only cultural, but also political nationalist fires and communicate a sense of duty and loyalty to the nation, spurring revolutionary action.

9

Storytellers and Schoolbooks

THIS FINAL CHAPTER explores how the Fianna have adapted to shifting circumstances in their homelands and beyond since the Irish nation won its freedom. While the late nineteenth- and early twentieth-century Celtic Revival fixed them in a symbolic network that ensured their ongoing relevance, different groups have had dissimilar relationships with them over the ensuing decades. Among the modern regions of the once culturally cohesive Gaelic world, Ireland is unique in its persistent attention to the Fianna, and they have maintained a multifaceted presence there. Our heroes' ideological utility to the new Irish state saw them take up residence in schoolbooks and contributed to the collection of thousands of Fenian folktales in the mid-twentieth century. Post-independence authors and dramatists also took inspiration from the Fenian cycle in creative new ways, albeit in somewhat reduced numbers from the Revival's peak. Not all of the Fianna's stories enjoyed the same attention in the Irish public sphere, however, and outside of Ireland, their recession to their familiar Gaelic haunts persisted. But change is always on the horizon. A reinvigorated late twentieth- and early twenty-first-century wave of Celticism, combined with the economic Celtic Tiger phenomenon and globalization, have recently seen Fionn and his brethren extend their wanderings at home and abroad. In the latest reverberations of their narratives, the Fianna's ability to acclimate to vastly different social, political, and even geographical environs—to become the go-to heroes for an eclectically wide range of people across time—has never been more evident.

Fionn in the Free State

The Fianna found themselves in a familiar position upon the establishment of the Irish Free State in 1922: at the beck and call of those in charge, or wishing to be in charge, of an Irish government. The early years of the new state were contentious. A civil war (1922–23) erupted, and although this conflict was brief, divisions remained after its resolution. In 1926 a large segment of the anti-Treaty Sinn Féin party peeled away to form a new party under Éamon de Valera.[1] When determining what to call themselves, these nationalist republicans looked to the Fianna, just as revolutionaries before them had done. While John O'Mahony adopted our heroes' English name for his Fenian Brotherhood, de Valera opted for the Irish Fianna Fáil, often translated 'Soldiers of Destiny' but more literally rendered 'the Fianna of Fál' (Fál being a poetic name for Ireland).[2] As de Valera himself explained in *An Phoblacht*, "The name Fianna Fáil has been chosen to symbolise a banding together of the people for national service, with a standard of personal honour for all who join as high as that which characterised the ancient Fianna Eireann, and a spirit of devotion equal to that of the Irish Volunteers from 1913 to 1921."[3] De Valera's statement calls to mind the ideal of national service of the youth group Fianna Éireann, so many of whose members went on to serve in the revolutionary units of the War of Independence: "To be a member of the Fianna means that you have devoted yourself to the service of Ireland," the *Fianna Handbook* states.[4] It echoes, too, the newly established Irish national anthem *Amhrán na bhFhiann* (literally "The Fianna's Song," but more commonly "The Soldiers' Song"). Originally penned in English by an IRB member in the early years of the century and regularly employed as a Volunteers marching song, the opening line of the anthem proudly proclaims: "Sinne Fianna Fáil atá fá gheall ag Éirinn" ("We are the Fianna of Fál who are pledged to Ireland").[5]

Fianna Fáil's star rose swiftly, and in 1932 de Valera became the head of the Free State government, engineering the new constitution of 1937 that saw the nation operating as a republic in nearly all but name.[6] Under his conservative, protectionist administration, many of the policies enacted in the early years of the Free State that enshrined the Fianna as national symbols were extended. Michael Collins had declared in 1922 that "complete liberty—what it stands for in our Gaelic imagination—cannot be got until we have impregnated the whole of our people with the Gaelic desire. Only then shall we be worthy of the fullest freedom."[7] Following the lead of Pearse and the Gaelic League, the Free State sought to Gaelicize the nation by means of the educational system. In addition to the language policies discussed in the previous chapter, new Irish-medium schools were founded, such as Dingle's Coláiste Íde (est. 1927), whose mantra "glaine ár gcroí" ("the purity of our heart") is a pared down version of Pearse's Fenian motto,[8] and plans were drawn up to revise the teaching of literature and history "to develop the best traits of the national character and to inculcate national pride and self-respect."[9]

The Fianna were ideal figures to accomplish this goal, due as much to their already established popularity as to their remove from the more contentious political issues of the day. Indeed, one study has shown that Fenian topics were among the most commonly covered aspects of Ireland's cultural heritage in the course books of the redeveloped school system.[10] Like in Scoil Éanna (St. Enda's School), Fionn and his men were convened to impart moral lessons, as we see not only in the continued repetition of Pearse's Fenian motto but also in such claims as the following:

> To the Fianna the telling of a lie would have been as base and cowardly as turning their backs on an enemy. A promise was always sacred to them, no matter what trouble might arise in fulfilling it. They were noted for their kindness and courtesy to all, even to their foes. . . . Thus for many years did the Fianna watch over the safety and honour of Ireland, earning for themselves much glory and renown, the memory of which has come down through the ages as a fine example to the youth of our land.[11]

This passage is followed by a scenario in which children must pretend to be their Fenian heroes. Educational writers appear to have recognized that they could circumvent discussion of divisive issues by utilizing such characters to celebrate the new nation through pre-conquest and pre-conflict imagery. This helps to explain the Fianna's particularly strong presence in primary schoolbooks from the Free State period (see fig. 16).[12] Fenian narrative also continued to be used as advanced Irish-language reading material, and government presses published several new editions of Fenian romances in modernized language (and censoring any sexual or scatological content) specifically for use in secondary schools.[13] Since their introduction in 1924, moreover, certificate examinations in Irish have regularly included Fenian texts.[14]

The political need to affirm the new nation's identity is also reflected in the Free State's commitment to folklore collecting. Systematic collecting got off to a gradual start with the Irish Folklore Institute, which was formed as a government body in 1930. In 1935 under the de Valera administration, the Irish Folklore Institute was reconstituted as the Irish Folklore Commission (IFC) and collecting drastically increased.[15] The state's aims in funding these bodies were twofold: to gain textual material to support the ongoing Irish language revival efforts and to preserve evidence of the nation's unique heritage. Regarding the first aim, Minister for Finance Sean MacEntee (Seán Mac an

FIGURE 16. Fionn cooking the salmon of knowledge in *The Irish-World Readers*, Junior Book (c. 1933). (John J. Burns Library, Boston College.)

tSaoi), expressed his view that the collection and publication of accurate vernacular spoken Irish should "act as an auxiliary in improving the quality of the Irish taught in Schools."[16] De Valera and Minister for Education Tomás Ó Deirg, meanwhile, were just as deeply invested "in saving the traditions of Ireland" and fostering "Ireland's native culture."[17] The archival and published resources expected to result from systemized collecting were thus intended to fortify the new nation both linguistically and culturally.

The directorship of the IFC was granted to James Delargy (Séamus Ó Duilearga). Delargy had previously been an assistant to Douglas Hyde at University College Dublin and swiftly took up his mentor's mantle as "the central figure in Irish folkloristics."[18] Under his watch, the IFC maintained between four and nine full-time professional collectors for the duration of its existence (1935–70), an office manager, and an archivist, Sean O'Sullivan (Seán Ó Súilleabháin).[19] Amateur collecting also saw a large boost in popularity, and the IFC employed as many as two hundred and fifty voluntary part-time collectors at the peak of this trend in the late 1930s. Holdings further increased substantially due to the implementation in 1937–38 of the Schools Folklore Scheme in which fifth and sixth class students (ages 11–14) in numerous primary schools across the country collected from their families and neighbors.[20] As a result of these efforts, a remarkable amount of folklore was gathered in the first five years of the IFC's operations alone. What is more, greater accuracy than ever before was ensured by the provision of Ediphone audio recording machines to full-time collectors, allowing them to circumvent the imprecision of transcribing from dictation. Well attuned to advances in academic folkloristics, Delargy also required his full-time collectors to keep field diaries, through which means valuable contextual information was recorded, and all collectors were asked to document tradition bearers' names, ages, localities, and, when possible, the people from whom they heard each account.[21] Such measures ensured the high quality of the copious material collected, which has since been inscribed in the UNESCO Memory of the World register.

Conditions at the IFC were highly favorable to collecting Fenian folklore. Among the principal factors helping to privilege such material was an institutional preference for the folklore of the Irish-speaking west, which continued to be viewed as the most authentically 'Irish' part of the nation, and as in the Celtic Revival period, the Fianna's lengthy literary history lent additional prestige to the orally collected tales about them.[22] Delargy himself viewed such material as a genuine connection to an illustrious past—a means of "[bridging] the gap of centuries [to] hear the voice of the nameless story-tellers and creators of the heroic literature of medieval Ireland."[23] In such an atmosphere, bias toward this prestige genre seems all but inevitable, even though collectors were encouraged to gather a wide variety of material. Indeed, Delargy's successor Bo Almqvist noted that "the longer and most spectacular hero tales" were given preferential treatment in the early years of collecting.[24] The pressure to meet or exceed quotas would also have generated favorable conditions for gathering Fenian folklore, for collectors' notebooks were filled faster with long hero tales than shorter material that could require considerable interaction to elicit.[25] Taken together, these factors helped to usher nearly 1,800 orally collected stories and songs about the Fianna into the IFC's possession by 1940. While this initial flood subsided to a stream and then a trickle near the end of the century, over 2,300 oral Fenian texts would eventually come to rest in the IFC's archive, known since its transfer to University College Dublin in 1971 as the Irish National Folklore Collection.[26] In some of this material, we can detect the influence of the adapted stories that proliferated throughout Ireland via popular literature and the educational system, but the vast majority of Irish Fenian folklore remains deeply rooted in Gaelic tradition (see below). Relatively little has ever been edited or published, however, despite the Free State government's foundational desire for the IFC to produce print material for use in schools, and the impact of this body of Fenian narrative on wider public perception has consequently been limited.

The Revival's Afterlife

Beyond the Free State government and the Folklore Commission, the Fianna continued to maintain a presence in the popular sphere in Ireland and its diaspora, if rarely in any of the other Gaelic heritage regions. While fewer Irish Fenian literary works were published in English in this period than in the heyday of the Revival, some of them utilized these nationally significant heroes to take creative—even polemical—stances. Most notable in this regard is Darrell Figgis's sensational novel *The Return of the Hero,* first published in 1923 under the pseudonym 'Michael Ireland.' A reimagination of the debate between Oisín and Saint Patrick, the book has alternatively been read as a satirical critique of the Irish Catholic church, the British government, or the contemporary Sinn Féin leadership.[27] Each reading upholds the Fianna's valor while viewing the internally divided authority of the early church as analogous to the modern institution in question. Indeed, the bishops who accompany the benevolent Patrick seem principally concerned with the protection and advancement of the church's power, as demonstrated in their determination that Oisín's unbaptized and long deceased comrades' damnation to hell is essential "for the future of the Church," lest the unconverted, hoping to avoid hell simply by denying baptism, shun Christianity. Figgis's Oisín ultimately rejects such flawed mores and does not undergo baptism, instead wading into the sea to rejoin his condemned brethren.[28] We thus see in this creative adaptation a provocative reprisal of the Fianna's accustomed practice of either upholding or, as in this case, contesting authority.

While Figgis was well versed in Fenian literature and drew on multiple sources,[29] other creatives confined their focus to a single tale, *Tóruigheacht Dhiarmada agus Ghráinne* (The pursuit of Diarmaid and Gráinne). Readily available in translation, the *Tóruigheacht* was adapted frequently in the first half century of independence and has proved the most resonant Fenian story in mid-twentieth-century anglophone Irish literature. Perhaps the most inventive treatment is Eugene Rutherford Watters's (Eoghan Ó Tuairisc) kaleidoscopic narrative poem *The Week-End of Dermot and Grace*, published in 1964, in which versions of the protagonists of the classic tale navigate personal moral anxieties against the traumatic backdrop of the bombing of Hiroshima.[30] Motifs from the story also enter into Hugh Leonard's comedic play *The Patrick Pearse Motel* (1971), which explores marital infidelity in a similarly modern setting, and Austin Clarke's historical romance novel *The Bright Temptation* (1932), which concerns a wilderness-rambling couple in the Viking age; the latter was censored in Ireland for nearly two decades for indecency.[31] Other authors went in less allusive directions, such as Pádraic Fallon, whose radio play based on the story aired in 1950.[32] Shorter Diarmaid and Gráinne–inspired works emerged from the pens of literary dynamos like Frank O'Connor, moreover, and Jack Butler Yeats completed a pair of paintings inspired by the story in the 1940s.[33]

Other Fenian tales may lack such extensive creative engagement in this period, but our heroes' enduring symbolic resonance is evident referentially. Clarke's displeasure at the quarrying of the Hill of Allen in his 1957 poem "The Loss Strength," for instance, calls to mind Yeats's exuberant account of summitting the Fenian residential prominence in his preface to Lady Gregory's *Gods and Fighting Men*. For Yeats, the hill was emblematic of Ireland's national heritage. For Clarke, its destruction to fuel roadworks belied a creeping cultural apathy:

Gelignite has blown up
Too much: yet on the Hill of Allen,
The blasters are at work. Gallon
By gallon our roads go on. Stonecrushers
Must feed them. Fionn hunted here, Oisín
Complained of age.[34]

Concerns about the hill's lack of preservation continue to be voiced in the present century.[35]

Fenian echoes of a different sort feature in two novels by the great modernists James Joyce and Flann O'Brien (Brian O'Nolan / Ó Nualáin). In *Finnegans*

Wake, Joyce toyed with Fionn's heroic reputation first in the characterization of his liquor-logged and apparently deceased protagonist, lamented as "Macool, Macool," and later in a comically long-winded description of a seemingly all-encompassing figure who turns out to be "Finn MacCool." Joyce's bewildering Fionn is, among other things, "the first to rise taller through his beanstale than the bluegum buaboababbaun or the giganteous Wellingtonia Sequoia; . . . escapemaster-in-chief from all sorts of houdingplaces; . . . sponsor to a squad of piercers, ally to a host of rawlies; against lightning, explosion, fire, earthquake, flood, whirlwind, burglary, third party, rot, loss of cash, loss of credit, impact of vehicles."[36] O'Brien renders our hero equally absurdly in *At Swim-Two-Birds*. There we encounter Fionn as imagined by the narrator, a University College Dublin student, whose depiction—presumably derived from school instruction—is similarly parodically embellished: "Finn MacCool was a legendary hero of old Ireland. Though not mentally robust, he was a man of superb physique and development. Each of his thighs was as thick as a horse's belly, narrowing to a calf as thick as the belly of a foal. Three fifties of fosterlings could engage with handball against the wideness of his backside, which was large enough to halt the march of men through a mountain-pass." This Fionn goes on to tell of Fenian amusements in mock-*Acallam* fashion, but in addition to the traditionally heroic belling of stags, he elates in "the whinging of fauns," "cow-cries in pregnancy," and "the squeal of a troubled mare."[37] In both novels, Fionn's mock heroism reflects a mounting impulse in some circles to push back on nationalist representations of Irish culture. O'Brien's Fionn even complains that he has been "twisted and trampled and tortured for the weaving of a story-teller's book-web," appearing to criticize not oral *seanchaithe*, 'storytellers,' but rather the contemporary authors whose sanitized accounts in English had become far more well-known than their Gaelic sources. It is notable, in this light, that while O'Brien's Fionn is able to relate amusing versions of a handful of short Fenian episodes regularly retold in popular and educational literature, he cannot recall several lengthy, less commonly adapted Fenian narratives, including *Tóruigheacht an Ghiolla Dheacair* (The pursuit of the difficult servant), *Bruidhean Bheag na hAlmhaine* (The little brawl at Allen), and *Bodach an Chóta Lachtna* (The churl in the drab coat).[38]

The broader context for Joyce's and O'Brien's portrayals of Fionn was the ongoing discussion about what a national literature should look like in the newly independent Irish state, and this was being deliberated in Irish language circles as well. Some expressed strong opinions that the great works of the past should serve as a model for twentieth-century compositions. For instance,

O'Brien's brother Ciarán Ó Nualláin argued that "writers of Irish would have style and a good sense of writing if they would read the earlier literature: Geoffrey Keating, the principal Fenian stories and lays and the Three Sorrows of Storytelling, those would suffice. . . . [W]ithout doing that, they will not have the inspiration or the knowledge to write well."[39] Tomás Ó Floinn suggested, moreover, "making available modern versions of the ancient stories, literary modern versions."[40] And Fenian literature did indeed inspire adaptations in multiple forms. The most successful dramatic treatment was Mícheál Mac Liammóir's *Diarmuid agus Gráinne: Dráma Trí nGníomh* (Diarmuid and Gráinne: A play in three acts), which launched Galway's new Irish-language theatre An Taibhdhearc in August 1928, but plays based on a late damsel in distress lay and *Cath Fionntrágha* (The Battle of Ventry) also appeared in print.[41] A somewhat less successful opera, *Loscadh na Teamhrach* (The burning of Tara) was performed at the Oireachtas in 1943, moreover, and a handful of radio plays hit the airwaves in the following decade.[42]

Short stories incorporating Fenian characters also appeared in Irish-language periodicals, such as Ciarán Ó Nualláin's "Ais-Éirghe Fhinn Mhic Chumhaill" (The resurrection of Fionn mac Cumhaill). Inspired by the folktale *Na Fianna ina gCodladh Faoin Talamh* (The Fianna asleep underground), Ó Nualláin's story depicts an IRA member who discovers and chooses *not* to wake the slumbering ancient heroes to seek their aid, uncertain if they would be "chomh sibhialta agus chomh carthannach agus bhí cáil ortha a bheith" ("as civilised and friendly as they were famed for being")—a critique of the revivalist portrayal of the Fianna that aligns well with O'Brien's satirical caricature of Fionn.[43] Aodh de Blácam also approached this theme critically in his "Draoidheacht an Óir" (The enchantment of gold), in which the Fianna have awoken in twentieth-century Dublin and forgotten their identities, having been "bewitched by the degeneracy of the modern age."[44] To these Fenian drama and prose compositions can be added satirical portrayals by Brian Ó Nualláin (Flann O'Brien) in University College Dublin's student magazine *Comhthrom Féinne* (Fenian Fairness, i.e., justice, fair play) and his popular *Irish Times* column Cruiskeen Lawn, as well as the occasional poem.[45]

The more diverse range of topics addressed in Irish-language creative explorations of Fenian narrative than in their English-language counterparts is evident. In the adult market these were far outstripped by non-Fenian compositions, however, despite calls from the likes of Ó Nualláin and Ó Floinn to look to earlier literary models for inspiration. Indeed, in both languages, the Fianna's Revival-era migration to the realm of childhood continued.

Numerous retellings were published, the most enduring of which actually originated abroad, although they tended to view their subject matter as strictly Irish. The first of these was American author Harold F. Hughes's 1922 Fenian collection *Legendary Heroes of Ireland*. Hughes took inspiration from scholars like Jeremiah Curtin, Douglas Hyde, and Eleanor Hull, but he admits to heavily adapting his source material, "[leaving] out much unsuitable to children" and "[changing] some incidents to conform to the modern standards of morals"—practices that would have met with his revivalist predecessors' approval.[46] Popular English children's book author Rosemary Sutcliff similarly retouched the tales in her still-influential *The High Deeds of Finn MacCool* (1967), "adding a flicker or a flourish of my own from time to time—as everyone who has retold them in the past thousand years or so has done before me."[47] The American writer Ella Young's popular and frequently reprinted 1929 Fenian anthology *The Tangle-Coated Horse*, on the other hand, was drawn eclectically from scholarly sources and Lady Gregory's *Gods and Fighting Men*, and uniquely recognized both Ireland and Gaelic Scotland's claims to the Fianna, situating them in both regions: "If there is a gulch anywhere [Fionn] has leaped over it; if there is a huge stone it is one that he cast once-upon-a-time as a shoulder-stone; if there is a gap in a mountain-crest he has lifted the bit from it."[48] The implied cultural importance of the Fianna is evident in the inscription of their renowned deeds on the landscape itself.

Children growing up with Irish had additional resources, the most innovative of which was Cathal Ó Sándair's 1951 juvenile novel *Réics Carló san Aifric* (Réics Carló in Africa). Like some authors writing for older audiences, Ó Sándair engaged creatively with the Fenian tradition, imagining the formidable detective Réics Carló discovering the Fianna's descendants in a lost African city and regaling them with the tale of how the youth group Fianna Éireann alongside Óglaigh Éireann (the Irish Volunteers) recently secured Irish independence, then accompanying them home to Ireland.[49] Plays also continued to be seen as a useful tool for linguistic and cultural development, and children's dramas helped to reinforce a new generation's knowledge of the Fianna in modified form.[50] To these can be added plenty of bedtime story–length retellings, like those Séamas Ó Searcaigh published in language "so-thuigthe ag an aos óg atá ag foghlaim na Gaeilge ar an scoil" ("easily comprehensible to the youngsters learning Irish in school") in his 1945 collection *Laochas* (Heroism).[51]

Scholarly resources continued to expand too. By the final quarter of the century, published editions not only of most of the romances but also of the expansive late medieval *Agallamh na Seanórach* (The dialogue of the elders) were readily available, due in large part to the efforts of Máire Ní Mhuirgheasa and Nessa Ní Shéaghdha. Working under the direction of University College Dublin professor Gerard Murphy, the texts they produced for the Department of Education's series Leabhair ó Láimhsgríbhnibh (Books from Manuscripts), many of them previously unedited, remain the academic standards today.[52] The lays also received considerable attention, most notably from Murphy, whose work on *Duanaire Finn* (1933–53) marks the beginning of modern Fenian textual scholarship,[53] but Pádraig Ó Siochfhradha also edited a collection of lays from Irish sources,[54] and Reidar Thoralf Christiansen and Neil Ross completed influential work on the Scottish lays preserved in the Book of the Dean of Lismore and elsewhere.[55] Ó Siochfhradha's *Laoithe na Feinne* (Fenian lays, 1941) succeeded in bridging the gap between reference works for scholarly purposes and anthologies intended for a broader readership; one approving reviewer vigorously declared, "Let these lays be heard again on the stage at *feis* and Oireachtas, let them be recited by the hearth, let them be studied in the schools of the country."[56] That there was demand for such materials is evident, too, from the positive reception that met Niall Ó Domhnaill's three-volume *Seanchas na Féinne* (Fenian lore, 1942–43), which contained condensed adaptations of notable tales that even new Irish readers could tackle.[57] Interpretive literature for a popular audience also emerged, including Cormac Ó Cadhlaigh's monumental *An Fhiannuidheacht* (The Fenian tradition, 1936), a lengthy overview of the cycle in Modern Irish that went through multiple editions, and Murphy's slim but informative volume *The Ossianic Lore and Romantic Tales of Medieval Ireland* (1955).[58] The romances and their orally collected counterparts received protracted critical attention, moreover, in Alan Bruford's *Gaelic Folk-Tales and Mediaeval Romances* (1969).[59] For those wishing to know more about medieval and early modern Fenian literature, a large corpus of primary sources was not only easily accessible at last, but also contextualized in scholarly resources and readily comprehensible readers.[60]

Continued study brought early Irish history into somewhat clearer view, moreover, and academic belief in the Fianna's historicity further declined. Yet the notion that the Fianna actually lived has never been wholly overcome at the popular level. Thus, Seumus MacManus, in his oft-reprinted *Story of the Irish Race*, declared that "the man Fionn lived and died in the third century," while Stephen Gwynn, in his histories for adult readers and students, averred à la Eoin MacNeill that Fenian stories were probably fictional, but their basis was in a real standing army to which the Fianna actually belonged.[61] In academia, however, the interpretation of Fionn and others of his warrior band as euhemerized deities took prominence from the publication of Dublin Institute for Advanced Studies director T. F. O'Rahilly's *Early Irish History and Mythology* in 1946. O'Rahilly's opinion that "Finn and his fellows (Goll, Diarmait, Oisín, etc.) never existed" found favor with Murphy, who affirmed that "Fionn was originally a god."[62] By the early 1970s, Irish historians and Celticists were in agreement that the Fianna belonged to a "romantic-mythological tradition," as Proinsias Mac Cana wrote.[63]

The denouement of the Celtic Revival was thus no Fenian finale, although popular perceptions of Fionn and his men continued to shift. Their subsequent presence in adult literature and drama was diminished—perhaps due to a "growing ambivalence about heroic violence" that Philip O'Leary observes following the Civil War—but often markedly creative.[64] They remained culturally important aspects of children's literature, moreover, and scholarly interest continued, particularly in Ireland. There was only occasional creative engagement with the Fianna outside of Ireland, however. Even in Scotland, our heroes only made irregular appearances, as when the elderly orator of Cailein T. MacCoinnich's 1969 science fiction story "Searmon a' Bhodaich" (The old man's sermon) offers to tell *Fionn ann an Taigh a Bhlàir Bhuidhe* (Fionn in the house of the Blàr-Buidhe) to young listeners who opt for a Biblical legend over "silly stories . . . about old warriors . . . who never existed."[65] George Campbell Hay (Deòrsa Mac Iain Dheòrsa) did pen both a humorous modern dialogue between Oisean and Saint Patrick and a poem inspired by *Na Fianna ina gCodladh Faoin Talamh* in the 1930s, and scattered references to "Oisin *d'eis na Feine*" (i.e., *Oisean as déidh na Féinne*, "Oisean after the Fianna") and other tales crop up in his elder contemporary Hugh MacDiarmid's nationalist poetry.[66] In 1933 An Comunn Oiseanach / The Ossianic Society, a Gaelic debating club formed by University of Glasgow students, began publishing a magazine titled *Ossian*, and in 1940 our heroes lent their name to Fianna na h-Alba, a short-lived Irish-inspired republican youth organization in Glasgow that advocated "the restoration to the Youth of Scotland of cultural heritage based on native traditions and ideals" and urged members to "let 'Cothrom na Féinne' [the fairness of the Fianna] be your slogan."[67] In most instances, however, the level of interaction with Fenian narrative was not sustained. There was simply little in the contemporary Scottish sociopolitical atmosphere to support the persistent creative adaptation of Gaelic hero tales. As Liam McIlvanney and Ray Ryan note, although Scotland was historically "subject to so many of the same linguistic, religious, political and cultural pressures as

Ireland," the nation's post-Revival zeitgeist was "marked . . . by a breach with its Gaelic past and a philosophical and economic modernization around metropolitan markets."[68]

The Oral Fenian Tradition

While they only rarely appeared in popular media outside of Ireland in the post-Revival period, Fionn and the Fianna lived on in the oral traditions of Gaelic speakers the world over. The stratum of Gaelic oral narrative known in Irish as *fiannaíocht* and in Scottish Gaelic as *sgeulachdan gaisge,* 'hero tales,' which incorporates much Fenian material, has long been recognized within the storytelling community and by academics as the most prestigious oral literary form.[69] The most complex Fenian hero tales could take several nights to relate, and the public tellers of such lengthy pièces de résistance—generally elderly men—were once celebrated within their communities.[70] But women are known to have told versions of Fenian hero tales too, if more frequently to audiences of children than at the socially mixed evening gatherings that loom large in academic accounts of storytelling, and numerous Fenian lays have been collected from both women and men.[71] Less complex stories about the Fianna that fall outside the formal hero tale classification were common fare for amateur and star storytellers alike, moreover, and were collected from men, women, and even children.[72]

Collecting at this time differs from the premodern period in that modes of life were rapidly shifting across the Gaelic world by the second quarter of the twentieth century and many traditional opportunities for storytelling, such as the evening gatherings in the Irish *teach airneáin* or Scottish *taigh céilidh,* 'visiting house,' had all but disappeared.[73] Nonetheless, as we have already seen in the Irish context, a great store of Fenian folklore came to rest in numerous archives across two continents in the twentieth century.

Over 90 percent of the known Irish corpus is concentrated in the Irish National Folklore Collection and is the result of government sponsored collecting by the Irish Folklore Commission in the early years of independence.[74] A much smaller proportion of Irish material has come to light in other archives and print sources, and more archival material remains to be discovered by researchers working with the ongoing Fionn Folklore Database project.[75] Scottish Fenian folklore similarly saw an increase in collecting in the twentieth century with the founding of the School of Scottish Studies in 1951, which took inspiration from the Irish Folklore Commission, but operated on a much smaller scale. In its early years, the school shared the Folklore Commission's bias in favor of older forms of tradition perceived to be in rapid decline and thus, despite not having the same nation-building imperative, conditions were favorable for the collection of Fenian folklore.[76] Nearly three hundred Fenian stories and songs came to rest in the school's archives at the University of Edinburgh, supplementing a larger store of previously collected Scottish Fenian material housed in other archives across the country.[77] Collecting efforts in Ireland and Scotland also inspired limited collecting among the Gaelic diasporas in Canada and the United States toward the end of the twentieth century, resulting in the documentation of a small number of Irish and Scottish Gaelic Fenian tales and lays on the North American continent.[78] The Isle of Man has likewise only seen minimal collecting. At the urging of Irish President de Valera, the Folklore Commission dispatched a collector to the island for two weeks in the spring of 1948, but nothing Fenian was documented at that time, and the small store of Manx Fenian folklore that has come to light is nearly all of an earlier date.[79] (See the appendix.)

Of the over 3,600 oral Fenian texts that have been documented to date, circa 2,500 were collected in Ireland, circa 1,000 in Scotland, and the small remainder elsewhere. Given the regional discrepancies that we have seen in folklore collecting, the vastly larger proportion of Irish material is not reflective of greater or more persistent popularity of Fenian tales and lays in Ireland. More significant is the fact that oral accounts of Fionn and the Fianna could be found as late as the final quarter of the twentieth century when complex storytelling was waning in traditional practice.[80] Our tenacious and ever-adaptive heroes continued to serve the needs of a wide variety of people in varied social and cultural circumstances as long as such entertainment practices persisted.

Because the corpus is so large and varied—approximately two hundred story and song types have now been identified—only a brief overview is possible here.[81] The Irish material is largely comprised of prose, while nearly half of the Scottish material consists wholly or partly of song, reflecting the far greater presence of Fenian lays in collected folklore from Scotland than from Ireland. This is partly for technological reasons: the gramophones the Irish Folklore Commission used in its most productive early decades of operation were less effective at capturing the upper melodic range than the tape recorders of the second half of the century, which contributed to a neglect of song.[82] Even so, the prolonged public and academic interest in lays in Scotland over the course of the long Ossianic controversy likely buoyed their popularity there relative to Ireland. (Indeed, Fenian lays are still sung in Scotland.) The

Scottish material also has a high prevalence of multiply recorded items from the same tradition bearer, reflecting a later twentieth-century folkloristic interest in memory and performance.[83]

Much of the material in the corpus represents versions of tales and lays also found in manuscript contexts. Some of the most expertly told Fenian hero tales are lengthy adventure stories that bear a close resemblance to extant written recensions, suggesting relatively recent oral-literary interaction. These often display similar stylistic features, including not only their multiepisodic structure, but also the distinctive formulaic passages known as 'runs' that punctuate star performers' tellings. While the same tales may circulate orally and in writing, however, a far greater degree of multiformity is present in orally collected Fenian tales and their plots and casts tend to be more straightforward.[84] Aspects of well-known tales and lays may also be localized to a particular region, and an eye to heroic geography can further be observed in hundreds of short accounts explicating nearby places associated with the Fianna. This *seanchas* or local lore may pertain to one of the notorious beds erected by Diarmaid and Gráinne during their flight—the folk interpretation of the distinctive prehistoric dolmens that dot the Irish landscape (fig. 17)—or massive stones thrown by the Fianna in conflicts, or other distinctive landscape features. Near Oban in Argyll, for instance, there is a grooved boulder called Clach a' Choin (The Dog Stone) to which Fionn is said to have chained Bran, the chain wearing the groove, while legend has it that the lake atop Mount Gabriel in Co. Cork was formed when Fionn dislodged a large rock and launched it into the sea, where it is still visible.[85] Such accounts belong to the oral corpus alone, as do a number of stories that are less well-known to us today due to lack of academic analysis and publication. The tragic story of a young Fenian recruit called the Feardhamhan is one such tale. On his journey home after his period of service, the Feardhamhan is killed by a wild sow he was warned to avoid, while his sister drowns coming to his aid upon hearing his dying cry.[86] The pair are said to have been from Co. Donegal, where the tale has primarily been collected.

Scholars have long regarded Fenian hero tales highly, but the study of regional variations is in its infancy. While Irish oral versions of *Bruidhean Eochaidh Bhig Dheirg* (Little red Eochaidh's enchanted hall) are often strongly reminiscent of manuscript recensions, for instance, a distinctive Scottish Gaelic ecotype (i.e., regional variant) has been documented not only in the Highlands and Islands but also in Nova Scotia. Known as *Fionn ann an Taigh a Bhlàir Bhuidhe*, this variant preserves the theme of poor hospitality in a

FIGURE 17. Poulnabrone Dolmen in the Burren, County Clare, Ireland. (Alamy. Photo by David Lyons.)

dwelling to which Fionn and several men have been lured, as well as their rescue by another group of Fianna in response to Fionn sounding his horn. The host's name—the Blàr Buidhe—differs here, however, and he is accompanied by a kindly wife inspired by friendly female helper characters in international wonder tales. Other incidents vary somewhat too, such as the prominent burning of Fionn's legs, which are then pierced with a roasting skewer in the Scottish ecotype. This likely derives from violence originally experienced by Conán, who is showered with hot coals while attempting to roast a boar and later has his toe burnt off in the romance.[87] The Scottish folktale about Fionn's birth also contrasts with Irish accounts. While the death of Fionn's father Cumhall at the hand of Goll mac Morna shortly after Fionn's conception is generally maintained in Irish oral versions, Scottish versions introduce a Norse element to the tale. According to storytellers like Angus MacLellan of South Uist, the Fianna under Cumhall have become rebellious, and so the kings of Ireland and Lochlann conspire to put him to death by treacherous means. The deed is accomplished following Cumhall's wedding to the king of Lochlann's daughter at the hand of an Irish outlaw named Arca Dubh, 'Dark-haired Arca', who fatally stabs the Fenian in his wedding bed with his own sword. As in Irish versions, the resultant son (Fionn) is secreted away by a female protector.[88] The Scottish ecotype appears to have been influenced by the great popularity there of the Cath Gabhra lays, which incorporate Lochlanners and describe the Fianna's final falling-out with the Irish high king (see chapter 3). The abundant multiformity of the Fenian folklore corpus, which extends far beyond these two examples, is a testament to the oral tradition's vigor even in decline.

Much academic work remains to be done to describe and contextualize this rich body of material. Analysis of the extensive biographical traditions about principal characters like Fionn, Oisín, Oscar, Goll, and Bran would reveal not only how the perception of our heroes has developed in modern times, but likely also the preservation of all but forgotten links to much earlier lore, as we saw in chapter 1 with regard to Oisín's shapeshifting mother. Detailed studies of oral reflexes of well-established categories—*bruíon* ('otherworldly dwelling'), *toraíocht* ('pursuit'), overseas adventure, damsel in distress, magical helper, invasion / battle, internecine strife—would help us to further understand the inner workings of the cycle through the more accurate delineation of structural patterns and characterological trends centuries in the making. Close examination of the context of individual Fenian folktales, moreover—including the course of and motivations for transmission, as well as individual tradition bearers' interpretations of these enduring texts—would enable a more detailed understanding than ever before of the social implications of Fenian narrative. The large-scale collection of the folktales and lays, primarily in the mid-twentieth century, and their more recent classification in the Fionn Folklore Database, which launched in 2023, are merely the first steps in our investigation of the vast but poorly appreciated oral Fenian tradition.[89]

Fianna for a New Century

While oral narratives about our heroes still frequently fly under the radar, the Fianna have not gone unnoticed in recent decades. To the contrary, Fionn and his followers have enjoyed renewed regard both within and outside of their regions of origin, due in part to an emergent post-Revival interest in 'things Celtic' in the latter part of the twentieth century—what Richard Barlow dubs "late Celticism."[90] This reinvigorated interest is reflected, for instance, in the foundation of the Celtic League in 1961 and the emergence of Celtic popular music in the folk, rock, and punk scenes of the 1960s, '70s, and beyond.[91] The new wave of Celtic bands—some of them internationally acclaimed—penned Fenian-inspired songs in the mid-1970s. Horslips's album *The Book of Invasions*,

FIGURE 18. Scottish folk band Ossian's eponymous album (1977). (By permission of Springthyme Music.)

which reached thirty-ninth in the UK Top 40 in 1977, included the *Tóruigheacht Dhiarmada agus Ghráinne*–inspired "Warm Sweet Breath of Love" and "King of Morning, Queen of Day"; Planxty composed and played the music for Seán MacCarthy's drama *The Fantastical Feats of Finn MacCool*, performed at the Royal Lyceum Theatre in Edinburgh in 1974; and the multi-artist Welsh-language rock opera *Nia Ben Aur* (Niamh of the golden hair) premiered at the National Eisteddfod in Carmarthen, Wales the same year.[92] The Glasgow-based folk band Na h-Òganaich also adapted the waulking song *Cumha Dhiarmaid* (The lament of Diarmaid) for their 1975 album *Scot-Free*, and the Scottish folk group Ossian took its name from Caledonia's most controversial Fenian-inspired masterpiece (fig. 18).[93]

The greatest recent surge in interest in Celtic heritage is centered squarely upon Ireland, however, and correlates with the end of the violent Troubles of the 1970s–90s in Northern Ireland and the beginning of the Celtic Tiger in the 1990s, which led not just to a fiscal turnaround in the Republic, but also contributed to a global revitalization of the Irish image.[94] As lingering negative stereotypes of poverty and purported backwardness were overwritten by a new image of prosperity and progress, Irishness became not only desirable, but coveted. As Gearóid Ó hAllmhuráin comments, "Irish identity—however spurious or fragmented—became an ethnic identity of choice for multicultural Americans, Canadians, Australians, and others eager to claim an Irish past."[95] This shifting perception was supported by an ongoing and concerted effort to market Irish culture. The promotion of the 'traditional'—no longer connected with an anti-imperialist struggle for nationhood—now serves as a mode of ethnocultural expression in both local and global contexts.

The commodification of Irishness is perhaps most observable in the tourism industry, which has in some cases coopted the Fianna to present a version of Gaelic heritage to travelers originating both within and beyond the island.[96] The most prominent example is the use of a variant of the story of *Fionn sa Chliabhán* (Fionn in the cradle) to promote the Giant's Causeway, a geographical feature consisting of forty thousand volcanic basalt columns that extend outward from the Co. Antrim coast in the direction of Scotland (see fig. 19). According to the story, Fionn constructed the causeway as a bridge to Scotland, and soon found himself in a predicament when a larger and more powerful Scottish warrior crossed over to challenge him. At the instigation of his clever wife, however, he was able to escape through trickery by pretending to be his own baby. Upon observing the enormous infant's strength and hearing of the superhuman feats of the child's purportedly gigantic father, the warrior fled back to Scotland tearing up columns as he went, leaving only the surviving portion.[97] The Causeway's Fenian connection has been presented in interpretive materials since the area was designated a UNESCO World Heritage Site in 1986 and the first visitor center was constructed. Today visitors can book a day trip to the site with Finn McCools Tours or stay locally in a hotel or hostel named after Fionn.[98] While other Fenian tourist locations are less well-known, the Fianna's wide-ranging traditional association with the Irish landscape presents similar heritage marketing opportunities. For instance, the tourism website for the Ballyhoura region in Co. Limerick associates the area with the story of Oisín's centuries-long sojourn with the otherworldly Niamh in Tír na nÓg, proclaiming that when he returned home on his magical horse, it was in

FIGURE 19. Fionn at the Giant's Causeway, Co. Antrim, Northern Ireland. (Alamy. Photo by Paul Faith.)

Glenosheen (Gleann Oisín) that he accidentally touched the ground and transformed into a decrepit old man; the townland now features as a stop on the Slí Finn (Fionn's Way) Drive.[99] Somewhat more ambitiously, a proposed visitor center at a Co. Cavan landmark intends to use augmented reality to promote "the history and heritage of the site including lore tracing back to the legendary Finn MacCool and the Fianna."[100]

The celebration of Irish cultural heritage during the Celtic Tiger period and beyond has also accelerated Fenian narrative production, expanding this seemingly perpetually malleable cycle in new ways. In 2011, for instance, the Fianna's ongoing presence in Irish schoolbooks and certificate examinations led the Irish-language summer school Coláiste Lurgan in Connemara to produce a musical theater adaptation of *Tóruigheacht Dhiarmada agus Ghráinne* for their YouTube channel to aid pupils' exam preparation.[101] A considerable amount of new children's literature has also been published, although both educational and popular resources largely focus on the same few stories: the salmon of knowledge and burning of Tara episodes from *Macgnímartha Finn* (The boyhood deeds of Fionn), *Oisín i dTír na nÓg* (Oisín in the Land of Youth), *Tóruigheacht Dhiarmada agus Ghráinne*, and the now ubiquitous Giant's Causeway variant of *Fionn sa Chliabhán*.[102] Even so, some excellent retellings have appeared, such as Ronan Moore's English-language juvenile novels (2020–21) tracing Fionn's boyhood and assumption of the leadership of the Fianna and Colmán Ó Raghallaigh's *An Tóraíocht* (2002), which artfully presents the story of Diarmaid and Gráinne in the medium of a graphic novel.[103] Highly creative adaptations have emerged too, like American author Megan Chance's interweaving of the Diarmaid and Gráinne tale with the story of the sleeping Fianna against the backdrop of Fenian Brotherhood activity in nineteenth-century New York City in her Fianna trilogy (2014–15) for young adults.[104] Other books bring modern characters into the world of the stories, as in American author Mary Tannen's *The Wizard Children of Finn* (1981), in which a pair of young siblings are transported back to the time of Fionn's boyhood, or English-Irish author Kate Thompson's Liddy trilogy (2005–7), which features sojourns in Tír nan Óg.[105] This theme extends into new media in *Cormac agus Órla agus Fionn mac Cumhaill* (2001), a well-orchestrated interactive storybook on CD-ROM, while further interaction with our heroes is encouraged in *Ardrí* (2011), a multilingual board game that incorporates a handful of Fenian plotlines.[106] A team of Irish animators also brought the Diarmaid and Gráinne story to the screen in a cartoon broadcast in both Ireland and Scotland in 2002.[107] As ever, innovation melds with tradition to extend our heroes' relevance to new generations.

Beyond the realm of childhood, although Fenian-inspired literature for the general reader is still significantly less frequent, growth is evident here too. Successful novel-length creative adaptations of the Fianna's adventures have emerged from the pens of Irish American author Morgan Llywelyn and New Zealand–resident Irish author Brian O'Sullivan.[108] O'Sullivan's two series reimagining Fionn's boyhood and the life of one of his guardians, Liath Luachra, have each extended to five books and counting. The Fianna also still find their way into short stories,[109] and Fenian texts have likewise continued to inspire poetry, such as Eavan Boland's "Once" and "Embers," which hark to *Tóruigheacht Dhiarmada agus Ghráinne* and *Laoidh Cholann gan Cheann* (The lay of the headless body).[110] Literary offerings in Irish can also be found, although they are somewhat more traditional: both Darach Ó Scolaí and Pádraig Ó Fiannachta have published book-length texts that closely approximate the style of early modern romances and lays.[111] Reminiscent of the earlier abundance of new Fenian editions for a growing Irish-language readership, these go some way toward realizing Ó Nualláin's and Ó Floinn's calls for a heroically inspired modern literature in Irish.

In the performing arts, moreover, there has been no lack of Fenian creativity in both Irish and English. *Tóruigheacht Dhiarmada agus Ghráinne*'s outsized influence persists, having inspired a range of adaptations, including plays, a radio comedy, a dance production, a chamber opera, songs, and a feature film.[112] The latter, Paul Mercier's 2015 gangland thriller *Pursuit*, was developed from an earlier play and features internationally acclaimed actors Liam Cunningham as Fionn and Brendan Gleeson as the Searbhán, one of the Tuatha Dé Danann.[113] Composers and directors have also looked to other texts. *Acallam na Senórach* and *Cath Fionntrágh* have inspired choral and orchestral scores, Fionn's boyhood has formed the subject of a rock musical, a handful of creatives have taken cues from *Oisín i dTír na nÓg* in musical productions, and the Giant's Causeway story was recently presented as an Irish-language pantomime.[114] There has been growing interest in professional storytelling too, and several storytellers can be hired to tell Fenian tales in English and, less frequently, in Irish.[115]

The enduring Irish interest in the Fianna coupled with the present motivation to promote the nation's cultural heritage has further led to numerous public commemorations of these beloved cultural icons in both the north and the south in recent decades. Among the public artworks that have been erected near important sites in the most commonly adapted Fenian tales, perhaps the most famous is Lynn Kirkham's larger-than-life steel rendering of Fionn and his hounds (fig. 20). Installed in 2010 at the Ballymany roundabout near the Hill of Allen in Co. Kildare, the sculpture evokes popular accounts of Fionn's boyhood ending in his taking up residence there, and the battle-ready figures' outward gaze and alert posture also suggest the Fianna's ongoing protection of Kildare and beyond.[116] Other notable artworks include Robin Buick's 1988 bronze relief of the fleeing Diarmaid and Gráinne opposite Sligo's Hughes Bridge, not far from Benbulbin where Diarmaid met his tragic death; Jim Connolly's 1992 bronze sculpture of Diarmaid and Gráinne in the Searbhán's tree in Kilbaha, Co. Clare; Ciaran Dunlevy's 2022 mural of the salmon of knowledge on the Fitzwilliam Court building in Drogheda, Co. Louth; John Kindness's 1999 ceramic-tiled salmon of knowledge sculpture in Belfast; the impressionistic 2022 statue of Fionn throwing a clod of earth that once occupied Lough Neagh, Co. Antrim; and the oversized model of Fionn erected in 2019 in the Belfast airport.[117] In the world of modern sport, several Gaelic Athletic Association teams are named after the Fianna, and Fionn has become the mascot for a Belfast hockey team established in 2000 and the inspiration for the Finn McCool Virtual Challenge, which encouraged people to run the equivalent of thirty-two marathons during the COVID-19 pandemic. The Irish Strength Association's award for Ireland's Strongest Man is also fittingly the Finn McCool Trophy.[118] As a giant puppet, he is known to march in parades,

FIGURE 20. Lynn Kirkham, *Fionn Mac Cumhail and His Hounds*, Ballymany roundabout, Co. Kildare. (Ronan McCormick.)

and a forty-foot animatronic version of him rides a motorcycle to the Wake the Giant music festival each year in Warrenpoint, Co. Down, where he then sleeps until an appointed time, evoking the folktale *Na Fianna ina gCodladh Faoin Talamh*.[119] Until the pandemic, the village of Ardpatrick near Glenosheen and Seefin (Suí Finn) in Co. Limerick also hosted an annual festival where, in the early 2000s, a young woman would be selected for the Niamh of Na Fianna crown.[120] This practice appears to have shifted with the times, as have many other aspects of the representation of our heroes, helping them to maintain their evident and ongoing prominent place in Irish cultural expression.

In contrast with Ireland, while Scottish heritage has also been both celebrated and commodified in the present age of globalization, our heroes' Caledonian public presence remains muted. In the rare instances when they are promoted as Scottish cultural symbols, they tend to don their Ossianic guises: a visitor to Edinburgh can stay aboard Fingal, a luxury floating hotel, or enjoy Inveralmond Brewery's Ossian beer.[121] Although Fionn does turn up on bookstore shelves in two recently published children's books, both present versions of the Giant's Causeway narrative that draw on Irish accounts rather than the

Scottish Gaelic Fenian tradition, and depict Fionn as Irish rather than pan-Gaelic.[122] But Scotland's Gaels still claim and commemorate the Fianna. William Sweeney's opera *An Turus Sìos gu Tìr nam Marbh* (The journey down to the land of the dead), a gritty modern take on the Diarmaid and Gráinne story with a libretto by Skye poet Aonghas MacNeacail, entertained onlookers in 1998; Robbie MacLeòid penned a song inspired by *Duan a' Mhuileartaich* (The lay of the Muileartach) in 2016; and during the pandemic, Ceit Langhorne imagined the Fianna in lockdown in a brilliantly parodic new lay published to YouTube.[123] However infrequently, moreover, oral Fenian narratives continue to pass down to new generations. For instance, Essie Stewart, the granddaughter of the great Gaelic Traveler storyteller Ailidh Dall Stiùbhart, learned tales from her grandfather's recordings in the School of Scottish Studies and has since told them professionally in both Gaelic and English.[124] Events centering the performance of Fenian story and song have also begun to take place with some regularity. In 2018, the Scottish International Storytelling Festival's opening event at Stirling Castle, Ossian: The Pipes and the Story, included renditions of Fenian tales and lays by several modern practitioners, and the 2019 festival included a Fenian folklore workshop, Sgeulachdan na Fèinne san Latha An-Diugh (Stories of the Fianna in a Modern World), led by broadcaster and author Ruairidh MacIlleathain (Roddy Maclean). Following the pandemic, the 2023 festival built on its earlier momentum with Alba agus Èirinn: Òrain agus Sgeulachdan na Fèinne / Scotland and Ireland: Songs and Stories of the Fianna, featuring tales and lays in Scottish Gaelic and Irish, with English explanations, by Màrtainn Mac an t-Saoir (Martin MacIntyre), Màiri NicIlle-Mhaoil (Màiri Macmillan), Mhairi Hall, and Gráinne Holland.[125] NicIlle-Mhaoil also performed a new arrangement of lays by Ned Bigham at the National Library of Scotland in conjunction with Sgeul | Story, a 2023–24 exhibition of John Francis Campbell's nineteenth-century folklore collection. The exhibition spotlit the tradition bearers and their tales and lays, and included in its audiovisual component an extract of a Fenian tale told by Mac an t-Saoir.[126] All of this bodes well for the continuation of the Scottish Gaelic Fenian tradition, despite a lack of public promotion akin to that in Ireland. Indeed, if the student turnout to the University of Edinburgh launch of the Fionn Folklore Database in November 2023 is anything to go by, interest is growing among a youthful, university-educated, Gaelic-speaking or -learning demographic.

That such interest is perceptible among students is undoubtedly the result of multiple factors, not least the latest wave of scholarship in what has emerged over the past half century as an academic field of Fenian studies. The pioneering criticism of mid-century researchers and the considerable number of textual editions available by the 1980s enabled scholars like Joseph Nagy, Máirtín Ó Briain, Dáithí Ó hÓgáin, and Donald Meek to view the cycle with fresh eyes. With attention to parallel literary, mythological, and folkloric traditions and informed by contemporary theoretical perspectives, they and others laid the groundwork for a modern scholarship of Fionn and the Fianna.[127] Not only does the growing cohort of academics who have completed Fenian postgraduate theses since the early 2000s—myself included—trace their inspiration to this earlier generation's work, many of us have gone on to take up lectureships and design university courses about Fenian narrative.[128] The continuing expansion of the field is due in no small part to this cohort's publications, including a growing number of Fenian essay collections, not to mention the awareness generated by the series of Fíanaigecht conferences that have been periodically organized since 2009.[129] While the field is still relatively young and there is much work to do, academic readers have greater opportunities for exposure than ever before. The effects of late Celticism must also be considered, for regardless of how readily available Fenian scholarship is becoming, many of our students *first* encounter Gaelic cultural symbols like the Fianna in modern, adapted guises, and thus tempted, find their way to Celtic and thence to Fenian studies to experience the 'real deal': traditionally produced Fenian narrative. The broad reach of such cultural symbols helps to account for the interest among a growing number of non-Irish or Gaelic Scottish students in texts that might otherwise have escaped their notice.

Indeed, the modern promotion of Gaelic cultural symbols has had ripple effects internationally, not only in prominent diaspora regions, but also in more distant locales. The tale of the Giant's Causeway has become so well-known on account of its use by the tourism industry that it is now a go-to story when showcasing Irish heritage, even featuring in some American cities' cultural programming for Saint Patrick's Day, for which accounts of Oisín and the saint would be more topical.[130] The salmon of knowledge from *Macgnímartha Finn* has also found a place abroad, particularly in culturally connected spheres; it features on the Graduate Student Life crest at the University of Notre Dame in Indiana, which has had a vibrant Institute for Irish Studies since 1992, and the Gaelic Council of Nova Scotia (Comhairle na Gàidhlig) adopted Fionn's salmon for its logo in 2008.[131] Further afield, the plot of *Tóruigheacht Dhiarmada agus Ghráinne* has been adapted in the popular Japanese light novel, manga, and anime series *Fate / Zero*, which also features a grail quest borrowed from

Arthurian legend.[132] Somewhat loosely Fenian-inspired characters appear in online role playing games,[133] moreover, and Fionn and the Fianna have lent their names to commercial and cultural ventures. Irish pubs named after Fionn can be found across North America and Australia, from Fionn MacCool's in the Toronto Pearson International Airport to Finn McCool's in New Orleans and Brisbane,[134] and Irish athletic organizations worldwide have taken Fenian monikers.[135] In modern international contexts, then, Fionn and his Fianna can hark to a broader narrative tradition, albeit sometimes heavily obscured by adaptation, or he can function as a detached marker of Irishness. The globalized cultural environment of the past half century has enabled both forms of Fenian reconceptualization.

The century preceding this book has ushered the Fianna on forays that would have been inconceivable to the founders of the Irish Free State, let alone the authors of medieval and early modern manuscripts. Pressed to service for myriad purposes, in the modern era these once-ancient characters have crowded as comfortably around cottage hearths as they have school classrooms and bookstore shelves. Although the immediate post-Revival period saw a decline in the composition of new Fenian literature, some very good creative fiction emerged in the initial decades of Irish independence, and authors like James Joyce, Flann O'Brien, and Ciarán Ó Nualláin engaged critically with revivalist portrayals of the Fianna. The sanitized, child-friendly portrayals pioneered by S. J. O'Grady and Lady Gregory found renewed expression in still-popular collections by the likes of Rosemary Sutcliff and Ella Young, and more recently, authors like Ronan Moore and Colmán Ó Raghallaigh have reinvigorated the juvenile market. Expanded global interest in Irish heritage since the Celtic Tiger period has led to adaptations in other media too, from public art to music to film, and our heroes have even taken to marketing tourist experiences and pub-style dining. And while their long association with Irish cultural identity has garnered them far greater public recognition below the North Channel than above, the Fianna do continue to be known in Gaelic Scotland. Recent attention to Scottish Gaelic Fenian folklore serves as a reminder that storytelling still persists, despite the great decline in folklore collecting since the mid-twentieth century. Not only do professional storytellers in both Ireland and Scotland count Fenian tales among their repertoires, parents still tell the well-loved stories to children, as Donegal-born Fionn Folklore Project researcher Dubhán Ó Longáin (Duane Long) can attest.[136] In the academic sphere, moreover, Fenian scholarship is more vibrant than ever, and a growing field of Fenian studies has emerged. From an auspicious start at the founding of a new nation to the present day, Fionn and his followers have thus characteristically risen to meet each new challenge of the past century, emerging as premodern heroes for a modern age. Only time will tell where they go from here.

Epilogue

THE STORY OF THE FENIAN narrative tradition is long and complex. It is a tale of adaptation and migration, perseverance and survival. It is something of a hero tale in its own right. To tell it properly, it has been necessary to take into account multiple historical periods and survey a wide geographical area; to navigate the twisted pathways and troubled seas of invasion and conquest, international relations, national politics, and the negotiation of cultural identity; to consider language shift and multilingualism, and account for privilege and power dynamics; and above all, to spin an interesting and accurate yarn out of the materials at hand. I have tried to do the story justice. If the preceding nine chapters are taken as the several-nights-long version, what follows is the consolidated account—the one that could neatly fill a break in conversation.

The Fenian narrative tradition has been an integral part of Gaelic culture and a means through which Gaelic-speaking societies have expressed themselves for many centuries. The earliest extant references to Fionn depict him as the leader of a *fían*—a migrant warrior band—and, in fact, one of several such leaders about whom bodies of story had formed. Such warrior bands, which are thought to have existed at the time of Christian conversion and for some time thereafter, would have been integral to the maintenance of social order, providing a means of dealing with potentially disruptive young men by their temporary removal from the legitimate social sphere. In Fenian literature from the seventh to ninth centuries, Fionn and his men conduct themselves much like early *fénnidi*, 'fenian warriors,' might have behaved, living a life of hunting and warfare and emerging from the wilderness to lead raiding parties and abduct women. Such stories generally present heroic reflections of the *fían* and, in addition to providing entertainment, would have been a means of reinforcing the value of this social practice.

By the tenth century, Fenian narrative began to take on new meanings, in the process shedding its association with certain aspects of the declining fenian practice that the medieval church found to be disreputable. Raiding and the abduction of women were largely jettisoned, the lives of Fionn and members of his Fianna were more clearly fleshed out, and they were drawn more closely into the social sphere—and into the purview of national politics. This is the point at which Fionn started to become associated with the legendary third-century high king Cormac mac Airt, taking on a new role as commander of a national defense force. Historians describe a growing tendency among kings of this period to employ standing armies and hire mercenaries, and Fionn's new position can be seen to represent contemporary military practices. The adaptation of Fionn from *fían* leader to the head of the high king's forces helped his body of story to remain relevant within a changing society. Moreover, Fionn's association with Cormac solidified his position as a national rather than a local hero. From the tenth century, Fionn began to be consistently depicted as the national protector of Ireland, defending against external—and generally supernatural—invasion.

As Fenian narrative continued to develop, a new strand emerged bringing the Fianna into the sphere of Ireland's most venerated cleric, Saint Patrick. The Patrician dialogue lays, the earliest extant of which date to the late tenth or eleventh century, established a narrative frame that allowed for seemingly infinite expansion—and expand is precisely what the cycle did. As national heroes associated with the Irish patron saint, the Fianna's literary presence increased exponentially from the thirteenth century onward, and extended prosimetrum and prose texts became commonplace from the appearance circa 1225 of the significant, if highly adapted, *Acallam na Senórach* (The dialogue of the elders). The *Acallam* idiosyncratically brings our pagan heroes in close alignment with church doctrine. Not only is the deceased Fionn said to have been given prophetic knowledge of the Christian God's existence, but the small number of heroes who survive to meet Saint Patrick are also baptized and made to advocate for religious reformist principles that would have been matters of quotidian relevance to the unknown monk who penned the *Acallam*. In an environment of growing hostility to secular literary production in monastic scriptoria, this proto-Christian portrayal would have helped to sanction the Fianna as an acceptable literary topic. Beyond anxieties of early thirteenth-century religious life, the text also reflects broader concerns of post-conquest Ireland, with Caoilte's and Oisín's sorrowful reactions to the redistribution and redesignation of the Fenian landscape calling to mind the complex contemporary social and political dynamics. While not an anticolonial text per se, the depiction of the Fenian-Patrician relationship does appear to promote integrative settlement practices conducive to maintaining positive Gaelic and Anglo-Norman relations. Such engagement with central concerns of the time can only have contributed to the *Acallam*'s appeal.

The maintenance or disruption of social order are prominent issues in much of the copious store of Fenian narrative composed over the course of the next five hundred or so years. After the removal of secular literature from its earlier monastic context, the cycle flourished in Gaelic-speaking Ireland and Scotland, evolving to suit the tastes of late medieval and early modern audiences. Subsequent *Acallam* recensions and hundreds of Fenian lays were composed, and lengthy Fenian stories emerged that were regularly invested with features of the heroic romance genre, which was prevalent not just in the Gaelic world, but across Europe. This vibrantly productive period in the Fianna's history saw the thematic expansion of the cycle and the interrogation of what constitutes effective leadership, at times even questioning Fionn's wisdom. We see, too, an unprecedented frequency of conflict with foreigners, most often against a standardized Scandinavian foe. Tales of foreign invasion would have afforded a space to process the collective trauma of persistent waves of invaders, colonizers, and settlers in once Gaelic-controlled lands. The strong resonance of this topic during a lengthy tumultuous period for both Irish and Scottish Gaels helps to explain the intense popularity of Fenian literature. Specific regional concerns were undoubtedly echoed and explored in Fenian plots too, although at this distance and given the limited scholarly attention most lays and romances have received, many historical reverberations remain unrecognized. That the texts continued to serve contemporary sociopolitical functions is evident in aspects of their transmission, moreover, as the compilation of *Duanaire Finn* in early seventeenth-century Flanders shows: its patron, Somhairle Mac Domhnaill, was an exiled rebel whose militant activities spanned both Ireland and Scotland and who likely had a personal affinity for our peripatetic Gaelic heroes. MacDomhnaill's admiration led to the preservation of a substantial body of Fenian narrative—including some of the earliest known lays—in danger of being swept away with the remains of the Gaelic systems of learning and governance. Just over a century later, a substantially different but similarly sociopolitically motivated Fenian project got underway in Scotland—one that would have profound implications.

The 1760s were a watershed moment for the perception of Fenian narrative and people's ideological investment in it. This is when James Macpherson published his English-language epics known collectively as *Ossian*, which he adapted from the Scottish Gaelic Fenian tradition. Instant international bestsellers, Macpherson's works rocketed Fenian plots and characters—albeit in the much-altered guise of sentimental heroes of a valiant but long-lost golden age—into the public consciousness. They spurred international interest in all things Celtic and had an immense effect on the perception of Fenian narrative and the path of scholarship in Ireland and Scotland. Fenian narrative, of both indigenous and Ossianic varieties, was effectively transformed into a symbol not just of Gaelic ethnic identity, but of Irish and Scottish national identity. Widespread interest in—and criticism of—Macpherson's epics soon led to efforts to collect the Gaelic oral and written lays on which he claimed to have based his texts. The epics also sparked historical debates and antiquarian research, particularly in Ireland, and led to the translation and publication of manuscript-derived Fenian texts. From the mid-eighteenth century until at least the mid-nineteenth century, Gaelic Fenian narrative was considered almost solely with regard to Macpherson's epics and the claims he made about them. Even modifications to his views tended in the same romanticist direction, such as the popular Anglo-Irish, antiquarian reconception of Fionn and his men as early, chivalric knights. The way non-Gaels and Gaels alike wrote and thought about the tradition was forever altered in the ongoing identity renegotiation process then taking place in Scotland and Ireland. In this era of burgeoning cultural nationalism, the terms for the perception of Fenian narrative were set by Macpherson, and they persisted long after his time.

While in the mid-eighteenth century, few non-Gaelic speakers in Ireland and Scotland would have known who the Fianna were, by the mid-nineteenth century, they were recognized as important elements within the newly conceived national heritages of both countries. This was the dawn of the period of major folklore collecting in Scotland and Ireland, and the beginning of sustained interest in Fenian oral prose. When John Francis Campbell began his pioneering, systematized folklore collecting project in Gaelic Scotland in 1859, he and his collectors still worked under the long shadow of *Ossian*. Although his subsequent revelations of stark differences between the Ossianic and native Fenian material were largely ignored by incipient Celtic revivalists during his lifetime, his comparative work did eventually temper claims of the absolute authenticity of Macpherson's 'translations.' Moreover, his collecting efforts resulted in the documentation of a considerable store of oral Fenian tales and lays. During the late nineteenth- and early twentieth-century Celtic Revival, greater focus tended to fall on other aspects of the nation's Celtic identity than the Fianna, however, and although Revival-era collectors did gather some additional Scottish Fenian folklore, Fenian narrative largely faded into the background of the public national consciousness.

The situation in Ireland during the Celtic Revival period was rather different. There, the symbolic value of the Fianna soared to new heights and Fenian narratives once again entered a period of major ideological reinvestment. Both Anglo-Irish and Gaelic revivalist approaches were strongly culturally nationalist, and Fenian narrative became an important topic of literature in both languages during this period. The most enduringly popular were English-language creative adaptations for younger audiences, which were bowdlerized to present an ideal image of Irish morality to be emulated for the betterment of the contemporary Irish nation. For their part, Gaelic revivalists edited primary texts and encouraged the collection and publication of folklore, and unprecedented numbers of Fenian literary and oral texts—some of them also bowdlerized—began to be published by revivalist presses for a growing audience of Irish speakers and learners. Revolutionary activists employed Fenian narratives in boys' educational and recreational activities, moreover, where they became entwined with propagandist messages affirming a saga-oriented ideal Irish masculinity. Taught to model themselves after versions of our heroes in Scoil Éanna (St. Enda's School) and Na Fianna Éireann, many boys went on to participate in armed conflict pursuing the right to national self-determination on the basis of cultural distinctiveness. The place where the Fianna lay sleeping until the time came to restore Irish sovereignty was not any far-flung cave, as it turned out, but the minds and hearts of Irish youth.

From the second quarter of the twentieth century within the newly free Irish state, sanitized and simplified forms of Fenian narrative became regular components in school curricula, so that to this day Irish children learn versions of Fenian stories as part of a standard, culturally informed education. In this period, too, large-scale, government sponsored folklore collecting was initiated to preserve the nation's oral traditions. Conditions for the collection of Fenian folklore were favorable, and over two thousand oral Fenian texts were deposited in the Irish National Folklore Collection by the end of the century. Ireland's collecting scheme also led to the launch of similar, if smaller, projects in Scotland and Nova Scotia that used modern recording techniques to document a reasonably substantial body of modern Scottish Gaelic Fenian folklore. The collection and production of Fenian narrative remained stronger in Ireland, where such cultural promotion supported nation-building efforts, than in other regions of the former Gaelic world, however. While the Hibernian post-Revival period saw the continuation, on a reduced but often delightfully creative scale, of Fenian literary composition in both English and Irish, in Caledonian climes the Fianna quietly withdrew to western shores.

Our heroes are not ones to languish for long, though. With the approach of the twenty-first century, they saw their star rise once again, buoyed by a late wave of Celticism, the Celtic Tiger, and globalization. In Ireland, heritage symbols like the Fianna are now a mode of ethnocultural expression visible in the marketing of tourist locations like the Giant's Causeway and the erection of Fenian public artworks, but also reflected in accelerated narrative production incorporating contemporary media from the CD-ROM to YouTube to film. Both Ireland and Scotland have seen the emergence of professional storytelling, moreover, and Scottish Fenian folklore has enjoyed increased public attention. Fenian scholarship, which saw tremendous growth in the late nineteenth and early twentieth centuries, has also increased substantially in recent decades, such that an academic field of Fenian studies has now emerged—to which this book contributes. Even while acknowledging ongoing and significant scholarly gaps, it is safe to say that the history of Fionn and the Fianna is better understood now than ever before.

Like all heroes, the Fianna persist in cultural memory as long as they are needed. From the earliest extant manuscript texts to the most recently told tales, Fenian narrative has endured by means of constant adaptation. The meanings this eminently malleable corpus has taken on from region to region over the centuries are countless. Not simply (that is, not solely) entertainers, the Fianna have often stood for something greater, and if we only look to the ideals they have upheld over time, we can perceive the power they are capable of wielding, even now. The story must end here, but unlike Oisín's plaintive adieu in *Caoidh Oisín i ndiadh na Féinne* (Oisín's lament for the Fianna), our final farewell to the Fianna, their heroic exploits, and their real-world reverberations is yet to come.

Slán le suirghe is le seilg, slán le meisce is le saor-cheol
Slán le cathaibh is le trodaibh, slán le lannaibh géara fós.
Slán le lúth agus le neart, slán le cead is le saorghuibh,
Slán le cian agus le teacht, slán le malairt is le gléagaibh
Slán le biadh agus le digh, slán le rith is le léimneach,
Slán le fiadhach gach garbh-chnuic, slán le curaidhe na dtréanfhear.
. . .
Slán leat, a Fhinn, arís is arís, céad slán leat, a rí na Féinne.

Farewell to wooing and hunting, to intoxication and natural music,
Farewell to battles and conflicts, to sharp-edged lances.
Farewell to agility and strength, to freedom and privilege,
Farewell to distant travel and return, to destruction and contention,
Farewell to food and drink, to running and leaping,
Farewell to coursing every rugged hill, to the champion strongmen.
. . .
Farewell Fionn, again and again, a hundred times farewell,
oh leader of the Fianna.[1]

APPENDIX

Documented Fenian Folklore as of December 2024[1]

Tradition Bearer's Region of Residence	Archive (number of items)
Ireland (island)	Irish National Folklore Collection (2,299)
	Royal Irish Academy (11)
	Trinity College, Dublin, Manuscripts and Archives Research Library (9)
	James Hardiman Library, National University of Ireland, Galway (3)
	Belfast Central Library (8)
	School of Scottish Studies (1)
	Harvard University Libraries (7)
	Raidió Teilifís Éireann (1)
	Private Collection (1)
	Print (189)
Scotland	School of Scottish Studies (295)
	Edinburgh University Library Special Collections (135)
	National Trust for Scotland, Canna Collection (50)
	University of Glasgow Special Collections (4)
	The Highland Council, Highland Archive Centre (2)
	National Library of Scotland (336)
	Inveraray Castle Archive (37)
	Digital Archive of Scottish Gaelic (5)
	Irish National Folklore Collection (14)
	Library of Congress, American Folklife Center (2)
	Print (193)

(*Continued*)

(*Continued*)

Tradition Bearer's Region of Residence	Archive (number of items)
Isle of Man	Manx National Heritage Library (7)
	British Library (1)
	Royal Irish Academy (1)
	Österreichische Akademie der Wissenschaften, Vienna (1)
	Private Collection (1)
	Print (6)
England	Irish National Folklore Collection (1)
	School of Scottish Studies (3)
	National Library of Scotland (1)
North America	Angus L. MacDonald Library, St. Francis Xavier University (20)
	St. Francis Xavier University, Celtic Department (7)
	Cape Breton University, Beaton Institute (4)
	Memorial University of Newfoundland, Folklore and Language Archive (1)
	Harvard University Libraries (3)
	University of Washington, Seattle, Ethnomusicology Archives (10)
	Irish National Folklore Collection (2)
	National Library of Ireland (1)
	School of Scottish Studies (1)
	National Trust for Scotland, Canna Collection (3)
	National Library of Scotland (1)
	Private Collection (3)
	Print (6)

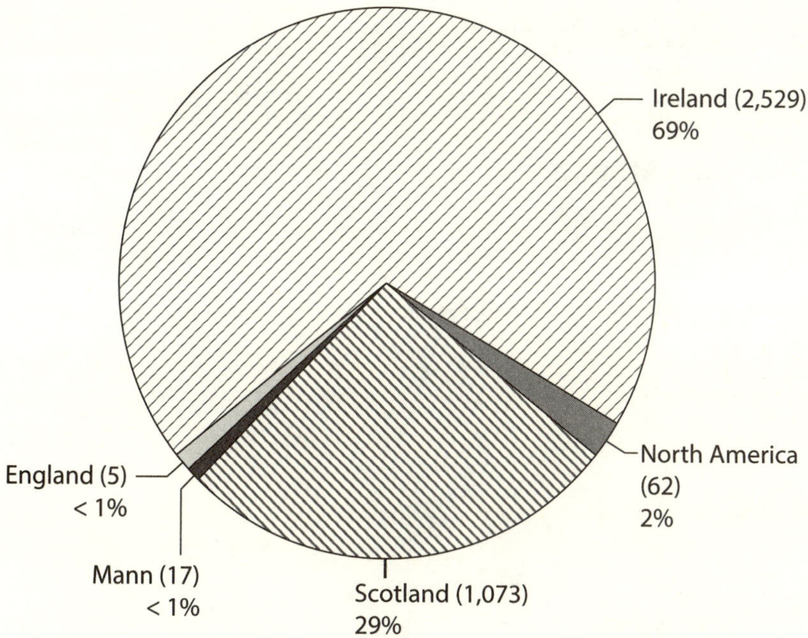

Distribution by tradition bearer's region of residence at time of collection

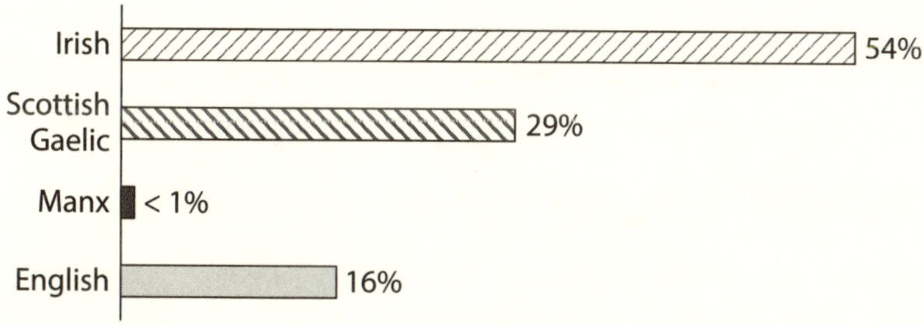

Distribution by language

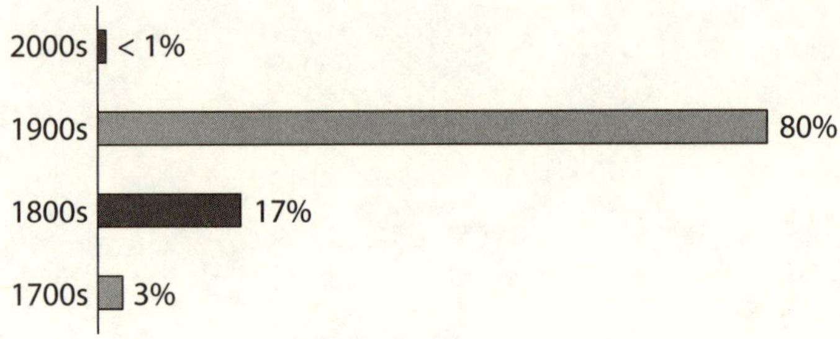

Distribution by century

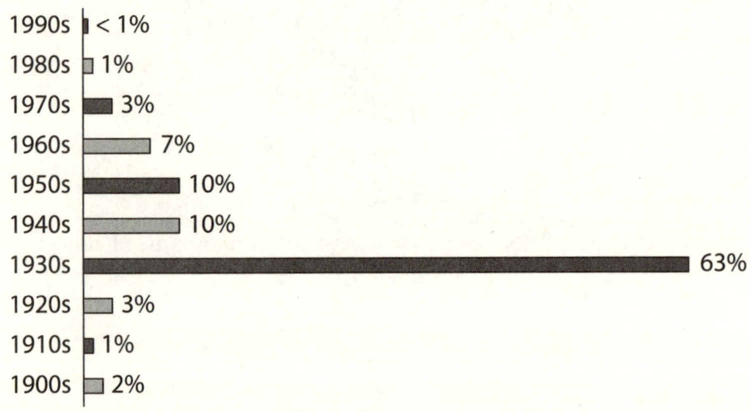

Distribution within the twentieth century

GUIDE TO GAELIC NAMES

THIS GUIDE IS INTENDED for readers who are unfamiliar with the Gaelic languages and their spelling conventions. Because it is difficult to represent sounds from one language in the orthography of another, and impossible to adequately account for dialectal differences, the pronunciations given are necessarily approximate.

Name	Historical Form(s)	Approximate Pronunciation
Aichleach Mór	Aichlech Mór	Akh-lekh More
Ailbhe	Ailbe	Al-yuh-vuh
Aillén	Aillenn	Al-yayn
Aodh	Aed	Eey
Aodh Beag	Aed Bec	Eey Byuhg
Art mac Morna	Art mac Morna	Art mac More-nuh
Bearrach Bhreac	Berrach Brecc	Bya-rahkh Vrak
Badhamair	Badamair	Ba-ghuh-muhr
Banbha	Banba	Ban-vuh
Blaoi Dhearg	Blai Derg	Blee Ya-rug
Bodhmall	Bodbmall	Boh-mull
Bran	Bran	Brahn
Cairbre	Cairbre	Kar-uh-bruh
Caireall		Kar-al
Caoilte	Caílte	Kweel-tuh / Kuhl-chuh
Clann Bhaoiscne	Clan Báiscne	Klown Weeshk-nuh
Clann Mhorna	Clan Morna	Klown Wore-nuh
Conán mac Morna	Conán mac Morna	Kuhn-ahn mac More-nuh
Conchúr mac Nessa	Conchobar mac Nessa	Con-khoor mac Nes-uh
Conn	Conn	Kahn
Corca Laoidhe	Corcu Loígde	Kohr-kuh Lee-yuh
Cormac mac Airt	Cormac mac Airt	Cormac mac Art
Cruithgheal	Cruithgheal	Cruh-yal

(*Continued*)

(*Continued*)

Name	Historical Form(s)	Approximate Pronunciation
Cuirreach Life	Cuirrech Life	Kur-ekh Liff-uh
Cúldubh	Cúldub	Kool Duhv
Cumhall	Cumall	Koo-wuhl
Dál nAraidhe	Dál nAraidi	Dahl Na-ri-yuh
Daolghas		Duhl-ghus
Daorghlas		Duhr-ghlus
Deimhne	Demne	Dev-nuh
Déise	Déisi	Day-shuh
Dearc Corra	Dercc Corra	Dyarc Kor-ruh
Dearg	Derg	Dya-rug
Diarmaid ua Duibhne	Diarmaid ua Duibne	Dyeer-mid Oo-uh Div-nuh
Diorraing mac Doghair		Dyir-rang mac Do-ghuhr
Dubh ua Duibhne	Dub ua Duibne	Duv Oo-uh Div-nuh
Donn ua Duibhne	Donn ua Duibne	Down Oo-uh Div-nuh
Earc	Erc	Ark
Faolán		Fwee-lahn
Fearghus Finnbhéil	Fergus Fínbél	Far-uh-ghus Feen-vale
Fearchess mac Commáin	Ferchess mac Commáin	Far-uh-khes mac Kom-mahn
Fianna Eireann	Fíana Erenn	Fee-yuh-na E-rin
Fionn mac Cumhaill	Finn / Find mac Cumaill	Fyuhn mac Koo-wuhl
Fionn mac Eassamain	Find mac Eassamain	Fyuhn mac Ass-uh-mun
Fothadh Canainne Fathadh Canainn	Fothad Canainne	Faw-hugh Ka-nee-nuh Fa-hugh Ka-nunn
Garadh mac Morna	Garad mac Morna	Gar-uh mac More-nuh
Glais Díge	Glasdic	Glash Dee-guh
Glas	Glas	Glas
Goll mac Morna	Goll mac Morna	Gawl mac More-nuh
Gráinne	Graindi	Grahn-yuh
Iollann		Uhl-lahn
Leathdhearg	Lethderg	La-yar-ug
Liath Luachra	Liath Luachra	Lee-yuh Loo-uh-khruh
Lomnochtán		Lum-nokh-tahn
Luaighne	Luigni	Loo-ugh-nuh
Lughaidh Mac Con	Lugaid Mac Con	Luh-ghee Mac Con
Mac Lughach	Mac Lugach	Mac Luh-ghukh
Mac Reithe		Mac Rey-huh
Mongfhind	Mongfind	Mung-ind
Oilill mac Eoghain	Ailill mac Eogain	Ahl-yil mac Oh-uhn
Oilill Flann Beag	Ailill Flann Bec	Ahl-yil Flahn Byuhg

Name	Historical Form(s)	Approximate Pronunciation
Oilill Ólom	Ailill Ólomm	Ahl-yil Oh-lum
Oisín, Oisean	Oisín, Ossine	Ah-sheen, Ah-shun
Oscar, Osgar	Oscar	Uhs-kur
Raighne	Raigne	Rye-nuh
Sadhbh	Sadb	S-aye-uv
Sceólang	Sceolaing	Shkyo-lung
Seandlach		Shand-lukh
Searbhán		Shar-uh-vahn
Smiorghad	Smirghat	Smer-ghud
Smiornad	Smirnat	Smer-nud
Uí Fhailghe	Uí Failge	Ee Al-uh-ghuh
Uirghriu	Uirgriu	Uhr-ghroo
Uí Thairsigh	Uí Thairsig	Ee Har-shee
Ulaidh	Ulaid	Uh-lee

NOTES

Introduction

1. Blair 1996a [1763], 364.

2. While it is impossible to know when the first stories about either hero were told, the earliest references to King Arthur in the Welsh corpus date to circa 800–1200: Lloyd-Morgan and Poppe 2019, 3–4.

3. Jefferson 1950 [1773], 96; Ferguson 1998a, 241. Napoleon sought poets to accompany his forces to Egypt and document his exploits in the manner of those of the Fianna.

4. Robert A. Segal (1990) and Tomás Ó Cathasaigh (1977, 1–23) discuss several influential theories of the hero in literature and folklore, while Kristian Frisk (2019) explores sociological understandings of heroes and heroism. As Ó Cathasaigh notes, martial excellence is not the defining quality of all heroes, although for those considered here it is (10–11). It should also be recognized that from the mid-twentieth century, the referential field of the term 'hero' expanded to include "relatively mundane figures" seen to exhibit subtle heroic qualities in everyday life (Frisk 2019, 90). Such comparatively banal heroism has limited relevance to a discussion of the protagonists of a heroic narrative tradition, however, and is omitted from consideration here.

5. See, e.g., *Find Taulcha* (Find [and] Taulcha) (Meyer 1910, xvii–xviii).

6. Murray 2017a, 141–42. Fionn's father's name was initially Umall. The 'c' of 'mac' in the patronymic 'mac Umall' appears to have been duplicated to form Cumall (later Cumhall).

7. See, e.g., Rees and Rees 1961, 242.

8. Murray 2017a, 140–41. In Old Irish these names are Demne and Glasdic.

9. Both of these incidents are described in *Macgnímartha Finn* (The boyhood deeds of Fionn): Meyer 1881–83, 199, 201; trans. Nagy 1985, 212, 214. See chapter 1 regarding Fionn's receipt of prophetic knowledge.

10. See chapter 3. Regarding Oscar's name in orally collected sources, see, e.g., MacNeil 1987, 62–65. Similar stories can be found in the Fionn Folklore Database under story type *Ainm Oscair* (Oscar's Name): https://fionnfolklore.org/#/lays/aos.

11. For various reasons, manuscript circulation remained common in the Gaelic world—Ireland especially—even after the introduction of the printing press. See Mac Craith 2006.

12. Regarding earlier scholarship, see chapters 7, 8, and 9.

13. See "Gaelic Terminology" in the "Technical Matters" section regarding the term *fíanaigecht.*

14. Arbuthnot and Parsons 2012, 10.

15. Grainger 2023; Stokes 1900.

16. This is evident in ventures like the 2000–2008 Bardic Poetry Project at Trinity College Dublin and the 2019 Seimineár Taighde ar na Scéalta Rómánsaíochta / Research Seminar on the Irish Romantic Tales at University College Cork.

17. See, e.g., Sneddon 2023. Ó Briain's articles remain insightful and influential; his early passing in 2004 was an outsized loss to the field of Fenian studies. Bruford's Fenian articles are similarly perceptive, and his *Gaelic Folk-Tales and Mediaeval Romances* (1969) remains the only concentrated analysis of Fenian romance literature and associated heroic folktales. In completing the latter, however, he was hindered by the finding aids then available, and both his literary and oral source inventories are incomplete. The Fionn Folklore Database now supersedes his highly commendable folklore cataloguing efforts.

18. See, e.g., the work of Fiona Stafford and Howard Gaskill.

19. See, e.g., the work of Donald Meek and Mícheál Mac Craith.

20. Kearney 2002, quoted at 3, 12.

21. Blieler and Blieler 1990, 740; Pilkington 2017, 18.

22. Nutt 1899, 4.

23. As Ted Underwood explains, distant reading studies "pose broad historical questions about literature, and answer them by studying samples of social or textual evidence" (2017, § 10). While influenced by distant reading, my methodology is less systematic or quantitative than most recent work in that field.

Technical Matters

1. Murray 2012, 34–44; Murphy 1953, lv–lx; Meyer 1910, xviii–xxx.

2. "In am fadó, bhí ceann feadhna clúiteach ós cionn slua Tíre na h-Éireann air go dtugaidís Fionn mac Cumhail, agus tugtaí Féinne mar ainm don tslua bhí faoi, ó ainm an ghaiscígh seo": Lyons 1891, collected from a Co. Sligo woman and reprinted from the *Tuam News*. I have normalized the spelling. In standard Irish, *Féinne* is the genitive case of *Fianna*, but it is used here as a nominative.

3. McCone 2012, 21; cf. the medieval explanation of Fianna in *Cóir Anmann* (The suitability of names): Arbuthnot 2007, 133.

4. MacInnes 1987, 103.

5. O'Brien 1768, 46; cf. *Oxford English Dictionary*, s.v. "Fenian."

6. O'Halloran 1772, 57; cf. Ó hÓgáin 1988, 317.

7. Vallancey 1782, 2; cf. Quinlivan 1994, 139.

8. Walker 1786, 41, 43, 110; cf. Quinlivan 1994, 139.

9. Brooke 2009 [1789], 158n.

10. See chapter 6.

11. Scott 2002 [1816], 295.

12. Quinlivan 1994, 141–42. Regarding the mid-nineteenth-century adoption of the name by the Irish Republican Brotherhood (IRB)'s North American branch, the Fenian Brotherhood, see chapter 7. It has been variously claimed that the word originated with or was first popularized by the Fenian Brotherhood: e.g., Comerford 2004; MacKillop 1986, 106. This is clearly not the case.

13. Bruford 1969, 61.

14. Cf. O'Leary 1994, 18.

15. Regarding oral literature, see Sumner forthcoming-c.

16. See, e.g., Barthes 1975, 237.

17. Anderson 1983, 15–16.

18. Hutchinson 1987, 2–3.

19. Regarding premodern Irish national identity, see Wadden 2017; McQuillan 2019. Regarding eighteenth-century developments in Ireland and Scotland, see chapters 5 and 6.

20. See chapters 7 and 8 and cf. Hutchinson 1987, 9, 15–16.

21. Foley 1991, 6n12.

Chapter 1. Fionn and the Fianna

1. McCone 2012, 15–18; Murray 2017a, 60–61.

2. McCone 1986, 6–8. Mercenary activities are represented in fictional accounts, but they may have been undertaken by actual *fénnidi*: see Nagy 1997, 295; 1985, 43. The wisdom text *Tecosca Cormaic* (Cormac's instructions) suggests that kings were expected to have spent time as *fénnidi* themselves: Fomin 2022.

3. McCone 1986, 3–6; 1990, 218–19; Ó Riain 1972, 18–19. Attitudes expressed toward *fénnidi* in early ecclesiastical literature and hagiography range from blatant hostility to ambivalence.

4. Recorded in the Annals of Ulster entry is an attack on a large host of *fénnidi* who had been raiding excessively (Mac Airt and Mac Niocaill 1983, 306).

5. See Tírechán's *Collectanea* (Collections) (Bieler 1979, 154–55). It is possible that Mac Con himself was meant, and not his son: see Murray 2017a, 88. See also the ninth-century reference to this event in *Sanas Chormaic* (Cormac's glossary), s.v. "mug éme" (Meyer 1912c, 75; trans. Russell 2008, 38).

6. O Daly 1975, 84. The tale is known as *Scéla Moshauluim* (The story of Moshaulum). Regarding its date, see Murray 2021, 60. The episode in which Fionn appears is also summarized in a ninth- or tenth-century anecdote in *Sanas Chormaic*, s.v. "rincne" (O Daly 1975, 15).

7. O Daly 1975, 84–85. Fearchess's name is likely a compound of *fer* and *ces*, meaning 'spear man' (Arbuthnot 2012, 64). Modern oral versions of this story have been collected in Ireland, but Fionn only rarely appears in these, and when he does, his role differs. The folktales are more closely related to the Early Modern Gaelic version of the tale, *Cath Mhaighe Mochruimhe* (The Battle of Magh Mucramha), for which see Ó Dúnlainge 1907; 1908.

8. Senior *fénnidi* may have filled the role of *fergniae*, 'champion,' acting within the *túath* as the king's personal enforcer, and that of *aire échta*, 'nobleman of slaughter,' who could be sent with a small *fían* to exact legally sanctioned vengeance beyond the boundaries of the *túath* (McCone 1990, 211–12). Legal evidence also suggests that the *túath*-resident *fergniae* could be dispatched to collect a *coibche*, 'bride price' (Murray 2017a, 59).

9. See *Find Taulcha* (Find [and] Taulcha) (Meyer 1910, xvi–xviii).

10. O Daly 1975, 52; McCone 1986, 12.

11. McCone 1990, 205. Perhaps this woman therefore ought to be considered a concubine. Yet there is no insinuation that she is one of a multitude of Fionn's transitory lovers—a situation described in a text dubbed "Fionn and the Jester Lomna" by Kuno Meyer (1910, xix). Rather, she is said to cohabit with him: "bói ina farrud" (Meyer 1893a, 242; cf. Hull 1941, 323).

12. An eleventh-century poem beginning *Ligi Guill i mMaig Raigni* ("The grave of Goll in Mag Raigne") alternatively attributes Badhamair's death to Goll mac Morna and his family, for whom see chapter 3 (Ó Murchadha 2009, 6–9).

13. Additional references to Cuirreach's beheading occur in the Middle Irish *dinnshenchas*, 'onomastic lore,' of Currech Life (Gwynn 1913, 234–35; Stokes 1894, 442–44) and *Acallam na Senórach* (The dialogue of the elders) (Stokes 1900, 221 [l. 7919]; cf. Dooley and Roe 1999, 221). The onomastic account claims that Fionn initiated the conflict by killing Dubh, who is there said to be Cuirreach's son-in-law. According to another Middle Irish onomastic story, the *dinnshenchas* of Tipra Sengarmna, Fionn also killed Cuirreach's wife and son after they embarked upon a campaign of reaving, killed Fionn's foster mother, and kidnapped Fionn's son, Oisín, to avenge Cuirreach's death (Gwynn 1913, 242–53; Stokes 1894, 446–48).

14. Hull 1941, 323–29. A different manuscript witness has one of Fionn's men kill Fothadh Canainne's relatives without realizing their kinship to him (Meyer 1893a, 243). They are killed in order to satisfy a *geis*, 'binding injunction,' upon Fothadh Canainne not to drink ale without the presence of severed heads.

15. The Middle Irish poetic *dinnshenchas* of Carraic Lethderg also depicts Fothadh Canainne eloping with a woman, this time the legendary Ulster king Conchúr mac Nessa's daughter Leathdhearg (Gwynn 1924, 120; Stokes 1895, 43). This indicates an uncertain timeline for Fothadh Canainne, since Conchúr mac Nessa figures in the Ulster story cycle, which takes place in an earlier period than the Fenian cycle—yet Fothadh Canainne appears alongside Fenian characters in other texts.

16. See "The Death of Fothadh Canainne" (Hull 1936, 401–4). The Old Irish prose text is followed by one stanza of the poem, *Reicne Fothaid Canainne*, which is preserved in full elsewhere.

17. The term *reicne* may underscore the extempore nature of Fothadh Canainne's poem, which is addressed to the woman with whom he eloped. Joseph Falaky Nagy analyzes his interactions with the woman and her role as witness to this testimony (1997, 299–301). Kristen Mills explores gender dynamics in the portrayal of both characters (2018).

18. Meyer 1910, 10–13, stanzas 8–19, 21–22.

19. Meyer 1910, 14–17, stanzas 24–40. Fidchell was a medieval Irish board game.

20. There are further references to Fothadh Canainne and his two brothers, also *fénnidi* named Fothadh, but no significant later body of literature about him is extant. His brothers are listed in the Middle Irish version of the prose tale, and they also turn up in a Middle Irish treatise on names; see *Aithed Mná Ailella mac Eógain la Fothad Canainne* (The elopement of Oilill mac Eoghain's wife with Fothadh Canainne) and *Cóir Anmann* (The suitability of names), s.vv. "Tri Fothaidh," "Fothad Canann," "Fothad Airgthech," and "Fothad Cairpthech" (Meyer 1910, 4–7; Arbuthnot 2007, 59–60).

21. Two versions of this story have survived. The first, called "Fionn and the Man in the Tree" by Meyer, dates to the eighth century (Binchy 1978, 3:879 [ll. 23–880, l. 14]; trans. Meyer 1904b), and the second, incorporated in *Faghbal in Fesa do Finn agus Marbad Cúlduib* (How Fionn obtained knowledge and the slaying of Cúldubh), dates to the eighth or ninth century (Hull 1941, 329–33).

22. Such residences were thought to be located in the Neolithic burial mounds that dot the Irish landscape.

23. According to one of the two extant versions, Fionn only succeeds after the failure of both his son Oisín and his equally famous young *fían* companion Caoilte (Hull 1941, 329, 330–31). Fionn slays Cúldubh with a spear, an action he repeats in contentions with lone otherworldly aggressors in subsequent medieval texts: see Murray 2017a, 77–79.

24. As the later account in *Macgnímartha Finn* (The boyhood deeds of Fionn) states, "an tan do bered a ordain i n-a beolu . . . faillsithea do iarum in ni no bid 'n-a ainfis" ("for whenever he would put his thumb in his mouth . . . that which he did not know would be revealed to him") (Meyer 1881–83, 201; trans. Nagy 1985, 214). Other texts have him chew his thumb to the bone—a certain deterrent against overuse of the gift. For a discussion of the mythological significance of Fionn's thumb of knowledge, see Nagy 1985, 21–26.

25. Binchy 1978, 3:879 (l. 39)–880 (l. 14); trans. Meyer 1904b, 347–49. The episode containing this example is only included in one of the two versions of the story. Regarding Dearc Corra's name (Dercc Corra in the Old Irish text), see Carey 2005, 120–23; Sayers 2013, 45.

26. Although the earliest manuscript witness of *Tóruigheacht Dhiarmada agus Ghráinne* (The pursuit of Diarmaid and Gráinne) dates to 1651, Nessa Ní Shéaghdha points out numerous references in the poems of Gearóid Iarla (Gerald Fitzgerald) that attest to the circulation of a similar plotline in the fourteenth century (1967, xiii–xiv). See also Murray 2018, 17–18.

27. Gregory Toner contends that the original list "was almost certainly created as a catalogue of the main tales of its day" (2000, 114). While some accretion is probable in the later lists, according to Toner's analysis, *Aithed Gráinne ingine Corbmaic la Díarmait húa nDuibni* likely appeared in the original list (109–10; see also Mac Cana 1980, 86, 105–6). There is no way of

knowing how closely related this lost tale might have been to any of the other texts referencing the elopement of Diarmaid and Gráinne.

28. Murphy 1956, 160; Stokes 1899, 154–66, 264. The *Amra Choluim Chille* is an early religious poem that is partially dated to the seventh century. The quatrains attributed to Diarmaid and Gráinne appear in separate locations in the commentary. One depicts Gráinne, presumably prior to eloping, pining after someone, presumably Diarmaid. In the other, which must take place after the elopement, Diarmaid proclaims the nobility of wild game and mead to Gráinne. The former quatrain has been dated to the ninth or tenth century, while the latter may be as late as the eleventh century (Ó Cathasaigh 2013, 452, 469). While the former quatrain is generally seen as our earliest evidence for the Diarmaid and Gráinne story, Kevin Murray notes that the attributions may not accurately reflect these quatrains' original context (2017a, 98).

29. See *Cotail becán becán bec* (Sleep a little, a little little) (Murphy 1956, 160–64). Regarding the date of this poem, see Carey 2003b, 11.

30. Ní Shéaghdha 1967, 130–37. This story—unnamed in its manuscript contexts—has long been identified with the title *Úath Beinne Étair*, which appears in one of the two extant medieval tale lists (Toner 2000, 116). Bearing in mind Caoimhín Breatnach's caution against too ready acceptance of this identification (2020, 77–81), I use the title in keeping with current scholarly practise.

31. Stokes 1900, 43 (ll. 1514–17, 191, ll. 6895–96); cf. Dooley and Roe 1999, 47, 194. Gerard Murphy understands Diarmaid's death to be already part of the framework of the tale at this point (1953, xxxvi). Tomás Ó Cathasaigh points out that it may not yet be, since the connection between the elopement and Diarmaid's death is not explicitly made, although from a comparative structural perspective it is likely (2013, 454–55, 457, 471–72, 474).

32. On the dating of the text, see Meyer 1910, xxiv; Thurneysen 1920–21, 253; Corthals 2004, 1. The title *Tochmarc Ailbe* is included in the two extant medieval tale lists, and it was likely also in the earlier list from which they derive (Toner 2000, 102, 115).

33. Some textual contradiction must be admitted. Although in the opening section of the story, Cormac gives his blessing to any of his daughters who might wish to sleep with Fionn (Thurneysen 1920–21, 254 [ll. 17–18]), he subsequently opposes Ailbhe's intention to marry the *fían* leader.

34. The opening section of *Tochmarc Ailbe* refers to the divorce (Thurneysen 1920–21, 254 [l. 17]). The terms of both the marriage and the divorce are given in a short Middle Irish story known as "Finn and Gráinne" (Corthals 1997–98). According to *Tochmarc Ailbe*, the dissolution of the marriage caused a temporary rift between Fionn and Cormac that was repaired when the divorce was finalized.

35. "Fearr mur Temrach fuair i sen / Demin as buan a tuillem / Asdas in rait nuae inde / Ro-clas la mac n-Arrtaile" ("Better Tara's aged rampart—undoubtedly its merit is enduring—than yesterday's new rampart that was razed by Arrtaile's son") (Thurneysen 1920–21, 266 [ll. 5–6]; trans. Ní Dhonnchadha 2002, 208). This quatrain has been attributed to Ailbhe in the published translation, but the speaker is clearly Cormac. The reference to Arrtaile's son is unclear.

36. "Dofersuind due umromalt airinsetho ad-connarc" ("I would give up the place where I was reared for the treasures I have seen") (Thurneysen 1920–21, 260 [l. 4]). In her description she relates a dream vision given to her by a druid.

37. Dobbs 1931, 178, 214; see also Dobbs 1930, 301–2, 327. The eight wives are Gráinne; Ailbhe; Badhamair (killed by Cuirreach Life); Mongfhind daughter of the king of the Uí Fhailghe (killed by a daughter of Diarmaid); Bearrach Bhreac daughter of the king of the Ulaidh (killed by Art mac Morna; see *Acallam na Senórach*: Stokes 1900, 61 [ll. 2155–61]; cf. Dooley and Roe 1999, 66); Sadhbh daughter of Conn (see also *A Rí richid, réidig dam*, "Oh King of Heaven, explain to me": Meyer 1910, 46); Seandlach daughter of Fionn mac Eassamain; and Smiornad (or

Smiorghad) daughter of Fothadh Canainne. Also listed are two consorts who bore him sons: Blaoi (Oisín's mother) and a woman known as the daughter of Earc. Several other wives and consorts appear in other texts. Ó hÓgáin discusses some of these (1988, 107–8, 152–55).

38. See "Fionn and the Man in the Tree" (Binchy 1978, 3:879 [ll. 32–34]; trans. Meyer 1904b, 347).

39. See *Cóir Anmann*, s.v. "Lugna Fer Trí" (Arbuthnot 2005, 181–82). The woman in question is Cormac mac Airt's mother, and the man his foster father, Lughna. The assault is said to have happened during Cormac's youth. While the rape attempt does not reflect negatively on Oscar, the physical deformity he receives during his struggle with Lughna is a source of humiliation. An alternate version in the fourteenth- or fifteenth-century *Agallamh na Seanórach* has Oscar lose his testicle in battle with a different man whose wife he is trying to abduct (Ní Shéaghdha 2014 [1942–45], 3:54–62; Arbuthnot 2006, 70).

40. "Ém cach roilbe 7 cach rofid nognāthaiged Finn cona fēin nobīth ben aurdalta ar a chind in cach thīr ba nessam dō beus" (Meyer 1910, xix; translation adapted from Russell 2008, 39). The story in which this statement appears, known as "Fionn and the Jester Lomna," relates the infidelity of one of these women and the murder of Fionn's jester for informing on her. The quoted statement is absent from the Middle Irish version of the story preserved in a law tract beginning *Cuaille fedha i feilm n-airgit* ("A wooden stake into a fence of silver") (Binchy 1978, 6:2115 [l. 38], 6:2116 [l. 27]; trans. Dillon 1932, 58–61).

41. Thurneysen 1920–21, 260 [l. 3].

42. "Ni-caistide fri liatu / Cia do-neidis cronan coir / Ni-eigid doib a fiachu" (Thurneysen 1920–21, 264 [ll. 3–4]).

43. Thurneysen 1920–21, 264 [ll. 7–8].

44. "Is de álchaib ind ḟir léith / Labrad a cobreth a scéith" (Stifter forthcoming, §12). David Stifter titles this story *Acaldam Ḟind ocus Oiséni* (The dialogue of Fionn and Oisín); scholars have previously followed Meyer (1910, 22) in referring to it as "The Quarrel between Fionn and Oisín."

45. "Ó foruban crith cech cnáim / Ní goirt in gáe asa láim" (Stifter forthcoming, §10).

46. According to Fionn: "Inna huile immallé / Níbad messa doïb dé / Dia mbem inar comardus / Ó ascomartmar ar nglé" ("All this [taken] together, none will be the worse for it, if we are equals, since we have fought our fight") (Stifter forthcoming, §17).

47. Thurneysen 1920–21, 264 (ll. 5–6, 9–10).

48. "Ro-cuala cor na-bi gaet / Ingen do dul co rolaec / Nimti at-agar de" (Thurneysen 1920–21, 266 [ll. 1–2, 13]; translation adapted from Ní Dhonnchadha 2002, 208). Rendered literally, *liathaínech* means 'grey (of hair) faced.'

49. See, for instance, the late ninth- or early tenth-century story, *Fingal Rónáin* (The kin-slaying of Rónán), in which a tragic series of events is initiated when Rónán, a powerful but aging man, ignores proffered advice and takes a much younger wife (Greene 1955, 1–15).

50. Thurneysen 1920–21, 270–74. Versions of this Fenian riddling sequence have been traced in early modern literature and modern Scottish Gaelic folklore: see Stewart and Stewart 1804, 545–47; Campbell 1872, 150; and Innes 2016.

51. Meyer 1897, 464–65. As Fionn recognizes, "áes airighit na fir forum-sa" ("it is [old] age that the men see in me") (464).

52. Three Middle Irish poems also document this tradition: *Fíana bátar i nEmain* ("The *fíana* who were in Emain") (Stokes 1902, 310); the *dinnshenchas* of Brug na Bóinne (Gwynn 1906, 12 [ll. 35–36]); and *Annálad anall uile* ("All the annal-writing heretofore") (Smith 2007, 190 [ll. 15, 522–23]). In addition, the fragmentary story of Fionn's leaping death has a party of Luaighne men come upon his body and behead him (Meyer 1897, 465); see also the marginal quatrain in the Book of Leinster beginning *Ro díchned Find, ba fer tend* ("Fionn was beheaded; he was a strong man") (Meyer 1910, xxv). We might infer that the author of the leaping death story

was attempting to unite two contradictory traditions. Alternatively, as Geraldine Parsons points out, the tradition of the leaping death could be taken as the primary one from which most other death accounts descend (2012, 86). For further references to medieval accounts of Fionn's death, see Parsons 2012, 91–96. On the opposition between Fionn and the Luaighne, see Murray 2017a, 89–91.

53. "Iar tiachtain foirbtechta 7 arrsaidechta cuice" (Meyer 1885, 73–74).

54. Meyer 1885, 74–75. An expanded but incomplete account of this battle features in the thirteenth- or fourteenth-century story dubbed "The Slaying of the Pig of Formaoíl and the Death of Fionn" by Murphy (1953, 136). Here, the Luaighne's messenger calls Fionn "senóir díblidi dolámaig" ("a debilitated, feeble-handed senior"), in response to which, Fionn pledges to give his enemies "cath gille óig" ("[the] battle of a young man") (Meyer 1910, 80, 82). He attempts this, but while his former valor has been established, as in the earlier account, his youth has been spent and his death foretold. The text breaks off with Fionn evidently not long for this world: having taken several spears to the chest, he understands "gur búaine bladh iná sháegal dó" ("that his fame is to be more lasting than his life") (94).

55. Stokes 1896, 21. Later accounts of Fionn's death are infrequent and not always in accordance with the Middle Irish accounts. In the modern folktale *Na Fianna ina gCodladh Faoin Talamh* (The Fianna asleep underground), rather than dying, Fionn is said to lie in enchanted sleep in a cave, awaiting a moment in time when he is to awaken and save Ireland / Scotland / the Gaels; in this international tale (ATU 766), Fionn parallels Arthur, Charlemagne, and other legendary figures, both historical and nonhistorical, for whom see Ó hÓgáin 1991.

56. See Tomás Ó Cathasaigh's *The Heroic Biography of Cormac mac Airt* (1977), the preeminent work on the concept of the heroic biography in early Irish literature.

57. Meyer 1881–83; Murray 2021, 17. See Joseph Falaky Nagy's landmark study, *The Wisdom of the Outlaw* (1985) for a detailed consideration of *Macgnímartha Finn* and related texts.

58. *Fotha Catha Cnucha* expands upon and quotes stanzas of verse from the Middle Irish *dinnshenchas* of Almu (later, Cnoc Almhaine, 'the Hill of Allen'): see Gwynn 1906, 72–77. Cnucha has been identified as Castleknock, County Dublin: Hennessy 1873–75, 92n1.

59. Hennessy 1873–75; Murray 2021, 27–28. Although *Fotha Catha Cnucha* indicates that Fionn makes peace with his father's killer, his assumption of Cumhall's position is not explicitly stated in this text. It can be inferred, however, from Fionn's regular portrayal in contemporary literature as the leader of the *fían*. Since the ending of *Macgnímartha Finn* is lost, that text sheds little light on the topic, but the fact that Fionn is on his way to meet a *fían* when the text breaks off suggests a forthcoming reintegration. In all likelihood, the story closed with Fionn's retaking of his father's position (see Ó hÓgáin 1988, 95). A mid-twelfth-century poem beginning *A Rí richid, réidig dam* provides the first extant account of the feat elsewhere connected with Fionn's taking control of the *fían*: his defeat of the otherworldly aggressor, Aillén, who had been burning Tara on an annual basis (Meyer 1910, 46; cf. *Acallam na Senórach*: Stokes 1900, 47–50 [ll. 1654–1769]; Dooley and Roe 1999, 47–55).

60. Cumhall is killed by Goll mac Morna in *Macgnímartha Finn* and *Fotha Catha Cnucha*, and both texts attribute the "fich bunad itir Finn ocus maccu Morna" ("hereditary feud between Fionn and the sons of Morna") to that act (Meyer 1881–83, 197; cf. Hennessy 1873–75, 90).

61. This is according to the *Macgnímartha Finn* version of the story of the Battle of Cnucha, which makes the leadership of the *fían* the primary issue of contention. In *Fotha Catha Cnucha*, the Luaighne rival, Uirghriu, is listed alongside prominent Clann Mhorna men in the troops opposing Cumhall. *Tesmolta Cormaic ui Chuinn ocus Aided Finn meic Cumaill* relates that Fionn killed Uirghriu and was, in turn, killed by Uirghriu's grandson, Aichleach Mór. In the fragmentary story of Fionn's leaping death, Aichleach beheads Fionn post mortem. Conversely, later texts will deemphasize Fionn's death and bring the feud—by then intergenerational—to a close at the Battle of Gabhair, for which see chapter 3.

62. See *A Rí richid, réidig dam,* attributed to Gilla in Chomded hÚa Cormaic: "Se fichit findscél na Fiann / foclas cech fili fírían" ("Every proper poet tells one hundred and twenty Fenian tales") (Best and O'Brien 1957, 587 [ll. 18, 161–62]).

63. Nagy 1985, 229n18; Stern 1897, 473. Regarding lists of heroes' names in early Irish literature, see Hillers 1994, 105–6.

64. "Friusin at-berat in daescar-sluag Fianna Find" (Stern 1897, 472).

65. "Fian-shruth Find, fáth cen dochta" (Gwynn 1913, 20). Regarding the date of the *dinnshenchas* of Carmun, see Ó Concheanainn 1981–83, 99.

66. Nagy 1995, 93; Stokes 1900, 95 (ll. 3345–62); cf. Dooley and Roe 1999, 101–2. The performer, Cas Corach, is called an *airfitech* multiple times in the text; see, e.g., Stokes 1900, 125 (l. 4612); cf. Dooley and Roe 1999, 129.

67. See Johnston 2013, 157, 160 and Finnegan 1977, 16–24. The third aspect of the medieval oral tradition noted above—the oral performance of written texts—exemplifies one way in which written texts could have initially entered the oral sphere. Elva Johnston's work on the earliest Irish literature shows distinct delineations between primarily literary and oral secular narrative texts to be largely superficial, given the likelihood of constant cross-influence.

68. Diarmaid is named as the descendent of Duibhne in a gloss to *Bruiden Átha Í,* the *dinnshenchas* of Currech Life, *Tochmarc Ailbe, Úath Beinne Étair,* and the title *Aithed Gráinne ingine Corbmaic la Díarmait húa nDuibni* in the medieval tale lists. Specific details about his lineage and upbringing are less consistent and may reflect variant or developing traditions. According to the glossed *Bruiden Átha Í,* Diarmaid's father, Dubh son of Duibhne, was the murdered foster brother of Fionn's wife, Badhamair (Hull 1941, 325). The *dinnshenchas* of Currech Life instead lists Dubh as Cuirreach Life's son-in-law (Stokes 1894, 442–43), and marginal quatrains in the Book of Leinster beginning *Máthair Díarmata ón Dáil* ("The mother of Diarmaid from the Deel") claim that Cuirreach's daughter was Diarmaid's mother (Best and O'Brien 1957, 728 [ll. 21, 821–22]). *Úath Beinne Étair* gives Diarmaid's father's name as Donn, rather than Dubh, which accords with later accounts (Ní Shéaghdha 1967, 84, 130; Stokes 1900, 7 [ll. 206–7]; cf. Dooley and Roe 1999, 9). *Acallam na Senórach* makes Diarmaid and Oisín foster brothers (Stokes 1900, 142 [l. 5206]; cf. Dooley and Roe 1999, 145).

69. See *Find Taulcha* (Meyer 1910, xvii–xviii).

70. See "Finn and Gráinne" (Corthals 1997–98, 76 [l. 11]), *A Rí richid, réidig dam* (Meyer 1910, 48), and the genealogical material in the Book of Leinster about Fionn and his family (Atkinson 1880, 379 [col. a, ll. 20–25]). As Meyer notes, the circumstances of Caoilte's birth are identical to the birth of the twins of Macha in an earlier, Ulster-cycle tale. The motif may have been directly borrowed (1885, x). Two different fathers are named in these texts, neither of whom is associated with Caoilte elsewhere. Later sources refer to him as either the son or the grandson of Rónán; see, e.g., *Acallam na Senórach* (Stokes 1900, 1 [l. 5], 3 [l. 73], 182 [l. 6578]; cf. Dooley and Roe 1999, 3, 5, 184). The Old Irish *Scél asa mberar combad hé Find mac Cumhaill Mongán* (A story in which it is said that Fionn mac Cumhaill was Mongán) describes him as *dalta Find* ("Fionn's foster son") (White 2006, 74).

71. See *Scél asa mberar combad hé Find mac Cumhaill Mongán* (White 2006, 73–74); *Échta Lagen for Leth Cuind* ("The Laigin's slaughters upon Leth Cuind") (Best et al. 1954, 238 [l. 7038]); "Finn and Gráinne" (Corthals 1997–98, 76 [l. 10]); and *Eól dam i ndairib dréchta* ("I am skilled in dense masses of compositions") (Meyer 1912a, 118). On the early references to Caoilte's speed, see Ó hÓgáin 1988, 177–80. This defining characteristic is also reflected in Caoilte's adapted name in Middle Welsh, Scilti Scawntroet, 'Caoilte Lightfoot': see Sims-Williams 2011, 173–74. Further discussion of Caoilte's characterization in the early sources can be found in Ó Síocháin 2021, 188–247.

72. See *Ogam i llia, lia uas lecht* ("An Ogham in a stone, a stone over a grave") (Windisch 1880, 158) and the *dinnshenchas* of Glaisse Bulga (Gwynn 1924, 288–89). Later, more detailed

descriptions of the Battle of Gabhair exist in prose and poetry; see, e.g., the heroic romance *Cath Gabhra* (O'Kearney 1854, 134–52). The modern folktale about the birth of Oscar follows the international tale type ATU 873.

73. See *Máthair Díarmata ón Dáil*: "... / is Blai Derg din Banbai braiss / mathair Ossine amnaiss. / Ticed i rricht elite / hi comdáil na díbergge; / Co ndernad Ossine de / ri Blai ṅDeirgg i rricht eilte" ("... and Blaoi Dhearg from great Banbha was the mother of strong Oisín. She used to come in the shape of a hind to meet the brigands; consequently, Oisín was begotten on Blaoi Dhearg when she was in the shape of a hind") (Best and O'Brien 1957, 728–29 [ll. 21, 823–28]; translation adapted from Ó Briain 1994, 465–66). Oisín's mother is alternatively called Cruithgheal daughter of Dearg in a Middle Irish poem beginning *Fíamhain mac Foraigh go fíor* ("Fiamhain son of Forach, in truth") (Murphy 1933, 122). In some modern accounts, she is known as Sadhbh (Kennedy 1866, 236; cf. Gregory 1970a [1904], 150).

74. Baumgarten 1987, 5. The suggestion that Oscar's name may be similarly derived from *os*, 'deer,' and *caraid*, 'loves,' meaning 'deer-loving' in relation to the *fían*'s hunting activities, has been discredited (Uhlich 1993, 288–89). Instead, Sharon Arbuthnot posits that an early iteration of the story of Oscar's lost testicle (see the previous section) may have explained the derivation of his name from *og*, 'testicle,' and *scaraid*, 'separates' (2006, 68–69, 72–73). The name could also simply reflect the noun *oscar*, 'outsider, foe' (69n8).

75. Ó Briain 1994, 460, 467. While the story of Oisín's birth to a deer-mother is not mentioned elsewhere in the early literature, details regarding his place of birth and fosterage are found in texts associated with *Acallam na Senórach* (464–65).

76. Baumgarten 1987, 16; Murray 2017a, 53–54.

77. Fionn has also been compared with the deity Lugus. See O'Rahilly 1946, 277–81; Murphy 1953, lxx–lxxxvii; Mac Cana 1987, 76–83; Ó hÓgáin 1988, 3–26; cf. Carey 2002, 118–19.

78. Carey 2002, 108–19; Flahive 2017, 2.

79. The evidence upon which this theory rests—the place name *buvinda* on Ptolemy's map—has also been interpreted differently. See Ó hÓgáin 1988, 325n55; 1994, 17–24; cf. Dillon 1975, 122.

80. Ó hÓgáin 1988, 33. Ó hÓgáin goes on to read the Luaighne's role in the Middle Irish accounts of Fionn's birth and death as reflections of the same conflict, the Luaighne being vassals of the Uí Néill (84–85, 108). The opposition between Fionn and the Luaighne can be traced back as far as the ninth century in "Fionn and the Jester Lomna"; see Ó hÓgáin 1988, 45 and Murray 2017a, 90–91. Whether these stories build on themes developed at the turn of the sixth century cannot be known.

81. Ó hÓgáin 1988, 27–31, 33, 43. Ó hÓgáin reiterates this developmental model in later publications: 1994, 24–27; 1999, 121; 2002, 131; 2006, 238–39.

82. See *Macgnímartha Finn* (Meyer 1881–83, 197); *Tesmolta Cormaic ui Chuinn ocus Aided Finn meic Cumaill* (Meyer 1885, 76); and *Acallam na Senórach* (Stokes 1900, 181 [l. 6548]; cf. Dooley and Roe 1999, 183). These texts portray Fionn as a member of the Uí Thairsigh, apparently a sept of the Uí Fhailghe. Other contemporary sources associate Fionn with different kin groups. Ó hÓgáin acknowledges that "conclusive proof is lacking" for his Fenian origin narrative (1988, 30). See also Ó Briain 1989a.

83. The first definitive association of Fionn with the Hill of Allen occurs in the tenth-century poetic *dinnshenchas* of Almu (Gwynn 1906, 72–77). Diarmuid Ó Murchadha has suggested a possible oblique reference to Fionn's association with the Hill of Allen in a seventh-century text, but this early reference remains uncertain (Ó Murchadha 2009, xxiii; Parsons 2014, 215).

84. Murray 2017a, 74, 85–89. From Munster, see *Bruiden Átha Í* (Hull 1941, 323–29), "Fionn and the Man in the Tree" (Binchy 1978, 3:879 [l. 23] to 880 [l. 14]; trans. Meyer 1904b), and *Faghbal in Fesa do Finn agus Marbad Cúlduib* (Hull 1941, 329–33), set in the region of the river Suir in Déise territory, and *Scéla Moshauluim*, set in the southwest in Corca Laoidhe territory

(O Daly 1975, 74–86). From Ulster, see *Scél asa mberar combad hé Find mac Cumhaill Mongán*, concerning the seventh-century Dál nAraidhe king Mongán mac Fiachna's knowledge of the details of a Fenian fight (White 2006, 73–74). While this story may be the sole surviving early Ulster example, as Mac Cana recognizes, it "takes for granted an easy familiarity on the part of readers or hearers with the general content of *fían* lore" (1987, 87).

85. Although somewhat tenuous, the assertion in the early eleventh-century *Liber Hymnorum* version of the preface to the *Amra Choluim Chille* that *fían* stories were being written down in Ulster in the early seventh century can also be noted: see Mac Cana 1987, 88–89. On the date of this text, see Herbert 1989, 68, 72.

86. *Fianna Éireann* is the modern spelling. In Middle Irish they are *Fíana Érenn*: see, e.g., *Tochmarc Ailbe* (Thurneysen 1920–21, 268 [l. 17]).

87. "Is de adbertæi fiana friu, ar ba siad fenidi 7 milid in ri iad" (Thurneysen 1920–21, 254 [ll. 6–7]).

88. "Cec æn tra do feraib Eirenn no-bid for dimfeirg on ri, is a tig Find no-bidis" (Thurneysen 1920–21, 254 [ll. 11–12]). I understand *dimferg* to mean a state of strife, but the word also suggests the sort of marauding band of outlaws (*díberga*) with which we are now familiar.

89. "Ro ordaigh didiu rig Erenn a amsaig for feraib Erenn. Ro ordaigh tri. L. rígfeindidh forro-side fri commus a cheana 7 a smachta 7 a fiadhaig. Dorat a chendacht uile 7 ardmæraidhecht Erenn d' Fhind Ua Baiscne" (Stokes 1891, 199, 217; translation adapted from Stokes); this text is titled *Echtra Cormaic i Tír Tairngiri* (Cormac's adventure in land of promise).

90. See Murray 2015 and Murray 2021, 42–46 for broader discussions of onomastics in early Fenian narrative.

91. See the *dinnshenchas* of Almu (Gwynn 1906, 72–77).

92. Ó Cathasaigh 1977, 64–65, 98–101; Byrne 2001 [1973], 266–69.

93. "Is e ropa thaisech teglaig 7 ropa cheand deorad 7 amhus 7 cech ceithirne archena la Cormac Find mac Cumhaill" (Stern 1897, 472).

94. McCone 1986, 1, 6.

95. Ó Corráin 1987, 29; Simms 1996, 99–100.

96. Simms 1996, 102.

97. See, for example, Mac Cana's comparison between Fionn and Mac Con (1987, 83).

Chapter 2. Saint Patrick and the Pagans

1. Poppe contrasts immanent cycles with "cycles-by-transmission," which comprise similarly interrelated texts that are grouped sequentially in one or more manuscripts (2008, 16, 22). For a formative exploration of immanence and its foundational "traditional referentiality," which "entails the invoking of a context that is enormously larger and more echoic than the text or work itself," see Foley 1991, 7, 10.

2. Poppe 2008, 12; cf. Staines 1996, 25–29. Poppe derives the concept of a "common, fixed point of reference" from the early nineteenth-century French literary critic Claude Charles Fauriel. Fauriel's *point fixe commun* appears to have been flexible enough to accommodate individual or collective central heroes: compare his metonymic evocation of *la Table ronde* as the *point fixe commun* of the Arthurian cycle with his identification of Charlemagne as the *point fixe* of that eponymous cycle: Poppe 2008, 4; Staines 1996, 27. Barbara Hillers has also highlighted the tendency for cycles to evoke a "circle of heroes, gathered around the central figure" (1994, 99). While Hillers focuses on the Irish Ulster cycle, her observation is equally applicable to the Fenian cycle.

3. Stokes 1900, 181 [l. 6538] and 182 [l. 6563]; cf. Dooley and Roe 1999, 183, 184.

4. While the Fenian narrative universe would have been familiar to contemporary audiences, we should bear in mind that the 'cycle' is a modern classification.

5. Staines 1996, 36; cf. Poppe 2008, 12, 22. According to Staines, "the beginning and the end [of the cycle] are often fixed and determined; the middle is the area of flexibility and creativity."

6. While Oscar's death in *Cath Gabhra* is fixed, Fionn's death is not a stable point of reference, as Geraldine Parsons (2012) has discussed.

7. Dumville 1993; Stokes 1896, 21 (Annals of Tigernach).

8. Flahive 2015, 139–40. Joseph Falaky Nagy (1997) explores several such saintly dialogues. Influence from secular dialogue texts is also likely: Flahive 2004, 32–33.

9. Stokes 1886; Murray 2021, 25. This poem is also known as "Fionn and the Phantoms." A prose version, *Echtra Finn* (Fionn's adventure), dated perhaps to the late eleventh century also exists: see Stern 1892, 5–7, 12–17; Meyer 1910, xxiii; Murray 2021, 20–21. The prose version and the poem are related, but the beginning of the former is lost, and it lacks the implicit dialogue structure of the poem. A partial prosimetrum adaptation of the poem appears in *Acallam na Senórach* (c. 1225), and Early Modern Gaelic versions are included in the fourteenth- or fifteenth-century *Agallamh na Seanórach* and in *Duanaire Finn* (*Áonach so a Moigh Eala in rí*, "This was a fair in Magh Eala of the king"): Stokes 1900, 45–46 (ll. 1595–1618); Dooley and Roe 1999, 50; Ní Shéaghdha 2014 [1945], 173–82; MacNeill 1908, 28–30.

10. Oisín's identity is also notably obscured at the beginning of the poem. He first calls himself *Guaire dall*, 'blind Guaire,' only later revealing the name he bore in his heroic youth (Stokes 1886, 290, 300).

11. Murphy 1971 [1955], 19–21; 1953, cxvi; 1943, 74. Cf. Shields 1993, 39–40.

12. Linguistic analyses of a handful of the copious number of Fenian dialogue poems edited by Murphy (1933; 1953) have led John Carey to suggest that "Murphy's dates may often have been too late, sometimes by a century or more" (2003b, 18); see also Murray 2017a, 130–32; Mac Eoin 2012.

13. Shields 1993, 4–5, 40; cf. Gearóid Mac Eoin's disputation of Shields's definition of ballads (2012, 304–6, 319). Among the few Fenian poems that share subject matter with the European ballad corpus is the fifteenth-century *Laoidh an Bhruit* (Lay of the mantle), in which the titular mantle is used in a magical fidelity test for the Fenian wives. The only woman found to have been completely faithful is the one whom the garment fully covers: the wife of a Fenian named Mac Reithe in the earliest extant texts, but Oisín's wife in an expanded nineteenth-century version: Ross 1939, 30–35; Murphy 1933, 330–35; Robinson 1903–4, 145–57. The plot is similar to that of the English Arthurian ballad "The Boy and the Mantle" (Child no. 29), and the Fenian poem is "recognizably a borrowed product," although the subject need not have been adapted directly from the Arthurian ballad (Shields 1993, 11–12). See also Murphy 1943, 75; 1953, 155–58.

14. Shields 1993, 11. See also Meek 1987, 132; Ó hUiginn 1995, 49. In modern Scottish Gaelic, the terms *laoidh* ('lay'), *duan* ('ode, rhyme'), and *dàn* ('poem, song') are all used to describe Fenian lays.

15. Ó hAodha 1991, 212.

16. Murray 2017a, 55–56; Shields 1993, 13. Nagy's suggestion that lower orders of performers sustained the early Fenian tradition accords well with this theory (1995, 93; and see chapter 1).

17. Flahive 2015, 141.

18. Flahive 2015, 143, 147–53. This poem is representative of a subgroup of early lays that center upon objects of importance to the Fianna. Similar object 'genealogies' are presented for Fionn's *corrbholg*, 'crane bag,' Caoilte's drinking vessel, Oscar's sword, and Caoilte's sword (*Laoidh an Chorr-Bholga*, *Laoidh Síthil Caoilti*, *Laoidh Cloidhimh Oscair*, and *Laoidh Colga Chaoilti*): see Flahive 2015, 140–41; MacNeill 1908, 21–22, 38–45, 49–55; Murphy 1933, 124–41. Other early Fenian lays also incorporate learned material, such as the list of Fenian gravestones in *A*

lia Thulcha Tuaithe shuas ("Oh stone above on Tulach Thuaithe") and the genealogies (of heroes) in *Fiond File ba fer go lí* ("Fionn the Poet was a man of beauty") and *Fégthar tech Finn a nAlmhain* ("Let us behold Fionn's house in Allen"), and Murray notes "strong legal overtones" in *Eól damh senchus Feine Finn* ("I know the story of Fionn's Fianna") (Murray 2017a, 132–33; 1933, 66–99; MacNeill 1908, 1–3, 24–27). Less erudite early lays are also extant.

19. Flahive 2017, 32. Regarding early non-Fenian narrative verse, see Clancy 2008.

20. Stern 1905; MacNeill 1908, 14–17; Murray 2021 33, 39. In the latter, Oisín addresses not Saint Patrick, but a woman who is washing his head.

21. Stokes 1894, 437. The phrase occurs in a short prose introduction to a late twelfth-century poem concerning the onomastic lore of Tonn Clidna. Meyer considered the introduction to be concurrent with the poem, but Nollaig Ó Muraíle posits that it might have been a later interpolation: Meyer 1910, xxx; Ó Muraíle 1995, 107; cf. Murray forthcoming. The poem was later incorporated into *Acallam na Senórach*: Stokes 1900, 109 (ll. 3833–3853); cf. Dooley and Roe 1999, 115–16. The considerable amount of material in the *Acallam* that presumably derives from preexisting lays (see below) sufficiently attests to the breadth of the dialogue tradition by the thirteenth century, in any case.

22. Medieval Irish literati regularly employed the prosimetrum form. *Tochmarc Ailbe* (The wooing of Ailbhe) and *Úath Beinne Étair* (The cave of Howth), discussed in chapter 1, are both prosimetrum texts. For discussion of the form's use in the *Acallam*, see Parsons 2009.

23. The size of the retinue fluctuates somewhat throughout the text. Only eleven of the men are named, all of them king's sons, and none of them recognizable members of the *gnáthfhiann*: Stokes 1900, 9–10 [ll. 305–13]; cf. Dooley and Roe 1999, 12.

24. "Ní roiched acht co tana a tháibh nó co formna a ghualand in bhfer ba mó dona cléirchibh don ḟir dhibh sin 7 iat ina súidhi" (Stokes 1900, 3 [l. 61, 76–78]; cf. Dooley and Roe 1999, 5).

25. Stokes 1900, 10 (ll. 314–24); cf. Dooley and Roe 1999, 12.

26. "Ocus scríbhthar na scéla sin letsa i támlorguibh filed 7 i mbriathraibh ollaman ór budh gairdiugudh do dronguibh 7 do degdáinibh deridh aimsire éisdecht frisna scéluib sin" (Stokes 1900, 9 [ll. 300–2]; translation adapted from Nagy 1995, 85; cf. Dooley and Roe 1999, 12).

27. McCone 1986, 1.

28. All five manuscript witnesses lack an ending, and nearly all of them differ to a greater or lesser degree. Given this complexity, Kevin Murray suggests that it may be problematic to treat the *Acallam* "as a single unitary text" (2017a, 22–23; see also Murray 2022). My analysis is dependent upon Whitley Stokes's 1900 edition, which remains the academic standard.

29. Kühns 2005; Ní Shéaghdha 2014 [1942–45]. While the *Acallam Bec* is usually presented as being contemporary with or slightly later than *Acallam na Senórach*, the possibility that it predates the latter has not been ruled out, nor has the prospect of a lost version from which both derive. Despite the close date and shared interlocutor of the two early texts, the *Acallam Bec* correlates more closely with *Agallamh na Seanórach*, the author of which clearly drew on both thirteenth-century versions. *Agallamh na Seanórach* is also known as the Reeves *Agallamh* or the *Agallamh Déanach* (Late dialogue). For discussions of the relationship between these texts, see Mills forthcoming, Flahive 2014, Kühns 2012, and Ó Muraíle 1995.

30. Ní Mhurchú 2014, 185–86. The *Agallamh Nua* has yet to be edited in full.

31. See, e.g., Nutt 1899, 18, 20–21; MacNeill 1908, xlvi; Rees and Rees 1961, 67; Murphy 1971 [1955], 24–29. Although preexisting sources are often not extant, it is broadly accepted that the *Acallam*'s author paraphrased multiple lays and incorporated segments of earlier verse (e.g., the late twelfth-century poem concerning the onomastic lore of Tonn Clidna footnoted above). That said, some of the verse is almost certainly original to the text. See Flahive 2017, 24–25; Dooley 2012, 97–98; Parsons 2009; Dooley and Roe 1999, xvii, xxvi; Ó hUiginn 1995, 55. The *Acallam Bec* and *Agallamh na Seanórach* also integrate earlier Fenian texts, some of which are extant (e.g., *Óenach indiu luid in rí*, discussed above).

32. Regarding the *Acallam*'s date of composition, see Murray 2017a, 24–28 and Toner 2022.

33. Simms 1992 [1989], 52–55; Ó Néill 1997, 177, 179–80; Nicholls 2003, 5. Prior to the conquest, Gaels and Norse settlers felled wood for architecture, shipbuilding, and trade, but not at the scale of the late medieval Anglo-Normans (Everett 2014, 24–25; Lehmann 2019, 239).

34. Ó Murchadha and Murray 2000, 148.

35. Regarding onomastic formulae, see Ó hUiginn 2007 and Murray 2017b, 14.

36. "Cret má tucad Fert Fiadmoir ar in n-inad-so, 7 créd 'ma tucad Cnocc in chircaill ar in ard-so thiar, 7 cred fa tucad Cnoc in chongna ar in cnoc-sa re thaob? . . . tucad na tri cind sin ar na tri tulchaib-seo, conid uatha atáit na hanmanna sin orro" (Stokes 1900, 178–80 [ll. 6445–48, 6524–25]; translation adapted from Dooey and Roe 1999, 181, 183).

37. "Is annsin tangadur na sluaig reompo co Breicsliab . . . risa raiter Sliab Formaile i Connachtaib isin tan-so, 7 co Suide Find a mullach in tṡleibe, 7 mar do tṡuidhidur ann ro moidedur déra co tróm falcmur tar a gruaidib do Chailti ac feicail inn inaid a ṁbíth Find mac Cumaill ina tṡuidhe. 'Ocus crét dobeir cáí ort, a m'anam, a Chailti?' ar rí Connacht, '7 in ac feicail in inaid a ṁbid Find ina tṡuidhe 7 Formaile na Fiann?' 'Iss ed immorro,' ar Cailte, 'uair rogha selga na gnathḞeinde in sliab-so, 7 Loch na n-eillted, risa raiter Loch Formaile isin tan-so, 7 Cluain na damraide, risa raiter Cell tulach isin tan-so, 7 baile sin Conain Máil meic Morna, 7 Ros na hechraide-'risa [*sic*] raiter inn Airm isin tan-so, bail a ṁbídis drong d'echaib na Feinde, 7 Dún Saltrain Sálḟata, risa raiter Cell Chaimin ar Succa, 7 co Moin na fostada, risa raiter Moin in tachair conneda isi[n] tan-so, 7 co Carraic ind ḟomorach, risa raiter Dún mor isin tan-so" (Stokes 1900, 181 [ll. 6530–45]; translation adapted from Dooey and Roe 1999, 183). Regarding these locations, see Connon 2013, 75–80; Connon 2014, 47, 50–51; Fitzpatrick 2013, 102–10.

38. Stokes 1900, 163–68 (ll. 5917–6082); cf. Dooley and Roe 1999, 166–70.

39. Stokes 1900, 88–90 (ll. 3114–95); cf. Dooley and Roe 1999, 94–97. See also Stokes 1900, 35–37 (ll. 1246–1309) (cf. Dooley and Roe 1999, 39–41) for the story of another king of Lochlann's son who comes to seize the kingship of Ireland and is defeated by the Fianna. Regarding the significance of invaders from Lochlann, see chapter 3.

40. Dooley 2004, 98. This is hardly surprising; Anglo-Normans rarely feature in medieval Irish literature, excepting post-conquest political poetry, some of which was composed for Anglo-Norman-descendant patrons. Anglo-Normans only make overt appearances in Fenian literature in two prophetic lays that foretell their coming, *A bhean labhrus rinn an laoidh* ("Woman who recites the lay to us") and *A Oissín in ráidhe rinn* ("Oisín can you tell us"): Ó Néill 1997, 178–79; MacNeill 1908, 85; Murphy 1933, 154–66.

41. Martyn 2016, 35; Mohr 2015, 50; McNeill 1997, 132. Richard de Burgh was granted Connacht in 1227.

42. Stokes 1900, 20–21, 26 (ll. 708–9, 906); cf. Dooley and Roe 1999, 23, 29. Regarding the location of Cenn Abrat Sléibe Cáin, see Ó Riain et al. 2011, 74, s.v. "Ceann Eabhradh."

43. *Bethu Phátraic* (The Life of Patrick, also called *Vita Tripartita Sancti Patricii*) attributes the founding of Árd Pátraic to the saint and locates *lecc Pátraic*, 'Patrick's flagstone,' there: Mulchrone 1939, 124 (l. 212); Gwynn and Hadcock 1970, 29. Harry Roe (1992) explores the *Acallam* author's engagement with the early Patrician Lives.

44. Empey 1981, 6, 21n49. William de Burgh's possession of the region was confirmed in a grant dated 1199.

45. Stokes 1900, 27 (l. 950); cf. Dooley and Roe 1999, 30; Connon 2021. De Burgh's installation in Munster was intended to strengthen the crown's position in the frontier zone between the Uí Bhriain (O'Briens) of Thomond and the Mic Chárthaigh (MacCarthys) of Desmond. The opening years of the thirteenth century found him campaigning to disrupt the Gaelic kingship of Connacht: Martin 1987, 124, 128, 131.

46. Stokes 1900, 27–28 (ll. 952–95); cf. Dooley and Roe 1999, 30–32.

47. Stokes 1900, 10 (ll. 314–24); cf. Dooley and Roe 1999, 12; Mills forthcoming, 6, 19.

48. Kühns 2005, 19–23, 43–44 (ll. 5–130, 673–79), quoted at 19 (ll. 16, 29–30); translation adapted from 87–88.

49. "'Truag dono sin,' ar Cailte, '7 missi do gabail deilbe druidechta umum. Ní géb acht in delb tuc mo Déntaid 7 mo Dúilem 7 in fírDia fororda dam, 7 iris chredme 7 crabaid in Táilgind intí tarrus a nEirinn.' Ocus adubradur Túath dé Danann: 'Guth fírlaich 7 fírgaiscid sin!'" (Stokes 1900, 196 [ll. 7039–43]; translation adapted from Dooley and Roe 1999, 197–98). See also Mulligan 2019, 163; Carey 2014, 85.

50. Mulligan 2019, 156–58. See, e.g., Stokes 1900, 217 (ll. 7766–67, 7774–75); cf. Dooley and Roe 1999, 216.

51. Mulligan 2019, 152. Saint Patrick's former enslavement in Ireland is referenced in the *Acallam*, but not his place of origin: Stokes 1900, 105 (ll. 3689–91); cf. Dooley and Roe 1999, 112.

52. Mulligan 2019, 170.

53. Dooley 2004, 120–21; Connon 2014, 52.

54. O'Keeffe 2011, 473.

55. Ó Néill 1997, 179; Simms 1994, 27–28.

56. "Acht min bhudh coll crábaid, 7 min bhudh maidnechtnaighi urnaigthi . . . dhúin é" (Stokes 1900, 9 [ll. 287–89]; trans. Dooley and Roe 1999, 11). Máire Ní Mhaonaigh refers to this as the "saint as mediator" motif and identifies similar uses of the motif in other contemporaneous texts, suggesting a broader literary reaction against the pressure to abandon secular topics (2006b, 147). As others have observed, the *Acallam* further situates itself within a dialogue of contemporary church politics in its opening pages with a conspicuous reference to one of the earliest and most fervent reformist foundations in Ireland, the Cistercian Mellifont Abbey, known here as Mainistir Droichit Átha (the monastery of Drogheda): Stokes 1900, 2 (l. 53); cf. Dooley and Roe 1999, 4; Nagy 1997, 319–20; Dooley 2004, 99–100.

57. Ó Néill 1997, 175.

58. Ní Mhaonaigh 2006b, 151–53, quoted at 151; Parsons 2008, 28–38. For instance, the twelfth-century Breton theologian Peter Abelard argued that pagans could be virtuous and could therefore be saved through baptism and the knowledge of Christ (Marenbon 2012, 50–52). As Harry Roe points out, the salvation of virtuous Irish pagans such as Cormac mac Airt, Mórann, Conchúr mac Nessa, and Cú Chulainn is also a strand in earlier Irish writings (1992, 338).

59. "'Cia ro choimét sibhsi mar sin,' ar Pátraic, 'in bar mbeathaidh?' Ocus ro frecair Cáilte.i. 'Fírinde inár croidhedhaibh 7 nertt inár lámhaibh, 7 comall inár tengthaibh'" (Stokes 1900, 4 [ll. 118–20]; translation adapted from Dooley and Roe 1999, 6).

60. "Dámadh ór in duille donn / chuiris di in caill, / dámad airget in gheal tonn / ro thidhluicfed Find" (Stokes 1900, 4 [ll. 116–17]; cf. Dooley and Roe 1999, 6).

61. Stokes 1900, 17–18 (ll. 580–605); cf. Dooley and Roe 1999, 19–20. Here Mac Lughach is born of drunken incest and misbehaves until Fionn redeems him through his tutelage. A late twelfth-century lay beginning *A lía Thulcha Tuaithe shuas* ("Oh stone above on Tulach Thuaithe") alternatively depicts Mac Lughach as the product of a tryst between one of Fionn's men and a fairy woman; prior to joining the Fianna, his mother is said to have raised him "samalta d'adhbar airdríogh" ("like a candidate for high-kingship") (Murphy 1933, 78). In the *Acallam* version, some critics perceive the influence of Continental concepts of chivalry in Fionn's counsel to Mac Lughach, which Ann Dooley observes is "different in quality from the more customary Irish examples of 'advice to a prince' hitherto in circulation" (Dooley 2004, 106; see also Ó Corráin 1987, 36; Nagy 2008, 68–69). Regarding chivalric influence in the later *Agallamh na Seanórach*, see Arbuthnot 2006.

62. "Ni ḟetar locht ar Ḟeind Ḟind / dar in Ri[g] [ḟ]uil os mo chind / acht, a Dé tadhaill talman / gan in Mac do moradhrad" (Stokes 1900, 73 [ll. 2571–72]; cf. Dooley and Roe 1999, 79; translation adapted from Harmon 2001, 69).

63. Stokes 1900, 41 (ll. 1453–58) (God), 52 (ll. 1832–56) (Saint Ciarán), 68–69 (ll. 2408–32) (Saint Caoimhín [Kevin]), 74 (ll. 2606–24) (Saint Máedóc), 75–76 (ll. 2660–87) (Saint

Moling); cf. Dooley and Roe 1999, 45, 56–57, 74–75, 80, 81–82. Caoilte himself spends time with Saint Colmán Éla, from whom he learns to observe the canonical hours (Stokes 1900, 81–84 [ll. 2882–969]; cf. Dooley and Roe 1999, 88–90), and Saint Patrick rescues Fionn's soul from hell, along with members of Caoilte's family (Stokes 1900, 117 [ll. 4116–22]; cf. Dooley and Roe 1999, 122).

64. Stokes 1900, 47–50 (ll. 1659–767); cf. Dooley and Roe 1999, 51–55.

65. See Parsons 2008, 18–28. The story of Garadh mac Morna and the Fenian women (Stokes 1900, 38–41 [ll. 1362–448]; cf. Dooley and Roe 1999, 42–45) is a particularly striking example of the author's reworking of source material pertaining to the hereditary feud to communicate a moral message. For analysis, see Connon 2014, 39–41; Parsons 2008, 19–21; Dooley 2004, 106; Nagy 1989, 151–52. Regarding the lays associated with the story, see chapter 3.

66. Stokes 1900, 55–57, 64–65 (ll. 1943–2033, 2253–305); cf. Dooley and Roe 1999, 60–62, 70–71. Elsewhere we are shown that the leadership of the Fianna alternated between Clann Bhaoiscne and Clann Mhorna, further legitimizing Donn mac Aoidh's assumption of the role: Stokes 1900, 71–72 (ll. 2507–40); cf. Dooley and Roe 1999, 77–78.

67. Stokes 1900, 2, ll. 50–52; cf. Dooley and Roe 1999, 4; Murray 2017a, 32. *Sídh* is a later spelling of *síd*, cited in chapter 1.

68. Dooley 2012, 98.

69. Stokes 1900, 192–203 (ll. 6900–7283); cf. Dooley and Roe 1999, 194–204. The raiders are three exceptionally long-lived sons of the King of Ulster who seek compensation for the death of their grandfather. Caoilte also helps to defeat trios of hostile and exceptionally powerful ravens and does, which have been periodically plaguing the *sídh*. Despite the resolution of these conflicts, we later learn that Patrick will forever banish the Tuatha Dé Danann "ind-étnaib cnocc 7 carracc" ("into the steep slopes of hills and rocks"), neutralizing any remaining threat they and their magic may pose (Stokes 1900, 210 [l. 7535]; trans. Dooley and Roe 1999, 210).

70. See also Carey 2014 on interactions among the Fenian, otherworldly, and Patrician 'worlds.'

71. Flanagan 2010, 184–95.

72. Stokes 1900, 34 (ll. 1205–36); cf. Dooley and Roe 1999, 38.

73. "Ro chindistar in rí do Dia 7 damsa . . . a beith ar aenmnái chengailti, 7 ní ḟuil acainde dul tar in cinded sin" (Stokes 1900, 176–78 [ll. 6361–437, quoted at ll. 6406–7]; trans. Dooley and Roe 1999, 180).

74. Stokes 1900, 216, 219 (ll. 7731–4, 7820–43); cf. Dooley and Roe 1999, 215, 217–18. For further textual and historical analysis, see Dooley and Roe 1999, xxviii–xxx; Dooley 2004, 98, 104–5; Roe 1992, 341–45. Regarding echoes of similar reformist concerns in other contemporary Irish literature, see Ní Mhaonaigh 2006b.

75. Stokes 1900, 219 (l. 7834); cf. Dooley and Roe 1999, 218.

76. Stokes 1900, 25–26 (ll. 872–929, quoted. at l. 923); cf. Dooley and Roe 1999, 28–30. A norm of taxation having thus been established, the reward in this case is merely the wayward man's physical relief.

77. Ecclesiastical patronage was also a virtue promoted by the reformers; see Flanagan 2010, 196–98.

78. Connon 2014, 21–52; Dooley 2004, 112, 120–21. Dooley has suggested the monastery of Achadh Fhabhair (Aghagower) in Co. Mayo as the *locus* of production, while Connon views the monastery of Ros Comáin (Roscommon) in Co. Roscommon as a more likely place of composition. Connon also highlights Roscommon's close affiliation with Clonmacnoise.

79. Connon 2014, 53–56; Dooley 2004, 102–3; Dooley and Roe 1999, xx–xxi, xxix–xxx; Ó Briain 1989b, 185–86; cf. Carey 2014, 76–78. As Dooley argues, social commentary on Cathal Croibhdhearg's marital fidelity—and his brother Ruadhrí's infamous infidelity—is almost certainly embedded in the characterization of Aodh mac Muireadhaigh.

80. See Dooley 2004, 112–13, 122–23.

81. Mulligan 2019, 169. Mulligan posits instead the creation of a space of "virtual travel or mental pilgrimage through landscapes made of words," accessible to audiences who are as likely to be sedentary as traveling (165).

Chapter 3. Heroes of the Gael

1. Caball and Hollo 2006, 78–79, 111; McLeod 2004, 59–60; Mac Cana 1974, 126–27. With regard to poetic learning, it is unclear "whether the emergent poets of the twelfth century simply incorporated the vernacular scholarship of the monastic schools within their repertoire or whether the pre-classical [i.e., early medieval] *filid* and the monastic scholars effectively combined their scholarly expertise in a creative act of cultural self-determination" (Caball and Hollo 2006, 79).

2. Caball and Hollo 2006, 81, 112; Nagy 2003, 39. A temporary recession of English power in fourteenth-century Ireland contributed to the revitalization of the secular literary tradition.

3. McLeod 2004, 55–107.

4. Meek 2003, 19–20, 36; Flahive 2017, 36–37, 40. Sixty-nine lays are preserved in *Duanaire Finn*, while the Book of the Dean of Lismore contains roughly twenty-five Fenian lay texts and fragments. Only four lays appear in both compilations (Meek 2003, 23–28).

5. Meek 2003, 28–32; Flahive 2017, 47–48. Late Scottish collections of lays tend to be orally derived; see chapters 4 and 5.

6. Flahive 2017, 48.

7. While the oral collection of the lay *Dóiteán Tighe Fhinn* (The burning of Fionn's house) in the Isle of Man in the eighteenth century is the only available evidence for the circulation of Fenian lays there, caution must be taken regarding any conclusion reached *in absentia*, given the paucity of sources. See Ó Muircheartaigh 2016.

8. Although less common, learned aspects can still occasionally be observed. See, for instance, *Cairdius Logha ré droing don Fhéin* ("Lugh's kinship with some of the Fianna") and *Innis a Oisín echtaigh* ("Tell, mighty Oisín"), two circa fourteenth-century lays with a genealogical focus, or *Atá fán tulaigh-se thuaidh* ("Beneath this mound to the north"), which consists of a short list of Fenian grave mounds: Murphy 1933, 114–21; Ross 1939, 2–3.

9. MacNeill 1908, 28–30. This is a later version of *Óenach indiu luid in rí* ("Today the king went to a fair").

10. Shields 1993, 4. Fenian lays are sometimes furnished with prose introductions in their manuscript and oral contexts, presumably for this reason. Lays that are "wholly self-contained in their story-line" also exist (Meek 1987, 135).

11. Flahive 2017, 32, 48; Meek 1987, 132–33.

12. Ó Siochfhradha 1941, 277–78; Murphy 1971 [1955], 56–58. The topic of the sweetest sounds is recurrent in the lays.

13. See, e.g., *Do-chonnaic mé teaghlach Finn* ("I have seen the household of Fionn"), *Urnuigh Oisein* (Oisean's prayer), *Oisín is fada do shuan* ("Oisín your slumber is long"); and *Caoidh Oisín i ndiadh na Féinne* (Oisín's lament for the Fianna): Ross 1939, 6–7, 124–35; Murphy 1933, 204–15; Ó Siochfhradha 1941, 227–40.

14. See, e.g., *Rosg Ghoill mhic Mhorna* (The incitement of Goll mac Morna) and *Rosg Osguir mhic Oisín re hucht Chatha Gabhra* (The incitement of Oscar son of Oisín before the Battle of Gabhair): Ross 1939, 60–69; Ó Siochfhradha 1941, 198–99.

15. Bruford 1969, 1, 5, 9–11, 27, 33, 36–40; Flahive 2017, 49–50. See also Nagy 1987.

16. Ó hUiginn 1995, 61. For instance, the late seventeenth-century romance *Eachtra Thailc mhic Thréin* (The adventure of Tailc mac Tréin) was based on the popular circa sixteenth-century lay *Cath Chnoic an Áir* (The Battle of the Hill of Slaughter): Ní Mhuirgheasa 1952, xiii, xiv; Murphy 1971 [1955], 58.

17. When verse is incorporated, it tends to be confined to passages of dialogue that have already been summarized or introduced in prose, a pattern descendent from the early literature (Bruford 1969, 34, 42n13).

18. Alan Bruford's bibliography of heroic romances provides a helpful but incomplete record of manuscript copies. While Bruford lists seventy-eight source entries for *Bruidhean Chaorthainn* (The enchanted hall of the rowan tree), for instance, Breandán Ó Cróinín has more recently documented ninety copies (Bruford 1969, 251–52; Ó Cróinín 1995, 12–33). Most romances are preserved in late manuscripts and their dates of composition are difficult to determine, but Bruford posits that "the best of them can probably be assigned to the late fifteenth and sixteenth centuries" (Bruford 1969, 5, 47–48, 70, quoted at 5; see also Murphy 1971 [1955], 49).

19. The pre-Christian setting of Fenian romance marks yet another difference from European (and particularly French) courtly romance, in which religious sentiment is prominent; see Bruford 1969, 24–26.

20. The title assigned by Murphy, "The Slaying of the Pig of Formaoíl and the Death of Fionn," is more appropriate than the one given by Kuno Meyer, "The Chase of Síd na mBan Finn and the Death of Finn," which invites comparison with an unrelated later lay, *Seilg Sléibhe na mBan* (The chase on Slievenamon) (Murphy 1953, 136; Meyer 1910, xxxi, 52–99). The story is an expanded version of the account of Fionn's death in battle with the Luaighne discussed in chapter 1. The text is incomplete and Fionn's death is omitted.

21. "Dosuidhighedh ocus dosrethnaigedh in tsealg leó fo ḟeadhuibh 7 fo ḟásaigibh 7 fo ḟánglenntuiph na ferann ba coimnesa dóip 7 fo muighib réidhe roáilli ocus fo chailltib clithardlúithe ocus fó dhoiredhuib dosleathna dímóra. Ocus dochúaid gach duine fo leth d' fíanaib hÉrenn ina dumha sealga 7 ina láthair licthe 7 ina berna báegail mar no gnáthaighdís cosgur gacha sealga do chur roimi sin. Ocus nírb inonn dóip in lá-sin 7 gach lái ele, oir do ceiled in selg-sin orra, co nách fúaratur mucc ná míl ná brecc [i.e., bréch] ná brocc ná dam ná eilit ná mang ná ógláegh allaid asa ndergfad nech díb a lá[i]m in lá-sin" (Meyer 1910, 52–53; translation adapted from Meyer). Regarding contemporary hunting practices, see Fitzpatrick 2013, 111–17 and McManus 2018. McManus contends that *láthair licthe* is a place where hounds would be slipped from their leashes, while *berna báegail* is a gap in the pass through which the quarry would be driven (161n32, 171).

22. Bruford 1969, 1, 5, 46–47; Ní Mhunghaile 2010b, 21; Ní Mhunghaile 2012, 224–26.

23. Shields 1993, 16, 18; Bruford 1986. Regarding oral collecting, see part three.

24. Nagy 1987, 12–13; Meek 1987, 138. Compare Bruford's claim that the length, complexity, and minimal divergences among manuscript copies shows that the romances were intended to be transmitted in written form rather than via oral narration. The stark distinction he draws between upper-class literary and lower-class oral traditions prior to the seventeenth century is difficult to accept. He may have been overstating his case in reaction to Gerard Murphy's claims of oral origins for several Fenian romances (or parts thereof), some of which he refutes. See Bruford 1969, 2–5; Murphy 1953, xiii–xxxvii; Nagy 1987, 11.

25. Caball and Hollo 2006, 94, 111; Gunderloch 2013, 74. There are rare exceptions to the tendency not to ascribe authorship. For instance, the circa fifteenth-century *Laoidh Dhiarmaid* (The lay of Diarmaid) and *Tuarasgabháil Chatha Gabhra* (The account of the Battle of Gabhair) are said to have been composed by Ailéin mac Ruaidhrí, an otherwise unknown poet, but these ascriptions are uncertain (Ross 1939, 70, 152; Meek 1990, 350, 358). *Filí* is the modern form of the Old Irish word *filid*, for which see chapter 1.

26. Authors with less formal training than the *filí* are also known to have composed in Early Modern Gaelic. For instance, Gearóid Iarla (Gerald FitzGerald), third Earl of Desmond, composed courtly love poetry in *ógláchas* meters in the fourteenth century. Although he made a point of referencing Diarmaid and Gráinne's flight from Fionn numerous times in his poems, he is unlikely to have composed extended Fenian material: Mac Niocaill 1963; Ní Shéaghdha 1967, xiii–xiv; Ó hUiginn 2018, 48–52.

27. Flahive 2004, 103; Flahive 2017, 32.

28. Ó Caithnia 1984, 20–21, 74–78. Donald Meek suggests that lays with "unusually strict metrical form[s]" may have originated as apologues (1987, 135).

29. McManus 2017, 194–201; McLeod 2004, 179–82.

30. Meek 1987, 136. It is notable that eighteenth- and nineteenth-century poets like Aindrias Mac Craith and Tomás Rua Ó Súilleabháin listed Fenian lays and romances among the most esteemed contents of their manuscript collections, and the accomplished late seventeenth- to early eighteenth-century poet Dáibhí Ó Bruadair was said to be an eloquent teller of Fenian tales: Ó hÓgáin 1990, 3–4; Griffin-Wilson 2010, 13.

31. Ó hUiginn 2003, 99.

32. Late lays include, among others, *Laoidh Oisín i dTír na nÓg* (Lay of Oisín in the Land of Youth, tenuously ascribed to Mícheál Coimín); *Suirghe Ghuill* (Goll's courting, by Seán Ó Neachtain); *Lá dhúinne ar Sliabh Fuaid* ("One day as we were on Sliabh Fuaid"), which differs from *Seilg Sléibhe Fuaid* (The chase on Sliabh Fuaid) and may have been composed by Muiris Ó Gormáin; *Laoidh Chab an Dosáin* (The lay of Cab an Dosáin); *Suirghe Fhinn go Críocha Lochlann* (Fionn's courting in Lochlann); *Laoidh Cholann gan Cheann* (The lay of the headless body); *Laoidh Mheargaigh na Lann* (The lay of Meargach of the blades); *Laoidh Mná Mheargaigh* (The lay of the wife of Meargach); and *Laoidh na h-Ighinne* (The lay of the maiden): Ó Briain 1989b, 181–83; Ó Briain 1984, 160; Ó Dubhthaigh 1958, 35; McCann 2012; Ó Briain 1995, 72; Ní Mhunghaile 2009a, II. 62; Ní Mhuirgheasa 1952, xiii. *Laoidh na h-Ighinne* was composed in Scottish Gaelic; the others were composed in Irish.

33. See Ní Mhurchú 2012 for a discussion of this sequence of lays, which was named after the title of the first text.

34. Ó Briain 1989b, 182.

35. Ó hÓgáin 1988, 270, 274; Bruford 1969, 50–51, 259, 262. *Eachtra an Deirg* remains unedited. This Dearg is Fionn's son.

36. Cf. Flahive 2017, 34, 37.

37. The circumstances surrounding Fionn's birth and youth are described in the expanded romance *Cath Cnucha* and in four lays postdating the fourteenth century: *Sgríobh sin a Bhrógain sgribhinn* ("Write that, Brógan, a composition"), *Turas Fhinn go Teamhraigh* (Fionn's foray to Tara), *Mar Chaidh Cumhall a Mharbhadh* (The death of Cumhall), and *Laoidh na Buadhachta* (The lay of the victory): Maignéar 1884–85; MacNeill 1908, 33–34; Murphy 1933, 336–61; Ross 1939, 184–89; Anon. 1825, 36–39. Regarding the death tale, see Meyer 1910, xxxi, 52–99. Other early stories expanded into romances include *Cath Mhaighe Mochruimhe* (The Battle of Magh Mucramha) and *Tóruigheacht Dhiarmada agus Ghráinne* (The pursuit of Diarmaid and Gráinne).

38. Propp 1968, 26–65; Barbara Hillers, personal communication, February 25, 2014; cf. Nagy 1987, 12–13. Northrop Frye similarly posited that romance literature "descended from [the] folktale" (1976, 6–15, quoted at 15). Others have noted the "universality of romance structures," and have therefore found it useful to examine heroic romance from a Proppian structuralist perspective (Saunders 1993, xii). While the search for oral or literary origins may ultimately be counterproductive, such studies provide yet another reminder of the regular interplay between orality and literacy not only in heroic romance, but in Fenian literature generally.

39. See also Sumner 2024.

40. Pearse 1908. See also Ó Cróinín 2013, 487–94; Ó hÓgáin 1988, 212–16; Murphy 1971 [1955], 53; Bruford 1969, 115–16, 251–52.

41. Ní Mhuirgheasa 1941. See also Ó Cróinín 2013, 494–97; Ó hÓgáin 1988, 207–12, 288–89; Bruford 1969, 117–18, 257–58.

42. Joynt 1936, 14–20 (ll. 471–659). See also Ó hÓgáin 1988, 234–36, 238–41; Bruford 1969, 118, 261; Christiansen 1931, 30–33.

43. Ní Shéaghdha 1941, 3–15. See also Ó Cróinín 2013, 483–86; Ó hÓgáin 1988, 204–5; Bruford 1969, 116–17, 252; Christiansen 1931, 30. Breandán Ó Cróinín posits that *Bruidhean Chéise Corainn* may have been composed as early as the turn of the fourteenth century, given that the thirteenth- or fourteenth-century lay beginning *Uathadh damh sa coirthe-so* ("Alone am I on this crag") appears to reference the story: MacNeill 1908, 91–92; Ó Cróinín 2013, 486; cf. Murphy 1953, 79. We do not know whether the poet's referend was this literary romance or an earlier version of the tale, however. Assuming the latter, Ó hÓgain dates *Bruidhean Chéise Corainn* "some centuries later" than *Uathadh damh sa coirthe-so* (1988, 204).

44. Hyde and Ó Caomhánaigh 1930. See also Ó hÓgáin 1988, 270–72; Bruford 1969, 50, 262. *Cuireadh Mhaoil Uí Mhanannáin* dates to the eighteenth century.

45. Ó Siochfhradha 1941, 93–110. See also Ó hÓgáin 1988, 266. According to Ó hÓgáin, Sliabh Fuaid is Deadman's Hill in Co. Armagh.

46. Ó Siochfhradha 1941, 137–45. See also Ó hÓgáin 1988, 266–27. *Seilg Ghleanna an Smóil* is also known as *Laoidh na Mná Móire* (The lay of the big woman).

47. McCann 2012. See also Ó hÓgáin 1988, 272–73. *Laoidh Chab an Dosáin* probably dates to the eighteenth century.

48. Ó Gallchobhair et al. 1915, 17–46. See also Ó hÓgáin 1988, 224–26; Bruford 1969, 109–11, 266; Murphy 1971 [1955], 50.

49. Ó Siochfhradha 1939b. See also Ó hÓgáin 1988, 228–32; Bruford 1969, 111–12, 261; Murphy 1971 [1955], 50.

50. Ní Shéaghdha 1967. See also Murray 2018; Ó hUiginn 2018; Ó hÓgáin 1988, 170–77; Bruford 1969, 106–9, 265–66.

51. Love triangles are certainly found elsewhere in medieval romance, however. Regarding potential intertextual or developmental relationships among the story of Diarmaid and Gráinne and other triadic tales, see Shercliff 2022, 94–98; Velasco López 2018; Theuerkauf 2017; Nagy 2015. In *Tóruigheacht Dhiarmada agus Ghráinne,* the love triangle is sublimated to an inverted *toraíocht* plot.

52. Ó Siochfhradha 1941, 24–31. See also Ó hÓgáin 1988, 223–24, 267–69. *Cath Chnuic an Áir* is also known as *Laoidh Thailc mhic Thréin* (The lay of Tailc [strong one] son of Tréan [powerful one]). It inspired several sequels, all of which are included in the late *Agallamh Oisín agus Phádraig: Laoidh Mheargaigh na Lann, Laoidh Mná Mheargaigh, Anmanna na Laochra do thit ar Chnoc an Áir* (The names of the warriors who fell at the hill of slaughter), *Anmanna na nGadhar is na gCon* (The names of the dogs and hounds), and *Seilg Sléibhe Fuaid*; see Ní Mhurchú 2012, 196–97. See further *Eachtra Thailc mhic Thréin*, a prose expansion of *Cath Chnoic an Áir*: Ní Mhuirgheasa 1952, xiii, xiv.

53. Ross 1939, 136–47; Ó Siochfhradha 1941, 151–54. *Cath Rìgh na Sorcha* is also known as *Eas Ruaidh* (Assaroe) and *Laoidh an Mhoighre Bhoirb* (The lay of Moighre Borb [handsome fierce one]).

54. Campbell 1872, 133, 135–37.

55. *Suirghe Ghuill* was composed by Seán Ó Neachtain in March 1713, according to a colophon in the author's hand in National Library of Ireland MS G 62, pp. 80–81: Ní Shéaghdha 1961, 92. Standish Hayes O'Grady (1926, 637) summarized it, but I am not aware of a published edition. There is a note of burlesque in that the distressed damsel is a Trojan who brings Goll, her champion, home to meet her father.

56. For a similar episode in the *Acallam* (noted in chapter 2), see Stokes 1900, 163–68 (ll. 5917–6082); cf. Dooley and Roe 1999, 166–70. Unfortunately, the women in such circumstances usually die, whether of shame or in the proximate armed conflict.

57. Bruford 1969, 8; Murphy 1953, xiii.

58. Pearse 1906. See also Ó hÓgáin 1988, 258–61, Bruford 1969, 129, 252–53; Murphy 1971 [1955], 50.

59. Ó hÓgáin 1988, 257–58; Bruford 1969, 123–27, 258. Although only three unedited nineteenth-century manuscript witnesses of *Eachtra Chéadaigh Mhóir* are extant, the tale's widespread popularity in the oral tradition suggests an earlier date of composition, as Dáithí Ó hÓgáin recognizes. Bruford dubs it a folktale, while Ó hÓgáin posits a lost literary text from which all known versions descend. The extent of initial literary or oral composition is likely unknowable and arguably irrelevant to an appreciation of the story in its extant literary and oral forms.

60. See also the episode in the *Acallam* in which three specially skilled sons of the king of a land called Irúaith, along with a wondrous hound that vomits liquor and emits magically fatal flatus, serve the Fianna as helpers in a battle against three Tuatha Dé Danann aggressors: Stokes 1900, 149–50, 152–53, 154, 168–73 (ll. 5452–86, 5555–88, 5617–24, 6083–269); cf. Dooley and Roe 1999, 152–53, 155–56, 157, 171–76. This episode is related to the twelfth-century lay beginning *Dám thrír táncatar ille* ("A company of three thus came"), for which see Stern 1900a; Christiansen 1931, 78–83.

61. Bergin and MacNeill 1905. See also Ó hÓgáin 1988, 261–63; Bruford 1969, 115, 262. *Eachtra Lomnochtáin* also displays aspects of a *bruíon* tale in that the Fianna are incapacitated by a drink at Lomnochtán's house and require the help of a local woman to escape. Although Lomnochtán means 'naked one,' this antagonist is not nude.

62. Ní Mhuirgheasa 1954. See also Hoyne 2015; Ó hÓgáin 1988, 263–65; Bruford 1969, 267.

63. Connellan 1829a, 6–8. See also Ó Briain 1995; Christiansen 1931, 183–88, 195–96. *Suirghe Fhinn go Críocha Lochlann* is an expansion of the earlier *Laoidh Chrumlinn na gCath* (Lay of Crumlann of the battles), for which see Campbell 1872, 83–86; Ó Briain 1995.

64. MacNeill 1908, 61–75; Christiansen 1931, 94–95. Sorcha is a variously located land of wonder; see Bruford 1969, 21, 22, 29n1.

65. See Bruford 1969, 8–9, 20–22, 24. Bruford views the *bruíon* tale as a sub-form of the overseas adventure tale, the travel location in this case being an otherworldly abode. Since most *bruíon* stories entail an accidental rather than purposeful journey into the otherworld and confinement to a single space rather than free exploration, I am more inclined to view the *bruíon* and overseas adventure themes as unrelated, if occasionally coexistent.

66. Regarding the shoreline, see Nicolaisen 1983, 157–58.

67. Bruford 1969, 8–9.

68. O'Rahilly 1962. See also Ó hÓgáin 1988, 146–49, 289; Bruford 1969, 118–20, 253. Early references appear in *Laoidh Scéith Fhinn* (The lay of Fionn's shield), *Laoidh Colga Chaoilti* (The lay of Caoilte's sword), and *A lia Thulcha Tuaithe shuas*: MacNeill 1908, 37; Murphy 1933, 86, 124. Compare the description of the Battle of Ventry in the *Acallam*: Stokes 1900, 21–25 (ll. 718–868); cf. Dooley and Roe 1999, 24–28.

69. MacNeill 1908, 55–57; Christiansen 1931, 91–93. The earliest version of *Cath na bPunann*, dated to circa 1200, takes place in Ireland, but modern Scottish versions localize the invasion to Tiree.

70. Murphy 1933, 362–69; Christiansen 1931, 97–131, 249–83. Some translators anglicize Airgheann's name as Erragon.

71. Ó Siochfhradha 1941, 155–60; Christiansen 1931, 131–56. Mánus is also found elsewhere in the tradition, including in an incomplete prose text preserved in the same manuscript as *Duanaire Finn*. His name sometimes appears as Magnus in translation, and the character may ultimately derive from the historical king Magnus Barelegs of Norway who invaded Ireland circa 1100; see Christiansen 1931, 88, 90, 156–71, 401–6.

72. Campbell 1872, 59, 68–71, 80–82, 223–24; Christiansen 1931, 215–31. Hags like the Muileartach invariably possess dangerous magical abilities.

73. For *Laoidh an Deirg mhic Droichil*, see Murphy 1933, 298–317; Ó hÓgáin 1988, 218. For *Laoidh Choinn mhic an Deirg*, see Campbell 1872, 113–21; Thomson 1952, 56. There is also a late

lay, *Dearg mac Deirg* (Dearg son of Dearg), that purports to be a lament composed by Dearg's wife after his friends have tried to test her love by pretending he has been killed by a boar. It is unclear if this is meant to be the same Dearg (Campbell 1872, 113; Thomson 1952, 56–57).

74. Ní Shéaghdha 1941, 16–39. See also Ó Cróinín 2013, 498–99; Ó hÓgáin 1988, 196–98; Bruford 1969, 120, 251. *Bruidhean* can refer to a dwelling or a fight; the homonymic wordplay in the title *Bruidhean Bheag na hAlmhaine* is almost certainly intentional.

75. See the twelfth- or thirteenth-century *Bás Ghuill mhic Morna* (The death of Goll mac Morna) and the modern Scottish Gaelic *Bàs Chairill* (The death of Caireall): MacNeill 1908, 58–61; Murphy 1953, 49–52; Campbell 1872, 166–72. Elsewhere, Caireall is said to have fallen in the Battle of Gabhair; see *Laoidh Chatha Gabhra* (The lay of the Battle of Gabhair): Ó Siochfhradha 1941, 204. He first appears as the son or grandson of Fionn's cousin Conbhrón, later as the son of Fionn, and he is said to have been fostered by the king of Scotland, where he subsequently resides: see Ó Briain 2003, 68; MacNeill 1908, 9, 60.

76. Bruford did not prioritize battle tales and appears to have disregarded the early modern *Cath Cnucha* (1969, 1, 129). Over forty manuscript copies survive, but the only published text is Daniel Magner's serialized edition in the *Irish-American* (Briody 1995; Flower 1926, 397–98; Maignéar 1884–85).

77. See *Mallacht Ghuill mhic Morna* (Goll mac Morna's malediction), *Tiomna Ghuill mhic Morna* (The testament of Goll mac Morna), *Bás Ghuill mhic Morna*, and *Uathadh damh sa coirthe-so*, and compare the account in the *Acallam*: MacNeill 1908, 22–24, 58–61, 86–92; Stokes 1900, 56 (ll. 1965–71); cf. Dooley and Roe 1999, 60. Goll's wife's role in bearing witness to his final words is comparable to that of Fothadh Canainne's consort in *Reicne Fothaid Canainne* (The *reicne* of Fothadh Canainne), discussed in chapter 1.

78. See Mac Cana 1980, 41–81; cf. Rees and Rees 1961, 207–11.

79. Meyer 1904b, 346. *Roscad* is a deliberately obscure style of early Irish poetry, features of which are the "use of language as a means for asserting dominance or exercising power; and a concern with the future, whether descriptive or prescriptive" (Carey 1996, 24).

80. See *Cétemain* (May Day): Meyer 1881–83, 201–2; Nagy 1985, 214–15. See also Carey 1997, 41, 47; Nagy 1985, 17–40.

81. Joynt 1936, 38 (l. 1287), 40–41. Fionn does recite poetry in *Feis Tighe Chonáin*, but not as a demonstration of inspired wisdom.

82. See *A bhean labhrus rinn an laoidh* and *A Oissín in ráidhe rinn* (MacNeill 1908, 85; Murphy 1933, 154–66).

83. Pearse 1908, 15–16. Ó Cróinín's edition from the earliest manuscript copy uses the same phrase for the revelation of knowledge as *Feis Tighe Chonáin*: namely, *fios 7 fíoreolas* (1995, 169 [l. 164]).

84. E.g., the circa twelfth-century poem *Bec innocht lúth mo dá lúa* ("Small tonight the vigour of my heels") is voiced by Caoilte (Meyer 1904a, 72–73).

85. "Ní gabthái fer díb so co mbo rífili dá leabar déc na filidheachta" ("Not a man of these was taken until he was a prime poet versed in the twelve books of poetry") (O'Grady 1892a, 92; translation adapted from O'Grady 1892b, 100). That Geoffrey Keating (Seathrún Céitinn) included this requirement in his early seventeenth-century *Foras Feasa ar Éirinn* (Compendium of knowledge about Ireland) suggests that it may have been broadly known in the late medieval and early modern periods (1908, 332).

86. See, e.g., *Ro loiscit na láma-sa* ("These hands have been withered"); *A bhen dén folcadh mo chinn*; *Do bhádhusa úair fa folt buidhe cas* ("Once I was yellow-haired, ringleted"); *Is fada anocht a n-Oil Finn* ("This night is long in Elphin"): Murphy 1956, 166–67; MacNeill 1908, 14–17, 80; Murphy 1933, 194–96.

87. Indeed, in *Eachtra Iollainn Iolchrothaigh* (The adventure of Iollann Iolchrothach [handsome Iollann]), Cormac mac Airt defers an invader by informing him that Fionn is the true king

of Ireland: Ó Gallchobhair et al. 1915, 51. This ruse becomes a serious query in some modern folklore versions of the story; see, e.g., Fear na Muintire 1900.

88. Murphy 1933, 230–231; translation adapted from Murphy.

89. Meyer 1910, 84.

90. Ross 1939, 154–55 (ll. 1955–57); translation adapted from Ross. Compare the circa sixteenth-century *Oisín is fada do shuan*, in which Oisín tells Saint Patrick, "Do bhí in domhan fa chíos . . . ní fhacus rí os a chionn" ("the world paid him tribute . . . I have seen no greater king than him") (Murphy 1933, 209).

91. Owen and Davidson 2009. The tendency of power to corrupt has also been observed in business and military environments.

92. See, e.g., *Laoidh Laighne Mhóir*, where "do-rinne sé sith go cóir" ("he made peace righteously") (Murphy 1933, 230–31); and the fifteenth-century *bruíon* lay *Cliabhán cuill cía do-róine* ("Who made a hazel [bird] crib"), where Fionn is described as a ruler (*flaith*) who exhibited such great clemency (*iocht*) "[nach raibh] commaith einigh Finn a nduine re a linn a celí" ("[that] no one living in his age had nobility equal to that of Fionn") (Murphy 1933, 64–65; translations adapted from Murphy).

93. Ó Gallchobhair et al. 1915, 52–53. See also Ó hÓgáin 1988, 220–21; Bruford 1969, 120, 262–63.

94. Sumner 2018, 122, 134. See also the thirteenth- or fourteenth-century lay *Éuchtach inghen Díarmatta* (Éuchtach daughter of Diarmaid), in which Diarmaid's sons, under the command of his daughter, pursue a campaign of vengeance against Fionn for his role in Diarmaid's death (MacNeill 1908, 45–47). Regarding the death by boar motif, see Carey 2022.

95. Ní Shéaghdha 1967, 94–96.

96. The location of Gabhair is uncertain. Eighteenth- and nineteenth-century scholars accepted the historicity of the battle and presumed it to have taken place in Counties Meath or Dublin (Gunderloch 1997, 161).

97. O'Kearney 1854, 134–36. See also Ó hÓgáin 1988, 149–50. *Cath Gabhra* is atypical in that it portrays Diarmaid and Goll as still living and fighting alongside the Fianna. O'Kearney dates the text to the fifteenth or sixteenth century based on its literary style. It likely postdates at least some of the lays about the battle (Gunderloch 1997, 170–71).

98. See *Tuarasgabháil Chatha Gabhra* and *A Oisín, cía in feart dona* ("Oisín, what is the unfortunate grave") (Ross 1939, 152; Murphy 1933, 38–40).

99. According to some sources, the Fianna are also lacking a leader, Fionn having either died or departed on an anachronistic pilgrimage (*oilithre*); see, e.g., *A Oisín, cía in feart dona* (Murphy 1933, 34). In *Laoidh Chatha Gabhra* this power vacuum leads to bickering about who will lead the Fianna into battle (Ó Siochfhradha 1941, 201–2). The romance conversely has Fionn commanding a still-united Clann Mhorna and Clann Bhaoiscne, while Geoffrey Keating centers the Fenian dynastic conflict in his seventeenth-century retelling by aligning Clann Mhorna with Cairbre for seven years prior to the battle, which they incite in order to get Clann Bhaoiscne banished (O'Kearney 1854, 134–52; Keating 1908, 354).

100. Murphy 1933, 40–52; Ross 1939, 152–66; cf. Ross 1939, 148–50 (*Bàs Oscair* [The death of Oscar]) and Campbell 1872, 182–85 (*Cath Ghabhra nam Beumannan* [The Battle of Gabhair of the Blows]). Other accounts of the battle differ in making another warrior responsible for Cairbre's death; see Gunderloch 1997, 160–69. Some sources also reference a subsequent battle fought by the remaining Fianna—Cath Ollarbha—in which Caoilte kills Fothadh Canainne's brother Fothadh Airgtheach, then high king of Ireland; see *Scél asa mberar combad hé Find mac Cumhaill Mongán* (A story in which it is said that Fionn mac Cumhaill was Mongán), *Acallam na Senórach*, and Keating's *Foras Feasa ar Éirinn*: White 2006, 74, 81; Stokes 1900, 31–32 (ll. 1093–144); cf. Dooley and Roe 1999, 35–36; Keating 1908, 356.

101. Ó Siochfhradha 1941, 142–43.

102. MacNeill 1908, 57.

103. Murphy 1933, 12. See also Ó hÓgáin 1988, 205–6; Christiansen 1931, 197–215. *Laoidh na Ceardcha* is known in Scottish Gaelic as *Duan na Ceàrdaich*. Before his rechristening, Caoilte was known variably as Daolghas or Daorghlas.

104. For the Middle Irish accounts of the birth of Mac Lughach, 'son of Lughach,' to an otherworldly woman, or alternatively to Fionn's daughter, after whom he is known, see *A lia Thulcha Tuaithe shuas* and the *Acallam*: Murphy 1933, 66–78; Stokes 1900, 16–18 (ll. 536–605); cf. Dooley and Roe 1999, 18–20. See also *A Lorcáin mheic Luighdheach Lain* ("Oh Lorcán son of Lughaidh Lán") and *Cairdius Logha ré droing don Fhéin*: Murphy 1933, 24–30, 114. Although usually called Mac Lughach, his given name is Gaoine and he is sometimes referred to as Caol. Other characters who appear somewhat regularly include Fionn's sons Faolán, Aodh Beag, Raighne, and Iollann, as well as Caireall (known as a son of Fionn in Scottish but not Irish sources), Mac Reithe, and Fathadh Canainn (i.e., Fothadh Canainne, reinterpreted as one of the Fianna).

105. Joynt 1936, 21–23 (ll. 698–766). See also the short circa fourteenth-century account of this story in Murphy 1953, 103–4. Ó Briain notes comparable oral accounts (1996, 187–89).

106. Ó Siochfhradha 1941, 170–75; Christiansen 1931, 171–82. A version of this story also appears in *Bruidhean Eochaidh Bhig Dheirg*, where Bran's own special heroic attribute is revealed: a deadly right claw ordinarily sheathed in a silver shoe: Ní Mhuirgheasa 1941, 60. Bran appears in the literature as early as the late twelfth-century *Laoidh Síthil Caoilti* (The lay of Caoilte's drinking vessel): MacNeill 1908, 40; Ó Briain 1996, 180–81.

107. See Flahive forthcoming. For an analysis of Goll as a Connacht hero, see Ní Uigín 2009.

108. Meyer 1912c.

109. See *Macgnímartha Finn, Fotha Catha Cnucha* (The reason for the Battle of Cnucha), and *Cath Cnucha*: Meyer 1881–83, 197; Hennessy 1873–75, 88–92; Maignéar 1884–85 (January 3, 1885), 3. Compare *Mar Chaidh Cumhall a Mharbhadh*, in which Garadh claims broader culpability in Cumhall's death, alleging that each Clann Mhorna man struck him with a spear (Ross 1939, 184–89; Ó hÓgáin 1988, 144). See also the accounts of Fionn's assumption of the leadership of the Fianna in *Acallam na Senórach* and *Uathadh damh sa coirthe-so* (Stokes 1900, 50 [ll. 1756–65]; cf. Dooley and Roe 1999, 54; MacNeill 1908, 91). For a late medieval account of Goll's name, see *Sgéla Catha Cruinn-mhóna* ("Tidings of the Battle of Cronnmhóin"): MacNeill 1908, 12.

110. Ó Murchadha 2009. *Ligi Guill i mMaig Raigni* details great losses on both sides of a decisive battle between Clann Mhorna and Clann Bhaoiscne.

111. Ní Shéaghdha 1941, 7–14.

112. Murphy 1933, 366–68.

113. Ross 1939, 144.

114. Ó Gallchobhair et al. 1915, 26–42.

115. See, e.g., *A Oisín, cía in feart dona* (Murphy 1933, 34, 40, 48, 50).

116. MacNeill 1908, 10; Murphy 1953, 10. The account of this incident in the *Acallam* reworks the story to communicate a moral message: Stokes 1900, 38–41 (ll. 1362–448); cf. Dooley and Roe 1999, 42–45. Compare *A Gharaidh, triallmaoid go Fionn* ("Garadh, let us go to Fionn"), in which Goll's brothers alternatively plot to avenge his death by killing Oisín, Oscar, and Caoilte (Ross 1939, 4).

117. See *Dóiteán Tighe Fhinn* (Gwynn 1904). Modern Scottish accounts add that Garadh chooses both his executioner and the mode of execution: his head is to rest on Fionn's thigh and Fionn's sword, which must cut through what it strikes, is to be used. Although protective materials are placed upon Fionn's thigh, he is still injured, and some storytellers thus explain Fionn's absence from the Battle of Gabhair by his need to seek healing for his leg in Rome. Others relate Garadh's execution to *Duan na Ceàrdaich* (i.e., *Laoidh na Ceardcha*), stating that the damage done to Fionn's sword required its re-forging by the otherworldly smith. See, e.g., Campbell 1872, 178; MacLellan 1961, 14–19.

118. Twelfth- to thirteenth-century lays describe Conán as a foolhardy (*cennbhάoth*) but valiant (*go ngoil*) man, "nár sechain tegmháil enfhir" ("who shunned battle against no one"). While both Caireall and Conán were contrarian, moreover, "ba hé Cairioll bói for ceill / Conán ba ghnáth ar mícheill" ("Caireall was sensible [and] Conán generally lacked sense"); see *Bás Ghuill mhic Morna* and *Fleadh ros fúair Corbmac ó Fhionn* (Mac Neill 1908, 60, 62, 63). The *Acallam* adds that Conán was "mellgalach muintire . . . 7 trotach (airecht)a 7 deabthach laithrech, 7 nir' tsir cóir ar duine (riam, 7 tuc) a mallacht don duine doberad cóir dó" ("the rowdy one of the retinue, the quarrelsome one of the nobility, and the contentious one of the battle-line; he never treated anyone fairly, and he cursed anyone who treated him fairly") (Stokes 1900, 186 [ll. 6708–10]; translation adapted from Dooley and Roe 1999, 188). Compare, however, *Domhnach lodmair lar Lúachair* ("One Sunday we went over Luachair"), in which he is depicted hunting a magic boar alongside Fionn, with no negative associations (Murphy 1933, 190).

119. Pearse 1908, 27–33; Ó Cróinín 1995, 174–76. The denuding incident is incredibly popular in modern Fenian folklore. Ó hÓgáin also notes a classical Greek parallel (1988, 216). Regarding Patrick Pearse's bowdlerization of the incident in his edition, see Breatnach 2009, 198–99.

120. Bergin and MacNeill 1905, 11, 15–18, 21–22.

121. Ó Siochfhradha 1941, 105–7.

122. "Conán nár dhian i gcath / 's nár iarr cáil gaiscidh ná gnímh" (Ó Siochfhradha 1941, 38, quoted at 49).

123. See, e.g., Ó hÓgáin 1988, 261; Murphy 1971 [1955], 59.

124. Mac Cana 1975, 86, 96. While there are earlier depictions of hostile *Lochlannaigh* in Gaelic literature, the use of the motif is limited prior to its inclusion in the Fenian literary corpus (80–81). See also Ní Mhaonaigh 2006a.

125. As Reidar Thoralf Christiansen first noted, the *Lochlannaigh* in Gaelic texts can be seen to parallel the Saracens in medieval French romance (1931, 38). Early medieval sources depict the Tuatha Dé Danann and the Fomorians as earlier waves of settlers in Ireland who were subsequently overcome and displaced. In later texts, Fomorians may appear as generic giants, and may be aligned with the Tuatha Dé Danann; see, e.g., the "fomhóir ur-ghránna" ("very ugly Fomorian / giant") in *Bruidhean Eochaidh Bhig Dheirg* (Ní Mhuirgheasa 1941, 67, 71).

126. Mac Cana 1975, 94–96.

127. Mac Cana 1980, 129. Mac Cana is here interested in the production of Middle Irish metrical tracts and other expository texts that he maintains were intended to justify the learned classes' valued position in a time of great uncertainty. His observation can be extended, however.

128. See, e.g., Hirschberger 2018.

129. Ó Súilleabháin 1976, 474–82; Covington 2022, 262–81.

130. The situation is arguably more ideologically complex in Scotland, given the acknowledged Norse and Gaelic cultural integration in the Western Isles. Even so, the historical record, though meager, indicates that the early Norse raids on Scotland were just as devastating as those on Ireland (Duncan 1989, 56–57, 79, 83–86). Settlement and cultural integration also took place in Ireland, moreover, and the 'Viking' side in the Battle of Clontarf was more diverse than popular recollection holds.

131. See, e.g., Ó Giolláin 1994–95, 169.

132. Detailed exploration of the *Lochlannaigh* in individual texts as potential calques for contemporary foes will need to take into account the ethnic diversity of Gaelic-speaking people. While many might have associated the *Lochlannaigh* with an Anglo-Norman 'other,' for instance, Gaelicized Anglo-Normans must certainly have had more nuanced views. Such complexity is evident in Caoimhín Breatnach's discussion of *Cath Fionntrágha*, referenced below.

133. Ó Murchadha 2009, xxxii; cf. Flahive forthcoming.

134. Versions of the story of this battle date back at least to the twelfth century, as we have seen.

135. Breatnach 1994–95, 143–53, quoted at 153; Breatnach 1995; O'Rahilly 1962, vii–x.

136. Ó hUiginn 2018, 52–53, 56–57; Murray 2018, 41–42. Ruairí Ó hUiginn stresses the likelihood that other early modern versions of the Diarmaid and Gráinne story existed elsewhere, despite not being reflected in the extant manuscript tradition of *Tóruigheacht Dhiarmada agus Ghráinne*. Perhaps there was less inclination to commit such versions to parchment in regions in which those with the means to commission manuscripts had weaker ties to the subject matter.

137. Gillies 1987, 58–9, 61; see also Ó hUiginn 2018, 67–69. I owe this suggestion to Lorena Alessandrini. The Campbells' ancestral association with Diarmaid appears to have begun in the popular sphere, perhaps in association with the family's political ascendance from the fourteenth century. Although William Gillies notes that those of a scholarly caste largely avoided the association prior to the seventeenth-century disintegration of the Gaelic learned system, this hesitancy may not have precluded a poet from gesturing to it obliquely in a lay.

138. Regarding the compilation of the Book of the Dean of Lismore, see MacGregor 2012, 126. The material in the manuscript is diverse and it can be difficult to know why a given poem was included, but the compilers must have been aware of the genealogical claim.

139. Mackenzie 1805, appendix, 54–55. Regarding Rev. Alexander Pope, see chapter 4.

140. Canny 1987, 145–47, 162–225.

141. In the first couple decades of the seventeenth century, Irish colleges existed or were established in Paris, Salamanca, Lisbon, Douai, Seville, Rouen, Bordeaux, Rome, and Leuven. From the 1630s to the 1680s, new Irish colleges were founded in Madrid, Prague, Poitiers, Toulouse, and Nantes (Leerssen 1996, 255).

142. Ó hUiginn 2012, 160–63; Ní Shéaghdha 1985, 5–6.

143. The manuscript (University College Dublin, Franciscan MS A 20) was largely written by two scribes working at the Irish military garrison in Ostend and the Irish college in Leuven. A third scribe began to copy a story about the Fianna's journey to Lochlann to defeat Mánus, which remains unfinished. See Ó hUiginn 2010, 89–90, 99; Christiansen 1931, 90.

144. "Tar ceann gur scríobhadh iomad d'fhinnscéalaibh filidheachta ar Fhionn agus ar an bh-Féin . . . taris sin, is dearbh gur scríobhadh staire fírinneacha inchreidthe orra. . . . buannadha do ríoghaibh Éireann ré cosnamh agus ré caomhna na críche dhóibh" (Keating 1908, 326; trans. 327). Keating accepted the historicity of an exceptionally long-lived Caoilte who related the Fianna's deeds to Saint Patrick, but he believed that romances such as *Cath Fionntrágha*, *Bruidhean Chaorthainn*, and *Tóruigheacht an Ghiolla Dheacair* were composed for entertainment purposes and were not credible historical sources.

145. Less well-known collections could also be examined in this light. For instance, the earliest known copy of *Cath Chnoic an Áir*, alongside a selection of other Fenian lays, is contained in a manuscript prepared for publication (but not ultimately published) at the Irish college in Leuven in 1685 (Mac Craith 2007–8, 106).

146. Ó hUiginn 2010, 99; see also Ó hUiginn 2003, 98–99.

147. Ó hUiginn 2003, 84–93; Ó hUiginn 2010, 90–96.

148. Nagy 2003, 40; cf. Ó hUiginn 2012, 161.

149. Nagy 2001, 443.

Chapter 4. From Fionn to *Fingal*

1. See Barbour's *The Brus* (1980 [1375], 48, ll. 67–70); Douglas's "The Palis of Honoure" (1992 [c. 1501], 66 [ll. 1715–16]); Lindsay's "Ane Satyre of the Thrie Estaitis" (1989 [c. 1552], 75 [ll. 2093–95], 174 [ll. 257–58]) and "The Historie of Squyer Meldrum" (1931 [c. 1550], 154 [l. 317]); and "The Crying of ane Playe" by an anonymous author (Fisher 1999 [c. 1512–15], 36 [ll. 33–37],

38 [l. 81–88]). Further discussion of these Scots references can be found in MacKillop 1986, 72–73 and Christiansen 1931, 61–62.

2. Douglas 1992, 66 (l. 1716); Fisher 1999, 36 (l. 40).

3. A garbled, but possible, allusion to contemporary accounts of Fionn's sojourn in Hell occurs in the anonymous poem (Innes 2013). More readily apparent correspondences can be seen between the poets' portrayal of the Fianna as giants, including a reference to a Fenian biofact (Fionn's enormous jawbone), and orally collected lore from the past few centuries: see Christiansen 1931, 62; MacBain 1886, 194–96; cf. MacBain 1891–94, 99–102.

4. See Boece's *Scotorum Historiae a Prima Gentis Origine* (1526, 133r). Keating disputed Boece's assertion (in keeping with Scottish popular tradition) that Fionn was a giant (Keating 1908, 330).

5. Campion 1633, 23. Campion gave the giant's Latin name as Ruanus, following his source, Giraldus Cambrensis's *Topographia Hibernica* (1861 [c. 1200], 142). Keating later identified Ruanus with Caoilte mac Rónáin (1902, 150–52).

6. McGowan-Doyle 2011, 135.

7. Fischer 2019; Brewer 1871, 2–15. Valerie McGowan-Doyle assigns responsibility for the many additions and adaptations in the Book of Howth to its compiler, the seventh Baron of Howth (2011, 75).

8. Hanmer 1633, 23–32. Hanmer's version found its way into print just in time for Geoffrey Keating to integrate criticism of its reworking of Fenian narrative into his counter-history (completed 1634): see Keating 1902, 48, 50.

9. See Walsh's *A Prospect of the State of Ireland* (1682, 51–53) and O'Flaherty's *Ogygia* (1685, 153–54, 338, 341–42). Walsh's argumentation follows that of Keating, who rejected the portrayal of the Fianna as giants (as in *Acallam na Senórach* [The dialogue of the elders] and oral tradition). Additional Fenian references appear in Raphael Holinshed's *Chronicle*, John Leslie's *De Origine, Moribus et Rebus Gestis Scotorum*, and William Camden's *Britannia*: see Holinshed 1577, 2.108, 3.17r (Description) and 3.17 (History); Leslie 1675 [1578], 131; and Camden 1587 [1586], 604. Details concerning Fionn's death and the requirements for entry into the Fianna also occur in a translation of the Annals of Clonmacnoise (Mageoghagan 1896 [1627], 61–62).

10. O'Connor 1726 [1723], 267–75, 286. Translations of Keating's history also circulated in manuscript form in the seventeenth century: see Caball and Hazard 2013.

11. See Farewell's *The Irish Hudibras* (1689, 85–86).

12. Martin 1703, 152–53, 217, 219, 220.

13. The last professionally trained poets in Gaelic Scotland belonged to the MacMhuirich learned family and ceased practicing in the early eighteenth century (see Grant and Cheape 1987, 175–76).

14. Thomson 1992–94, 407.

15. Meek 1996, 260; cf. Withers 1984, 23–24. Prejudicial views of Lowlanders can also be found in Scottish Gaelic sources.

16. Sher 1991, 214.

17. Campbell 1872, 218–24; Cameron 1892, 393–99. Pope also referenced an unnamed collaborator (Mackenzie 1805, appendix, 52–53).

18. Cameron 1894, 310, 371–96.

19. Thomson 1992–94, 406–7.

20. Thomson 1953, 181–82; Cameron 1892, 295–370. McLagan gathered multiple versions of some of these. Three of his lays are in the style of *Ossian* rather than traditional (Thomson's item nos. 40, 87, and 94). Derick Thomson counted forty-eight different heroic lays and related items (1953, 181). The discrepancy between his count and mine can be explained by irregularities in Thomson's title index to McLagan's heroic material. The index includes both standard and alternative titles. Standard titles are cross-referenced with item numbers, while alternative titles

are not. Thomson cross-references forty-eight items with item numbers, suggesting that the collection contains that many unique lays and related items. However, he lists the two variants of item 40 separately, while item 92, *Cath Ghabhra nam Beumannan* (The Battle of Gabhair of the Blows), is titled *Bàs Oscair* (The death of Oscar) elsewhere. The number of unique lays and related items should therefore be forty-six. It can also be noted that items 25 and 52 are omitted from the title index (218–21).

21. Henderson 1908–11, 343; Thomson 1952, 7–8; Campbell 1872, v, xvi. Campbell's items 1 and 31; 10 and 13; and 21 and 28 are translated or variant versions of the same lays (v).

22. Thomson 1952, 7; Campbell 1872, v–vi, xvi–xvii.

23. Thomson 1953, 179.

24. Mackinnon 1887; Stone 1756; cf. Mackenzie 1805, appendix, 99–117.

25. Stone died young of illness and his treatise was never published, but drafts survive among his papers (Mackinnon 1887, 315–16, 319). William Ferguson has outlined his historical claims (1998a, 214–17).

26. Blackwell 1735, 34.

27. Stone 1756, 15.

28. Gaskill 1986, 123.

29. Moore 2004a, xxxiii–xxxvi; Kristmannsson 2017, 43–44.

30. Thomson 1987, 248–50. Fiona Stafford analyzes these two early poems (1988, 42–47). For the influence of Blackwell's theories on Macpherson's *Ossian*, see Bysveen 1982 and Stafford 1988, 28–34.

31. Thomson 1998, 17; Stafford 1996a, viii–x.

32. Among the only things that the English planter and poet Edmund Spenser praised about the Irish Gaels in *A View of the Present State of Ireland* was their poetry, which he heard being sung, and which was translated for him. However, he criticized their use of such well-crafted poetry to praise subjects he deemed unworthy (Spenser 1997, 75–77).

33. Lamont 1968, 140 (ll. 13–17, 36, 39–43). Collins's poem can be seen in light of an appreciation for 'things Celtic' that began to take hold in Europe in the mid-eighteenth century, and that has come to be known as the first Celtic Revival (Deane 1985, 20; cf. Snyder 1923, 4–7; O'Halloran 1989, 73). For an analysis of the portrayal of Highland culture in the poem, see Stafford 1996b, 82–84.

34. This image is very similar to the way in which Ossian would come to be depicted in artists' renderings.

35. Stafford 1988, 77–78.

36. Among modern commentators, see most notably Hugh Trevor-Roper (1983; 1985; 2008) and, more recently, Thomas Curley (1987; 2009). Howard Gaskill refutes many of their claims concerning Macpherson's *Ossian* (1986; 1988a).

37. Regarding Macpherson's reluctance, see Mac Craith 2015, 167–68. The June edition was followed in October by a second, emended edition that also contained an additional 'fragment.' Prior to the publication of these editions, extracts had been forwarded to a number of prominent English writers to pique their interest—which they succeeded in doing. After publication, extracts also appeared in the *Scots Magazine* and the English *Gentleman's Magazine* (Stafford 1988, 78–79, 96, 113).

38. Blair 1996b [1760], 5–6. Blair's preface was initially published anonymously. He would later greatly expand upon these statements in his "Critical Dissertation on the Poems of Ossian" (1996a [1763]).

39. Blair later acknowledged that the preface to *Fragments* was the result of conversations between himself and Macpherson (Mackenzie 1805, appendix, 57–58).

40. Sher goes so far as to portray the young Macpherson as something of a "victim" who would have felt forced to produce the desired text (1982, 59). Perhaps—but since his name did

not appear in the earliest editions of *Fragments* (Gaskill 1991, 2), presumably he could have backed away from the project without losing face, even if it meant forfeiting eminent literary connections.

41. Macpherson obtained perhaps thirteen lays from McLagan by referencing their shared ethnic pride. In October, 1760, Macpherson wrote: "I am informed, that you have a good collection of poems of the kind I want.—It would be, therefore, very obliging, you should transmit them to me as soon as convenient . . . I shall not make any apology for this trouble, as it will be for the honour of our ancestors, how many of their pieces of genius will be brought to light" (Mackenzie 1805, appendix, 153–54).

42. Not having any formal training in Early Modern Gaelic language or orthography, Macpherson turned to his relatives and acquaintances, Ewan Macpherson, Lachlan Macpherson, Capt. Alexander Morison, and Rev. Andrew Gallie, to help him interpret the manuscript texts. He was likely "of middling or better proficiency when it comes to writing near contemporary language," however, and therefore quite capable of working with the orally collected texts (McKean 2001, 454). Regarding Macpherson's research travels and the scholars he enlisted to help him, see Stafford 1988, 116–23.

43. 'Temora' is Macpherson's adapted form of the Irish toponym Teamhair (Tara).

44. Macpherson 1996, 49–51. In the preface to *Fragments*, Blair also asserted that the texts "were handed down . . . some in manuscript, but more by oral tradition" (1996b [1760], 5).

45. While Macpherson acknowledged his use of Keating and O'Flaherty as sources, he rejected numerous aspects of their version of Irish history (see, e.g., Macpherson 1996, 211, 450n33, 525n9). Cf. Thomson 1952, 69–72; MacQueen 1998.

46. Locke 1975, 664; cf. Stafford 1988, 82.

47. Mackenzie 1805, appendix, 153–54. The surviving collection record of eighteenth-century Fenian lays indicates that the oral tradition was strong when Macpherson was collecting. He is likely to have gathered excellent versions of the most popular lays, even if his search for epic qualities tempered his appreciation of them.

48. These dates range from *A*^{o} *D*^{ni} *millesimo quin*^{mo} *duodecimo*, or 1512, to *a*^{o} *xlii*, or [15]42 (NLS Adv. MS 72.1.37, pp. 82, 144). While Macpherson may not have known the precise ages of some of his other manuscript sources, not all of which have survived, he never claimed to have early medieval manuscripts. Regarding the Book of the Dean of Lismore, the clearly legible dates may hold a clue to the circumstances through which the Ossianic epics emerged. It has been posited that Macpherson acquired the Book of the Dean of Lismore very early in his Fenian research. The scenario most strongly endorsed by the manuscript's modern cataloguer, Ronald Black, is that while Macpherson was employed as a private tutor to Graham of Balgowan (c. 1758–60, the same period in which he met Home), he acquired the Book of the Dean of Lismore and other Gaelic manuscripts from his pupil's uncle, Rev. Thomas Fraser (see Ronald Iain Black, 2010, "The Book of the Dean of Lismore," *Catalogue of Gaelic Manuscripts in the National Library of Scotland*, Irish Script on Screen: National Library of Scotland Adv. MS 72.1.37, [Gaelic MS XXXVII], https://www.isos.dias.ie, accessed August 29, 2017). For Howard Gaskill, Macpherson's, Blair's, and others' early and consistent references to more modern—and in their opinion, corrupt—Fenian texts as originating in the fifteenth century, further supports the theory that this manuscript was in Macpherson's possession from the very beginning, since the early sixteenth-century dates in the Book of the Dean of Lismore could easily have suggested that the material in the book dated to the century prior (Gaskill 1990, 75–77). Indeed, even with help, Macpherson may not have understood much in the Book of the Dean of Lismore apart from the dates; highly competent Gaelic scholars still struggle with the manuscript's nonstandard orthography. Yet, as illegible as he may have found it, he would have recognized that it contained a large number of Fenian texts, and he might even have thought the Book of the Dean of Lismore contained the text of the epic he sought (Thomson 1952, 80, 83). While

these ideas must remain in the realm of conjecture, they are compelling, particularly when considered together. If Macpherson had the Book of the Dean of Lismore from the start and presumed it contained a fairly complete text of an Ossianic epic (albeit in a corrupted, fifteenth-century form), then the conviction expressed by Blair in his preface to the *Fragments* that such an epic could be recovered is far more grounded than it has generally appeared to be.

49. Macpherson 1996, 51. Macpherson circumvented the problem posed by continuous textual degeneration by arguing that transmitters' modernizing tendencies were relatively recent; in the period prior to contact with other ethnic groups and the advent of literacy—which was considerably late, according to his historical schema—a great degree of fidelity to the posited original text was possible: "The ancient Scots, a people so free of intermixture with foreigners, and so strongly attached to the memory of their ancestors, had the works of their bards handed down with great purity" (50).

50. One might even call *Ossian* a "transcreation"—a translation that "fails to adhere to the 'original,' but uses it as a starting point for its own literary creation." As Cordula Lemke explains, this process of rewriting "addresses both contemporary structures of power and questions of tradition and influence" (2017, 53).

51. Thomson 1952, 14; Thomson 1987, 259–61. Thomson presents evidence that Macpherson had recourse to fourteen or fifteen Gaelic lays, and notes Macpherson's familiarity with material derived from the early Irish *Táin Bó Cúailnge* (The cattle raid of Cooley), the cornerstone of the Ulster cycle (1952, 10, 26–28). Donald Meek points out that the lays Macpherson used are linked by the theme of foreign invasion, and further notes structural similarities between *Fingal* and *Cath Fionntrágha* (The Battle of Ventry), a comparison first made by Macpherson's Irish contemporary, Bishop John O'Brien of Cloyne (Meek 1991, 40–41, 47–48n57; O'Brien 1764, 850).

52. Macpherson 1996, 5.

53. Macpherson 1996, 50.

54. Sher 1991, 212–13. Bute was to become the principal patron of Macpherson's *Ossian* (Sher 1982, 59).

55. See chapter 6.

56. Contemporary authors who argued for the Gaels' ancient history within Scotland, from whence they claimed Ireland was colonized, included Jerome Stone, in his unpublished treatise, and John Macpherson, in *Critical Dissertations on the Origin, Antiquities, etc. of the Caledonians* (1768), both of whose manuscripts James Macpherson is likely to have read. Their views derive from those of Sir George Mackenzie in the seventeenth century, whose account modified those of John of Fordun, Hector Boece, and George Buchanan. This model of history had been challenged, but it was popular in Scotland, and others had taken similar positions. See Ferguson 1998a, 212–17, 239; O'Halloran 2004, 29–30, 32.

57. For Macpherson's engagement with *Paradise Lost*, see Stafford 1998, 168–72.

58. Sher 1982, 57.

59. Sher 1982, 57–58; Stafford 1988, 114.

60. Mac Craith 1998, 66–67.

61. The latter complaint was most strongly voiced by Irish commentators, although it was also picked up by other skeptics. The Irish reaction is considered in chapter 6.

62. Doubts regarding *Ossian*'s authenticity had begun to be expressed privately, but they were not yet prominent in print, and their influence was still not widely felt. We know from later publications that Samuel Johnson formed his opinion of the inauthenticity of *Ossian* prior to departing for the Highlands in 1773. Also during this early period, Scottish philosopher David Hume, who would write (but not publish) a critique in the 1770s, is known to have probed Blair for textual evidence showing the origin of Macpherson's *Ossian* in Gaelic tradition. This is likely what prompted Blair to broach the topic in 1765 in a revised version of his "Critical Dissertation" that included accounts of oral recitations of the original poems. Published claims countering

Blair's assertion of authenticity would emerge in the following decade. See Ferguson 1998a, 243; Moore 2004a, lxxiii, lxxvi.

63. Johnson 1971, 114–15. Johnson was aware of Gaelic religious books such as the 1653 translation of the Shorter Catechism and the 1659 translation of the Psalms. As several commentators have pointed out, his view of other aspects of Highland society was more favorable: see Gaskill 1986, 130–31 and Thomson 1963, 16–17.

64. Johnson, of course, knew nothing about the developmental stages of the Gaelic languages or the details of their relationship to one another: cf. Ferguson 1998b, 190–91.

65. Johnson 1971, 118; Boswell 1964, 95; Boswell 1963, 133. Johnson did acknowledge the possibility that Macpherson used oral source material, writing: "He has doubtless inserted names that circulate in popular stories, and may have translated some wandering ballads, if any can be found" (1971, 118). However, in addition to his mistrust of the fidelity of oral transmission, he may well have thought that all Scottish Gaelic songs resembled waulking songs (sung by women while fulling tweed). Having been told about the nonsensical vocables that often turn up in the refrains of such songs, he assumed the subjects of these to be trivial (Boswell 1964, 241, cf. 178).

66. Johnson 1971, 209–10.

67. MacNicol 1779, 346. It has been noted that Macpherson had access to MacNicol's manuscript prior to publication, and that he may have added "some crude innuendo about Johnson and a scathing attack on Boswell, as well as some of the more bitter reflections on Johnson's attitude to Macpherson" (Moore 2004a, lxxviii). Some of these additions were apparently removed or amended, while others are thought to remain in the text. If true, this is one of the few contributions that Macpherson made to the controversy. However, it is worth bearing in mind William Ferguson's cautionary note that the assertions regarding Macpherson's contributions to MacNicol's manuscript remain unsubstantiated (1998b, 185). We do know that shortly after the publication of Johnson's *Journey to the Western Islands of Scotland* in 1775, Macpherson contacted Johnson personally to ask him to retract some of his more caustic statements. The missive in which the English critic indignantly refused is famous, and so is the suggestion that Macpherson's lost letter(s) to Johnson may have contained a challenge to a duel. Only Johnson's reply is extant, and some time ago Fiona Stafford identified an inconsistency in the commonly cited form of this reply and the original; specifically, she noted a change from "his intention to repel 'whatever insult' may be offered" in the original to repelling "'violence'" in the version he dictated to friends (1989, 76). The rumor that Macpherson challenged Johnson to a duel also remains unsubstantiated, but it appears that Johnson encouraged the belief that he did. See Metzdorf 1970, 49–58 and Stafford 1989, 70–77.

68. MacNicol 1779, 350–351, 361. Today the supposition that a tradition bearer could not recall something as lengthy as an epic poem is easily refuted with reference to Milman Parry and Albert Lord's work with South Slavic tradition bearers (Lord 2019). MacNicol is certainly correct that no complete rendition of an Ossianic epic could be collected in the Scottish Gaelic oral tradition, but the reason was not because no contemporary tradition bearer could remember such a lengthy poetic text in its entirety, but rather because no such oral text ever existed.

69. Sher 1991, 208–9; Gaskill 1988b, 15–16. Several of the texts pertaining to the controversy are included in Edward Snyder's lists by decade of publications concerning *Ossian* and the late eighteenth-century interest in Celtic cultures (1923, 93–189). Extracts from the most salient contemporary commentary appear in the third volume of Dafydd Moore's *Ossian and Ossianism* (2004).

70. Rev. John Smith in Mackenzie 1805, appendix, 75. In the 1780s, Smith published his own derivative Ossianic verses, seeking Macphersonic fame and fortune: see chapter 5. Adam Ferguson was among those who argued that Macpherson's actions resembled those of Homer: "I am ready to admit, that after collecting all the scattered fragments, he tied them together in form

of heroic poems, as Homer is said to have done when he collected the songs of the bards of Greece" (Mackenzie 1805, appendix, 67). See also Sher 1991, 236.

71. Mackenzie 1805, 151–52. This judgment appears to be most applicable to *Fingal*. Later in the committee's conclusions it is strongly suggested, if not stated outright, that much of *Temora* is an original composition (154).

72. Laing 1971. See also the dissertation on *Ossian* he appended to his major work, a history of Scotland (Laing 1800).

73. Thomson 1958, 177, 186; Thomson 1987, 254–57. See Thomson 1952, 85–90 for an analysis of the language of the Gaelic *Ossian*. See Gaskill 1988b, 20–21 for thoughts on its composition over a long period of time, and the possible loss of some portions.

74. Macpherson 1996, 33.

75. MacNicol 1779, 243, 246; Gaskill 1991, 3, 11, 13.

76. As Thomson notes, the Gaelic *Ossian* "was for long regarded with respectful doubt" (1952, 85); yet for some, particularly Scottish Gaels, it was surrounded with "an aura of sanctity" (Meek 2013).

77. See Black 2001, 328–37 for a lament by Donnchadh MacAoidh (Duncan MacKay) of Badenoch.

Chapter 5. Romantic Highlands and Godly Fingalians

1. Leask 2016, 184.

2. Dafydd Moore has called the Ossianic controversy a "loud and eye-catching side-show to the true story and importance of *Ossian*'s reception" (Moore 2004b, 29). In recent decades, Moore and others have helped to elucidate the texts' widespread and sustained appeal.

3. Moore 2004b, 32–36; Barnaby 2004. Three metrical editions of *Fingal* had appeared by 1776, and two different versifications of the complete works emerged in 1810 and 1817. While the positive creative literary response was large, a number of parodies satirizing or ridiculing aspects of *Ossian* were also published in Britain and abroad; see Bär 2012 for a consideration of these.

4. Barthélemon 1768; Reeve and Shield 1791; Moore 2004b, 35. *Oithóna* was staged in the Haymarket Theatre and *Oscar and Malvina* was performed at Covent Garden. John Home, Macpherson's supporter, also composed an Ossianic play, *A Fatal Discovery*, which was staged at Drury Lane in 1769.

5. Macdonald 2004, 394; Macdonald 2017, 98. For descriptions of the Penicuik ceiling, see Coltman 2019, 95–96; Cheape 1997, 9–10.

6. Gaskill 1994, 647–48, 657. The number of complete German translations by separate translators reached fourteen by 1924, far exceeding that of any other language. For an extensive list of European translations, criticism, and creative responses, see Barnaby 2004.

7. Gaskill 1994, 652.

8. Goethe 1774, 192–205, 206; trans. Constantine 2012, 96–102, 103.

9. Gaskill 2003, 108. Gaskill adds that while Macpherson was prone to foreignization, Goethe de-exoticized the text to achieve a desired effect within his own narrative (2013a, 318).

10. Gaskill 2001, 215; Gaskill 2013b, 297.

11. Gaskill 2013b, 297–98; Ó Dochartaigh 2004, 156–58, 173–75. It is unclear precisely what linguistic resources Goethe had, although Edward Lhuyd's *Archaeologica Britannica* (1707) and Bishop John O'Brien's *Focalóir Gaoidhilge-Sax-Bhéarla or an Irish-English Dictionary* (1768) were likely among them.

12. Barnaby 2004, xxv, xxvi.

13. Gaskill 2001, 212.

14. Herder 1773, 5, 28; trans. Bohlman 2016, 141, 157; Gaskill 2013b, 296.

15. Herder 1773, 17; trans. Bohlman 2016, 149.

16. Herder 1981 [1778–79], 2:130–39; Gaskill 2013b, 298; Gaskill 2001, 215; Ó Dochartaigh 2004, 172.

17. Gaskill 1989, 333; Gillies 1969, 62. Herder compiled an Ossianic Gaelic glossary and there is evidence that he expected to receive translation help from a Hebridean in Weimar, Rev. James MacDonald of Anstruther.

18. Christian Wilhelm Ahlwardt published the earliest and most popular complete translation of the Gaelic *Ossian* into any modern language in 1811; see Gaskill 1989, 335–36.

19. Wilson 1989, 23.

20. Gaskill 2003, 101–3.

21. Wilson 1989, 23–24. Herder was, of course, also influenced by numerous other scholars. Wilson draws particular attention to Montesquieu.

22. Gaskill 1994, 662.

23. Gaskill 2013b, 298; Gaskill 1989, 332; cf. Herder 1773, 5; Herder 1795, 87–95; trans. Bohlman 2016, 141, 173–77.

24. Wilson 1989, 28–29; Gaskill 2003, 99, 109.

25. "Wir Deutschen wohl mehr solche Gedichte hätten, als ich mit der schottischen Romanze angeführet. . . . In mehr als einer Provinz sind mir Volkslieder, Provinziallieder, Bauerlieder bekannt, die an Lebhaftigkeit und Rhythmus, und Naivetät und Stärke der Sprache vielen derselben gewiß nichts nachgeben würden; nur wer ist der sie sammle? der sich um sie bekümmre? sich um Lieder des Volks bekümmre? auf Strassen, und Gassen und Fischmärkten? im ungelehrten Rundgesange des Landvolks? um Lieder, die oft nicht skandirt, und oft schlecht gereimt sind? wer wollte sie sammlen" (Herder 1773, 51; translation adapted from Feldman and Richardson 1972, 229). Wilson notes that this essay "awakened an immediate interest in folklore" in Germany (1989, 30).

26. Gaskill 2003, 103.

27. Gaskill 1994, 659, 672.

28. Barnaby 2004; Porter 2019.

29. Stafford 1988, 177; Stafford 1996a, vi; Macdonald 2017, 92. Gérard's *Le Barde Ossian Évoquant les Fantômes sur le Bord du Lora* (Ossian evoking spirits on the bank of the Lora) (1801) and Girodet's *Les Ombres des Héros Français Morts pour la Patrie, Conduites par la Victoire, Viennent Visiter dans Leurs Nuages les Ombres d'Ossian et de Ses Guerriers, qui Leur Donnent la Fête de l'Amitié* (The ghosts of French war heroes, conducted by victory, come to visit in their clouds the ghosts of Ossian and his warriors, who receive them) (1802) were commissioned for Malmaison. Ingres's *Le Songe d'Ossian* (The dream of Ossian) (1813) graced the emperor's bedroom ceiling in the Palazzo di Monte Cavallo in Rome.

30. Stafford 1988, 177; Vance 1980, 221.

31. Jefferson 1950 [1773], 96. Although non-European responses to Macpherson's works have received less recognition, the Ossianic epics and literature influenced by them were being read, written, and performed in the Americas and the Caribbean in the late eighteenth and nineteenth centuries; see Carpenter 1931; Gaskill 1988b, 5; Gaskill 1994, 653, 660.

32. DeGategno 1991, 95, 98–102. Jefferson's letter was addressed to an acquaintance, Charles McPherson, with the request that Charles would communicate Jefferson's message to his relative, which Charles did. Jefferson later purchased Alasdair mac Mhaighstir Alasdair's collection of original Gaelic poetry, the first ever such collection to be printed.

33. See Snyder 1923, 93–189; Barnaby 2004.

34. Scott 1805; Moore 2004b, 31; Leask 2017. Scott even incorporated a fictionalized excerpt of a Fenian dialogue lay in a discussion of the controversy in his novel *The Antiquary*; see Scott 2002 [1816], 292–95.

35. Stafford 1991, 51, 53–55, 57–60, 64–67. Some of Wordsworth's early poems even show signs of direct influence. Although Coleridge looked positively on *Ossian* for many years, his opinion later shifted against Macpherson's epics.

36. Macdonald 2016, 237–39. Turner's first Ossianic landscape, *Ben Lomond Mountains, Scotland: The Traveller—Vide Ossian's 'War of Caros'* (1802) was thought to be lost for two centuries before its rediscovery by Murdo Macdonald and Eric Shanes in 2013.

37. Black 1986, 1–2, 8–9; Dingwall 1997, 65–66. Christopher Dingwall summarizes the Highland Society of London's cultural commitment as follows: "First among the Society's objects was 'the restoration of the Highland Dress' after which were listed 'the preservation of the ancient music of the Highlands; promoting the cultivation of the Celtic language; [and] the rescuing from oblivion the valuable remains of Celtic literature'" (1997, 65).

38. Cheape 1997, 11–13. The Society of Antiquaries of Scotland also provided a forum to discuss the authenticity of *Ossian.*

39. Regarding the late eighteenth- and nineteenth-century mass evictions known as the Highland clearances, see Richards 2005.

40. Scott 2015 [1814]; Harvie 1996, 238.

41. Cheape 1997, 11.

42. Leask 2016, 186. Leask notes the overwriting of sites previously associated with the Romans with Fenian toponyms. As recognized in chapter 4, Fingal's resistance is always noble and valorous rather than brutish and unbridled. For a fuller exploration of early Highland tourism, see Leask 2020.

43. Dingwall 1997, 62–63. Part of the hall was destroyed in 1869, and the painting of Ossian along with it.

44. Meek 2007, 254–55; Meek 2000, 40–41; Baines 1997, 45–46.

45. Macpherson 1807, 498–540. The map depicts "the region around Oban and Lismore Island in upper Loch Linnhe at the mouths of Loch Creran and Loch Etive" (Gidal 2015, 57). The Highland Society of London was responsible for publishing the Gaelic *Ossian* (1807), the financial backing for which had been raised some years prior by Sir John MacGregor Murray of Lanrick (Black 1986, 6).

46. Leask 2016, 187–88; Baines 1997; Wordsworth 1997 [1874], 139. Wordsworth was looking down Loch Etive, the Isle of Mull in the distance, in September 1803. Shortly thereafter, she and her illustrious brother were shown "the hills of Morven, so much sung of by Ossian" (141). Regarding Wordsworth and Pennant's Highland tours, see Leask 2020, 97–135, 171–217.

47. Smollett 1998 [1771], 240.

48. Baines 1997, 48–50, 52; Dingwall 1997, 64, 66.

49. Michael 2007, 3, 5; Baines 1997, 45–48. This site was immensely popular. Turner took it as the inspiration for his painting *Staffa, Fingal's Cave* (1832), while another tourist, German composer Felix Mendelssohn, adopted *Die Fingals-Höhle* (Fingal's Cave) as an alternate title for his overture, *Die Hebriden* (The Hebrides) (1833); see Macdonald 2016, 238–39 and Porter 2019, 113–22. The non-Fenian name (*an uamh bhinn*) also appeared in early nineteenth-century tourist literature; see Lizars 1830, 284.

50. Gidal 2015, 11; Baines 1997, 56. Initiated for the conveyance of military troops, by the late eighteenth century a network of roads, railways, and steamer lines enabled both resource extraction and leisure travel.

51. Baines 1997, 57.

52. Smollett 1998 [1771], 240.

53. Carswell 1970 [1567], 11; trans. Shaw 2004, 216.

54. Sher 1991, 214–15; Sher 2009; Oz-Salzberger 2009. Ferguson had been chaplain to the 42nd (Royal Highland) Regiment, i.e., the Black Watch, for several years before retiring from service to the church.

55. Blair 1996a [1763], 398–99.

56. McLauchlan 1859, vii.

57. On the European continent, see, e.g., the work of the sixteenth-century Magdeburg Centuriators (Meek 2000, 110).

58. Meek 2000, 104, 110–13, 215. Saint Columba was notably coopted and the teachings of his church on Iona were said to have differed considerably from standard Roman Catholicism.

59. Macpherson 1996, 45–46; Blair 1996a [1763], 349, 355–56, 370, 377–78, quoted at 395.

60. Meek 2000, 222.

61. Blair 1996a [1763], 353–56.

62. Rev. John Smith of Campbeltown quoted in Mackenzie 1805, appendix, 75–76. At issue was the fact that "different editions of the same poem were, as you may well suppose, very widely different, from their having been recited for ages by different persons and in different places." Modern folksong specialists would certainly affirm the existence of multiple versions of orally transmitted verse, including the Fenian lays—although we now know that the lays do not vary widely enough to exonerate Macpherson of textual meddling.

63. Campbell 1872, 168.

64. Rev. John MacDonald of Ferintosh quoted in Kennedy 1867, 44.

65. Rev. Dugald Buchanan quoted in Meek 2004, 45.

66. MacDiarmid's collection originally consisted of two manuscript volumes. The location of the first volume is now unknown. In addition to a large store of proverbs and riddles, it contained at least two Fenian lays, which are printed in J. F. Campbell's *Leabhar na Feinne* (Campbell 1872, vi, xvii, 71–74, 182–83). The second volume was rediscovered in 1968. It contains one or two additional Fenian lays, as well as other poetry (Thomson 1992, 1–3, 5, 167–91).

67. Gunderloch 2011, 55, 57–9, quoted at 67; Gunderloch 2012, 179; Campbell 1872, vi, xviii–xxiii.

68. Meek 2004, 46. While the Eigg Collection does not contain Fenian lays, the opening poem is Macphersonic in style.

69. Ludwig Christian Stern reported that the Gillies Collection was widely read in the Highlands in its time, but this is uncertain; it was not reprinted and J. F. Campbell considered it a rare book a century later (Stern 1900b, 291; Campbell 1872, xxiv). Included in the collection are versions of *Suire Oisein* (Oisean's courting), *Laoidh Mhághnuis Mhóir* (The lay of Mánus the Great), *Comhairle Fhinn air Oscar* (Fionn's advice to Oscar), *Rosg Ghoill mhic Mhorna* (The incitement of Goll mac Morna), *Laoidh na h-Ighinne* (The lay of the maiden), *Laoidh Choinn mhic an Deirg* (The lay of Conn son of Dearg [red one]), *Cath Rìgh na Sorcha* (The battle of the king of Sorcha), two versions of *Cath Ghabhra nam Beumannan* (The Battle of Gabhair of the Blows), *Mar Chaidh Bran a Mharbhadh* (The death of Bran), *Duan na Ceàrdaich* (The lay of the smithy, also known as *Laoidh na Ceardcha*), *Duan a' Mhuileartaich* (The lay of the Muileartach), *Laoidh Dhiarmaid* (The lay of Diarmaid), *Dearg mac Deirg* (Dearg son of Dearg), *Laoidh Laomuinn* (The lay of Laomann), and *Laoidh an Airghinn Mhóir* (The lay of Airgheann the Great) (Gillies 1786, 11–14, 18–24, 34–44, 162–72, 233–36, 250–53, 284–87, 300–21).

70. Gillies 1786, front matter (unpaginated).

71. Thomson 1992–94, 409. Derick Thomson located the originals of several Gillies Collection lays in McLagan's manuscripts at the University of Glasgow.

72. Hill 1784. Hill published *Laoidh Mhághnuis Mhóir, Laoidh Dhiarmaid, Mar Chaidh Bran a Mharbhadh, Duan a' Mhuileartaich, Laoidh an Airghinn Mhóir, Urnuigh Oisein* (Oisean's prayer), and *Cath Ghabhra nam Beumannan*. Only *Cath Ghabhra nam Beumannan* appears to have been orally collected. Because it was translated on the spot by the Lochaber tradition bearer's family members, the Gaelic is not given. Regarding a similar Highland collecting tour that Matthew Young, an Irish Protestant clergyman, embarked upon in 1784, see chapter 6.

73. See Faujas de Saint-Fond 1799, 290–92, 294; Leyden 1903 [1800], 86–89; Stoddart 1801, 275–81. MacNab also appeared as an authority in Rev. John Smith of Campbeltown's *Galic Antiquities* (1780).

74. Leask 2016, 192.

75. Mackenzie 1805, 2, 90.

76. Campbell 1872, vii, xxv–xxvi; Hogg 2011, 97–174.

77. Cameron 1892, 371–92; Campbell 1872, vii, xxvi–xxvii; Mackenzie 1805, advertisement. The lays in MacDonald of Staffa's collection are often incomplete. The collection also contains prose versions of *Bruidhean Eochaidh Bhig Dheirg* (Little red Eochaidh's enchanted hall) and *Dóitean Tíghe Fhinn* (The burning of Fionn's house).

78. Cameron 1892, 247–88, 400–24; Mackenzie 1805, advertisement. McLagan's and Fletcher's collections were also transmitted to the Highland Society at this time: Mackenzie 1805, 90. Only copies of Sage's and Mackenzie's manuscripts survive (Cameron 1892, xiv).

79. Campbell 1872, vii, xxvii; Cameron 1892, 167–246.

80. Gunderloch 1996, 50.

81. Kennedy 1867, 43–45, quoted at 43.

82. Cameron 1888; Campbell 1872, vii, xxix–xxx.

83. Dunbar 2013, 56–57.

84. The Stewarts published an eighteenth-century manuscript version of the riddling sequence in *Tochmarc Ailbe* (The wooing of Ailbhe), which was later orally collected on Barra (Stewart and Stewart 1804, 545–47; Campbell 1872, 150; Innes 2016, 277). They were also the first to publish *Duan Ghairbh mhic Stairn* (The lay of Garbh son of Starn), *Laoidh na Con Duibhe* (The lay of the black dog), and the popular puzzle *Àireamh Muinntir Fhinn agus Dhubhain* (The enumeration of Fionn and Dubhan's people), which is known internationally as *Ludus Sancti Petri* (Stewart and Stewart 1804, 547–48, 554–80).

85. Thomson 1958, 184. The MacCallums were the first to publish *Laoidh an Deirg mhic Droichil* (The lay of Dearg son of Droicheal), *Laoidh Chrumlinn na gCath* (The lay of Crumlann of the battles), *Na Brataichean* (The banners) (as a standalone lay; Gillies's and Hill's versions of *Laoidh an Airghinn Mhóir* incorporated it), *Dan Chiuthaich* (The lay of Ciuthach), and *Seilg Shléibhe na mBan* (The chase of Slievenamon): MacCallum and MacCallum 1816, 95–111, 118–23, 197–99. They also provided translations of versions of lays that Gillies and the Stewarts had printed in Gaelic only.

86. Cf. Campbell 1872, xxx.

87. Meek 2004, 41.

88. Smith 1780, 126. Smith occasionally quotes unaltered passages of lays in the notes to his text, although like Macpherson, he introduces these only to discredit them as late interpolations. Any oral transcriptions he may have made are lost.

89. Smith 1780, 126–27.

90. Gaskill 1986, 134.

91. Mackenzie 1805, appendix 89–91; Gaskill 2004, 16–18. Smith's *Galic Antiquities* was bound with *Ossian* in France, ensuring wide circulation there, as well as in Italy, Spain, and South America. It also gained a modest foothold in Germany and was occasionally read in Russia.

92. Smith 1787. Duncan Kennedy did call some passages into question, claiming to have composed them himself; see Gunderloch 2011, 71–72.

93. Gunderloch 2011, 55, 75, 82–89; Gunderloch 2012, 183–94. Gunderloch suspects that Kennedy's alterations were made in the spirit of youthful exuberance, given that he was a teenager (or possibly even a preteen) when he began collecting and he gave up the hobby around the age of twenty-five. Because his field notes appear to have been lost in his lifetime, no comparison can be done (2011, 55–56, 67).

94. Gunderloch 1996, 52–53.

95. Thomson 1958, 184. A few Macphersonic texts have been ascribed to Irvine, although it is unclear whether the responsibility for these lies with a source (Campbell 1872, xxvi; Thomson

1958, 184). MacDiarmid's collection also includes an Ossianic "fragment" and an extract from the seventh book of *Temora* (Thomson 1992, 3, 5–6).

96. Gunderloch 2011, 60, 76; 2012, 181, 185–86. The published arguments summarized the plot of the verse to follow. As Gunderloch points out, Gaelic lays can also include prose introductions or take a prosimetrum form, and some of Kennedy's prose may be adapted from traditional material (2011, 77–81). When prose accompanies traditional Fenian verse, it often sets the scene or links disparate events, although it may summarize.

97. Thomson 1958, 182–84, quoted at 184.

98. MacCallum and MacCallum 1816, v.

99. MacCallum and MacCallum 1816, lxxxii–lxxxvii.

100. MacCallum 1821, 1–67; Mackenzie 1841, 1–16. Regarding the initial English-language publication of two poems included by both MacCallum and Mackenzie by John Clark in 1778, see Meek 2004, 41–42.

101. Moore 2004b, 30.

102. "Chum gu'n deanta, le h-uirigleadh taitneach bhur Baird fein, a mòr aigne so altrum, abachadh, agus a shior-mhosgladh, feadh na linntean a tha ri teachd, gus an eirich e gu barr mhullach na mòralachd" (Macpherson 1818, 8).

103. Meek 2004, 43.

104. Meek 2004, 46–49, quoted at 49.

105. Meek 2004, 50–56. MacLeod edited the periodicals *An Teachdaire Gaelach* (1829–31) and *Cuairtear nan Gleann* (1840–43).

106. Macpherson 1996, 61, 158. Macpherson adapted his melancholy subject from the Gaelic narrative tradition, but the phrase "joy of grief" derives from the classics: Blair identified a comparable phrase in Homer's *Iliad* in his "Critical Dissertation" (1996a [1763], 381).

107. Arguments for authenticity do postdate the first decade of the century, but engagement from the other side was limited at this time. We will recall, for instance, that the MacCallums rehearsed the case for authenticity in their preface. One can also point to James Grant, who argued on behalf of *Ossian* in his *Thoughts on the Origin and Descent of the Gael* in 1814, adducing a small selection of primarily Macphersonic poetry to support his case, and Donald Campbell, who published a pamphlet using the evidence of eighteenth and early nineteenth-century publications to refute Samuel Johnson in 1825. See Grant 1814, 379–423; Campbell 1825.

108. Black 1989, 146–47; Black 1986, 4, 16, 32, 33. Scholars unassociated with the Highland Society's dictionary project also succeeded in producing useful lexicographical materials in the same period.

109. Black 1989, 147; Black 1986, 19.

110. McLauchlan 1862; Black 1989, 147.

Chapter 6. Ireland's Own *Fianna Éireann*

1. Clare O'Halloran identifies Gothism and Orientalism as strong influences in the emergence of this early Celticism, which has come to be known as the first Celtic Revival (O'Halloran 2004, 41; O'Halloran 1989, 73; cf. Snyder 1923, 4–7). The atmosphere of curiosity about the Celts no doubt contributed to Macpherson's popularity, which in turn generated much additional interest. By 1787, the decidedly hostile Lowland Scottish antiquarian John Pinkerton could complain that "this may be called the Celtic century, for all Europe has been inundated with nonsense about the Celts" (Pinkerton 1787, 123). Interestingly, at an earlier point, Pinkerton had been an Ossianic supporter and poetic imitator (Ferguson 1998a, 250; Snyder 1923, 132).

2. O'Conor 1753, v–xxxviii, 35, 37; O'Halloran 2004, 20, 24.

3. O'Halloran 2012, 194–95. Also relevant, though not as widely circulated in later centuries, are the depictions of the Irish in John Derricke's *Image of Ireland* (1581) and Sir John Davies's *A Discovery of the True Causes Why Ireland was Never Entirely Subdued* (1612).

4. O'Halloran 2004, 19.

5. Brown 1988, 4. Consider, for instance, this cautionary statement issued in the late eighteenth century by the Anglo-Irish Protestant antiquarian Edward Ledwich in a letter to Anglo-Irish Protestant but Catholic-sympathizing antiquarian Joseph Cooper Walker: "You are bound personally, politically, and patriotically to be polite to the English; and it is historically true that they under providence, humanized the Irish. Who otherwise at this day would be perfect barbarians even as it is they are half civilized" (quoted in Ní Mhunghaile 2008, 187).

6. O'Halloran 2004, 23. O'Conor was a descendant of Ruaidhrí Ó Conchobhair, the last holder of the title of Irish high king prior to the Anglo-Norman invasion. His father had been a patron of the arts, and gatherings that included the celebrated harpist Turlough Carolan (Toirdhealbhach Ó Cearbhalláin) had taken place in his childhood home (Ní Shéaghdha 1985, 9).

7. Macpherson 1996, 211.

8. Macpherson 1996, 217, 223.

9. Clare O'Halloran provides a succinct description of the claims about the origin of the Irish and Scottish Gaels advanced in this text (O'Halloran 2004, 32; cf. Kidd 1993, 230–32; Ferguson 1998a, 233–34).

10. [O'Halloran] 1763a; [O'Halloran] 1763b, quoted at 460. O'Halloran was preceded by an English ecclesiastical scholar, Ferdinando Warner, whose pamphlet, *Remarks on the History of Fingal, and Other Poems of Ossian* appeared in 1762. While Warner enjoyed Macpherson's poetry and believed that it derived from authentic sources, he argued that these were actually of Irish provenance. He further added that the *Poems of Ossian* chronologically conflated the historical narrative and should not have been taken as accurate historical sources. Warner published his own *History of Ireland* in 1763 which followed the historical framework set out by O'Conor.

11. With the help of scribes in his employ, O'Brien later authored the dictionary *Focalóir Gaoidhilge-Sax-Bhéarla* (1768), which Herder and presumably Goethe used. The dictionary includes references to his article on *Ossian* (O'Halloran 1989, 81; Ó Catháin 1993, 503, 512).

12. Diarmaid Ó Catháin notes quotations from over ninety different authors in O'Brien's approximately forty-thousand-word critique (1993, 508).

13. O'Brien 1764; Ó Catháin 1993, 499–504, 507–11; Mac Craith 2004, 103–4. O'Brien's commentary circulated in Amsterdam in a reprint of the *Journal* articles, and it was granted its own edition by a printer in Cologne in 1765. Extracts in German translation were also published in 1766—and rejected as insufficient by Herder (Ó Catháin 1993, 513–14, 516–17).

14. O'Halloran 1989, 76.

15. O'Conor 1766, 27. While calling the stories "vulgar" and not valuing them very highly, O'Conor did believe the historicity of their characters. For a detailed investigation of O'Conor's involvement in the Ossianic controversy, see Mac Craith 2015.

16. O'Halloran 1989, 78.

17. O'Halloran 1772, 310–13. O'Halloran also devoted a good deal of space in this chapter to a criticism of a history recently published by James Macpherson's cousin, John Macpherson, which advanced a similar perspective on early Irish and Scottish history; see Kidd 1993, 235–37.

18. O'Halloran went so far as to posit that Greek literacy could be traced to Phenius (i.e., Fénius Farsaid), the ancestor of the Gaels from whom he said the term Phenian (i.e., Fenian) derived. For him, the term originally denoted a proto-Gaelic population group (O'Halloran 1772, 64).

19. See, for instance, his statement that Ireland's "antient militia were, for comeliness of appearance, for activity and personal courage, equal to any troops in the world; and the proofs they were obliged to give of these qualifications to obtain admittance into the corps are surprising, and can only be accounted for, from the military genius of the people" (O'Halloran 1772, 124). The referenced "qualifications" can only have been the conditions for entry into the Fianna detailed by Keating, which were in turn summarized from the twelfth-century *Áirem Muintire Finn* (The enumeration of Fionn's people) (Keating 1908, 332–35).

20. O'Halloran 1772, 43–44, 163–64.

21. O'Halloran 2004, 109.

22. Ní Mhunghaile 2008, 184.

23. This was not, in fact, the earliest Anglo-Irish attempt to form an antiquarian society, but it was the first after a long hiatus. The Physico-Historical Society was formed in 1744 by a group of eminent Dublin men and it remained active until the mid-1750s (O'Conor 1949, 326).

24. O'Halloran 2004, 38; O'Conor 1949, 332–33; Ó Catháin 1993, 502–3, 519.

25. Love 1962, 419–28. Two members disagreed with the Phoenician origin hypothesis. As Clare O'Halloran notes, the position taken by Anglo-Irish academics was "linked directly to one of the major contemporary political issues of the second half of the eighteenth century—namely what to do about the panoply of discriminatory laws against Catholics" (2010, 330). Those for the repeal of the penal laws generally supported the Phoenician / civilized origin hypothesis, while those who still perceived Catholics as a serious threat and therefore saw the laws as justified supported the Northern European / barbaric origin hypothesis.

26. O'Conor 1949, 335–36; Love 1962, 429. The early surge of support for the Royal Irish Academy has been related to the optimistic—and patriotic—atmosphere accompanying the granting of legislative independence to Grattan's Parliament (Breatnach 1965, 89–90).

27. Ní Mhunghaile 2010a, 237.

28. While the Royal Irish Academy's collection would come to number in the hundreds in the mid-nineteenth century, Clare O'Halloran notes that as late as 1831, it only had four Gaelic manuscripts. However, she points out that the library at Trinity College "remained *the* library of Academy antiquaries down to the mid-nineteenth century" (2004, 173). Trinity College had been gathering manuscripts since the early seventeenth century, and in the 1780s it received the important gift of Edward Lhuyd's Irish manuscript collection, which included the Yellow Book of Lecan and the Book of Leinster; see O'Halloran 2004, 172; Ní Shéaghdha 1985, 4, 7–8.

29. Ní Mhunghaile 2008, 191–92; O'Halloran 2004, 173; O'Conor 1949, 333. In the first volume of the Royal Irish Academy's *Transactions*, another scholar-scribe, Theophilus O'Flanagan, famously publicized a forged ogham stone in Co. Clare said to mark the grave of Conán, inspiring much research into ogham; the stone was first noted in 1780 in a travel guide written by the poet John Lloyd (Seon Lúid). O'Flanagan was a close friend of Matthew Young and would go on to aid Joseph Cooper Walker and Charlotte Brooke (all discussed in this chapter). See Lloyd 1780, 9; O'Flanagan 1787; Ní Mhunghaile 2009b; Leaney 2009; McManus 1991, xi, 131.

30. This is hardly surprising; as Lesa Ní Mhunghaile's article on bilingualism and print culture during the period evidences, the Gaelic literati of the time straddled the Anglophone and Gaelophone public spheres. They kept abreast of news and publications in English and did not simply work for the benefit of others, but were actively involved in publication projects of their own (2012, 229–37).

31. Bruford 1969, 48, 251–67; Flahive 2017, 47. Alan Bruford discusses these scribes' activities in greater detail and notes the semiprofessional status of many of them. An examination of the dates (when given) in his inventory of Irish manuscript copies of Fenian romances reveals that nearly twice as many were penned after the publication of *Ossian* as before.

32. O'Halloran 2004, 101.

33. Breatnach 1965, 90–91. Walker was only twenty-six when this book was published.

34. Outwardly, Walker denounced Macpherson as an unfaithful adaptor of an already degenerate Scottish Fenian tradition (Walker 1786, 109–10; Mac Craith 2000, 8).

35. Walker 1786, 42–43; O'Halloran 1989, 85–86. Attributions to Fearghus are also included in the Book of the Dean of Lismore; see McLauchlan 1862, 1:43, 48.

36. Walker 1786, 111–20, appendix 57.

37. O'Halloran 2010, 333.

38. Gibbons 1998, 251; Stafford 1996b, 85–86.

39. Gibbons 1998, 231.

40. Edmund de Harold, also discussed in this section, dedicated a book of Ossianic-style poetry to Henry Grattan (Gibbons 1998, 233, 235).

41. Ní Mhunghaile 2008, 192; O'Halloran 1989, 84; Young 1787. By the time of printing, versions of all the lays in Young's collection had appeared previously in Scottish publications. The Scottish Gaelic volume of Rev. John Smith's Ossianic imitations was also published in 1787.

42. Young 1787, 44–45.

43. Young 1787, 50–51.

44. Young 1787, 45. Macpherson viewed the Patrician material as a late Irish accretion.

45. Harold 1787a; Harold 1787b. Harold had, in fact, contributed to that popularity by publishing his own German translation of Macpherson's *Ossian* in 1775.

46. Harold 1787a, iv; Gaskill 2004, 15.

47. Harold 1787a, iv–vi; Gibbons 1998, 234–35. Harold further pursued his creative engagement with *Ossian* by composing a German-language drama in the Macphersonic style, *Sulmora, Tochter Cuthullins,* published in 1802.

48. Gaskill 2004, 16.

49. Ní Mhunghaile 2009a, I. xxiii, xxv.

50. Walker 1786, 41–42, note 'p.' Walker reports a conversation with Brooke in which she described hearing one of her father's laborers reading poetry aloud from an Irish manuscript. She is said to have studied the language for a couple years, but little is known for certain about the type or duration of any formal training she may have received (Ní Mhunghaile 2009a, I. xxv–xxvi).

51. Mac Craith 2000, 16. Brooke included *Laoidh Mhághnuis Mhóir* (The lay of Mánus the Great), *Laoidh na Seilge, Cath Rìgh na Sorcha* (The battle of the king of Sorcha), *Rosg Osguir mhic Oisín re hucht Chatha Gabhra* (The incitement of Oscar mac Oisín before the Battle of Gabhair) and *Rosg Ghoill mhic Mhorna* (The incitement of Goll mac Morna) in her anthology (Brooke 2009 [1789], 37–134, 151–75, 271–93, 296–300). *Laoidh na Seilge* stands apart, bearing little resemblance to anything in *Ossian*.

52. Brooke's familiarity with other aspects of the Fenian tradition is evident in her notes, which include verses from Fenian lays not included in the collection; cf. Ní Mhunghaile 2009a, I. xxviii.

53. Leerssen 2004, 115. The formatting of the originals contributes to the appearance of greater authority; they are made to mimic early manuscript form, appearing in block text and Irish characters, rather than the stanzaic presentation of the English translations, and they occasionally include abbreviations (Ní Mhunghaile 2009a, I. xxix). Some years ago, Kenneth Gantz also noted that Brooke's careful provision of dates, delineation of customs, discussion of geography, and provision of manuscript references reflect a concern with her texts being recognized as authentic in light of the criticism of *Ossian* (1940, 140–41).

54. Brooke 2009 [1789], 27, vii.

55. O'Halloran 2004, 119.

56. O'Halloran 2004, 119. O'Halloran also comments on Brooke's greater propensity toward a primitivist view of early Irish culture than those who came before her, highlighting Brooke's assertion that to the early poets "both art and nature came arrayed in simple dignity; and afforded not that variety of circumstance, and appearance so calculated to call forth fancy, and diversify ideas" (O'Halloran 2004, 121; Brooke 2009 [1789], 237).

57. Ní Mhunghaile 2009a, I. xli. Ní Mhunghaile's edition includes new translations and commentary for each poem.

58. Ní Mhunghaile 2009a, I. xlii. O'Halloran's influence is readily apparent in his authorship of the introduction to the poem "Conlach."

59. O'Halloran 1989, 83.

60. Ní Mhunghaile 2010b, 28. Brooke was also responsible for translating two poems attributed to Carolan in Walker's *Historical Memoirs of the Irish Bards* (Ní Mhunghaile 2009a, I. xxvi).

61. Brooke 2009 [1789], 230–31; Ní Mhunghaile 2010b, 23, 26–27.

62. Ní Mhunghaile 2010b, 29. Ní Mhunghaile discusses manuscript circulation in eighteenth-century Ireland as a form of publication (2012, 227–29). For a discussion of the intersection of print and manuscript traditions in Ireland during the eighteenth and nineteenth centuries, see Ní Úrdail 2000, 204–25. Ní Mhunghaile also addresses the possibility that Brooke's texts may have reentered or bolstered the oral tradition (2010b, 31). The boundary between literary and oral texts was highly permeable; however, Brookeian resonances in orally collected Irish Fenian lays has not been studied.

63. O'Halloran 1989, 89. *Reliques of Irish Poetry* also bolstered the "'cult of Carolan'" (Ní Mhunghaile 2010b, 28).

64. Wilson's anthology of Irish and Scottish Gaelic poetry contained the text and a loose translation of *Cath Chnoic an Áir* (The Battle of the Hill of Slaughter), a loose translation of *Laoidh an Deirg mhic Droichil,* and a heavily adapted English version of *Laoidh Mná Mheargaigh* (The lay of the wife of Meargach) (Wilson [1792], 1–20, 59–63, 86–96; Mac Craith 2004, 93–96, 98–105).

65. Mary Helen Thuente explores the United Irishmen's use of cultural symbols. See, in particular, her discussion of Celticism and antiquarianism (1994, 26–34).

66. Glass 1792. A contribution influenced by *Ossian* also turned up on the third page of the antepenultimate issue of the *Northern Star* on May 12, 1797, where Thomas Moore's "Extract from a Poem in Imitation of Ossian" first appeared; see Thuente 1994, 118, 247–48. Moore would go on to publish the popular collection *Irish Melodies* in 1808. The *Northern Star* ceased publication due to the destruction of its printing presses in a raid (McDowell 1986, 353).

67. *Bolg an tsoláthair* suggests a bag of provisions or miscellaneous items, and in literary terms it has come to mean a miscellany; see Ó Dónaill 2005 [1977], 123, s.v. "bolg"; Dinneen 1934 [1927], 108, s.v. "bolg."

68. Thuente 1994, 9, 75–101; [Lynch] 1795, 73–101. The projected readership included people from all social classes and linguistic backgrounds.

69. Thuente 1994, 96. This significance was not heralded in commentary (of which there was none) but was left to readers to deduce on their own.

70. [Lynch] 1795, ix; Uí Chollatáin 2010, 51–52.

71. McDowell 1986, 294–302, 347–51, 353–69; O'Halloran 2010, 330.

72. O'Halloran 2010, 331; Ní Mhunghaile 2008, 194; Gibbons 1998, 242. Walker was one of the few antiquarians who maintained interest, now limiting his focus to the literary content of narratives like *Oisín i dTír na nÓg* (Oisín in the Land of Youth) and avoiding any suggestion of cultural continuity (O'Halloran 2004, 179–80).

73. Owenson 1999 [1807], 47; O'Halloran 2010, 332, 336.

74. Owenson 1999 [1807], 106–16; O'Halloran 1989, 91–92. Owenson turned to Keating for further information on "the *Finian* [*b*]*and,* or ancient militia of Ireland" (1999 [1807], 25n1).

75. O'Halloran 1989, 91.

76. O'Flanagan 1808, 189–223, quoted at 189. O'Flanagan also included a translation of the Ulster cycle story of Deirdre, drawing attention to the tale's resonances in *Ossian* (1808, 1–179).

77. The volume largely consisted of a chronology of Gaelic authors and their works compiled by lexicographer Edward O'Reilly, who accepted Fearghus Finnbhéil as a third-century poet but expressed doubt that poems attributed to Oisín were "the genuine compositions of that bard" (1820, xxiii, xxv).

78. Crofts 1819; [Griffin] 1832, 78–79; Sharpe and Hoyne 2020, 508–9, 701–702; Ó Ciosáin 1997, 57.

79. Anon. 1825, 3, 11–39; Sharpe and Hoyne 2020, 570–71. This anthology included *Geinealach Oisín* (Oisín's genealogy), *Laoidh Mhághnuis Mhóir* (reprinted from Brooke), *Laoidh na Seilge* (reprinted from Brooke), *Cath Rìgh na Sorcha* (reprinted from Brooke), and *Laoidh na Buadhachta* (The lay of the victory).

80. Connellan 1829a, 1–10, 20–22; Connellan 1829b, part 2: 6, 20, 50–60, 74–84. The former included six Fenian lays: *Laoidh an Doirn* (The lay of the fist), *Duan Ghairbh mhic Stairn* (The lay of Garbh son of Starn), *Suirghe Fhinn go Críocha Lochlann* (Fionn's courting in Lochlann), *Seilg Tuirc Ghleanna an Scáil* (The hunt for the boar of Gleann an Scáil), *Cath Chnoic an Áir*, and *Laoidh na Seilge* (the same version as in Brooke's anthology and the anonymous *Reliques of Irish Poetry*). The latter contained four lays—*Lon Doire an Chairn, Laoidh an Deirg mhic Droichil, Tuarasgabháil Chatha Gabhra* (The account of the Battle of Gabhair), and *Laoidh Chatha Gabhra* (The lay of the Battle of Gabhair)—as well as a three-stanza fragment of a lay not yet identified. A Protestant convert, Connellan also produced several Irish language learning texts for the purpose of proselytization, and he may have been involved in the preparation of the second edition of Brooke's *Reliques of Irish Poetry* (Ní Mhunghaile 2009a, I. xxxii, n51).

81. Drummond 1830; O'Reilly 1830; O'Halloran 1989, 94. Drummond was the Royal Irish Academy's librarian. He had earlier commented on Macpherson's "fictions" in notes to his poem *The Giants' Causeway*, which incorporates the legend of Fionn's construction of this Co. Antrim geological feature (1811, 9–17, 110). He would go on to produce *Ancient Irish Minstrelsy* (1852), an anthology of translated lays. O'Reilly had earlier expressed skepticism about the language of the Gaelic *Ossian* in the *Transactions of the Iberno-Celtic Society* (1820, xxiii).

82. O'Grady 1926, 642; Hardiman 1831. The lay is *Laoidh Bhinne Boilbin* (The lay of Benbulbin). The British Library copy of the collection is MS Egerton 144; the Royal Irish Academy copy is MS 12 I 16 (O'Grady 1926, 642–44; Ó Briain 2013, 264).

83. Connellan 1829a; Connellan 1829b; Ó Briain 2013, 262–63.

84. Ó Buachalla 1968, 69–80, 95–101. See also Hughes 1998; Ó Giolláin 2000, 98–99. MacAdam is known today for amassing the largest single collection of Irish proverbs.

85. *Laoidh na Mná Móire thar Lear* (The lay of the big woman beyond the sea), *Laoidh na Seilge*, and a proverb beginning "bhí oiread Osgair ann a dá bhonn" are contained in MS 31 of the Bryson and MacAdam Collection, catalogued in Ó Buachalla 1962, 28, 29, 31; see also Hughes 1998, 144, 157. While MacAdam reported being told of people in Inishowen, Donegal who could "repeat old poems and Fenian tales" and he was "particularly desirous to see these preserved and published," I have not located any such tales in the Belfast Central Library; they may yet turn up elsewhere (Ó Buachalla 1962, 96).

86. Croker 1824, 14, 99; O'Halloran 2012, 202–4. Croker referred approvingly to Giraldus Cambrensis's disparaging assessment of Irish character in his *Researches in the South of Ireland*, published one year before *Fairy Legends and Traditions of the South of Ireland* (1824, 13).

87. Croker 1825 28; Dorson 1966, v; Markey 2006, 21, 25–26. Croker subsequently published two additional volumes of *Fairy Legends and Traditions*. Less than a year after the first volume was published, Jacob Grimm translated it for a German popular market.

88. [Otway] 1827, 181–200; Carleton 1845, 97–112. Otway's version of *Macgnímartha Finn* was reprinted in the *Dublin Penny Journal* (Otway 1832). Carleton's version of *Fionn sa Chliabhán*, which set the tale at the Giant's Causeway, was first published in *Chambers' Edinburgh Journal* (Carleton 1841).

89. Ó Cadhla 2007, 25–26, 152, 238.

90. Boyle 1992, 52.

91. Doherty 2004, 15, 29–32.

92. Leerssen 1997, 101–2.

93. Sheehy 1980, 20. Petrie is now principally remembered as a collector of traditional airs due to the popularity of *The Petrie Collection of the Ancient Music of Ireland* (1855).

94. Leerssen 1997, 106–7; O'Halloran 2004, 38; Murray 2000, 23–25, 30–31.

95. For example, the first volume of the *Transactions of the Kilkenny Archaeological Society* contains a short summary of the story of Diarmaid and Gráinne and information about some "leapacha Dhiarmada agus Ghráinne" ("beds of Diarmaid and Gráinne"), as the distinctive prehistorical dolmens scattered throughout Ireland are known colloquially (Prim 1849, 18–20).

The Kilkenny Archaeological Society eventually became the Royal Society of Antiquaries of Ireland.

96. Ó Catháin 2009.

97. O'Curry 1861, 301, 304.

98. O'Curry 1861, 319. O'Curry also dedicated part of his nineteenth lecture to prophecies attributed to Fionn.

99. Nicholas O'Kearney penned an earlier scholarly introduction to the Fenian cycle in the first Ossianic Society volume (1854, 9–67), but O'Curry's overview was more authoritative. Subsequent introductions by Standish Hayes O'Grady and Owen Connellan also went to print before O'Curry's lecture was published (O'Grady 1857, 15–39; Connellan 1860).

100. Connolly 1989a, 79–82, 93–94; Connolly 1989b, 56–58, 70–71.

101. O'Halloran 2010, 343; Leerssen 1997, 158. O'Connell's position on the Irish language was pragmatic; English was increasingly seen by Gaels as a means of social advancement. See Doyle 2015, 108–13; Leerssen 1997, 157.

102. Sheehy 1980, 30; Thuente 1994, 193, 222–23.

103. Donnelly 1989, 361–69.

104. As one collector of Fenian traditions lamented, "My researches cannot be now made with such facility as in by-gone days—and those not remote either . . . Now, alas! the storytelling peasant is in his grave, the poor-house, or the wilds of America" (Dunne 1851, 334).

105. The Trinity College chair was created for the purpose of proselytism and located in the Divinity School. Its first occupant was Rev. Thomas Coney (Walsh 2007, 156, 160–62). John O'Donovan was appointed to the Belfast chair, Owen Connellan to the Cork chair, and Cornelius Mahony to the Galway chair (167, 169).

106. These followed Belfast native Henry R. Montgomery's *Specimens of the Early Native Poetry of Ireland*, an anthology of previously published translations of "historical interest" situated within "a running commentary . . . to illustrate the ages to which they respectively belong" (1846, iv). Alongside two Fenian lays extracted from Brooke's collection, Montgomery reaffirmed Fionn's Irish lineage and denounced the "daring and ingenious attempt of Mr. Macpherson to impose upon public credulity" (26, 29).

107. Simpson 1856.

108. Simpson 1857, 10. Simpson appears to have encountered a manuscript collection of lays in the *Agallamh Oisín agus Phádraig* (Dialogue between Oisín and Patrick) sequence. It is likely that some of his orally collected material was transmitted in prose rather than in verse.

109. Drummond 1852, ix. Drummond was aided in his translations and research by Eugene O'Curry and Nicholas O'Kearney (59, 61, 65, 88).

110. See Drummond 1852, 14–18, 133–38, 272–74 for translations of Kennedy's *Laoidh Mhághnuis Mhóir*, *Bàs Chairill* (The death of Caireall), and *Bàs Oisein* (The death of Oisean). John Francis Campbell suspected *Bàs Oisein* had been "made up of fragments and mended" by Kennedy (1872, 196). Drummond also adapted part of Rev. John Smith of Campbeltown's "Manos" (Drummond 1852, 139–40; Smith 1780, 260–61).

111. The orally collected specimen was a version of *Turas Fhinn go Teamhraigh* (Fionn's foray to Tara). Drummond used a more complete manuscript witness for his translation, which is the earliest published one (1852, 171–82).

112. Drummond 1852, 172.

113. O'Daly 1853, 3.

114. O'Kearney 1854, 134–53; O'Kearney 1855, 117–99; O'Grady 1857, 40–211; O'Donovan 1859; O'Daly 1859, 1–226; O'Daly 1861.

115. Connellan 1860, 172. O'Kearney also railed against Macpherson's descriptions of ghosts in his introduction to the first volume, claiming of one such description, "This impudent piece of forgery, of itself, is sufficient to damn for ever any pretension to authenticity that

Macpherson's supporters can claim for his poems" (1854, 30). Others rarely mentioned him or his works.

116. Murray 2000, 74, 78. The cost of publications was included in the society's very reasonable annual membership fee of five shillings.

117. O'Kearney 1855, 9; cf. O'Grady 1857, 15.

118. O'Daly 1853, 3. Drummond had likewise suggested that "every genuine patriot" should take an interest in Fenian literature (1852, xv).

119. O'Grady 1857, 9; O'Daly 1861, ix; Murray 2000, 75, 92–93.

120. Murray 2000, 108–9; Davis 2009. O'Brien was not a supporter of the IRB. One IRB member, James O'Mahony of Bandon, Co. Cork, was an officer in the Ossianic Society.

121. O'Mahony 1857a, 345n64; Uí Fhlannagáin 2008, 1, 10–11. Cognizant of the Ossianic controversy, O'Mahony also referenced Macpherson and his supporters and derided their "surreptitious attempts to rob Ireland of Finn and his heroes" (1857a, 347n65). That same year he began coediting the nascent Gaelic Department in the *Irish-American* (New York), contributing commentary to the Fenian lay *Lon Doire an Chairn* in the first column: O'Mahony 1857b; see also Knight 2021.

122. O'Keeffe 1878. Fionnuala Uí Fhlannagáin questions O'Keeffe's reliability (2008, 26).

123. O'Mahony 1860.

124. O'Mahony 1859.

125. Hayes-McCoy 1979, 155–57; Anon. 2016. The *Gal Gréine* is alternatively known as *Glas Gréine, Gath Gréine, Dealbh Grèine,* and *Deò-Ghrèine* in the lays; see, e.g., Campbell 1872, 73, 98; MacNeill 1908, 13; Laoide 1916, 76; Ross 1939, 88.

126. See Uí Fhlannagáin 2008, 25, 328–31.

127. Cf. Steward and McGovern 2013, 23. This folktale is known as *Na Fianna ina gCodladh Faoin Talamh* (The Fianna asleep underground).

128. O'Curry thought little of O'Kearney and had nothing positive to say about O'Grady's *Tóraidheacht Dhiarmada agus Ghráinne*; see O'Curry 1858.

129. Sommerville-Woodward 2004, 142–45, 147, 149–56; Murray 2000, 126–28.

130. Steward and McGovern 2013, 194, 200–11. For the IRB, which persisted considerably longer than its American counterpart; see chapter 8.

131. Anon. 1867.

132. Sommerville-Woodward 2004, 157.

133. See chapter 8.

134. Walsh 2007, 167–71, 174.

Chapter 7. Scottish Gaelic Folklore in an Ossianic Shadow

1. Campbell's father was forced to give up Islay to resolve his debts in 1847, at which point the family departed from the island (Thompson 1985, 7).

2. Campbell 1994a [1860], 10; Campbell 1870b, 325–26. As Frank Thompson observes, Campbell's memories of the bagpiper are from a very early period in his life, since he would not yet have been ten years of age when the bagpiper died in 1831 at the age of thirty-six (Thompson 1985, 3).

3. Campbell 1870b, 326. Elsewhere Campbell is more circumspect, writing to his aunt, for instance, "I only happened to know of [the] existence [of Gaelic folktales] from having heard a few from my nurse John Campbell the piper" (J. F. Campbell to [Lady Caroline Charteris], draft, June 19, 1859, NLS Adv. MS 50.1.14, f. 201a).

4. Campbell 1994a [1860], 28.

5. Dorson 1968, 393.

6. Campbell 1994a [1860], 6–9, 78. In a draft of a letter to Dasent dated February 23, 1859, Campbell wrote: "If the Celts did come from the East their traditions should be worth getting

together" (NLS Adv. MS 50.1.14, f. 2; cf. Campbell 1994a [1860], 42). He would go on to write a comparative theoretical monograph titled "Oral Mythology" (NLS Adv. MS 50.3.2), which was rejected by a publisher in 1870, but which, in the opinion of prominent turn-of-the-century English folklorist Alfred Nutt, could have had a significant impact on the emerging discipline (Nutt 1890a, 370–71). Campbell's views on contemporary folklore theory and his own ideas about the emergence of folklore are summarized in a paper he read before the Ethnological Society of London in March 1870 (Campbell 1870b, 329–30, 332–39). For more on Campbell's unpublished monograph and his engagement with the work of Dasent and the Grimms, see Shaw 2022.

7. Campbell 1994a [1860], 12. Campbell's written Gaelic had improved immensely by the later, Fenian-focused stage of his folklore research, as his journals and notes evidence.

8. The most productive of Campbell's collectors were Hector MacLean of Islay, Hector Urquhart of Argyll, John Dewar of Argyll, and Alexander Carmichael of Lismore, who altogether covered a large swath of the Highlands and Islands.

9. According to Donald A. MacDonald, Campbell's complete collection contains "over a million and a quarter words of oral tradition" (MacDonald 1985, 14). Campbell himself ascertained that the collecting project, which ran from 1859–60, resulted in the transcription of 791 stories (Campbell 1862, 464).

10. Draft copies of the letters in which Campbell advised his collectors are preserved in NLS Adv. MS 50.1.14.

11. Campbell 1994a [1860], x–xvii; 6; Campbell 1994b [1860–62], vi–xiii.

12. Campbell 1994a [1860], 82–83.

13. G. W. Dasent to J. F. Campbell, February 17, 1859, NLS Adv. MS 50.1.14, f. 3.

14. Campbell 1994a [1860], 10, 50–56.

15. Campbell 1994a [1860], 90; cf. J. F. Campbell to H. MacLean, draft, July 7, 1860, NLS Adv. MS 50.1.14, f. 479a. While there is immense value in having paradigms that enable the identification of structural similarities and aid the comparative study of folktales, the search for ancient *ur*-forms of tales has long since been abandoned in favor of the study of living folklore "as an integral, inseparable constituent of culture" (Dégh 1995, 263–64).

16. Campbell 1994a [1860], 3.

17. Cf. Campbell 1978, 9; Stiùbhart 2013, 30–31.

18. J. F. Campbell to G. W. Dasent, draft, February 19, 1859, NLS Adv. 50.1.14, ff. 4–4a.

19. G. W. Dasent to J. F. Campbell, March 6, 1859, NLS Adv. 50.1.14, ff. 5a-6.

20. Campbell 1994a [1860], 9–10.

21. Campbell 1994a [1860], 19.

22. J. F. Campbell to H. MacLean, draft, May 19, 1859, NLS Adv. MS 50.1.14, ff. 165–165a; J. F. Campbell to H. Urquhart, draft, May 19, 1859, NLS Adv. MS 50.1.14, f. 170; J. F. Campbell to the Duke of Manchester, draft, June 5, 1859, NLS Adv. MS 50.1.14, f. 177.

23. W. F. Skene to J. F. Campbell, May 12, 1859, NLS Adv. MS 50.1.14, ff. 142–43. Campbell put Skene in touch with the Duke of Manchester.

24. J. F. Campbell to G. W. Dasent, draft, June 7, 1859, NLS Adv. MS 50.1.14, f. 191a.

25. J. F. Campbell to G. W. Dasent, draft, September 11, 1859, NLS Adv. MS 50.1.14, f. 275a. Campbell describes this lay, a version of *Duan a' Mhuileartaich* (The lay of the Muileartach) and its reciter in the first volume of *Popular Tales of the West Highlands* (Campbell 1994a [1860], 18).

26. Campbell 1994a [1860], 22.

27. Campbell 1994a [1860], 19, 20, 22.

28. Campbell 1994a [1860], 22–24.

29. Campbell 1862, 5. See, e.g., J. D. Dougall to J. F. Campbell, December 3, 1860, NLS Adv. MS 50.2.1, ff. 258–258a: "In any future editions could you possibly publish the originals of any of Ossian's poems side by side with Macpherson's paraphrase in translation? Or, do such

originals not exist?" See also the response of Duncan Campbell, secretary of the Glasgow Celtic Society, written December 28, 1860, NLS Adv. MS 50.2.1, ff. 276–276a.

30. D. Douglas to J. F. Campbell, November 14, 1860, NLS Adv. MS 50.2.1, f. 213a. Douglas envisioned a volume of lays that "would come out best after the publication of the Deans book had proved uncontestably that there was a *written Gaelic* literature in the 16th century" (D. Douglas to J. F. Campbell, January 4, 1861, NLS Adv. MS 50.2.1, ff. 115a–116). McLauchlan's edition of the Book of the Dean of Lismore was published in 1862. McLauchlan had edited a new edition of the Gaelic *Ossian* three years previously for a different press.

31. Campbell had already received roughly twenty items about the Fianna that Hector MacLean collected in September and October 1860. The bulk of the Fenian material he received in 1861—approximately thirty items—came from Alexander Carmichael, who noted that he "might have got a great deal of Ossianic Poetry" prior to that point, "were it not that I thought you did not care much for it" (A. Carmichael to J. F. Campbell, November 19, 1861, NLS Adv. MS 50.1.11, f. 429).

32. D. Douglas to J. F. Campbell, April 12, 1761, NLS Adv. MS 50.2.1, f. 132; T. McLauchlan to D. Douglas, n.d. [May 1761], NLS Adv. MS 50.2.1, f. 140.

33. Campbell 1862, 10–34. Campbell was critical of the Irish cultural nationalist perspective outlined by Owen Connellan in the fifth Ossianic Society volume. He was far more approving of Eugene O'Curry's scholarship.

34. *Laoidh Dhiarmaid* relates the death of the Fenian warrior Diarmaid in a treacherous hunt for a poisonous boar; see chapter 3, as well as Sumner 2018 and Meek 1990.

35. Campbell 1862, 130–35.

36. Campbell printed statements by Hector MacLean, John Dewar, Donald K. Torrie, Alexander Carmichael, and Glasgow Gaelic publisher Archibald Sinclair. The originals of these are in NLS Adv. MS 50.1.6. MacLean's statement takes the form of an academic essay. Among his observations, he provides an analysis of the language of the Gaelic *Ossian* (Campbell 1862, 173–77).

37. Campbell 1862, 248–50, cf. 6–7.

38. Campbell 1862, 252.

39. J. F. Campbell, note to "A Chaora Bhoidheach Ghlas," NLS Adv. MS 50.1.11, f. 326.

40. Campbell 1862, 233, 239–47.

41. Note to "Osein na Sheann Aois," NLS Adv. MS 50.1.12, f. 222. Carmichael knew Macpherson's *Ossian* well—so well that it may have affected the accuracy of some of the material he transcribed. Unlike the other collectors, Carmichael was pressed to send Campbell copies of his field notes. Even so, Campbell printed very little of the substantial amount of material that Carmichael sent him, likely due to his enduring uncertainty about Carmichael's methodology; see Stiùbhart 2008, 25.

42. "A Mhuireartach," NLS Adv. MS 50.1.12, ff. 161–63. The lay in question, *Duan a' Mhuileartaich*, has only been collected in Scotland.

43. A. Carmichael to J. F. Campbell, December 19, 1861, NLS Adv. MS 50.1.12, f. 214.

44. Arnold 1867, 152–53. Arnold was not necessarily aware of Campbell's recent reappraisal, tucked away as it was in a folklore series. As Patrick Sims-Williams has noted, the folklore of modern Celtic peoples was of less interest to Arnold than it would be to later revivalists; Arnold focused solely on "an idealized Celtic past" (Sims-Williams 1986, 86).

45. Sims-Williams 1986, 72.

46. Arnold 1867, 106–7.

47. Arnold 1867, 107, 111, 115–16, 177–78, quoted at 107.

48. Arnold 1867, 123–35, 152–58, quoted at 134.

49. Sims-Williams 1986, 73–74. Sims-Williams is essentially paraphrasing John Kelleher's earlier statements regarding Arnold and the Celtic Revival here; see Kelleher 1950, 200, 212.

50. Williams 2006, 43. As Daniel Williams shows, however, Arnold was not committed to the Celts' inferiority being an inherent quality; rather, he noted the ability of Celts to "become English," and strongly advocated such assimilation, both linguistically and culturally (44–45, 51–52).

51. Champion 1996, 71.

52. Sims-Williams 1986, 74.

53. Campbell jotted on the title page of his copy of MacNeill's booklet, "This has nothing new + ignores me altogether" (NLS Cam.2.c.13).

54. Campbell 1869. MacNeill's publisher acknowledged in a letter to Campbell dated January 27, 1869 that it was printed "for private circulation." Campbell first offered his review to Edmonston and Douglas in Edinburgh, whose rejection led him to rewrite it for the *Times*, where it appeared several months later; see the letters bound into the back of his copy of MacNeill's booklet (NLS Cam.2.c.13).

55. Clerk 1869. Campbell suspected "the minister" of authoring the piece; see the clipping bound into the front of his copy of MacNeill's booklet (NLS Cam.2.c.13).

56. Clerk 1870, xxii–xxiii, li–lii, lvi. Clerk went so far as to present Campbell's work as though it supported his argument (1870, lii), which Campbell declared "unfair" in the marginal notes to his copy (NLS Cam.1.b.3–4).

57. Campbell 1871; Shairp 1871. Campbell's contributions to the press were often anonymous. In this instance, he may have preferred to go unnamed because the book had been sent to him at Clerk's request, and Clerk had asked him "to call attention" to it (NLS Adv. MS 50.4.6, f. 2). Nonetheless, Clerk learned the truth and was "very bitter," according to Campbell (NLS Adv. MS 50.4.6, f. 1). Shairp was clearly unaware of the author's identity, praising Campbell's collecting work, but viewing the *Times* piece as an example of the "arrogant bigotry" of "some English, or at least Sassenach, critics" (Shairp 1871, 113–14).

58. Campbell 1871. Later that year one of Campbell's Irish correspondents, the scholar W. M. Hennessy, also criticized Clerk's position on authenticity in the *Academy*, accusing him of committing "very serious philological heresies" under the influence of an "Ossianic mania" (Hennessy 1871, 394).

59. Nearly all of the texts are of Scottish provenance, Irish manuscript collections not being well-known or readily accessible to Campbell. Apart from the Book of the Dean lays, he did not include material from publications that were not rare.

60. Campbell set out in August 1870 with folktales in mind; he was then completing a monograph titled "Oral Mythology" that would never be published (NLS Adv. MS 50.3.2). His focus shifted to the Fenian Cycle in early September, as Dòmhnall Uilleam Stiùbhart has noted (Stiùbhart 2014). In October he published an anonymous article in the *Inverness Courier* attempting (but largely failing) to turn up additional Fenian stores; see Campbell 1870a. Upon his return to the Highlands in autumn 1871, he was joined for a portion of his trip by Alexander Carmichael, who acted as a guide and introduced him to informants known to have Fenian material. Stiùbhart points out that this was "quite possibly the only time these two giants of Gaelic folklore collecting actually met" (Stiùbhart 2008, 6).

61. Collecting journal entry, September 17, 1870, NLS Adv. MS 50.2.2, f. 190 (punctuation added).

62. Campbell 1870a.

63. Collecting journal entry, September 30, 1871, NLS Adv. MS 50.2.4, ff. 199–202.

64. Campbell 1872, xxxv.

65. Cf. Campbell 1862, 134–36.

66. Campbell 1872, 212.

67. A. Carmichael to J. F. Campbell, November 4, 1872, NLS Adv. MS 50.2.17, ff. 25–25a. Nonetheless, Carmichael could not relinquish his belief that "Macpherson must have had much

more to go upon than anything that has been yet discovered" (A. Carmichael to J. F. Campbell, October 31, 1873, NLS Adv. MS 50.2.9, f. 174).

68. See Campbell's correspondence pertaining to *Leabhar na Féinne* in NLS Adv. MS 50.2.17; J. F. Campbell to A. Nicolson, draft, March 24, 1873, bound into the front of Campbell's copy of *An Gaidheal* 1 (NLS Cam.1.d.8); note, May 25, 1877, NLS Adv. MS 50.2.11, f. 252.

69. J. F. Campbell to C. S. Jerram, draft, March 12, 1874, written on the flyleaves of his copy of Jerram's *Dàn and Deirg, agus Tiomna Ghuill* (NLS Cam.1.g.48). Jerram would go on to express his opinion about *Ossian* to the Gaelic Society of Inverness in April 1876, there communicating a preference for Campbell's 1862 views over those more recently expressed (Jerram 1876, 104).

70. He did not see this a problematic; see Waddell 1878, 64.

71. Waddell 1875, 38. Waddell argued that *Ossian* contains accurate descriptions of topographical and geological features in Ireland, Scotland, the Orkneys, and Iceland, some of which would have been present only in the era in which the text is set. Since neither Macpherson nor any other person within the preceding half century could have known about these, he claimed that the text must therefore be an authentic composition of the third century or earlier. The actual geographical vagueness of *Ossian* lends an air of absurdity to Waddell's analysis.

72. MacLeod 2013, 34–37.

73. See Campbell's copy of Waddell's *Ossian and the Clyde*, NLS Cam.1.b.17, half title, p. 3, and p. 32. The choice to send Waddell a copy of *Leabhar na Féinne* was likely motivated as much by Campbell's aggravation as by Waddell's own initiative in first sending Campbell a copy of *Ossian and the Clyde*. Waddell's letter to Campbell preceding the arrival of the book is bound into the front of Campbell's copy.

74. Waddell, Clerk, Campbell, and Hector MacLean all participated in exchanges in the pages of the *Scotsman* (Edinburgh), the *Highlander* (Inverness), the *Coleraine Chronicle*, and the *Celtic Magazine* (Inverness) at this time. See the *Scotsman* of August 30, 2, 21; September 28, 11, 25, 28; October 29, 8, 12, 13; November 18, 1875; the *Highlander* of September 4, 1875; and the *Coleraine Chronicle* of May 13 and 27; June 17, 1, 8, 15; July 29, 5, 12, 19; August 26, 2, 16; September 30, 7, 21; October 28, 11; November 25; December 9, 1876. Some of the correspondence in the *Coleraine Chronicle* was reprinted in *Celtic Magazine* 1 (1876): 313–50 and 372–78; *Celtic Magazine* 2 (1877): 32–36. Waddell continued to write to the *Coleraine Chronicle* in 1878 and 1879, after his critics had ceased to respond. An earlier exchange between Campbell and Clerk, and columns by Waddell (after he had been shut out of the *Scotsman*), also appeared in *Celtic Magazine* 1 (1876): 18–22, 35–39, 67–71, and 99–105.

75. Note, May 25, 1877, NLS Adv. MS 50.2.11, f. 252. See also J. F. Campbell to W. F. Cumming, draft, December 20, 1872, NLS Adv. MS 50.2.16, ff. 17–18; J. F. Campbell to A. Nicolson, draft, March 24, 1873, bound into the front of Campbell's copy of *An Gaidheal* 1 (NLS Cam.1.d.8); and J. F. Campbell to the Highland Society of London, draft, July 16, 1873, written on the endpapers of Campbell's copy of the 1873 edition of *The Highland Society of London, and Branch Societies* (NLS Cam.1.f.13).

76. Note, January 3, 1874, NLS Adv. MS 50.3.9, f. 7. The article, which argued against contemporary (inaccurate) beliefs about clan tartans, was rejected in 1872; see NLS Adv. MS 50.3.9, f. 3.

77. A. Nicolson to J. F. Campbell, March [17?], 1873 and J. F. Campbell to A. Nicolson, draft, March 24, 1873, bound into the front of Campbell's copy of *An Gaidheal* 1 (NLS Cam.1.d.8).

78. Quoted in Kennedy 1892, clxiii–clxiv. Cameron, not having been slighted (as Campbell felt he had been) and with his passion for Gaelic studies intact, was not dissuaded from his plan.

79. See NLS Adv. MSS 50.2.11–50.2.16.

80. Note, May 15, 1876, NLS Adv. MS 50.2.11, f. iii; cf. note, June 12, 1876, NLS Adv. MS 50.2.9, f. 1; note, December 22, 1878, NLS Adv. MS 50.2.9, f. 24. Following the rejection, Campbell discussed the translation project with Whitley Stokes in India, opining that "nobody cares for

the subject except a few bookworms, Philologers and 'Keltomaniacs'" (note, May 25, 1877, NLS Adv. MS 50.2.11, f. 252; cf. note, July 11, 1877, NLS Adv. MS 50.2.16, f. 65).

81. Note, July 22, 1881, NLS Adv. MS 50.2.14, ff. 2–3.

82. Thompson 1984–86, 20; cf. Hunter 2000 [1976], 185–86.

83. Campbell's father had been the landlord on Islay until his financial insolvency forced him to give up the island. While on Islay he had, in fact, employed Murdoch's father; Campbell describes Murdoch as the "son of my Father's gamekeeper" (note, October 1, 1883, written on the endpapers of Campbell's copy of *Transactions of the Gaelic Society of Inverness* 1 [1872], NLS Cam.2.e.8).

84. Note, January 3, 1874, NLS Adv. MS 50.3.9, f. 7. "Home Rule" refers to the emerging campaign for parliamentary devolution in Ireland. This campaign would be reformulated and strengthened under the leadership of Charles Stewart Parnell in the 1880s. "Fenianism" by this time had come to refer to support of the Irish Republican Brotherhood, which had an interest in the Home Rule movement (Hutchinson 1987, 157). A similar campaign would soon emerge in Scotland and Blackie would become the first chair of the Scottish Home Rule Association in 1886 (Hunter 1975, 189). "The abolition of Game and Landlords" and "the Commune" refer to the promotion of an idealized Highland communal system of landholding over the landlord-dominated crofting system; this was a feature of the Scottish crofters' rights movement and the subject of a pamphlet authored by Blackie in 1880 (Harvie 1996, 248). Some of the scholarly work in this area was also done by Alexander Carmichael, whose appendix on Hebridean land customs in the third volume of W. F. Skene's *Celtic Scotland* led to his being asked to contribute appendices on the topic to the report of the Napier Commission on crofters' rights in 1883 (Stiùbhart 2008, 15).

85. Thompson 1984–86, 21–23.

86. J. F. Campbell to J. S. Blackie, April 17, 1871, NLS MS 2630, f. 31; note, NLS Adv. MS 50.4.6, f. 81.

87. J. F. Campbell to J. S. Blackie, January 9, 1876, NLS MS 2632, f. 9; note, July 22, 1881, NLS Adv. MS 50.2.14, f. iii.

88. Note, January 10, 1876, NLS Cam.1.b.3–4, p. lxvi.

89. Note, September 4, 1876, NLS MS Adv. 50.2.16, f. 167: "I wished to see Hector MacLean amongst those who are to lecture from the chair knowing him to be the fittest in Scotland by knowledge."

90. Kennedy 1892, clxviii–clxix; Mackechnie 1964, 52–53.

91. Meek 2004, 61; note, July 30, 1883, NLS MS Adv. 50.2.14, f. iii; cf. Mackechnie 1964, 54.

92. Note, October 1, 1883, written on the endpapers of Campbell's copy of *Transactions of the Gaelic Society of Inverness* 1 (1872) (NLS Cam.2.e.8), punctuation and capitalization adjusted.

93. See, for instance, Blackie's essay on Scottish nationality and Mackinnon's comments regarding "the northern Celt" in his inaugural address as Chair of Celtic (Blackie 1890; Mackinnon 1883, 8 et passim; cf. Kidd 1995, 64–66). In 1875, Blackie commissioned a translation of German scholar August Ebrard's essay supporting *Ossian*'s authenticity for publication in *An Gaidheal* 4 (279–88), which evoked further discussion in Scottish periodicals: see Maier 2022, 188–89.

94. In 1876 Blackie tried to goad Campbell into a public debate about *Ossian*. Campbell reflected, "I did not want to fight Blackie because to conquer him would be to damage the credit of the man who is working for the Celtic chair which I wish to see established" (note, September 4, 1876, NLS Adv. MS 50.2.16, f. 167; cf. Blackie 1876a; Anon. 1876). While Campbell's correspondence with Blackie was candid, he limited his public engagement with the professor to a polite exchange in the *Scotsman*, which he averred was intended "to kick up a dust in order that you might more easily pick the public pockets for a good cause" (J. F. Campbell to J. S. Blackie, July 21, 1877, NLS MS 2632, f. 231; Blackie and Campbell 1875a; 1875b).

95. Blackie 1876b, 226, 232–33.

96. "Coma an traths' co-dhiu is e Mac Mhuirich e fein a rinn 'Oisean' no nach e. B'fhior Ghaidheal e a dh'aon chor" (Mackinnon 1877, 356; translation adapted from Meek 2004, 62; cf. Mackinnon 1883, 33–34).

97. Meek 2004, 63. Nonetheless, some, like Carmichael's friend Keith Norman MacDonald of Skye and Edinburgh, and Rev. Duncan Blair of Barney's River, Nova Scotia, persisted in arguing for authenticity; see MacDonald 1904–5; MacDonald 1906; and Blàrach 2013 [1895].

98. Sharp published both under his own name and under the pseudonym, 'Fiona Macleod,' having derived the name 'Fiona' from Macpherson's spelling of 'Fianna' in *Ossian* (Pittock and Jack 2007, 342–43). Also significant is the depiction of Macpherson's Fingal, Ossian, Malvina, and Cuchullan alongside other Gaelic cultural symbols in artist John Duncan's *Anima Celtica,* published in the first issue of Geddes's periodical, the *Evergreen* (Duncan 1895; Macdonald 2003, 32–33).

99. Sharp 1896b, ix. Sharp was confused about the order in which Campbell's publications appeared, referring to *Leabhar na Féinne* as though it preceded *Popular Tales of the West Highlands,* and recommending that his readers consult only the fourth volume of the latter series because there Campbell's views "were more fully matured" (xiii).

100. Sharp 1896b, xxiii–xxiv.

101. Campbell 1907; Oates 2013, 147–61. The Marquis of Lorne, John G.E.H.D.S. Campbell, married Princess Louise, served as the fourth Governor General of Canada, and later succeeded his father as the ninth Duke of Argyll. He wrote the libretto and Hamish McCunn composed the score. The Campbells had long seen Diarmaid as an ancestor figure, which may explain Lorne's particular interest in the Diarmaid and Gráinne story: Gillies 1987, 60–61. Two additional Fenian operas were planned, but not completed: Oates 2013, 162–63.

102. Sharp 1896a, xxxvii–xxxviii. *Lyra Celtica* included translations of *Cétemain* (May Day), *Géisid cúan* (Créide's lament for Cáel, extracted from *Acallam na Senórach* [The dialogue of the elders]), *Na Brataichean* (The banners), and *Binn guth duine i dTír an Óir* ("Sweet is man's voice in the Land of Gold").

103. See chapter 8.

104. Stern 1895; Stern 1900b. Meyer would later address *Ossian* in one of a series of lectures at the University of Glasgow; see Anon. 1906.

105. Waddell 1878.

106. Kennedy 1892, clxiv–clxv. Preexisting Scottish journals were aimed at a more general readership.

107. Kennedy 1892, clxv–clxvii.

108. MacBain and Kennedy 1892, xii–xiv.

109. MacBain 1886 [paper presented in 1885], 207, 209, 211. See also MacBain 1887, in which he discussed *Ossian* at length. In his view, Macpherson innovated far more than Tennyson (with whom Campbell compared Macpherson) in the latter's adaptation of Arthurian legend (MacBain 1887, 254).

110. MacBain 1886, 194, 203–6; cf. MacBain 1891–94, 88–92. MacBain reached his conclusion by plotting Fionn's biography according to Alfred Nutt's reinterpretation of J. G. von Hahn's sixteen-stage 'Expulsion and Return' formula, which documented common incidents in Indo-European heroes' biographies; see Nutt 1881. Campbell, on the other hand, had invoked solar mythology; see Campbell 1862, 322. MacBain did not reference Campbell's work.

111. Henderson 1905–6. To complement his observations, Henderson transcribed and printed Campbell's consolidated narrative of Fionn's birth and boyhood from NLS Adv. MS 50.2.14.

112. It might be argued that such investigations of the historicity of the Fianna were themselves limited, concentrating narrowly on the origins of the tradition. Some, like W. A. Craigie, Professor of Latin at the University of St. Andrews, did approach the tradition from different angles. Highlighting a gap in Fenian scholarship as practiced by philologists, Craigie complained about the neglect of late manuscripts of great literary but little philological interest (Craigie 1894, 271). In other essays he explored Fenian lays (Craigie 1899) and Fenian references in Scottish Gaelic poetry of the preceding few centuries (Craigie 1908).

113. Lord Archibald Campbell was the brother of the Marquis of Lorne and the son of George Campbell, the eighth Duke of Argyll. The eighth Duke had also sponsored a collecting project, employing J. F. Campbell's collector John Dewar for a period after the completion of *Popular Tales of the West Highlands* to collect clan traditions and other folklore in Argyllshire, Arran, West Perthshire, and Lochaber; see Black 2016, 63. The Dewar manuscripts in the Inveraray Castle Archives contain a number of Fenian tales and lays.

114. MacInnes 1890; MacDougall 1891; Campbell 1891.

115. Nutt 1890b, 430n1. Nutt later condensed the commentary he made in the *Waifs and Strays* volumes into a pamphlet (Nutt 1899).

116. Nutt 1891, xxxvii–xxxviii.

117. The most substantial creative work was Donald Mackenzie's *Finn and His Warrior Band*, a 1911 retelling of Fenian tales for a juvenile audience. Appin-born author Katherine Whyte Grant also composed her children's play *Dùsgadh na Féinne* (The awakening of the Fianna), based on the folktale *Na Fianna ina gCodladh Faoin Talamh* (The Fianna asleep underground), in Sydney, Australia early in the century; see Grant 1908; Innes 2022; Innes and Mathis 2019.

118. Stiùbhart 2008, 13; Stiùbhart 2013, 50.

119. Only the first two volumes appeared during Carmichael's lifetime, both in 1900; the remaining four were published posthumously from additional material in his papers. On Carmichael's reworking of texts in *Carmina Gadelica* and the controversy surrounding this collection, see Black 2008 and Stiùbhart 2008.

120. These volumes were published posthumously, but the manuscript had been ready for the press since the mid-1870s (Black 2008, 61). The Gaelic texts were cut by the publisher, but they have been restored in the modern, combined edition, *The Gaelic Otherworld* (2005), edited by Ronald Black.

121. Stiùbhart 2008, 20.

122. Black 2008, 60.

Chapter 8. Fionn at the Birth of an Irish Nation

1. Campbell 1862, 435. Campbell also visited the Isle of Man in 1860 to search for and compare Gaelic folklore. While he failed to gather much material due to linguistic differences and his inability to gain Manx tradition bearers' confidence, he concluded that the tradition there was similar to that of Ireland and Scotland (Campbell 1994a [1860]: 30–34; cf. 23–24). As with Irish folklore, he expressed his "hope that some Manksman may be induced to gather the popular lore of his own country" (32).

2. This request was issued under a pseudonym, and readers were directed to send traditions to "Kennedy's Library, Angles-street." Underlying Kennedy's wish to publish folktales was his perception that "in the present transition state of the country, they are likely to be lost" ([Kennedy] 1851). He had witnessed the population decline in his own region as a result of "want and emigration," and he recognized that people's ways of life had changed since the famine (Kennedy 1866, vii–viii). Yet his nostalgia was limited to the loss of story material and did not reflect

a romanticized longing for an idealized, former way of life, as was the case among many later revivalists; so long as the tales were published, Kennedy asserted that "The loss after all is not so great. The curious will still have access to them, and if religion and sound knowledge take the place of idle and superstitious ideas in the minds of the populace, society will be the gainer" (Kennedy 1862b, 247).

3. Kennedy 1862a, 321–22. Kennedy also displayed his familiarity with collections by "Vellemarck, Souvestre, Grimm, Croker, Campbell, Keightley, Dasent, and others" in a *Dublin University Magazine* article (1862b, 247). For his understanding of comparative folkloristics, see Kennedy 1862a, 318–20.

4. Kennedy 1866, viii.

5. Campbell 1862, 435. In Kennedy's defense, there is reason to believe that he had not yet read this admonition in the final volume of *Popular Tales of the West Highlands*. In an 1866 letter to Campbell he asked to exchange two of his books for the third and fourth volumes of Campbell's series, which he said he had not been able to purchase in Dublin; see P. Kennedy to J. F. Campbell, December 12, 1866, bound into the front of Campbell's copy of *Legendary Fictions of the Irish Celts* (NLS Cam. 2.f.22). Despite Kennedy's stylistic interference, folklorists have determined that structurally, his recollected versions are likely to have been relatively accurate. As Bo Almqvist notes, Kennedy tended "to elaborate on his raw material and bestow upon it a literary style. He is also particularly fond of introducing extra humorous elements . . . and he has a tendency to heap hibernicism on hibernicism, all of which creates an absurd stage-Irish effect. There is nothing to indicate that Kennedy took major liberties with the content of his stories, however" (1991, 10–11; see also Delaney 1983, 35).

6. Kennedy 1866, viii–ix. Kennedy's literary sources included the editions of manuscript texts in the second and third volumes of the *Transactions of the Ossianic Society*, published in 1855 and 1857 (220, 223, 224).

7. Cf. Kennedy 1866, 196–202. Even Campbell was more concerned with structural than literal accuracy, although Kennedy's methodology certainly fell short of Campbell's standards. We can infer that Campbell informed him of this from Kennedy's response, dated December 19, 1866 and bound into the front of Campbell's copy of *Legendary Fictions of the Irish Celts* (NLS Cam. 2.f.22).

8. Kennedy 1866, 22–3, 208–9.

9. Language shift is not the only way Fenian folklore could become current in Anglic languages, as the early knowledge of Fenian lore in Scots-speaking regions attests (see chapter 4). The collection of Fenian tales from Scottish travelers who frequented both Gaelophone and Anglophone areas, and who could tell the tales in either language, evidences another available mode of linguistic transference; see, e.g., tellings of *Oisean as déidh na Féinne* (Oisean after the Fianna) recorded from 'Ailidh Dall' Stewart in July 1955 (SSS tapes SA1955.074.A2a and A2b). That said, the majority of Fenian folklore that has been collected in Ireland and Scotland is in Irish or Scottish Gaelic; see chapter 9.

10. Kennedy 1859. The length of Kennedy's review was due to his practice of quoting or retelling large portions of the Fenian material published in the volumes. Nonetheless, he showed familiarity with other Irish manuscript-based scholarship and his commentary was learned; no less a judge than J. F. Campbell commented positively on the copy that Kennedy sent him; see the title page of Campbell's copy (NLS Cam.2.e.3[9]).

11. Kennedy 1859, 73, 75–76.

12. Steward and McGovern 2013, 179; Anon. 2016.

13. Anon. 1867. Given the topic and newspaper, the reviewer is likely to have been J. F. Campbell, although he would not admit this to Kennedy; see J. F. Campbell to P. Kennedy, draft, May 24, 1867, bound into the front of Campbell's copy of *Legendary Fictions of the Irish Celts*

(NLS Cam. 2.f.22). Compare the accusation leveled at the Fenian Brotherhood in America by Ontario-resident Scottish Gaelic and English-language poet Eòghann MacColla (Evan MacColl) in 1868:

> The Fenian Brotherhood! the phrase sounds well,
> But what's *your* right to such a title, tell?
> Strangers alike to honor, truth, and shame—
> Conspirators to aim at Fenian fame!
> If truly sang the bard of Selma old,
> The Fenian race were of no cut-throat mould:
> . . .
> Fenians, indeed! all true men of that race
> Fraternity with you would deem disgrace. (MacColl 1883, 288)

14. Comerford 1989a, 33, 35–36, 45.

15. Comerford 1989a, 35, 42–52; Comerford 1989b, 53–56, 61–64, 69–76. While the Land League's goal of converting tenants into proprietors was not adequately met under Parnell's leadership, the agitation it prompted during the period known as the Land War (1879–82) did lead to a significant amelioration of tenant grievances in an 1881 act that fixed rents and prohibited evictions without cause.

16. Leerssen 1997, 158–59; O'Leary 2006, 226.

17. Ó Cuív 1989, 403.

18. Ó Cuív 1989, 400, 403–5, 411–12.

19. However, few schools were able to offer Irish until after 1897 when teacher training was made available; prior to that, the test to obtain the teaching certificate was seen by many to be too difficult. See Ó Buachalla 1984, 78–79; Ó Murchú 2001, 157–66, 177–85, 241–43.

20. O'Leary 1994, 230; cf. Ó Séaghdha 1912, 450.

21. O'Grady 1880–81 [1857]; Comyn 1880; Comyn 1881.

22. O'Grady 1880–81 [1857], 1:138–40. These and other Fenian texts also found their way onto university syllabi. For instance, John Millington Synge studied *Tóruigheacht Dhiarmada agus Ghráinne* in an Irish course at Trinity College, Dublin in 1892 (Kiberd 2009). They were used in Gaelic League courses, too; see, e.g., "Lee Gaelic League" 1899, which reports the use of *Laoidh Oisín i dTír na nÓg* in instruction.

23. Ó Briain 1893; Bergin and MacNeill 1905; Ua hÓgáin and Laoide 1905; Pearse 1906; Pearse 1908; Ó Siochfhradha 1911; O'Kelly 1911; Laoide 1916. Earlier editions of *Bodach an Chóta Lachtna, Bruidhean Chaorthainn, Cath Fionntrágha, Tóruigheacht an Ghiolla Dheacair,* and *Eachtra Lomnochtáin* had been published by John O'Daly (1858; 1871), J. F. Campbell (1872, 86–88), Kuno Meyer (1885), Standish Hayes O'Grady (1892a, 257–75, 289–96), and Thomas D. Norris (1893).

24. Knight 2021, 416–17; O'Leary 1994, 7–8, 230. *An Claidheamh Soluis* absorbed the separately founded newspaper *Fáinne an Lae* (1898) in 1900. The *Irish-American* was the first newspaper ever to publish a Gaelic column, and it is the only place the Early Modern Gaelic romance *Cath Cnucha* (The Battle of Cnucha) has been published.

25. The Gaelic program for the Belfast *tableaux vivants* was printed in the nationalist periodical *Shan Van Vocht*; see [Milligan] 1898. See also Tymoczko 1993, 47–50.

26. Pádraig Ó Séaghdha (P. J. O'Shea), a teacher with the Belfast Gaelic League, was 'Conán Maol'; Diarmuid Ó Súilleabháin of the Killarney chapter was 'Diarmuid Ó Duibhne'; Micheál Ó Máille, secretary of the Cornamona chapter, was 'Diarmuid Donn'; Diarmuid Ó Foghludha (Dermot Foley) of the Galway and Belfast chapters was 'Fearghus Finnbhéil'; one Micheál Ua Murchadha was 'Caol an Iarainn' (a common Fenian foe); and other correspondents in nationalist periodicals claimed monikers such as 'Goll Mac Móirne' and 'Oscar.'

27. O'Leary 1994, 278–79.

28. Wilson 1989, 23–24; see chapter 5. Herder's ideas about national expression and the right of culturally distinct nations to self-determination were at the heart of several cultural nationalist movements that developed alongside literary romanticism in nineteenth-century Europe.

29. This concern also played into contemporary debates about the path new creative literature in Irish should take, for which see O'Leary 1994, 19–90; 2006.

30. "Ag clos mórán sgeul dom agus mé go han-óg adubhart féin dá mbaileóchaidhe iad, agus iad do chlóbhualadh go dtairbheóchadh sé d'á lán. . . . B'fhiosach mé go rabhadar luachmhar, óir taisbeánaid dúinn intinn agus intleacht na nGaodhal níos soléire solusmhaire, b'fhéidir, ná aonnidh eile atá fágtha anois againn, agus aonrud soillsigheas ar a nósaibh-san is cóir dúinn bheith suimeamhuil ann" (Ó Laoghaire 1895, iii; translation adapted from O'Leary 1994, 92).

31. O'Leary 1994, 93–96, 232–33; Ó Giolláin 2000, 119, 121–22.

32. Nutt 1891, xxxvii.

33. Fr. Richard Henebry quoted in Sheehan 1912, vii.

34. Dunleavy and Dunleavy 1980, 70–71.

35. Curtin 1940, 62; Dunleavy and Dunleavy 1980, 68–69, 73, 86; Bourke 2009, 160.

36. Curtin 1890; Curtin 1894; Curtin 1895. Curtin's collected stories in the *Sun* appeared in 1892–93. His papers are housed at the Milwaukee County Historical Society. According to Janet and Gareth Dunleavy, these contain a number of folktales in various stages of editing, but for the most part, his field notes are not extant (1980, 76–77).

37. Curtin 1940, 385. Curtin acknowledged receiving help from individuals such as J. J. MacSweeney of the Royal Irish Academy and Bryan O'Looney, editor of *Laoidh Oisín i dTír na nÓg* in the Ossianic Society's fourth volume; he asserted that O'Looney's "knowledge of ancient Gaelic lore is unmatched" (Curtin 1894, l, li). His memoirs record meetings with these and other Gaelic scholars and visits to the Royal Irish Academy to consult its manuscript collection (Curtin 1940, 397–99, 457, 763, 766). In the introduction to *Myths and Folk-Lore of Ireland*, he also mentioned having read published Irish folklore and done preliminary collecting among the Irish in the United States, which led him to believe that he might find "some myth tales in a good state of preservation" in Ireland (Curtin 1890, 7–8). For more on Curtin's influences and motivations see Bourke 2009, 145–49.

38. That Curtin was able to gather a considerable amount of Fenian material is interesting given John Francis Campbell's observation a couple decades prior that in Ireland, "questions about Fin Mac Cowl were regarded with suspicion. In regions where 'the Fenians' had been active a few years earlier, caution was natural" (Campbell 1873, 50). Certainly, the social climate had changed in the intervening years, but as an American of Irish descent, Curtin may also have been perceived as a less threatening foreigner; Campbell was, after all, a Scottish aristocrat affiliated with the British state. Moreover, Curtin's use of local guides and translators would have helped him gain storytellers' trust.

39. Hyde also published under the names "An Craoibhín Aoibhinn" and Dúbhglas de h-Íde.

40. Hyde was critical of Curtin's lack of attributions and methodological explanations, and noted that the literary style of his translations surely deviated from the unavailable originals (1890, xv–xvi). Indeed, in their examination of Curtin's papers, Janet and Gareth Dunleavy found that some of the manuscript texts are a good deal shorter than their published counterparts (1980, 82, 84).

41. Hyde 1890, xvi–xvii.

42. Fenian texts in *An Sgéaluidhe Gaedhealach* were first published with French translations in *Annales de Bretagne* from 1896 to 1901; see Hyde 1901. Hyde's *Legends of Saints and Sinners* (1915) is exceptional in that it is entirely in English translation; however, he references published originals.

43. Hyde 1890, x.

44. Matthew Arnold similarly deplored modern materialism, but for him, England's culture, as evidenced by its literature, was not only vibrant, but the best in Europe thanks to its assimilation of Celtic cultural traits.

45. Hyde 1890, xli.

46. Dégh 1995, 263.

47. Hyde 1890, xxxiv–xxxv.

48. Hyde 1889, 217.

49. Hyde 1890, xlv. Hyde's points of reference included the hedge schoolmasters common earlier in the century who could still read Gaelic manuscripts; he would have also had in mind more well-established Gaelic literati, who he knew had existed into the nineteenth century (cf. Hyde 1894, 129–33).

50. Hyde 1894, 125.

51. Hyde 1894, 128. Hyde wrote extensively about the Fenian literary record in *The Story of Early Gaelic Literature* (1895, 59, 82–106, 121–35). Adaptations of his writings about Fenian literature were also included in his *Literary History of Ireland* (1899, 363–86, 498–513).

52. Hyde 1895, 90.

53. O'Leary 1994, 229.

54. For Fenian folklore collected and published by Hyde, see Hyde 1890, 14–19; 1901, 240–47, 306–11, 358–73; 1906, 208–13, 217; and 1939b, 200–21. Hyde also published Fenian material collected or recalled by Próinsias Ó Conchubhair in Hyde 1901, 294–305, 374–401, 468–89.

55. Larminie collected in Donegal and western Connacht. He published a Fionn cycle story from Achill Island, County Mayo in Larminie 1893, 64–84.

56. See Ó Fotharta 1892, 5–15; adapted in Ó Fotharta 1912, 39–48. Ó Fotharta's published material was edited and glossed for use in schools. He was among the earliest instructors certified to teach Irish, having qualified circa 1880 (Ó Murchú 2001, 161).

57. See Ó Tiománaidhe 1906, 8–13, 21–22; Ó Tiománaidhe and Ó Fotharta 1910, 46–56; Ó Tiománaidhe 1935, 139–63.

58. See, e.g., Laoide 1901, 64–66, 77–80, 85–87, 92–94; Laoide 1908, 29–31; Laoide 1913, 14–38, 51–55, 94–98, 107–14. Laoide also published under the pseudonym 'Mac Tíre na Páirce.' In addition to material from Donegal and Monaghan, he gathered one story about the Fianna from a Co. Galway resident.

59. Ó Muirgheasa published under the name Fearghus Mac Róigh. See, e.g., Mac Róigh 1911; Mac Róigh 1913, 34–37; Mac Róigh 1924, 49–53.

60. Ó Tuathail's earliest Fionn cycle material was collected in Counties Monaghan and Donegal several years prior to its publication in Ó Tuathail 1927 and Ó Tuathail 1931, 129–30. He conducted fieldwork in County Tyrone later, between 1929 and 1932; see Ó Tuathail 2015 [1933], xiv, 158–67.

61. See Hyde 1934; 1936; 1937. Mac Diarmada collected these tales circa 1903 from Bean an tSáirséalaigh (Mary Ellen Sarsfield) of Castlerea and gave them to Douglas Hyde, who published them after the collector's death.

62. See Hyde 1931, 188–94; 1932; 1939a, 9–11. Hodgson collected this material circa 1903 from Éamonn Ó Cuanaigh (Ned Cooney) and Pádraig Ó hAllmhuráin (Pat Halloran) of Oughterard and gave it to Douglas Hyde.

63. Briody 2007, 78, 529, cf. 101; Almqvist 1977–79, 12. Tales about the Fianna also appeared in Irish-language newspapers and periodicals not specifically dedicated to folklore, like *An Lóchrann*, *An Stoc*, and *An t-Ultach*. Some early collections from this era that may have contained Fenian material were unfortunately lost "in the troubled years 1916 to 1922" (Ó Giolláin 2000, 131).

64. O'Grady 1918, 3.

65. O'Grady 1918, 4–5; cf. O'Grady 1878, xiv–xv, xviii–xix.

66. Leerssen 1997, 154. The three volumes were subtitled *The Heroic Period* (1878), *Cuculain and His Contemporaries* (1880), and *Critical and Philosophical* (1881). O'Grady subsequently reformatted his Ulster cycle material to publish *Cuculain: An Epic* (1882).

67. O'Grady 1878, iii, v.

68. O'Grady 1878, 22.

69. Yeats 1999 [1938], 183.

70. O'Grady 1878, xiii. O'Grady also wrote a Fenian drama, *The Masque of Finn*, first published in 1907 and later appended to an edition of *Finn and His Companions*; see O'Grady 1921.

71. S. J. O'Grady 1892, 62, 65–66, 84, 162–63. O'Grady's Ulster cycle heroes are likewise depicted as chivalrous knights.

72. MacKillop 1986, 108.

73. S. J. O'Grady 1892, x–xi.

74. Others have further examined the portrayals of the Fianna and the Ulster heroes in O'Grady's works; see, e.g., Tymoczko 1999, 171–72, 174; MacKillop 1986, 108–110; Seaman 1992, 454–56; Maume 2004, 15–16.

75. Cf. Tymoczko 1999, 180.

76. O'Grady maintained a classist belief that only members of the aristocracy were suited to rule; in his view, Ireland would falter under Home Rule due to inadequate leadership; see Maume 2004, 17, 30.

77. Joyce 1879, viii.

78. Ó Murchadha and Murray 2000, 150.

79. Breatnach 2009, 196–97, 199. The most notable excised passage is the humorous incident in which the process of pulling Conán Maol from a surface to which he has been magically affixed leaves him with a skinned rear, for which reason he is called *maol*, 'bare.' Joyce's Conán remains wholly intact (Joyce 1879, 216; Breatnach 2009, 199). As Alan Bruford points out, Patrick Pearse also altered this passage in his later, Irish edition of the text, but he did not omit it entirely (Bruford 1969, 3–4; cf. Breatnach 2009, 198–99).

80. Joyce 1879, vii.

81. Sims-Williams 1986, 73–74. See chapter 7.

82. O'Grady 1878, 22; Watson 1996, 209.

83. Joyce 1879, iii.

84. Arnold 1867, 106–7.

85. Breatnach 2009, 197; Joyce 1879, 178.

86. Yeats 2007 [1898], 130–32. Daniel Williams critiques both Yeats's engagement with Arnoldian Celticism and modern criticism of the same (2006, 127–28, 130–33).

87. Versions of the first two lands are also found in Yeats's source text in the fourth Ossianic Society volume; the third is his own interpolation and is clearly inspired by the folktale *Na Fianna ina gCodladh Faoin Talamh* (The Fianna asleep underground), according to which the Fenian heroes were not dead but merely sleeping, and would arise once again to save Ireland. In Yeats's version, the sleeping warriors are not named as the Fianna and do not arise before he departs, although he does briefly rouse one of them by blowing a horn—an episode that parallels the early, partial awakening of the Fianna in the folktale (Yeats 1997 [1889], 380–85). For a detailed consideration of Yeats's sources, see Parsons 2023, 125–32.

88. Yeats 1989 [1888], 4.

89. In 1893, Yeats also published *The Celtic Twilight*, into which he wove renditions of supernatural lore that had been told to him.

90. Yeats 1989 [1888], 8.

91. Yeats 1989 [1888], 7.

92. Yeats 2007 [1898], 132. Yeats also composed a play based on *Tóruigheacht Dhiarmada agus Ghráinne* in collaboration with George Moore, which was performed in Dublin's Gaiety Theatre in 1901 (Yeats and Moore 2005).

93. Lady Gregory adapted the stories in this collection from print sources in Irish and in translation from Irish and Scottish Gaelic, occasionally incorporating orally gathered "parts of stories, or comments on them" (1970a [1904], 355, 363–64; quoted at 364). Her tales are thus creative, composite versions "more the product of her own taste and genius than of tradition" (MacKillop 1986, 112). She wrote in an earlier collection of folklore about gathering Fenian folklore during a few days spent visiting a workhouse: "I was looking for legends of those shadow-heroes, Finn and his men, to help me in writing their story; and I heard many tales and long poems about fair-haired Finn, who 'had all the wisdom of a little child'; and Conan of the sharp tongue, who was 'some way cross in himself,' and who had a briar on his shield; and their adventures beyond sea, and their hunting after deer that were 'as joyful as the leaves of a tree in summer time'" (Gregory 1974 [1903], 98). None of her folklore material was attributed or conformed to the methodological rigors by then current.

94. Tymoczko 1999, 175.

95. MacKillop 1986, 113. Gregory also reimagined *Tőruigheacht Dhiarmada agus Ghráinne* in her play *Grania*, which was not performed in her lifetime (Gregory 1970b [1912]).

96. Gregory 1970a [1904], 356.

97. Gregory 1970a [1904], 356.

98. Yeats 1970 [1904], 19–20. The former triad of names relates to major Fenian tale locations; the latter relates to the body of story surrounding Cú Chulainn, already known from Lady Gregory's and O'Grady's earlier publications.

99. Cf. O'Leary 1994, 226–27, 232, 286–88; Hutchinson 1987, 119–20.

100. O'Leary 1994, 290, 343.

101. Tymoczko 1999, 173.

102. Gregory 1970a [1904], 356.

103. James MacKillop (1986) explores Anglo-Irish creative adaptations of Fenian literature in detail. Prominent imitators include T. W. Rolleston (*High Deeds of Finn*, 1910) and Scottish author Donald Mackenzie (*Finn and His Warrior Band*, 1911). Short stories, poems, and plays inspired by the Fenian cycle were also composed by Anglo-Irish revivalists not discussed above, including Alice Milligan and 'Ethna Carbery' (Anna MacManus). In addition, the Fianna were regularly referenced in the pages of nationalist periodicals. Imagining themselves in the ranks of the "new Fianna Eirinn" and feeling "the impulse of higher ideals, of yearnings after nobler ends," contributors longed to see "fair Ireland's sons in tongue and soul, GAELIC, UNBRANDED, FREE!" (Aileach 1898; Mac 1897).

104. O'Leary 1994, 232.

105. Cf. Frehan 2014, 159.

106. Gregory 1970a [1904], 356.

107. Breen 2009a; Meyer 1881–83; Meyer 1885.

108. Clinton and Sturgeon 2009; Stokes 1900. The earliest edition of the *Acallam* appeared in S. H. O'Grady's *Silva Gadelica*, but Stokes's edition is superior and remains unsurpassed.

109. Ó Raghallaigh and Ní Mhunghaile 2009a; Hennessy 1873–75. A correspondent of J. F. Campbell, Hennessy was assistant deputy keeper in the Public Record Office of Ireland.

110. Hourican 2009; Windisch 1880; Windisch 1893. Windisch also reedited *Fotha Catha Cnucha* in 1879.

111. Breathnach and Ní Mhurchú 2020; Stern 1897; Stern 1905. Stern coedited the prestigious journal *Zeitschrift für Celtische Philologie* with Meyer.

112. Ní Mhunghaile 2013; O'Grady 1892a. Early in Meyer's career, O'Grady had taken issue with his work on *Cath Fionntrágha*, and when O'Grady published *Silva Gadelica*, Meyer repaid him the favor with a poor review; see O'Grady 1887; Meyer 1893b. *Silva Gadelica* also contained the first ever edition of the *Acallam*, which was later superseded by Stokes's edition.

113. Giffney 2014; Gwynn 1904; Gwynn 1906; Gwynn 1913; Gwynn 1924.

114. O'Curry 1861, 303.

115. Arbois de Jubainville 1892, 375–77.

116. Campbell 1862, 322; MacBain 1886, 194, 203–6; Henderson 1905–6, 1:196–207; see chapter 7. Nutt argued that Fionn's "myth has been rationalised into history. And it may be denied, with fair show of reason, that such a person as Fionn ever did live" (Nutt 1881, 12–21, 38–40, quoted at 39). See also Nutt 1890b, 409–10, 425, and Douglas Hyde's reaction in Hyde 1895, 100–101 and Hyde 1899, 371. In his later writings, while Nutt did not entirely rule out the possibility that a third-century Fionn had existed, he argued forcefully that the extant body of Fenian narrative was mythical rather than historical (cf. Flahive 2017, 68–69). Rhys (1888) related legendary Irish heroes, including the Fianna, to the Greek pantheon.

117. Skene 1862, lxxiii–lxxviii. Skene's theory was later adopted and modified by David MacRitchie (1890, 46–49).

118. Zimmer 1887; 1891a; 1891b. While Zimmer's schema did not hold up under scrutiny, it does bear some resemblance to the Fenian origin narrative in the sixteenth-century Book of Howth (see chapter 4); he was not the first to grant the Fianna Norse heritage.

119. MacNeill 1908, xxix–xxxiv; 1919, 150; 1941, 7–9. See also Flahive 2017, 64–68. Scottish antiquarian John Pinkerton first proposed that the Fianna were modelled on Roman British legions in the late eighteenth century. His fellow countryman Duncan Campbell further developed this idea a century later, suggesting that 'Fionn' was a title rather than a personal name, such that there was more than one historical Fionn (Pinkerton 1789, 76–77; Campbell 1889). Eoin MacNeill was appointed to the Chair of Early Irish History in the new University College, Dublin in 1909 and would go on to become Minister for Education in the Irish Free State (Maume and Charles-Edwards 2013).

120. Hyde 1899, 42.

121. Hyde 1899, 382–83; cf. Hyde 1895, 106. Cormac mac Airt is now seen as a legendary rather than historical person. Hyde was appointed to the Chair of Irish in the new University College, Dublin in 1909 (Hutchinson 1987, 121–22).

122. Hull 1908, 3, 40. Hull studied under both S. H. O'Grady and Kuno Meyer (Ó Raghallaigh and Ní Mhunghaile 2009b).

123. Hull 1926.

124. Hull 1904, 210.

125. Hutchinson 1987, 170, 173, 181, 188–89.

126. Nolan 1999, 354; O'Leary 1983, 26; Breatnach 2009, 196.

127. Pearse's lecture outlined the extant primary sources and summarized contemporary scholarly opinion. It was published in *Irisleabhar na Gaeidhilge*; see Pearse 1900.

128. For evidence of bowdlerization in *Bruidhean Chaorthainn*, see Breatnach 2009, 198–99.

129. "Badh dheacair [í] a shárughadh ar áilneacht smaointe ná ar bhinneas focal agus litridheacht na hEorpa a chuarthughadh" (Pearse 1908, viii; trans. Breatnach 2009, 197). Pearse similarly claimed of *Bodach an Chóta Lachtna*: "Badh dheacair í shárughadh ar ghontacht 7 ar fuinneamh" ("It would be difficult to surpass it in precision and energy") (Pearse 1906, iii).

130. Hutchinson 1987, 153.

131. Ó Buachalla 1984, 78–79.

132. Ó Buachalla 1984, 81–82; Hutchinson 1987, 179.

133. Walsh 2007, 180–87; Buttimer and Ní Annracháin 2003, 542–43; Laukaitis 2010, 230–31. The National University, established in 1908 with colleges in Dublin, Cork, and Galway, was the successor to the Royal University, founded in 1882, which in turn was the successor to the Queen's Colleges and the Catholic University (Coolahan 2003, 757–59).

134. Pearse 1916, 3–4, 16–17. See also Walsh 2007, 122–26.

135. Walsh 2007, 126; Hutchinson 1987, 245.

136. Pearse 1905, 6.

137. Pearse 1916, 9.

138. Pearse 1916, 17.

139. Frehan 2012, 103; Pearse 1914, 161; 1916, 16. The phrase adopted as the school motto derives ultimately from *Acallam na Senórach*; see Stokes 1900, 4 (ll. 119–20). It was also promoted by others for its educational merit; see M. C. Ó Connghalaigh's query in an article on "The Educational Value of National History" whether there was "any better way to make an Irish boy a lover of truth and manly courage than, after narrating the great and heroic deeds of the Fianna na hEireann [*sic*]," to tell him about Oisín professing those values to Saint Patrick (1905, 8).

140. O'Leary 1983, 23–24; Sisson 2004, 57, 58, 83. "The Coming of Fionn" was extracted from O'Grady's longer pageant *The Masque of Finn*. Both S. J. O'Grady and Yeats were in attendance at the 1909 performance by St. Enda's students; see Nolan 1999, 354. Pearse's plays included *Macghníomhartha Chúchulainn* (1909), *The Defence of the Ford* (1913), *The Fianna of Fionn* (1913), and *Fionn: A Dramatic Spectacle* (1914). The latter three plays, one dealing with Ulster cycle material and two Fenian, were unscripted; see Pearse 2013, 65–89, 293–305.

141. Sisson 2004, 123, 126; Hay 2011, 442.

142. Pearse 1914, 151.

143. Patrick Pearse quoted in Anon. 1939, 65, cf. 68–69; Sisson 2004, 126; Hay 2011, 448; Walsh 2007, 97, 269.

144. Hay 2011, 446.

Chapter 9. Storytellers and Schoolbooks

1. Fitzpatrick 1992 [1989], 212–16. The establishment of the Irish Free State followed the 1921 partitioning of the six counties of Northern Ireland, which remain part of the United Kingdom to this day.

2. Compare, e.g., *rí fionn Fáil* ("fair-haired king of Fál") in Keating 1908, 350.

3. De Valera 1926, 3.

4. Anon. 1914, 14.

5. Sherry 1996, 39, 42.

6. Fitzpatrick 1992 [1989], 216, 218.

7. Collins 1996 [1922], 132.

8. Anon. 2020.

9. National Programme Conference 1922, 5. This statement was made about primary school history instruction, but it is broadly descriptive of the ideals motivating both the new primary and secondary school programs. Compare then–Minister of Education Eoin MacNeill's statement only three years later that "the chief function of Irish educational policy is to conserve and develop Irish nationality, that is, the form and kind of civilization distinctive of the Irish people" (MacNeill 1925, 200). See also McManus 2014, 21–25.

10. Frehan 2012, 35.

11. Anon. 1933[?], 53–54; Frehan 2012, 241–42. This does not accord with the countless tales in which deceitful manipulation constitutes a legitimate display of heroic Fenian savvy. However, as noted in the last chapter, Fenian material in Irish schoolbooks often derives from Revival-era adaptations more suited to the educators' ideological purposes than the original Gaelic sources.

12. Frehan 2012, 28–29.

13. Fenian texts in modernized language for use in schools were published by the Educational Company of Ireland, Browne and Nolan, and the National Press. These include: *Tóruigheacht an Ghiolla Dheacair* (The pursuit of the difficult servant) (Ó Canainn 1939, 66–108; Ó Siochfhradha 1939b), *Tóruigheacht Dhiarmada agus Ghráinne* (The pursuit of Diarmaid and

Gráinne) (Ó Canainn 1939, 9–65; Ó Siochfhradha 1939a; Ní Shéaghdha 1944), *Bodach an Chóta Lachtna* (The churl in the drab coat) (Ó Canainn 1939, 109–15), *Bruidhean Eochaidh Bhig Dheirg* (Little red Eochaidh's enchanted hall) (Ní Mhuirgheasa n.d.; Ó Siochfhradha 1947), and *Bruidhean Chaorthainn* (The enchanted hall of the rowan tree) (Pearse n.d., adapted posthumously from Pearse 1908). Shorter selections from Fenian romances and lays were also printed in *Prós na Fiannaidheachta* (Breathnach 1932) and *Filidheacht Fiannaigheachta* (Ó Donnchadha 1933).

14. McManus 2014, 39. *Tóruigheacht Dhiarmada agus Ghráinne* was introduced to Irish-language secondary education before independence, as noted in the previous chapter, and others have been included since. In 1945, for instance, Ciarán Ó Nualláin complained about the inclusion of *Bruidhean Eochaidh Bhig Dheirg*—to his mind, an inferior text—on the leaving certificate exam (O'Leary 2010, 349). *Oisín i dTír na nÓg* (Oisín in the Land of Youth) presently appears as the folklore text in the prose section and *Tóruigheacht Dhiarmada agus Ghráinne* is one of the additional prose options for those sitting the higher-level exam.

15. The Irish Folklore Institute grew out of the Folklore of Ireland Society, established in 1927. For more about these organizations, see Briody 2007; Ó Giolláin 2000, 130–36.

16. Quoted in Briody 2007, 112.

17. Briody 2007, 106, 109; cf. Briody 2005, 27.

18. Briody 2007, 79, 83–84, quoted at 79. Hyde had held a chair in Irish Studies at University College Dublin since 1909.

19. Briody 2007, 232–33, 241, 323, 526.

20. Briody 2007, 260–61, 528. An earlier, more limited schools scheme was also implemented in 1934.

21. Briody 2007, 244–45, 344–47, 418–19. From the 1960s, the use of cassette tape recorders became common.

22. Ó Giolláin 2000, 141.

23. Delargy 1969 [1945], 9; cf. Ó Giolláin 2000, 136–38. It is noteworthy that only three years after Patrick Pearse's edition of *Bruidhean Chaorthainn* was printed in 1908, Fearghus Mac Róigh (1911) published a lengthy oral telling of the same Fenian tale collected in Donegal.

24. Almqvist 1977–79, 14; Briody 2007, 248–49, 445.

25. Briody 2007, 249, 251–52.

26. Briody 2007, 214. Numerical data derives from the Fionn Folklore Database in December 2024. At that time, a considerable amount of background information and place lore (i.e., *seanchas*) had not yet been catalogued and was therefore excluded from the count. See the database for the most current oral corpus data.

27. Lanters 1995, 206. Figgis had served as a Volunteer and was a disillusioned Independent parliamentarian when the book reached store shelves.

28. Figgis 1923, 176, 234–42, 248–53, quoted at 176; cf. 225 for Saint Patrick's alternate view.

29. Figgis appears to have worked most closely with O'Daly 1859, O'Daly 1861, and Whitley Stokes's 1887 edition of the Tripartite Life of Patrick (Lanters 1995, 205). His incorporation of the rarely retold *bruíon* lay *Seilg Sléibhe Fuaid* (The chase on Sliabh Fuaid) is noteworthy (Figgis 1923, 182–88).

30. Watters 1964.

31. Leonard 1971; Clarke 1932; Harmon 1974, 20, 23. Clarke had earlier imagined the characters of the *Tóruigheacht* at middle age in a lengthy poem, "The Vengeance of Fionn," first published in 1917 at the tail end of the Revival (Clarke 1974, 3–40).

32. Fallon's radio play was aired by Radio Teilifís Éireann (RTÉ) in 1950 and the British Broadcasting Corporation (BBC) in 1956, but only an extract was published (Fallon 1951). Additional poetic adaptations of *Tóruigheacht Dhiarmada agus Ghráinne* by English poets John Redwood Anderson and John Masefield appeared in the same decade, the latter paired with Masefield's take on *Laoidh Oisín i dTír na nÓg* (The lay of Oisín in the Land of Youth): Anderson

1950; Masefield 1959. Tomás Ó Ceallaigh and Geoffrey Molyneux Palmer also composed an opera in the 1920s, *Grania Goes*, which was never published or performed, and an English translation of a Revival-era Czech play about the tragic lovers by Julius Zeyer, *Legenda z Erinnu* (Legend of Erin), appeared in 1938: O'Leary 2004, 369–70; Rapall Noyes and Mezirka 1938.

33. O'Connor 1932; O'Connor 1989 [1959]; Chamot, Farr, and Butlin 1964, 789.

34. Clarke 1974, 212–17, quoted at 216; cf. Yeats 1970 [1904].

35. See, e.g., Doyle 2017; Kedzierska 2008.

36. Joyce 1999 [1939], 6, 126–39, quoted at 6, 126, 127, and 133. *Tóruigheacht Dhiarmada agus Ghráinne* is also evoked in the portrayal of the Prankquean, who arrives "be dermot" and proceeds to wash "the blessing of the lovespots" off an abducted child before transforming into a different Gráinne, the sixteenth-century pirate Grace O'Malley, and leaving the heroic age behind (21). For additional Fenian echoes in *Finnegans Wake*, see Benstock 1978; MacKillop 1986, 163–93.

37. O'Brien 1998 [1939], 2, 6–7. For additional Fenian echoes in *At Swim-Two-Birds*, see Wäppling 1984, 38–51; MacKillop 1986, 133–43.

38. O'Brien 1998 [1939], 11–12, 13, quoted at 13.

39. "Bheadh stíl agus ciall don deagh-scríobhnóireacht ag scríobhnóirí na Gaeilge dá léighfeadh siad an tsean-litríocht: Seathrún Céitinn, príomh-scéalta agus laoithe na Fiannaíochta agus Trí Truaighe na Scéalaíochta, ba leor iad san. . . . [G]an sin a dhéanamh ní bhéidh an spreagadh nó an t-eolas acu le scríobhadh go maith" (quoted and translated in O'Leary 2010, 362, 572n64).

40. "Nua-leaganacha de na seanscéalta a chur ar fáil, nua -leaganacha liteartha" (quoted and translated in O'Leary 2010, 348, 566n8).

41. Mac Liammóir 1935; M. G. 1932–33; Ó Néill 1936 [1933–34]; O'Leary 2004, 371–74. Mac Liammóir's play was also performed in English translation at the Gate Theatre in Dublin in 1928, and J. E. Caerwyn Williams later translated it into Welsh as *Seren Serch* (Love star). M. G.'s *Goll Mac Móirne* was adapted from *Suirghe Ghuill* (Goll's courting), an eighteenth-century lay by Seán Ó Neachtain; the playwright may have been working from a manuscript copy, since I am not aware of a published edition. A 1944 translation by "Torna" (Tadhg Ó Donnchadha) of Alice Milligan's 1917 English-language dramatic adaptation of *Oisín i dTír na nÓg* also won critical approval, and Welsh poet T. Gwynn Jones's adaptation of the same Fenian tale in his influential 1926 dramatic poem *Tir na n-Óg*, reworked in 1930 as an operatic libretto, is worth mention too, despite not being Irish (Ó Leary 2010, 380; Ifan 2015, 89–90). The modern Welsh personal names Osian and Nia (i.e., Oisín and Niamh) derive from this.

42. O'Leary 2010, 378. In addition, short dramas were performed but not published. O'Leary documents Fenian *geamaireachtaí*, 'pantomimes,' performed at An Taibhdhearc, including a "brief dialogue between St Patrick and Oisín as part of their St Patrick's Day programme" in 1931, Diarmuid Ó Murchadha and Seán Ó Neachtain's *Tóraidheacht an Ghiolla Dheacair* in 1939, and *Cúirt an Ghrádha* (The court of love) in 1946, as well as others at Dublin's Abbey Theatre in the 1940s and '50s (O'Leary 2004, 371, 628n113; 2010, 387).

43. Quoted and translated in O'Leary 2004, 371.

44. O'Leary 2004, 371. De Blácam was well versed in Fenian literature; see his *Gaelic Literature Surveyed*, where he described it as "pre-eminently the national literature" (1973 [1929], 57–86).

45. See O'Leary 2010, 381; Flahive 2017, 83. Both Ó Nualláin brothers wrote for *Comhthrom Féinne*. The phrase—also the university's motto—is presently echoed in the Cothrom na Féinne scholarship program.

46. Hughes 1922, 4.

47. Sutcliff 2001 [1967], 8.

48. Young 1929, front matter. This collection is primarily Irish but contains one tale from John Francis Campbell's *Popular Tales of the West Highlands*.

49. Ó Sándair 1951, 52–53; O'Leary 2010, 381–82. Ó Sándair's racist depictions of most of his Black African characters as superstitious primitives is problematic.

50. O'Leary (2004, 628n114) evidences children's dramas that were performed but not published, such as *Niamh Chinn Óir* (Niamh of the golden hair) and *Laoi Oisín* (The lay of Oisín) at Feis Charman in 1934.

51. Ó Searcaigh 1984 [1945], vii.

52. These include the first editions of *Eachtra Thailc mhic Thréin* (The adventure of Tailc mac Tréin), *Tóruigheacht Taise Taoibhghile* (The pursuit of Taise Thaoibhgheal [soft bright-sided one]), and *Agallamh na Seanórach*: Ní Mhuirgheasa and Ó Ceithearnaigh 1952, 241–99; Ní Mhuirgheasa 1954; Ní Shéaghdha 2014 [1942–45]. The pair also reedited *Bruidhean Bheag na hAlmhaine, Bruidhean Chéise Corainn* (The enchanted hall at Keshcorann), and *Bruidhean Eochaidh Bhig Dheirg* for Leabhair ó Láimhsgríbhnibh and *Tóruigheacht Dhiarmada agus Ghráinne* for the Irish Texts Society, while Maud Joynt and Cecile O'Rahilly reedited *Feis Tighe Chonáin* (The feast at Conán's house) and *Cath Fionntrágha* for the Dublin Institute for Advanced Studies' Mediaeval and Modern Irish Series: Joynt 1936; Ní Shéaghdha 1941; Ní Mhuirgheasa 1941; O'Rahilly 1962; Ní Shéaghdha 1967.

53. MacNeill 1908; Murphy 1933; Murphy 1953. The first volume of *Duanaire Finn* was edited by Eoin MacNeill. Murphy edited the second and produced a third volume of scholarly notes, the sizable introduction to which contains a seminal study of the Fenian cycle.

54. Ó Siochfhradha 1941. Ó Siochfhradha frequently published under the pen name 'an Seabhac.'

55. Christiansen 1931; Ross 1939. Christiansen also worked with Irish manuscript sources.

56. "Cloistear na laoithe seo fós ar árdán feise is Oireachtais, aithristear iad cois teallaigh, déantar staidéar ortha i sgola na tíre" ('P. Ó F.' quoted and translated in O'Leary 2010, 369, 575n85).

57. Ó Domhnaill 1996 [1942–43].

58. Ó Cadhlaigh 1936; Murphy 1971 [1955].

59. Bruford 1969.

60. Editions of Irish and Scottish Gaelic folktales also continued to appear, but as previously noted, the majority of Fenian folklore remains unedited to this day.

61. MacManus 1977 [1921], 64; Gwynn 1923, 14–15; Gwynn 1925, 14. MacManus, principally a fiction author, married the revivalist writer 'Ethna Carbery' (Anna MacManus), while Gwynn was brother of E. J. Gwynn, the editor of the metrical *dinnshenchas*, 'onomastic lore' (see chapter 8).

62. O'Rahilly 1946, 277; Murphy 1953, lxxxv–lxxxvi. For the present scholarly view of the origin of the Fianna, see chapter 1.

63. Mac Cana 1970, 110. Similarly, Irish historian Francis J. Byrne wrote of "the predominately magical milieu of . . . Finn and the Fianna" and called the stories about them "mythological tales" (Byrne 2001 [1973], 49, 54).

64. O'Leary 2004, 374–75. When Irish heroism *was* broached, authors could now proudly hark to "the courage, nobility, and self-sacrifice of those who fought for national independence," as indeed Ó Sándair felt the need to do even when tackling a Fenian topic.

65. "Sgialachdan faoin . . . mu sheann ghaisgich . . . nach robh riamh ann" (MacCoinnich 1969, 112–13, 123). I owe this reference to Duncan Sneddon. *Fionn ann an Taigh a Bhlàir Bhuidhe* is a Scottish ecotype of *Bruidhean Eochaidh Bhig Dheirg*; see below.

66. Campbell Hay 2000, 26–31, 51; MacDiarmid 1967 [1932], 249. Fenian references can be found in other poets' works too, and one of Campbell Hay's late poems appears to evoke Oisean's lament for Oscar (2000, 401).

67. MacCoinnich 2016; and "Constitution of Fianna na h-Alba," 1940–50, Leaflet, Duke University, Broadsides and Ephemera Collection, folder 15, https://idn.duke.edu/ark:/87924/

r4610xw5h (accessed 22 March 2025). Earlier militant organizations by the name Fianna na h-Alba were established in Glasgow in 1910 to support the Irish revolution and in the 1920s with the soon-dashed aim of securing Scottish independence. The 1940s Fianna na h-Alba was avowedly nonsectarian, but members did engage in violence in 1943–44. The group's lasting legacy was its piping college, which long outlived it. See Watts 1981, 387; Brooke 2018, 18. *An Comunn Oiseanach* was reconstituted at the University of Glasgow in the present century as a Gaelic student society.

68. McIlvanney and Ryan 2005, 13.

69. Regarding the Modern Irish translation of *fiannaíocht* as 'hero tales' rather than 'the Fenian tradition,' as we might accurately translate the earliest form of the word, see Bruford 1969, 61 and the introduction.

70. Delargy 1969 [1945], 7, 19–20, 21; Zimmermann 2001, 448–49, 451; Briody 2007, 464.

71. Hillers 2007, 162; Sumner 2025. As Zimmermann (2001, 431) notes, women telling stories to children "could be talented but were generally not counted as 'storytellers' in the same sense of the word." Their lower traditional status and lack of publicity undoubtedly led to many being overlooked by collectors.

72. See the Fionn Folklore Database (https://fionnfolklore.org).

73. Delargy 1969 [1945], 18–19.

74. A comparatively small amount of material pre-dating the Irish Folklore Commission has also been incorporated into the Irish National Folklore Collection.

75. The Fionn Folklore Database, which I direct, is funded by Harvard University and the Government of Ireland.

76. Sanderson 1957, 3, 6.

77. The School of Scottish Studies archives also house some earlier collections in which Fenian material can be found.

78. Regarding Canadian Fenian folklore, see Sumner forthcoming-a. Next to no collecting was ever undertaken in other regions of considerable diasporic settlement like England or Australia.

79. Briody 2007, 298; Ó Súilleabháin 1957, 456. See Sumner 2022 for a detailed collecting history of Fenian folklore.

80. Folklore collectors very likely prolonged the telling of complex tales in Gaelic by providing an audience after traditional opportunities for storytelling had become infrequent (Ó Giolláin 2000, 141).

81. The story and song types used in the Fionn Folklore Database are modeled on the categorical system for international folktales and form the first comprehensive classification of Fenian folklore.

82. Briody 2007, 271, 275–76.

83. See, e.g., Bruford 1981. In some cases, the same lay was recorded from a tradition bearer as many as ten times.

84. Regarding the variations that tend to occur in oral circulation, see Bruford 1969, 167–249.

85. Sumner 2018, 125; Faichney 1897, 30; NFC, Schools Manuscript Collection, MS 1128, p. 41 (Fionn Folklore Database ID 3525). Much Fenian place lore is still in the process of being catalogued and added to the expanding Fionn Folklore Database by project staff.

86. See, e.g., NFC, Main Manuscript Collection, MS 180, pp. 174–86 (Fionn Folklore Database ID 1113).

87. For further discussion of the relationship between *Fionn ann an Taigh a Bhlàir Bhuidhe* and *Bruidhean Eochaidh Bhig Dheirg*, see Sumner forthcoming-a.

88. MacLellan 1961, 3–6 (Fionn Folklore Database ID 2285). Numerous Scottish versions of this story have been collected.

89. Grainger 2023.

90. Barlow 2023, 17. Michael Dietler (2006) subdivides this modern phenomenon into the categories "Celticism," "Celtitude," and "Celticity," concepts that would nuance a more detailed discussion than space permits here.

91. Berresford Ellis 1985, 193–94; Ó hAllmhuráin 2016, 215–16.

92. Horslips 1976; Official UK Charts Company 2023; Playography Ireland, play ID 32285; Elis et al. 1975; Anon. n.d.-k. MacCarthy's production combined themes from *Oisín i dTír na nÓg* and *Tóruigheacht Dhiarmada agus Ghráinne* and *Nia Ben Aur* was inspired by T. Gwynn Jones's 1926 adaptation of *Oisín i dTír na nÓg*. The latter was reinterpreted by director Angharad Lee for the 2024 Eisteddfod in Pontypridd, Wales: Anon. 2024. Eoghan Ó Tuairisc's Irish-language pantomime *Oisín* was also performed at the Abbey Theatre in Dublin in 1978: Playography Ireland, play ID 30514.

93. Òganaich 1975. More recently, Boston's Celtic punk rock band the Dropkick Murphys released "The Legend of Finn MacCumhail" on their 2001 album *Sing Loud, Sing Proud*.

94. Coulter 2003, 15; Zuelow 2009, 226.

95. Ó hAllmhuráin 2016, 217.

96. Coulter 2003, 25; Zuelow 2009, xxiii.

97. See, e.g., Causeway Coast and Glens Heritage Trust n.d. While the earliest version of *Fionn sa Chliabhán* to appear in print was set at the Giant's Causeway (Carleton 1841), most of the numerous orally collected accounts are localized to other Irish regions. This discrepancy is explicable by the very limited amount of folklore collecting undertaken in Northern Ireland.

98. Boyd and Timothy 2006, 64; Finn McCools Tours (https://www.finnmccoolstours.com/), Finn MacCool's Guest House (https://www.bushmillsvillage.com/finnmccools.html), and Finn McCool's Hostel (https://finnmccoolshostel.com/), accessed December 11, 2023.

99. Anon. 2023b. Fenian place lore about Glenosheen also features in the primary school textbook *An Stair Mórthimpeall Orm* 5 (Anon. 2004, 2–3).

100. Heavey 2021.

101. TG Lurgan 2011. In another notable creative project, 2010 Co. Laois Writer-in-Residence Ann Egan led Fenian-focused writing projects in schools and published a collection of their compositions (Egan 2010).

102. For an exploration of twenty-first-century Fenian educational and popular texts for children in the Republic of Ireland, see Sumner 2017, 89–95, 100–102. Steps have also been taken to introduce the Fianna to school children in regions in which the Fianna's educational presence has been limited. For instance, Philip Hammond was commissioned to compose an instrumental piece based on *Oisín i dTír na nÓg* for primary school workshops in Northern Ireland in 1980 (Horgan Goff 2017, 94–96). More recently, the Northern Irish Council for the Curriculum, Examinations and Assessment partnered with Stòrlann Nàiseanta na Gàidhlig / The National Gaelic Resource Agency in Scotland to produce a collection of children's stories in Irish and Scottish Gaelic, accompanied by a teaching guide and drama scripts. Three Fenian tales are included (Kidd 2011; Stòrlann Nàiseanta na Gàidhlig n.d.).

103. Moore 2021; Moore 2020; Ó Raghallaigh and the Cartoon Saloon 2002. The Fenian content included in Marie Heaney's well-loved *Over Nine Waves* has also been influential, and popular American author Rick Riordan of Percy Jackson fame recently presented the tale of Fionn's boyhood in a compelling short story that he and Element Pictures are adapting to pitch as a television series (Heaney 1994; Riordan 2021; Riordan 2023).

104. Chance 2014; Chance 2015a; Chance 2015b.

105. Tannen 1981; Thompson 2005; Thompson 2007; Thompson 2009. Also notable are Irish author and professional storyteller Eddie Lenihan's children's books, many of which present original Fenian compositions; see, e.g., Lenihan 2006.

106. Mac Cárthaigh at al. 2001; Anon. 2011a.

107. Fleming 2002; West Highland Animation 2014.

108. Llywelyn 1994; O'Sullivan 2014; O'Sullivan 2015. O'Sullivan publishes under his own imprint. For other novels in these series, see O'Sullivan 2023.

109. See, e.g., Adrian McKinty, Garbhan Downey, and Brian McGilloway's Fenian-inspired stories in Brennan and Stone 2010, 187–202, 231–65.

110. Boland 2001, 16, 20. Boland earlier engaged with *Tóruigheacht Dhiarmada agus Ghráinne* in "Listen: This is the Noise of Myth" (Boland 1987, 47–49).

111. Ó Scolaí 1999; Ó Fiannachta 2014. Ó Scolaí's *Feis Tigh Chonáin* corresponds closely with the most recent edition of the early modern text, apart from two apparently newly composed interpolations; see Sumner 2017, 97–98.

112. Paul Mercier's *Diarmuid and Gráinne* took to the stage at An Taibhdhearc in 2001, Fíbín performed Philip Doherty's *Tóraíocht* at the Town Hall Theatre, also in Galway, in 2016, and Zoë Seaton and Briona Corrigan's *The Pursuit of Diarmuid and Grainne* opened in Derry in the University of Ulster's Riverside Theatre in 1999: Playography Ireland, play IDs 30324, 60331, and 30515. Aisling Bea and Yasmine Akram's comedic "Diarmuid and Grainne" first aired on the BBC Radio 4 program Irish Micks and Legends in 2015. Jean Butler and Colin Dunne's Riverdance-adjacent *Dancing on Dangerous Ground* was performed at Theatre Royal in London in 1999 and Radio City Music Hall in New York in 2000, and a commercial DVD was also released (Byrne 2000). Dana Lyn and Loius de Paor's in-progress chamber opera *Mise Gráinne* was workshopped during a residency at the Baryshnikov Arts Center in New York in 2017, and director Caitríona McLaughlin's interpretation of Lady Gregory's play *Grania* opened at Dublin's Abbey Theatre in September of 2024 (de Paor and Lyn 2022; Hayes 2024).

113. Mercier 2015. *Pursuit* played in theatres in Ireland and Northern Ireland and subsequently on Irish television, but it received lukewarm reviews and was not released commercially.

114. Tarik O'Regan's choral work *Acallam na Senórach; An Irish Colloquy* was performed by the National Chamber Choir of Ireland in 2010 and is available on compact disc (O'Regan 2011). Rachel Holstead's symphony "Cath Fionntrá" was performed by the Kerry School of Music Orchestra in 1995: Choral Music Catalogue, https://www.cmc.ie/music/cath-fionntra. Paul Boyd's musical *McCool XXL* showed at the Lyric Theatre in Belfast in 2002 (Playography Ireland, play ID 32896). *Oisín i dTír na nÓg* inspired Elaine Agnew's symphony "Tír na nÓg," which debuted in Downpatrick in 1992, Eric Sweeney's cantata "Níamh of the Golden Hair," performed in Waterford in 2005, and Vincent Kennedy's symphony "Legends and Lore," performed at Dublin's Civic Theatre in 2019: Horgan Goff 2017, 88–94; Choral Music Catalogue, https://www.cmc.ie/music/tir-na-nog, https://www.cmc.ie/music/niamh-golden-hair, and https://www.cmc.ie/music/legends-and-lore-south-county-dublin. Fíbín performed Séamus McHugh's pantomime *Fionn agus Clochán an Aifir* at An Taibhdhearc in December 2023 (Ní Fhlatharta 2023).

115. Professional storytellers whose repertoires incorporate Fenian tales include, for instance, Eddie Lenihan (https://eddielenihan.weebly.com), Niall de Búrca (https://storyteller.ie), Randall Stephen Hall (https://randallstephenhall.com), and Eithne Ní Ghallchobhair (https://fairycouncil.ie/eithne-ni-ghallchobhair).

116. Kirkham 2010.

117. Buick 1988; Connolly 1992; McCambridge 2022; Corr 2021; Anon. 2022b; "Pmaupin" 2022. The statue at Lough Neagh references an episode in some versions of the Giant's Causeway story.

118. Anon. 2022a; McMullan 2020; Irish Strongman Association 2016. Since approximately the beginning of the Celtic Tiger, Gaelic football and hurling teams named after the Fianna have been established in Wexford (est. 1987), Kildare (est. 1999), Enfield, Co. Meath (est. 2000), and Clodiagh, Co. Offaly (est. 2015): Anon. n.d.-l.; Anon. n.d.-h.; Anon. n.d.-f.; Anon. n.d.-b. The

prominent Dublin club Na Fianna, Glasnevin (est. 1955) predates these, as do hurling teams in Middletown, Co. Armagh (est. 1900) and Coalisland, Co. Tyrone (est. 1903) in Northern Ireland: Anon. n.d.-m.; Anon. n.d.-d.; Anon. n.d.-c.

119. Anon. 2011b; Anon. 2023a.

120. McGrath 2004.

121. See Fingal Hotel (https://www.fingal.co.uk) and Innes & Gunn (https://www.innisandgunn.com/beer/inveralmond-ossian), accessed December 20, 2023. Calum Colvin's 2002–3 photography exhibition *Ossian: Fragments of Ancient Poetry / Oisein: Bloighean de Sheann Bhàrdachd* at the Scottish National Portrait Gallery also drew public attention to Macpherson's infamous epics, taking inspiration from *Ossian* to investigate Scottish national identity (Normand and Colvin 2002).

122. Don 2022; Breslin and Leiper 2015. I perused the shelves of Waterstones, Blackwell's Bookshop, and the Scottish Storytelling Centre in Edinburgh in November 2023 looking for Fionn, much as I had done earlier in Dublin (Sumner 2017). In these shops, Fenian stories could also be found in folklore collections and academic publications.

123. MacNeacail 1999; MacLeòid 2016; Langhorne 2021. Safety restrictions prevented the Muileartach from invading during the COVID-19 pandemic, Langhorne informs us.

124. Stewart 1996, 13; McDermitt 1999, 292; Am Baile, AB_Essie_Stewart_Oisean_01–03 and AB_Essie_Stewart_Cochulla_01–06 (Fionn Folklore Database IDs 69 and 1082). Essie Stewart had heard her grandfather telling the tales when she was young, but only made a concerted effort to learn them later in life. She has performed professionally in both Gaelic and English. Professional Skye storyteller George W. Macpherson has also told and published Fenian stories in English, aspects of which lack traditional analogues in the Fionn Folklore Database (Macpherson 2016). A lack of analogues may result from conscious adaptation or composition on the part of a storyteller or their source(s). Gaelic translations of some of Macpherson's stories are available from Ruairidh MacIlleathain's website *Sgeulachdan nan Gaisgeach*, created in 2019 (https://gaisgeach.com).

125. See the Scottish International Storytelling Festival's event listings (https://www.sisf.org.uk/event/?eventid=16713; https://www.sisf.org.uk/event/?eventid=20740, and https://sisf.online.red61.co.uk/event/913:5073/913:21626, accessed December 31, 2023). The 2019 and 2023 events took place at the Scottish Storytelling Centre in Edinburgh.

126. Bigham's arrangement paired NicIlleMhaoil's vocals with a string quartet (Mannion 2023). Irish professional storyteller Eddie Lenihan also told Fenian tales at a subsequent event associated with the exhibition (Muscio 2023). The exhibition displays included Campbell's own field notes about Fenian lays he had heard performed, as well as lays others gathered for him for inclusion in *Leabhar na Féinne* (1872). An earlier exhibition at the National Library of Scotland in 1985, *Lamplighter and Story-Teller: John Francis Campbell of Islay 1821–1885*, focused more broadly on Campbell's life (Thompson 1985).

127. See, e.g., Ó Briain 1984; Nagy 1985; Meek 1987; Ó hÓgáin 1988. Nagy's sizable body of Fenian scholarship has had an outsize impact on the field. Notable researchers who joined the relatively small cohort working in the field in the 1990s include Caoimhín Breatnach, Ann Dooley, Anja Gunderloch, and Ruairí Ó hUiginn.

128. See the work of Geraldine Parsons, Síle Ní Mhurchú, Joseph Flahive, Julia Kühns, and Deirdre Nic Chárthaigh, among others. Kevin Murray also became a prominent voice in the Fenian field at this time.

129. Recent essay collections include Carey 2003a, Arbuthnot and Parsons 2012, Arbuthnot et al. 2022, Doyle and Murray 2014, and others currently in preparation (see the introduction). Prior to this were only Almqvist et al. 1987 and Ó Fiannachta 1995.

130. Readings of Charlotte Guillain's "Finn MacCool and the Giant's Causeway" were performed on Saint Patrick's Day, March 17, 2022 and 2023 at the Children's Museum of Atlanta in

Georgia, and on March 18, 2023, Pleasantville Music Theatre, Inc. in Ossining, New York staged Dean Friedman's children's musical theater adaptation of the tale. A version of the tale by Sabina Hahn also featured on the American National Public Radio program Circle Round in April 2021, and Academy Theatre in Hapeville, Georgia produced an adaptation by Rob Shaw-Smith on June 16–25, 2023. See Central Atlanta Progress n.d.; Newmark 2023; Mileo n.d.; Sheir 2021; Reitzes and Shaw-Smith 2023.

131. Graduate Student Life 2023; Gaelic Affairs 2008; Comhairle na Gàidhlig 2021.

132. Urobuchi and Shinjiro 2016 [2011], 74.

133. For Fionn's characterization in the online role-playing games Shin Megami Tensei V and Fate/Grand Order, see Fandom n.d.-a. and Fandom n.d.-b.

134. Some of the restaurants named after Fionn are franchises, while others appear to be independent. Regarding franchises, see, e.g., Fionn MacCool's (https://fionnmaccools.com/restaurants/), Finn McCool's (https://finnmccools.com/), and Finn McCool's [Australia] (https://finnmccools.com.au/). Restaurant marketing generally displays little understanding of the character or the broader Fenian Cycle.

135. Gaelic football, hurling, and camogie organizations founded in the United States, Canada, Australia, and the Middle East since the 1990s include Na Fianna, New York (est. 1992), Na Fianna, San Diego (est. 1997), Na Fianna Katarokwi, Kingston, Ontario (est. 2019), Na Fianna, Port Adelaide, South Australia (est. 1999), and Na Fianna, Abu Dhabi (est. 1995): Anon. n.d.-j; Anon. n.d.-i; Anon. n.d.-g; Anon. n.d.-e.; Anon. n.d.-a.

136. Ó Longáin 2023.

Epilogue

1. Ó Siochfhradha 1941, 227; translation adapted from O'Kelly 1911, xxxv.

Appendix: Documented Fenian Folklore as of December 2024

1. The data in the appendix derive from the Fionn Folklore Database and reflect total catalogued items. Duplicate copies and multiply recorded tellings from the same tradition bearer have not been removed.

BIBLIOGRAPHY

Aileach [pseud.]. 1898. "Day Dreams on an Irish Hillside." *Shan Van Vocht* 3, no. 10: 185.

Almqvist, Bo. 1977–79. "The Irish Folklore Commission: Achievement and Legacy." *Béaloideas* 45/47: 6–26.

———. 1991. "Irish Migratory Legends on the Supernatural: Sources, Studies and Problems." *Béaloideas* 59: 1–43.

Almqvist, Bo, Séamas Ó Catháin, and Pádraig Ó Héalaí, eds. 1987. *Fiannaíocht: Essays on the Fenian Tradition of Ireland and Scotland*. Dublin: The Folklore of Ireland Society.

Anderson, Benedict. 1983. *Imagined Communities*. London: Verso.

Anderson, John Redwood. 1950. *The Pursuit of Diarmuid and Graunia*. London: Oxford University Press.

Anon. 1825. *Reliques of Irish Poetry: Consisting of Heroic Poems, Songs, Elegies, &c. of the most Approved Ancient and Modern Irish Bards*. Dublin: Thomas Courtney.

Anon. 1867. "Legendary Fictions of the Irish Celts." *Times* [London]. April 26, 7.

Anon. 1876. "Professor Blackie on Ossian." *Scotsman*. May 2, 2.

Anon. 1906. "Macpherson's 'Ossian': Lecture by Professor Meyer." *Glasgow Herald*. March 12, 12.

Anon. 1914. "Na Fianna Eireann." *Fianna Handbook* [Dublin: The Central Council], 12–24.

Anon. 1933[?]. "Fionn and the Fianna." *The Irish-World Readers*, Junior Book [Dublin: Browne and Nolan], 49–54.

Anon. 1939. "Fianna Eireann (Boy Scouts of Ireland)." *Inis Drong Átha Cliath / Dublin Brigade Review* [Dublin: National Association of the Old IRA], 65–70.

Anon. 2004. *An Stair Mórthimpeall Orm* 5. Dublin: Comhlacht Oideachais na hÉireann.

Anon. 2011a. *Ardrí*. Indreabhán: Leabhar Breac. Board game.

Anon. 2011b. "St Patrick's Day Carnival Line Up." *Northern Ireland World*. March 10. https://www.northernirelandworld.com/news/st-patricks-day-carnivalline-up-2804682. Accessed December 8, 2023.

Anon. 2016. "History: Remembering an Gal Gréine." *Dublin People*. March 6. https://dublinpeople.com/news/entertainment/articles/2016/03/06/history-remembering-an-gal-greine. Accessed December 30, 2023.

Anon. 2020. "Mar Gheall Orainn." *Coláiste Íde All Irish Boarding School for Girls*. https://colaisteide.com/mar-gheall-orainn/. Accessed September 22, 2023.

Anon. 2022a. "Belfast Giants Debut New Mascot for 2022/23 Season." *Belfast Live*. October 1. https://www.belfastlive.co.uk/sport/other-sport/belfast-giants-debut-new-mascot-25154945. Accessed November 10, 2023.

Anon. 2022b. "Long Awaited Finn McCool Statue Is Set to Stride into Borogh This Week." *Antrim Guardian*. May 3. https://www.antrimguardian.co.uk/news/2022/05/03/gallery/long-awaited-finn-mccool-statue-is-set-to-stride-into-borough-this-week-24529/. Accessed November 10, 2023.

Anon. 2023a. "Fionn Rocks the Lough—Wake the Giant Festival, Warrenpoint, County Down." *Mourne Mountains and Ring of Gullion* (blog). August 3. https://www.visitmournemountains.co.uk/blog/read/2023/08/fionn-rocks-the-lough-wake-the-giant-festival-warrenpoint-county-down-b371. Accessed November 10, 2023.

Anon. 2023b. "Slí Finn Drive." *Visit Ballyhoura.* https://visitballyhoura.com/days-out/sli-finn-drive. Accessed December 11, 2023.

Anon. 2024. "Eisteddfod Choir Brings Tir na nÓg Back to Life." *Eisteddfod.* June 12. https://eisteddfod.wales/node/1747. Accessed October 6, 2024.

Anon. n.d.-a. "Abu Dhabi Na Fianna." *Middle East GAA.* https://middleeastgaa.com/content_page/296029/. Accessed November 3, 2024.

Anon. n.d.-b. "About." *Clodiagh Gaels GAA.* https://clodiaghgaels.gaa.ie/about/. Accessed November 3, 2024.

Anon. n.d.-c. "Coalisland Fianna." *Tyrone GAA.* https://tyronegaa.ie/clubs/coalisland-fianna/. Accessed November 3, 2024.

Anon. n.d.-d. "Middletown." *Armagh GAA.* https://armaghgaa.net/middletown/. Accessed November 3, 2024.

Anon. n.d.-e. "Na Fianna." *GAA International.* https://gaa.international/clubs/australia/south-australia/na-fianna/. Accessed November 3, 2024.

Anon. n.d.-f. "Na Fianna." *Meath G.A.A.* https://meath.gaa.ie/clubs/na-fianna/. Accessed November 3, 2024.

Anon. n.d.-g. *Na Fianna Katarokwi.* https://www.nafiannakatarokwi.com/nafiannakatarokwi/. Accessed November 3, 2024.

Anon. n.d.-h. "Na Fianna, Kildare." *Finalwhistle.* https://www.finalwhistle.ie/ladiesfootball/team/kildare/na-fianna-kildare/. Accessed November 3, 2024.

Anon. n.d.-i. *Na Fianna Ladies Gaelic Athletic Club.* https://www.nafianna.com/. Accessed November 3, 2024.

Anon. n.d.-j. "Na Fianna NY." *New York GAA.* https://gaanewyork.com/clubs/2563. Accessed November 3, 2024.

Anon. n.d.-k. "Rock Opera and Musicals." The Welsh Music Archive, Llyfrgell Genedlaethol Cymru / The National Library of Wales. https://www.library.wales/catalogues-searching/about-our-collections/archives/the-welsh-music-archive/rock-opera-and-musicals. Accessed October 6, 2024.

Anon. n.d.-l. "Our History." *Na Fianna Cluain Ard CLG.* https://nafiannaclonard.ie/club-history/. Accessed November 3, 2024.

Anon. n.d.-m. 'Who Are the Fianna?' *CLG na Fianna 1955.* https://clgnafianna.com/who-are-na-fianna/. Accessed October 17, 2024.

Arbois de Jubainville, Henri d'. 1892. *L'Épopée Celtique en Irlande.* Cours de Littérature Celtique 5. Paris: Ernest Thorin.

Arbuthnot, Sharon J. 2005. *Cóir Anmann: A Late Middle Irish Treatise on Personal Names.* Vol. 1. Irish Texts Society 59. London: Irish Texts Society.

———. 2006. "On the Name Oscar and Two Little-Known Episodes Involving the *Fían.*" *Cambrian Medieval Celtic Studies* 51: 67–81.

———. 2007. *Cóir Anmann: A Late Middle Irish Treatise on Personal Names.* Vol. 2. Irish Texts Society 60. London: Irish Texts Society.

———. 2012. "Finn, Ferchess and the *Rincne*: Versions Compared." In *The Gaelic Finn Tradition,* edited by Sharon J. Arbuthnot and Geraldine Parsons, 62–80. Dublin: Four Courts.

Arbuthnot, Sharon J., Síle Ní Mhurchú, and Geraldine Parsons, eds. 2022. *The Gaelic Finn Tradition II.* Dubin: Four Courts.

Arbuthnot, Sharon J. and Geraldine Parsons, eds. 2012. *The Gaelic Finn Tradition.* Dublin: Four Courts.

Arnold, Matthew. 1867. *On the Study of Celtic Literature*. London: Smith, Elder and Co.

Atkinson, Robert, ed. 1880. *The Book of Leinster: sometimes called the Book of Glendalough*. Dublin: Royal Irish Academy.

Baines, Paul. 1997. "Ossianic Geographies: Fingalian Figures on the Scottish Tour, 1760–1830." In "Macpherson's Ossian." Special issue, *Scotlands* 4, no. 1: 44–61.

Bär, Gerald. 2012. "Ossian—No Laughing Matter?" In *Ossian and National Epic*, edited by Gerald Bär and Howard Gaskill, 29–53. Passagem Studies in Cultural Sciences 6. Frankfurt am Main: Peter Lang.

Barbour, John. 1980. *Barbour's Bruce*. Edited by Matthew P. McDiarmaid and James A. C. Stevenson. Vol. 2. Edinburgh: Scottish Texts Society.

Barlow, Richard Alan. 2023. *Modern Irish and Scottish Literature: Connections, Contrasts, Celticisms*. Oxford: Oxford University Press.

Barnaby, Paul. 2004. "Timeline: European Reception of Ossian." In *The Reception of Ossian in Europe*, edited by Howard Gaskill, xxi–lxviii. London: Thoemmes Continuum.

Barthélemon, François-Hippolyte. 1768. *Oithóna: A Dramatic Poem Taken from the Prose Translation of the Celebrated Ossian*. London: T. Becket and A. de Hondt.

Barthes, Roland. 1975. "An Introduction to the Structural Analysis of Narrative." Translated by Lionel Duisit. *New Literary History* 6, no. 2: 237–72.

Baumgarten, Rolf. 1987. "Placenames, Etymology and the Structure of *Fianaigecht*." In *Fiannaíocht: Essays on the Fenian Tradition of Ireland and Scotland*, edited by Bo Almqvist, Séamas Ó Catháin, and Pádraig Ó Héalaí, 1–24. Dublin: The Folklore of Ireland Society.

Benstock, Bernard. 1978. "A Setdown Secular Phoenish: The Finn of 'Finnegan's Wake.'" *The Crane Bag* 2, no. 1: 22–28.

Bergin, Osborne [*recte* Osborn] J., and John [Eoin] MacNeill, eds. 1905. *Eachtra Lomnochtáin*. Dublin: Gaelic League.

Berresford Ellis, Peter. 1985. *The Celtic Revolution: A Study in Anti-Imperialism*. Talybont: Y Lolfa.

Best, Richard Irvine, Osborn Bergin, and M. A. O'Brien, eds. 1954. *The Book of Leinster, formerly Lebar na Núachongbála*. Vol. 1. Dublin: Dublin Institute for Advanced Studies.

Best, Richard Irvine, and M. A. O'Brien, eds. 1957. *The Book of Leinster, formerly Lebar na Núachongbála*. Vol. 3. Dublin: Dublin Institute for Advanced Studies.

Bieler, Ludwig, ed. and trans. 1979. *The Patrician Texts in the Book of Armagh*. Dublin: Dublin Institute for Advanced Studies.

Binchy, D. A., ed. 1978. *Corpus Iuris Hibernici*. 7 vols. Dublin: Dublin Institute for Advanced Studies.

Black, Ronald Iain. 1986. "The Gaelic Academy: The Cultural Commitment of the Highland Society of Scotland." *Scottish Gaelic Studies* 14, no. 2: 1–38.

———. 1989. "The Gaelic Manuscripts of Scotland." *Gaelic and Scotland / Alba agus a'Ghàidhlig*, edited by W. Gillies, 146–74. Edinburgh: Edinburgh University Press.

———, ed. 2001. *An Lasair: Anthology of 18th Century Scottish Gaelic Verse*. Edinburgh: Birlinn.

———. 2008. "I Thought He Made It All Up: Context and Controversy." In *The Life and Legacy of Alexander Carmichael*, edited by Dòmhnall Uilleam Stiùbhart, 57–81. Port of Ness, Lewis: The Islands Book Trust.

———. 2016. "The Gaelic Manuscripts at Inveraray Castle." In *Cànan & Cultar / Language & Culture: Rannsachadh na Gàidhlig 8*, edited by Wilson McLeod, Anja Gunderloch, and Rob Dunbar, 55–70. Edinburgh: Dunedin.

Blackie, John Stuart. 1876a. "Is the Gaelic Ossian a Translation from the English?" *Celtic Magazine* 1: 267–75, 299–303.

———. 1876b. *The Language and Literature of the Scottish Highlands*. Edinburgh: Edmonston and Douglas.

———. 1890. "Scottish Nationality." In *Essays on Subjects of Moral and Social Interest*, 170–227. Edinburgh: David Douglas.

Blackie, John Stuart, and John Francis Campbell. 1875a. "The Ossianic Question." *Scotsman*, September 21, 3.

———. 1875b. "The Ossianic Controversy." *Scotsman*, October 11, 6.

Blackwell, Thomas. 1735. *An Enquiry into the Life and Writings of Homer*. London: n.p.

Blair, Hugh. 1996a [1763]. "A Critical Dissertation on the Poems of Ossian." In *The Poems of Ossian and Related Works*, by James Macpherson, edited by Howard Gaskill, 345–99. Edinburgh: Edinburgh University Press.

———. 1996b [1760]. Preface to "Fragments of Ancient Poetry, Collected in the Highlands of Scotland, and Translated from the Galic or Erse Language." In *The Poems of Ossian and Related Works*, by James Macpherson, edited by Howard Gaskill, 5–6. Edinburgh: Edinburgh University Press.

Blàrach, An t-Urr. Donnchadh [Rev. Duncan Blair]. 2013 [1895]. "The Poems of Ossian / Dàin Oisein." In *Fògradh, Fàisneachd, Filidheachd / Parting, Prophecy, Poetry*, edited and translated by John A. Macpherson and Michael Linkletter, 200–205. Sydney, Nova Scotia: Cape Breton University Press.

Blieler, Everett F., and Richard Blieler. 1990. *Science-Fiction: The Early Years*. Kent, OH: Kent State University Press.

Boece, Hector. 1526. *Scotorum Historiae a Prima Gentis Origine*. Paris: Badius Ascensius.

Bohlman, Philip V., ed. 2016. *Song Loves the Masses: Herder on Music and Nationalism*. Oakland: University of California Press.

Boland, Eavan. 1987. *The Journey and Other Poems*. Manchester: Carcanet.

———. 2001. *Code*. Manchester: Carcanet.

Boswell, James. 1963. *Boswell: The Ominous Years, 1774–1776*. Edited by Charles Ryskamp and Frederick A. Pottle. New York, Toronto, and London: McGraw-Hill Book Company.

———. 1964. *Boswell's Life of Johnson*. Vol. 5, *The Tour to the Hebrides and the Journey into North Wales*, edited by George Birkbeck Hill and L. F. Powell. 2nd ed. Oxford: Clarendon Press.

Bourke, Angela. 2009. "The Myth Business: Jeremiah and Alma Curtin in Ireland, 1887–1893." *Éire-Ireland* 44, nos. 3–4: 140–70.

Boyd, Stephen W., and Dallen J. Timothy. 2006. "Marketing Issues and World Heritage Sites." In *Managing World Heritage Sites*, edited by Anna Leask and Alan Fyall, 55–68. Oxford: Elsevier.

Boyle, James. 1992. "Memoir by James Boyle, May 1835, with Additions from Draft." In *Ordnance Survey Memoirs of Ireland*, vol. 13, *Parishes of County Antrim IV: 1830–8*, edited by Angelique Day and Patrick McWilliams, 42–53. Belfast: The Institute of Irish Studies.

Breathnach, Diarmuid, and Máire Ní Mhurchú. 2020. "Stern, Ludwig Christian (1846–1911)." *Ainm.ie: An Bunachar Náisiúnta Beathaisnéisí Gaeilge*. https://www.ainm.ie/Bio.aspx?ID=680. Accessed March 3, 2020.

Breathnach, Micheál. 1932. *Prós na Fiannaidheachta*. Dublin: Comhlucht Oideachais na hÉireann.

Breatnach, Caoimhín. 1994–95. "The Historical Context of Cath Fionntrágha." *Éigse* 28: 138–55.

———. 1995. "Cath Fionntrágha." In *An Fhiannaíocht*, edited by Pádraig Ó Fiannachta, 128–43. Léachtaí Cholm Cille 25. Maynooth: An Sagart.

———. 2009. "Exploiting the Past: Pearse as Editor and Interpreter of *Fiannaíocht* Literature." In *The Life and After-Life of P. H. Pearse: Pádraic Mac Piarais: Saol agus Oidhreacht*, edited by Roisín Higgins and Regina Uí Chollatáin, 195–207. Dublin: Irish Academic Press.

———. 2020. "Explanations of Three Rare Words in the Tale Known as *Úath Beinne Étair* and a Re-Assessment of this Title." *Ériu* 70: 73–81.

Breatnach, R. A. 1965. "Two Eighteenth-Century Irish Scholars: J. C. Walker and Charlotte Brooke." *Studia Hibernica* 5: 88–97.

Breen, Aidan. 2009a. "Meyer, Kuno." *Dictionary of Irish Biography* online, edited by James McGuire and James Quinn. http://dib.cambridge.org/viewReadPage.do?articleId=a5810. Accessed March 3, 2020.

———. 2009b. "Windisch, Wilhelm Oscar Ernst." *Dictionary of Irish Biography* online, edited by James McGuire and James Quinn. http://dib.cambridge.org/viewReadPage.do?articleId=a9085. Accessed March 3, 2020.

Brennan, Gerard, and Mike Stone, eds. 2010. *Requiems for the Departed.* Norrköping, Sweden: Morrigan Books.

Breslin, Theresa, and Kate Leiper. 2015. "The Story of the Giant's Causeway." In *An Illustrated Treasury of Scottish Mythical Creatures,* 37–53. Edinburgh: Floris Books.

Brewer, J. S., ed. 1871. "The Book of Howth." In *Calendar of the Carew Manuscripts Preserved in the Archiepiscopal Library at Lambeth,* vol. 5, 1–260. London: Longman and Co. and Trübner and Co.

Briody, Mícheál. 1995. "Cath Cnucha: Medieval Romance and Modern Folktale." Unpublished paper given at the fifth Symposium of Societas Nordica Celtologia, Helsinki.

———. 2005. "'Publish or Perish': The Vicissitudes of the Irish Folklore Institute." *Ulster Folklife* 51: 10–33.

———. 2007. *The Irish Folklore Commission 1935–1970: History, Ideology, Methodology.* Studia Fennica Folkloristica 17. Helsinki: Finnish Literature Society.

Brooke, Charlotte. 2009 [1789]. *Reliques of Irish Poetry.* Edited by Lesa Ní Mhunghaile. Dublin: Irish Manuscripts Commission.

Brooke, Nick. 2018. *Terrorism and Nationalism in the United Kingdom.* Cham, Switzerland: Palgrave Macmillan.

Brown, Terence. 1988. "Saxon and Celt: The Stereotypes." In *Ireland's Literature: Selected Essays,* 3–13. Mullingar, Ireland: The Lilliput Press.

Bruford, Alan. 1969. *Gaelic Folk-Tales and Mediaeval Romances.* Dublin: The Folklore of Ireland Society.

———. 1981. "Memory, Performance and Structure in Traditional Tales." *Arv* 37: 103–9.

———. 1986. "The Singing of Fenian and Similar Lays in Scotland." In *Ballad Research: The Stranger in the Ballad Narrative and Other Topics,* edited by Hugh Shields, 55–70. Dublin: Folk Music Society of Ireland.

Buick, Robin. 1988. "The Pursuit of Diarmuid and Grainne." Per Cent for Art Sculpture Commissions. Sligo County Council Arts Service. http://www.sligoarts.ie/PublicArt/PerCentforArtCommissions/PerCentforArtSculptureCommissions/Name,14123,en.html. Accessed November 10, 2023.

Buttimer, Neil, and Máire Ní Annracháin. 2003. "Irish Language and Literature." *A New History of Ireland,* vol. 7, edited by J. R. Hill, 538–86. Oxford: Oxford University Press.

Byrne, Darragh, dir. 2000. *Dancing on Dangerous Ground.* Paris: NVC Arts. DVD.

Byrne, Francis John. 2001 [1973]. *Irish Kings and High Kings.* 2nd ed. Dublin: Four Courts.

Bysveen, Josef. 1982. *Epic Tradition and Innovation in James Macpherson's Fingal.* Uppsala: Ubsaliensis S. Academiae.

Caball, Marc, and Benjamin Hazard. 2013. "Dynamism and Decline: Translating Keating's *Foras Feasa ar Éirinn* in the Seventeenth Century." *Studia Hibernica* 39: 49–69.

Caball, Marc, and Kaarina Hollo. 2006. "The Literature of Later Medieval Ireland, 1200–1600: From the Normans to the Tudors." *The Cambridge History of Irish Literature,* vol. 1, edited by Margaret Kelleher and Philip O'Leary, 74–139. Cambridge: Cambridge University Press.

Camden, William [Guilielmo Camdeno]. 1587 [1586]. *Britannia.* London: [Eliot's Court Press].

Cameron, Rev. Alexander. 1888. "Poems of Ossian Collected by John M'Donald in the Western Parishes of Strathnaver, Ross, and Inverness-shire, in September and October, 1805." *Transactions of the Gaelic Society of Inverness* 13: 269–300.

———. 1892. *Reliquiae Celticae: Texts, Papers, and Studies in Gaelic Literature and Philology left by the late Rev. Alexander Cameron, L.L.D.* Vol. 1, *Ossianica*, edited by Alexander Macbain and Rev. John Kennedy. Inverness: Northern Chronicle.

———. 1894. Reliquiae Celticae: *Texts, Papers, and Studies in Gaelic Literature and Philology left by the late Rev. Alexander Cameron, L.L.D.* Vol. 2, *Poetry, History, and Philology*, edited by Alexander Macbain and Rev. John Kennedy. Inverness: Northern Counties Newspaper and Printing and Publishing Co.

Campbell, Donald. 1825. *An Essay on the Authenticity of Ossian's Poems.* Ayr: McCormick and Carnie.

Campbell, Duncan. 1889. "The Imperial Idea in Early British History." *Transactions of the Gaelic Society of Inverness* 14: 276–97.

Campbell, John Francis. 1862. *Popular Tales of the West Highlands.* Vol. 4. Edinburgh: Edmonston and Douglas.

[———]. 1869. "Ossian Redivivus." *Times* [London]. October 14, 4.

——— [Sail Dhiarmaid]. 1870a. "Gaelic Legends." *Inverness Courier.* October 6, 3.

———. 1870b. "On Current British Mythology and Oral Traditions." *Journal of the Ethnological Society of London*, n.s., 2, no. 3: 325–40.

[———]. 1871. "Ossian Redressed." *Times* [London]. April 15, 6.

———. 1872. *Leabhar na Féinne: Heroic Gaelic Ballads Collected in Scotland Chiefly from 1512 to 1871.* London: Spottiswoode and Co.

———. 1873. "A Turn Through Gaelic Ireland in 1872." *Fraser's Magazine* [n.s., vol. 8], 50–56.

———. 1994a [1860]. *Popular Tales of the West Highlands.* Vol. 1. Edinburgh: Birlinn.

———. 1994b [1860–62]. *Popular Tales of the West Highlands.* Vol. 2. Edinburgh: Birlinn.

[Campbell, John George Edward Henry Douglas Sutherland], Duke of Argyll. 1907. "Diarmid." In *Passages from the Past*, vol. 2, 652–72. London: Hutchinson.

Campbell, John Lorne. 1978. "Notes on Hamish Robertson's 'Studies in Carmichael's Carmina Gadelica.'" *Scottish Gaelic Studies* 3, no. 1: 1–17.

Campbell, Rev. John Gregorson, ed. 1891. *Waifs and Strays of Celtic Tradition: Argyllshire Series.* Vol. 4, *The Fians; or, Stories, Poems, and Traditions of Fionn and His Warrior Band.* London: David Nutt.

Campbell Hay, George. 2000. *Collected Poems and Songs of George Campbell Hay (Deórsa Mac Iain Dheòrsa).* Vol. 1. Edited by Michel Byrne. Edinburgh: Edinburgh University Press.

Campion, Edmund. 1633. "Campion's Historie of Ireland." Edited by James Ware. In *The Historie of Ireland, Collected by Three Learned Authors viz. Meredith Hanmer, Doctor in Divinitie: Edmund Campion, Sometime Fellow of St Johns Colledge in Oxford: and Edmund Spenser, Esq.* Dublin: Society of Stationers.

Canny, Nicholas. 1987. *From Reformation to Restoration: Ireland, 1534–1660.* Dublin: Helicon.

Carey, John. 1996. "Obscure Styles in Medieval Ireland." *Mediaevalia* 19: 25–39.

———. 1997. "The Three Things Required of a Poet." *Ériu* 48: 41–58.

———. 2002. "Nōdons, Lugus, Windos." In *Dieux des Celtes, Goetter der Kelten, Gods of the Celts*, edited by Charles-Marie Ternes and Hartmut Zinser, 99–126. Études Luxembourgeoises d'Histoire et de Science des Religions 1. Luxembourg: Association Européenne pour l'Étude Scientifique des Religions.

———, ed. 2003a. *Duanaire Finn: Reassessments.* Irish Texts Society Subsidiary Series 13. Dublin: Irish Texts Society.

———. 2003b. "Remarks on Dating." In *Duanaire Finn: Reassessments*, edited by John Carey, 1–18. Irish Texts Society Subsidiary Series 13. Dublin: Irish Texts Society.

———. 2005. "Two Notes on Names." *Éigse* 35: 116–24.

———. 2014. "*Acallam na Senórach*: A Conversation Between Worlds." In *In Dialogue with the Agallamh: Essays in Honour of Seán Ó Coileáin*, edited by Aidan Doyle and Kevin Murray, 76–89. Dublin: Four Courts.

———. 2022. "The Death of Diarmaid: Pessinus to Ben Bulben?" In *The Gaelic Finn Tradition II*, edited by Sharon J. Arbuthnot, Síle Ní Mhurchú, and Geraldine Parsons, 126–39. Dubin: Four Courts.

Carleton, William. 1841. "A Legend of Knockmary." *Chambers' Edinburgh Journal*. January 16, 409–11.

———. 1845. *Tales and Sketches Illustrating the Character, Usages, Traditions, Sports and Pastimes of the Irish Peasantry*. Dublin: James Duffy.

Carpenter, Frederic I. 1931. "The Vogue of Ossian in America: A Study in Taste." *American Literature* 2, no. 4: 405–17.

Carswell, John. 1970 [1567]. *Foirm na n-Urrnuidheadh: John Carswell's Gaelic Translation of the Book of Common Order*. Edited by R. L. Thomson. Edinburgh: Scottish Gaelic Texts Society.

Causeway Coast, and Glens Heritage Trust. n.d. *Giant's Causeway and Causeway Coast World Heritage Site*. Promotional video. https://giantscauseway.ccght.org/. Accessed December 11, 2023.

Central Atlanta Progress. n.d. "St. Patrick's Day Programming." *Atlanta Downtown*. https://www.atlantadowntown.com/do/st-patricks-day-programming. Accessed December 13, 2023.

Chamot, Mary, Dennis Farr, and Martin Butlin. 1964. *The Modern British Paintings, Drawings and Sculpture*. Vol. 2. London: Oldbourne Press.

Champion, Timothy. 1996. "The Celt in Archaeology." In *Celticism*, edited by Terence Brown, 61–78. Studia Imagologica: Amsterdam Studies on Cultural Identity 8. Amsterdam: Rodopi.

Chance, Megan. 2014. *The Shadows*. Fianna Trilogy 1. New York: Skyscape.

———. 2015a. *The Veil*. Fianna Trilogy 3. New York: Skyscape.

———. 2015b. *The Web*. Fianna Trilogy 2. New York: Skyscape.

Cheape, Hugh. 1997. "The Culture and Material Culture of Ossian, 1760–1900." In "Macpherson's Ossian." Special issue, *Scotlands* 4, no. 1: 1–24.

Christiansen, Reidar Thoralf. 1931. *The Vikings and the Viking Wars in Irish and Gaelic Tradition*. Oslo: I Kommisjon Hos Jacob Dybwad.

Clancy, Thomas Owen. 2008. "Before the Ballad: Gaelic Narrative Verse before 1200." In "Caindel Alban: Fèill-Sgrìobhainn do Dhòmhnall E. Meek." Special issue, *Scottish Gaelic Studies* 24: 115–36.

Clarke, Austin. 1932. *The Bright Temptation*. London: Allen and Unwin.

———. 1974. *Collected Poems*. Edited by Liam Miller. London: Dolmen Press and Oxford University Press.

Clarke, D. V. 1981. "Scottish Archaeology in the Second Half of the Nineteenth Century." In *The Scottish Antiquarian Tradition: Essays to Mark the Bicentenary of the Society of Antiquaries of Scotland and Its Museum, 1780–1980*, edited by A. S. Bell, 114–41. Edinburgh: J. Donald.

[Clerk, Rev. Archibald]. 1869. "'Ossian Redivivus' Retractatus." *London Scotsman*. October 30, 269.

———. 1870. *The Poems of Ossian in the Original Gaelic with a Literal Translation into English and a Dissertation on the Authenticity of the Poems*. Vol. 1. Edinburgh: William Blackwood and Sons.

Clinton, Georgina, and Sinéad Sturgeon. 2009. "Stokes, Whitley." *Dictionary of Irish Biography* online, edited by James McGuire and James Quinn. http://dib.cambridge.org/viewReadPage.do?articleId=a8335. Accessed March 3, 2020.

Collins, Michael. 1996 [1922]. *The Path to Freedom*. Cork: Mercier Press.

Coltman, Viccy. 2019. *Art and Identity in Scotland: A Cultural History from the Jacobite Rising of 1745 to Walter Scott*. Cambridge: Cambridge University Press.

Comerford, R. V. 1989a. "The Land War and the Politics of Distress, 1877–82." *A New History of Ireland*, vol. 6, edited by W. E. Vaughan, 26–52. Oxford: Oxford University Press.

———. 1989b. "The Parnell Era, 1883–91." *A New History of Ireland*, vol. 6, edited by W. E. Vaughan, 53–80. Oxford: Oxford University Press.

———. 2004. "O'Mahony, John (1815–1877)." *Oxford Dictionary of National Biography* online. http://www.oxforddnb.com/view/article/20751. Accessed May 3, 2015.

Comhairle na Gàidhlig. 2021. "The Gaelic Image." *Comhairle na Gàidhlig / The Gaelic Council of Nova Scotia*. https://www.gaelic.ca/salmon-image. Accessed December 14, 2023.

Comyn, David, ed. and trans. 1880. *Laoidh Oisín air Thír na n-Óg*. Dublin: Chamney, for the Society for the Preservation of the Irish Language.

———, ed. and trans. 1881. *Mac-ghníomhartha Fhinn (Sliocht Saltrach Chaisil) / The Youthful Exploits of Fionn*. Dublin: M. H. Gill and Son, for the Gaelic Union.

Connellan, Owen. 1860. "The Poems of Ossian by Macpherson." In *Imtheacht na Tromdhaimhe; or, the Proceedings of the Great Bardic Institution*, edited by Owen Connellan, 171–204. Transactions of the Ossianic Society 5. Dublin: John O'Daly.

Connellan, Thaddeus. 1829a. *An Duanaire: Fiannaigheacht, Danta, agus Ranna le'r tTeanga Mhin Bhinn Mhilis a Léigheadh / A Selection of Irish Poems, and Moral Epigrams; Collected from Ancient Manuscripts and Oral Tradition; For the Use of Schools, and Learners of the Irish Language*. Dublin: M. Goodwin.

———. 1829b. *An Duanaire: Fonna Seanma, Danta, agus Ranna le'r tTeanga Mhin Bhinn Mhilis a Léigheadh / A Selection of Irish Melodies, Poems and Moral Epigrams, Collected from Ancient Manuscripts and Oral Tradition; For the Use of Schools, and Learners of the Irish Language*. Dublin: M. Goodwin.

Connolly, Jim. 1992. "Diarmuid and Grainne." *Clare Public Art*. https://clarearts.ie/sites/public-art/diarmuid-and-grainne-jim-connolly/. Accessed November 10, 2023.

Connolly, S. J. 1989a. "Mass Politics and Sectarian Conflict, 1823–30." In *A New History of Ireland*, vol. 5, edited by W. E. Vaughan, 74–107. Oxford: Oxford University Press.

———. 1989b. "Union Government, 1812–23." In *A New History of Ireland*, vol. 5, edited by W. E. Vaughan, 48–73. Oxford: Oxford University Press.

Connon, Anne. 2013. "Plotting *Acallam na Senórach*: The Physical Context of the 'Mayo' Sequence." In *Gablánach in Scélaigecht: Celtic Studies in Honour of Ann Dooley*, edited by Sarah Sheehan, Joanne Findon, and Westley Follett, 69–102. Dublin: Four Courts.

———. 2014. "The Roscommon *Locus* of *Acallam na Senórach* and Some Thoughts as to *Tempus* and *Persona*." In *In Dialogue with the Agallamh: Essays in Honour of Seán Ó Coileáin*, edited by Aidan Doyle and Kevin Murray, 21–59. Dublin: Four Courts.

———. 2021. "Weaving Norman Families into the Irish Landscape: The Threading of Colonial Dynastics into the *Dindshenchas* of *Acallam na Senórach*." Paper presented at the Celtic Studies Association of North America's online lecture series.

Constantine, David, trans. 2012. *The Sorrows of Young Werther*, by Johann Wolfgang Goethe. Oxford: Oxford University Press.

Coolahan, John. 2003. "Higher Education in Ireland, 1908–84." In *A New History of Ireland*, vol. 7, edited by J. R. Hill, 757–95. Oxford: Oxford University Press.

Corr, Shauna. 2021. "The Story behind Belfast's 'Big Blue Fish' on the Bank of the River Lagan." *Belfast Live*. March 19. https://www.belfastlive.co.uk/whats-on/arts-culture-news/story-behind-belfasts-big-blue-20216794. Accessed November 10, 2023.

Corthals, Johan, ed. and trans. 1997–98. "Die Trennung von Finn und Gráinne." *Zeitschrift Für Celtische Philologie* 49/50: 71–91.

———. 2004. "Ailbe's Speech to Cithruad (*Tochmarc Ailbe*)." *Éigse* 34: 1–9.

Coulter, Colin. 2003. "The End of Irish History? An Introduction to the Book." In *The End of Irish History? Critical Reflections on the Celtic Tiger*, edited by Colin Coulter and Steve Coleman, 1–33. Manchester: Manchester University Press.

Covington, Sarah. 2022. *The Devil from Over the Sea: Remembering and Forgetting Oliver Cromwell in Ireland*. Oxford: Oxford University Press.

Craigie, W. A. 1894. "Three Tales of the Fiann." *Scottish Review* 24: 270–97.

———. 1899. "The Ossianic Ballads." *Scottish Review* 34: 260–90.

———. 1908. "The Legend of the Fiann in the Highland Bards." In *The Old Highlands: Being Papers Read before the Gaelic Society of Glasgow, 1895–1906*, 131–68. Glasgow: Archibald Sinclair.

Crofts, Christopher, trans. 1819. *The Battle of Ventry Harbour: Which Took Place in the Fourth Century; And Which Continued without Intermission for 366 Days!* Cork: n.p.

Croker, Thomas Crofton. 1824. *Researches in the South of Ireland, Illustrative of the Scenery, Architectural Remains and the Manners and Superstitions of the Peasantry*. London: John Murray.

———. 1825–28. *Fairy Legends and Traditions of the South of Ireland*. 3 vols. London: John Murray.

Curley, Thomas. 1987. "Johnson's Last Word on Ossian: Ghostwriting for William Shaw." In *Aberdeen and the Enlightenment*, edited by Jennifer J. Carter and John H. Pittock, 375–431. Aberdeen: Aberdeen University Press.

———. 2009. *Samuel Johnson, the Ossian Fraud and the Celtic Revival in Great Britain and Ireland*. Cambridge: Cambridge University Press.

Curtin, Jeremiah. 1890. *Myths and Folk-Lore of Ireland*. Boston: Little, Brown, and Co.

———. 1894. *Hero-Tales of Ireland*. London: Macmillan and Co.

———. 1895. *Tales of the Fairies and of the Ghost World*. Boston: Little, Brown, and Co.

———. 1940. *Memoirs of Jeremiah Curtin*. Edited by Joseph Schafer. Wisconsin Biography Series 2. Madison: State Historical Society of Wisconsin.

Davis, Richard P. 2009. "O'Brien, William Smith." *Dictionary of Irish Biography* online, edited by James McGuire and James Quinn. http://dib.cambridge.org/viewReadPage.do?articleId=a6507. Accessed May 24, 2020.

Deane, Seamus. 1985. *Celtic Revivals: Essays in Modern Irish Literature, 1880–1980*. London: Faber and Faber.

de Blácam, Aodh. 1973 [1929]. *Gaelic Literature Surveyed*. Dublin: Talbot Press.

deGategno, Paul J. 1991. "'The Source of Daily and Exalted Pleasure': Jefferson Reads the Poems of Ossian." In *Ossian Revisited*, edited by Howard Gaskill, 94–108. Edinburgh: Edinburgh University Press.

Dégh, Linda. 1995. *Narratives in Society: A Performer-Centred Study of Narration*. Folklore Fellows Communications 255. Helsinki: Suomalainen Tiedeakatemia.

Delaney, James G. 1983. "Patrick Kennedy, Folklorist: A Preliminary Assessment." *Past* 14: 49–66.

Delargy, James Hamilton [Séamus Ó Duilearga]. 1969 [1945]. *The Gaelic Story-Teller*. Reprints in Irish Studies / American Committee for Irish Studies 6. Chicago: University of Chicago. [Sir John Rhys Memorial Lecture. Reprinted from the *Proceedings of the British Academy* 31.]

de Paor, Louis, and Dana Lyn. 2022. "A Poetry and Music Collaboration." *Louis de Paor and Dana Lyn* (blog). https://www.poetandmusician.com/. Accessed November 9, 2023.

de Valera, Eamon. 1926. "Eamon de Valera's View: Aims of Fianna Fáil (Amplified Interview to U.P.)." *An Phoblacht*. April 23.

Dietler, Michael. 2006. "Celticism, Celtitude, and Celticity: The Consumption of the Past in the Age of Globalization." In *Celtes et Gaulois dans l'Histoire, l'Historiographie et l'Idéologie Moderne*, edited by S. Rieckhoff, 237–48. Glux-en-Glenne: Bibracte, Centre Archéologique Européen.

Dillon, Myles, ed. and trans. 1932. "Stories from the Law Tracts." *Ériu* 11: 42–65.

———. 1975. *Celts and Aryans: Survivals of Indo-European Speech and Society*. Rashtrapati Nivas, Simla: Indian Institute of Advanced Study.

Dingwall, Christopher. 1997. "Ossian and Dunkeld: A Hall of Mirrors." In "Macpherson's Ossian." Special issue, *Scotlands* 4, no. 1: 62–70.

Dinneen, Patrick S. 1934 [1927]. *Foclóir Gaedhilge agus Béarla / An Irish-English Dictionary*. Dublin: Irish Texts Society.

Dobbs, Margaret. 1930. "The Ban-Shenchus." *Revue Celtique* 47: 283–339.

———. 1931. "The Ban-Shenchus (Suite)." *Revue Celtique* 48: 163–234.

Doherty, Gillian M. 2004. *The Irish Ordnance Survey: History, Culture and Memory*. Dublin: Four Courts.

Don, Lari. 2022. *The Tall Tale of the Giant's Causeway: Finn McCool, Benandonner and the Road between Ireland and Scotland*. Edinburgh: Kelpies.

Donnelly, James S., Jr. 1989. "A Famine in Irish Politics." In *A New History of Ireland*, vol. 5, edited by W. E. Vaughan, 357–71. Oxford: Oxford University Press.

Dooley, Ann. 2004. "The Date and Purpose of *Acallam na Senórach*." *Éigse* 34: 97–126.

———. 2012. "The Deployment of Some Hagiographical Sources in *Acallam na Senórach*." In *The Gaelic Finn Tradition*, edited by Sharon J. Arbuthnot and Geraldine Parsons, 97–110. Dublin: Four Courts.

Dooley, Ann, and Harry Roe, trans. 1999. *Tales of the Elders of Ireland*. Oxford: Oxford University Press.

Dorson, Richard M. 1966. "Foreword." In *Folktales of Ireland*, edited by Sean O'Sullivan [Seán Ó Súilleabháin], v–xxxii. Chicago and London: University of Chicago Press.

———. 1968. *The British Folklorists: A History*. Chicago: University of Chicago Press.

Douglas, Gavin. 1992 [c. 1501]. *The Palis of Honoure*. Edited by David Parkinson. Kalamazoo, MI: Medieval Institute Publications.

Doyle, Aidan. 2015. *A History of the Irish Language from the Norman Invasion to Independence*. Oxford: Oxford University Press.

Doyle, Aidan, and Kevin Murray, eds. 2014. *In Dialogue with the Agallamh: Essays in Honour of Seán Ó Coileáin*. Dublin: Four Courts.

Doyle, Linda. 2017. "Concern for the Future of the Hill of Allen." *Kildare Nationalist*. March 1. https://kildare-nationalist.ie/2017/03/01/concern-for-future-of-the-hill-of-allen. Accessed December 26, 2023.

Dropkick Murphys. 2001. *Sing Loud, Sing Proud*. Los Angeles: Hellcat. Compact disc.

Drummond, William Hamilton. 1811. *The Giants' Causeway, A Poem*. Belfast: Joseph Smyth.

———. 1830. "Subject Proposed by the Royal Irish Academy—To Investigate the Authenticity of the Poems of Ossian, both as Given in Macpherson's Translation, and as Published in Gaelic, London, 1807, under the Sanction of the Highland Society of London; And, on the Supposition of Such Poems not Being of Recent Origin, to Assign the Probable Era and Country of the Original Poet or Poets." *Transactions of the Royal Irish Academy* 16, part 2: 3–161.

———. 1852. *Ancient Irish Minstrelsy*. Dublin: Hodges and Smith.

Dumville, David N. 1993. "The Date 432." In *Saint Patrick, A.D. 493–1993*, edited by David N. Dumville, 39–43. Woodbridge, UK: Boydell Press.

Dunbar, Robert. 2013. "Vernacular Gaelic Tradition." In *The Edinburgh Companion to Scottish Traditional Literatures*, edited by Sarah Dunnigan and Suzanne Gilbert, 51–62. Edinburgh: Edinburgh University Press.

Duncan, A.A.M. 1989. *Scotland: The Making of the Kingdom*. The Edinburgh History of Scotland 1. Edinburgh: Mercat Press.

Duncan, John. 1895. "Anima Celtica." *Evergreen* 1: 106–7.

Dunleavy, Janet Egleson, and Gareth W. Dunleavy. 1980. "Jeremiah Curtin's Working Methods: The Evidence from the Manuscripts." *Éigse* 18: 67–86.

Dunne, John. 1851. "The Fenian Traditions of Sliabh-na-m-ban." *Transactions of the Kilkenny Archaeological Society* 1, no. 3: 333–62.

Egan, Ann, ed. 2010. *Laois Echoes with Fionn MacCumhaill*. Portlaoise: The Arts Office, Laois County Council.

Elis, Hefin, et al. 1975. *Nia Ben Aur*. Llandwrog, Caernarfon: Sain. Vinyl LP.

Empey, C. A. 1981. "The Settlement of the Kingdom of Limerick." In *England and Ireland in the Later Middle Ages: Essays in Honour of Jocelyn Otway-Ruthven*, edited by James Lydon, 1–25. Dublin: Irish Academic Press.

Everett, Nigel. 2014. *The Woods of Ireland: A History, 700–1800*. Dublin: Four Courts.

Faichney, Alexander Mailer. 1897. *Mackay's Complete Tourists' Guide to Oban and Vicinity*. Oban: D. Mackay.

Fallon, Padraic. 1951. "The Death of Diarmuid, from Diarmuid and Grainne: A Play." *Dublin Magazine* 26, no. 1: 4–15.

Fandom. n.d.-a. "Fionn mac Cumhaill." *Megami Tensei Wiki*. https://megamitensei.fandom.com/wiki/Fionn_mac_Cumhaill. Accessed December 14, 2023.

———. n.d.-b. "Fionn mac Cumhaill." *Fate / Grand Order Wiki*. https://fategrandorder.fandom.com/wiki/Fionn_mac_Cumhaill. Accessed December 14, 2023.

Farewell, James. 1689. *The Irish Hudibras, or Fingallian Prince*. London: Richard Baldwin.

Faujas de Saint-Fond, Barthélemy. 1799. *Travels in England, Scotland, and the Hebrides; Undertaken for the Purpose of Examining the State of the Arts, the Sciences, Natural History and Manners, in Great Britain*. Vol. 1. London: James Ridgway.

Fear na Muintire [pseud.]. 1900. "An Machaidhe Mór." In *Imtheachta an Oireachtais, 1899*, edited by S. J. Barrett, 70–86. Dublin: The Gaelic League.

Feldman, Burton, and Robert D. Richardson, trans. 1972. "From 'Excerpt from a Correspondence on Ossian and the Songs of Ancient Peoples' (1773)," by Johann Gottfried Herder. In *The Rise of Modern Mythology 1680–1860*, edited by Burton Feldman and Robert D. Richardson, 228–30. Bloomington: Indiana University Press.

Ferguson, William. 1998a. *The Identity of the Scottish Nation: An Historic Quest*. Edinburgh: Edinburgh University Press.

———. 1998b. "Samuel Johnson's Views on Scottish Gaelic Culture." *The Scottish Historical Review* 77, no. 204: 183–98.

Figgis, Darrell [Michel Ireland]. 1923. *The Return of the Hero*. London and Sydney: Chapman and Dodd.

Finnegan, Ruth. 1977. *Oral Poetry: Its Nature, Significance and Social Context*. Cambridge: Cambridge University Press.

Fischer, Lenore. 2019. "Fionn mac Cumhaill among the Old English. Some Comments on *The Book of Howth*." *North American Journal of Celtic Studies* 3, no. 1: 65–84.

Fisher, Keely. 1999. "The Crying of ane Playe: Robin Hood and Maying in Sixteenth-Century Scotland." *Medieval and Renaissance Drama in England* 12: 19–33, 35–58.

Fitzpatrick, David. 1992 [1989]. "Ireland Since 1870." In *The Oxford History of Ireland*, edited by R. F. Foster, 174–229. Oxford: Oxford University Press.

Fitzpatrick, Elizabeth. 2013. "Formaoil na Fiann: Hunting Preserves and Assembly Places in Gaelic Ireland." *Proceedings of the Harvard Celtic Colloquium* 32: 95–118.

Flahive, Joseph J. 2004. "The Relic Lays: A Study of the Development of Late Medieval Gaelic Fianaigheacht." PhD diss., University of Edinburgh.

———. 2014. "Revisiting the Reeves *Agallamh*." In *In Dialogue with the Agallamh: Essays in Honour of Seán Ó Coileáin*, edited by Aidan Doyle and Kevin Murray, 164–84. Dublin: Four Courts.

Flahive, Joseph J. 2015. "The Shield of Fionn: The Poem *Uchán a sciath mo rígh réigh* in Leabhar Ua Maine." In *Sacred Histories: A Festschrift for Máire Herbert*, edited by John Carey, Kevin Murray, and Caitríona Ó Dochartaigh, 139–60. Dublin: Four Courts.

———. 2017. *The Fenian Cycle in Irish and Scots-Gaelic Literature*. Cork: Cork Studies in Celtic Literatures.

———. Forthcoming. *Fenian Tradition and Gaelic Identity from Past to Present*. Edited by Natasha Sumner and Joseph Nagy.

Flanagan, Marie Therese. 2010. *The Transformation of the Irish Church in the Twelfth and Thirteenth Centuries*. Studies in Celtic History 29. Woodbridge, UK: Boydell Press.

Fleming, Eileen, dir. 2002. *The Journey West*. Episode 4, *Betwixt the Betweens*. Balquhidder, Perthshire: West Highland Animation.

Flower, Robin. 1926. *Catalogue of Irish Manuscripts in the British Museum*. Vol. 2. London: British Museum, Department of Manuscripts.

Foley, John Miles. 1991. *Immanent Art: From Structure to Meaning in Traditional Oral Epic*. Bloomington: Indiana University Press.

Fomin, Maxim. 2022. "*Tecosca Cormaic* and *Fíanaigecht* Tradition." *The Gaelic Finn Tradition II*, edited by Sharon J. Arbuthnot, Síle Ní Mhurchú, and Geraldine Parsons, 114–25. Dubin: Four Courts.

Frehan, Pádraic. 2012. *Education and Celtic Myth: National Self-Image and Schoolbooks in 20th Century Ireland*. Studia Imagologica 20. Amsterdam: Rodopi.

———. 2014. "National Self-Image: The Imagological Impact and Subsequent Contemporary Permeations of Celtic Mythology in Ireland's School Literature from 1924." In *Ireland and Popular Culture*, edited by Sylvie Mikowski, 157–79. Reimagining Ireland 54. Bern: Peter Lang.

Frisk, Kristian. 2019. "What Makes a Hero? Theorising the Social Structuring of Heroism." *Sociology* 53, no. 1: 87–103.

Frye, Northrop. 1976. *The Secular Scripture: A Study of the Structure of Romance*. Cambridge, MA: Harvard University Press.

Gaelic Affairs. 2008. "New Gaelic Symbol for Nova Scotia to be Launched." Government of Nova Scotia. May 22. https://novascotia.ca/news/release/?id=20080522003. Accessed December 14, 2023.

Gantz, Kenneth F. 1940. "Charlotte Brooke's *Reliques of Irish Poetry* and the Ossianic Controversy." *Studies in English* 20: 137–56.

Gaskill, Howard. 1986. "'Ossian' Macpherson: Towards a Rehabilitation." *Comparative Criticism* 8: 113–46.

———. 1988a. "On the Continuing Sorrows of 'Ossian' Macpherson." *Eighteenth-Century Scotland* 2: 15–17.

———. 1988b. "'Ossian' at Home and Abroad." *Strathclyde Modern Language Studies* 8: 5–26.

———. 1989. "German Ossianism: A Reappraisal?" *German Life and Letters* 42, no. 4: 329–41.

———. 1990. "What Did James Macpherson Really Leave on Display at His Publisher's Shop in 1762?" *Scottish Gaelic Studies* 16: 67–89.

———. 1991. "Introduction." In *Ossian Revisited*, edited by Howard Gaskill, 1–18. Edinburgh: Edinburgh University Press.

———. 1994. "Ossian in Europe." *Canadian Review of Comparative Literature* 21: 643–78.

———. 2001. "'Aus der Dritten Hand': Herder and his Annotators." *German Life and Letters* 54, no. 3: 210–18.

———. 2003. "Ossian, Herder, and the Idea of Folk Song." In *Literature of the Sturm und Drang*, edited by David Hill, 95–116. The Camden House History of German Literature 6. Rochester, NY: Camden House.

———. 2004. "Introduction: 'Genuine poetry . . . like gold.'" In *The Reception of Ossian in Europe*, edited by Howard Gaskill, 1–20. London: Thoemmes Continuum.

———. 2007–8. "'The Homer of the North.'" In "Ossian: Then and Now," edited by Frédéric Ogée and Maurice Géracht. Special issue, *Interfaces: Image Texte Language* 27: 13–24.

———. 2013a. "'Arise, O Magnificent Effulgence of Ossian's Soul!': Werther the Translator in English Translation." In "Versions of Ossian: Receptions, Responses, Translations," edited by Howard Gaskill. Special issue, *Translation and Literature* 22, no. 3: 302–21.

———. 2013b. "Introduction: The Translator's Ossian." In "Versions of Ossian: Receptions, Responses, Translations," edited by Howard Gaskill. Special issue, *Translation and Literature* 22, no. 3: 293–301.

Gibbons, Luke. 1998. "From Ossian to O'Carolan: The Bard as Separatist Symbol." In *From Gaelic to Romantic: Ossianic Translations*, edited by Fiona Stafford and Howard Gaskill, 226–51. Amsterdam: Rodopi.

Gidal, Eric. 2015. *Ossianic Unconformities: Bardic Poetry in the Industrial Age*. Charlottesville: University of Virginia Press.

Giffney, Noreen. 2014. "Gwynn, Edward John." *Dictionary of Irish Biography* online, edited by James McGuire and James Quinn. http://dib.cambridge.org/viewReadPage.do?articleId=a3692. Accessed March 3, 2020.

Gillies, Alexander. 1969. *A Hebridean in Goethe's Weimar: The Reverend James MacDonald and the Cultural Relations Between Scotland and Germany*. Oxford: Basil Blackwell.

Gillies, John [Eoin], ed. 1786. *Sean Dain, agus Orain Ghaidhealach, air an Tabhairt o Dhaoin Uaisle Araid an Gaeltachd Alba / A Collection of Ancient and Modern Gaelic Poems and Songs, Transmitted from Gentlemen in the Highlands of Scotland*. Perth: John Gillies.

Gillies, William. 1987. "Heroes and Ancestors." In *Fiannaíocht: Essays on the Fenian Tradition of Ireland and Scotland*, edited by Bo Almqvist, Séamas Ó Catháin, and Pádraig Ó Héalaí, 57–73. Dublin: The Folklore of Ireland Society.

Giraldus Cambrensis. 1861. *Giraldi Cambrensis Opera*. Vol. 5, *Topographia Hibernica et Expugnatio Hibernica*, edited by James F. Dimock. Rerum Britannicarum Mediiaevi Scriptores. London: Longmans, Green, Reader, and Dyer.

Glass, Rev. James. 1792. "The Irish Bard." *Northern Star*. May 19, 4.

Goethe, Johann Wolfgang. 1774. *Die Leiden des Jungen Werthers*. Leipzig: Weygandschen Buchhandlung.

Graduate Student Life. 2023. "Why the Salmon?" *Salmon Tales: A Graduate Student Life Blog* (blog). https://sites.nd.edu/ask-the-salmon/why-the-salmon/. Accessed December 14, 2023.

Grainger, Laura. 2023. "Irish Government Collaborates with Harvard University to Fund New Fionn mac Cumhaill Folklore Database." *Irish Star*. April 23. https://www.irishstar.com/culture/nostalgia/irish-government-collaborates-harvard-university-29775495. Accessed December 20, 2023.

Grant, I. F., and Hugh Cheape. 1987. *Periods in Highland History*. London: Shepheard-Walwyn.

Grant, James. 1814. *Thoughts on the Origin and Descent of the Gael: With an Account of the Picts, Caledonians, and Scots; And Observations Relative to the Authenticity of the Poems of Ossian*. Edinburgh: Archibald Constable and Co.

Grant, Katherine Whyte. 1908. *Dùsgadh na Féinne*. Paisley: J. and R. Parlane.

Greene, David, ed. 1955. *Fingal Rónáin and Other Stories*. Dublin: Dublin Institute for Advanced Studies.

Gregory, Lady Isabella Augusta. 1970a [1904]. *Gods and Fighting Men: The Story of the Tuatha De Danaan and of the Fianna of Ireland*. Coole Edition 3. New York: Oxford University Press.

———. 1970b [1912]. "Grania." *Collected Plays*, vol. 2, edited by Ann Saddlemyer, 11–46. New York: Oxford University Press.

———. 1974 [1903]. *Poets and Dreamers: Studies and Translations from the Irish*. Coole Edition 10. New York: Oxford University Press.

[Griffin, Gerald]. 1832. *The Invasion*. Vol. 2. London: Saunders and Otley.

Griffin-Wilson, Margo, ed. 2010. *The Wedding Poems of Dáibhí Ó Bruadair*. Dublin: Dublin Institute for Advanced Studies.

Gunderloch, Anja. 1996. "18th Century Literary Fraud and Oral Tradition: The 'Real' Ossian." In *Orality, Literacy, and Modern Media*, edited by Dietrich Scheunemann, 44–61. Columbia, SC: Camden House.

———. 1997. "The Cath Gabhra Family of Ballads: A Study in Textual Relationships, Vol. 1." PhD diss., University of Edinburgh.

———. 2011. "Duncan Kennedy: Poet and Collector of Heroic Ballads." *Scottish Gaelic Studies* 28: 55–95.

———. 2012. "Duncan Kennedy and His Heroic Ballads." In *The Gaelic Finn Tradition*, edited by Sharon J. Arbuthnot and Geraldine Parsons, 179–94. Dublin: Four Courts.

———. 2013. "The Heroic Ballads of Gaelic Scotland." In *The Edinburgh Companion to Scottish Traditional Literatures*, edited by Sarah Dunnigan and Suzanne Gilbert, 74–181. Edinburgh: Edinburgh University Press.

Gwynn, Aubrey, and R. Neville Hadcock. 1970. *Medieval Religious Houses: Ireland*. London: Longman.

Gwynn, Edward J., ed. and trans. 1904. "The Burning of Finn's House." *Ériu* 1: 13–17.

———, ed. and trans. 1906. *The Metrical Dindshenchas*. Vol. 2. Todd Lecture Series 9. Dublin: Hodges and Figgis.

———, ed. and trans. 1913. *The Metrical Dindshenchas*. Vol. 3. Todd Lecture Series 10. Dublin: Hodges and Figgis.

———, ed. and trans. 1924. *The Metrical Dindshenchas*. Vol. 4. Todd Lecture Series 11. Dublin: Hodges and Figgis.

Gwynn, Stephen. 1923. *The History of Ireland*. New York: Macmillan.

———. 1925. *The Student's History of Ireland*. New York: Macmillan.

Hanmer, Meredith. 1633. "The Chronicle of Ireland." Edited by James Ware. In *The Historie of Ireland, Collected by Three Learned Authors viz. Meredith Hanmer, Doctor in Divinitie: Edmund Campion, Sometime Fellow of St Johns Colledge in Oxford: and Edmund Spenser, Esq.* Dublin: Society of Stationers.

Hardiman, James, ed. 1831. "Laoidh Bhin Bhoilbin." Translated by Rev. William Hamilton Drummond. In *Irish Minstrelsy, or Bardic Remains of Ireland with English Poetical Translations*, 386–89. Vol. 2. London: Joseph Robins.

Harmon, Maurice. 1974. "Notes towards a Biography." *Irish University Review* 4, no. 1: 13–25.

———, trans. 2001. *The Colloquy of the Old Men (Acallam na Senórach)*. Dublin: Maunsel and Company.

Harold, Edmund de. 1787a. *Poems of Ossian*. Düsseldorf: John Cretien Daenzer.

———. 1787b. *Neu Entdeckte Gedichte Ossians*. Düsseldorf: John Cretien Daenzer.

Harvie, Christopher. 1996. "Anglo-Saxons into Celts: The Scottish Intellectuals 1760–1930." In *Celticism*, edited by Terence Brown, 231–56. Studia Imagologica: Amsterdam Studies on Cultural Identity 8. Amsterdam: Rodopi.

Hayes, Katy. 2024. "Grania: Lady Gregory's Difficult Play Gets a Gutsy Outing at the Abbey." *Irish Independent*. September 30. https://www.independent.ie/entertainment/theatre-arts/grania-lady-gregorys-difficult-play-gets-a-gutsy-outing-at-the-abbey/a278125276.html. Accessed October 6, 2024.

Hayes-McCoy, G. A. 1979. *A History of Irish Flags from Earliest Times*. Dublin: The Academic Press.

Hay, Marnie. 2011. "Moulding the Future: Na Fianna Éireann and Its Members, 1909–1923." *Studies: An Irish Quarterly Review* 100, no. 400: 441–54.

Heaney, Marie. 1994. *Over Nine Waves: A Book of Irish Legends*. London: Faber and Faber.

Heavey, Fiona. 2021. "World-Class Visitor Attraction to Put West Cavan 'On the Map.'" *Leitrim Observer*. June 10. https://www.leitrimobserver.ie/news/cavan/640284/world-class-visitor-attraction-to-put-west-cavan-on-the-map.html. Accessed December 11, 2023.

Henderson, Rev. George. 1905–6. "The Fionn Saga." *Celtic Review* 1: 193–207, 352–66; 2: 1–19, 135–53, 255–72, 351–59; and 3: 56–61.

———. 1908–11. "Lamh-Sgrìobhainnean Mhic-Neacail." *Transactions of the Gaelic Society of Inverness* 27: 340–409.

Hennessy, W. M. 1871. Review of *The Poems of Ossian*, edited and translated by Rev. Archibald Clerk. *The Academy: A Record of Literature, Learning, Science, and Art* 2: 365–67.

———, ed. and trans. 1873–75. "The Battle of Cnucha." *Revue Celtique* 2: 86–93.

Herbert, Máire. 1989. "The Preface to *Amra Coluim Cille*." In *Sages, Saints and Storytellers: Celtic Studies in Honour of Professor James Carney*, edited by Donnchadh Ó Corráin, Liam Breatnach, and Kim R. McCone, 67–75. Maynooth Monographs 2. Maynooth: An Sagart.

Herder, Johann Gottfried. 1773. "Auszug aus einem Briefwechsel über Ossian und die Lieder alter Völker." In *Von Deutscher Art und Kunst: Einige Fliegende Blätter*, 1–70. Hamburg: Bey Bode.

———. 1795. "Homer und Ossian." *Die Horen* 4, no. 10: 86–107.

———, ed. 1981 [1778–79]. *Volkslieder*. Hildesheim: Georg Olms Verlag.

Hillers, Barbara. 1994. "The Heroes of the Ulster Cycle." In *Ulidia: Proceedings of the First International Conference on the Ulster Cycle of Tales*, edited by J. P. Mallory and Gerard Stockman, 99–106. Belfast: December Publications.

———. 2007. "Storytelling and the International Folktale in Scotland." In *Scottish Life and Society: A Compendium of Scottish Ethnology*, vol. 10, *Oral Literature and Performance Culture*, edited by John Beech et al., 153–70. Edinburgh: John Donald.

Hill, Thomas Ford, ed. 1784. *Antient Erse Poems, Collected in the Scottish Highlands, in Order to Illustrate the Ossian of Mr. Macpherson*. London: n.p.

Hirschberger, Gilad. 2018. "Collective Trauma and the Social Construction of Meaning." *Frontiers in Psychology* 9, no. 1441: https://doi.org/10.3389/fpsyg.2018.01441.

Hogg, Ulrike. 2011. "The Life and Papers of the Rev. Dr Alexander Irvine." *Scottish Gaelic Studies* 28: 97–174.

Holinshed, Raphaell, ed. 1577. *The Firste Volume of the Chronicles of England, Scotlande, and Irelande*. London: n.p.

Horgan Goff, Angela. 2017. "Musical Interpretations of Fenian Literature by Contemporary Irish Composers." In *New Crops, Old Fields: Reimagining Irish Folklore*, edited by Conor Caldwell and Eamon Byers, 83–98. Reimagining Ireland 80. Oxford: Peter Lang.

Horslips. 1976. *The Book of Invasions: A Celtic Symphony*. London: DJM Records. Vinyl LP.

Hourican, Bridget. 2009. "Russell, Thomas O'Neill (Tomás Ó Néill Ruiséal)." In *Dictionary of Irish Biography* online, edited by James McGuire and James Quinn. https://dib.cambridge.org/viewReadPage.do?articleId=a7847. Accessed March 3, 2020.

Hoyne, Mícheál. 2015. "*Imtheacht an Dá Nónmhar agus Tóraigheacht Taise Taoibhghile*: An Early Modern Irish Exemplary Tale." *Ériu* 65: 1–47.

Hughes, A. J. 1998. *Robert Shipboy MacAdam (1808–95): His Life and Gaelic Proverb Collection*. Belfast: Institute of Irish Studies, Queen's University Belfast.

Hughes, Harold F. 1922. *Legendary Heroes of Ireland*. San Francisco: Harr Wagner.

Hull, Eleanor. 1904. *Pagan Ireland*. Epochs of Irish History 1. London: David Nutt; Dublin: M. H. Gill and Son.

———. 1908. *A Text Book of Irish Literature*. Vol. 2. Dublin: M. H. Gill and Son.

———. 1926. *A History of Ireland and Her People*. Vol. 1. London: George Harrap.

Hull, Vernam, ed. and trans. 1936. "The Death of Fothath Cananne." *Zeitschrift Für Celtische Philologie* 20: 400–404.

Hull, Vernam, ed. and trans. 1941. "Two Tales about Find." *Speculum* 16, no. 3: 322–33.

Hunter, James. 1975. "The Gaelic Connection: The Highlands, Ireland and Nationalism, 1873–1922." *The Scottish Historical Review* 54, no. 158: 178–204.

———. 2000 [1976]. *The Making of the Crofting Community*. Edinburgh: Birlinn.

Hutchinson, John. 1987. *The Dynamics of Cultural Nationalism: The Gaelic Revival and the Creation of the Irish Nation State*. London: Allen and Unwin.

Hyde, Douglas [Dúbhghlas de h-Íde], ed. 1889. *Leabhar Sgeulaigheachta*. Dublin: Gill.

———, ed. 1890. *Beside the Fire: A Collection of Irish Gaelic Folk Stories*. London: David Nutt.

———. 1894. "The Necessity for De-Anglicising Ireland." In *The Revival of Irish Literature*, 117–61. London: T. Fisher Unwin.

———. 1895. *The Story of Early Gaelic Literature*. London: T. Fisher Unwin.

———. 1899. *A Literary History of Ireland from Earliest Times to the Present Day*. London: T. Fisher Unwin.

——— [Dúbhglas de h-Íde], ed. 1901. *An Sgéaluidhe Gaedhealach*. Dublin: M. H. Gill and Son.

———, ed. 1906. *Abhráin Diadha Chúige Connacht / The Religious Songs of Connacht*. Vol. 1. Dublin: M. H. Gill and Son.

———, ed. 1915. *Legends of Saints and Sinners*. London: T. Fisher Unwin.

——— [An Chraoibhín], ed. 1931. "Báirne Mór." *Béaloideas* 3, no. 2: 187–95.

——— [An Craoibhín], ed. 1932. "Cailleach an Teampuill." *Béaloideas* 3, no. 4: 447–55.

——— [An Craoibhín], ed. 1934. "Diarmuid agus Gráinne." *Béaloideas* 4, no. 4: 425–30.

——— [An Craoibhín], ed. 1936. "An Sean-Duinín a Tháinig chuig na Fianntaibh." *Béaloideas* 6, no. 1: 104–7.

——— [An Craoibhín], ed. 1937. "Leath a' Duine." *Béaloideas* 7, no. 2: 180–84.

——— [An Craoibhín], ed. 1939a. "Laoi na Con Duibhe: I." *Béaloideas* 9, no. 1: 3–12.

———, ed. 1939b. *Sgéalta Thomáis Uí Chathasaigh*. Irish Texts Society 36. Dublin: Educational Company of Ireland.

Hyde, Douglas [An Craoibhín], and Tomás Ó Caomhánaigh, eds. 1930. "Cuireadh Mhaoil uí Mhananáin ar Fionn mac Cumhaill agus Fiannaibh Éirionn." *Lia Fáil* 3: 87–114.

Ifan, Elan. 2015. "T. Gwynn Jones' 'Tir na n-Óg': The Irish Origins of a Welsh Classic." *Proceedings of the Harvard Celtic Colloquium* 34: 87–111.

Innes, Sìm. 2013. "Fionn in Hell." *Scottish Gaelic Studies* 29: 21–53.

———. 2016. "Fionn and Ailbhe's Riddles between Ireland and Scotland." In *Ollam: Studies in Gaelic and Related Traditions in Honor of Tomás Ó Cathasaigh*, edited by Matthieu Boyd, 271–85. Madison, NJ: Fairleigh Dickinson University Press.

———. 2022. "*Dùsgadh na Fèinne* (1908): Katherine Whyte Grant's Scottish Gaelic Kinderspiel." In *The Gaelic Finn Tradition II*, edited by Sharon J. Arbuthnot, Síle Ní Mhurchú, and Geraldine Parsons, 197–210. Dubin: Four Courts.

Innes, Sìm, and Kate Louise Mathis. 2019. "Gaelic Tradition and the Celtic Revival in Children's Literature in Scottish Gaelic and English." In *The Land of Story-Books: Scottish Children's Literature in the Long Nineteenth Century*, edited by Sarah Dunnigan and Shu-Fang Lai, 107–57. Glasgow: Scottish Literature International.

Irish Strongman Association. 2016. "ISA Strongman Results Since 2000." *Irish Strongman Association*. February 16, https://irishstrongman.com/strongman-results/. Accessed November 10, 2023.

Jefferson, Thomas. 1950 [1773]. "To Charles McPherson." In *The Papers of Thomas Jefferson*, vol. 1, edited by Julian P. Boyd et al., 96–97. Princeton, NJ: Princeton University Press.

Jerram, C. S. 1874. *Dàn an Deirg, agus Tiomna Ghuill (Dargo and Gaul)*. Edinburgh: MacLachlan and Stewart.

———. 1876. "Some Causes of the Imperfect Appreciation by Englishmen of the Ossianic Poems." *Transactions of the Gaelic Society of Inverness* 5: 97–110.

Johnson, Samuel. 1971. *A Journey to the Western Islands of Scotland*. Edited by Mary Lascelles. The Yale Edition of the Works of Samuel Johnson 9. New Haven, CT: Yale University Press.

Johnston, Elva. 2013. *Literacy and Orality in Early Medieval Ireland*. Studies in Celtic History. Woodbridge, UK: Boydell Press.

Joyce, James. 1999 [1939]. *Finnegans Wake*. New York: Penguin.

Joyce, Patrick Weston, trans. 1879. *Old Celtic Romances*. London: C. Kegan Paul and Co.

Joynt, Maud, ed. 1936. *Feis Tighe Chonáin*. Mediaeval and Modern Irish Series 7. Dublin: The Stationary Office.

Kearney, Richard. 2002. *On Stories*. London: Routledge.

Keating, Geoffrey [Seathrún Céitinn]. 1902. *Foras Feasa ar Éirinn*. Vol. 1, edited and translated by David Comyn. Irish Texts Society 4. London: Irish Texts Society.

———. 1908. *Foras Feasa ar Éirinn*. Vol. 2, edited and translated by Patrick S. Dinneen. Irish Texts Society 8. London: Irish Texts Society.

Kedzierska, Aleksandra, et al. 2008. "Quarrying at Historic Hill of Allen." *Irish Times*. August 16. https://www.irishtimes.com/opinion/letters/quarrying-at-historic-hill-of-allen-1.931173. Accessed December 26, 2023.

Kelleher, John V. 1950. "Matthew Arnold and the Celtic Revival." In *Perspectives of Criticism*, 197–221. Cambridge, MA: Harvard University Press.

[Kennedy, Patrick]. 1851. "The Whitney Papers—No. 3." *Independent* [Wexford]. September 20, 1.

———. 1859. *Fictions of Our Forefathers: Fion Mac Cumhail and His Warriors*. Dublin: M'Glashan and Gill, James Duffy, W. B. Kelly, and P. Kennedy.

[———]. 1862a. "Norse and Gaelic Popular Tales." *Duffy's Hibernian Sixpenny Magazine* 1, no. 4: 317–28.

[———]. 1862b. "Pagan Relics and Fairy Lore in a County of the Pale." *Dublin University Magazine* [59, no. 350], 239–47.

———. 1866. *Legendary Fictions of the Irish Celts*. London: Macmillan and Co.

Kennedy, Rev. John. 1867. *The "Apostle of the North": The Life and Labours of the Rev. Dr. M'Donald*. London: T. Nelson and Sons.

———. 1892. "Memoir of Dr. Cameron." *Reliquiae Celticae: Texts, Papers, and Studies in Gaelic Literature and Philology left by the late Rev. Alexander Cameron, L.L.D.*, vol. 1, *Ossianica*, edited by Alexander MacBain and Rev. John Kennedy, xvii–clxxi. Inverness: Northern Chronicle.

Kiberd, Declan. 2009. "Synge, (Edmund) John Millington." In *Dictionary of Irish Biography* online, edited by James McGuire and James Quinn. http://dib.cambridge.org/viewReadPage.do?articleId=a8429. Accessed October 4, 2019.

Kidd, Colin. 1993. *Subverting Scotland's Past: Scottish Whig Historians and the Creation of an Anglo-British Identity, 1689–c. 1830*. Cambridge: Cambridge University Press.

———. 1995. "Teutonist Ethnology and Scottish Nationalist Inhibition, 1780–1880." *The Scottish Historical Review* 74, no. 1: 45–68.

Kidd, Màiri. 2011. *Mar a Chuala Mise E*. Stornoway: Stòrlann Nàiseanta na Gàidhlig.

Kirkham, Lynn. 2010. "Fionn Mac Cumhaill and His Hounds." *Publicart*. [Irish Department of Culture, Heritage and the Gaeltacht]. https://publicart.ie/main/directory/directory/view/fionn-mac-cumhaill-and-his-hounds/ea2774fe8a999138e5cdc129c53b897f/. Accessed November 10, 2023.

Knight, Matthew. 2021. "'Our Gaelic Department': The Irish-Language Column in the New York *Irish-American*, 1857–1896." PhD diss., Harvard University.

Kristmannsson, Gauti. 2017. "Ossian and the State of Translation in the Scottish Enlightenment." In *The International Companion to James Macpherson and The Poems of Ossian*, edited by Dafydd Moore, 39–51. Glasgow: Scottish Literature International.

Kühns, Julia S., ed. 2005. "An Edition and Translation of the *Agallamh Bheag* from the Book of Lismore." MPhil thesis, University of Glasgow.

———. 2012. "Some Observations on the *Acallam bec*." In *The Gaelic Finn Tradition*, edited by Sharon J. Arbuthnot and Geraldine Parsons, 122–38. Dublin: Four Courts.

Laing, Malcolm. 1800. "An Historical and Critical Dissertation on the Supposed Authenticity of Ossian's Poems." In *The History of Scotland from the Union of the Crowns on the Accession of James VI. to the Throne of England, to the Union of the Kingdoms in the Reign of Queen Anne*, 377–453. London: A. Strahan.

———, ed. 1971 [1805]. *Poems of Ossian*, by James Macpherson. 2 vols. Edinburgh: Mercat Press.

Lamont, Claire. 1968. "William Collins's 'Ode on the Popular Superstitions of the Highlands of Scotland'—A Newly Recovered Manuscript." *Review of English Studies*, n.s., 19, no. 74: 137–47.

Langhorne, Ceit. 2021. "An Duan fo Ghlas: The Fianna in a Time of COVID." *YouTube* video. December 28. https://www.youtube.com/watch?v=YNbWQ4h70zw. Accessed November 9, 2023.

Lanters, José. 1995. "Darrell Figgis, *The Return of the Hero*, and the Making of the Irish Nation." *Colby Quarterly* 31, no. 3: 204–13.

Laoide, Seosamh, ed. 1901. *Sgéalaidhe Fearnmhuighe*. Dublin: Connradh na Gaedhilge.

———, ed. 1908. *Éan an Cheoil Bhinn agus Sgéalta Eile*. Imtheachta an Oireachtais 1901, book 2, part 3. Dublin: Connradh na Gaedhilge.

———, ed. 1913. *Cruach Chonaill*. Dublin: Connradh na Gaedhilge.

———, ed. 1916. *Fian-Laoithe*. Dublin: Clódhanna, Teo.

Larminie, William, ed. 1893. *West Irish Folk-Tales and Romances*. London: Elliot Stock.

Laukaitis, John. 2010. "The Politics of Language and National School Reform: The Gaelic League's Call for an Irish Ireland, 1893–1922." *American Educational History Journal* 37, no. 1: 221–35.

Leaney, Enda. 2009. "Young, Matthew." In *Dictionary of Irish Biography* online, edited by James McGuire and James Quinn. http://dib.cambridge.org/viewReadPage.do?articleId=a9175. Accessed April 29, 2020.

Leask, Nigel. 2016. "Fingalian Topographies: Ossian and the Highland Tour, 1760–1805." *Journal for Eighteenth-Century Studies* 39, no. 2: 183–97.

———. 2017. "Sir Walter Scott's *The Antiquary* and the *Ossian* Controversy." *Yearbook of English Studies* 47: 189–202.

———. 2020. *Stepping Westward: Writing the Highland Tour c. 1720–1830*. Oxford: Oxford University Press.

"Lee Gaelic League." 1899. *Shan Van Vocht* 4, no. 3: 52.

Leerssen, Joep. 1996 [1986]. *Mere Irish and Fíor-Ghael: Studies in the Idea of Irish Nationality, Its Development and Literary Expression Prior to the Nineteenth Century*. Field Day Monographs 3. Cork: Cork University Press.

———. 1997. *Remembrance and Imagination: Patterns in the Historical and Literary Representation of Ireland in the Nineteenth Century*. Field Day Monographs 4. Cork: Cork University Press.

———. 2004. "Ossian and the Rise of Literary Historicism." In *The Reception of Ossian in Europe*, edited by Howard Gaskill, 109–25. London: Thoemmes Continuum.

Lehmann, Edyta. 2019. "'If We Settled in the Forest . . .': Tracing the Function of Wooded Spaces from Old Irish Literature to Contemporary Poetry." In *Landscape and Myth in Northwestern Europe*, edited by Matthias Egeler, 239–56. Borders, Boundaries, Landscapes 2. Turnhout: Brepols.

Lemke, Cordula. 2017. "Nostalgic Ossian and the Transcreation of the Scottish Nation." In *The International Companion to James Macpherson and The Poems of Ossian*, edited by Dafydd Moore, 52–64. Glasgow: Scottish Literature International.

Lenihan, Eddie. 2006. *Irish Tales of Mystery and Magic*. Cork: Mercier Press.

Leonard, Hugh. 1971. *The Patrick Pearse Motel: A Comedy*. London: Samuel French.

Leslie, John. 1675. *De Origine, Moribus et Rebus Gestis Scotorum Libri Decem*. 2nd ed. Rome: n.p.

Leyden, John. 1903 [1800]. *Journal of a Tour in the Highlands and Western Islands of Scotland in 1800*. Edited by James Sinton. Edinburgh: Blackwood.

Lindsay, David. 1931. "The Historie of ane Nobil and Wailȝeand Squyer, William Meldrum." In *The Works of Sir David Lindsay of the Mount, 1490–1555*, edited by Douglas Hamer, vol. 1, 145–88. Scottish Texts Society 1, 3rd series. Edinburgh: William Blackwood and Sons.

———. 1989. *Ane Satyre of the Thrie Estaitis*. Edited by Roderick Lyall. Edinburgh: Canongate.

Lizars, W. H. 1830. *The Scottish Tourist, and Itinerary; or, A Guide to the Scenery and Antiquities of Scotland and the Western Islands*. 3rd ed. Edinburgh: Stirling and Kenney.

Lloyd, John. 1780. *A Short Tour; or, an Impartial and Accurate Description of the County of Clare with Some Particular and Historical Observations*. Ennis: John Busteed and George Trinder.

Lloyd-Morgan, Ceridwen, and Erich Poppe. 2019. "Introduction." In *Arthur in the Celtic Languages: The Arthurian Legend in Celtic Literatures and Traditions*, edited by Ceridwen Lloyd-Morgan and Erich Poppe, 1–10. Cardiff: University of Wales Press.

Llywelyn, Morgan. 1994. *Finn Mac Cool*. New York: Tom Doherty Associates.

Locke, John. 1975. *An Essay Concerning Human Understanding*. Edited by Peter H. Nidditch. Oxford: Clarendon Press.

Lord, Albert B. 2019. *The Singer of Tales*. Edited by David F. Elmer. 3rd ed. Hellenic Studies Series 76. Publications of the Milman Parry Collection of Oral Literature 4. Cambridge, MA: Harvard University Press.

Love, Walter D. 1962. "The Hibernian Antiquarian Society: A Forgotten Predecessor to the Royal Irish Academy." *Studies: An Irish Quarterly Review* 51, no. 203: 419–31.

[Lynch, Patrick], ed. 1795. *Bolg an Tsolair: Or, Gaelic Magazine* 1.

Lyons, J. J., ed. 1891. "Fionn Mac Cumhail agus Ridire 'n Gháire." *Monitor* [San Francisco], June 10; June 17; July 1; July 8; July 15.

Mac [pseud]. 1897. "To Young Irishmen." *Shan Van Vocht* 2, no. 8: 51.

Mac Airt, Seán, and Gearóid Mac Niocaill, eds. and trans. 1983. *The Annals of Ulster, to AD 1131*. Dublin: Dublin Institute for Advanced Studies.

MacBain, Alexander. 1886. "The Heroic and Ossianic Literature." *Transactions of the Gaelic Society of Inverness* 12: 180–211.

———. 1887. "Macpherson's Ossian." *Celtic Magazine* 12: 145–54, 193–201, 241–54.

———. 1891–94. "Who Were the Feinn?" *Transactions of the Gaelic Society of Glasgow* 2: 67–106.

MacBain, Alexander, and Rev. John Kennedy. 1892. "Preface." In *Reliquiae Celticae: Texts, Papers, and Studies in Gaelic Literature and Philology left by the late Rev. Alexander Cameron, L.L.D.*, vol. 1, *Ossianica*, edited by Alexander MacBain and Rev. John Kennedy, xi–xvi. Inverness: Northern Chronicle.

[MacCallum, Duncan], ed. 1821. *Co-chruinneacha Dhan, Orain, Etc., Etc.: A Collection of Original Poems, Songs, Etc. Taken from Oral Recitation in Various Parts of the Highlands and Islands of Scotland, during the Last Twenty Years*. Inverness: Seumas Friseal.

MacCallum, Hugh, and John MacCallum, eds. 1816. *An Original Collection of the Poems of Ossian, Orrann, Ulin, and Other Bards who Flourished in the Same Age / Comh-Chrunneachadh Taghta de Shaothair Oisian, Orrann, Ullinn, agus Baird Eile Bha Ann ri an Linn*. Montrose: James Watt.

Mac Cana, Proinsias. 1970. *Celtic Mythology*. London: Hamlyn.

———. 1974. "The Rise of the Later Schools of *Filidheacht*." *Ériu* 25: 126–46.

———. 1975. "The Influence of the Vikings on Celtic Literature." In *The Impact of the Scandinavian Invasions on the Celtic-Speaking Peoples c. 800–1100 A.D.*, edited by Brian Ó Cuív, 78–118.

Proceedings of the International Congress of Celtic Studies 1. Dublin: Dublin Institute for Advanced Studies.

Mac Cana, Proinsias. 1980. *The Learned Tales of Medieval Ireland*. Dublin: Dublin Institute for Advanced Studies.

———. 1987. "*Fianaigecht* in the Pre-Norman Period." In *Fiannaíocht: Essays on the Fenian Tradition of Ireland and Scotland*, edited by Bo Almqvist, Séamas Ó Catháin, and Pádraig Ó Héalaí, 75–99. Dublin: The Folklore of Ireland Society.

Mac Cárthaigh, Maitias, et al. 2001. *Cormac agus Órla agus Fionn mac Cumhaill*. Baile an Fheirtéaraigh, Co. Chiarrai: Fios Feasa. CD-ROM.

MacCoinnich, Aonghas. 2016. "19th & 20th Century: The Ossianic Society." *The Gaelic Story at the University of Glasgow* (blog). March 3. https://sgeulnagaidhlig.ac.uk/ossianic-society/?lang=en. Accessed April 13, 2024.

MacCoinnich, Cailein T. 1969. "Searmon a' Bhodaich." In *Oirthir Tím*, 111–25. Glasgow: Gairm.

MacColl, Evan. 1883. "A Word with the Fenian Brotherhood." In *The English Poetical Works of Evan MacColl*, 288–89. Toronto: Hunter, Rose, and Co.

Mac Craith, Mícheál. 1998. "*Fingal*: Text, Context, Subtext." In *From Gaelic to Romantic: Ossianic Translations*, edited by Fiona Stafford and Howard Gaskill, 59–68. Amsterdam: Rodopi.

———. 2000. "Charlotte Brooke and James Macpherson." *Litteraria Pragensia* 10: 5–17.

———. 2004. "'We Know all These Poems': The Irish Response to *Ossian*." In *The Reception of Ossian in Europe*, edited by Howard Gaskill, 91–108. London: Thoemmes Continuum.

———. 2006. "Literature in Irish, c. 1550–1690: From the Elizabethan Settlement to the Battle of the Boyne." In *The Cambridge History of Irish Literature*, vol. 1, edited by Margaret Kelleher and Philip O'Leary, 191–231. Cambridge: Cambridge University Press.

———. 2007–8. "'Beathaíonn na Bráithre na Briathra': The Louvain Achievement." *Seanchas Ardmhacha: Journal of the Armagh Diocesan Historical Society* 21, no. 2 / 22, no. 1: 86–123.

———. 2015. "Charles O'Conor of Ballinagare and the Macpherson Controversy." In *Charles O'Conor of Ballinagare, 1710–91: Life and Works*, edited by Luke Gibbons and Kieran O'Conor, 165–85. Dublin: Four Courts.

MacDiarmid, Hugh. 1967. *Collected Poems of Hugh MacDiarmid*. Revised ed. New York: Macmillan.

MacDonald, Donald A. 1985. "Campbell and Gaelic Oral Tradition." In *Lamplighter and Storyteller: John Francis Campbell of Islay 1821–1885*, 10–15. Edinburgh: National Library of Scotland.

MacDonald, Keith Norman. 1904–5. "The Reasons Why I Believe in the Ossianic Poems." *Celtic Monthly* 12: 7–8, 27–29, 47–49, 76–78, 98–99, 104–5, 128–29, 130, 156–58, 168–69, 187–88, 218–20, 234–36; and 13: 16–18, 35–36, 58–60, 72–73, 95–96, 102–4, 133–34, 154–55, 199–200, 204–6, 227–29.

———. 1906. *In Defence of Ossian: Being a Summary of the Evidence in Favour of the Authenticity of the Poems*. Oban: Oban Times.

Macdonald, Murdo. 2003. "Anima Celtica: Embodying the Soul of the Nation in 1890s Edinburgh." In *Art, Nation and Gender: Ethnic Landscapes, Myths and Mother-Figures*, edited by Tricia Cusack and Síghle Bhreathnach-Lynch, 29–37. Aldershot, UK: Ashgate.

———. 2004. "Ossian and Art: Scotland into Europe via Rome." In *The Reception of Ossian in Europe*, edited by Howard Gaskill, 393–404. London: Thoemmes Continuum.

———. 2016. "Ossian and Visual Art: Mislaid and Rediscovered." *Journal for Eighteenth-Century Studies* 39, no. 2: 235–48.

———. 2017. "The Significance of James Macpherson's *Ossian* for Visual Artists." In *The International Companion to James Macpherson and The Poems of Ossian*, edited by Dafydd Moore, 92–104. Glasgow: Scottish Literature International.

MacDougall, Rev. James, ed. 1891. *Waifs and Strays of Celtic Tradition: Argyllshire Series*. Vol. 3, *Folk and Hero Tales*. London: David Nutt.

Mac Eoin, Gearóid. 2012. "Early Irish Narrative Verse." In *Atlantic Currents: Essays on Lore, Literature and Language / Sruthanna an Aigéin Thiar / Aistí ar Sheanchas, ar Litríocht agus ar Theanga*, edited by Bo Almqvist, Críostóir Mac Cárthaigh, Liam Mac Mathúna, Séamus Mac Mathúna, and Seosamh Watson, 303–21. Dublin: University College Dublin Press.

MacGregor, Martin. 2012. "The Campbells: Lordship, Literature, and Liminality." *Textual Cultures: Texts, Contexts, Interpretation* 7, no. 1: 121–57.

MacInnes, John. 1987. "Twentieth-Century Recordings of Scottish Gaelic Heroic Ballads." In *Fiannaíocht: Essays on the Fenian Tradition of Ireland and Scotland*, edited by Bo Almqvist, Séamas Ó Catháin, and Pádraig Ó Héalaí, 101–30. Dublin: The Folklore of Ireland Society.

MacInnes, Rev. Duncan, ed. 1890. *Waifs and Strays of Celtic Tradition: Argyllshire Series*. Vol. 2, *Folk and Hero Tales*. London: David Nutt.

Mackechnie, John. 1964. "Introduction: John Francis Campbell (Iain Og Ile) and His Place in the Literary History of the Highlands." In *The Dewar Manuscripts*, vol. 1, 17–56. Glasgow: William MacLellan.

Mackenzie, Donald A. 1911. *Finn and His Warrior Band, or, Tales of Old Alban*. London: Blackie and Son.

Mackenzie, Henry, ed. 1805. *Report of the Committee of the Highland Society of Scotland Appointed to Inquire into the Nature and Authenticity of the Poems of Ossian*. Edinburgh: Archibald Constable & Co.

Mackenzie, John, ed. 1841. *Sar-Obair nam Bard Gaelach: or, the Beauties of Gaelic Poetry and Lives of the Highland Bards*. Glasgow: Macgregor, Polson, and Co.

MacKillop, James. 1986. *Fionn mac Cumhaill: Celtic Myth in English Literature*. Syracuse, NY: Syracuse University Press.

Mackinnon, Donald. 1877. "Litreachas nan Gaidheal: XIII. Bardachd Naduir." *An Gaidheal* 6.72: 353–58

———. 1883. *University of Edinburgh Celtic Chair: Inaugural Address*. Edinburgh: MacLachlan and Stewart.

———, ed. 1887. "Collection of Ossianic Ballads by Jerome Stone." *Transactions of the Gaelic Society of Inverness* 14: 314–69.

MacLellan, Angus. 1961. *Stories from South Uist*. Translated by John Lorne Campbell. London: Routledge and Kegan Paul.

MacLeod, Anne. 2013. "Painting Time: The Highland Journals of John Francis Campbell of Islay." *Scottish Archives* 19: 25–38.

MacLeòid, Robbie Anndra. 2016. "Èistibh Beag Mas Àill Leibh Laoidh." *Steall* 1: 71–77.

Mac Liammóir, Mícheál. 1935. *Diarmuid agus Gráinne: Dráma Trí nGníomh*. Dublin: Oifig Díolta Foillseacháin Rialtais.

MacManus, Seumus. 1977 [1921]. *The Story of the Irish Race: A Popular History of Ireland*. New York: Devin-Adair.

MacNeacail, Aonghas. 1999. "Bho An Turas Sìos gu Tìr nam Marbh / from The Journey Down to the Land of the Dead." In *An Tuil*, edited by Ronald Black, 580–83, 803. Edinburgh: Polygon.

MacNeil, Joe Neil. 1987. *Tales Until Dawn / Sgeul gu Latha: The World of a Cape Breton Gaelic Story-Teller*. Edited and translated by John Shaw. Edinburgh: Edinburgh University Press.

[MacNeill, Archibald]. 1868. *Notes on the Authenticity of Ossian's Poems*. Edinburgh: William Blackwood and Son.

MacNeill, Eoin, ed. and trans. 1908. *Duanaire Finn: The Book of the Lays of Fionn*. Vol. 1, *Irish Text, with Translation into English*. Irish Texts Society 7. Dublin: David Nutt.

———. 1919. *Phases of Irish History*. Dublin: M. H. Gill and Son.

———. 1925. "Irish Educational Policy—II." *Irish Statesman* 5, no. 7: 200–201.

———. 1941. "Military Service in Medieval Ireland." *Journal of the Cork Historical and Archaeological Society* 46, no. 163: 6–15.

MacNicol, Rev. Donald. 1779. *Remarks on Dr Samuel Johnson's Journey to the Hebrides*. London: T. Cadell.

Mac Niocaill, Gearóid. 1963. "Duanaire Ghearóid Iarla." *Studia Hibernica* 3: 7–59.

Macpherson, George W. 2016. *The Old Grey Magician: A Scottish Fionn Cycle*. Edinburgh: Luath Press.

Macpherson, James. 1771. *An Introduction to the History of Great Britain and Ireland*. London: T. Becket and P. A. de Hondt.

———. 1807. *The Poems of Ossian in the Original Gaelic*. Vol. 3. London: W. Bulmer and Co.

———. 1818. *Dàna Oisein Mhic Fhinn, air an Cur amach airson Maith Coitcheanntа Muinntir na Gaeltachd*. Edinburgh: Tearlach Stiubhart.

———. 1996. *The Poems of Ossian and Related Works*. Edited by Howard Gaskill. Edinburgh: Edinburgh University Press.

MacQueen, John. 1998. "*Temora* and Legendary History." In *From Gaelic to Romantic: Ossianic Translations*, edited by Fiona Stafford and Howard Gaskill, 69–78. Amsterdam: Rodopi.

MacRitchie, David. 1890. *The Testimony of Tradition*. London: Kegan Paul, Trench, Trübner and Co.

Mac Róigh, Fearghus [Énrí Ó Muirgheasa], ed. 1911. *Bruidhean Chaorthainn*. Dublin: M. H. Gill and Son.

———, ed. 1913. *Maighdean an tSoluis agus Sgéalta Eile*. Dundalk: Dundalgan Press.

———, ed. 1924. *Oidhche Áirneáil i dTír Chonaill*. Dundalk: Preas Dhún Dealgan.

Mageoghagan, Conell, trans. 1896 [1627]. *The Annals of Clonmacnoise*. Edited by Rev. Denis Murphy. Dublin: The University Press.

Maier, Bernhard. 2022. "Late Victorian Ideas about *Ossian* and the Origins of Celtic Studies." In *The Gaelic Finn Tradition II*, edited by Sharon J. Arbuthnot, Síle Ní Mhurchú, and Geraldine Parsons, 187–96. Dubin: Four Courts.

Maignéar, D. [Daniel Magner], ed. 1884–85. "Cath Cnocha." *Irish-American* [New York]. October 4, 3; October 11, 3; October 18, 3; November 22, 3; November 29, 3; December 6, 3; December 13, 3; December 20, 3; December 27, 3; January 3, 3; January 10, 3.

Mannion, Kimberley. 2023. "National Library to Host Rare Performance of Medieval Gaelic Ballads." *Herald*. August 14. https://www.heraldscotland.com/news/23722430.national-library-host-rare-performance-medieval-gaelic-ballads. Accessed December 31, 2023.

Marenbon, John. 2012. "A Problem of Paganism." In *Paganism in the Middle Ages: Threat and Fascination*, edited by Carlos Steel, John Marenbon, and Werner Verbeke, 39–54. Mediaevalia Lovaniensia 1, no. 43. Leuven: Leuven University Press.

Markey, Anne. 2006. "The Discovery of Irish Folklore." *New Hibernia Review / Iris Éireannach Nua* 10, no. 4: 21–43.

Martin, F. X. 1987. "Overlord Becomes Feudal Lord, 1172–85" and "John, Lord of Ireland, 1185–1216." In *A New History of Ireland*, vol. 2, edited by Art Cosgrove, 98–155. Oxford: Oxford University Press.

Martin, Martin. 1703. *A Description of the Western Islands of Scotland*. London: Andrew Bell.

Martyn, Adrian. 2016. *The Tribes of Galway, 1124–1642*. [Galway]: Adrian Martyn.

Masefield, John. 1959. *The Story of Ossian*. London: Argo. Vinyl record.

Maume, Patrick. 2004. "Standish James O'Grady: Between Imperial Romance and Irish Revival." *Éire-Ireland* 39: 11–35.

Maume, Patrick, and Thomas Charles-Edwards. 2013. "MacNeill, Eoin (John)." In *Dictionary of Irish Biography* online, edited by James McGuire and James Quinn. http://dib.cambridge.org/viewReadPage.do?articleId=a5283. Accessed March 5, 2020.

McCambridge, Jonathan. 2022. "New Murals Embrace Ireland's Mythological Past." *Breaking News*. May 2. https://www.breakingnews.ie/entertainment/new-murals-embrace-irelands-mythological-past-1298344.html. Accessed November 10, 2023.

McCann, James. 2012. "Laoidh Chab an Dosáin." MA thesis, University of Aberystwyth.

McCone, Kim. 1986. "Werewolves, Cyclopes, *Díberga*, and *Fíanna*: Juvenile Delinquency in Early Ireland." *Cambridge Medieval Celtic Studies* 12: 1–22.

———. 1990. *Pagan Past and Christian Present in Early Irish Literature*. Maynooth: An Sagart.

———. 2012. "The Celtic and Indo-European Origins of the *Fían*." In *The Gaelic Finn Tradition*, edited by Sharon J. Arbuthnot and Geraldine Parsons, 14–30. Dublin: Four Courts.

McDermitt, Barbara. 1999. "Storytelling Traditions in Scotland." In *Traditional Storytelling Today: An International Sourcebook*, edited by Margaret Read MacDonald, 289–300. Chicago: Fitzroy Dearborn.

McDowell, R. B. 1986. "The Age of the United Irishmen: Reform and Reaction, 1789–94" and "The Age of the United Irishmen: Revolution and the Union, 1794–1800." In *A New History of Ireland*, vol. 4, edited by T. W. Moody and W. E. Vaughan, 289–373. Oxford: Clarendon Press.

McGowan-Doyle, Valerie. 2011. *The Book of Howth: The Elizabethan Re-Conquest of Ireland and the Old English*. Cork: Cork University Press.

McGrath, Michael. 2004. "Hairdresser Yvonne Takes Niamh of Na Fianna Crown." *Irish Independent*. July 28. https://www.independent.ie/regionals/cork/news/hairdresser-yvonne-takes-niamh-of-na-fianna-crown/27057370.html. Accessed November 10, 2023.

McIlvanney, Liam, and Ray Ryan. 2005. "Introduction." In *Ireland and Scotland: Culture and Society, 1700–2000*, edited by Liam McIlvanney and Ray Ryan, 11–22. Dublin: Four Courts.

McKean, Thomas A. 2001. "The Fieldwork Legacy of James Macpherson." *Journal of American Folklore* 114, no. 454: 447–63.

McLauchlan, Rev. Dr. Thomas, ed. 1859. *The Poems of Ossian / Dàna Oisein Mhic Fhinn*. Edinburgh: MacLachlan and Stewart.

———, ed. 1862. *The Dean of Lismore's Book: A Selection of Ancient Gaelic Poetry from a Manuscript Collection Made by Sir James McGregor, Dean of Lismore, in the Beginning of the Sixteenth Century*. 3 vols. Edinburgh: Edmonston and Douglas.

McLeod, Wilson. 2004. *Divided Gaels: Gaelic Cultural Identities in Scotland and Ireland c. 1200–c. 1650*. Oxford: Oxford University Press.

McManus, Antonia. 2014. *Irish Education: The Ministerial Legacy, 1919–99*. Dublin: The History Press Ireland.

McManus, Damian. 1991. *A Guide to Ogam*. Maynooth Monographs 4. Maynooth: An Sagart.

———. 2017. "Celebrating the Canine: An Edition of *Slán dona Saoithibh Sealga* 'Farewell to the Masters of the Hunt,' an Elegy for Diarmaid Mág Carthaigh's (†1368) Hound." *Ériu* 67: 187–213.

———. 2018. "Celebrating the Canine II: The Hunt in Medieval Ireland, with Special Reference to the Evidence of Classical Irish Poetry." *Ériu* 68: 145–92.

McMullan, Michael. 2020. "Sperrin Harriers in Pre Winter Lockdown Action." *Derry Now*. December 21. https://www.derrynow.com/news/athletics/597281/sperrin-harriers-in-pre-winter-lockdown-action.html. Accessed November 10, 2023.

McNeill, Tom. 1997. *Castles in Ireland: Feudal Power in a Gaelic World*. London: Routledge.

McQuillan, Peter. 2019. "'Nation' as *Pobal* in Seventeenth-Century Irish." In *Early Modern Ireland: New Sources, Methods, and Perspectives*, edited by Sarah Covington, Vincent P. Carey, and Valerie McGowan-Doyle, 113–29. London: Routledge.

Meek, Donald. E. 1987. "Development and Degeneration in Gaelic Ballad Texts." *Fiannaíocht: Essays on the Fenian Tradition of Ireland and Scotland*, ed. Bo Almqvist, Séamas Ó Catháin, and Pádraig Ó Héalaí (Dublin: The Folklore of Ireland Society), 131–60.

———. 1990. "The Death of Diarmaid in Scottish and Irish Tradition." *Celtica* 21: 335–61.

———. 1991. "The Gaelic Ballads of Scotland: Creativity and Adaptation." *Ossian Revisited*, ed. Howard Gaskill (Edinburgh: Edinburgh University Press), 19–48.

Meek, Donald. E. 1996. "The Scots-Gaelic Scribes of Late Medieval Perthshire: An Overview of the Orthography and Contents of the Book of the Dean of Lismore." *Stewart Style, 1513–1542: Essays on the Court of James V*, ed. Janet Hadley Williams (East Linton: Tuckwell Press), 254–72.

———. 2000. *Celtic Christianity* (Edinburgh: Hansel Press).

———. 2003. "*Duanaire Finn* and Gaelic Scotland." Duanaire Finn*: Reassessments*, ed. John Carey. Irish Texts Society Subsidiary Series 13 (Dublin: Irish Texts Society), 19–41.

———. 2004. "The Sublime Gael: The Impact of Macpherson's *Ossian* on Literary Creativity and Cultural Perception in Gaelic Scotland." *The Reception of Ossian in Europe*, ed. Howard Gaskill (London: Thoemmes Continuum), 40–66.

———. 2007. "Gaelic Literature in the Nineteenth Century." *The Edinburgh History of Scottish Literature*, vol. 2: Enlightenment, Britain and Empire (1707–1918) (Edinburgh: Edinburgh University Press), 253–66.

———. 2013. "Nineteenth-Century Studies: Ossian and Gaelic Scholarship." *Passages from Tiree* (blog). 15 March. http://meekwrite.blogspot.com/2013/03/romanticism-and-revivalossian-and.html. Accessed 3 Jan. 2015.

Mercier, Paul, dir. 2015. *Pursuit*. Carraroe, Ireland: An Pointe Productions. Feature film.

Metzdorf, Robert F. 1970. "M'Nicol, Macpherson, and Johnson." In *Eighteenth-Century Studies in Honor of Donald F. Hyde*, edited by W. H. Bond, 45–61. New York: Grolier Club.

Meyer, Kuno, ed. 1881–83. "Macgnímartha Find." *Revue Celtique* 5: 195–204.

———, ed. 1885. *Cath Finntrága*. Anecdota Oxoniensia: Texts, Documents, and Extracts chiefly from Manuscripts in the Bodleian and other Oxford Libraries: Mediaeval and Modern Series, vol. 1, part 4. Oxford: Clarendon Press.

———, ed. and trans. 1893a. "Two Tales About Finn." *Revue Celtique* 14: 241–48.

———. 1893b. Review of *Silva Gadelica*, edited by Standish H. O'Grady. *Revue Celtique* 14: 321–37.

———, ed. and trans. 1897. "The Death of Finn Mac Cumaill." *Zeitschrift für Celtische Philologie* 1: 462–65.

———, ed. and trans. 1904a. "Cáilte Cecinit." *Ériu* 1: 72–73.

———, ed. and trans. 1904b. "Finn and the Man in the Tree." *Revue Celtique* 25: 344–49.

———. 1910. *Fianaigecht*. Royal Irish Academy: Todd Lecture Series 16. Dublin: Hodges, Figgis, and Co.

———, ed. 1912a. "Mitteilungen aus Irischen Handschriften: Do chomramaib Laigen inso sís." *Zeitschrift für Celtische Philologie* 8: 117–19.

———, ed. 1912b. "Mitteilungen aus Irischen Handschriften: Cath Sléphe Cáin inso." *Zeitschrift für Celtische Philologie* 8: 105.

———, ed. 1912c. *Sanas Cormaic: An Old-Irish Glossary Compiled by Cormac úa Cuilennáin, King-Bishop of Cashel in the Tenth Century*. Edited by Osborn Bergin, R. I. Best, Kuno Meyer, and J. G. O'Keeffe. Anecdota from Irish Manuscripts 4. Dublin: Hodges, Figgis, and Co.

M. G. [pseud.]. 1932–33. "Goll Mac Móirne." *Ar Aghaidh* 2, no. 6 (December): 6, 8; 2, no. 7 (January): 7; 2, no. 8 (February): 7–8.

Michael, Jennifer Davis. 2007. "Ocean Meets Ossian: Staffa as Romantic Symbol." *Romanticism* 13, no. 1: 1–14.

Mileo, Brenda. n.d. "The Legend of Finn McCool (A Silly Tall Tale of Giant Proportions)." *Patch*. https://patch.com/new-york/rivertowns/calendar/event/20230318/082efe5e-b8af-46d3-9719-6cc83630a8e3/the-legend-of-finn-mccool-a-silly-tall-tale-of-giant-proportions. Accessed December 13, 2023.

[Milligan, Alice L.]. 1898. "Gaelic Tableaux in Belfast." *Shan Van Vocht* 3, no. 6: 114–15.

Mills, Kristen. 2018. "Death, Women, and Power: Theme and Structure in *Reicne Fothaid Canainne*." *Ériu* 68: 65–98.

———. Forthcoming. *Fenian Tradition and Gaelic Identity from Past to Present*. Edited by Natasha Sumner and Joseph Nagy.

Mitchell, Sebastian. 2012. "Macpherson, Ossian, and Homer's *Iliad*." In *Ossian and National Epic*, edited by Gerald Bär and Howard Gaskill, 55–71. Passagem Studies in Cultural Sciences 6. Frankfurt am Main: Peter Lang.

Mohr, Paul. 2015. "The de Berminghams, Barons of Athenry: A Revised and Supplemented Lineage." *Journal of the Galway Archaeological and Historical Society* 67: 48–68.

Montgomery, Henry R. 1846. *Specimens of the Early Native Poetry of Ireland in English Metrical Translations*. Dublin: James McGlashan.

Moore, Dafydd. 2004a. "General Introduction." In *Ossian and Ossianism*, edited by Dafydd Moore, vol. 1, xxi–cxxx. London: Routledge.

———. 2004b. "The Reception of *The Poems of Ossian* in England and Scotland." In *The Reception of Ossian in Europe*, edited by Howard Gaskill, 21–39. London: Thoemmes Continuum.

Moore, Ronan. 2020. *Young Fionn*. Dublin: Gill.

———. 2021. *Fionn and the Fianna*. Dublin: Gill.

Mulchrone, Kathleen, ed. and trans. 1939. *Bethu Phátraic: The Tripartite Life of Patrick*. Vol. 1, *Text and Sources*. Dublin: Hodges and Figgis.

Mulligan, Amy C. 2019. *A Landscape of Words: Ireland, Britain and the Poetics of Space, 700–1250*. Manchester: Manchester University Press.

Murphy, Gerard, ed. and trans. 1933. *Duanaire Finn: The Book of the Lays of Fionn*. Vol. 2. Irish Texts Society 28. London: Irish Texts Society.

———. 1943. Review of *European Balladry*, by William J. Entwistle. *Éigse* 3, no. 1: 74–76.

———. 1953. *Duanaire Finn: The Book of the Lays of Fionn*. Vol. 3, *Introduction, Notes, Appendices and Glossary*. Irish Texts Society 43. Dublin: Irish Texts Society.

———, ed. and trans. 1956. *Early Irish Lyrics: Eighth to Twelfth Century*. Oxford: Oxford University Press.

———. 1971 [1955]. *The Ossianic Lore and Romantic Tales of Medieval Ireland*. Revised ed. Irish Life and Culture 11. Dublin: Mercier Press.

Murray, Damien. 2000. *Romanticism, Nationalism and Irish Antiquarian Societies, 1840–80*. Maynooth Monographs Series Minor 3. Maynooth: The Department of Old and Middle Irish, National University of Ireland, Maynooth.

Murray, Kevin. 2003. "A Reading from *Scéla Moshauluim*." *Zeitschrift für Celtische Philologie* 53: 198–201.

———. 2012. "Interpreting the Evidence: Problems with Dating the Early *Fianaigecht* Corpus." In *The Gaelic Finn Tradition*, edited by Sharon J. Arbuthnot and Geraldine Parsons, 31–49. Dublin: Four Courts.

———. 2015. "The Treatment of Place-Names in the Early *Fíanaigecht* Corpus." In *Clerics, Kings and Vikings: Essays on Medieval Ireland in Honour of Donnchadh Ó Corráin*, edited by Emer Purcell et al., 452–57. Dublin: Four Courts.

———. 2017a. *The Early Finn Cycle*. Dublin: Four Courts.

———. 2017b. "Genre Construction: The Creation of the *Dinnshenchas*." *Journal of Literary Onomastics* 6, no. 1: 11–21.

———. 2018. "*Tóruigheacht Dhiarmada agus Ghráinne*: The Manuscript Tradition." In *Tóruigheacht Dhiarmada agus Ghráinne: Reassessments*, edited by Kevin Murray, 17–42. Irish Texts Society Subsidiary Series 30. Dublin: Irish Texts Society.

———. 2021. *The Early Fenian Corpus*. Cork: Cork Studies in Celtic Literatures.

———. 2022. "Editing *Acallam na Senórach*: A Test Case Based on the *Mucc Shlánga* Episode." In *The Gaelic Finn Tradition II*, edited by Sharon J. Arbuthnot, Síle Ní Mhurchú, and Geraldine Parsons, 24–38. Dubin: Four Courts.

Muscio, Manon. 2023. "National Library of Scotland Teams up with Musicians for Beacon." *National*. September 18. https://www.thenational.scot/news/23797450.national-library-scotland-teams-musicians-beacon. Accessed December 31, 2023.

Nagy, Joseph Falaky. 1985. *The Wisdom of the Outlaw: The Boyhood Deeds of Finn in Gaelic Narrative Tradition*. Berkeley: University of California Press.

———. 1987. "In Defense of Rómánsaíocht." *Ériu* 38: 9–26.

———. 1989. "Compositional Concerns in the *Acallam na Senórach*." In *Sages, Saints and Storytellers: Celtic Studies in Honour of Professor James Carney*, edited by Donnchadh Ó Corráin, Liam Breatnach, and Kim R. McCone, 149–58. Maynooth Monographs 2. Maynooth: An Sagart.

———. 1995. "Oral Tradition in the *Acallam na Senórach*." In *Oral Tradition in the Middle Ages*, edited by W.F.H. Nicolaisen, 77–95. Medieval and Renaissance Texts and Studies 112. Binghamton, NY: Medieval and Renaissance Texts and Studies.

———. 1997. *Conversing with Angels and Ancients: Literary Myths of Medieval Ireland*. Ithaca, NY: Cornell University Press.

———. 2001. "Observations on the Ossianesque in Medieval Irish Literature and Modern Irish Folklore." In "James Macpherson and the Ossian Epic Debate." Special issue, *Journal of American Folklore* 114, no. 454 (Autumn): 436–46.

———. 2003. "The Significance of the *Duanaire Finn*." In *Duanaire Finn: Reassessments*, edited by John Carey, 39–50. Irish Texts Society Subsidiary Series 13. Dublin: Irish Texts Society.

———. 2008. "*Acallam na Senórach*, a 'tri-cycle'?" In *Essays on the Early Irish King Tales*, edited by Dan Wiley, 68–83. Dublin: Four Courts.

———. 2015. "The Celtic 'Love Triangle' Revisited." In *Proceedings: XIV International Congress of Celtic Studies*, edited by Liam Breatnach, Ruairí Ó hUiginn, Damian McManus, and Katharine Simms, 221–44. Dublin: Dublin Institute for Advanced Study.

National Programme Conference. 1922. *National Programme of Primary Instruction*. Dublin: Educational Company of Ireland.

Newmark, Avery. 2023. "Family-Friendly St. Patrick's Day Activities in Atlanta to Unleash the Fun." *Access Atlanta*. March 13. https://www.accessatlanta.com/atlanta-things-to-do/family-friendly-st-patricks-day-activities-in-atlanta-to-unleash-the-fun/4P4FDVJBDVAY3IB2JBFDEYSERY/. Accessed December 13, 2023.

Nicholls, K. W. 2003. *Gaelic and Gaelicized Ireland in the Middle Ages*. Dublin: The Lilliput Press.

Nicolaisen, W.F.H. 1983. "Concepts of Time and Space in Irish Folktales." In *Celtic Folklore and Christianity: Studies in Memory of William W. Heist*, edited by Patrick K. Ford, 150–58. Santa Barbara: McNally and Loftin.

Ní Dhonnchadha, Máirín, trans. 2002. "Tochmarc Ailbe: The Wooing of Ailbe." In *The Field Day Anthology of Irish Writing*, vol. 4, edited by Angela Bourke et al., 206–10. Cork: University of Cork Press.

Ní Fhlatharta, Bernie. 2023. "Irish Mythology the Perfect Basis for Panto Fare." *Connacht Tribune*. December 15. https://connachttribune.ie/irish-mythology-the-perfect-basis-for-panto-fare/. Accessed January 9, 2024.

Ní Mhaonaigh, Máire. 2006a. "Literary Lochlann." In *Cànan & Cultar / Language & Culture: Rannsachadh na Gàidhlig*, edited by Wilson McLeod, James E. Fraser, and Anja Gunderloch, 25–37. Edinburgh: Dunedin Press.

———. 2006b. "Pagans and Holy Men: Literary Manifestations of Twelfth-Century Reform." In *Ireland and Europe in the Twelfth Century: Reform and Renewal*, edited by Damian Bracken and Dagmar Ó Riain-Raedel, 143–61. Dublin: Four Courts.

Ní Mhuirgheasa, Máire, ed. 1941. "Bruighean Eochaidh Bhig Dheirg." In *Trí Bruidhne*, edited by Nessa Ní Shéaghdha and Máire Ní Mhuirgheasa, 40–91. Dublin: Oifig an tSoláthair.

———. 1952. "Introduction." In *Sgéalta Románsaíochta*, edited by Máire Ní Mhuirgheasa and Séamus Ó Ceithearnaigh, viii–xv. Leabhair ó Láimhsgríbhnibh 16. Dublin: Oifig an tSoláthair.

———, ed. 1954. *Imtheacht an Dá Nónbhar agus Tóraigheacht Taise Taoibhghile*. Leabhair ó Láimhsgríbhnibh 16. Dublin: Oifig an tSoláthair.

———, ed. n.d. *Bruidhean Eochaidh Bhig Dheirg.* Téacsaí Fianaigheachta do Scoláirí na Meán-scoileanna. Dublin: Brún agus Ó Nualláin.

Ní Mhuirgheasa, Máire, and Séamus Ó Ceithearnaigh, eds. 1952. *Sgéalta Románsaíochta.* Leabhair ó Láimhsgríbhnibh 16. Dublin: Oifig an tSoláthair.

Ní Mhunghaile, Lesa. 2008. "Anglo-Irish Antiquarianism and the Transformation of Irish Identity, 1750–1800." In *Anglo-Irish Identities, 1571–1845,* edited by David A. Valone and Jill Marie Bradbury, 181–98. Lewisburg, PA: Bucknell University Press.

———. 2009a. "Introduction" and "New Translations and Commentaries." In *Reliques of Irish Poetry,* by Charlotte Brooke, edited by Lesa Ní Mhunghaile, xxi–xliv, 4–163. Dublin: Irish Manuscripts Commission.

———. 2009b. "O'Flanagan, Theophilus." In *Dictionary of Irish Biography* online, edited by James McGuire and James Quinn. http://dib.cambridge.org/viewReadPage.do?articleId=a6757. Accessed April 28, 2020.

———. 2010a. "Anglo-Irish Antiquarianism in County Longford in the 1780s: The Case of Charlotte Brooke." In *Longford: History and Society,* edited by Fergus O'Ferrall and Martin Morris, 237–58. Dublin: Geography Publications.

———. 2010b. "The Intersection Between Oral Tradition, Manuscript, and Print Cultures in Charlotte Brooke's *Reliques of Irish Poetry* (1789)." In *Oral and Printed Cultures in Ireland, 1600–1900,* edited by Marc Caball and Andrew Carpenter, 14–31. Dublin: Four Courts.

———. 2012. "Bilingualism, Print Culture in Irish and the Public Sphere, 1700–c. 1830." In *Irish and English: Essays on the Irish Linguistic and Cultural Frontier, 1600–1900,* edited by James Kelly and Ciarán Mac Murchaidh, 218–42. Dublin: Four Courts.

———. 2013. "O'Grady, Standish Hayes." In *Dictionary of Irish Biography* online, edited by James McGuire and James Quinn. http://dib.cambridge.org/viewReadPage.do?articleId=a6772. Accessed March 3, 2020.

Ní Mhurchú, Síle. 2012. "*Agallamh Oisín agus Phádraig*: Composition and Transmission." In *The Gaelic Finn Tradition,* edited by Sharon J. Arbuthnot and Geraldine Parsons, 195–208. Dublin: Four Courts.

———. 2014. "An tAgallamh Nua: Athleagan Déanach d'Agallamh na Seanórach." In *In Dialogue with the Agallamh: Essays in Honour of Seán Ó Coileáin,* edited by Aidan Doyle and Kevin Murray, 164–84. Dublin: Four Courts.

Ní Shéaghdha, Nessa, ed. 1941. "Bruighion Chéisi Coruin" and "Bruighion Bheag na hAlmhan." In *Trí Bruidhne,* edited by Nessa Ní Shéaghdha and Máire Ní Mhuirgheasa, 3–39. Dublin: Oifig an tSoláthair.

———, ed. 1944. *Tóraigheacht Dhiarmada agus Ghráinne.* Téacsaí Fianaigheachta do Scoláirí na Meán-scoileanna. Dublin: Brún agus Ó Nualláin.

———. 1961. *Catalogue of Irish Manuscripts in the National Library of Ireland.* Fascicle 2. Dublin: Dublin Institute for Advanced Studies.

———, ed. 1967. *Tóruigheacht Dhiarmada agus Ghráinne.* Irish Texts Society 48. Dublin: Irish Texts Society.

———. 1985. "Collectors of Irish Manuscripts: Motives and Methods." *Celtica* 17: 1–28.

———, ed. 2014 [1942–45]. *Agallamh na Seanórach: Trí hImleabhair.* Dublin: Irish Texts Society.

Ní Uigín, Noelle. 2009. "Goll mac Morna: Laoch Connachtach na Fiannaíochta agus Ceist an Chúigeachais." In *Diasa Díograise: Aistí i gCuimhne ar Mháirtín Ó Briain,* edited by Mícheál Mac Craith and Pádraig Ó Héalaí, 237–55. Indreabhán: Cló Iar-Chonnachta.

Ní Úrdail, Meidhbhín. 2000. *The Scribe in Eighteenth- and Nineteenth-Century Ireland.* Studien und Texte zur Keltologie 3. Münster: Nodus Publikationen.

Nolan, Jerry C. M. 1999. "Standish James O'Grady's Cultural Nationalism." *Irish Studies Review* 7, no. 3: 347–57.

Normand, Tom, and Calum Colvin. 2002. *Ossian: Fragments of Ancient Poetry*. Edinburgh: Scottish National Portrait Gallery.

Norris, Thomas D., ed. 1893. "Eachtradh Lomnochtain Sléibe [*sic*] Riffi." *Irish-American* [New York]. November 20, 8; November 27, 8; December 4, 10; December 11, 8; December 18, 8.

Nuner, Robert D. 1958–59. "The Verbal System of the *Agallamh na Senórach*." *Zeitschrift für Celtische Philologie* 27: 230–310.

Nutt, Alfred. 1881. "The Aryan Expulsion-and-Return-Formula in the Folk and Hero Tales of the Celts." *Folk-Lore Record* 4: 1–44.

———. 1890a. "The Campbell of Islay MSS. at the Advocates' Library, Edinburgh." *Folklore* 1, no. 3: 369–83.

———. 1890b. "Development of the Fenian or Ossianic Saga." In *Waifs and Strays of Celtic Tradition: Argyllshire Series*, vol. 2, *Folk and Hero Tales*, edited by Rev. Duncan MacInnes, 399–430. London: David Nutt.

———. 1891. "Introduction." In *Waifs and Strays of Celtic Tradition: Argyllshire Series*, vol. 4, *The Fians; or, Stories, Poems, and Traditions of Fionn and His Warrior Band*, edited by Rev. John Gregorson Campbell, ix–xxxviii. London: David Nutt.

———. 1899. *Ossian and the Ossianic Literature*. Popular Studies in Mythology, Romance, and Folklore 3. London: David Nutt.

Oates, Jennifer L. 2013. *Hamish MacCunn (1868–1916): A Musical Life*. Surrey: Ashgate.

Ó Briain, Máirtín. 1984. "Micheál Coimín agus Oisín i dTír na nÓg." In *Macalla*, edited by Aingeal Ní Chualáin and Gearóid Denvir, 158–75. Galway: An Cumann Éigse agus Seanchais, Coláiste na hOllscoile, Gaillimh.

———. 1989a. Review of *Fionn Mac Cumhaill: Images of the Gaelic Hero*, by Dáithí Ó hÓgáin. *Béaloideas* 57: 174–83.

———. 1989b. "Some Material on Oisín in the Land of Youth." In *Sages, Saints and Storytellers: Celtic Studies in Honour of Professor James Carney*, edited by Donnchadh Ó Corráin, Liam Breatnach, and Kim McCone, 181–99. Maynooth: An Sagart.

———. 1994. "Oisín's Biography: Conception and Birth." In *Text und Zeittiefe*, edited by Hildegard L. C. Tristram, 455–86. ScriptOralia 58. Tübingen: G. Narr.

———. 1995. "Suirghe Fhinn." In *An Fhiannaíocht*, edited by Pádraig Ó Fiannachta, 69–95. Léachtaí Cholm Cille 25. Maynooth: An Sagart.

———. 1996. "The Conception and Death of Fionn Mac Cumhaill's Canine Cousin." In *Celtica Helsingiensia: Proceedings from a Symposium on Celtic Studies*, edited by Anders Ahlqvist et al., 179–202. Commentationes Humanarum Litterarum 107. Helsinki: Societas Scientiarum Fennica.

———. 2003. "*Duanaire Finn* XXII: Goll and the Champion's Portion." In *Duanaire Finn: Reassessments*, edited by John Carey, 51–78. Irish Texts Society, Subsidiary Series 13. Dublin: Irish Texts Society, 51–78.

———. 2013. "Ginealach 'Geinealach Oisín.'" In *Saltair Saíochta Sanasaíochta agus Seanchais: A Festschrift for Gearóid Mac Eoin*, edited by Dónall Ó Baoill, Donncha Ó hAodha, and Nollaig Ó Muraíle, 261–73. Dublin: Four Courts.

Ó Briain, Padruig, ed. 1893. "Sgeul Fiannuidheachta: Bruighean Eochaidh Bhig Dheirg." In *Bláithfhleasg de Mhílseáinibh na Gaoidheilge*, 129–57. Dublin: Patrick O'Brien.

O'Brien, Flann [Brian O'Nolan / Ó Nualláin]. 1998 [1939]. *At Swim-Two-Birds*. Dublin: Dalkey Archive Press.

[O'Brien, John]. 1764. "Mémoire de M. de C. a Messieurs les Auteurs du Journal des Sçavans, au Sujet des Poëmes de M. Macpherson." *Journal des Sçavans*: 277–92, 353–62, 408–17, 537–55, 604–17, 845–57.

———. 1768. *Focalóir Gaoidhilge-Sax-Bhéarla*. Paris: Nicolas-Francis Valleyre.

Ó Buachalla, Breandáin. 1962. *Clár na Lámhscríbhinní Gaeilge i Leabharlainn Phoiblí Bhéal Feirste*. Dublin: An Clóchomhar.

———. 1968. *I mBéal Feirste Cois Cuain*. Dublin: An Clóchomhar.

Ó Buachalla, Séamas. 1984. "Educational Policy and the Role of the Irish Language from 1831 to 1981." *European Journal of Education* 19, no. 1: 75–92.

Ó Cadhlaigh, Cormac. 1936. *An Fhiannuidheacht*. Dublin: Oifig an tSoláthair.

Ó Cadhla, Stiofán. 2007. *Civilizing Ireland: Ordnance Survey 1824–1842; Ethnography, Cartography, Translation*. Dublin: Irish Academic Press.

Ó Caithnia, Liam. 1984. *Apalóga na bhFilí, 1200–1650*. Dublin: An Clóchomhar.

Ó Canainn, Pádraig [Patrick Francis Garrett Cannon], ed. 1939. *Diarmuid agus Gráinne; An Giolla Deacair; Bodach an Chóta Lachtna*. Dublin: An Press Náisiúnta.

Ó Catháin, Diarmaid. 1993. "An Irish Scholar Abroad: Bishop John O'Brien of Cloyne and the Macpherson Controversy." In *Cork: History and Society: Interdisciplinary Essays on the History of an Irish County*, edited by Patrick O'Flanagan and Cornelius G. Buttimer, 499–533. Dublin: Geography Publications.

———. 2009. "O'Curry (Curry, Ó Comhraí), Eugene (Eoghan)." In *Dictionary of Irish Biography* online, edited by James McGuire and James Quinn. http://dib.cambridge.org/viewReadPage.do?articleId=a6664. Accessed March 3, 2020.

Ó Cathasaigh, Tomás. 1977. *The Heroic Biography of Cormac mac Airt*. Dublin: Dublin Institute for Advanced Studies.

———. 2013. "*Toraíocht Dhiarmada agus Ghráinne* / The Pursuit of Diarmaid and Gráinne." In *Coire Sois, The Cauldron of Knowledge: A Companion to Early Irish Saga*, edited by Matthieu Boyd, 449–83. Notre Dame, IN: University of Notre Dame Press.

Ó Ciosáin, Niall. 1997. *Print and Popular Culture in Ireland, 1750–1850*. London: MacMillan.

Ó Concheanainn, Tomás. 1981–83. "The Three Forms of *Dinnshenchas Érenn*." *Journal of Celtic Studies* 3: 88–101.

Ó Connghalaigh, M. C. 1905. "The Educational Value of National History II." *An Claidheamh Soluis* 7, no. 15: 8–9.

O'Connor, Dermod, trans. 1726 [1723]. *The General History of Ireland*, by Geoffrey Keating. 2nd ed. Westminster: J. Cluer and A. Campbell.

O'Connor, Frank. 1932. "Lullaby of Adventurous Love (from Diarmuid and Grania)." In *The Wild Bird's Nest: Poems from the Irish*, 6–9. Dublin: Cuala Press.

———. 1989 [1959]. "Grania." In *Kings, Lords, and Commons: An Anthology from the Irish*, 49–50. Van Nuys, CA: Ford and Bailie.

O'Conor, Charles. 1753. *Dissertations on the Antient History of Ireland: Wherein an Account is Given of the Origine, Government, Letters, Sciences, Religion, Manners and Customs, of the Antient Inhabitants*. Dublin: James Hoey.

———. 1766. *Dissertation on the First Migrations, and Final Settlement of the Scots in North-Britain; with Occasional Observations on the Poems of Fingal and Temora*. Dublin: G. Faulkner.

O'Conor, Charles. 1949. "Origins of the Royal Irish Academy." *Studies: An Irish Quarterly Review* 38, no. 151: 325–37.

Ó Corráin, Donnchadh. 1987. "Legend as Critic." In *The Writer as Witness: Literature as Historical Evidence*, edited by Tom Dunne, 23–38. Historical Studies 16. Cork: Cork University Press.

Ó Cróinín, Breandán. 1995. "Bruidhean Chaorthainn ón Lámhscríbhinn is Sine i Leabharlann Náisiúnta na hAlban." MA thesis, NUI Maynooth.

———. 2013. "Bruíonta na Féinne." In *Séimhfhear Suairc: Aistí in Ómós don Ollamh Breandán Ó Conchúir*, edited by Seán Ó Coileáin, Liam P. Ó Murchú, and Pádraigín Riggs, 480–501. Dingle, Kerry: An Sagart.

Ó Cuív, Brian. 1989. "Irish Language and Literature, 1845–1921." In *A New History of Ireland*, vol. 6, ed. W. E. Vaughan, 385–435. Oxford: Oxford University Press.

[O'Curry, Eugene]. 1858. "Review, *Transactions of the Ossianic Society* (Vol. III.) for the Year 1855." *Tablet* [London]. January 30, 74.

———. 1861. *Lectures on the Manuscript Materials of Ancient Irish History*. Dublin: James Duffy.

O'Daly, John. 1853. "The Ossianic Society." *Transactions of the Kilkenny Archaeological Society* 2, no. 2: 1–3.

———, ed. 1858. "Eachdra agus Imtheachta Bhodaig an Chota Lachtna." *Nation*, n.s., 16, no. 11: 171; 16, no. 12: 187; 16, no. 13: 203; 16, no. 14: 219.

———, ed. and trans. 1859. *Laoithe Fiannuigheachta; or, Fenian Poems*. Transactions of the Ossianic Society 4. Dublin: John O'Daly.

———, ed. and trans. 1861. *Laoithe Fiannuigheachta; or, Fenian Poems*. Transactions of the Ossianic Society 6. Dublin: John O'Daly.

———, ed. 1871. "Eachtra agus Imtheachta Bhodaigh an Chota Lachtna." In *Self-Instruction in Irish: Or, A Primer of Spelling and Pronunciation with Easy Reading Lessons for Beginners*, 41–54. Dublin: John O'Daly.

O Daly, Máirín, ed. and trans. 1975. *Cath Maige Mucrama*. Irish Texts Society 50. Dublin: Irish Texts Society.

Ó Dochartaigh, Caitríona. 2004. "Goethe's Translation from the Gaelic *Ossian*." In *The Reception of Ossian in Europe*, edited by Howard Gaskill, 156–75. London: Thoemmes Continuum.

Ó Domhnaill, Niall. 1996 [1942–43]. *Seanchas na Féinne*. Dublin: An Gúm.

Ó Dónaill, Niall. 2005 [1977]. *Foclóir Gaeilge-Béarla*. Dublin: An Gúm.

Ó Donnchadha, Tadhg [Torna]. 1933. *Filidheacht Fiannaigheachta*. Dublin: Comhlucht Oideachais na hÉireann.

O'Donovan, John, ed. and trans. 1859. "Mac-Gnimartha Finn Mac Cumaill: The Boyish Exploits of Finn Mac Cumhaill." In *Laoithe Fiannuigheachta; or, Fenian Poems*, edited by John O'Daly, 281–304. Transactions of the Ossianic Society 4. Dublin: John O'Daly.

Ó Dubhthaigh, Bearnárd. 1958. "Agallamh Oisín agus Phádraig: Lá dhúinne ar Sliabh Fuaid." *Éigse* 9: 34–52.

Ó Dúnlainge, Micheál, ed. 1907. "Cath Mhuighe Macroimhe." *Irisleabhar na Gaedhilge* 17: 385–87, 406–8, 427–31, 434–39.

———, ed. 1908. "Cath Mhuighe Macroimhe." *Irisleabhar na Gaedhilge* 18: 30–34, 75–82, 180–81.

Official UK Charts Company. 2023. "Horslips." *Official Charts*. https://www.officialcharts.com/artist/3012/horslips/. Accessed November 9, 2023.

Ó Fiannachta, Pádraig, ed. 1995. *An Fhiannaíocht*. Léachtaí Cholm Cille 25. Maynooth: An Sagart.

———. 2014. *Fianna Éireann: Eipic ar an bhFiannaíocht idir Laoithe agus Scéalta*. An Daingean: An Sagart.

O'Flaherty, Roderic 1685. *Ogygia: seu Rerum Hibernicarum Chronologia*. London: R. Everingham.

O'Flanagan, Theophilus. 1787. "An Account of an Antient Inscription in Ogam Character on the Sepulchral Monument of an Irish Chief." *Transactions of the Royal Irish Academy* 1, part 3: 3–16.

———. 1808. "Deirdri, or, the Lamentable Fate of the Sons of Usnach, an Ancient Dramatic Irish Tale, One of the Three Tragic Stories of Eirin." *Transactions of the Gaelic Society of Dublin* 1: 1–235.

Ó Fotharta, Domhnall, ed. 1892. *Siamsa an Gheimhridh; nó, Cois an Teallaigh in Iar-gConnachta.i: Sceulta, Dánta, Abhráin, Tomhsanna, 7c*. Dublin: Patrick O'Brien.

———, ed. 1912. *Fuigheall Sgéal ó'n tSean-Aimsir*. Dublin: Patrick O'Brien.

Ó Gallchobhair, Tomás, Pádraig Ua Cuain, and Tadhg Mac Giolla-Fhionnain, eds. 1915. *Gadaidhe Géar na Geamh-Oidhche*. Dublin: Dollard and Gill.

Òganaich, na. 1975. *Scot-Free*. London: Beltona Sword. Vinyl LP.

Ó Giolláin, Diarmuid. 1994–95. "The Image of the Vikings in Irish Folk Legends." *Béaloideas* 62 / 63: 163–70.

———. 2000. *Locating Irish Folklore: Tradition, Modernity, Identity*. Cork: Cork University Press.

O'Grady, Standish Hayes, ed. and trans. 1857. *Tóruigheacht Dhiarmuda agus Ghráinne; or The Pursuit after Diarmuid O'Duibhne, and Grainne the Daughter of Cormac mac Airt, King of Ireland in the Third Century*. Transactions of the Ossianic Society 3. Dublin: John O'Daly.

———, ed. and trans. 1880–81 [1857]. *Tóruigheacht Dhiarmuda agus Ghráinne: The Pursuit of Diarmuid and Grainne*. 2 vols. Dublin: Society for the Preservation of the Irish Language.

———. 1887. "Remarks on the Oxford Edition of the Battle of Ventry." *Transactions of the Philological Society* 20: 619–46.

———, ed. 1892a. *Silva Gadelica (I–XXXI): A Collection of Tales in Irish*. Vol. 1. London: Williams and Norgate.

———, trans. 1892b. *Silva Gadelica*. Vol. 2. London: Williams and Norgate.

———. 1926. *Catalogue of Irish Manuscripts in the British Museum*. Vol. 1. London: British Museum, 1926.

O'Grady, Standish James. 1878. *History of Ireland*. Vol. 1, *The Heroic Period*. London: Sampson Low, Searle, Marston, and Rivington.

———. 1892. *Finn and His Companions*. New York: Cassell Publishing Company.

———. 1918. *Standish O'Grady: Selected Essays and Passages*. Edited by Ernest A. Boyd. Dublin: Talbot; London: T. Fisher Unwin.

———. 1921. "The Masque of Finn." *Finn and His Companions*. Dublin: Talbot.

Ó hAllmhuráin, Gearóid. 2016. *Flowing Tides: History and Memory in an Irish Soundscape*. Oxford: Oxford University Press.

O'Halloran, Clare. 1989. "Irish Re-Creations of the Gaelic Past: The Challenge of Macpherson's Ossian." *Past & Present* 124 (August): 69–95.

———. 2004. *Golden Ages and Barbarous Nations: Antiquarian Debate and Cultural Politics in Ireland, c. 1750–1800*. Critical Conditions: Field Day Monographs 14. Cork: Cork University Press and Field Day.

———. 2010. "Harping on the Past: Translating Antiquarian Learning into Popular Culture in Early Nineteenth-Century Ireland." In *Exploring Cultural History: Essays in Honour of Peter Burke*, edited by Melissa Calaresu, Filippo de Vivo, and Joan-Pau Rubies, 327–43. Farnham: Ashgate.

———. 2012. "Negotiating Progress and Degeneracy: Irish Antiquaries and the Discovery of the 'Folk,' 1770–1844." In *Folklore and Nationalism in Europe During the Long Nineteenth Century*, edited by Timothy Baycroft and David Hopkin, 193–206. National Cultivation of Culture 4. Leiden: Brill.

[O'Halloran, Sylvester]. 1763a. "The Poems of Ossine, the Son of Fionne Mac Comhal, Re-Claimed." *Dublin Magazine* (January): 21–23.

[———]. 1763b. "A Letter to Mr Macpherson, Occasioned by His Dissertation on the Poems of *Temora*." *Dublin Magazine* (August): 457–60.

———. 1772. *An Introduction to the Study of the History and Antiquities of Ireland: in which the Assertions of Mr. Hume and Other Writers are Occasionally Considered*. London: J. Murray.

Ó hAodha, Donncha. 1991. "The First Middle Irish Metrical Tract." In *Metrik und Medienwechsel / Metrics and Media*, edited by Hildegard L. C. Tristram, 207–44. Tübingen: Gunter Narr.

Ó hÓgáin, Dáithí. 1988. *Fionn mac Cumhaill: Images of the Gaelic Hero*. Dublin: Gill and Macmillan.

———. 1990. "Folklore and Literature: 1700–1850." In *The Origins of Popular Literacy in Ireland: Language Change and Educational Development 1700–1920*, edited by Mary Daly and David Dickson, 1–13. Dublin: Department of Modern History, Trinity College.

Ó hÓgáin, Dáithí. 1991. "'Has the time come?' (MLSIT 8009): The Barbarossa Legend in Ireland and Its Historical Background." *Bealoideas* 59: 197–207.

———. 1994. "The River Boyne and the Ancient Seers." *Studia Celtica Japonica* 6: 13–35.

———. 1999. *The Sacred Isle: Belief and Religion in Pre-Christian Ireland.* Woodbridge, UK and Cork: The Boydell Press and the Collins Press.

———. 2002. "Fenian Cycle [Fianna Cycle]." In *Medieval Folklore: A Guide to Myths, Legends, Tales, Beliefs, and Customs*, edited by Carl Lindahl, John McNamara, and John Lindow, 131–33. Oxford: Oxford University Press, 2002.

———. 2006. "Fionn mac Cumhaill." In *The Lore of Ireland: An Encyclopaedia of Myth, Legend and Romance*, 235–49. Woodbridge, UK: Boydell Press.

Ó hUiginn, Ruairí. 1995. "Duanaire Finn." In *An Fhiannaíocht*, edited by Pádraig Ó Fiannachta, 47–68. Léachtaí Cholm Cille 25. Maynooth: An Sagart.

———. 2003. "*Duanaire Finn*: Patron and Text." In *Duanaire Finn: Reassessments*, edited by John Carey, 79–106. Irish Texts Society Subsidiary Series 13. Dublin: Irish Texts Society.

———. 2007. "Onomastic Formulae in Irish." In *Proceedings of the Seventh Symposium of Societas Celtologica Nordica*, edited by Mícheál Ó Flaithearta, 53–70. Studia Celtica Upsaliensia 6. Uppsala: University of Uppsala.

———. 2010. "Captain Somhairle and His Books Revisited." In *The Book of the O'Conor Don: Essays on an Irish Manuscript*, edited by Pádriag Ó Macháin, 88–102. Dublin: School of Celtic Studies, Dublin Institute for Advanced Studies.

———. 2012. "*Fiannaigheacht*, Family, Faith and Fatherland." In *The Gaelic Finn Tradition*, edited by Sharon J. Arbuthnot and Geraldine Parsons, 151–62. Dublin: Four Courts.

———. 2018. "*Tóruigheacht Dhiarmada agus Ghráinne*: Characters, Themes and History." In *Tóruigheacht Dhiarmada agus Ghráinne: Reassessments*, edited by Kevin Murray, 43–71. Irish Texts Society Subsidiary Series 30. Dublin: Irish Texts Society.

O'Kearney, Nicholas, ed. and trans. 1854. *The Battle of Gabhra: Garristown in the County of Dublin, fought A.D. 283*. Transactions of the Ossianic Society 1. Dublin: John O'Daly.

———, ed. and trans. 1855. *Feis Tighe Chonain Chinn-Shleibhe; or the Festivities at the House of Conan of Ceann-Sleibhe, in the County of Clare*. Transactions of the Ossianic Society 2. Dublin: John O'Daly.

O'Keeffe, David. 1878. "The 'N. Y. Ossianic Society.'" *Irish-American* [New York]. November 23, 4.

O'Keeffe, Tadhg. 2011. "Augustinian Regular Canons in Twelfth- and Thirteenth-Century Ireland: History, Architecture, and Identity." In *The Regular Canons in the Medieval British Isles*, edited by Janet Burton and Karen Stöber, 469–84. Medieval Church Studies 19. Turnhout: Brepols.

O'Kelly, J. J. 1911. *Leabhar na Laoitheadh: A Collection of Ossianic Poems*. Dublin: M. H. Gill and Son.

Ó Laoghaire, Pádruig. 1895. "Roimh-Rádh." In *Sgeuluidheacht Chúige Mumhan*, iii–iv. Dublin: Pádruig Ó Briain.

O'Leary, Philip. 1983. "'What Stalked through the Post Office?': Pearse's Cú Chulainn." *Proceedings of the Harvard Celtic Colloquium* 3: 21–38.

———. 1994. *The Prose Literature of the Gaelic Revival, 1881–1921: Ideology and Innovation*. University Park: Pennsylvania State University Press.

———. 2004. *Gaelic Prose in the Irish Free State, 1922–1939*. University Park: Pennsylvania State University Press.

———. 2006. "The Irish Renaissance, 1880–1940: Literature in Irish." In *The Cambridge History of Irish Literature*, vol. 2, edited by Margaret Kelleher and Philip O'Leary, 226–69. Cambridge: Cambridge University Press.

———. 2010. *Irish Interior: Keeping Faith with the Past in Gaelic Prose: 1940–1951*. Dublin: University College Dublin Press.

Ó Longáin, Dubhán. 2023. "Oidhreacht." *Strabane Chronicle*. October 12, 19.

O'Mahony, John, trans. 1857a. *Foras Feasa Ar Éirinn do réir an Athar Seathrún Céiting, Ollamh Ré Diadhachta / The History of Ireland, from The Earliest Period to the English Invasion*, by Seathrún Céitinn. New York: P. M. Haverty.

———. 1857b. "Lon-Dubh Dhoire an Chairn." *Irish-American* [New York]. July 25, 4.

———. 1859. "To Correspondents." *Phoenix* [New York]. June 4, 4.

——— [Maelguala]. 1860. "The New York Ossianic Society." *Pilot* [Boston]. June 23, 2.

Ó Muircheartaigh, Peadar. 2016. "*Fin as Ossian* Revisited: A Manx Ballad in Belnagare and Its Significance." *Zeitschrift für Celtische Philologie* 63, no. 1: 95–128.

Ó Muraíle, Nollaig. 1995. "Agallamh na Seanórach." In *An Fhiannaíocht*, edited by Pádraig Ó Fiannachta, 96–127. Léachtaí Cholm Cille 25. Maynooth: An Sagart.

Ó Murchadha, Diarmuid, ed. 2009. *Lige Guill / The Grave of Goll: A Fenian Poem from the Book of Leinster*. Irish Texts Society 62. Dublin: Irish Texts Society.

Ó Murchadha, Diarmuid, and Kevin Murray. 2000. "Place-Names." In *The Heritage of Ireland*, edited by Neil Buttimer, Colin Rynne, and Helen Guerin, 146–55. Cork: Collins.

Ó Murchú, Máirtín. 2001. *Cumann Buan-Choiméadta na Gaeilge: Tús an Athréimnithe*. Lúb ar Phár 4. Dublin: Cois Life.

Ó Néill, Pádraig. 1997. "The Impact of the Norman Invasion on Irish Literature." *Anglo-Norman Studies* 20: 171–85.

Ó Néill, Séamus. 1936 [1933–34]. *Buaidh an Ultaigh: Dráma Nua*. Dublin: Oifig an tSoláthair.

Ó Raghallaigh, Colmán, and the Cartoon Saloon. 2002. *An Tóraíocht*. Clár Chlainne Mhuiris: Cló Mhaigh Eo.

Ó Raghallaigh, Eoghan, and Lesa Ní Mhunghaile. 2009a. "Hennessy, William Maunsell (Ó hAonghusa, Liam M." In *Dictionary of Irish Biography* online, edited by James McGuire and James Quinn. https://dib.cambridge.org/viewReadPage.do?articleId=a3935. Accessed March 3, 2020.

———. 2009b. "Hull, Eleanor Henrietta." In *Dictionary of Irish Biography* online, edited by James McGuire and James Quinn. http://dib.cambridge.org/viewReadPage.do?articleId=a4151. Accessed March 6, 2020.

O'Rahilly, Cecile, ed. 1962. *Cath Finntrágha*. Mediaeval and Modern Irish Series 20. Dublin: Dublin Institute for Advanced Study.

O'Rahilly, Thomas F. 1946. *Early Irish History and Mythology*. Dublin: Dublin Institute for Advanced Studies.

O'Regan, Tarik. 2011. *Acallam na Senórach: An Irish Colloquy*. Los Angeles: Harmonia Mundi USA. Compact disc.

O'Reilly, Edward. 1820. "A Chronological Account of Irish Writers, and Descriptive Catalogue of Such of Their Works as Are Still Extant in Verse or Prose." *Transactions of the Iberno-Celtic Society* 1, no. 1: xi–ccxxxiii.

———. 1830. "Essay 'to Investigate the Authenticity of the Poems of Ossian, both as Given in Macpherson's Translation, and as Published in Gaelic in 1807, under the Sanction of the Highland Society of London; And, on the Supposition of Such Poems not Being of Recent Origin, to Assign the Probable Era and Country of the Original Poet or Poets.' Proposed by the Royal Irish Academy." *Transactions of the Royal Irish Academy* 16, part 2: 163–336.

Ó Riain, Pádraig. 1972. "Boundary Association in Early Irish Society." *Studia Celtica* 7: 12–29.

Ó Riain, Pádraig, Diarmuid Ó Murchadha, and Kevin Murray, eds. 2011. *Historical Dictionary of Gaelic Placenames / Foclóir Stairiúil Áitainmneacha na Gaeilge*. Fascicle 4. Dublin: Irish Texts Society.

Ó Sándair, Cathal. 1951. *Réics Carló san Aifric*. Dublin: Oifig an tSoláthair.

Ó Scolaí, Darach. 1999. *Feis Tigh Chonáin*. Indreabhán: Leabhar Breac.

Ó Séaghdha, Pádraig ["Conán Maol"]. 1912. "Fian Poetry." *Catholic Bulletin* 2: 449–55.

Ó Searcaigh, Séamus. 1984 [1945]. *Laochas: Scéalta as an tSeanlitríocht*. Dublin: An Gúm.

Ó Síocháin, Tadhg. 2021. *Caoilte sa Luath-Fhiannaíocht*. Dublin: Coiscéim.

Ó Siochfhradha, Pádraig [An Seabhac], ed. 1911. *Cath Fionntrágha: Aith-Innsint ar an Seinsgéal as Gaedhilg na hAimsire seo*. Dublin: Connradh na Gaedhilge.

——— [An Seabhac], ed. 1939a. *Tóraidheacht Dhiarmada agus Ghráinne*. Dublin: Comhlucht Oideachais na hÉireann.

——— [An Seabhac], ed. 1939b. *Tóraidheacht an Ghiolla Dheacair*. Dublin: Comhlucht Oideachais na hÉireann.

——— [An Seabhac], ed. 1941. *Laoithe na Féinne*. Dublin: An Cumann le Béaloideas Éireann.

———. 1943. "Appendix: Notes on Some of Jeremiah Curtin's Storytellers." In *Irish Folk-Tales*, by Jeremiah Curtin, edited by Séamus Ó Duilearga, 152–57. Dublin: Folklore of Ireland Society.

——— [An Seabhac], ed. 1947. *Bruighean Eochaidh Bhig Dheirg*. Dublin: Comhlucht Oideachais na hÉireann.

Ó Súilleabháin, Seán [Sean O'Sullivan]. 1957. "The Collection and Classification of Folklore in Ireland and the Isle of Man." *Folklore* 68, no. 4: 449–57.

———. 1976. "Oliver Cromwell in Irish Oral Tradition." In *Folklore Today: A Festschrift for Richard M. Dorson*, edited by Linda Dégh, Henry Glassie, and Fexlis J. Oinas, 473–83. Bloomington: Indiana University, Research Center for Language and Semiotic Studies.

Ó Súilleabháin, Seán, and Reidar Th. Christiansen. 1963. *The Types of the Irish Folktale*. FF Communications 188. Helsinki: Suomalainen Tiedeakatemia.

O'Sullivan, Brian. 2014. *Fionn: Defence of Ráth Bládhma*. Wellington, NZ: Irish Imbas Books.

———. 2015. *Liath Luachra: The Grey One*. Wellington, NZ: Irish Imbas Books.

———. 2023. "Featured Books." *Irish Imbas*. https://irishimbasbooks.com. Accessed November 7, 2023.

Ó Tiománaidhe, Mícheál [Michael Timony], ed. 1906. *Sgéalta Gearra So-Léighte an Iarthair, an Darna Saothar / Short Easy Stories of the West, Part II*. Dublin: M. H. Gill and Son.

———, ed. 1935. *An Lampa Draoidheachta agus Naoi Sgéalta Eile*. Dublin: Oifig Díolta Foillseacháin Rialtais.

Ó Tiománaidhe, Mícheál, and Domhnall Ó Fotharta, eds. 1910. *Sgéalta Gearra an Iarthair / Western Folk-Reports*. Dublin: Patrick O'Brien.

Ó Tuathail, Éamonn, ed. 1927. "An Feardhamhan." *Béaloideas* 1, no. 1: 54–57.

———, ed. 1931. "Measgradh ó Fhearnmhuigh." *Béaloideas* 3, no. 2: 121–34.

———, ed. 2015 [1933]. *Sgéalta Mhuintir Luinigh / Munterloney Folktales: Irish Tradition from County Tyrone*. Translated by S. Watson. Dublin: Four Courts.

[Otway, Caesar]. 1827. *Sketches in Ireland: Descriptions of Interesting, and Hitherto Unnoticed Districts in the North and South*. Dublin: William Curry, Jun. and Co.

———. 1832. "Legend of Fin M'Coul." *Dublin Penny Journal*. September 29, 110–11.

Owen, David, and Jonathan Davidson. 2009. "Hubris Syndrome: An Acquired Personality Disorder? A Study of US Presidents and UK Prime Ministers Over the Last 100 Years." *Brain* 132, no. 5 (May): 1396–406.

Owenson, Sydney, Lady Morgan. 1999 [1807]. *The Wild Irish Girl*. Oxford: Oxford University Press.

Oz-Salzberger, Fania. 2009. "Ferguson, Adam (1723–1816), Philosopher and Historian." *Oxford Dictionary of National Biography* online. https://doi.org/10.1093/ref:odnb/9315. Accessed October 6, 2020.

Parsons, Geraldine. 2008. "The Structure of *Acallam na Senórach*." *Cambrian Medieval Celtic Studies* 55: 11–39.

———. 2009. "*Acallam Na Senórach* as Prosimetrum." *Proceedings of the Harvard Celtic Colloquium* 24–25: 86–100.

———. 2012. "Breaking the Cycle? Accounts of the Death of Finn." In *The Gaelic Finn Tradition*, edited by Sharon J. Arbuthnot and Geraldine Parsons, 81–96. Dublin: Four Courts.

———. 2014. "Revisiting Almu in Middle Irish Texts." In *Authorities and Adaptations: The Reworking and Transmission of Textual Sources in Medieval Ireland*, edited by Elizabeth Boyle and Deborah Hayden, 211–31. Dundalk: Dundalgan Press.

———. 2023. "Ancient Ireland." In *The Oxford Handbook of W.B. Yeats*, edited by Lauren Arrington and Matthew Campbell, 115–33. Oxford: Oxford University Press.

Pearse, Patrick H. 1898. "Gaelic Prose Literature." In *Three Lectures on Gaelic Topics*, 9–31. Dublin: M. H. Gill and Son.

——— [Pádraig Mac Piarais]. 1900. "An Fhiann⁊ an Fhiannaidheachd." *Irisleabhar na Gaedhilge* 10: 532–38.

[———]. 1905. "The Secondary School." *An Claidheamh Soluis* 7, no. 37: 6–7.

——— [Pádraig Mac Piarais], ed. 1906. *Bodach an Chóta Lachtna*. Dublin: Connradh na Gaedhilge.

——— [Pádraig Mac Piarais], ed. 1908. *Bruidhean Chaorthainn: Sgéal Fiannaidheachta*. Dublin: Connradh na Gaedhilge.

———. 1914. "The Fianna of Fionn." In *Fianna Handbook*, 151–65. Dublin: The Central Council.

———. 1916. *The Murder Machine*. Dublin: Whelan and Son.

———. 2013. *Patrick Pearse: Collected Plays / Drámaí an Phiarsaigh*. Edited by Róisín Ní Ghairbhí and Eugene McNulty. Sallins, Co. Kildare: Irish Academic Press.

——— [Pádraig Mac Piarais], ed. n.d. *Bruíon Chaorthainn: Scéal Fiannaíochta*. Dublin: Comhlacht Oideachais na hÉireann.

Pilkington, Ace G. 2017. *Science Fiction and Futurism: Their Terms and Ideas*. Jefferson, NC: McFarland.

Pinkerton, John. 1787. *A Dissertation on the Origin and Progress of the Scythians or Goths: Being an Introduction to the Ancient and Modern History of Europe*. London: John Nichols.

———. 1789. *An Enquiry into the History of Scotland Preceding the Reign of Malcom III: or the Year 1056, Including the Authentic History of that Period*. Vol. 2. London: John Nichols.

Pittock, Murray, and Isla Jack. 2007. "Patrick Geddes and the Celtic Revival." In *The Edinburgh History of Scottish Literature*, vol. 2, *Enlightenment, Britain and Empire (1707–1918)*, 338–46. Edinburgh: Edinburgh University Press.

Pmaupin [pseud.]. 2022. "Finn McCool - Belfast International Airport, Northern Ireland." *Waymarking*. May 6. https://www.waymarking.com/waymarks/wm164YG_Finn_McCool_Belfast_International_Airport_Northern_Ireland. Accessed November 10, 2023.

Poppe, Erich. 2008. *Of Cycles and Other Critical Matters: Some Issues in Medieval Irish Literary History and Criticism*. E. C. Quiggin Memorial Lectures 9. Cambridge: Department of Anglo-Saxon, Norse, and Celtic, University of Cambridge.

Porter, James. 2019. *Beyond Fingal's Cave: Ossian in the Musical Imagination*. Rochester, NY: University of Rochester Press.

Prim, John G. 1849. "Giants' Graves. No. II." *Transactions of the Kilkenny Archaeological Society* 1, no. 1: 14–22.

Propp, Vladimir. 1968. *Morphology of the Folktale*. Edited by Louis A. Wagner. Translated by Laurence Scott. 2nd ed. American Folklore Society Bibliographical and Special Series 9. Austin: University of Texas Press.

Quinlivan, Patrick J. 1994. "Hunting the Fenians: Problems in the Historiography of a Secret Organisation." In *The Irish World Wide: History, Heritage, Identity*, vol. 3, edited by Patrick O'Sullivan, 133–53. Leicester: Leicester University Press.

Rapall Noyes, George, and Vera Mezirka, trans. 1938. "Diarmuid and Grainne: A Drama in Four Acts." *Poet Lore* 44, no. 4: 289–343.

Rees, Alwyn, and Brinley Rees. 1961. *Celtic Heritage: Ancient Tradition in Ireland and Wales.* London: Thames and Hudson.

Reeve, William, and William Shield. 1791. *The Airs, Duets, Choruses, and Argument, of the New Ballet Pantomime, (Taken from Ossian), Called Oscar and Malvina; or, The Hall of Fingal.* London: W. Woodfall.

Reitzes, Lois, and Rob Shaw-Smith. 2023. "Play 'The Legend of Finn McCool' Brings the Magical Irish Tale to Life at Academy Theatre." *WABE.* June 13. https://www.wabe.org/play-the-legend-of-finn-mccool-brings-the-magical-irish-tale-to-life-at-academy-theater/. Accessed December 13, 2023.

Rhys, John. 1888. *Lectures on the Origin and Growth of Religion as Illustrated by Celtic Heathendom.* The Hibbert Lectures. London: Williams and Norgate.

Richards, Eric. 2005 *The Highland Clearances: People, Landlords and Rural Turmoil.* Edinburgh: Birlinn.

Riordan, Rick. 2021. "My Life as a Child Outlaw." In *The Cursed Carnival and Other Calamities: New Stories about Mythic Heroes,* edited by Rick Riordan, 382–438. Los Angeles: Disney Hyperion.

———. 2023. "Ár coicís in Éirinn (Our fortnight in Ireland)." *Rick Riordan* (blog). April 22. https://rickriordan.com/2023/04/ar-coicis-in-eirinn-our-fortnight-in-ireland/. Accessed November 13, 2023.

Robinson, Fred Norris. 1903–4. "A Variant of the Gaelic 'Ballad of the Mantle.'" *Modern Philology* 1, no. 1: 145–57.

Roe, Harry. 1992. "*Acallamh na Senórach*: The Confluence of Lay and Clerical Oral Traditions." In *Celtic Languages and Celtic Peoples: Proceedings of the Second North American Congress of Celtic Studies,* edited by Cyril J. Byrne, Margaret Harry, and Pádraig Ó Siadhail, 331–46. Halifax: D'Arcy McGee Chair of Irish Studies, Saint Mary's University.

Rolleston, T. W. 1910. *The High Deeds of Finn and Other Bardic Romances of Ancient Ireland.* London: G. G. Harrap.

Ross, Neil, ed. and trans. 1939. *Heroic Poetry from the Book of the Dean of Lismore.* Edinburgh: Oliver and Boyd.

Russell, Paul. 2008. "Poets, Power and Possessions in Medieval Ireland: Some Stories from Sanas Cormaic." In *CSANA Yearbook 7: Law, Literature and Society,* edited by Joseph F. Eska, 9–45. Dublin: Four Courts.

Sanderson, Stewart F. 1957. "The Work of the School of Scottish Studies." *Scottish Studies* 1: 3–13.

Saunders, Corinne. 1993. *The Forest of Medieval Romance: Avernus, Broceliande, Arden.* Cambridge: D. S. Brewer.

Sayers, Peig. 1938. *Scéalta ón mBlascaod.* Edited by Kenneth Jackson. Dublin: An Cumann le Béaloideas Éireann.

Sayers, William. 2013. "'Finn and the Man in the Tree' Revisited." *e-Keltoi* 8, no. 2: 37–55. http://www4.uwm.edu/celtic/ekeltoi.

Scott, Sir Walter. 1805. "*Report of the Highland Society,* ed. by Henry Mackenzie, and *The Poems of Ossian,* ed. by Malcolm Laing." *Edinburgh Review* 6: 429–62.

———. 2002 [1816]. *The Antiquary.* Edited by Nicola J. Watson. Oxford: Oxford University Press.

———. 2015 [1814]. *Waverley; or, 'Tis Sixty Years Since.* Edited by Claire Lamont. Oxford: Oxford University Press.

Seaman, A. T. 1992. "Celtic Myth as Perceived in Eighteenth and Nineteenth-Century Literature in English." In *Celtic Languages and Celtic Peoples: Proceedings of the Second North American Congress of Celtic Studies,* edited by Cyril J. Byrne, Margaret Harry, and Pádraig Ó Siadhail, 443–60. Halifax, NS: D'Arcy McGee Chair of Irish Studies.

Segal, Robert A., ed. 1990. *In Quest of the Hero.* Princeton, NJ: Princeton University Press.

Shairp, [John Campbell]. 1871. "Ossian." *Macmillan's Magazine* 24: 113–25.

Sharpe, Richard, and Mícheál Hoyne. 2020. *Clóliosta: Printing in the Irish Language, 1571–1871*. Dublin: Dublin Institute for Advanced Study.

Sharp, William. 1896a. "Introduction." In *Lyra Celtica: An Anthology of Representative Celtic Poetry*, edited by Elizabeth A. Sharp, xix–li. Edinburgh: Patrick Geddes and Colleagues.

———, ed. 1896b. *The Poems of Ossian*. Translated by James Macpherson. Edinburgh: Patrick Geddes and Colleagues.

Shaw, John. 2004. "Oral Traditions / Folklore of Argyll." In *The Argyll Book*, edited by Donald Omand, 213–22. Edinburgh: Birlinn.

———. 2022. "The Grimms, Scotland and 'This New Science of "Storyology."'" In *Grimm Ripples: The Legacy of the Grimms' Deutsche Sagen in Northern Europe*, edited by Terry Gunnell, 288–315. Leiden: Brill.

Sheehan, Rev. Michael. 1912. *Gile na mBláth*. Dublin: M. H. Gill and Son.

Sheehy, Jeanne. 1980. *The Rediscovery of Ireland's Past: The Celtic Revival 1830–1930*. London: Thames and Hudson.

Sheir, Rebecca. 2021. "The Giant's Causeway." WBUR, National Public Radio. April 13. https://www.wbur.org/circleround/2021/04/13/the-giants-causeway-circle-round. Accessed December 13, 2023.

Sher, Richard B. 1982. "'Those Scotch Imposters and Their Cabal': Ossian and the Scottish Enlightenment." *Man and Nature: Proceedings of the Canadian Society for Eighteenth-Century Studies* 1: 55–63.

———. 1991. "Percy, Shaw and the Ferguson 'Cheat': National Prejudice in the Ossian Wars." In *Ossian Revisited*, edited by Howard Gaskill, 207–45. Edinburgh: Edinburgh University Press.

———. 2009. "Blair, Hugh (1718–1800), Church of Scotland Minister and Literary Critic." *Oxford Dictionary of National Biography* online. https://doi.org/10.1093/ref:odnb/2563. Accessed October 6, 2020.

Shercliff, Rebecca. 2022. "The Narrative Unity of 'Finn and the Man in the Tree.'" In *The Gaelic Finn Tradition II*, edited by Sharon J. Arbuthnot, Síle Ní Mhurchú, and Geraldine Parsons, 87–99. Dubin: Four Courts.

Sherry, Ruth. 1996. "The Story of the National Anthem." *History Ireland* 4, no. 1: 39–43.

Shields, Hugh. 1993. *Narrative Singing in Ireland: Lays, Ballads, Come-All-Yes and Other Songs*. Dublin: Irish Academic Press.

Simms, Katharine. 1992 [1989]. "The Norman Invasion and the Gaelic Recovery." In *The Oxford History of Ireland*, edited by R. F. Foster, 44–87. Oxford: Oxford University Press.

———. 1994. "An Eaglais agus Filí na Scol." In *An Dán Díreach*, edited by Pádraig Ó Fiannachta, 21–36. Léachtaí Cholm Cille 24. Maynooth: An Sagart.

———. 1996. "Gaelic Warfare in the Middle Ages." In *A Military History of Ireland*, edited by Thomas Bartlett and Keith Jeffery, 99–116. Cambridge: Cambridge University Press.

Simpson, John Hawkins. 1856. *An Englishman's Testimony to the Urgent Necessity for a Tenant Right Bill for Ireland: After a Residence of Five Years in That Country*. London: W. and F. G. Cash.

———. 1857. *Poems of Oisin, Bard of Erin. "The Battle of Ventry Harbour," etc. from the Irish*. London: Bosworth and Harrison.

Sims-Williams, Patrick. 1986. "The Visionary Celt: The Construction of an Ethnic Preconception." *Cambridge Medieval Celtic Studies* 11: 71–96.

———. 2011. *Irish Influence on Medieval Welsh Literature*. Oxford: Oxford University Press.

Sisson, Elaine. 2004. *Pearse's Patriots: St. Enda's and the Cult of Boyhood*. Cork: Cork University Press.

Skene, William Forbes. 1862. "Introduction." In *The Dean of Lismore's Book: A Selection of Ancient Gaelic Poetry from a Manuscript Collection Made by Sir James McGregor, Dean of Lismore, in the Beginning of the Sixteenth Century*, vol. 1, edited by Rev. Dr. Thomas McLauchlan, i–xc. Edinburgh: Edmonston and Douglas.

Smith, John. 1780. *Galic Antiquities: Consisting of a History of the Druids, Particularly of Those of Caledonia; a Dissertation on the Authenticity of the Poems of Ossian; and a Collection of Ancient Poems, Translated from the Galic of Ullin, Ossian, Orran, etc.* Edinburgh: Charles Elliot.

———. 1787. *Sean Dana; le Ossian, Orran, Ullin, etc. Collected in the Western Highlands and Isles.* Edinburgh: Charles Elliot.

Smith, Peter J. 2007. *Three Historical Poems Ascribed to Gilla Cóemáin: A Critical Edition of the Work of an Eleventh-Century Irish Scholar*. Studien und Texte zur Keltologie 8. Münster: Nodus.

Smollett, Tobias. 1998 [1771]. *The Expedition of Humphry Clinker*. Edited by Lewis M. Knapp. Oxford: Oxford University Press.

Sneddon, Duncan. 2023. "Laoidh Chaolte ann an Uibhist a Deas anns na 1860an." *Scottish Gaelic Studies* 32: 23–40.

Snyder, Edward D. 1923. *The Celtic Revival in English Literature, 1760–1800*. Cambridge, MA: Harvard University Press.

Sommerville-Woodward, Robert. 2004. "The Dublin Ossianic Society, 1853–63." In *The Remaking of Modern Ireland 1750–1950: Beckett Prize Essays in Irish History*, edited by Raymond Gillespie, 138–63. Dublin: Four Courts.

Spenser, Edmund. 1997. *A View of the State of Ireland*. Edited by Andrew Hadfield and Willy Maley. Oxford: Blackwell.

Stafford, Fiona J. 1988. *The Sublime Savage: A Study of James Macpherson and the Poems of Ossian.* Edinburgh: Edinburgh University Press.

———. 1989. "Dr. Johnson and the Ruffian: New Evidence in the Dispute between Samuel Johnson and James Macpherson." *Notes and Queries* 36, n.s.: 70–77.

———. 1991. "'Dangerous Success': Ossian, Wordsworth, and English Romantic Literature." In *Ossian Revisited*, edited by Howard Gaskill, 49–72. Edinburgh: Edinburgh University Press.

———. 1996a. "Introduction: The Ossianic Poems of James Macpherson." In *The Poems of Ossian and Related Works*, by James Macpherson, edited by Howard Gaskill, v–xxi. Edinburgh: Edinburgh University Press.

———. 1996b. "Primitivism and the Primitive Poet: A Cultural Context for Macpherson's Ossian." In *Celticism*, edited by Terence Brown, 79–96. Studia Imagologica: Amsterdam Studies on Cultural Identity 8. Amsterdam: Rodopi.

———. 1998. "*Fingal* and the Fallen Angels: Macpherson, Milton and Romantic Titanism." In *From Gaelic to Romantic: Ossianic Translations*, edited by Fiona Stafford and Howard Gaskill, 163–82. Amsterdam: Rodopi.

Staines, David. 1996. "The Medieval Cycle: Mapping a Trope." In *Transtextualities: Of Cycles and Cyclicity in Medieval French Literature*, edited by Sara Sturm-Maddox and Donald Maddox, 15–37. Binghamton: Center for Medieval and Early Renaissance Studies, State University of New York at Binghamton, 1996.

Stern, Ludwig Christian. 1892. "Le Manuscrit Irlandais de Leide." *Revue Celtique* 13: 1–30.

———. 1895. "Die Ossianischen Heldenlieder." *Zeitschrift für Vergleichende Litteraturgeschichte* 8: 51–86, 143–74.

———, ed. and trans. 1897. "Fiannshruth." *Zeitschrift für Celtische Philologie* 1: 471–73.

———, ed. and trans. 1900a. "Eine Ossianische Ballade aus dem XII. Jahrhundert." In *Festschrift Whitley Stokes zum Siebzigsten Geburtstage am 28 Februar 1900*, edited by Kuno Meyer et al., 7–19. Leipzig: Otto Harrassowitz.

———. 1900b. "Ossianic Heroic Poetry." Translated by J. L. Robertson. *Transactions of the Gaelic Society of Inverness* 22: 257–325.

———, ed. 1905. "Die Bekehrung der Fianna." *Zeitschrift für Celtische Philologie* 5: 179–83.

Steward, Patrick, and Bryan McGovern. 2013. *The Fenians: Irish Rebellion in the North Atlantic World, 1858–1876*. Knoxville: University of Tennessee Press.

Stewart, Alexander, and Donald Stewart, eds. 1804. *Cochruinneacha Taoghta de Shaothair nam Bard Gaëleach: A Choice Collection of the Works of the Highland Bards, Collected in the Highlands and Isles*. Edinburgh: T. Stiuart.

Stewart, Essie. 1996. "Essie Stewart: The Blind Man's Daughter." In *The Summer Walkers: Travelling People and Pearl-Fishers in the Highlands of Scotland*, edited by Timothy Neat, 3–17. Edinburgh: Canongate Books.

Stifter, David. Forthcoming. "The Language of the *Cín Dromma Snechtai* Texts." In *23 N 10: The Book of Ballycummin*, edited by Elizabeth Boyle. Codices Hibernenses Eximii 4. Dublin: Royal Irish Academy.

Stiùbhart, Dòmhnall Uilleam. 2008. "Alexander Carmichael and *Carmina Gadelica*." In *The Life and Legacy of Alexander Carmichael*, edited by Dòmhnall Uilleam Stiùbhart, 1–39. Port of Ness, Lewis: The Islands Book Trust.

———. 2013. "The Making of a Charm Collector: Alexander Carmichael in Uist, from 1864 to 1882." In *The Power of Words: Studies on Charms and Charming in Europe*, edited by James Kapalo and Eva Pocs, 27–70. Budapest: Central European University Press.

———. 2014. "Heroic Cycles in the Nineteenth-Century Hebrides: The Work of John Francis Campbell and Alexander Carmichael." Paper given at Fíanaigecht: The Second International Finn Cycle Conference, University of Glasgow.

Stoddart, John. 1801. *Remarks on Local Scenery and Manners in Scotland during the Years 1799 and 1800*. Vol. 1. London: William Miller.

Stokes, Whitley, ed. and trans. 1886. "Find and the Phantoms." *Revue Celtique* 7: 289–307.

———, ed. and trans. 1891. "The Irish Ordeals, Cormac's Adventure in the Land of Promise, and the Decision as to Cormac's Sword." In *Irische Texte*, vol. 3.1, ed. W. H. Stokes and E. Windisch, 183–229. Leipzig: S. Hirzel.

———, ed. and trans. 1894. "The Prose Tales in the Rennes Dindṡenchas." *Revue Celtique* 15: 272–336, 418–84.

———, ed. and trans. 1895. "The Prose Tales in the Rennes Dindṡenchas." *Revue Celtique* 16: 31–83, 135–67, 269–312, 468.

———, ed. and trans. 1896. "The Annals of Tigernach: Second Fragment. A.D. 143–A.D. 361." *Revue Celtique* 17: 6–33.

———, ed. and trans. 1899. "The Bodleian Amra Choluimb Chille." *Revue Celtique* 20: 30–55, 132–83, 248–89, 400–37.

———, ed. 1900. *Acallam na Senórach. Irische Texte*. Vol. 4.1. Edited by W. H. Stokes and E. Windisch. Leipzig: S. Hirzel.

———, ed. and trans. 1902. "On the Deaths of Some Irish Heroes." *Revue Celtique* 23: 303–48.

Stone, Jerome. 1756. "Albin and the Daughter of Mey: An Old Tale, Translated from the Irish." *Scots Magazine* 18: 15–17.

Stòrlann Nàiseanta na Gàidhlig. n.d. "Co-Obrachadh eadar Alba is Èirinn airson 'Mar a Chuala Mise E' Fhoillseachadh." *Stòrlann Nàiseanta na Gàidhlig*. https://www.storlann.co.uk/goireasan/Mar-a-chuala-mise-e.html. Accessed November 10, 2023.

Sutcliff, Rosemary. 2001 [1967]. *The High Deeds of Finn MacCool*. London: Random House.

Sumner, Natasha. 2017. "Fionn mac Cumhaill in Twenty-First-Century Ireland." *North American Journal of Celtic Studies* 1, no. 1: 82–106.

———. 2018. "Diarmaid and Gráinne in Oral Tradition." In *Tóruigheacht Dhiarmada agus Ghráinne: Reassessments*, edited by Kevin Murray, 107–58. Irish Texts Society Subsidiary Series 30. Dublin: Irish Texts Society.

———. 2022. "The Fianna and the Folklore Collectors." In *The Gaelic Finn Tradition II*, edited by Sharon Arbuthnot, Síle Ní Mhurchú, and Geraldine Parsons, 159–73. Dublin: Four Courts.

Sumner, Natasha. 2024. "Trapped and Transported: The Fianna from the *Bruíon* to Boston." *Proceedings of the Harvard Celtic Colloquium* 41: 1–34.

———. 2025. "Fionn among the Women: A Re-evaluation of Irish Women's Fenian Tales." In *Imagination and Innovation in Medieval Celtic Literatures*, edited by Georgia Henley and Helen Fulton, 180–90. Cardiff: University of Wales Press.

———. Forthcoming-a. "Oisean Overseas: Fenian Folklore from Canada." In *Proceedings of Ulidia-Finn 2018*, edited by Ralph O'Connor, Abigail Burnyeat, Geraldine Parsons and Domhnall Uilleam Stiùbhart. Woodbridge, UK: Boydell Press and Brewer.

———. Forthcoming-b. "Gender and Genre: Female Storytellers' Approaches to Irish Fenian *Bruíon* Tales." In *Essays in Memory of Professor Anders Ahlqvist*, edited by Pamela O'Neill, Arwen Smith, and Dan Anlezark. Sydney Series in Celtic Studies. Sydney, Australia: Celtic Studies Foundation, University of Sydney.

———. Forthcoming-c. "Oral Tradition." In *The International Companion to Scottish Gaelic Literature*, edited by Sìm Innes and Sheila Kidd. Glasgow: Association for Scottish Literary Studies.

Tannen, Mary. 1981. *The Wizard Children of Finn*. New York: Alfred A. Knopf.

TG Lurgan. 2011. "Tóraíocht Lurgan." YouTube video. October 9. https://www.youtube.com/watch?v=YZOCARj__oY. Accessed October 20, 2023.

Theuerkauf, Marie-Luise. 2017. "Tristan and Early Modern Irish Romances: James Carney's *Ur-Tristan* Revisited." In *The Matter of Britain in Medieval Ireland: Reassessments*, 92–121. Irish Texts Society Subsidiary Series 29. Dublin: Irish Texts Society.

Thompson, Frank G. 1984–86. "John Francis Campbell." *Transactions of the Gaelic Society of Inverness* 54: 1–57.

———. 1985. "J. F. Campbell: Victorian Polymath." In *Lamplighter and Storyteller: John Francis Campbell of Islay 1821–1885*, 7–9. Edinburgh: National Library of Scotland.

Thompson, Kate. 2005. *The New Policeman*. London: Bodley Head.

———. 2007. *The Last of the High Kings*. London: Bodley Head.

———. 2009. *The White Horse Trick*. London: Bodley Head.

Thomson, Derick S. 1952. *The Gaelic Sources of Macpherson's 'Ossian'*. Edinburgh and London: Oliver and Boyd.

———. 1953. "A Catalogue and Indexes of the Ossianic Ballads in the McLagan MSS." *Scottish Gaelic Studies* 8, no. 2: 177–224.

———. 1958. "Bogus Gaelic Literature, c. 1750–c. 1820." *Transactions of the Gaelic Society of Glasgow* 5: 172–88.

———. 1963. "'Ossian' Macpherson and the Gaelic World of the Eighteenth Century." *Aberdeen University Review* 40: 7–20.

———. 1987. "Macpherson's *Ossian*: Ballads to Epics." In *Fiannaíocht: Essays on the Fenian Tradition of Ireland and Scotland*, edited by Bo Almqvist, Séamas Ó Catháin, and Pádraig Ó Héalaí, 243–64. Dublin: The Folklore of Ireland Society.

———, ed. 1992. *The MacDiarmid MS Anthology: Poems and Songs, Mainly Anonymous, from the Collection Dated 1770*. Edinburgh: Scottish Gaelic Texts Society.

———. 1992–94. "The McLagan MSS in Glasgow University Library: A Survey." *Transactions of the Gaelic Society of Inverness* 58: 406–24.

———. 1998. "James Macpherson: The Gaelic Dimension." In *From Gaelic to Romantic: Ossianic Translations*, edited by Fiona Stafford and Howard Gaskill, 17–26. Amsterdam: Rodopi.

Thuente, Mary Helen. 1994. *The Harp Re-Strung: The United Irishmen and the Rise of Irish Literary Nationalism*. Syracuse, NY: Syracuse University Press.

Thurneysen, Rudolf, ed. and trans. 1920–21. "Tochmarc Ailbe 'Das Werben um Ailbe.'" *Zeitschrift für Celtische Philologie* 13: 251–82.

Toner, Gregory. 2000. "Reconstructing the Earliest Irish Tale Lists." *Éigse* 32: 88–120.

———. 2022. "The Dating of the *Acallam*." In *The Gaelic Finn Tradition II*, edited by Sharon J. Arbuthnot, Síle Ní Mhurchú, and Geraldine Parsons, 15–23. Dubin: Four Courts.

Trevor-Roper, Hugh. 1983. "The Invention of Tradition: The Highland Tradition of Scotland." In *The Invention of Tradition*, edited by Eric Hobsbawn and Terence Ranger, 15–41. Cambridge: Cambridge University Press.

———. 1985. "The Ossian Forgeries: Wrong but Romantic." *Spectator*. March 16, 14–15.

———. 2008. *The Invention of Scotland: Myth and History*. New Haven, CT: Yale University Press.

Tymoczko, Maria. 1993. "Amateur Political Theatricals, *Tableaux Vivants*, and *Cathleen ni Houlihan*." *Yeats Annual* 10: 33–64.

———. 1999. *Translation in a Postcolonial Context: Early Irish Literature in English Translation*. Manchester: St. Jerome Publishing.

Ua hÓgáin, Seaghán, and Seosamh Laoide, eds. 1905. *Teacht agus Imtheacht an Ghiolla Dheacair agus Tóruidheacht Chonáin agus A Chuideachtan*. Dublin: Connradh na Gaedhilge.

Uhlich, Jürgen. 1993. *Die Morphologie der komponierten Personennamen des Altirischen*. Witterschlick, Bonn: Wehle.

Uí Chollatáin, Regina. 2010. "Crossing Boundaries and Early Gleanings of Cultural Replacement in Irish Periodical Culture." *Irish Communications Review* 12: 50–64.

Uí Fhlannagáin, Fionnuala. 2008. *Fíníní Mheiriceá agus an Ghaeilge*. Dublin: Coiscéim.

Underwood, Ted. 2017. "A Genealogy of Distant Reading." *Digital Humanities Quarterly* 11, no. 2. https://digitalhumanities.org/dhq/vol/11/2/000317/000317.html#. Accessed March 12, 2024.

Urobuchi, Gen and Shinjiro. 2016 [2011]. *Fate / Zero*. Vol. 2. Milwaukie: Dark Horse.

Uther, Hans-Jörg. 2004. *The Types of International Folktales: A Classification and Bibliography*. 3 vols. FF Communications 284–86. Helsinki: Suomalainen Tiedeakatemia.

Vallancey, Charles. 1782. *A Grammar of the Iberno-Celtic, Or Irish Language*. 2nd ed. Dublin: R. Marchbank.

Vance, Norman. 1980. "Celts, Carthaginians and Constitutions: Anglo-Irish Literary Relations." *Irish Historical Studies* 22, no. 86: 216–38.

Velasco López, Henar. 2018. "Diarmaid and Gráinne in the Light of Classical Mythology." In *Tóruigheacht Dhiarmada agus Ghráinne: Reassessments*, edited by Kevin Murray, 72–106. Irish Texts Society Subsidiary Series 30. Dublin: Irish Texts Society.

Waddell, Rev. Dr. Peter Hately. 1875. *Ossian and the Clyde, Fingal in Ireland, Oscar in Iceland, or Ossian Historical and Authentic*. Glasgow: James Maclehose.

———. 1878. "Dr. Hately Waddell on the Authenticity of Ossian." *Transactions of the Gaelic Society of Inverness* 6: 63–87.

Wadden, Patrick. 2017. "Church, Apostle and Nation in Early Ireland." *Medieval Worlds* 5: 143–69.

Walker, Joseph Cooper. 1786. *Historical Memoirs of the Irish Bards, Interspersed with Anecdotes of, and Occasional Observations on the Music of Ireland*. London: T. Payne and Son and G.G.J. and J. Robinson.

Walsh, Brendan. 2007. *The Pedagogy of Protest: The Educational Thought and Work of Patrick H. Pearse*. Bern: Peter Lang.

Walsh, Peter. 1682. *A Prospect of the State of Ireland*. London: Johanna Broom.

Wäppling, Eva. 1984. "Four Irish Legendary Figures in At Swim-Two-Birds: A Study of Flann O'Brien's Use of Finn, Suibhne, the Pooka and the Good Fairy." PhD diss., Uppsala University.

Warner, Ferdinando. 1762. *Remarks on the History of Fingal, and Other Poems of Ossian*. London: H. Payne and W. Cropley.

Watson, George. 1996. "Celticism and the Annulment of History." In *Celticism*, edited by Terence Brown, 207–20. Studia Imagologica: Amsterdam Studies on Cultural Identity 8. Amsterdam: Rodopi.

Watters, Eugene Rutherford. 1964. *The Week-End of Dermot and Grace*. Dublin: Allen Figgis.

Watts, John R. 1981. "Na Fianna Eireann: A Case Study of a Political Youth Organisation." PhD diss., University of Glasgow.

West Highland Animation. 2014. "Journey West . . ." *West Highland Animation*. https://www.westhighlandanimation.co.uk/Projects_JourneyWest.html. Accessed November 6, 2023.

White, Nora. 2006. *Compert Mongáin and Three Other Early Mongán Tales: A Critical Edition with Introduction, Translation, Textual Notes, Bibliography and Vocabulary*. Maynooth: Department of Old and Middle Irish, National University of Ireland, Maynooth.

Williams, Daniel G. 2006. *Ethnicity and Cultural Authority from Arnold to Du Bois*. Edinburgh: Edinburgh University Press.

Williams, Fionnuala. 1995. "Six Hundred Gaelic Proverbs Collected in Ulster by Robert Mac Adam." *Proverbium* 12: 343–51.

Wilson, Charles Henry. [1792]. *Select Irish Poems Translated into English*. Dublin: Joseph Hill.

Wilson, William A. 1989. "Herder, Folklore and Romantic Nationalism." In *Folk Groups and Folklore Genres: A Reader*, edited by Elliott Oring, 21–37. Logan: Utah State University Press.

Windisch, Ernst, ed. 1879. "Fotha Catha Cnucha in so." In *Kurzgefasste Irische Grammatik mit Lesestücken*, 121–23. Leipzig: Verlag von S. Hirzel.

———, ed. 1880. "Drei Gedichte aus der Finnsage." In *Irische Texte*, vol. 1, edited by E. Windisch, 146–64. Leipzig: S. Hirzel.

———. 1893. "Ancient Irish Legendary Literature and Ossianic Poetry." Translated by Thomas O'Neill Russell. *Irish Echo* [Boston], April [vol. 4, no. 1], 4–16.

Withers, Charles W. J. 1984. *Gaelic in Scotland 1698–1981: The Geographical History of a Language*. Edinburgh: John Donald.

Wordsworth, Dorothy. 1997 [1874]. *Recollections of a Tour Made in Scotland*. Edited by Carol Kyros Walker. New Haven, CT: Yale University Press.

Yeats, William Butler. 1970 [1904]. "Preface." In *Gods and Fighting Men: The Story of the Tuatha De Danaan and of the Fianna of Ireland*, by Lady Isabella Augusta Gregory, 11–20. Coole Edition 3. New York: Oxford University Press.

———. 1989 [1888]. "Introduction and Headnotes to *Fairy and Folk Tales of the Irish Peasantry*, ed. W. B. Yeats." In *Prefaces and Introductions*, edited by William H. O'Donnell, 3–22. The Collected Works of W. B. Yeats 6. New York: Scribner.

———. 1997 [1889]. "The Wanderings of Oisin." In *The Poems*, edited by Richard J. Finneran. 2nd ed. The Collected Works of W. B. Yeats 1. New York: Scribner.

———. 1999 [1938]. *Autobiographies*. Edited by William H. O'Donnell and Douglas N. Archibald. The Collected Works of W. B. Yeats 3. New York: Scribner.

———. 2007 [1898]. "The Celtic Element in Literature." In *Early Essays*, edited by George Bornstein and Richard J. Finneran, 128–38. The Collected Works of W. B. Yeats 4. New York: Scribner.

Yeats, William Butler, and George Moore. 2005. *Diarmuid and Grania: Manuscript Materials*. Edited by J.C.C. Mays. Ithaca, NY: Cornell University Press.

Young, Ella. 1929. *The Tangle-Coated Horse and Other Tales: Episodes from the Fionn Saga*. New York and Toronto: Longmans, Green and Co.

Young, Matthew. 1787. "Antient Gaelic Poems Respecting the Race of the Fians, Collected in the Highlands of Scotland in the Year 1784." *Transactions of the Royal Irish Academy* 1, part 3: 43–119.

Zimmer, Heinrich. 1887. Review of *Essai d'un Catalogue de la Littérature Épique de l'Irlande*, by H. d'Arbois de Jubainville. *Göttingische Gelehrte Anzeigen*: 153–99.

———. 1891a. "Keltische Beiträge III: Weitere Nordgermanische Einflüsse in der Ältesten Ueberlieferung der Irischen Heldensage." *Zeitschrift für Deutsches Altertum und Deutsche Literatur* 35: 1–172.

———. 1891b. "Ossin und Oscar: Ein Weiteres Zeugnis für den Ursprung der Irisch-Gälischen Finn -(Ossian-)Sage in der Vikingerzeit." *Zeitschrift für Deutsches Altertum und Deutsche Literatur* 35: 252–55.

Zimmermann, Georges Denis. 2001. *The Irish Storyteller*. Dublin: Four Courts.

Zuelow, Eric G. 2009. *Making Ireland Irish: Tourism and National Identity since the Irish Civil War*. Syracuse, NY: Syracuse University Press.

Archives

Irish National Folklore Collection (NFC), University College Dublin.
National Library of Scotland (NLS), Edinburgh.
National Museum of Ireland (NMI), Dublin.
Pearse Museum, Dublin.
School of Scottish Studies Archives (SSS), University of Edinburgh.
Special Collections, University College Cork Library.
Special Collections, University College Dublin Library.

Online Databases and Dictionaries

Am Baile, Highland Archive Centre, The Highland Council / Comhairle na Gàidhealtachd. https://www.ambaile.org.uk. Accessed December 31, 2023.

Choral Music Catalogue, The Contemporary Music Centre, Ireland. https://www.cmc.ie/music, Accessed November 9, 2023.

Fionn Folklore Database. https://fionnfolklore.org. Accessed September 6, 2023.

Oxford English Dictionary online, Oxford University Press. https://doi.org/10.1093/OED/5658621893. Accessed March 24, 2024.

Playography Ireland, Irish Theatre Institute. https://www.irishplayography.com. Accessed November 9, 2023.

INDEX

Page numbers in italics indicate figures.

Abbreviations

BDL	Neil Ross, *Heroic Poetry from the Book of the Dean of Lismore* (1939)
DF	Eoin MacNeill and Gerard Murphy, *Duanaire Finn*, 3 vols. (1908–53)
EFC	Kevin Murray, *The Early Fenian Corpus* (2017)
F.	Kuno Meyer, *Fianaigecht* (1910)